UNDERSTANDING ECONOMICS

Economic issues exert a considerable pressure on everyday life. Yet, economic theory is often communicated as removed and difficult with little relation to real-life situations. *Understanding Economics* shows that this is not the case. In so doing, the book presents an accessible and alternative introduction to economics.

The book is designed to illustrate the usefulness, versatility and relevance of economics. The author conveys how economics is concerned with a broad range of diverse matters, from economic systems as a whole, to particular issues, such as family planning, the stock market, pricing of shares or the non-market allocation of education and blood. The work provides an alternative view of traditional issues as well as an analysis of areas not normally covered. The key topics include:

- Time – throughout time is presented as a key theme, with an emphasis on risk and uncertainty;
- Institutional rules, such as laws and customs;
- Market and non-market allocation;
- Internal working of households, business firms and non-profit organizations;
- Investment analysis with an illustration of investment decision-making techniques and risk and uncertainty in different contexts.

Understanding Economics is reader-friendly in both style and content and requires no prior knowledge of economics and minimal mathematics.

Vicky Allsopp is senior lecturer in Economics at Middlesex University where she teaches economics and finance to social science, humanities and business studies students. She has extensive teaching and consultancy experience both in this country and abroad.

UNDERSTANDING ECONOMICS

VICKY ALLSOPP

 LONDON AND NEW YORK

First published 1995
by Routledge
11 New Fetter Lane, London EC4 4EE

Simultaneously published in the USA and Canada
by Routledge
29 West 35th Street, New York, NY 10001

Typeset in Times by Datix International Limited, Bungay, Suffolk
Printed and bound in Great Britain by T J Press Ltd, Padstow, Cornwall

British Library Cataloguing in Publication Data
A catalogue record for this book is available from the British Library

Library of Congress Cataloging in Publication Data

Allsopp, Vicky, 1946–
Understanding economics / Vicky Allsopp.
  p.   cm.
Includes bibliographical references and index.
ISBN 0–415–09132–2. — ISBN 0–415–09133–0
1. Economics. I. Title
HB171.A467   1995   95–11819
330—dc20   CIP

ISBN 0–415–09132–2
ISBN 0–415–09133–0 (pbk)

In memory of
Sidney Childs, Ronald Meek and Aubrey Bruce

Contents

List of figures

Preface

Economics is never short of critics and often receives a bad press. It is not unusual for disdainful strangers to dismiss it – out of hand. This book is written in retaliation. But its aim is to help and encourage those who are starting their first course in economics – to give a different approach – to pass on ideas.

In the writing of this book I have received generous gifts of time and energy from so many people. Although I cannot mention everyone, I have appreciated their help and encouragement.

First, I must thank the Allsopp family, in particular, J.G. and J.R. who have been prominent readers and great supporters, and Siân for the Incas, and Huw for endless coffee; and my sister who always said 'keep going'.

I wish to record my special thanks to Sheila Dow for all her advice, encouragement and very valuable comments on so many draft chapters. This made an immense difference. Also, particular thanks must go to the following: Alex Rebmann, Atai Winkler, Professor Michael Driscoll, Maria Moschandreas, Sue Glycopantis, Colin Sparks, John Cole, Maureen Spencer, Liz Allison, the library staff, particularly Maggie Jesson and Pauline Hollis at the Middlesex University Business School and Barbara Waine from the University; Murray Glickman, University of East London; Professor Alistair Dow and Bob Arnot at Glasgow Caledonian University; also, Beverley Winkler and John Skinner.

Sadly, and very recently, Professor Barry Turner has died. He encouraged this project and gave me interesting ideas on risk.

I must also thank my ex-students for their help, especially, from the distant past, Paul Olliver, for his unfailing support and good examples and Angela Genn-Bash for her kick in the right direction; and more recent students Nicola Board, Matthieu Georgelin and Alicia Pi. Finally, to those at Routledge, particularly Alan Jarvis, the editor, for all his help and good faith in taking a risk and Alison Kirk whose calm assistance never failed.

Part I

BASIC CONCEPTS

1

Introduction

ABOUT THE BOOK AND ITS READERS

Understanding Economics aims to give a readily accessible and an interesting introduction to key economic ideas. We illustrate some of the ways in which economists work, and plan to give readers the confidence to analyse key economic issues, important matters which impinge upon us all. Pick up today's newspaper, listen to the radio or watch television news: economic matters are always topical because they are important. When you have studied economics you will be surprised to find how many different facets of your own life have a significant economic dimension.

The book is written for those with no prior knowledge of formal economic theory, indeed no background in economics save that afforded to anyone living in a late twentieth-century modern economy. *Understanding Economics* is designed for those who want an understanding of what economics is about and what economists can contribute. The majority of readers will not intend to become professional economists. None the less we hope that the reader-friendly approach and content will encourage people to delve into the wide range of economic literature, to acquire an enthusiasm for economics, and to see the world through different eyes.

In particular, this book is written for humanities and social science students studying introductory undergraduate economics courses. However, *Understanding Economics* will appeal to those business studies, engineering and accounting students who want a different perspective from that offered by the usual text. Moreover, this book will give a clear starting point and a useful basis for those who come to postgraduate courses with little or no knowledge of economics, where students are required to grapple with more advanced economic concepts and methods, whether on human resource management or social administration courses. *Understanding Economics* provides a beginning.

WITH WHAT IS ECONOMICS CONCERNED?

People often have preconceived ideas about the concerns of economics. Many seem to believe that economics is simply a study of business, banking and markets. Indeed, those who scratch the surface might be convinced that economics is a subject concerned primarily with a competitive 'market man', who works in a commercial environment, actively engaging in market transactions, buying and selling commodities for individual consumption. He is assumed to live in a world where people are merely market players engrossed in the ubiquitous, everlasting pursuit of the best buy; where governments are on the sidelines merely intervening in the market process; and where there is little past to consider, except for the briefest 'economic history' of recent times.

Economics is in fact very much more than that. Economics is not just the study of how people gain their living whether by ordinary or extraordinary means, but how they use their time and resources, how they spend their lives, not just their money. People make decisions in market and non-market situations; they are more than market players. And there are often very real differences in the ways in which people and their organizations use resources and time, whether from one generation to another, from country to country, or over the sweep of history. Economics has important ideas to bring; it involves much more than explaining the workings of money and banking, or a study of markets and business, albeit important concerns in the modern economy.

Economics is concerned with *identifying* and *clarifying choices*; the range of possibilities which face us *over time*. On a personal level the choice might be between buying a book or a compact disc; training to be a teacher, social worker or financial analyst; saving for retirement or spending on a holiday now, using our time for leisure, D-I-Y or the washing up. At the level of the organization, such as a business firm, the choice could be between investing in a new computer system or retaining and up-grading existing equipment. In a health care charity the choice might manifest itself as the option of spending donations to reduce the suffering of chronically sick people now or investing those limited funds for research into prevention and cure in the future. In practice, these can be agonizingly difficult choices. At the national level, in Britain, the choice could be between increasing government expenditure on motorways and ring roads or expanding the number of National Health Service beds. Indeed, there is also the need to choose between alternative methods of financing such increased expenditure.

No individual, nor organization can avoid making choices about the use of limited resources, including the time required to meet competing alternative ends. There is *scarcity*: never enough of everything to go around, even amongst the richest communities. Despite rapid technological and organizational change, in the late twentieth century all wants and needs just cannot be satisfied. As knowledge evolves the ability to satisfy old desires may improve but new wants are created. And as time is strictly rationed – all of us must die – we need to think about the different ways in which we can spend our time. Of course, some individuals, social groups and organizations have more choices available than others, for these depend on the distribution of resources, income and wealth; this raises important issues, dependent on a variety of factors.

Economics aims to clarify and explain the pattern of available possibilities, the options open to us now and to give insights into how these might change in the future. Economists can look backwards and forwards through time, searching for information from the past and present, imagining the future. The determination is to make sense of a highly complex reality, explaining the range of options and the consequences of making different choices. Choices always have to be made, whether, for example, by rational calculation, the use of routines and customary responses or simply by default. Economic theories provide a basis for analysing such issues.

Economics is essentially concerned with *human behaviour*, for in order to make the best use of limited resources and time to produce output or to enjoy leisure, agreements have to be made amongst people. Human beings *co-operate* together in very different types of organizations. These range from the relatively intimate social grouping of the family, to giant corporations like British American Tobacco (BAT), British Telecom (BT) or General Motors (GM). Moreover, people can belong to the smallest local charity or voluntary group. People co-operate with each other to bring about a variety of ends, from the production of high-tech products like space shuttles, to the provision of 'meals on wheels'. Individuals have to form agreements with each other. When we recognize this 'economics then becomes the study of the social mechanisms which facilitate such agreements' (Ricketts 1987: 4).

Economics is also concerned with *competition* both amongst people and between their organizations. Much traditional theory lays great emphasis on the role of competition and has a great deal to say on such matters. Moreover, economics can consider situations of *conflict* where there may well be confrontation and contention. Yet whether we focus on competition, co-operation or conflict, the economist has to observe and explain human relationships. For those with preconceived notions, economics is very much more than detailing and explaining the price of pork chops or British Gas shares.

ECONOMIC PERSPECTIVES

Economics provides different windows on the world – it takes distinctive routes and reaches the parts which no other discipline can. However, its applications and insights are of necessity limited. All disciplines by their very nature concentrate and specialize. As with other areas of study, economics presents a partial view. Moreover, it does not provide unique easy answers to highly complex problems. Economics gives vital insights and prompts important questions. It has many faces and is surprisingly versatile. Whatever the context – from family planning, the problem of AIDS, to the take-over of one company by another – economists have distinct knowledge to bring and different stories to tell. Certainly, economics has overlapping boundaries with a wide range of other disciplines, from politics and sociology to mathematics. Indeed, some claim that economics provides the bridge between the humanities and the sciences – it draws from both.

Economics facilitates an understanding of real problems which are inevitably multi-faceted. The claim for economics is not that this subject can give 'the' diagnosis or 'the' prescription, a unique solution for any particular problem. Rather, economic thinking helps us to clarify the possibilities, to identify and think systematically about problems and the alternative ways of dealing with them, to predict the outcomes of different scenarios given different starting points. Within economics there are overlapping and competing ideas and theories, for nobody has a monopoly of truth. There are always alternative explanations and it is debate which helps to make economics lively and exciting.

Economics encompasses a series of different perspectives, built on views which share some important common method or object of study. There are different schools of thought, but the dominant orthodoxy in microeconomics is known as *neo-classical*. This camp lays much store on rational maximizing individuals and relies heavily on mathematical techniques. We shall contrast this approach with other views: for economics is not a seamless web of ideas. Economics is rather like a kaleidoscope – change the position, then new perspectives on old problems are illuminated and new questions surface. The beauty is that we see things in different ways. Economists have different views and follow different lines of arguments, but they interact, stimulate and pose conundrums for each other. Different perspectives overlap and mingle – they are not always easy to pigeon-hole. Economists have many issues to debate, and distinct ideas to bring. This book aims to give the reader an awareness of that. For those who are keen to explore the nature of the different schools of thought and how they relate to each other, Mair and Miller's *A Modern Guide to Economic Thought* 1991 will prove a very useful opening. However, before you do that, we must turn to introductory ideas.

THE SCOPE AND DISTINCTIVE FEATURES OF *UNDERSTANDING ECONOMICS*

Understanding Economics is essentially concerned with the study of people and their organizations, including households, firms and markets. We are concerned with economic behaviour, whether on the domestic scene, in an individual market context, within the business firm, government organization or charity. This places the book within a *microeconomics* mould.

There is a major standard divide in economics between microeconomics and macroeconomics. *Macroeconomics*, in contrast, is concerned with the workings of an economy as a whole, dealing with broad aggregates, examining such issues as national income, output and employment, inflation (the general movements in prices) and economic growth. Macroeconomic theories provide explanations about how an economy works overall; all the components of an economy operating together as a whole.

In practice, it is not always easy or useful to draw a clear dividing line between the areas of micro- and macroeconomics. Money and investment topics, both of which fall within the sphere of macroeconomics, feature prominently in *Understanding Economics*, for they are just as important in a microeconomic context. However, this text is not intended as an all embracing traditional introductory economics reference book covering both macro- and microeconomics. No general macroeconomic models, such as those of income and employment determination, are developed here.

In contrast, we provide an introduction which emphasizes economic history and economic development, drawing attention to the way in which economies and institutions have evolved over time. Given the constraints of time and space, this inevitably means that the choice of particular examples is limited. The reader must appreciate that this is perforce a selective account.

What are the key distinguishing features of *Understanding Economics?*

Time and the different ways in which economists consider time provides the recurrent theme. Looking back through time past, incorporating an evolutionary perspective is part of that special feature. However, when people contemplate the present and the prospect of the future – time to come – considerations of *risk* and *uncertainty* are very significant. We give an explicit treatment of risk and uncertainty, introducing these notions simply and at an early stage, as basic key elements. An appreciation of the nature and significance of risk and uncertainty is useful for understanding many new theoretical developments in economics. But risk and uncertainty are especially relevant to the problems which people actually face in real-world decision-making, whatever roles they play.

With few exceptions most introductory texts have relatively little to say about time. They ignore risk and uncertainty, or essentially marginalize these topics, often subsuming uncertainty under a heading of risk, dealing with such issues in self-contained sections or chapters which can be readily omitted or overlooked. In this book time, risk and uncertainty figure as inescapable features, just as they do in life. We make clear the importance of time in different contexts. Moreover, we distinguish between risk and uncertainty, explaining how people and their organizations cope with these problems.

Following on from our treatment of time, risk and uncertainty, *institutional factors* are explicitly recognized and explained. We emphasize the importance of the evolving institutional backdrop. The economic significance of laws and customs, the so-called 'rules of the game', are underlined, for they are vital in a world of imperfect knowledge, uncertainty and the human limited ability to process information. Given these essential rules, economic actors can take some things 'as read'. Moreover, law and custom can bring solace in uncertain times.

Non-market allocation and the importance of the *internal workings* of organizations such as the household, the business firm and the charity are examined here. Indeed, whilst we recognize the importance of the business firm seeking profit, we draw attention to the amazing range of different organizations with distinct and often complex missions. The inside workings of households and their non-market relationships very rarely surface in conventional introductory treatments, where individuals and households are perceived as mere market players. The inclusion of a discussion of the economic aspects of organizations like charities which operate in non-market contexts, indeed voluntary sector groups from the 'third sector', and public sector non-trading organizations such as the National Health Service, also represents an important departure. Usually the internal workings of organizations and non-market activities are largely ignored despite their significance and interest to the economist.

HOW THE BOOK IS ORGANIZED AND AN OVERVIEW OF CONTENT

Understanding economics is divided into three parts. Part I explains basic economic concepts, and introduces the notions of *time, risk* and *uncertainty*. It provides essential ideas and analytical tools required for the rest of the book. The first three chapters particularly emphasize an evolutionary view of different economic systems, focusing on the nature of change through historical time. Chapter 2 examines scarcity and choice, introducing key concepts and analytical tools which will be used extensively in later chapters. Here we introduce different notions of time and give an insight into economic method. Chapter 3 examines the fundamental economic concepts of specialization and exchange and shows how these work, and their importance in different time contexts. The nature of uncertainty and risk are introduced at this stage, important fundamental concepts which we shall repeatedly use in later analysis. Chapter 4 introduces the reader to the vital nature of the 'rules of the game', the laws and customs necessary for any economy regardless of time and place, indispensable for coping with an uncertain world. The different types of laws relating to property are introduced. Money itself is an example of one such important rule – a convention, which has important functions and which can provide a refuge in uncertainty. Chapter 5 focuses on the nature of markets, prices and the way in which the price mechanism works to allocate and distribute resources and output. The chapter puts markets into context and uses what can be thought of as the economists' 'ideal type' market as a bench mark. Chapter 6 highlights the evolving role of the State, its integral position in the economic system and its different relationships with markets. We examine alternative possibilities for allocating and distributing resources, those non-market means where political and administrative procedures take prominence, or where gift relationships are important.

Part II focuses on the *economics of organizations*, building on and developing ideas introduced in the first part. Here we pay attention to the different ways in which economists have treated key socio-economic groupings of the household/family in Chapter 7, and the business firm in Chapters 8 and 9. Chapter 8 gives an introduction to the traditional theory of the firm, whilst Chapter 9 asks different questions, looking at the firm's internal workings and its legal structure. Non-profit organizations, whether creatures of the state, like the army or civil service, or 'third sector' private organizations, are highlighted in Chapter 10. The NHS and charities figure prominently in this discussion.

Again, the different ways of using time feature conspicuously in our explanations. And whilst in Part II we are, in the main, concerned with organizations in a late twentieth-century, industrialized context, there is still an important evolutionary view.

Part III examines economic approaches, in particular, to *investment decision-making*, where the passage of time is an essential feature and risk and uncertainty are of the essence. We emphasize that investments can be made in quite different organizational contexts and in many forms. Here the concepts of risk and uncertainty are developed in greater depth and we gain insights into the ways in which economists model such pervasive facts of life. People cannot see into the future; they lack omniscience, at once a boon and a burden.

Chapter 11 sets the scene and introduces analytical tools for dealing with the passage of time and the different methods for distinguishing between projects within a business context. Chapter 12 focuses on risk and uncertainty, examining in greater depth how economists explain these notions in different situations, and delving more extensively into the ways in which people and their organizations cope with such problems. Chapter 13 examines investment decision-making in non-commercial contexts and introduces the tool of cost benefit analysis, again examining how risk and uncertainty may be handled. Chapter 14 brings us to the question of investment in people, where we explore human capital theory and the different ways in which economists can examine investment in people.

THE LANGUAGE OF ECONOMICS AND TECHNICAL CONTENT

Before we begin it is important to note that through the process of specialization, economists use language in a specific way. Everyday words like 'costs' and 'investment' are used in subtly different ways. The economist distinguishes carefully, using precise terms in order to separate different concepts, to make these quite distinct for analysis. That can be confusing for the first time reader. Here every effort is made to explain the technical idioms, for like any other discipline, as economics has developed, so its language has become more intricate. A term which sounds difficult may reflect a simple but precise idea. Expressions have to be created to convey such ideas – customary terminology – to which only the initiated are privy. Moreover, economic language has many interesting nuances which often reflect the inclinations of authors. The reader should be aware that economics has a language which can be at once persuasive as well as technical.

Indeed, in order to explain the contribution and value of economics, and to provide the foundation for an understanding of more advanced ideas, this book must give an introduction to more than the words of economics. The majority of chapters contain, in part, an explanation of key economic techniques; they use graphs, figures and in a few cases straightforward, basic algebra. Wherever possible simple figures have been included to help the reader – not as a stumbling block. Graphical analysis and simple mathematical notation are customary mainstream tools. The important point is to understand the ideas behind the graphs and figures. Economists use these to convey ideas and help their thought processes. But they are an aid – not the be-all-and-end-all – it is an *understanding* of the ideas which ultimately matters.

2

Scarcity, choice and time

INTRODUCTION

This chapter aims to explore the nature of scarcity and choice; and to emphasize that scarcity and the range of choices available to people and society will vary over time and place. Wants and needs are, in part, culturally determined; they evolve over time. Indeed, not all economies are organized in the same way, there are different types of economic systems meeting the production and distribution problems which societies must face. The different economic systems of the present, just like those of the past, have to cope with scarcity; but they do so in distinctive ways.

From our own experience, given limited resources and time, we cannot do all the things we would like; and the same goes for society as a whole. Our concern here is to clarify the nature of the overall production constraint which confronts any society, and to explain how a society's production options can be changed over time. Key economic concepts will be explained in this chapter as a basis for what is to follow. We shall discuss time – the linchpin of our account. We shall underline the importance of different treatments of time and the ways in which economists work. The aim is ultimately to throw light on the real economic problems faced by individuals, their organizations and society.

SCARCITY, WANTS AND TIME

We have said that scarcity is the result of unlimited wants set against limited resources and time. People, regardless of the society in which they live, its historical time and place, have biological requirements for food, clothing and shelter. These necessities form the basis of a hierarchy of wants. Such basic needs have to be met before attempting to satisfy other wants. As people have larger incomes they are able to satisfy desires which were previously unattainable. Indeed, as society, its technology and the ability to produce change, wants change too.

The necessities of life are, in part, culturally determined; people do not live by bread alone. Time and place are important. Adam Smith regarded necessities as 'not only the commodities which are indispensably necessary for the support of life, but whatever the custom of the country renders it indecent for creditable people, even of the lowest order, to be without' (1776: Vol. 2 Ch. V: ii: 870). He took as one example, leather shoes, which at that time, 'custom has rendered . . . a necessary of life in England' where 'even the poorest creditable person of either sex would be ashamed to appear in publick without them' (ibid., 870). In contrast, in Scotland whilst the lowest ranks of men must have shoes, women of the same station could 'without discredit, walk about barefooted'. Similarly, in France, people of either sex could walk barefooted without disgrace. What Smith termed 'the established rules of decency' were not flouted. Rowntree, for example, tried to consider what would constitute the minimum necessities, in his surveys of poverty in York at the turn of this century and then again in 1936 and 1950; but each year the list of basic 'necessaries' grew longer. Despite its minimal nutritional value, tea, by the turn of the nineteenth century, was regarded as a necessity. Rowntree pinpointed tea as a basic requirement, even for the poorest. Without it people could not engage in essential social customs, offering tea to others. Hence they would not be 'creditable people' in Adam Smith's terms. However, in seventeenth-century Britain, tea was a luxury item consumed by the rich and kept in locked caddies to ensure its safe keeping, for it was highly prized amongst the servants too. Over time the luxury purchase of the relatively few became the necessity of the many.

Additional examples are not hard to come by – the car, once the status symbol of the rich, in Britain, now could be regarded as the necessity of the rural poor. The colour television and washing machine, once rare, are commonplace, basic wants, even for those on relatively low incomes. Ninety-one per cent of all the households in Britain have colour televisions (Government Statistical Office 1991), and even in the lowest paid group, unskilled workers, 90 per cent have colour televisions, and 83 per cent have washing machines.[1] Also, our wants for services, once impossible to supply, quickly grow – whether for foetal monitoring, organ transplants or fax facilities. The success of human organ transplants, now a commonplace medical procedure, in Britain, depends in part on people's gifts. The nature of gift giving will be discussed in greater detail in Chapter 6. However, given the dramatic increase in transplants and the increasing lengths of waiting lists for such operations, we can see that the call for these procedures is growing over time.

The hierarchy of wants dictates a ranking of goods and services, at any time, in terms of the 'satisfaction', 'happiness' or 'utility' they provide. People have similar wants, but may rank items differently. Many women, for example, in modern economies might place a high ranking for child-care facilities, or pre-cooked foods.

People follow different lifestyles. But whatever the society, no matter how affluent, there will be some who are disappointed; for as a result of scarcity, all wants cannot be met. Looking backwards through time, *survival* has always been the essential concern of the majority of the world's population. Scarcity did not manifest itself in a choice between the purchase of a new car or a foreign holiday, extra leisure time or more consumer goods, the options of the relatively rich in historical terms. Enough food, shelter and clothing to keep alive, given the vagaries of the natural elements, disease and political upheavals, was as much as many could hope for. Choice for the vast majority on a personal level was minimal. Both now and in the past many societies have been unable to provide the basic necessities, for appreciable numbers, and a short life expectancy was and is, the norm for many. Despite sophisticated technological advances of the twentieth century, affluence is still relatively limited on the global stage and even in the richest nations there are many who in terms of their consumption possibilities, fall below the poverty line. Women and children figure prominently in the ranks of the poor, whether in the Third World or in relatively rich countries such as Britain.

ALTERNATIVE ECONOMIC SYSTEMS

As a result of scarcity, decisions have to be made about the following problems:

1 What goods and services to produce, i.e., which wants to satisfy?
2 How to produce such output?
3 How to distribute the output, i.e., whose wants to meet?

Whatever the historical setting, societies as widely different in their socio-economic and political structures as ancient Egypt, tenth-century Britain, or late twentieth-century Russia have to make such allocative choices. Different methods have been used for addressing the questions of production and distribution: what, how and for whom? Although we shall have much to say about late twentieth-century modern industrialized *market* economies, it is important to note that not all economies are or were organized on the same lines. It is usual to classify economies into different types, according to the predominant way in which they deal with the economic problem. Economies can be categorized as: traditional, market or planned economies.

Looking backwards through time, in *traditional* pre-industrial societies, production and distribution decisions were based on procedures evolved through a long course of trial and error. The procedures were maintained rigidly by the sanctions of law, custom and belief. The bulk of the population worked on the land meeting most of their own needs, as typified by peasant agriculture. Markets did exist, but these were places where people came together to buy and sell a relatively restricted range of products; where goods and services were either swapped or exchanged for money. However, they were not the modern sophisticated markets of today, those which we shall examine in later chapters. Relatively few of society's resources were allocated by markets. Most people produced for their own needs, they did not supply their labour for money wages in labour markets.

Elements of planning or command, the central direction of resources by government, did exist. Ancient Egypt provides an interesting example of an economy with a traditional base, but where the Pharaohs ensured resources were directed into 'public' works. Pyramids, and other amazing engineering feats were accomplished with the central direction of slave labour. Resources were thus set aside for consumption, by the Pharaohs, for their afterlife; diverted from alternative uses. Indeed, central direction ensured the construction of road systems, public buildings and fortifications in ancient empires, all very different in time and place. Whether we consider the ancient empires of China, Rome or of the Incas, all displayed remarkable public works.

India under the caste system, or feudal Britain, would have had different, but essentially traditional solutions to the economic problem. Under the caste system, rigidly stratified, there was very little labour mobility, certainly between castes. Fathers were followed by sons into the same occupation and the role of women was heavily circumscribed by custom, practice and religious belief. In feudal Britain labour was tied to the land, which was largely owned by the church, king and nobility. Although monasteries were often relatively large-scale planning units, 'corporate' bureaucratic administrative structures making important allocative decisions, there was no emphasis on rapid economic change. The traditional solutions to questions of production and distribution gave static results, with relatively little development over time.

Contemporary Third World economies, like Zambia, Kenya and Bolivia, with relatively small market enclaves, still function on a traditional basis. And in the Third World today, custom and tradition ensure that the general pattern of economic life goes on in much the same way as in the past for the bulk of the population.

The *market* economy in contrast uses the market mechanism to find solutions to questions of production and distribution. In Britain, for example, the Industrial Revolution, the move from an agrarian to an industrial society, came about in an economy which had private ownership of resources, and a growing reliance on the workings of supply and demand – the market mechanism. Here the activities of a large number of individuals and organizations, such as private business firms, acted in response to price changes in the market. The market mechanism co-ordinates the factors of production, and prices provide the market signals. Today in market economies, apparently unco-ordinated activities of individuals and firms are reconciled by Adam Smith's 'hidden hand' – the adjustment of prices in a wide range of markets. Self-interest and profit provide the incentives which are usually emphasized in much economic theory. Economies based on private ownership of resources and the workings of markets, include the USA, West Germany, Hong Kong, Britain, Australia and Japan. All of these countries use the market in different degrees, Hong Kong and the USA might be thought of as the archetypal market economies, with large proportions of their resources allocated by markets. The implication of privatization policies – the sale of state-owned assets, such as the sale of council housing or the gas industry, reflect the increased use of the market mechanism in Britain. But we shall have more to say on this issue in later chapters.

However, in practice, many vital elements of planning exist in market economies, with allocative decisions being made by governments and, for example, within business firms. Governments affect production and distribution decisions, through a variety of means, whether, for example, by taxation and expenditure or by regulation of the competitive process. Whether through social security or welfare payments, by taxation on income or expenditure, the provision of goods and services such as defence or the judiciary, governments play a vital part in the economic system. Indeed, governments in any economy have an important role to play in setting 'the rules of the game', the laws and regulatory framework of an economic system. At the same time, the giant corporation, the huge bureaucratic firm often straddling many national boundaries, depends on its internal planning mechanism.

Elements of tradition, custom and practice from the past are still important in allocative decisions. Whether in the workings of markets, or in the internal arrangements of organizations like households and firms, custom and convention have an important role to play. We shall explore the vital 'rules of the game' in Chapter 3, to see how they affect economic behaviour.

The *planned* or *command* economy, in contrast, does not rely on the workings of markets to solve the economic problem. It may have a central planning unit to decide on production and distribution targets. Economic effort is directed towards goals administratively chosen by the State. In the USSR planning was intended to bring about rapid economic development and equality; to industrialize an essentially traditional economy. Resources were directed into the mechanization of agriculture, investment in heavy industry, the military and, latterly, into space research. Although there is a limited use of the market in any planned economy, major decisions about what and how to produce, and for whom, are made administratively.

The command mechanism can be a powerful force for change, but the central planners, despite much power, have an enormous task, particularly as the range of possibilities for production grow. As people want a greater choice of consumer goods, and the economy develops, relying less on heavy industry where outputs can be easily specified, difficulties in setting and meeting planning targets increase. *Perestroika* in the Soviet Union resulted, in part, from the inability of the economy to provide for a rapid growth in the standard of living of the people, hence the move towards a greater use of the market mechanism. State ownership of non-human resources, and central direction have given way to a greater acceptance of private ownership and the use of the price mechanism, to allocate scarce resources and goods. Indeed, the break up of the USSR and the reunification of Germany underline the desire for fundamental economic change.

There are different 'brands' of planning. In Albania, for example, the economy was, and still is, relatively highly centralized, the archetypical command economy. In China there has been a less centralized approach, with resources communally owned.

However, throughout the planned economies there is now a move to make greater use of markets. The stark gap in economic performance between the economies of East and West Germany before and after reunification, bear witness to some of the difficulties of central planning. The movement towards an economy on West German lines, whilst bringing a greater range of consumer goods for some, also brings unemployment, a price that is paid as outdated East German productive power and organization meets competition from the West.

The privatization of East German, state-owned firms involves the encouragement of foreign investors to make acquisitions of such companies. Poland has had no stock exchange since the Second World War, but in the early 1990s reinstated trading in the shares of companies, previously owned by the state. The move from the state to private ownership, whether in Germany, Poland or Albania, and the use of market incentives for allocating and co-ordinating resources, reflect the effort to improve economic performance and, particularly, to provide for growing consumer aspirations. However, as time unfolds, it becomes clear that drastic changes do not deliver western production and consumption patterns over night. Economic growth is not so easily engineered. There are no simple blueprints.

Emphasis must be placed on the concept of the *mixed economy* where a combination of different responses are used to tackle the economic problem; where elements of planning and tradition combine with the market to provide solutions to the problems of choice and constraints. *All societies are unique in time and place.* All but the most basic of economic systems are mixed, where Adam Smith's 'hidden hand' of market forces works alongside government – elements of central direction, and traditional rules and procedures. The actual combination of these factors and how they have evolved over time, varies between nations. But in practice, any society has complex sets of interwoven relationships between people and a wide variety of organizations, including markets – *the economic system.*

We shall have much more to say about the role of markets, laws, custom, convention and planning in subsequent chapters. But now we turn to the important economic concepts of production constraints and choice to show how economists often display basic ideas.

THE PRODUCTION CONSTRAINT: PRODUCTION CHOICES

Although there are different ways to tackle the economic problem – scarcity – all societies face a production constraint. In order to explore and clarify the nature of that constraint and to show how it might be changed through time – increasing the range of production choices – we must first examine the inputs of the production process, *the factors of production.* Both the quantity and quality of such resources must be considered. These inputs, which are used to produce outputs are usually divided into three broad categories: land, capital and labour.

Land This has a much wider meaning than is normal in everyday speech. The economist uses land to refer to gifts of the environment, which include not simply farmland or the industrial site, but minerals underground, resources like North Sea oil and natural gas, even fish stocks in the sea. Such resources can be separated into those which are renewable and those which are not; mineral reserves can be mined once only, oil supplies cannot be recreated, given current technical 'know-how'. Contrast these with water which may flow continuously for the generation of hydroelectric power. Conservationists, in particular, draw attention to the depletion and destruction of natural resources, which often comes hand-in-hand with economic growth.

Capital   This is the produced means of production and refers to such items as plant and equipment, factories, warehouses, or the infrastructure which includes, for example, roads, schools and hospitals. Capital embodies a particular level of technical 'know-how'; for example, in British industry, some capital equipment is at least fifty years old, acquired from Germany at the end of the war. Clearly, this embodies a very different technology from that of sophisticated computerized equipment of the 'best practice' plant, just brought into production. In some countries the range of technical 'know-how' embodied in capital is very wide. In parts of the developing world in agriculture, for example, late twentieth-century equipment is used on highly mechanized farms; others employ ploughs and oxen, techniques largely unaltered for centuries.

The term capital is another example of the economist using language in a technical way, one which is different from common usage. Capital is a factor required as a physical input in the production process; to be clearly distinguished from financial capital – pieces of paper such as ordinary shares in Marks and Spencer or British Telecom, which promise future dividend payments and a potential selling price; or Local Authority Bonds, and Government Gilt edged securities, which give entitlements to receive future interest payments and a redemption value, the amount paid when this loan to the government or a local authority is paid back. Subsequent chapters will give a greater understanding of such financial assets. *Real capital* goods produce for wants indirectly, for who wants to consume a lathe or fork lift truck, or live in a warehouse? Physical capital is used to help produce output for final consumption, in these examples: to manufacture, move and store goods. Resources have to be set aside from current consumption to make capital goods, i.e., physical investment; time has to pass before goods for final consumption are made.

Labour   This is the human resource, the people who use the land and capital to produce output. Labour can embody very different physical and mental talents, reflecting differences in innate abilities and, more importantly, large variations in the type and levels of education and training -- investments in *human capital*. The labour resource is often divided into broad categories: unskilled, semi-skilled, skilled, professional and managerial, depending on training levels and function. There are different types of labour, from the highly trained engineer, quantity surveyor, accountant to the manual labourer or machine operative. In modern Britain there are new training needs, for example, old heavy industries of iron and steel have declined and the leisure industry and financial services make new demands for investment in people. And unlike capital in the production process, labour can provide services to satisfy wants directly. The doctor and the hairdresser do that, although now, often with the aid of sophisticated equipment.

The managerial function is vital, although as we shall see there are inequalities of access to many different jobs, including those in management. Class, gender and race have an important part to play. Women and those from some minority groups, for example, often have less education and training than their counterparts. In many communities worldwide, for example, girls rarely go to school, and so women have higher illiteracy rates than men. Even in western economies, like Britain, women receive less higher education and employment training than their male counterparts. Ethnic minority groups face discrimination and class is still an important element in explaining inequalities in access to education and health care. Custom and convention and inequalities of income and wealth still play an important part in the differential demand for education. Tradition and differential market earnings still ensure that women provide the majority of domestic work within the household, although changing labour market opportunities and attitudes have brought about some modifications on the domestic scene (Chapters 6 and 14).

Entrepreneurs   These are usually singled out from the factor 'labour', for special emphasis. Particularly in the market economy, these are the people who organize and co-ordinate the other factors, take risks and innovate new ideas and make new investments in products, machinery and people. They are alert to gaps in the market for new products and processes and take advantage of new opportunities. The entrepreneur has the energy and foresight to overcome individual and institutional resistance to change. Their ultimate goal is usually seen as one of self-interest. In Britain, for example, Alan Sugar, the founder of Amstrad, brought together a high-powered technical and marketing team to look for niches in the consumer market and to develop new products, like home computers, satellite dishes and user-friendly video recorders. Anita Roddick who founded Body Shop, seized an opportunity to fill a market need with cosmetic products not tested on animals, and made with natural products. She stands out as an example, for there are relatively few women entrepreneurs in the business world.

Entrepreneurs have to base their decisions on limited information about the present and the future. They face uncertainty by going into uncharted fields where there is no previous experience. They are not always successful – but they provide a key driving force within the economy. Indeed, 'entrepreneurial' type talents of innovation, organizational skills and energy may be needed in a variety of contexts in the mixed economy, including the setting up of new charities, spotting areas of particular need, as yet not met by other organizations, inadequately catered for by the market or government agencies. Here the goal could be that of 'creative altruism', a concept used by Richard Titmuss (1970). A small group of individuals set up the Terence Higgins Trust with 'entrepreneurial' type talent, to help AIDS sufferers. People with foresight, determination, organizational and managerial skills have set up many voluntary groups. The Fawcett Society is an example of a women's organization, a charity for women's equality with men. Private charity often works alongside government agencies and sometimes mobilizes resources very rapidly. The Romanian Orphans Fund became one of Britain's most successful fund raisers in a very short time (The Charities Aid Foundation 1992). In Chapter 10, we shall emphasize the wide range of non-profit organizations, and, indeed, how government may augment or set up private charitable organizations and their links with households and business firms.

In summary, all of the factors of production are combined together to produce output, the goods and services which give satisfaction to people. At any time the resources may differ in terms of both quantity and quality. The level of technology – the range of technical 'know-how' in the community – is of great importance. The automated factory will give a far greater productivity, as measured by output per person per hour, than people using nineteenth-century technology. But in addition, the social, political and legal institutions, the custom and practice in society are highly significant; for they determine, in part, how the inputs will be brought together and hence the nature of the overall production constraint facing society. As we shall argue in Chapter 4, these laws and customs provide the necessary 'rules of the game', whatever the nature of human society. Changes in the society's political and social structure can herald important changes in the ability to produce; they move in a symbiotic pattern.

Time   Last but not least, time is a vital limited resource, a necessity in the production process; an indispensable component in all human activity. Whilst we shall have much more to say on the subject of time, given these basic concepts, we are now in a position to explain a useful economic abstraction. This initial simplification is one which we shall use in a variety of different contexts.

The production function

Clearly, any economic system is very complex. Economists use simplifications to express ideas and relationships, such as 'shorthand notation' in algebraic form. One example of such functional notation is given as:

$$Q = f(L,N,K,T) \tag{2.1}$$

Where Q is simply the total quantity of all goods available to a hypothetical society in a particular year, f means depends on, and L, N and T respectively, represent land, labour and technology.

The equation simply says that the amount of output available in a particular year depends on the land, labour and capital available, embodying the technology given in that particular time period. The *f* sign or *function* is simply a mathematical convention which tells us that there exists a *systematic relationship* between inputs and outputs. But it has only been specified in general terms not in a precise way. It is an abstraction from reality. We shall see that if we change one of the inputs, holding everything else constant (*ceteris paribus*) then a change occurs on the other side of the equation too. For example, an increase in the quantity of capital could increase output, other things being equal.

The *Production Possibility Curve* gives a simplified snapshot view of the range of production options, or choices open to a society. It shows the best possible output combinations that can be achieved, given a society's limited resources. Anywhere on the curve all resources are used fully and efficiently. The production possibility curve marks the boundary between what is possible and what is not. To derive this curve, imagine that we have full information – perfect knowledge of the qualities and quantities of the resources available at any time, and the different ways in which these can be combined to give various production outcomes. In a modern economy, there is an enormous range of outputs – both for final consumption and intermediate capital goods. So, for simplicity, assume only two goods, margarine and missiles, to symbolize the basic needs for food and security, or private consumption versus defence. (In a health conscious age, margarine is no longer an inferior substitute for butter.) The data for an imaginary economy is summarized in Table 2.1. Moreover, as we have only two dimensions, to illustrate graphically, in a stylized picture form, this additional simplification is necessary. Now it is possible to illustrate a production possibility curve, as shown in Figure 2.1 the 'picture' which sets out the society's production constraint, at *a point in time*. Missiles are measured on the vertical axis and margarine is measured on the horizontal axis both in straightforward units to keep the exposition simple (a unit of missiles could represent a million missiles, a unit of margarine, a million tonnes).

Take the extreme position where all resources are used in missile production. In Figure 2.1, point P, on the vertical axis, marks the maximum achievable output of missiles, 5 units with zero margarine production. At the other extreme point T, on the horizontal axis, all resources would be utilized for margarine production, 6 units in total coupled with a zero missile production. Given an initial starting point at P, some resources could be switched from missile to margarine production, enough to

Table 2.1   Missile and margarine production: increasing costs

Missiles Output (millions)	Margarine Output (million tonnes)	Change in Missile Output
5	0	—
4	2.5	2.5
3	4.0	1.5
2	5.0	1.0
1	5.75	0.75
0	6.0	0.25

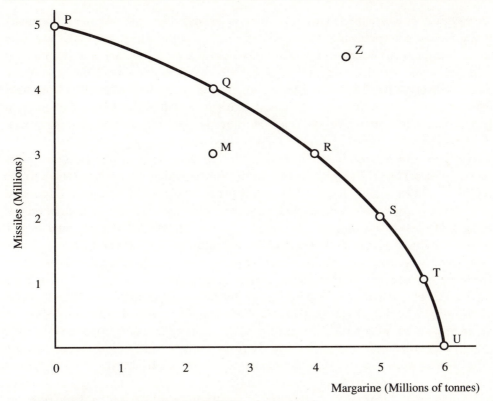

Figure 2.1   A production possibility curve (ppc)

give the combination of output at point Q on the production possibility curve. At this point a total of 4 units of missiles and 2.5 units of margarine would be produced. Points R, S and T represent different output combinations and each implies a different resource combination. Resources are progressively moved into margarine production as we move along the curve from point P towards point U, where all the resources are used in margarine production. The combinations of output are given in Table 2.1. Any point on the boundary shows combinations of output where all of society's resources are used to their best. Note that more margarine output can only be achieved at the 'expense' of missile production, or vice versa.

Opportunity Cost tells us the cost of one item in terms of the best alternative foregone. Given that the economy is at point P in Figure 2.1, a hypothetical extreme, on the boundary, in order to increase margarine output – moving society to point Q, then resources have to be switched from making missiles. Weaponry has to be reduced. The missiles foregone represent the opportunity cost, the sacrifice that society makes for additional margarine output. We are costing margarine output gained in terms of missile output lost. One unit of missiles is relinquished for 2.5 units of margarine. Therefore, the cost of 1 additional unit of margarine is only 0.4 missile units. Note that here cost is measured in physical units, not in money terms.

Opportunity cost is a key concept in economics and one which we shall use many times – a concept applicable in a variety of contexts. Opportunity cost does not have to be expressed in money terms. The opportunity cost of reading this chapter, for example, could be identified as the best alternative use for your time and effort. There will of course be many alternatives, but it is the best alternative sacrificed which gives opportunity cost. The best alternative will be different for different people, and hence subjective. We shall return to the opportunity cost concept in later chapters.

Increasing Opportunity Costs are depicted by the slope of the production possibility curve, as displayed in Figure 2.1. The production possibility curve is concave to the origin, an outward bow shape. It illustrates the principle that if the society proceeds to switch resources from missiles into margarine production, every additional unit of margarine costs more in terms of missile output foregone. For each time missile output is reduced by one unit, when additional resources are switched into margarine production, smaller increases in extra margarine output are achieved. There is an *increasing opportunity cost* of missiles in terms of margarine.

This can be illustrated with a simple arithmetic example using the data in Table 2.1. We have seen that the first one million missiles sacrificed, enabled society to move to point Q, with a total production of 2.5 units of margarine. On average each unit of margarine costs 0.4 units. A move from point Q to R adds an additional 1.5 units to margarine output and reduces missile production by 1 unit. Total output of margarine now stands at 4 units, total output of missiles is 3 units. Effectively, each additional unit of margarine in this case, costs 0.666 missile units, an increase in the opportunity cost at the margin. A move to point S, by transferring additional resources, giving up an equal amount of missiles once more – a further one unit of missiles, this time increases margarine output by only 1 unit. To achieve this change, the cost of the margarine is exactly 1 unit of missiles. The move from point S to T gives an increase of only 0.75 of a unit of margarine, thus for a 1 unit in missile output here, the cost of margarine is 1.33 units. The final move to point U on Figure 2.1 switches all the remaining resources into margarine production. This gives only a relatively tiny increment in margarine of 0.25 units and leaves us with no missile production. The cost of the last unit of margarine is effectively 4 units of missiles. The process can be put in reverse, starting from Point U. You will find that the opportunity cost of expanding missile production, switching resources back into missiles, increases.

This increasing opportunity cost is a reflection of the specialized characteristics of the resources employed. They are not assumed to be completely adaptable to margarine or missile production – not perfectly transferable, not equally productive in each use. The increasing costs reflect the fact that workers manufacturing missiles would be highly trained and specialized and could not easily or immediately transfer their skills to margarine production. Some production would be lost as resources are transferred from what they produce relatively well, to what they do relatively badly. As society switches less suitable resources into margarine production they are less productive at the margin. Also, each type of output would utilize resources in different combination, for example, margarine production would require the greater use of land. As extra resources are transferred to margarine production, at a point like T to move society to U, this would add very little additional margarine output. As shown on the diagram, the cost in terms of missiles foregone would be high, for only a small additional increase in margarine production would be gained by transferring the final remaining resources from missile manufacture. Each time society forgoes an equal number of missiles the size of the gain in margarine output is smaller. You can put this process into reverse, beginning at point U, giving up equal units of margarine production, each additional increase in missile output will be smaller than the last.

So the production possibility curve reflects the way society 'trades-off' or transforms output from missiles to margarine and vice versa. The rate of transformation is not constant but changes. The smooth curve tells us that infinitesimally small changes, *marginal* changes in output combinations can be achieved, by making infinitesimally small changes in the inputs between the two outputs. There is no 'lumpiness' in the production process, that is, no large minimum amounts of capital required, for example, in the manufacture of either output. Theoretically, infinitesimally small changes in all resources can be made, clearly, this is, in reality, not possible.

Efficiency means the most output for given inputs, i.e., using resources to their best. It can only be defined with reference to the state of knowledge. The production possibility curve is useful for illustrating this concept. Production efficiency is achieved at any point on the boundary. At points R or S, for example, no possible rearrangement of inputs could produce more missiles without forgoing some margarine – or vice versa. Points inside the curve represent *inefficient* but *feasible* combinations of goods, within society's capacity to produce. Beyond the boundary lie currently unattainable options, such as point Z – combinations of goods as yet inaccessible because of limited resources and technological 'know-how'. A community producing an output combination such as M, inside the constraint, operates inefficiently. Here resources are either used ineffectively, that is underemployed or wasted by being left idle – unemployed. At point M, it could be that the skills of some people are underutilized as a result of discrimination either because of sex, race or age. In world trade downturns, during a recession, unemployment would be the cause of wasted resources. Some readily identified groups in society will suffer more frequently and for a longer duration than others. For certain categories of workers, like older workers, a bout of unemployment can herald the end of employment in the formal paid sector, with the loss of human skills that this entails. If people are unemployed in the long term their human capital may decline as they gradually lose their confidence and skills; the production possibility curve shifts inwards, to the left, as a result.

Society operates inefficiently because it could increase output of one or both goods, and move to a position on the boundary, from a point like M. All the slack in the economy could be used to increase margarine output for example, with no reduction in missile production, or vice versa. Alternatively, formerly idle/under-utilized resources could be divided between the two, giving more missiles and margarine. Society, by using the resources to their full, and efficiently, would move to the boundary.

The production possibility curve says nothing about the desirability of the various options. Different societies may choose different combinations of output. A society keen on defence (or attack) could be shown at a position where resources were used mostly for missiles at the expense of margarine. Some might make the value judgement that a society that was inefficient, operating inside the boundary, with most resources devoted to margarine production, and a minimum resource input into weaponry, is preferable to one that was efficient, operating on the boundary, but using the bulk of its resources for missiles, as at point Q. The achievement of efficiency does not necessarily imply an equality of income distribution within the society. Given income equality as a goal, a society which achieves a boundary position, only with an unequal distribution of income, faces a clash of objectives.

PRODUCTION POSSIBILITY CURVES: FURTHER APPLICATIONS

The production possibility curve can be used to show the 'trade-off' between two goods, but it can also illustrate the choices available between outputs from two sectors of the economy, for example, industrial and service sector output, the public and private sectors or education and health care. The concept of the production possibility curve can be used to illustrate the options available in many diverse settings. We shall use this as a theoretical underpinning in following chapters, for example, in our explanations of the rationale for modern investment criteria. However, initially we can use the analysis to illustrate different scenarios, where we build-in additional constraints.

Closing options

A production possibility boundary can be drawn to illustrate the 'trade-off' between industrial and service sector output. The range of choice open to a society could then be limited, by imposing a minimum level of industrial production in one year, to Ob units on Figure 2.2. This could be a necessary requirement, to make capital goods, to meet depreciation – the wearing out of capital equipment. Without this provision productive potential would decline over time as capital was depleted, if the society located between A and B. This allowance for depreciation closes off some options by setting a minimum target for industrial output. At the same time, the range of choice could be further constrained by arguing that a community has to provide a minimum level of services for education to maintain human capital. The area over which society can choose to locate is now restricted.

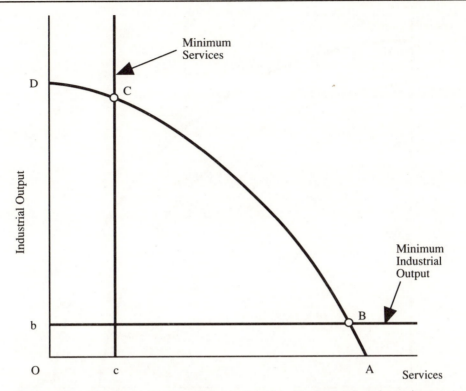

Figure 2.2 Closing options: minimum levels of industrial and service sector output required to maintain physical and human capital. Without these minimum levels the ppc would shrink. Choices in future would decline, *ceteris paribus*

Moving constraints: growth and decline

The production constraint facing society could be tightened, in other words, the boundary shifted inwards as shown in Figure 2.3 by a failure to replace worn out capital, and maintain education levels. Failure to make good and maintain the levels of human as well as non-human resources would lead to a leftward shift in the boundary. There would be economic decline, *ceteris paribus*. Choices in the future would be reduced. However, by ensuring worn out capital was replaced, and increasing the amount of capital equipment, over and above that previously available, and at the same time ensuring not only the maintenance of human capital but also increasing education and training expenditure, economic growth could also be achieved. This means an improvement in the range of options open to society over time; an expansion of productive capacity, as shown in Figure 2.4. Now if all resources were used in either sector, a larger output could be achieved. This is shown as a shift in the whole curve to the right as in the production possibility curve in Figure 2.4.

Indeed, changing the quantity and/or quality of the inputs would affect the position of the frontier. Long-term increases in population, raising work hours, the

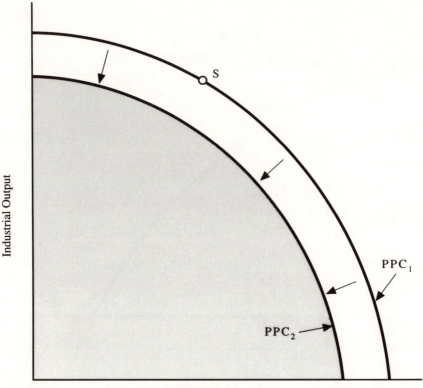

Figure 2.3 Economic decline: the production possibility curve PPC₁ shifts to the left. Given the new PPC₂ combinations of goods and services such as S are no longer available

use of more and better capital equipment – embodying new technology and the development of human resources – through education and training, all could achieve this end. Indeed, increasing the inputs would shift the production possibility curve to the right – improving society's productive capacity and the options open. Technological change and new capital equipment are important sources of growth, but so too are investments in the skills and talents of people.

Economic decline in absolute terms, represented by a shift of the boundary inwards would happen if depreciation were not covered or if resources were destroyed by war. Some African countries currently facing famine, and, for example, Iraq and Kuwait, Serbia and Croatia, and Rwanda face reduced production possibilities as a result of war. Also, if non-renewable resources were depleted and technological changes were insufficient to compensate for this, or climatic changes brought drought, the constraint would tighten. Indeed, in economies where AIDS is reducing the young productive labour supply, then production possibility curves will shrink; shift to the left. This is particularly alarming in Africa, where many countries are already beset

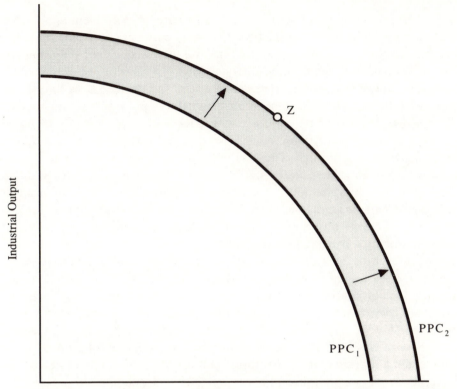

Figure 2.4   Economic growth: The production possibility curve shifts to the right from PPC$_1$ to PPC$_2$. Combinations of goods and services previously unobtainable such as Z are now available

by serious economic difficulties. Here AIDS has equally affected women and men. Not only is there a possibility of transmission to babies, affecting future labour supplies, but also it impairs the multi roles of women – as carers for children, the elderly and the sick, and as producers of food (Garcia Moreno 1989). In Uganda, for example, the most productive group in the community between the ages of 15 and 40 have been severely affected, with as many as one-fifth of this age range in some communities affected by HIV. Income has fallen, there are at times insufficient people to harvest crops and families affected by the disease are less capable of sending their children to school. This will have long-run implications. 'On a national scale, the cumulative costs of AIDS to Uganda will soon be 12 per cent of its GDP [Gross Domestic Product]', Bellos (1994).[2]

TIME AND METHOD

Now we have explained a standard economic model, it is useful to distinguish explicitly between different concepts of time. This will help us to see how economists work, and give an insight into the benefits and limitations of different approaches in general, and the value of the production possibility curve in particular. Initially, we can begin with the notions of '*analytical*' time and '*perspective*' time (Winston 1988). 'Time orders events.' Analytical time abstracts from experiencing events, it enables us to pull events out of time, so that patterns of causes and consequences can be found. All the points on the production possibility boundary, and inside it, are simultaneously available. We have been able to move backwards and forwards to different points without changing anything which could occur afterwards. We simply take up a series of *hypothetical* positions. This method enables us to play the role of an all-seeing God, to stand aside from events, with *full information* about all the different possibilities before, now and after. The production possibility curve is an example of a traditional economic model, set in analytical time, with known inputs, outputs and technologies, where we always know the best options for combining resources – given complete information in a hypothetical mode.[3]

In perspective time, we see events as people experience them. Events have occurred in the past, they occur in the present or are expected to happen in the future. Individuals cannot control events fully. People and their organizations attempt to modify their environment; but whether through advertising, taking over a rival business firm, buying insurance or getting married, people cannot recreate the past or completely map out the future. In reality, only one option can be taken and this decision could have ramifications for future choices. When we think of people acting in perspective time, we are thinking about the time of decision, when people have to make choices on the basis of limited and sometimes ill-digested information.

It would not be possible to give an exact production boundary for Britain, Bangladesh or Hong Kong. In perspective time information about the present is imperfect. To search for the mass of information required to approximate a multi-dimensional production possibility curve for any economy would be very expensive – even given modern computing facilities. Our models could not exactly replicate reality. The cost would be immense in terms of resources, including the time required to generate the data. Certain individuals or groups might wish to deceive the information collectors, fearing they were business rivals or from the Inland Revenue. Even with the aid of computers, the human limitations in our understanding and processing capacity would give us imperfect information. Yet even more telling – the future is unknowable – for it is yet to happen. No amount of time, effort and money spent on searching for information, would enable us to predict the future with certainty.

By using analytical time and abstracting from the horrendous real-world complexity, with a production possibility boundary, we can think about the essential features of a production constraint and the choices available. It enables us to juxtapose different situations and analyse. It helps to clarify concepts such as opportunity cost and economic growth. Like a map, it picks out the salient features. But it is not intended to be an exact replica of reality, if it were so, it would be as confusing as reality; and so useless.

However, as we move to situations of greater realism and complexity, we shall assess the ways in which people and their organizations try to cope with the problems of imperfect information about the present and the unknowable future. The simple model developed here has given a clear picture of the choices available now and in the next periods, based on different assumptions. It is easy with analytical omniscience or the advantage of hindsight to say how people and society should have behaved in various circumstances. The problem, which we should not forget, is that all of us make decisions in perspective time. We shall continue to use the notion of analytical time throughout the book, as we explain, for example, the workings of markets, and the behaviour of firms and households. These two distinct time modes help to explain the different perspectives which economists can bring.

However, time passes and economies evolve. It is important to have a view of how economies have changed in *historical time.*[4] Pictures of the past may well shed light on the present and help us to consider the future. In what is to follow we shall focus attention on the way people and their organizations have *changed* over the passage of time; this gives us a very valuable dimension for understanding economics.

SCARCITY, CHOICE AND TIME – SUMMARY

- Scarcity faces societies where wants and needs outstrip limited resources, including time.
- Wants and needs evolve over time; they are, in part, culturally determined.
- There is a hierarchy of wants – a ranking of goods and services. People rank items differently.
- Survival has been the essential concern of the majority of the world's population.
- All societies have to answer questions about production and distribution. Alternative economic systems provide answers to these questions.
- Economies can be categorized into traditional, planned or market economies – although in reality all economies are mixed. There are no pure types. All have interwoven socio-economic and political relationships. Societies are unique in time and place.
- The production constraint facing any society depends on the factors of production, the level of technology and the way in which they are combined together – the rules of the game.
- Time is a vital component of all economic activity.
- The production possibility curve gives a graphical representation of the production function and a range of output choices. It can be used to illustrate the important concepts of opportunity cost, efficiency and inefficiency.
- With the production possibility curve we can illustrate economic growth

and decline and how options can change when we add further limitations on choice.

- Time has a key relevance in economics, economists use different concepts of time – they look at time in different ways. Analytical time is used in hypothetical models. Perspective time is the time of decision, where people have limited knowledge and understanding. Historical time gives us the time of the past.

SCARCITY, CHOICE AND TIME – QUESTIONS FOR DISCUSSION

1 Draw a production possibility curve to illustrate the trade-off between education and health care services. Ensure that this displays increasing costs. Analyse the following changes explaining whether or not they imply a change in the position of or a movement along the boundary or a movement from within the boundary.

   a) the early retirement of a significant number of teachers;
   b) new technology, including laser surgery, as applied to health care;
   c) unemployed workers in both sectors are re-employed;
   d) new schools are built;
   e) switching resources from education to health care;
   f) an increased number of doctors and medical workers are trained.

2 Despite improvements in health care technology, an economy's health care output remains static – although educational services have expanded. Some medical commentators argue that technological break throughs in health care have been wasted. Do you agree? Use the production possibility curve from question 1 to illustrate your answer. Make your assumptions clear.

3 'It is impossible to draw a production possibility curve which exactly matches the reality of an actual situation, but that does not render it useless.' Discuss.

4 'The problem for some poorer countries is that they cannot provide the basic necessities to feed the population, never mind about putting resources into physical capital and human investment.'

   What might this signify for the position of the production possibility curve? Will the production possibility curve stay in the same position, shift to the left or to the right? By what means might the situation be changed for the better? Can you provide examples of real economies which might fall into this category?

5 Given the concept of scarcity and opportunity cost, explain and comment on the following statements:

   I work for a voluntary group for nothing, after all my time is free.

   Woman voluntary worker

   Accident and emergency services are costless in Britain.

   Tourist

AIDS is a problem for those who do not practice safe sex or have contaminated blood transfusions – it will not affect me.

Senior citizen

I use my free time for studying.

Part-time mature student

6 'Opportunity cost, like beauty, is dependent on the view of the beholder.' Discuss.
7 What can be said if a position of efficiency on the production boundary is associated with a very unequal distribution of income and wealth? What can be said if a more equal distribution of wealth and income coincides with superior economic growth?
8 What do you understand by the concepts of:

a) analytical time;
b) perspective time;
c) historical time?

Why are they important and how can they help you to understand economics? Answer now and come back to this question after you have read the book.

3

Specialization, exchange and uncertainty

INTRODUCTION

This chapter is concerned with one of the most important discoveries in economics. Whatever the context, whether we focus our attention on individuals, regions or nations, we can show that more can be achieved by specializing and co-ordinating activity with others than by operating independently. Within modern economies people are clearly not self-sufficient, producing everything they need. We make and consume a myriad of different products and services. We are certainly not the Robinson Crusoe of conventional introductory analysis. For any individual to follow a policy of splendid self-sufficient isolation would be, for the most part, impossible and certainly inefficient. By and large, the same argument goes for regions and nation states too. Indeed, specialization – the concentration of time, effort and resources into a particular task – is not just a feature of modern life in rich economies. Specialization and the co-operation that this requires has always played an important role in human activity.

Given this starting point, we develop the basic theoretical rationale for both specialization and voluntary exchange. Ultimately, specialization requires exchange to take place because, as we shall see, this is how people are able to reap the benefits of their concentrated work. With the help of a simple model we can begin to explore in what circumstances and on what terms exchange or trade will take place. As we move from the analytical time mode of the basic model, we can begin to analyse the costs that specialization and exchange may impose. Indeed, an understanding of the benefits and costs of specialization and exchange provides some of the fundamental concepts required to explain the workings of organizations like households, firms and markets, themes to be developed further in later chapters. Moreover, we can look back through historical time to give a view of the changing nature, extent and intensity of specialization, co-operation and exchange; an insight into the process of economic development.

To aid our analysis we shall call upon the theoretical techniques developed in Chapter 2, in particular the powerful conceptual tool of the production possibility boundary. We shall continue to distinguish between the different concepts of time. Of course, actual decisions about specialization and exchange are made in real or perspective time. As such, they are inextricably linked with the unknowable future, where the outcomes of human behaviour and of the world around us are uncertain. There are different levels of doubt about how the future might unfold. As such, a closer examination of the nature of risk and uncertainty will prove invaluable for understanding the behaviour of economic actors and systems, and the importance of organizations and institutionalized rules. Such a discussion is vital for seeing economic models and economic systems in a clearer light.

THE GAINS FROM SPECIALIZATION AND EXCHANGE

If we look backwards through historical time, complete self-sufficiency for individuals, families, tribes, even, in later years, nation states, has been vary rare. There have always been specialists. Even in pre-history, palaeolithic times, men are said to have concentrated their efforts on hunting. Women specialized as the gatherers; their functions ascribed according to sex. The neolithic revolution brought a more settled, agricultural life with the majority of people working as farmers in small units, but still toiling to satisfy most of their own needs. Nevertheless, with the evolution of early agriculture and the gradual development of trade between peoples and regions, the opportunities for other types of work gradually developed. There were skilled craftsmen, individual artisans plying their different crafts, and merchants specializing in trade – buying and selling. Scribes and teachers, usually men of religion – and even court jesters all had particular roles to fulfil, along with the soldiers and administrators. As time passed the majority of people still made a living from the land. Even with the decline of ancient civilization, through feudal times, specialization and exchange, although very limited by modern standards, still continued.

However, after the Agrarian Revolution, bringing with it increased agricultural output, it was the Industrial Revolution which saw the spread of the great seachange in technological know-how and in the nature and extent of specialization and co-operation. This revolution, rooted in eighteenth-century Britain, but then taking hold in parts of Western Europe and North America, saw the birth and growth of firms specializing in the production of goods as different as wrought iron, fine china, textiles and machine tools; a rapidly growing array of both old and new products, many made with innovative techniques and processes. There was a gradual movement of people from the land to industry. Manufacturing work at home, for example, spinning and weaving, often organized through a putting-out system where individual contractors supplied raw materials and equipment to home workers, became less significant as factory work expanded. But the practice of putting-out still continues to-day for activities such as machining and the assembly of Christmas crackers. Workers, often women with children, made nails and chains, for example, in small workshops, well into the twentieth century. Furthermore, many non-manufacturing organizations, such as specialist merchant, insurance and shipping firms developed to take advantage of the increased opportunities and to fulfil specialized functions required in the expanding markets. For coupled with the significant change in production was the rapid development of trade. The industrializing nations saw the expansion of their own home markets and the trade between many nations flourished. The rapidly industrializing nations were powerful in terms of their trading relationships and for Britain, for example, the Empire served as a ready market for new products, often in exchange for raw materials.

Specialization, so prevalent throughout history, does not occur by accident. There are good reasons, as we can show, for concentrating resources and effort, for co-operating and then exchanging or trading. Such activity can provide the following benefits:

1 A greater variety of goods and services.
2 Increased efficiency – more goods with the same total resources.
3 The enhancement of economic growth.

The first advantage of specialization and trade, the increased variety of goods and services, is relatively easy to explain. Even the simple subsistence economies of the past benefited by exchanging their own produce for goods which they just could not produce for themselves, given resources such as natural gifts of climate or mineral reserves. Precious metals, spices, tea or whatever, the trade routes of the past were busy. Despite all the advances in technology, for example, modern day Japan has no oil reserves to speak of, and Britain cannot naturally produce bananas or citrus fruits. One good reason for trade is to acquire the products which cannot be produced by the group or nation. Yet that is not the only, or indeed the major reason for trade. Even where countries could readily produce the same goods, differences in the opportunity costs of production by different nations can render trade very worthwhile.

It was David Ricardo, writing in the nineteenth century, who first formally analysed the impact of specialization and exchange or trade. He took an example of two nations, Britain and Portugal, with different endowments of resources which included the natural conditions such as climate. By careful analysis he showed that if each nation concentrated all resources on doing what it did best, where it had the lowest opportunity cost, and then traded with the other, both nations could benefit. Each country would ultimately have more commodities giving an increase in combined total output, and following on from this an increase in consumption possibilities. More goods would be available than would be the case under a regime of self-sufficiency, even though one nation was the superior producer. An understanding of his theory of specialization and trade between nations gives valuable insights which can be readily transferred to explain the behaviour of individuals, organizations and the process of exchange. The explanatory power and versatility of Ricardo's analysis is very important. It explains the benefits of specialization where individuals, groups or countries concentrate on what they do best. Ricardian analysis shows that specialization and exchange can promote economic efficiency and mutual benefit, ultimately the possibility of more consumption (or leisure).

In order to capture Ricardo's key insights we can work with a traditional economic model, using analytical time. We focus on two individuals each of whom wants to obtain the best possible personal result – their own individual self-interest. By building the basic model we can show precisely how the gains from specialization and exchange arise in particular circumstances. To do this, compare the productive potential of two women whom we assume have different endowments of human and physical resources. These differences can arise from a variety of factors. Human capital disparities, for example, could be due to inherited physical or psychological characteristics, such as strength, manual dexterity or even determination. Individuals could have different levels of education and training which augment inherited characteristics. Indeed, they may have different quantities of physical resources at their disposal. However, at this stage the nature and source of the differences in physical and human resources need not concern us, although in later chapters we shall return to the origins and significance of such disparities.

Imagine that the women, Maureen and Mary, are both able to produce only two products, beer and bread, unsophisticated goods, chosen to keep the analysis straight-forward. More complex goods like televisions or washing machines would bring us squarely into the twentieth century. However, in reality the chances of producing a complete product of such a complex nature are virtually nil, a feature of modern production to which we shall turn our attention in later sections of this chapter. For simplicity, we shall work with relatively basic products. Further assume that Mary, if she puts *all* her resources, which include time, effort and physical resources into *either* beer *or* bread production can produce more than Maureen. Mary can always, in overall terms, outperform Maureen, no matter how the two women allocate their resources. Mary has the greater production potential. In Ricardo's terminology this means that Mary has an *absolute advantage* in the production of both goods.

Ricardo's analysis shows us that rather than plying both trades, brewing and baking, Maureen and Mary could both be better off in ultimate consumption terms, by concentrating their resources where they personally produce at best, in other words where each has what Ricardo termed a *comparative advantage*. If Maureen and Mary want to achieve their own individual best possible consumption levels, the first step must be for each to specialize in the activity where she has a comparative advantage, to concentrate all her resources in producing where she has the greatest relative efficiency. That simply means each should make only the product which she can produce with the *smallest opportunity cost* to herself. The final step to achieve maximum consumption levels would involve a swap or an exchange of output.

Despite the fact that Mary can always outperform Maureen in the manufacture of both goods, it will benefit Mary to concentrate in her area of relative strength. Maureen should do likewise and concentrate her resources in her own personal best production activity, where she is relatively efficient, or where she has the least disadvantage in comparison with Mary. The overall result of such specialization and exchange would be an increase in combined total output and thus joint consumption possibilities.

For each to gain the maximum satisfaction from all of this, we would have to make the further assumption that the women have no special preference for working at brewing or baking, that they find each occupation equally satisfying, or, indeed, that they prefer to work in their field of comparative advantage. Additionally, we would have to believe that they have no idiosyncratic production practices which lead them to have a strong preference for their own produce; neither has a secret beer recipe nor bread baking technique which renders her own batch or brew overwhelmingly 'best' in her own estimation. We abstract from all such complications.

The concepts of comparative and absolute advantage and the gains from specialization and exchange can be clarified by using numerical and graphical examples. In Chapter 2, we drew a production possibility boundary for the economy as a whole, a stylized picture. Now we can use this adaptable concept to illustrate Ricardo's analysis by showing the individual's production possibility frontiers or 'productivity profiles'. These display the productive potential of the two individual workers at a point in time. The examples, although highly simplified, will enable us to illustrate Ricardo's enduring analysis of specialization and trade, to show clearly the important production and consumption benefits which follow on from such activity.

Productivity profiles: individual production possibilities

In analytical time we have complete knowledge of both women's productive potential. In order to illustrate Mary's situation in greater detail we can draw her individual production possibility boundary from the data given in Table 3.1, which shows the alternative combinations of output which she can obtain by dividing her resources in different ways. Bread output is measured on the vertical axis and beer on the horizontal axis. Take the extreme position where Mary puts all her inputs into bread

Table 3.1 Mary: Production possibilities

Bread (units)	Beer (units)
0	80
2	60
4	40
6	20
8	0

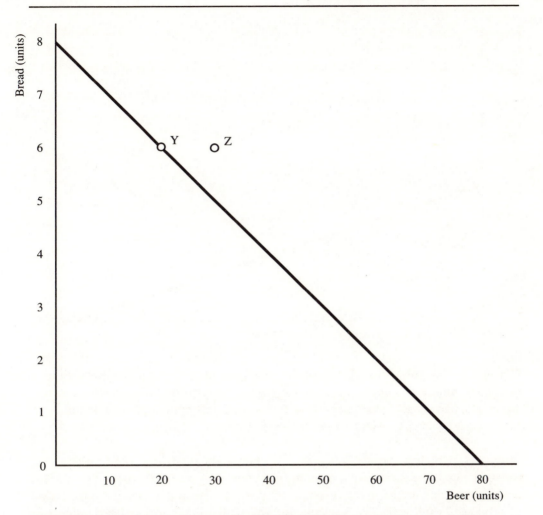

Figure 3.1   Mary: productivity profile. The individual's production possibility boundary. Mary's opportunity cost or the rate of transformation is constant at 1 unit of bread for 10 units of beer. Z is an unobtainable combination of goods. Mary prior to specialization and trade is at point Y

manufacture, she could produce 8 units of bread but no beer as shown on Figure 3.1. Other combinations of output, with fewer resource inputs in baking, and more in beer production can be plotted. At the other extreme, if she chooses to put all resources into beer production, she could have 80 units of beer but no bread.

We assume that Mary always knows precisely how much bread would have to be sacrificed if she wants to make more beer, by switching resources from bread to beer production. To simplify the analysis, the opportunity cost or the 'trade-off' is assumed to be *constant*. The data has been deliberately chosen to show that 1 unit of bread always has an opportunity cost of 10 units of beer as shown by the downward

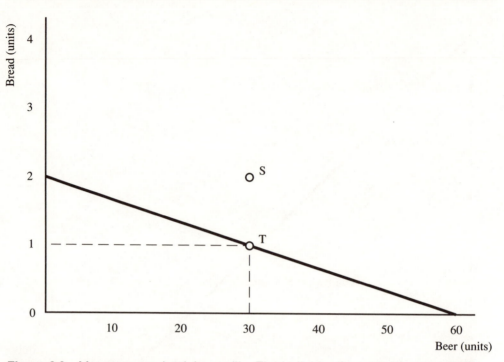

Figure 3.2   Maureen: productivity profile. The individual's production possibility boundary. Maureen's opportunity cost or the rate of transformation is constant at 1 unit of bread for 30 units of beer. S is an unobtainable combination of goods. Maureen prior to specialization and trade is at point T

sloping straight line, production possibility boundary in Figure 3.1. Mary faces a constant rate of transformation or uniform opportunity costs. The boundary divides obtainable from unobtainable production possibilities, and designates production possibilities at full capacity. We have not altered the model's essential feature as a constraint. It still displays all production options, albeit this time for an individual facing constant opportunity costs, assumed for ease of exposition. Note that this productivity profile or transformation boundary is simply a tool of illustration; if we change our assumptions, the trade-off is different and the picture changes. We could assume increasing opportunity costs which would give us a curved production possibility frontier, concave to the origin, analogous to the one we met in Chapter 2. Check that you could explain the reasoning for a situation of increasing opportunity costs.

Maureen has a different production possibility boundary as displayed in Figure 3.2. Her individual 'productivity profile' has been plotted from the data given in Table 3.2. This tells us that at most, Maureen can only produce 2 units of bread by concentrating all her resources and effort into baking. This course of action would leave her with no beer whatsoever, as shown on the diagram. If, on the other hand, she devoted all her resources to brewing, she could produce 60 units of beer but no

Table 3.2 Maureen: Production possibilities

Bread (units)	Beer (units)
2	0
1	30
0	60

bread. To increase bread production from 0 to 1 unit would require her to forgo 30 units of beer. Indeed, to produce an extra unit of bread, to make 2 units in total, would require switching resources yet again, and forgoing another 30 units of beer. Again, a constant opportunity cost of beer in terms of bread is assumed.

Now the numerical value of the slope and the position of Maureen's and Mary's production possibility constraint can be compared. They are quite different. If both are plotted in the same quadrant, clearly Maureen's production possibility boundary lies inside, that is, to the left of Mary's. This is shown in Figure 3.3. The different slopes display the different opportunity costs or relative efficiencies of the two producers. (The opportunity cost of beer is simply the inverse of the opportunity cost of bread.) We shall see that it is these *differences* in relative efficiencies or opportunity costs which make specialization and trade worthwhile through increased output and thus improved consumption possibilities. It will pay each person to produce output with the lower opportunity cost.

The information in the tables and diagrams displays the fact that Mary has an *absolute advantage* in the production of both beer and bread – she outperforms Maureen in both types of production. Her production possibility boundary lies to the *right* of Maureen's. In addition, both women have different opportunity costs for brewing and bread making as illustrated by the different slopes of their production possibility boundaries. However, it is the *difference in opportunity costs* which matter, for this forms the basis of *comparative advantage*. Ricardo's 'law' of comparative advantage tells us that although Mary can outperform Maureen in both types of activity, Mary's comparative or relative advantage, is in baking bread. Maureen is least disadvantaged in brewing and so her own comparative advantage is in brewing. If both women specialize in what they personally do best, where they have a comparative advantage, then total output will increase and *consumption possibilities will rise*. More output from the same total resources means an increase in economic efficiency. We can illustrate this by developing the numerical example. But for specialization and voluntary trade to take place we assume that both individuals must expect to be better off.

Production and consumption: before specialization

In order to show the production and consumption benefits we need to compare production and consumption levels both before and after specialization and trade.

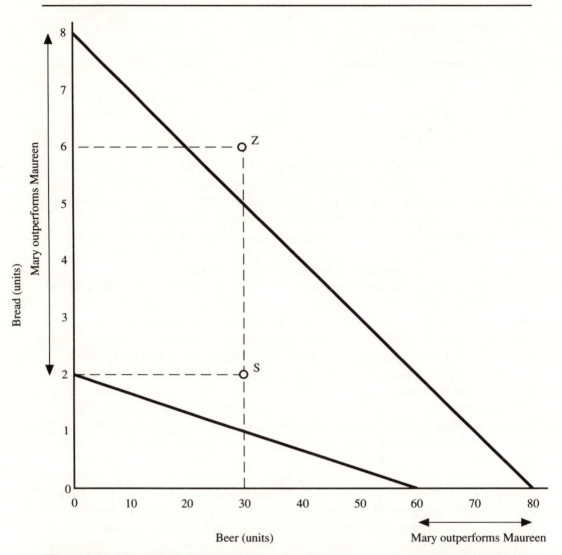

Figure 3.3 Absolute and comparative advantage. Mary has an absolute advantage in bread and beer production; and a comparative advantage in bread production. Maureen has a comparative advantage in beer production where she is least disadvantaged. Given the differences in opportunity costs and with a price ratio of 1 unit of bread for 15 units of beer – complete specialization enables each person to reach previously unobtainable consumption positions; Mary moves to Z and Maureen to S

Imagine an initial production and consumption position, *before* specialization and with no exchange. Each person produces both goods for her own consumption. Assume that Mary puts three-quarters of her resources into baking and one-quarter into brewing. Maureen, on the other hand, divides her resources equally between beer

Table 3.3 Maureen and Mary: total output and consumption, with and without specialization

Mary and Maureen	Bread	Beer
Without specialization	7	50
With specialization	8	60

and bread production. Given this hypothetical starting point, Mary produces, at full capacity on her production possibility boundary, 6 units of bread and 20 units of beer. Maureen produces, at full capacity, 30 units of beer and 1 unit of bread. Maureen's and Mary's combined full capacity output totals 7 units of bread and 50 units of beer. Table 3.3 gives a summary of this data. See Figures 3.1 and 3.2, respectively to confirm this.

Production: complete specialization

Now if Mary and Maureen concentrate *all* their resources in their own personal best occupation, Mary specializes completely in baking, Maureen in brewing, their *combined full capacity* total output would be 60 units of beer and 8 units of bread. Mary produces the bread, Maureen produces the beer. There is a greater quantity of goods available than would have been the case if both women had divided their resources, making both bread and beer. Note on the diagram in Figure 3.3 just how much extra bread Mary can produce over and above Maureen when each puts all resources into bread production. Mary produces three times as much again as Maureen. When we compare the other extreme, where each produces beer, the relative gap between the two women is much smaller. Mary produces only one-third as much again. This makes the comparative advantage quite clear and shows us where each individual should specialize to maximize the gain. Compared with pre-specialization production totals, there has been a 14 per cent increase in bread output and a 20 per cent increase in beer output.

Without trade Mary would have no beer and Maureen no bread. To enjoy the benefits of their specialization each must trade. After trade has taken place, we can display the consumption gains.

The consumption gains from specialization and trade

Assume the women agree to trade with each other on mutually beneficial terms, where each makes a gain. Suppose that Mary is willing to swap 2 units of bread for 30 units of beer and Maureen finds this 'trade off' acceptable. In effect, the 'price' of bread per unit is 15 units of beer. If Mary sells 2 units of bread for 30 units of beer she can maintain her original consumption of bread. But she is now better off than in her pre-specialization position. Her beer consumption can increase by 10 units, giving her a total of 30 units. Post specialization and trade, Mary has a consumption point, **Z** on Figure 3.1, beyond her personal productivity constraint, a combination of goods previously unobtainable.

After specialization and trade Maureen is also better off. She gives up 30 units of beer in exchange for 2 units of bread. She too moves to a consumption point beyond her personal productivity boundary, a combination of goods previously out of the question, but now available as a direct result of concentrating her resources in brewing and engaging in exchange. She consumes the same level of beer as before but she now has 2.0 units of bread as at point **S** in Figure 3.2.

The key message is that both women have improved their consumption possibilities despite the fact that their production potential remains static. Their production boundaries have not improved; shifted to the right. But when each specializes and co-operates in exchange, so that each 'puts all her eggs into one basket' Mary and Maureen both do better than before. Given the same total resources, a greater quantity of goods has been produced, overall efficiency has improved and each person has gained. These increases in bread consumption have been made without any reduction in beer drinking. To eat more bread without specialization and trade would of course have required both to reduce beer consumption. Whatever the source of the differences in relative efficiencies, for example, better training, equipment or innate ability or 'flair', both workers have improved their consumption, even though Mary is both a better baker and brewer than Maureen. Despite Mary's absolute advantage, there are gains to be made provided there are differences in opportunity costs – different relative efficiencies. *Unless* the individuals have the same opportunity cost, provided each has a comparative advantage, it can pay to specialize.

The terms of trade: the division of the benefits

What determines the division of the extra output produced – who gains what? Will it always be worthwhile for the two individuals to specialize and trade, given that each has a comparative advantage? To answer these questions we must examine the 'prices' at which the individuals are willing and able to swap their goods. Such relative prices are known as *the terms of trade*. These will determine how much each person actually gains from the deal. The result which leaves Maureen with an additional 1 unit of bread, and Mary with an extra 10 units of beer, is certainly not the only possible outcome of exchange. We predetermined that exchange would be worthwhile for both and the relative size of the individual's gain by setting a particular price ratio. Note that there is no reference to money, monetary exchange will be examined in Chapter 4. In this example, the price of 1 unit of bread is expressed as 15 units of beer. Put the other way round, the price of one unit of beer is 0.066 units of bread.

The terms of trade for beer and bread actually depend on the relative willingness and ability of the two parties to trade. There are a series of prices which could exist.

There will be more to say about what affects the terms of trade later in this chapter, how relative prices are influenced by an interplay of factors which determine bargaining power. Here we note that at some prices exchange will not occur. Moreover, when exchange takes place, relative prices critically determine the division of benefits. Maureen might insist on 1 unit of bread as the necessary compensation to induce her to part with 10 units of beer. This price ratio would leave Mary no better off, still on her original boundary. She would not benefit from the transaction, for without specialization she could achieve 6 units of bread and 20 units of beer. If Mary traded on Maureen's terms, then Maureen would capture all the gain from specialization. The price simply reflects Mary's own opportunity cost in the absence of specialization – her marginal rate of transformation.

Likewise, if Mary refused to pay more than 1 unit of bread for 30 units of beer, then Maureen would be no better off. At such a low price there would be no incentive for Maureen to specialize or trade. This price exactly matches the opportunity cost which she would have to pay in the absence of specialization – her marginal rate of transformation. Mary would capture all the gains. There would be no incentive for Maureen to specialize.

If we could argue, for example, that Maureen finds bread making a much more exciting prospect than brewing, then of course our conclusion might be different. Indeed, if we could argue that Maureen wants to make a gift to Mary then exchange might take place. However, assuming that the two women have no particular preference for working in either occupation and that each wishes to do the best for herself, motivated by self-interest, specialization and voluntary exchange will not take place at the prices considered above.

There are other prices at which one of the individuals will be worse off. For example, Mary could ask for 40 units of beer in order to induce her to exchange 1 unit of bread. Such a price would obviously make her much better off, if the deal were accepted. But a moment's reflection shows that this would be an unacceptable price for Maureen, it would leave her worse off. She would have to pay 40 units of beer simply to achieve her pre-specialization bread consumption level. She would then be left with a mere 20 units of beer, a reduction of 10 units on her pre-specialization level.

Acceptable prices to both parties will lie between the bounds of their respective opportunity costs of transforming one good into the other, the slopes of their production possibility boundaries. In this example the price of one unit of bread must be set somewhere *between* 10 and 30 units of beer. Any price outside this range will not make it worthwhile for *both* individuals to specialize and exchange.

The impact of relative prices on the actual division of the benefits can be shown starkly in the following situation. Assume both women produce 30 units of beer initially. Their total bread output is 6 units, 5 from Mary, 1 from Maureen. After complete specialization, bread output stands at 8 units, beer output remains the same. Given a price ratio of 2 units of bread for 30 of beer, then both gain 1 unit of bread each, 50 per cent of the overall gain. But if the price of beer falls, for example,

Mary pays only 1.5 units of bread for 30 of beer, then Maureen's share is reduced. Mary gains 1.5 units, that is 75 per cent of the total gain. Maureen's share is 25 per cent. The absolute and percentage size of Maureen's share has fallen, Mary's has risen.

In summary, by operating in analytical time, we have the benefit of moving backwards and forwards in order to examine different possibilities. Our results critically depend on the assumptions we have made. By using the production possibility boundaries we have been able to illustrate the moral of Ricardo's story in the context of two individuals, abstracting from real-world complexities. In analytical time there is perfect information and all production plans are achieved with certainty. This is a conventional approach, where we have no problems in formulating agreements between people, because information is perfect and so acquired without cost and equally available to both parties. Everything turns out exactly as planned – a convenient story. In reality, this is not always, if ever, so. As Alchian once asked 'are there many choices – or actions – in life in which the consequences can be predicted with absolute certainty? Even the act of purchasing a loaf of bread has an element of uncertainty in its consequences' (1969: 75).

We have somewhat unrealistically assumed that the women have not improved their productivity by specialization. Their personal productivity profiles remain static, the rate of transformation between the goods are unchanged. They have not learned by experience for they are assumed to know already the best way of doing things. We have shown the gains from specialization and trade given differences in comparative advantage; and that at some prices no deal will take place because one of the potential traders will be, at best, no better off as a result of exchange. The terms of trade actually acceptable to both Maureen and Mary will determine the division of the benefit. Our useful fiction of two isolated individuals co-operating goes some way toward illustrating the sources of the gains from specialization and exchange; and in what circumstances these will take place. But this is by no means a complete picture.

SPECIALIZATION AND THE DIVISION OF LABOUR: FURTHER GAINS

In historical time, even in the simplest subsistence societies there was specialization, a division of labour into specialized functions and some exchange. The type of exchange which distinguished most of economic history has been personalized exchange involving small scale production and local trade, a feature to which we shall return in Chapter 4. Our example of two individual specialists engaging in face to face trade is by no means wholly removed from reality of the past. But the segregation of workers into *different* trades, is only one way of dividing labour. The example of the brewer and baker enables us to formally identify the improvement in consumption possibilities, where we have assumed that there is no change in productive potential as a result of specialization. But specialization could go further; there are more potential gains to be had. The brewer's work could be split into a series of mini-tasks, basic steps in production to be undertaken by different people. This further *specialization* and the *division of labour* creates additional benefits in terms of enhanced production and economic growth.

It was Adam Smith, in *The Wealth of Nations* (1776) who examined what were in fact the dynamic effects of specialization and the division of labour. With his insights we can go on to explain how further gains can be made from intensifying specialization. Smith noticed that those who specialized in a particular task, for example, people who spent all their time making nails could produce them much more rapidly than the first rate blacksmith who made nails infrequently. Women and boys with little overall training and experience who made only nails, could turn out much greater quantities than highly skilled blacksmiths who produced a range of products. A major reason for this was that as people became more practised and learned by experience, they became quicker and more skilful at their work. They 'mastered' a particular task for intensive practice made perfect. Indeed, labour could be divided further still. Instead of making a complete product, like a nail, individual workers would only complete a small stage in its production. Manufacturing could be sub-divided into a number of basic stages, so that raw materials could gradually be turned into a finished article via a sequence of relatively simple steps undertaken by different individuals. In addition, the breaking down of complex overall tasks into relatively simple procedures made it easier to train people.

Additionally, gains could be made by economizing on the time used in production. Time would be saved by individual workers, for they would not have to move from one stage of production to the next – there would be no need to change tools for example – they would stick with one aspect of the process. Nor would workers have to have different sets of specialist tools for making different items. So the nailer's work too could be further divided, different people would make the head, a shank and a point. So 'many hands make light work'. People worked together in business firms, *not* as isolated artisans. They co-operated in the manufacturing process where a particular activity was split into a number of discrete tasks, where resources, including people, were co-ordinated and organized.

The production process which Adam Smith observed took time to complete. Over a longer time period, people's production was enhanced by working with new machinery. When the various tasks had been reduced to relatively simple routine repetitive actions, then machinery could take over. Indeed, the division of labour acted as a spur to invention and mechanization, for it was easier to devise machinery for straightforward routine basic procedures. Examples of industries and trade transformed by such a division of labour abound. Adam Smith's famous pin factory is the classic illustration of how a relatively complicated process, just like nail making, could be broken down into small parts. This not only enabled people to gain expertise and speed but also encouraged the application of machinery. Whether we look at the steel and cotton mills or the chocolate factories of Britain in the nineteenth and twentieth centuries, an increasing division of labour revolutionized productivity. Entrepreneurs competed with each other to enhance and improve production, to supply the market with cheaper, better, more novel products than their rivals. They often did so by extending the intensity and scope of specialization and the division of labour.

Economies of Scale could be reaped. Going hand in hand with the division of labour was large scale production. This often enabled dramatic reductions in the costs of production per item. It was much cheaper per unit to produce chocolate, for example, in large vats rather than small saucepans. When production levels were increased the costs of increasing vat sizes would not rise proportionately with production. The area of a vat could be doubled but its capacity, its volume, would increase threefold. This is an example of an *internal economy of scale*. Managers could oversee large outputs as well as small, so *managerial economies* could be made as output increased. *External pecuniary economies of scale* could be made as the scale of production increased. These pecuniary economies arise from the advantages of buying inputs in bulk at lower prices. Economies could be made in the cost of training people, human capital investment and on the purchase of physical capital. Borrowing money to fund investments might be had more cheaply as the scale of borrowing grew (see Chapter 11). In short, all of these changes stimulated *economic growth* by encouraging improvements in both human and physical capital. Invention and innovation gathered pace. Even though no individual or firm had a comparative advantage in producing a particular product at the outset, by specializing and gaining the benefits of the division of labour and economies of scale, a comparative advantage could be promoted. Production potential was enhanced for existing products, and changes in capacity were needed for the plethora of new goods and services which evolved over time. In analytical time, we could illustrate this by shifting production possibility curves to the right.

At this point it is useful to remember that specialization within the firm, the division of labour, involves no internal exchange of commodities between its members. There is no swapping of goods as in the case of Maureen and Mary – no market exchange. Within the manufacturing firm there would simply be the passing of semi-finished items along a production line. Resources are allocated within the organization without the use of the market mechanism. We shall examine the internal workings of the firm in Chapter 9. In relatively simple processes it was possible to clearly pick out the contribution of workers within the firm. But in the modern economy, particularly for sophisticated products, production processes are often extremely complex, requiring a highly involved division of labour. In these circumstances it may not be possible to identify and separate any one person's contribution. Teams of people are involved in production and any team member's output cannot be readily isolated and measured, an important feature of modern production.

One hallmark of the industrial revolution was the rapid spread and refinement of specialization and the division of labour in manufacturing industry. But in addition, the *scope* of this process evolved over time. The new administration factories producing services, including banks, building societies, insurance firms, even government departments can employ an intensifying division of labour. Many workers in the modern economy may now deal with only one small aspect of a highly involved production process. They acquire an in-depth knowledge and dexterity in only a narrow aspect of production. People are not the 'Jacks and Jills of all trades', but neither are they 'master or mistress of one'. And whether working in highly interrelated production processes, individually on their own account, or in production teams, people increasingly depend on each other.

Limitations to the division of labour

There are limitations to the division of labour and economies of scale and the extent varies from industry to industry. The extent of specialization and division of labour is determined in part by technological factors and the size of the market. If there were a small market demand for a product there would be no good reason to produce large outputs, which could not be sold. This restricted demand would not warrant an intensified division of labour so would limit this process. In certain industries only large-scale output can be cost effectively produced, for example, mass car production, electricity generation. Certainly, small-scale enterprise is still commonplace in the highly industrialized nations and of course in the Third World. In Britain, individual small-scale bakers exist side by side with modern day mass production bakeries. Here the bakery process is sub-divided into a number of discrete separate steps, undertaken by different workers and machines. Similarly, breweries sub-divide work for the mass production of beer, making it possible to achieve economies of scale and huge production runs. But this is a far cry from small independent brewers like Ma Pardo in Netherton, West Midlands, who produced beer at her own premises and on a very small scale.

However, overall, specialization and the division of labour have increased over time, hand in hand with the growth of markets and economies. The division of labour has deepened and widened. Now firms will often produce one part, say a microchip – the tiny component used in a host of complex end-products from word processors to washing machines. Amstrad, the trailblazer for the low-cost personal computer have chips made in the Far East and are essentially an import and assembly company. Indeed, now many firms are themselves part of a wider division of labour. They buy-in semi-finished products, often in the world market-place and sell to other firms as they complete only part of the manufacturing process. Large multinationals, giant corporations, often bypass the market by undertaking different stages of the manufacturing process in different countries. There is an interdependent web of production activity.

Specialization within a whole geographical area, such as Silicon Valley in the US, has encouraged high levels of invention and innovation in the computing industry. And as modern economies evolve, the division of labour widens and deepens not just in manufacturing but in some agricultural sectors and service sectors such as banking, financial services, tourism and education. The gains from trade have in turn depended on the increasing size of markets. As the division of labour becomes ever more specific, specialization and exchange, most particularly for the rich economies, but also for Third World nations, is increasingly played out on a global stage, with worldwide production and trade.

THE COSTS OF SPECIALIZATION, THE DIVISION OF LABOUR AND EXCHANGE

There can be little doubt about the advantages of concentrating resources, time and effort. Certainly, without specialization and exchange on a very wide scale, modern economies would not have developed to give us such historically unprecedented income, wealth and consumption benefits. We have focused our attention on the indisputable gains. But there are drawbacks. The wealth of some nations cannot be so dramatically enhanced without cost. Working in analytical time, assuming away most of the real-world problems, we have been able to ignore the costliness of the actual production and exchange process. In simple economies the costs associated, for example, with organizing, co-ordinating and planning production and exchange activities are relatively small. Yet as the production and exchange process develops, particularly as it becomes more complex and interdependent through time and space – the costs of organization change too.

The orthodox, two person model, set in analytical time, is very useful for explaining some of the key features of specialization and trade. It provides a fundamental understanding, made possible by working in an uncluttered situation. Given this starting point, we have already referred to the actual problems encountered in perspective time. We have also illustrated how the gains from specialization and trade can be seen in an evolutionary context. Nevertheless, to explore the costs of specialization and exchange, we shall go back to the simple static model. In the example of Maureen and Mary, we assume that each person is indifferent about the type of work, brewer or baker, it does not matter. Perfect knowledge and so the exact outcome of any decision is seen fully and in advance. All potential costs and benefits are known without a shadow of doubt. No one needs to worry, for example, about whether agreements or bargains will be honoured, goods of the appropriate standard will be delivered because everyone meets their production and exchange plans and the nature of all goods is known exactly. In this straightforward account, the costs of engaging in economic relationships with others are zero. Given an appropriate price, Maureen and Mary have a clear and assured benefit – a positive consumption gain derived from specialization and exchange. It is as if production and exchange were instantaneous. Analytical time gives us what Shackle (1965) terms a timeless and mechanical time, 'a rational, sure and pre-reconciled world', where we can move backwards and forwards abstracting from the experiencing of events, seeing all the different possibilities, picking out just some of the salient features. It is only when we relax the assumptions of the basic model that we can address important problems which have so far been safely ignored, and specify some of the costs of engaging in more complex economic relations with others. For whether we focus attention on individuals, groups or nations, there are costs.

Monotony

For an individual, the boredom resulting from the repetitive nature of production can be seen as a key cost of specialization and the division of labour. Maureen and Mary completely concentrate their work efforts in order to achieve full consumption gains. However, in reality, people do derive satisfaction from their work, a factor assumed away in the basic model. Indeed, if 'variety is the spice of life' then concentrating on just one activity implies a cost in terms of lost satisfaction. Additionally, 'a change may be as good as a rest' and monotonous working may eventually lead to declining productivity, absenteeism and ill health. Personal productivity profiles could shift to the left as a result of boredom. Marx highlighted these problems. The worker 'becomes an appendage of the machine, and it is only the most simple, most monotonous, and most easily acquired knack, that is required of him' (Marx and Engels 1872: 41). Workers would be de-skilled, interchangeable cogs in a production process.

Smith had also been worried, long before Marx, about the adverse effects of the division of labour. He felt that:

> The man whose whole life is spent in performing a few simple operations, of which the effects too are, perhaps, always the same, or very nearly the same, has no occasion to exert his understanding, or to exercise his invention in finding out expedients for removing difficulties which never occur. . . . His dexterity at his own particular trade seems . . . to be acquired at the expense of his intellectual, social and martial virtues.
>
> (1776: 782)

So whilst the division of labour brought great material gain, it also arrested the development of the personality of many workers. This qualified Smith's view of the advantages professed for the division of labour. In fact, he argued that the great body of people would fall into this diminished state, 'unless government takes some pains to prevent it' (ibid.). A public authority would need to provide an element of education to offset the stultifying effects of a working life spent performing a few simple procedures.

There are no clear cut answers about the costs of intensifying the division of labour or indeed their relationship to the benefits. Of course, deepening the division of labour and increasing the use of machinery has enabled many boring and often very dangerous jobs to be replaced. There are plenty of examples from industries as different as candle making to mining. In the late twentieth century the process of specialization is still evolving. An increasing division of labour within some banks has been heralded as a means of combating boredom. As it takes a shorter time to train people for increasingly divided functions, staff can be rotated between tasks in order to combat tedium, or indeed to hire and fire with greater ease. As the economy evolves, jobs change, new functions and interests are created. Moreover, the decline in the length of the working week, made possible in part by increased specialization, provides more leisure time. But the process of technological change and innovation still throws up new tedious tasks and potential occupational dangers. Those tied to the word processor or the automated supermarket check out may find their work no more stimulating than did those in the factories of the past; albeit cleaner and safer.

Organization/Co-ordination

At whatever the level of specialization and exchange, even in the simplest of societies, these activities have to be *organized* and *co-ordinated*. In the straightforward story of Mary and Maureen, the gains from specialization and trade are achieved without such costs. But whether resources and goods are co-ordinated through *markets* on the one hand, or managed within *organizations*, such as private firms, public bodies or households, on the other, costs are involved. These *transaction costs* arise once we relax the assumption of omniscient people. Whether making exchanges in the market-place or working within firms, people do not know everything. They make decisions in perspective time, where they face imperfect information, complex masses of detail and uncertainty. They find difficulty in understanding and processing such information and are therefore said by some economists to face *bounded rationality*. They find difficulty in 'doing the best they can' and have to spend resources to tackle this problem.

Given the static model illustrating comparative advantage there is of course no need to spend anything on grading products, providing guarantees, trademarks or proof of ownership. There are no surprise attributes of beer or bread. Maureen and Mary meet all their production plans and obligations. In analytical time they have no need of trust, hope or legal enforcements. Certainty that both are willing and able to honour their production and exchange commitments prevails. Perfect information rules.

For specialization and exchange to be carried out in reality there have to be means by which one person's work efforts and consumption goals are made compatible with those of others; and so transaction costs are incurred. The exchange which occurred so easily between two people in what is effectively a simple two person world becomes complex when people have incomplete information about the production possibilities and the preferences of others. The economic actors themselves have different amounts and types of information about each other and the world at large. There is asymmetric information available to different parties. They may also interpret that information differently.

Adam Smith (ibid.) turned his attention both to markets and firms as the co-ordinators and organizers of economic activity. He talked about 'the invisible hand' of the markets as the co-ordinator, where each person following his or her own self-interest, and exchanging in markets would lead to generally beneficial results for society as a whole. Smith used evocative rhetoric to emphasize the potency of individual interest and the system of exchange. People would be moved by *mutual sympathy*. The system would be harmonious for individuals would be stirred by sympathy and the desire for the good opinion of others. They would usually be helpful to each other and avoid causing pain. Common self-interest and mutual sympathy would lead to the development of general practices which although not planned would lead to the common good. Indeed, whilst there are those who concentrate simply on the role of markets and the price system as the mechanism for co-ordinating human activity, Smith was more profound. He acknowledged the role of organizations, customs and the laws developed to aid the co-ordination of production and exchange. For Smith, the practices of economic life motivated by self-interest become established because they deliver general benefit; an unplanned result.

Organizations and institutional rules have evolved to aid co-ordination of production and exchange. Organization and co-ordination of the factors of production require an outlay of resources, there is a cost. Turn attention from the individual artisan in analytical time to real-world corporations, with involved production processes which take place over the passage of time. Then there have to be managers, planners organizing the factors of production and monitoring work. Certainly, as specialization and the division of labour becomes more complex, production and trade have to be organized more carefully. Appropriate rules of conduct and the means for enforcing such rules had to evolve, to cope with the costs of human interactions. Transactions costs had to be met.

Adam Smith could not have foreseen the extent to which the division of labour would grow (Rickets: 1987: 115). However, a central feature highlighted by Smith's work was the problem of achieving the co-operation amongst people which allowed the gains from increased specialization and trade to be secured. How could people and resources be brought together to work effectively? This was the key to the wealth of nations and it required organization and co-operation. Different legal organizational forms, like the joint stock company, had to evolve to enable the gains to be effectively reaped. 'Firms', as we shall see, changed their nature.

Ensuring the co-operation of people as the production process becomes more involved requires substantial costs of organizing, planning, monitoring, overseeing and policing workers. In addition, the firm itself has to be regulated and policed. The whole process of bringing resources effectively together, in so many different ways, gives rise to different organization costs. For example, individual craftsmen doing the whole job, taking a pride in the result of their efforts, need no monitoring. But once part of a group in a complex interrelated process, people would need to be monitored and encouraged, to ensure that they were working in the manner prescribed. Entrepreneurial and managerial talent would be required to achieve this, and resources would have to be spent on organizing and planning the production and exchange process. These are costs and considerations which go unnoticed in the traditional analytical models founded on the assumption of perfect information. These costs have important implications which will be developed in later chapters.

Dependency/vulnerability

In order to achieve the full benefits of specialization Maureen and Mary have to 'put all their eggs into one basket'. In our model they have to 'depend' on each other. Given perfect information they have no problem. Each knows the gain. However, in perspective time the outcome of specialization and exchange might be very different. Beer or bread production could be interrupted by some unforseen circumstances. A complete surprise happening or an event already perceived as an identifiable risk could render actual production well within the full potential level. Through no fault of their own, in the reality of perspective time, Mary and Maureen might be unable to fulfil their production plans. If manufacturing targets are not met by either party and there is an inability to exchange at an acceptable price, each could be left to make expensive alternative arrangements. A brew gone sour would leave someone to go without. It may be therefore perfectly rational for them to keep a hand in both lines of production. It may be more costly in terms of forgone alternatives to produce both goods – there is a loss of the potential consumption gains. But it keeps options open, hedges bets, in an uncertain world. That usually costs.

At the national level, Adam Smith was counselling caution about the extent of specialization some two hundred years ago. In the interest of national security, weaponry should be produced at home. That could not be left to the potential vagaries of trading partners whose future behaviour was uncertain. Even if others had a cost advantage in the manufacture of arms, a 'buy British' policy it was argued, would be more likely to ensure a continuous and uninterrupted supply of armaments. Essentially, the nation would pay more for the perceived security of supply, even though other nations have a comparative advantage in the production of weaponry, so that armaments could be obtained more cheaply. Again, forgoing some of the potential gains from specialization and trade might be the necessary but worthwhile price to pay for keeping options open and reducing the dependency on others for vital requirements. In reality, people and nations operate in perspective time where the future is unknowable. The need to keep open the loss making Royal Ordnance, the privatized small arms manufacturer now owned by British Aerospace has been put forward because its closure would mean that there was no longer any indigenous small arms capability to support any future requirement. The Ministry of Defence would have to rely on an offshore supplier whose political aims may not coincide with those of the British Government (Macrae 1992). We shall return to the notion of dependency and vulnerability in Chapter 6 when the division of labour in the household is explored.

To take a different example it may currently be cheaper to close British pits and import coal from other nations who may have a comparative advantage. But in the long term over real time this could lead to a dependency on other sources which might dry up or become exorbitantly expensive should the terms of trade become unfavourable. An assessment of the various possible scenarios is dependent on such factors as the estimated number of coal suppliers and the range of future substitutes for coal over time. Even if existing foreign supplies were completely cut-off in the future, it may be relatively easy to substitute new fuels – pure surprises as yet not imagined. We do not have crystal balls. We have to consider how the future may unfold; exact answers cannot be given. Moreover, disparate observers are likely to perceive and evaluate available information differently, thereby coming to different conclusions. Decision-making in perspective time about investment and disinvestment, as we shall see in later chapters, can be problematic. There are no neat solutions.

Fixed production roles

A fixed role in the production process could be sustained by specialization. People might be pigeon-holed into a particular task and their potential for other types of work could go unrecognized. In perspective time where there is imperfect information, and an unknowable future, Maureen might have a large potential comparative advantage for baking, given training. But she could not be certain of this. The potential might be lost by complete specialization in brewing and exchange with a stronger and more powerful trading partner, already secure in her current comparative advantage. This situation can be generalized and is recognized when a case is made for protecting a new or infant industry, by, for example, import controls. This is a defence against strong foreign competition which adversely affects the development of a potential comparative advantage. But in order to open options for the future, costs have to be met in terms of restricted trade now.

Review: link with uncertainty

We have an initial view of the types of benefits and costs which accrue from specialization and exchange. The concepts of comparative advantage, economies of scale and transactions costs are all important in developing an understanding of economic activity and how that changes through historical time. We have juxtaposed states of perfect information, *certainty*, with real situations where we lack complete knowledge of the past, present and future. Before concluding this chapter we will delve more deeply into the nature and significance of uncertainty.

UNCERTAINTY: A CLOSER LOOK

Uncertainty cannot be eradicated, for time cannot be reversed. Whilst many economists have explicitly recognized that incomplete foresight – uncertainty – is an important fact of life, much standard model building abstracts from this feature. Indeed, in most introductions to economics, risk and uncertainty are relegated to the sidelines. Even though Marshall stated clearly that:

> we cannot foresee the future perfectly. The unexpected may happen; and the existing tendencies may be modified before they have had time to accomplish what

appears now to be their full and complete work. The fact that the general conditions of life are not stationary is the source of many of the difficulties that are met with in applying economic doctrines to practical problems.

(1920a: 347)

Others have also recognized the importance of this feature, as Begg, Fischer and Dornbusch state in their much more recent text: 'Risk is a central characteristic of economic life. Every topic in this book could be extended to include uncertainty', (1994: 250). Yet it does not follow that such aspects of our economic life receive prominent treatment.

Even when the assumption of certainty is finally relaxed – that weighty, albeit very useful simplifying premise for modelling reality – the concepts of uncertainty and risk are often fused together. These terms are used synonymously to indicate that we are not sure of the future. Frequently, uncertainty is subsumed under a heading of risk as in the Begg, Fischer and Dornbusch approach. Given the central importance which we wish to give to such matters in explanations of economic reality, we shall examine these concepts carefully at the outset and discuss the distinctions between risk and uncertainty.

Certainty   This is the starting point of the basic traditional model, where all outcomes of any decision are known completely and in advance. Certainty tells us that only *one* result follows from any particular action – there are no alternative scenarios to ponder. Despite the old joke that 'only death and taxation are certain' the only certainty is our own demise. Death cannot be evaded. But even then, fortunately for people, the exact timing and usually the manner of this event are unknown. Given actual situations, economic decisions perforce are made with imperfect foresight. There may be several possible outcomes from any course of action and the one which will occur cannot be known in advance. Decision-makers may well have to fumble in circumstances far removed from the omniscience of our basic economic models.

Do all economic situations have the same type and degree of uncertainty? Are risk and uncertainty synonymous? Are there some circumstances in which we have more confidence or faith in our ability to make predictions about how we think future events might unfold? To answer these questions, we shall point to the importance of the quantity and quality of information available and how we perceive and evaluate this information. These matters will be discussed further in Chapter 12. Usually we are not totally *ignorant* about what might occur in the future, even though there is no crystal ball. Indeed, between the extremes of certainty and ignorance lie situations which embody different degrees of knowledge on which to base forecasts about the future.

Uncertainty and risk: a distinction

The distinction between risk and uncertainty hinges on knowledge, or the lack of it. No matter how much information we have from the past and present, we do not have

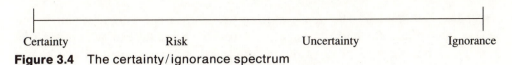

| Certainty | Risk | Uncertainty | Ignorance |

Figure 3.4   The certainty/ignorance spectrum

information from the future. The future is unknowable. Many economists, including Knight and Keynes, have separated the notions of risk and uncertainty.

Risk   This is measurable. It can be shown on the spectrum between certainty and ignorance. In Figure 3.4, risk falls much closer to the certainty of perfect knowledge than to ignorance. Some activities are repetitive and replicable, where all the possible outcomes are known. To give an initial basic example, in a game of chance the tossing of an unbiased coin can only give two outcomes, a head or tail. By the laws of probability we can know the likelihood of a particular result. So if it were heads to win, there is a 0.5 or a 50 per cent chance of losing and, of course, a 0.5 or 50 per cent chance of winning. The two possibilities must sum to an outcome of one, or 100 per cent. By flipping the coin we could come up with six heads on the run; but given a sufficiently large number of experiments the proportion will average at 50 per cent. Insurance companies, whilst not being able to repeat experiments with the same 'coin', for they are insuring different people or objects, keep information on claims from previous policy holders and any other relevant information. Here risk can be measured on an actuarial basis, where probabilities of future events occurring can be estimated on the basis of past information from similar circumstances. So an actuary can work out the probability of giving birth to triplets or having a heart attack.

However, there are many situations where, although we know all the possible outcomes, there is less comprehensive information, and we are not as confident about the probabilities we assign to various possible outcomes. (There will be far more to say on the gradations and measurement of risk in Chapter 12.) People often speak in terms of probabilities when they have little knowledge on which to base such figures. Prior to Black Wednesday, 16 September 1992, some City analysts thought that there was an 80 per cent chance that Britain would stay in the European Exchange Rate Mechanism, ERM, and a 20 per cent chance that sterling would leave the ERM. However, these probabilities were not based on repeated trials from the past. We had moved into the realm of uncertainty and gut reaction, based on individual perceptions of a unique historical situation. This introduces us to the question of uncertainty.

Uncertainty   In an *uncertain* situation we cannot provide neat probability measures. We may have no real idea of the precise structure of the problem, indeed all the possible types of outcome, how the future may 'pan out'. There is no longer any component of repetition to provide guidance, as in a situation of risk. There may be adverse or agreeable surprises in the future (Shackle 1972, 1983; Earl 1986). We have considerable ignorance about the situation and we certainly cannot measure the likelihood or probability of an event with any confidence. Information is lacking and expectations are unclear. The signposts from the past are either non-existent or too blurred to be of use. So when they opened new possibilities, the explorers of the past from Columbus, Cook or NASA (for the Apollo Moon Programme), took unknown paths where uncertainty was considerable. Those pioneering innovators with new technologies and products often had hazy ideas of the use or side effects of their activities. And people in the ordinary business of life, constantly face true uncertainty, that is, where they have no idea what the future will bring, where 'they haven't got a clue'.

Nearer home in terms of time and space, go back to the example of Black Wednesday.[1] There was heavy selling of Sterling on the foreign exchange markets. The Bank of England took the historically unprecedented action of increasing interest rates by 50 per cent, and it was argued that the British economy was 'moving into uncharted waters'. Uncertainty was high and people's confidence in the predictions of future changes, low. Past information and experience yielded relatively little insight into how the future might unfold. People saw interest rate changes which would have previously been considered, by many, as almost impossible over such a short period. New information alerted economic actors to new possibilities. But this creates problems for rational decision-making, even for those trying to hedge their bets on the foreign exchange markets. Uncertainty is far closer to ignorance on the certainty/ignorance spectrum as shown in Figure 3.4.

Certainty/ignorance spectrum

Now some situations of uncertainty can eventually be transformed into risky ones as time passes, with the accumulation of information and experience. The 'explorer' will map the new terrain. But there will always be the random unique event, the nature and/or timing of which cannot be foreseen. We should not ignore the possibility of such incidents, for they may well have far reaching ramifications. Historical shocks and unique events, such as the break up of the Soviet Union, perceived by some as a possibility indeed, but one whose actual timing and speed took the world by surprise, is a case in point.

The significance of uncertainty: an opening view

If uncertainty lies at the heart of the human condition, then it must be an essential element in our thinking. Much economic behaviour and the importance of organizations and institutional constraints take on a different light when the assumption of certainty is relaxed, as we shall see in following chapters. In perspective time, the issue is about making choices in situations which embody different grades of risk and uncertainty, not about making choices in certain, safe circumstances or indeed where we are completely ignorant. Uncertainty and risk are important features. This acknowledgment is required to make sense of the economic panorama.

CONCLUDING COMMENTS

We have shown the benefits of specialization and exchange and seen the central ideas of Ricardo's analysis and its versatility. In the light of Smith's observations, we can see how specialization and the division of labour works and the basic need for co-operation. Co-operation, no less than competition, is an essential requirement to ensure the gains from specialization and exchange. Indeed, when we move from analytical to perspective time, we examine the costs of economic interaction with others. It is then that we have to address the reality of dealing with information problems and uncertainty. In Chapter 4 we shall continue with these themes, by moving on to examine the role of laws, customs and money; institutionalized rules vital to coping with action in perspective time.

SPECIALIZATION, EXCHANGE AND UNCERTAINTY – SUMMARY

- There are gains to be had from specialization and exchange. Even given an absolute advantage, provided that each party to trade has a comparative advantage it can pay to specialize. Consumption possibilities can improve although individual production potential remains static.
- Comparative advantage reflects differences in opportunity costs – relative efficiencies. If opportunity costs are the same for individuals there will be no gain from trade.
- The terms of trade – relative prices – determine the division of benefits arising from specialization. There are price ratios at which no deal will take place.
- In historical time even in the simplest economies there was always some specialization and exchange – personalized exchange involving small scale production and local trade.
- Widening and deepening of specialization over a wide variety of areas in historical time has brought forth enormous gains. Specialization and trade increasingly played out on a global stage, increasing the interdependence amongst people and nations.
- The sources of gains came from a variety of factors including economizing on time, introduction of machinery, economies of scale and large-scale production.
- There are limitations to the division of labour and specialization; brought about in part by technology and the size of the market.
- There are costs of specialization in perspective time. Problems of monotony; organization and co-ordination; dependency and vulnerability: fixed production roles.
- The costs of specialization, the division of labour and exchange are linked with uncertainty. It costs to keep options open in an uncertain world.

> • Distinguishing between concepts of certainty risk, uncertainty and ignorance. In perspective time there are different grades of risk and uncertainty, not a certain world.

SPECIALIZATION, EXCHANGE AND UNCERTAINTY – QUESTIONS FOR DISCUSSION

1 Take the example of Maureen and Mary. Use the data from Tables 3.1 and 3.2 but assume that Maureen, if she puts all her resources into bread production can now produce 10 units. Her capacity to produce beer remains constant, if all resources were used here, output would be 60 units.

a) Draw Maureen's new productivity profile, production possibility curve and explain what it shows.
b) In which good does she have a comparative advantage in production?
c) Given complete specialization what would be the new joint total output and consumption?
d) Given that both individuals initially divide their resources equally into the production of both goods and that the terms of trade do not change from the original example, show how much each can gain.
e) In what circumstances will it not pay Maureen to trade?
f) What could cause the shift in Maureen's productivity profile?

2 'Transactions costs are an important feature of perspective time.' Explain and discuss.

3 You are the best financial analyst in town but also the most efficient user of the word processor. Does it make economic sense for you to do your own word processing? Would your answer change if you were:

a) freelance;
b) employed by a large investment trust company? Make your assumptions clear.

4 What are the key advantages of specialization and the division of labour? Explain how companies like ASDA, ICI or Cadbury Schweppes reap economies of scale. Distinguish between internal and external economies.

5 Why is co-operation an essential form of economic behaviour and by what kind of means can this be encouraged?

6 How can uncertainty be distinguished from risk? Illustrate your answer from current news items. Is it possible to transform uncertain situations into risky ones and vice versa?

4

Law, custom and money

INTRODUCTION

This chapter focuses on the 'rules of the game', *laws* and *customs*, essential integral features of *any* economic story, indispensable for people making decisions in a world of imperfect information and uncertainty. We explore and clarify how these rules may affect economic relationships and underline their significance. Rules provide the basic prerequisite, a key underpinning for all economic systems, affecting the way in which resources are co-ordinated and the rewards distributed.

In Chapter 2 we introduced a simplified classification of economic systems, all of which have distinctive institutionalized rules. Here we look more closely at the nature of these rules, whether formal or informal. Societies through historical time have evolved quite different dictates for ensuring the co-operation of people, necessary in order to organize and derive the benefits of the division of labour and specialization and to distribute the rewards. The extent and type of co-operation, competition and indeed the means for handling conflict, both within organizations like firms and in markets, depend on institutionalized rules. Their make-up is complex, dependent on socio-economic and political factors. Some rules foster an increasing division of labour, specialization and exchange; others hold this back. None the less, rules are vital for people coping with knowledge, ignorance and uncertainty.

The nature of law and custom is complicated and many-sided, often thought to be the preserve of lawyers, anthropologists and political scientists. But law and custom is also an appropriate focus for the economist. Once we leave the confines of the traditional economic model set in analytical time, where perfect information and certainty reign, then laws and customs become significant. People making economic decisions in perspective time, of necessity, require a framework of rules. Whilst we introduce the nature and effects of formal and informal rules in general, in particular we focus on property rights, a subset of these institutionalized rules. The mix of property rights, including personal, collective and communal rights, varies over time and place. These rules alter the costs and benefits involved in co-ordinating activity in different organizations. They interact in a symbiotic process of cause and effect, changing over time. We illustrate how 'the rules of the game' may promote the wealth of nations by making possible the economic gains emphasized in the last chapter. Moreover, we shall have more to say about the significance of law and custom in later chapters.

In the simple model of exchange developed in Chapter 3, set in analytical time, trade took place without any reference to rules in general and in particular without the use of money. But money itself serves as an important illustration of a legal rule or convention, an important economic institution. Money plays a key role in any developed economy. Here we ask: What is money? How did people in historical time manage without it? What does money do and how has it evolved through time? Money reduces the costs of human associations; it encourages the development of some organizations, in particular, markets and business firms and it facilitates the co-ordination of resources and the distribution of rewards. Money flows through markets, but it also moves directly between individuals and organizations, not as a direct result of market transactions. The discussion of the circular flow of money and real goods and resources in a market system forms the prelude to Chapter 5 when we focus attention on explaining how markets work, the price mechanism and market allocation. Finally, the relevance of trust will be underlined for rational economic people require trust.

RULES OF THE GAME – INSTITUTIONS

Definition and overview

In earlier chapters we have drawn attention to the impact of different property rights in particular and the diversity of laws and customs in general, in historical time and place. The laws and customs relating to property rights are part of an overall framework of rules, 'the rules of conduct' which structure human relationships. Whilst economists are concerned primarily with economic interactions, these need to be understood within the context of a framework of rules; the institutional backdrop and underpinning, significant for explaining economic behaviour and outcomes.

Whatever human society we spotlight, simple or technologically advanced, past or present, rules are necessary to order, constrain and guide people, in fact, to ensure the production and reproduction of the system itself. There must be a set of rules as Joan Robinson (1962: 10) said, 'to reconcile conflict between contrary tendencies, each of which is necessary for existence' – like self-interest and altruism. Rules exist because of the need to reduce the difficulties involved in human interaction, where people relate to each other and make decisions in perspective time. We have to cope with our own limitations in gathering, and making sense of information and dealing with fundamental uncertainty. As North maintains 'the major role of institutions in society is to reduce uncertainty by establishing a stable (but not necessarily efficient) structure to human interaction' (North 1990: 9).

The framework of rules or institutions, as North defines them is made up of both formal and informal rules and the additional rules of enforcement.

Formal rules   At one end of the spectrum these can include a written constitution, for example, as in the USA, common law which evolves over a period of time, built on custom and practice based on precedent cases, or statute law created by formal legislation. In addition, there are local by-laws and of course legal contracts between individuals, like marriage. At the other end of the spectrum formal rules incorporate taboos, custom and tradition of simpler societies. As economies become more complex, so do the required rules. Many of the intricate formal rules of modern economies are very different from the unwritten taboos and traditions of earlier societies, where modern legislation would be irrelevant. Formal rules are altered by studied action, an increasing volume of laws are set and changed by a State legislative process, in modern societies. Yet such laws are, in part, dependent on the formal and informal rules of both past and present. Many examples exist including: laws relating to property, patent and copyright laws, and the panoply of merchant, company and consumer law. The rules about who can and cannot hold shares in companies, are different in the USA, Japan and Germany for example (*Economist* October 1994).

However, human interaction is not simply affected by formal institutions. Informal pressures are also significant in determining behaviour.

Informal rules or constraints   These include conventions, norms of behaviour, and codes of conduct, some often ingrained as *habit* and *routine*. But all are based on traditions, customs and practices of the past. Some rules are complex, others symbolic expressing intent, for example, nodding the head at an auction. This is unwritten in any law but accepted as appropriate practice in auction markets to signify a bid. Certainly, the market player who does not understand or play by such rules might lose out. Customary pay differentials and tipping, although quite different in their impact, are part of these informal rules. Ethical codes of business conduct, indeed many voluntary standards of behaviour all help to order economic life. Language itself is an important convention. These standards and conventions are culturally determined, and very different, for example, between the British and Japanese, Nigerians and New Zealanders or between groups like the Quakers, Islamic or Jewish people. Such differences have important consequences for working practices and productivity, investment and consumption, indeed a very wide range of economic issues.

Yet unlike the act of parliament there is *no* formal edict which can change informal rules. What brings about change in norms and conventions is not easy to pinpoint and takes us well beyond the realms of economics. Informal rules may be modified through group pressure, changes in cultural or religious climates. Informal and formal rules interact with each other, evolving over time, affected by and affecting socio-economic and political realities. But informal rules may change very slowly; vestiges of the past lingering in the present, unlike the formal rule which can be altered by a parliamentary decree, or the change of a local authority by-law. Specific acts of parliament, in a British context, for example, the Equal Pay Act (1975), and the Sex Discrimination Acts (1975 and 1986) may formally outlaw unequal treatment between men and women. However, deep seated informal rules may continue at the work place and in society at large, perpetuating discrimination. Yet the passage of legislation may act, in part, to change underlying views, to highlight what are considered unacceptable practices. Changes in the law signal information and can affect values and norms in consequence. So informal rules evolve, often feeding back into the formal structure. Economies have unique blends of rules as a result of their different histories, their cultural, political and economic past and present.

The rules of enforcement   Both formal and informal rules require enforcement. Given 'rules of the game', there has to be the means to oversee and regulate them, to measure the extent of any breach or infringement, to police and correct. Indeed, the setting and large-scale enforcement of formal rules are important functions of the modern nation state and the supra-national organizations which provide international law and regulation in the late twentieth-century global economy. These are as diverse as, for example, NATO, the European Community parliament, the European Convention on Human Rights and the World Bank.

In contrast, informal constraints may be enforced by peer group pressure, by social sanction, the prospect of retaliation in the event of 'transgression' or self-monitoring and policing simply based on personal integrity. No matter what rules exist there will be those who break them. Moreover, what is illegal and/or informally unacceptable in one society at a particular historical time may be legal and acceptable in another. What is considered sharp business practice by one group may be considered acceptable by others. The legalization and legitimization of some activities can have a significant impact on economic behaviour, as we shall see in the case of Usury 'laws'. What are now illegal drugs in Britain were not always outlawed. Indeed, particular rule sets have varied considerably, in historical time and place. A comparison of contemporary societies alone illustrates a wide diversity. Contrast the 'rules of conduct' in a Third World country with those of the USA, the UK, Russia, Taiwan or Brazil, old and new industrial hands. Western economies with value systems descended in large part from a Graeco-Roman and Judaeo-Christian ancestry have different business practices when compared with the so-called Asian Tigers, for example, a modern successful economy like Taiwan, whose heritage is different – based on a Chinese culture and the religious thoughts of Confucianism and Daoism (Sheng, Chang and French 1994).

Institutional rules are significant. But what patterns of rules are best for encouraging economic development? How can these be engineered in practice? The very intricacy of rules and their sensitivity to time and place dashes the hope of a simple answer. However, we can consider the functions of such institutional rules in a time framework, inquiring further into the question of why rules are a critical, integral component of economic life; and how they evolve.

Institutional rules in analytical, perspective and historical time

To shed more light on the necessity of rules, take the model of simple exchange between Maureen and Mary from Chapter 3. In this hypothetical analytical time mode people have no need for a framework of rules. We implicitly assumed each individual had ownership rights over her output. Both were free to enter into voluntary exchange relationships with each other. Of course they had perfect information and the gains from their trade were acquired with zero search and transaction costs. Trade and production were instantaneous. There was no possibility that either would renege on the deal. No cheating nor unforseen event beyond their control would render the women incapable of meeting their mutual agreement. They would exchange specified quantities of a known quality product at an agreed price. There were no doubts, no need for trust, nor any third party to adjudicate or enforce their arrangements in a certain world. The contract is simple and complete. In analytical time, institutionalized rules for negotiating, organizing, regulating and policing exchange, would be superfluous. Moreover, to set aside resources as a precaution or for insurance would be unnecessary.

In *perspective time* the account is different. To understand individuals and their organizational behaviour we must consider the rules of conduct, formal and informal, which people invent as a necessary reaction to a complex reality. Such institutionalized rules can actually help to reduce the costs of human interaction by giving a framework for organizing human exchange, whether economic, social or political. Formal and informal rules help to reduce the impact of imperfect knowledge, the problems of risk and uncertainty. They help people to cope with their own limited ability to process the mass of information which they actually possess and allow for that which they cannot know. Institutions are datums, constraints which help decision-makers. Those engaged in an economic exchange are more confident about the actions of others if there are known laws, effectively enforced, and generally accepted conventions. These place boundaries on what people expect, and so limit the information needed for making decisions in new situations. Some elements can be 'taken as read', now and in the foreseeable future. Rules help to define the possibilities in any particular situation, in interpersonal exchange or interactions in a wider context. They provide economic players with a view of what is 'normal', so curtailing search and transaction costs. Rules reduce uncertainty by giving a secure structure to human transactions.

Economic interaction in perspective time may involve complex deals which often extend over long periods of time. Intentions and agreements in reality cannot be perfectly mapped out – not every eventuality can be specified. Contracts are perforce incomplete. Even in the case of exchange, where markets are well developed and private property rights are clearly specified and upheld, any contract – the result of the intentions and agreement of people – always carries uncertainty. There may be shocks and surprises. That applies whether the 'contract' is a verbal agreement between friends in a non-market context or a sophisticated legal document specifying terms of a billion pound agreement. Knowledge of formal laws at one extreme or the use of habitual routines at the other help decision-makers. And the order which rules bring helps to ensure production and survival of the system itself. The constraining institutional framework ensures connections between successive periods; whether in carrying debt contracts through time, the passing of wealth from one generation to another or the handing on of tacit knowledge.

Moreover, importantly, laws and customs also give an important measure of security and comfort in the face of fundamental uncertainty. Institutional rules can be a direct source of positive utility gains for people coping in an uncertain world. Age old practices, routines, conventions help people to cope in times of turbulence. They reassure and soothe, as vital in the modern technologically sophisticated world, as in ancient times.

Economic historians like North (1990, 1993) and evolutionary economists argue that institutionalized rules are significant for explaining individual and group economic behaviour and different levels of economic activity in economies over time. The existing rules of an economy at a point in historical time have a profound effect by helping to set the relative costs and benefits of different forms of production and exchange; structuring incentives and very importantly affecting whether resources are co-ordinated through markets or other organizations. Institutions ensure more than a guidance for individuals in perspective time. The production and reproduction of the overall system itself depends on orderliness (Carvalho 1983–4). Rules are themselves part of an intricate process of cause and effect in economic evolution. As North (1990: 6) states: '[t]hese cultural constraints not only connect the past with the present and future, but provide us with a key to explaining the path of historical change'. Indeed, North (1993) argues that institutional rules are the most important determinant of economic performance. Together with the factors of production and technology, the standard constraints of economic theory, 'the rules of the game', are key elements determining the production possibilities which face different societies. Economic development requires a stable underlying institutional framework which will bolster the incentives for individuals and organizations to engage in productive activity, to expand the division of labour specialization and trade. These require human co-operation.

To give institutional rules such prominence stands in sharp contrast to the orthodox economic approach, where institutional rules are imperfections, parameters held constant or factors simply ignored. Whilst working in an orthodox analytical time mode is useful for isolating certain key economic variables, we need a wider appreciation.

Economists can gain important insights into economic interactions by observing the *evolution of rules*. The consequences of institutions are always 'a mixed bag' (North 1990). Whilst some help to further the division of labour and co-operation, for example, the development of company law and money itself, or the Protestant ethic, others reduce it. The requirement to pay conventional bribes, which force up transaction costs in parts of the Third World, or outdated bureaucratic rules and procedures, hamper development. In a recent fascinating comparative study of national innovation systems, Nelson *et al.* (1993) link institutional arrangements to technological and economic performance. Distinctive national characteristics pervade firms, educational systems, the law, government 'all shaped by a shared historical experience and culture'. One of the factors cited for the relative decline in Britain's industrial standing in the twentieth century is said to be '[w]eakness in coordination, due *inter alia* to the strong tradition of individualism (at institutional as well as personal levels)' (Walker 1993: 188).

Over historical time societies had different cultural, religious, political even geographical features, associated with different mixes of formal and informal rules. In very early societies there were no formal rules as set by a strong centralized state, simply custom, convention and taboo. Rules were enforced by the group, often determined by a single ruler, perhaps with a council of elders, on a traditional basis. Tradition would have legitimized private property, such as it was. Production and exchange were guided by rules handed down over time, passed on by word of mouth. Neolithic farmers had no need for complex rules of procedure or enforcement, for exchange and production were on a small, personalized scale. The incentives to cheat or shirk were few and those who broke the basic unwritten rules would be dealt with by clearly defined traditional sanctions.

In contrast, the early civilizations, whether we think of those in Egypt, the Greek City States or China, had comparatively well developed, written formal laws. Their customs and conventions were quite different; each possessed a unique institutionalized order where unique myths and religion helped to shape the rules. In Rome, for example, a strong centralized state acted as an enforcer, providing a judiciary and policing. Roman order covered a wide geographical area providing the stable environment for amassing wealth and tribute. However, with the collapse of the Roman Empire, the strong centralized state in Europe disappeared, although Roman law and Christianity, for example, were passed on through time. Economic activity and trade shrank without the policing and protection of Rome.

The emergence of feudal Europe saw a rigid division of labour where people had very clearly defined roles set by law and custom. Serfs were not allowed to leave the land and required to give up a fixed portion of their output to their lords, both spiritual and temporal. There were feudal obligations for the owners of the land too. Feudal knights gave organization and protection in the absence of a secure, robust central government. As in earlier societies, religion helped to give the rationale and the guiding principles. Religion underpinned formal and informal rules, providing a large element of confidence and security in a world where people had no sophisticated scientific or technological know-how.

The laws and customs of the medieval world, whilst effective for structuring incentives in simple agrarian societies, were essentially inimical to the development of an extensive and changing division of labour. Making a profit from industry or trade was unacceptable. *Usury*, money lending, was offensive and the earning of interest 'unlawful'. Given usury laws, people would disguise interest payments in loan contracts as, for example, penalties for late payments (North 1990: 125). This made payment and enforcement of interest difficult and thus costly. It put a brake on the provision of capital for investment. In addition, the notion of a 'just price' was all important, a fair transaction, where to make a profit at someone else's expense, was seen as sinful.[1] The general attitudes, laws and conventions helped to sustain a static agrarian economy based on rigid lines, impeding commercial and industrial development. Islamic traditions in existence today take this view.

The incentives to invest and make profit were not developed. In the medieval world, the surplus output over and above that required for subsistence was generally spent by the clergy, nobility and princes. It was often consumed, spent on wars or set aside for God. Cathedrals and churches were important. The division of labour and specialization for the market or within other organizations was very limited. Markets and the market exchange process were confined to relatively small enclaves in society and wider trade was restricted. Change took place very slowly, but inexorably.

What rule changes were required for the development of markets and industrialization?

In historical time, various changes in the pattern of rules have clearly facilitated the division of labour, specialization and the growth of markets by lowering search and transaction costs. However, such alterations, influencing how things are done, form part of a complex process of cause and effect, interacting with many factors including technological change.

When trade grows beyond exchange in small personalized groups, then search and transactions costs can increase significantly. More resources have to be devoted to negotiation, measurement and the enforcement of deals. Religious codes were (and are) important, particularly in the absence of a well defined political structure or common formal rules. Extensive trade requires secure property rights and the political and judicial organization to enforce contracts; to protect property across international boundaries. Regular exchange existed without clearly defined nation states but the rules of exchange were enforced by threat of feuds between family and tribal groups (North 1990). As trade and production have developed, the constraining political order has become more complex and there has been a growth in impersonal forms of interaction. As global economic activities, whether in production, trade or investment, have become more widespread, supra-national government, international organizations and international laws have developed. This process is assisted by sophisticated technology. The supra-national government is a far cry from the localized authority of the tribal chieftain or council. Of course, in localized small-scale trading of simple products, on a personal face to face basis, complex contracting, legal rules and enforcement were unnecessary; and given the technology, impossible.

The Agrarian and Industrial Revolutions and the eventual rise of modern societies were associated with the development of increasingly complex formal institutional frameworks. These were required to structure the involved exchange and production processes in a world where technological and industrial changes were moving much more rapidly. Company, financial and labour law, indeed an evolving array of legislation was crucial for development. However, modifying informal rules – habits and conventions – takes time; people 'un-learn' slowly. Traditional values and ways of proceeding exist in the modern world, as an important part of the economic and social fabric. Groups of conventions may be beneficial in furthering both co-operation and competition, whether reducing conflict or not. An assessment of the effect of rules, in part, depends on the perspective of the observer.

In technologically advanced societies, complex contracts or agreements are necessary for decision-making. The growing number of formal rules, and the increasing involvement of state organizations operating in legal, judicial and regulatory guises, go hand-in-hand. 'Rolling back the State' with privatization, as in, for example, the sale of nationalized industries, has been accompanied by a proliferation of regulatory bodies such as: Ofwat, Oftel, Ofgas, designed to oversee and uphold the 'rules of the game' (for further discussions see Chapters 6 and 10). Increasingly the multidimensional attributes of complicated goods and resources have to be set out in exchange contracts. With the inability to identify every possible future eventuality, it is impossible to draw up contracts setting out all provisions. There has to be a third party adjudicator to enforce contracts; a secure and robust central government to provide stability. So in modern economies, the strong state is a key feature. The importance of religious codes and laws has declined although religious philosophies still have significance. Whilst the extent and particular details of state activity varies in different societies, in developed economies these activities are extensive.

Some institutional changes enable the lowering of transaction costs, like the long evolution of maritime and merchant law and the gradual spread of clearly defined property rights and international laws of protection. This helped to bring about the development of modern economic systems. Rules designed to improve the quantity and quality of information to buyers, whether, for example, through standardized weights and measures, or the Trades Description Act, all play a part. Over historical time, rules have evolved to enable people to spread the risks of their transactions, and to insure, for example, the development of Lloyds of London (see Chapter 12) and maritime insurance law. In more recent times, in Britain the advent of the Small Claims Courts, and the institution of an entitlement to legal aid for some groups who would otherwise be unable to enforce their contracts, has helped to reduce costs. We shall have much more to say about the development of standardized money later in this chapter, but note that the adoption of the metric system in Britain was undertaken to make trading easier, bringing production and exchange dealings into line with major trading partners who used metric measures. Sterling was decimalized, shillings and old pence are now a feature of the past. Moreover, the call for a single European currency is based, in part, on the desire to reduce transactions costs, to sweep away charges for changing money, converting one money price, say in Deutschmarks to another in Francs. This is to make economic life easier and facilitate exchange.

Formal and informal rules: speed of change and system intricacy

How quickly and effectively can the rules of the game be changed? In any economy, formal rules can change relatively quickly but informal conventions change much more slowly. Revolution may ensure the rapid change of written laws and a constitution, but 'old habits die hard'. The events surrounding the disintegration of the USSR give an insight into the unique intricacy of a particular system and the difficulty of engineering change in a specific direction. The move towards an economy based on western market lines is not simply a matter of edict. The Soviet economic structure evolved over a long period of time, with 'rules of the game' suitable for central planning. *Perestroika* and *glasnost* – the liberalization of the system – weakened the necessary co-ordination functions of central planning without providing a timely substitute. Market institutions and the organizational structures associated with them take time to develop. The changes introduced by Gorbachev led to an absolute fall in output and paved the way for political disintegration. The Gross Domestic Product, year on year, in 1992 fell by 30 per cent (Matthews 1993: 139). Even though this reduction in output was mostly in armaments and investment goods, further falls in output are feared. The Russian economy may take some considerable time to embrace market conventions.

Moreover, the path of change may be different from that expected by policy-makers and Western observers. Informal rules, for example, may still ensure that old patterns of behaviour continue. In the case of the Russian economy in recent time, Matthews notes

> (t)he economy might have collapsed even more completely had it not been that many government decisions were not carried out, and indeed were not capable of being carried out, as new laws piled on top of old unrepealed ones – a repetition of events in the years after 1917.
>
> (1993: 140)

Managers of old state enterprises have had to develop barter systems to survive but this 'does not guarantee the evolution of a stable interdependent decision-making system' (ibid). In what was the USSR people and their organizations continue to function by relying on the customs and conventions of the past in the face of rapid changes in the formal rules and the economy around them.

There are no clear blueprints for changing an economic system. Each economy is constrained to some extent by an inheritance from the past and also factors beyond its control in the present. But when the rules break down there can be disastrous consequences for economic production and exchange, particularly in a revolution or war. The horrendous uncertainties of civil war provide no firm basis for developing the benefits of specialization and exchange. Conflict prevails. Events in what was Yugoslavia, given the collapse of communism, have seen a distinct change in the institutional framework and a dramatic fall in output and living conditions, given the conflict which ensued.

The rise in nationalism in Eastern Europe and Russia, and the uncertainty about the new procedures have imposed extra costs. The hope is that long-term gains will outweigh short-term costs. Hodgson (Hodgson and Screpanti 1991: 163) discusses the views of several writers who argue that wars or revolutions – external shocks or internal discontinuities – may bring opportunities for restructuring an economy and its social fabric, thereby giving faster economic growth. As it is not possible to rerun historical time, we cannot be sure what the consequences of an alternative path would have been. Some would argue that a lack of disruption can be a partial explanation for the relative economic decline of both Britain and the USA. Countries which are contrasted with this include: Belgium, France, Germany, Italy and Japan. These nations have faced either war and occupation or revolutions in the last two centuries. Their frameworks of rules have been altered considerably, and have not been allowed to ossify. But it would be hard to sustain this case for Serbians, Bosnians and Croatians. In contrast, Sweden and Switzerland, countries not involved in war or revolution in such time, rank as economic success stories.

At any point in time the blend of customs and conventions, of formal and informal rules is a mixture; some will facilitate and enhance change, others will act as a hindrance. Every person and organization is circumscribed to a greater or lesser extent by traditions, which affect human interactions in the present and the way in which the future is created. Some environments may have rules of the game which foster technological change and rapid economic growth. But it is often just not possible to unravel cause and effect in a symbiotic process.

One aspect of the institutional framework which is particularly useful in understanding economic development are rules which relate to property; they are a central feature in economic life.

PROPERTY RIGHTS

Property rights, often taken for granted in orthodox approaches, have found considerable attention amongst some economists, who draw attention to their importance in structuring exchange and production. (For further discussion and references, see Ricketts 1987, 1994.) A pattern of property rights is important, for it specifies what people are entitled to do with resources and goods. Formal and informal rules which give rights over use, ownership and disposal may be more or less clearly defined. It is helpful to distinguish between different property rights structures and explore their attributes because this enables us:

1 to clarify situations where markets present the most appropriate co-ordinator and

allocator of goods and resources on the one hand, and on the other, where alternative organizational responses are either necessary or more efficient,

2 to distinguish those property rights structures which may favour an increasing division of labour and specialization from those which do not. A classification of rights shows the different prerogatives which people have over resources and goods. Maureen and Mary were implicitly assumed to have private ownership. Each had the right to use her own beer or bread, to exclude others from the use of her own goods, and the liberty to exchange such rights. We shall begin by examining private ownership in more detail.

Private rights

Private ownership is of major importance in the modern capitalist economy. It is possible to own land, buildings, machinery, consumer goods – an amazing array of articles and resources as a private individual. And with this ownership comes the right to exchange or to give away private property.

Significantly, people do not now have the right to own other human beings, for slavery is illegal, an important feature to which we shall return to in Chapter 14.

Private property rights provide the entitlement to use property only in circum-scribed ways. Even in economies with very well defined property rights people have a claim to do only certain things with the goods they have bought, been given or inherited. In modern day Britain, the purchase of a pint of beer or a car brings with it *exclusivity*. No one else is entitled to drink the beer or drive the car without the owner's consent. Whilst ownership gives the right to exclude others from use, it does not bring the right to do exactly as the purchaser pleases. The ownership of beer does not confer the right to squirt beer at a passing stranger. The ownership of the motor vehicle does not give the owner the right to drive it at excessive speed, and/or whilst under the influence of drink. There are clear rules relating to the use of a private car. The presence of well defined private property rights and the appropriate laws for policing such rights are of key importance and underpin market exchange and inheritance. If it were not possible to exclude others from the use of private goods few would be willing to purchase them. If 'ram raiding' were to reach extensive proportions in Britain, people would be reluctant to buy cars. The demand, particu-larly for new cars, would be reduced. There would be adverse effects for both production and consumption. The sanctity of private property and the traditional rules of private inheritance underpin the market mechanism. Private property rights are required because of *rivalry*. If there were an over abundance of goods and resources, there would be no need to protect what a family might have against the actions of others. Everyone could have exactly what they wanted. However, as a result of scarcity all desires cannot be met, so people want to have secure rights over their property. These secure rights reduce uncertainty.

Hunters and gatherers in simple societies and small traders involved in exchange, did not have well defined property rights with recourse to formal laws to protect them. They relied on custom and convention in small scale dealings. They would not have wanted to break religious codes or tribal practices, therefore despite the lack of a legal contract and the absence of any well defined state policing, an organized and secure trade could often take place. But in many societies, particularly those in the past, private property played a very much smaller role than it does in modern economies today. There are other types of property rights to consider:

Communal rights

In some situations people hold the rights to use a resource in common with others. Common lands used for grazing animals in feudal Britain enabled peasants to use a valuable resource. They did not own the common, they had no legal contract but custom and practice gave them rights of use, for example, to collect wood. The common land which still remains in existence is open to those who still have prescribed rights; they do not have to ask permission of another to use common land and cannot be excluded (see Chapter 6). Much agricultural land in Nigeria, for example, is communally owned. Indeed, if none can be excluded from the use of a resource it is by definition communal.

Collective rights

Collective rights are quite different from the two preceding forms. Given private or communal rights, the decisions about the use of the resource or good, are left to the individual, providing they are made within the circumscribed limits. A collective right involves a decision on behalf of the group. Monastic orders like the Cistercians, Carthusians and Benedictines 'owned' the land, buildings and other resources, but decisions about the use of these would either have to be taken by a 'manager', the Abbot, often with absolute control and/or by a select group or by a vote of all monks. Many monastic orders were part of the larger organization of the Roman Catholic church, where ultimately the Pope had the final word.

Over historical time the development of such rights has been important. The collective ownership of a public limited company, where shareholders leave managers to undertake the day-to-day running of the organization, is an important example which we shall develop in Chapter 9. In the modern economy, just as in past times, it can often be the case that concentrating property rights in a single holder is not necessarily the most efficient solution. Sometimes the *sharing* of property rights may be more suitable, as in the case of the joint stock company. In the large corporation a multitude of individuals own shares. There are costs and benefits to be found in different forms of ownership, and property rights laws evolve over time to reflect this.

Collective assets such as shares in public limited companies are *exchangeable*, they can be traded in well developed capital markets. However, not all collective assets are exchangeable. Assets taken into state ownership cannot be traded in markets. There were no markets for land and capital in the Soviet Union. Part ownership in state-owned companies could not be traded. Indeed, there are in any society rights which are not tradeable: 'inalienable rights'. Often items which are not sold on markets but are allocated to an individual by non-market means, at a zero or nominal price, like a university place, the right to adopt a child or citizenship granted to an immigrant, cannot be sold to someone else (see Chapter 6).

Transactions costs are not independent of the type of property rights in which trade takes place. If we look back through historical time we can see how these property rights have changed to facilitate development. Whether through the Enclosures in Scotland or the development of collective tradeable rights of the joint stock company, these evolved to allow the development of economies of scale and large-scale production. In some cases ownership rights were seized. One historical example is given by the dissolution of the monasteries, the wholesale grabbing of land and property by Henry VIII, at knock-down prices. Some abbots and clerics who co-operated were paid handsome pensions, others who tried to secure the church's property paid with their lives, in a one-sided power struggle.

Yet for economic growth, societies require well defined and enforceable property rights. This reduces risk and uncertainty, and can bring peace of mind to individuals. In twentieth-century Britain, assets have changed from private to public ownership, and then back again through privatization sales, instigated by economic change and the political decision-making process. The ownership of the means of production in the old Soviet world has changed. The appropriate mix of property rights for economic development is subject to change and debate. Money is another key socio-economic institution necessary for economic development and it is to this subject we now turn.

MONEY: DEFINITION AND SIGNIFICANCE – OVERVIEW

What is money and what does it do? Why does money matter? There is no mystery about money – it is anything which is commonly offered or accepted for buying and selling goods and services, and for settling debts – a means of payment. In a modern economy, money is used to pay people for their work, and to recompense them for the use of their resources.

Money can be legal tender or can simply take a customary form. It is a social invention and what functions as money depends in part on historical time and place. Money has taken many different forms and developed over time from the commodity money of antiquity, like gold, silver, barley, salt and even decorative shells. These had a use value apart from functioning as money. In some circumstances today, cigarettes and illegal drugs act as commodity money in prisons, or in countries where local currency is unacceptable, as in parts of Eastern Europe. In the modern economy, money has no intrinsic value except in fulfilling a role as money.

In late twentieth-century Britain we have cash in our pockets and money in the bank. *Notes* and *coins*, are acceptable to make everyday purchases, like payments in shops and restaurants, where relatively small value transactions are made. *Bank accounts* on which people draw cheques, form bank money, offered and accepted in exchange for all kinds of transactions. Indeed, cheques are currently the dominant form of payment in the UK (Henderson 1993). In modern economies the assets which function as money have increased. Given legislative change in Britain, The Building Societies Act 1986, allowed the societies to provide chequing accounts and to develop full banking services. Now building society accounts with checking facilities count as money, prior to this change such accounts could not be used directly as money.

Recent *technological changes* have helped to foster innovations. In Britain now, ATM (Automated Teller Machines), which dispense cash, adorn the high street, shopping precinct, even hospitals and universities. People can have ready access to their cash at any time. What is more, banks can be instructed to move funds, almost instantaneously, internationally from one account to another at a few taps on the computer keyboard. Technological developments have brought significant changes to the banking system and the way we use cash. Some observers even predict the eventual redundancy of cash. The electronic funds transfer at point of sale (EFT–POS), where the retailer's cash terminal is connected directly to the bank to transmit electronic messages, scraps the need for paper transactions (Henderson 1993). Indeed, such technology could enable the bulk of financial transactions to be made through advanced information networks. Although a cashless society may be an unlikely scenario given the existence of the 'under-cover' illegal economy, where people do not wish their financial transactions to be recorded or monitored. Certainly, technological change has allowed us to economize on the use of cash. Plastic credit cards, for example, enable us to shop without using money, although at the end of the month the credit card account has ultimately to be settled with money. For those living in any modern economy, whether paying in dollars or deutschmarks, francs or yen, it is difficult to imagine life without the sheer convenience of money.

Yet not all societies in the past used money. Moreover, even in the many societies where money circulated, the large majority of people would have used it on an irregular basis, if at all. In these societies money was important for denominating large contracts, measuring wealth and keeping account of debt. But to understand the importance of money in a modern economic system and its role in facilitating specialization, production and exchange, we ask why and how societies and individuals could manage without it.

Barter in analytical, perspective and historical time

In Chapter 3 we focused attention on the direct swapping of goods – barter – where no money changes hands and the price of one good is expressed in terms of another. In analytical time, Maureen and Mary have perfect knowledge and face no uncertainty. Production and exchange are effectively instantaneous in this hypothetical mode. They do not need money, as with other conventions, their exchange is achieved without it. We have to leave the analytical time mode to show when and where money matters.

Barter   This is exchange without money. A completely self-sufficient person has no need for money. In historical time those who were not self-sufficient, but who had quite an extensive division of labour and specialization, found it possible to do without such a convenience. Barter was used in the relatively simple economies of the past. Palaeolithic hunters and gatherers exchanged surplus skins for decorative jewellery, which small farming communities could not produce.[2] Neolithic farmers traded surplus produce with the specialist manufacturers of flint tools and weapons, which farming communities could not readily produce for themselves. The relatively advanced Inca empire thrived for many centuries despite the absence of money. It had some division of labour and specialization and was able to construct sophisticated road systems and buildings, which surpassed the engineering feats of the Romans. Yet no money was used despite the ready availability of gold. There was no private ownership of land, little personal property and no private business. Only small handicrafts, including household goods or utensils, made by craftsmen in their spare time were bartered at small local markets or occasionally at larger principal centres. Production was communal and periodic public distributions of goods from communal stores to households, if surplus to family needs, were also bartered (Alden Mason 1964).

Those living in simple societies, for example, the medieval monk living in a European monastic community, the indigenous American living in the tribe, had little need of money. Communal production prevailed for the consumption of the group, not for market sale. The feudal command economy in Europe was essentially non-monetary, although merchants and, for example, those frequenting markets and fairs would have used coinage. Only when in some parts of Western Europe feudal command eventually gave way to a capitalist economy, based on private ownership and the development of production for market exchange, did money became much more important in economic life. Such an evolutionary transformation was closely associated with the changing significance of money.

Countertrade   Barter, with its ancient pedigree, is still practised in small- and large-scale economic transactions in the Third World. It also occurs between industrialized nations and less developed countries. *Countertrade*, exchange without money, occurs between countries where at least one of the traders has a currency which is either non-convertible (of little value in relation to hard currencies), or has insufficient money to exchange. It is used when money transactions are not possible, as sometimes in Eastern Europe, and when countries are effectively bankrupt, unable to honour their financial commitments, as at times in Latin America. In the former USSR, where there is an inconvertible rouble and substantial supplies of raw materials, it is estimated that as much as one-third of total Western sales to Russia are financed through various countertrade deals (Thorniley and Reed 1993).

The principal Russian countertrade goods include oil, steel, chemical fertilizers, metals and scrap metals. They are swapped for a variety of western products. In Kazakhstan, for example, cotton is a popular countertrade commodity. With the decentralization in the region, oil, easy to ship in large volumes, is also frequently bartered. Some large multinational companies such as Fiat (Italy) and IBM (USA) have been organizing countertrade deals through their own specialist in-house departments. But there are significant transactions costs in perspective time. Often companies go to outside specialist countertrader houses or commodity brokers to organize, co-ordinate and monitor such deals. These firms can charge between 2–5 per cent of the value of the transaction. Why can bartering be costly?

The problems of barter and countertrade

In the modern world, as illustrated by many countertrade deals, barter is inconvenient and inefficient for large-scale deals. In fact, countertrade is often a last resort, to enable an exchange which would otherwise not happen. Just think of the difficulties of a farmer in a non-monetary, simple agrarian society. He has a cow surplus to requirements and wants to exchange it for goats. The first step is to find someone who wants to acquire a cow, and is willing and able to exchange an acceptable number of goats, in return. Suppose the cow owner wants three goats, but after searching locally – in perspective time he does not have perfect information – finds that no one is prepared and able to do such a swap. The search could be widened and/or the farmer could negotiate in order to make a deal. Perhaps a goat owner with *two* surplus animals, who also wants to take possession of a cow might be prepared to offer two goats plus five chickens. As a live cow is indivisible, to effect a deal the cow owner has to be prepared *either* to take less than he wanted, in effect making a part gift to the goat owner by swapping a cow for two goats and forgetting 'the change', *or* by accepting two goats and something in addition like chickens, in part exchange.[3]

A great deal of time could be wasted trying to match exactly the desires of would-be traders. A smooth and relatively cheap transaction would require:

A double coincidence of wants This would have to occur quickly. Luck may have to be with the farmer to find a trader with an exactly matching want. The cow owner may need to hunt about and possibly negotiate to effect a deal. The transaction can only take place if desires exactly match and each trader can deliver goods of the requisite quantity and quality (see Figure 4.1). To gain a simultaneous exchange in a world without money may entail significant search and transactions costs. Traders could not express these in monetary terms. But they could specify the opportunity

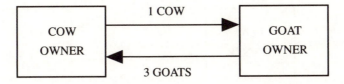

Figure 4.1 Barter and a double coincidence of wants: an exactly matching deal

cost of the time spent arranging such deals; time which might have been spent tending their animals or resting. Without a double coincidence of wants no exchange between two people can occur. But a solution might be achieved through negotiating with additional traders.

Triangular and multilateral trade   This occurs where more than two people are involved in joint multilateral swaps. This makes a double coincidence of wants unnecessary. Say that the first farmer cannot find an exactly matching deal. Suppose that the goat owner has only two goats and chickens to trade for a cow; no exchange can take place. But the cow owner, to complete a successful transaction, could search for, find and include another trader in the negotiations. This third person must be prepared to take chickens and simultaneously agree to offer a goat. The first farmer could take two goats from the second farmer in exchange for the cow. The second farmer could give his surplus chickens to the third farmer who in turn could give his surplus goat to the first farmer (see Figure 4.2). This completes a triangular simultaneous deal. The first farmer has sold the cow for three goats, two from the second farmer, one from the third. The second farmer has sold two goats and chickens and bought a cow. The third farmer has sold a goat and bought chickens.

However, the deal takes place in perspective time so hunting about for another potential trader, negotiating an additional agreement, would be even more complicated. The *multilateral barter*, including more than three traders would be more costly again in terms of time and effort. Furthermore, there are also increased potential risks. With more trading partners there are more possibilities for things to go wrong. Anyone who has been in a house purchasing chain, where all contracts have to be exchanged on the same date will realize the difficulties of completing simultaneous exchanges with multiple traders.

Whilst large groups could be involved in mutual swaps arranged at the same time, this would need careful co-ordination and planning; often very expensive in terms of

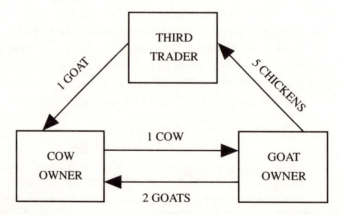

Figure 4.2   Barter but no double coincidence of wants: unnecessary with triangular trade

search and transactions costs. Complex arrangements are a barrier to trade, on anything but the most simple lines, an impediment to increasing specialization. Specialist firms of countertraders undertake such planning and co-ordination.

Without money there is no common unit of account. Keynes argued that the earliest money was not created to facilitate exchange but was devised as a unit of account, a numeraire (Davidson 1991b; Wray 1990). Without money there would be no way of simply and clearly expressing prices in terms of a common denominator. The permutations of price, the cow/goat exchange rate, the chicken/cow exchange rate and so on would involve a huge number of different rates as the number of goods increased. This difficulty would obscure information and cloud negotiations. When every price is expressed in one common unit, price information is transparent, allowing a ready comparison for traders.

Moreover, bartering does not divorce the act of buying and selling. 'Selling' a cow necessitates 'buying', other goods have to be accepted in return. At the same time, the buyer of a cow has to sell something too. Whether in bilateral or multilateral trade, everyone has to be *at one and the same time* both a buyer and a seller. Without money, no convenient mechanism exists for deferring or postponing purchase or sale to some future time. Moreover, a deal negotiated in such specific goods carries the risk that one of the traders might not be able to fulfil their agreements in a specific good. Thus a collapse (or disruption) of the whole deal is more likely, with no positive gain for the time and effort spent. This is a real problem faced by modern countertraders. Agreements are broken when goods of the appropriate quantity or quality are not delivered. Given the best intentions to honour a deal, unforseen problems can occur.

So in the late twentieth century where an acceptable currency is absent, but where there is the desire and ability to trade, it is not surprising that specialist countertrade organizations have evolved to cope with such problems. Search, co-ordination and negotiation costs are substantial. Nor should it be surprising that favourite modern countertrade goods are often basic commodities, such as cotton and oil. The nature of the product and monitoring its quality is relatively straightforward.

In economies based on tribal or feudal lines, exchange without money presented little problem amongst the members of relatively small, tightly knit groups. Information was easily available and therefore cheaply acquired. People either knew each other well or had a clear idea of what to expect of others. Swaps could be achieved at relatively low transaction and search costs. In any event, the need for exchange was limited. Output was produced by the family or local grouping for own consumption. There was nothing like the vast array of products facing rich twentieth-century consumers. With little or no private ownership, there were no land and capital markets. A collective security system existed. Borrowing and lending took place in times of need, but there was often no expectation of a money interest payment or even the return of what was lent – this was often a reciprocal gift. The fabric of life was not interwoven with monetary market exchange. Traditional communal or command allocation was all important and market transactions were insignificant.

For the basic commodities of a simple life, in small-scale local exchanges such monetary transactions were largely unnecessary.

The role of money in perspective and historical time

This is not to deny that trade has played an important part in historical time or that money has been absent. The rich cities and towns, the merchant classes and trading routes of past times bear witness to their importance. Money and its use have evolved over time, dependent, in part, on the particular laws and customs of the society in question. But whilst money was a feature of life in the past, most societies were not monetized. Whatever the 'coinage' of the tribal or feudal world, money was not essential to the everyday pattern of life of ordinary people. In contrast, modern industrialized systems could not function without money. The highly complex division of labour and specialization, the intricate web of economic relationships necessitates the use of money. With mass and highly specialized production, our increasing interdependency, and the associated need for money, grows.

Imagine the difficulties of paying late twentieth-century urban workers in terms of their own output. Feudal serfs produced simple agricultural produce for their own consumption, the manorial lord and the tithe for the church. They were 'paid' in kind with their agricultural produce. But in most cases it would be impossible to identify an individual's contribution to the production of complex goods and services. Individuals often work in teams to provide output of intricate indivisible commodities and services. Moreover, think of the problems of trying to sell a second-hand car in the absence of money, when the ultimate goal is to acquire a new personal computer and dancing lessons. In a different, yet still problematic scenario, the seller does not want to buy anything at the time of sale or is unsure of just what to acquire. There is only a desire to sell, immediately, for perhaps the car is troublesome.

Money is necessary where there are complex exchange and production relationships which extend widely over time and place. Money is *one* of the vital elements which enhance the division of labour, specialization and human economic interaction, by cutting down on search and transactions costs, facilitating human decision-making in perspective time. Yet how does money work and what does it require to work well? Economists put different emphasis on the importance and functions of money. We can examine the key roles which money fulfils in exchange and production. We have already identified the difficulties of 'money free' transactions in perspective time. This helps to illuminate the functions of money.

The functions of money

1 Money allows people to avoid the necessity of forming agreements to buy and sell goods simultaneously at one and the same time. By working as a *medium of exchange*, in fact, a means of payment, money enables a sequence of *bilateral* arrangements. A person with goods for sale can sell to anyone who has the money

to buy. No exchange of goods is required. Money frees the seller from the need to buy at the time of sale. Likewise, money emancipates the buyer from the need to sell at the time of purchase. A stock of money will enable people to obtain anything within their ability to pay (or borrow) from those with goods to sell. Money represents *general purchasing power*. It does not commit the holder to any specific item but can be given in exchange for a myriad of items. In a world of complex products, a double coincidence of wants in specific goods between two people would be rare indeed. Searching for them would be time consuming and frustrating. Think back to our examples of second-hand cars and dancing lessons. How could these sales and purchases be achieved without money in perspective time? Whilst multilateral trades might provide a solution, they could be hopelessly complex, particularly when dealing with intricate products and highly specialist services. The horrendous difficulties of arranging such deals would make them prohibitively expensive.

Money gives people the freedom to search for exactly what they want or at least a better deal. Money *reduces* search and transactions costs by reducing the time and effort that would otherwise be spent trying to synchronize acceptable and viable transactions. The use of money widens the possibilities open to both buyers and sellers.

2 In addition, and more importantly, according to Keynes, money acts as a single *unit of account*. It came into existence along with debts. Debts and price lists can only be expressed in the money of account. Money is delivered to discharge debt contracts and enables people readily to compute and compare the relative prices for the thousands of complex products. It would be almost impossible to work out the relative exchange values; the prices of millions of different products. This common denominator cuts transaction costs.

3 Money can be held as a *store of value*. It divorces the act of buying and selling. Money can be accepted at the point of one sale and stored to use at a later time; it enables a delay in committing real resources (Davidson 1991b). When goods are sold, money can be taken in exchange, saved to spend later: a cache of general purchasing power for use in the future. Moreover, money can be borrowed to spend now; to be paid back at a later date.

4 Once we recognize the possibilities of borrowing and lending money, moving purchasing power through time, we can underline the role of money as the *standard of deferred payment*. When people want to postpone the payment for goods or resources, they borrow. Debt contracts are the pledges to repay and the terms of these agreements are specified in money. This repayment includes the principal, the amount of money borrowed, plus an interest payment (see Chapter 11). The interest payment compensates lenders for forgoing the immediate use of their purchasing power, a return for waiting *and* an element to cover the risk and uncertainty. In perspective time the future is uncertain, the lender not only forgoes *liquidity* – the ability to have cash resources immediately, but also has to suffer the possibility of loss; borrowers might fall on hard times or cheat. Contracts made

now may not be honoured, if future expectations are not fulfilled. By issuing an IOU buying power can be transferred to the borrower. And as the mirror image, the holder of the IOU, that is the lender, obtains a claim on future buying power, a swap of purchasing power between different time periods – at some agreed rate of exchange – the interest rate – the price of the deal.

Money and production

Following on from this, it is important to understand that borrowing money is an essential element in the finance of production, not merely to enable people to bring forward the purchase of consumer goods. Money plays an important role in production, for all production takes time. The pin factory where Adam Smith observed the division of labour in the eighteenth century, was able to survive and prosper by selling its output in markets. But production for the market requires an entrepreneur to pay for resources *before* output can be finished and sold. Production does not occur instantaneously. Raw materials, capital equipment and people have to be brought together and services paid for usually *in advance* of sales. Some entrepreneurs had insufficient money of their own and loans were an answer to their cash shortage. They undertook debt commitments, specified in money. Even when finished goods were sold for cash so that more production could be paid for, the success of expanding order books necessitated yet more cash to finance increased purchases of raw materials, capital equipment and to pay the wages of more workers. A growth in market demand might require the entrepreneur to borrow again to pay for increased production in the drive to accumulate wealth.

The world of Adam Smith was some way from that of medieval serfs producing the bulk of their own requirements in an economic system where security came from the community and where communal property rights prevailed. But further back in historical time, in the Greek City State, there was private property and free men. Here producers borrowed money to finance production. Those who lent their stock of money, their own security, expected an interest to compensate them for their loss of *liquidity* (cash) and the inevitable uncertainties they shouldered. Borrowers wanted to enhance their production potential to ensure that they could make the repayments. If they could not repay debts with money, then they would have to pay with their own human capital. They would be taken into slavery, lawful at that time, locked into forced labour (Heinsohn and Steiger 1985).

Moreover, to reiterate, production for the market necessitates paying of people in money, as a basic financial claim; not in kind. In the modern economy, people often make a very small contribution to a complex product or service, and one which is impossible to isolate. They cannot be paid with the output of their administration factories, or fractional parts of indivisible, intricate, highly-specialized products and services.

Why have and hold money?

Money aids decision-making in perspective time. In both production and exchange activities money implies that a *discovery* process can be continued through time. People hold money to use as a *means of payment*, where it is impossible to synchronize all transactions. But people do not have perfect foresight about consumption and investment possibilities now and in the future. They also have to consider unexpected needs which might arise. Money as a store of value proves useful for what Keynes isolated as *speculative* and *precautionary* needs. He introduced the notion of speculative demand for money and explained how money would be held in preference to other financial assets, like government bonds, if speculators thought that bond prices were about to fall. Speculators wanted to avoid making a capital loss, so held money until they thought the price of bonds had bottomed out. They would buy bonds when they believed bond prices would rise. We can generalize this argument. A person may want to purchase a new car or house but instead of buying immediately may wait in order to take advantage of a possible price cut or a model change in the future. Some people in the early 1990s property slump in Britain refrained from buying and held out waiting for prices to fall further. In fact, money enables people to speculate on what might happen in a wide range of situations, to take advantage of development and learning, invention and innovation, in short, the process of change over time. Where we are unsure of the repercussions of consumption and investment expenditures and particularly where these are very expensive or impossible to reverse, money is a boon.

Money helps to provide insurance should the future turn out to be adverse for it can act as a precautionary balance. Accumulating money may bring a buffer against some of the vagaries of life, a security which can be readily transformed into goods. 'Money . . . is a means of handling the consequences of the excessive cost or the sheer impossibility of abolishing ignorance' (Loasby 1976). In a 'monetized' economy, money performs a vital function for people making production, investment and consumption decisions in perspective time. Money matters in modern economies. Yet in societies of the past, where there was also incomplete information, human fallibility and uncertainty, other social mechanisms provided security and most production was not for the market. Money was relatively insignificant.

Money: a pervasive feature of modern economies

Money is a pervasive feature of modern capitalist economies, characterized by private property, a complex division of labour, specialization and production for market exchange. In general, money facilitates a broader range of transactions both through time and place. The social institution of money *and* the civil law of contracts enables entrepreneurs and households to form sensible expectations about the certainty of cash flows (but not necessarily real outcomes) over time (Davidson 1991a and b). And to quote Sheila Dow:

[a]s the linchpin of the financial system – the means of payment and the last refuge of uncertainty – money plays a crucial role in the short run and in the long run. This role cannot however be disassociated from the setting of historical time and the formation of expectations under uncertainty that entails.

(1993: 23)

What does money require to function efficiently?

To fulfil its everyday function as a means of payment, money must have *portability*, *durability* and *divisibility*. Barley, for example, was too heavy in relation to its weight to fulfil this function. Precious metals like silver and gold were a more popular form of money through historical time. These did not rot if improperly stored. They had a high value to weight ratio and were also readily divisible, providing small change to facilitate a matching transaction. Modern money displays all of these attributes in varying degrees.

People must have *confidence* in money. They must believe that it will be readily acceptable to buy goods or settle debts in the future; that money will retain its value. This is a key element. Money is accepted in the expectation that it will allow the meeting of targets at later dates. Its very flexibility ensures that it can be accepted with no specific ideas about its future use. Yet people have to *trust* that money will be accepted by others and retain its value. The bank money of today cannot be consumed if things go wrong as could the commodity money of the past. Money becomes accepted habitually once trust is established. The longevity and permanence of the modern state helps to give money and the monetary system credibility. The *control of inflation* – where inflation is the general tendency for prices to rise – is often a key objective of government economic policy. The aim is to maintain confidence in money. Where that confidence is lost, for whatever reason, money ceases to function efficiently and people turn to other means, like countertrade. In dire circumstances of war, rampant inflation and economic breakdown people turn to bartering.

What is acceptable as money has to be an agreed social convention. In a move to reduce transactions costs in the European internal market, the European Bank wants to move to a common currency, the ECU. Whilst this could cut transactions costs, many people are wedded to their unique national currencies and traditions.

To understand the nature and role of money we have to leave the domain of analytical time. Money has no place in a situation where transactions are costlessly and instantaneously harmonized, information is perfect and individuals know exactly what they want. In perspective time, money is a convention, an established practice which allows people to cut down on the transactions costs and cope with fundamental uncertainty. Money enables a widening of trade and production, which otherwise would be impossible and permits the rearrangement of purchasing patterns through time. People make decisions in perspective time, where they do not have all the facts; they do not know exactly what the passage of time will bring or indeed what they will need or aspire to as the future unfolds. Money is a great advantage.

MONEY: A LINK BETWEEN INDIVIDUALS, ORGANIZATIONS AND MARKETS

Money provides market and non-market money links between individuals and organizations. The evolution of money and organizations, like business firms and markets go together. In a modern economy there are many different types of organizations, or 'societal units' (Fourie 1991) with purposeful intent and objectives. Economic aspects of these organizations will be examined in Part II, whilst the distinct nature of markets will be considered in the following chapter. Initially, however, notice the variety of 'societal units'. These include, for example: primarily social groupings, such as families, households, churches, voluntary groups; primarily economic groupings, such as business firms, trades unions or employer associations. Political organizations of the State, which include local councils, government departments, like the Inland Revenue and the DSS; educational bodies including schools and universities; health care organizations. These organizations can be highly complex. And all are externally linked to a greater or lesser extent by money flows. Money is also used *within* organizations, like the business firm as a unit of account.

In the rich and new industrializing countries, money links are strong, extensive and highly developed. Many money links are global, reflecting the growing importance of transnational transactions whether for trade, or the movement of international capital. Yet a significant amount of money flows in the form of *non-market* payments between individuals and different organizations. For example, the DSS pays money to households in child benefit, and the European Community pays money to Britain from the social fund.

Money flows link buyers and sellers in markets

Money exchange relationships provide an *external link* between individuals and organizations, like business firms and households. Money circulates between the households and firms who buy and sell in markets. There is a *circular flow relationship*, where money flows as the payments for goods and services on the one hand and the money rewards earned by the factors of production, like wages, salaries, rents and dividends on the other. These are matched respectively, by a flow of real goods and services and resources and factor services like labour. This relationship can be shown in a basic flow diagram Figure 4.3. Households buy in markets and pay the firms who supply them with money. Firms buy or rent the resource inputs required for production, so money flows back to the households, the ultimate owners of these productive inputs. Households receive wages, salaries, rents and dividends; *factor income payments*. In Figure 4.3 the flow of goods, services and resources is shown in the outer circuit. The reciprocal money payments are shown in the inner circuit. In reality, the money flows are often interwoven. Smaller sub-flows pass between firms, for some firms supply semi-finished products, or capital equipment items which would be of no use directly to the household, but which are sold to other enterprises.

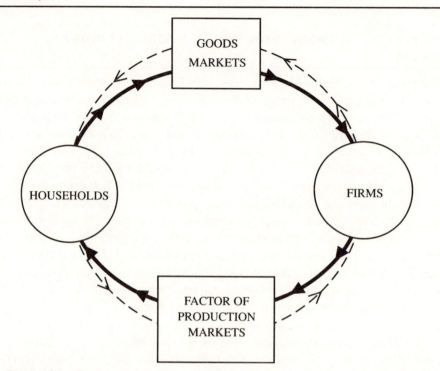

Figure 4.3 Basic circular flow: money links buyers and sellers through markets; it is exchanged for goods and services and the factors of production services

There are wholesalers who sell to retail firms not to the public. Organizations like banks and building societies dealing with currency and other financial claims, move money between themselves and households. In short, there is an entangled web of transactions. This simple flow diagram gives a view of the circular flow process in a *closed* economic system with no international transactions, but this could be widened with the introduction of international money and goods flows, which are increasingly important on the global scene.

Non-market money flows link individuals and organizations

Money flows also pass from one individual or organization to another by non-market routes (see Figure 4.4). These are often one way transfers. Money may go from state organizations to welfare recipients, in the form of income support benefits or to educational establishments as grants, or from private individuals to charities as donations (see Chapters 6 and 10). It circulates between people and groups as private gifts. These money flows do not entail market exchange (Boulding 1973).

Money is paid directly by state organizations as *transfer payments* – like an old age pension or a student grant. These are not related to current labour market work. Money also flows in the form of *taxation*. Much taxation is related to the volume of

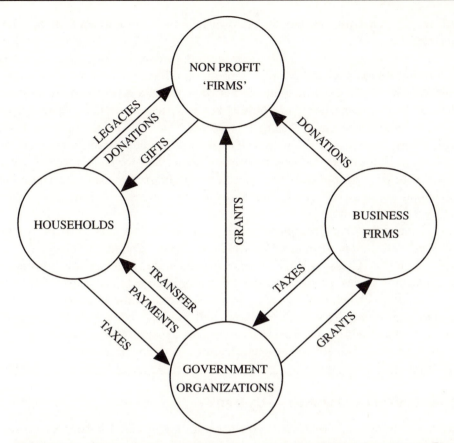

Figure 4.4 Money flows: a sample of non-market direct money flows. There are no matching real goods flows as in market exchange

market activity, like income tax or excise duties. However, the poll tax was a 'direct' tax, unrelated to market exchange, not as direct taxation like income tax, related to market paid work. These money flows link individuals/households to state organizations. Of course, in the modern world taxes are paid in money not in kind as was often the case for the tithes and taxes of the past.

In modern economies all organizations, whether households, business enterprises, government organizations, schools, churches or charities are joined to a greater or lesser extent by money in a complex web.

TRUST

Finally, we underline the significance of trust. People have to trust that money will be acceptable to others, otherwise they would not accept it. Regardless of legal rules and customary conventions *trust* is important. In reality, all human exchange has to be based, in part, on trust because of our own human limitations. We all operate in perspective time.

When we have repeated dealings with a trading partner over time, confidence grows in that person's reliability, more information is available to use as a guide for the future – *confidence* – can be built up. Yet when we have a first time exchange with trading partners about whom very little is known, particularly if they come from a different cultural background, then much less confidence may be placed in predictions of their future behaviour. Even with well established trading partners, an unforeseen surprise can always make outcomes better or worse than we had expected. We can never be sure how people will react; or draw up completely water-tight contracts. Transactions are often not synchronized at a particular point in time in the market. Trust is an essential feature.

Casson maintains that '[p]eople who are always selfish cannot trust one another. Only threats and financial inducements influence them. The law is invoked to give threats credibility' (Casson 1993). This creates inefficiency and increases transactions costs. In Casson's view, *ethical* as opposed to economic man can derive satisfaction from honouring obligations to others and can trade with a handshake, whilst economic man must draw up a contract and employ lawyers and accountants. Reciprocity allows informal transactions, which are cheaper. Organizations, including markets, require a considerable element of trust to function effectively.

LAW, CUSTOM AND MONEY – SUMMARY

- A framework of formal and informal rules are essential in any economy: they order, constrain and guide, ensuring the production and reproduction of the system itself. Rules interact with each other and evolve over historical time, unique in time and place.
- People require rules given the difficulties involved in perspective time. Rules reduce uncertainty – give a stable structure to transactions and human interrelationships. They bring security and comfort in the face of fundamental uncertainty.
- Rules are significant determinants of production possibilities facing different individuals and societies. Economies require stable rules for the development of production possibilities, to expand the division of labour specialization and trade. Some rules foster co-operation, set guidelines for competition and the means to handle conflict.
- Rules are a mixed bag. They can hold back economic development. There is no simple pattern of optimum rules. And informal rule changes may take a long time to evolve and cannot be easily engineered.
- Technology is an important factor in affecting the kind of rules in existence and their enforcement.
- Property rights are an important subset of institutionalized rules. Different mixes of private, collective and communal rights have evolved over time in different countries.

- Money is a powerful invention and a social convention. In historical time money played a much less prominent role although in different periods and places money had importance. Barter and countertrade are still used in some situations. But no modern economy functions without the extensive use of money and a well developed monetary system embodying rules and regulations.
- Money acts as a medium of exchange – a means of payment, a store of value, a unit of account, a standard of deferred payment.
- Money gives immediacy, allows direct deals without delay, saves time and cuts down on transactions costs. It helps to encourage the growth in production and consumption possibilities; an important social mechanism used to cope with uncertainty and ignorance.
- Trust is an essential feature of human interrelationships.

LAW, CUSTOM AND MONEY – QUESTIONS FOR DISCUSSION

1 What are the main functions of institutionalized rules and why do people require them for making decisions in perspective time? Use examples of both formal and informal rules to illustrate your answer.

2 USA Gun Laws, the licensing and ownership rights for firearms are different from those existing in Western Europe.

a) What reasons can you give for this?
b) Discuss the economic ramifications of such differences.

3 Distinguish between private, communal and collective property rights. Why and how has the mix of property rights evolved over historical time? How do they alter the costs and benefits of co-ordinating economic activity? Use examples.

4 The rules, both formal and informal, regarding the education, training and employment of girls and women have changed considerably over the last century in Britain. Of what changes are you aware? Consider the economic implications of such rule changes.

5 'The blueprint for Russian or Polish development is straightforward – introduce the market mechanism.' Critically appraise.

6 If the social convention of money cuts down on search and transaction costs, why do we see barter and countertrade used in late twentieth-century market transactions?

7 What are the functions of money? How can money reduce the impact of uncertainty?

8 'There is no such thing as a perfectly specified legal contract.' 'Trust is a necessary component of human economic interactions.' Discuss whether or not there is any link between these two statements.

5

Markets, prices and allocation

INTRODUCTION

This chapter explores the nature and workings of the market mechanism. We have already examined aspects of market exchange in previous chapters. Now we build on these foundations. Here we focus attention directly on markets and price theory, in order to put different markets, and the operation of the price mechanism into clearer perspective. We must understand what markets are, what they do, how they work, in order to assess their role in and contribution to the economic system. The chapter begins with an overview of the essential features and importance of markets, and how markets can be classified. Then to explain what determines market prices and what causes them to change, we examine what some still refer to as, 'the laws of supply and demand'. Initially, we use the 'ideal type' market model of perfect competition, developing a theory of price set in analytical time. This will help us to understand how the market mechanism provides one indispensable way of dealing with the problem of allocating resources and goods in the modern economy. But in reality markets do not match the economist's 'ideal type'. As we shall see, people acting in perspective time use markets which do not measure up to this yardstick. We shall discuss situations where prices do not move as in the perfectly competitive ideal. However, whatever the market type, in the modern economy as adults we are all market players; and price changes impinge upon everybody, one way or another. Markets are essential. We need insights into markets, prices and the allocative process. It is to these matters we now turn.

THE IMPORTANCE OF MARKETS AND PRICES

Markets and prices are usually at the top of the economist's standard agenda.

in the beginning there were markets.

(quoted in Williamson 1975: 20)

Albeit historically inaccurate, the biblical resonance of this quotation tells us much about the central importance actually accorded to markets in economic theory. Given a certain conviction, a view based on specific premises, we can show a flawlessly competitive market, an 'ideal' type, useful as a *starting point* to analyse the variety of real world markets in which people act in perspective time. In the standard 'ideal type' market, prices are the guiding light; the beacons which signal where resources are best used, other things being equal, to meet competing ends. Prices show producers which resources to use and what products to produce most profitably. Indeed, prices also give vital information to buyers, for prices guide and constrain their purchasing. In short the market price mechanism works to *allocate and co-ordinate* scarce goods and resources, and *rations* them between competing buyers, whether of final consumer products or raw materials for production. The market co-ordinates the activities of individuals and organizations and provides *incentives*. Markets can do many things; they work without an overseer, and no controller. These are powerful claims. They have to be evaluated carefully.

There can be no doubt that markets are an *essential feature* of any modern economy. We have seen that markets, working through a price mechanism, are not the only way of handling transactions and allocating resources and goods, nor are they the only means of providing incentives or rationing. However, markets are an integral part of modern economies, woven into the fabric of the economic system. At one extreme, they can have international significance linking people and their organizations globally, via international commodity and money markets. At the other extreme, they can be small local affairs, like car boot sales or street markets. In the contemporary industrialized economy we are all market participants.

Looking back through *historical time*, as we have emphasized, markets have often played an important, although much smaller role, whether in antiquity, through medieval times, even in the early phases of the Agricultural and Industrial Revolutions. Yet Adam Smith was already detailing the virtues of the market system in *The Wealth of Nations* (1776). Over time, markets have evolved and grown in complexity as economies have developed, in a symbiotic process.

Defining and categorizing markets

What is a market? Often markets are not defined, but seen as self-evident. We have an insight into what markets can do. Yet before we proceed to develop a theory of price determination, we need to consider the nature and essential features of markets.

Lipsey (1989: 52) defines the market as 'an area over which buyers and sellers negotiate the exchange of a well defined commodity'. He points out that buyers and sellers must be able to communicate with each other in the market, for worthwhile exchange to take place.

In fact, Hodgson (1988: 174) defines the market as 'a set of social institutions in which a large number of commodity exchanges of a specific type regularly take place, and to some extent are facilitated and structured by those institutions'. He emphasizes contractual agreements, the exchange of property rights in the market, where legal rules, customs and practices are set. Organizations of the market give information about products, prices, quantities and buyers and sellers, both actual and potential.

In fact, the key purpose of any market is *economic exchange*, which in order to take place, requires both buyers and sellers. There is an *indispensable reciprocity in the market* whether in a situation of barter or monetary exchange. There has to be a swap, *a payment*, either in money or goods; exchanged for well defined products or services, whether these are chocolates, haircuts or British Telecom shares. The payment is at a price which has been communicated – a mutually agreed and explicit exchange rate. Furthermore, the market transaction actually involves the *exchange of property rights*, not just goods and money. There is a straightforward exchange of private rights when the sale of such items as cars or chocolates takes place. In other situations there may be a partitioning of private rights. This gives the rights to use a good, in exchange for money, for example, where a landlord rents a property to a tenant. Or market exchange can involve the purchasing of a good with a collective right, like a share in a public quoted company such as BT or IBM, as we discussed in the previous chapter.

Market exchange is predominantly economic. There has to be an agreed price, a *quid pro quo* bond. Compare this with gift giving. Whilst there is reciprocity in gift giving, and often an exchange of property rights, the fundamental basis of the gift is not economic. There is no well defined, nor explicit price ratio. Certainly, the gift often brings no immediate need for reciprocity, and there is *no* market-like exchange. We shall return to the gift relationship in the following chapter.

Market exchange essentially requires a communication and information system and the rules of the game. Buyers and sellers may never meet – a telephone link and a means of transporting goods and payments will suffice. There may not be a particular geographical location, like Petticoat Lane, where buyers and sellers meet face to face. Market players can be quite anonymous doing deals through international cable links. Indeed, some see markets simply as the summation of multitudes of individuals, where there is no real difference between markets and firms, both simply combinations of individuals, contracting with each other.

However, markets are more usefully and realistically viewed as organizations themselves, inseparably intertwined with families and firms, organizations which are more than a collection of separate individuals. But the market is often not an identifiable unit like a firm or family. The market is a collection of relationships linking individuals usually in a non-collective, non-communal, independent sense.

Although, when people make a deal they are aware of other buyers and sellers (except where two individuals make an isolated exchange). The market is not a community or an organization like a firm or household which have an inner unity (Fourie 1991). Buyers and sellers often have diverse and opposing interests. People in markets, whilst being in some senses dependent on each other, are not bound as in the relative internal solidarity of a firm, or with the bonds of family.

Markets do not produce goods neither do they consume them. Markets are for exchange. People working within firms and sometimes households, make products for market exchange; without these markets would not exist. Moreover, whilst we know that buyers and sellers have different considerations in mind, in exchange there can be mutual benefit, even where a lower price for one person means more for another. We illustrated this in Chapter 3 with the example of Maureen and Mary and the division of the gains from specialization and exchange. We shall see that *co-operation* and *rivalry* occur in markets on different levels. Sellers in some markets, whilst being rivals, may still collude with other sellers in order to do the best they can for themselves.

Market organizations interlink the external relationships of private firms, households and public sector organizations with money and real goods flows. Moreover, there are different types of real markets, set in different institutional contexts and configurations, in different historical time periods and in very different economic systems.

Different market types: categorizing markets

Given their essential features, markets are diverse. The products traded, the market make-up and performance may vary considerably. We can categorize markets in many ways, according to the type of product traded, whether for delivery now or at some future date, whether new or second-hand. We can distinguish between spatial and institutional features of markets. We can classify markets according to:

The type of product or service traded

a) We shop in *consumer goods markets*, buying items as diverse as vegetables, personal computers and package holidays. Sometimes the deal is directly with a supplier, sometimes through a series of wholesalers, so there is also a further distinction between *wholesale markets* and *retail markets.*

b) *Factor markets* include those markets where resources, inputs in the production process, are traded. People offer to sell labour services in the *job market*, a vital factor market. Firms buy raw materials in *commodity markets*, rent land and capital equipment in markets. All this to make the final goods which we ultimately consume.

c) *Financial markets* include markets where firms and government organizations raise money to pay for investment by selling shares or bonds. Indeed, it is money itself which is the object of trade in the international currency markets, now dwarfing global international trade flows of goods in terms of turnover and value.

For delivery now or later

Futures and *options markets* are set up for exchanging forward contracts which enable the trade of physical commodities, currencies or the options to buy and sell shares *at some future date,* derivatives. These contracts are exchanged for money. The futures markets enable dealers to buy and sell a product for delivery at some time hence; not now. This is in contrast to a *spot market*, where goods and payment are exchanged, with people taking delivery immediately.

Primary and secondary markets

These are distinguished to give an important contrast between markets for *new and 'used'* products. *Primary markets* are for the purchase and sale of new products, like new share issues or new cars. Yet the buyers and sellers of used cars or second-hand shares can operate in *secondary markets*, where second-hand goods are exchanged. The London Stock Exchange acts mainly as a secondary market, almost all of the trading is in 'second-hand' shares, not new share issues. Of course, not all primary markets have a related secondary market. But whilst there is no second-hand trade in used hamburgers, used cinema tickets or flowers, we shall see the significance of secondary markets in some situations. The trading of second-hand shares is important for efficient primary market functioning as we shall show in Chapter 6.

Geographical dimension

We can categorize markets *spatially*, some markets are global, others national, regional or local.

Legal/institutional dimensions

Finally, markets can be classified by their *legal/institutional* dimensions. Markets can have different institutional frameworks, subject to different formal and informal rules of proceeding. The London Stock Exchange operates in a different institutional framework of formal and informal rules than say the French equivalent, the Bourse. Within the European Community, rules relating to the exchange of financial assets are gradually being harmonized so that some institutional rules of the Stock Exchange will change.

Moreover, whilst the bulk of markets are legitimate there is a significant volume of trade carried out in *illegal* markets. The international criminal undercover markets trading in drugs like crack or heroin and those dealing in human organs are unlawful, but nevertheless function as markets. They operate with the rules of procedure, custom and practice of the underworld, yet they require a set of rules to function, just as any legal market. There has to be some 'honour amongst thieves' for continued effective trade, even where honour is often backed by intimidatory power.

Classification by market structure

Clearly, markets may have combinations of different attributes. However, for the economist, seeking to explain the workings of any market, the fundamental distinguishing feature is the *type and extent of competition* which that market displays. To handle real-world complexity, economists have to make essential simplifications. The traditional neo-classical theories of markets abstract from the many differences of place and time, and institutional make-up. They take an ahistorical approach, set in *analytical time* to provide particular essential insights and explanations.

The *key classification* for any market in standard theory is given by the *degree of competition* which that market exhibits. Competition, or the lack of it, is what defines market structure. We can build an explanation of how prices and quantities are determined and how the price mechanism rations and allocates, by using the most highly competitive market scenario as the starting point. This 'ideal type' market is flawlessly competitive. It provides the yardstick of comparison for other market models embodying different levels of competition. This 'ideal type' market, set in analytical time, can be shown to give the most output for the least cost; to deliver the best possible result provided that appropriate conditions hold.

Market structure is specified by a series of salient features which include the number of buyers and sellers and market entry barriers. The *perfectly competitive* 'ideal type' market is assumed to have *many, many buyers and sellers both actual and potential*. There are always hoards of potential market players. Even though people may be buying or selling something else in other markets, they are ready and able to switch markets, should the price be right; if they can make a bigger profit or a better buy. Furthermore, every firm produces a well defined, uncomplicated *homogeneous good*, like a uniform vegetable – a carrot, or a commodity like tin or coal of either consistent quality, or readily gradable. Indeed, agricultural products and raw materials are traded in international markets which are said to fit the requirements of the 'ideal type' fairly closely.

As they operate in analytical time, market players have *perfect information* about all product qualities and prices. Moreover, no single buyer or seller can possibly affect the market price, because each is too small in relation to the market as a whole. *No individual player has power over price.* Sellers are small autonomous traders, not the giant multinational firm or a domineering powerful producer. And there are no big buyers. None can hold buyers to ransom by cornering the market, none can intimidate sellers by withholding demand. *Freedom of entry* prevails – no existing firms or buyers can bar new entrants. There is *free exit* – no potential costs of switching production for another market; nothing to act as a deterrent to those who wish to participate – no expensive unsaleable capital equipment for the producer to be stuck with should things go wrong.

Finally, all market players aim to do the best they can for themselves. This is the key underlying behavioural premise of all standard neo-classical models. For producers, this means seeking the biggest profits, for consumers securing the largest utility or satisfaction. Whilst we may deviate from the competitive 'ideal' by changing the assumptions to give different market forms, in orthodox analysis we are making the same behavioural assumptions. Individuals are assumed to be rational economic people (REP) – know-all, selfish maximizers.

Other theoretical market forms exist but these depart from the 'ideal type'. At the other extreme there are markets where *monopoly* prevails. The *monopolistic* market in sharp contrast to the perfectly competitive market, has only *one* seller. Here it is possible to keep would-be rivals out, by barring entry, whether by patents, large expensive capital equipment or the monopoly ownership of vital inputs. British Gas has a monopoly of the sale of gas in the domestic market. British Oxygen had a virtual monopoly on the sale of oxygen for medical purposes in Britain. An *oligopolistic market* is dominated by a *few* sellers, but is also characterized by entry barriers. In Britain, the markets for cars, white goods such as refrigerators and cookers, the wholesale market for petrol and the retail grocery trade are oligopolistic. Oligopolistic scenarios are highly pervasive in the modern economy.

Monopolistic competition is the market form closest to perfect competition, with many market sellers and buyers and *no* entry barriers. However, unlike in the perfectly competitive market, each individual firm produces a differentiated product or offers a slightly different service, not exactly matched by competitors. There are many small builders, motor vehicle maintenance firms, domestic appliance repairers, hairdressers in any locality. Entry into markets which can be categorized as such is easy.

THE TRADITIONAL MODEL: INTRODUCTION TO PRICE THEORY

If we work with the orthodox model of perfect competition, we can analyse what determines the behaviour of both buyers and sellers and how they respond to market changes. We can develop a theory which can explain and predict market price and quantity movements. To do this we examine:

a) the factors determining demand and supply, the responses from the two sides of a market.

b) how demand and supply interact together to give an equilibrium price, one which will bring about a balance in the market, by equating quantities supplied and demanded.

We start by looking at *demand*; the buyers' side of the market.

The theory of demand

When economists talk about demand, they mean *effective demand*, that is the *desire to buy*, backed by the *ability to pay*. Of course, effective demand may not coincide with needs or wants, but producers in the market only respond to those with the money to back their desires. For sellers want to cover their costs and make a profit from the sale of goods. They are commercial enterprises not charities. Effective demand has two essential conditions. First, the ability to pay: the buyer must have the wherewithal – the necessary purchasing power to buy. Second, the willingness to purchase must exist too. In reality, the low-income earner or unemployed window shopper with insufficient cash and an inability to borrow, may fervently want or need to purchase any one of a number of goods. But that person has no effective demand for them. These goods whether necessities or luxury items are beyond their reach. Regardless of the strength of desire or need, their limited real resources constrain them. The wealthier shopper, on the other hand, may have the ability to buy a whole range of expensive items. Yet this person may not have either the need or desire for such products. So, despite an ability to pay they have no effective demand for the good in question.

In fact, there are many underlying variables at work determining demand – a real-world tangle of different factors, often interrelated and pulling in different directions. These include prices, incomes and tastes. We can simplify the situation by working in analytical time. To unravel the factors influencing demand, we shall consider the impact of each factor in isolation. We shall take the example of the carrot, a simple good and initially focus attention on the price of carrots, to aid our understanding of buyers purchasing plans for this commodity.

Price and its impact on the quantity demanded

Price gives us the essential terms of market exchange, usually in the modern economy, a price expressed in monetary value. The money price has to be paid for a specified quantity of carrots, in this case, a standard measure in weight. Price is one determinant of demand, a vital piece of information; it tells us what money the buyer must give up to secure the product. It reflects the opportunity cost of the best alternative forgone for the consumer, for money handed over in exchange for one product, cannot be used by the buyer for anything else.

It is customary to display information about *demand* by listing a series of possible prices with the quantities which buyers plan to buy at each price in a particular time period. Such a list, as shown in Table 5.1, is known as a *demand schedule*. Note that the information given here is for the market as a whole. All of the purchasing plans of individuals or households in the market have been added together to give a total picture: *the market demand schedule*. What we can see from the data presented in Table 5.1 is interesting. As the price of carrots falls so the planned quantity demanded increases, and vice versa, rising prices are matched by reductions in the quantities that buyers plan to buy.

The schedule focuses attention *solely* on the way in which quantity demanded responds to changes in price. But remember that we are working in analytical time. All the prices given cannot co-exist at one and the same real time, they are simply hypothetical possibilities. And to handle the complexity of reality, we assume that, when the list of prices and corresponding quantities is drawn up, other factors which might influence demand are held constant. In this way we can safely display an uncluttered relationship between price and the quantity demanded.

The market demand curve

To illustrate the information more potently, economists display the relationship between the series of hypothetical prices and the quantities demanded, those amounts which buyers *plan* to buy in a particular time period, in graphical form. The *market demand curve* is shown in Figure 5.1. To transfer the schedule into graphical form, the price and quantity pairs are plotted from the information given in Table 5.1. Price, an *independent variable*, is measured on the vertical axis in pence per kilo. The quantity demanded of carrots, the *dependent variable* is measured on the horizontal axis, in tonnes, for a particular time period, a week or a month.[1]

Table 5.1 The market demand schedule: carrots

Price per kilo, pence	Quantity demanded (tonnes)
70	2,000
60	4,000
50	6,000
40	8,000
30	10,000
20	12,000
10	14,000

These price and quantity points are connected to form the demand curve. The demand curve simply shows the respective quantities demanded at each price over a given time period. The important proviso is that every other factor, which might affect demand over this analytical time period, is held constant – *ceteris paribus* holds. We are using the freeze-frame facility of analytical time. The most notable feature of this graphical picture is that the demand curve, as plotted in Figure 5.1, slopes downwards from left to right. In other words, there is an *inverse* or *negative relationship* between the price and the quantity demanded. When the price is high the quantity demanded is low. When price is low the quantity demanded is high. Changes in price lead to movements along the demand curve; so a price increase from 60 pence per kilo to 70 pence per kilo brings about a revision in buyers' plans and so a reduction in planned quantity demanded. We can read the exact quantity change

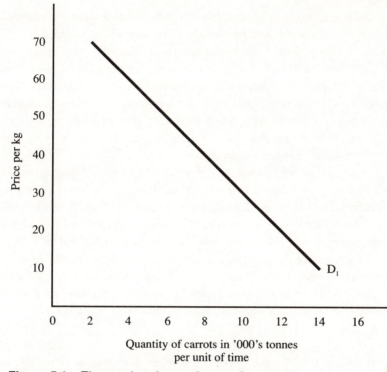

Figure 5.1 The market demand curve for carrots

from the information displayed on the horizontal axis. Quantity demanded falls from 4,000 tonnes to 2,000 tonnes.

Buyers, of course, will only pay one price at any particular moment in perspective time. But in analytical time we can change the price at will and see the impact of these changes on the quantities buyers *plan* to buy. We can now clearly see the impact of a change in price on the quantity demanded.

The demand schedule and the graphical representation display the fundamental hypothesis or principle often referred to as '*the law of demand*'. This holds that the higher the price, the lower the quantity demanded, assuming everything else is constant. We can also put the case into reverse. The lower the price, the higher the quantity demanded, again holding all else constant. This 'law of demand' enables us to predict that for any good, as price falls so there will be a planned increase in quantity demanded. The use of the term 'law' shows economists in their Newtonian mode. It was believed that economists could derive scientific immutable laws to explain economic reality, like those of physicists, for example, the Law of Gravity. In fact, we may say that the quantity demanded is usually inversely related to price; but this is not an immutable law for all situations.

How can the basic downward sloping demand curve, the inverse relationship between price and quantity demanded, be explained? We can begin to answer the question by initially looking at the individual consumer. We can take a variety of examples, but when prices are very high unless the person has a strong preference for a good, then cheaper *substitutes* will be bought. The consumer might buy turnips instead of carrots, or rice or bread instead of potatoes. Take the case of carrots, as their price falls individuals will be induced to buy more carrots. The absolute money and relative price of carrots has fallen, in comparison with substitute goods. Carrots will look a 'better' buy when compared with substitute goods whose money prices have not fallen. There is a substitution effect in favour of carrots as a result of the price change. And the £ in the pocket, *income*, will 'stretch' to buy more, for carrots are not as 'pricey'. Imagine that the money price of carrots falls from 70 pence to 35 pence per kilo. If a consumer had previously planned to purchase 10 kilos of carrots, then this admittedly dramatic price fall, would be equivalent to an increase in income of £3.50, for on each kilo of carrots, the consumer would save 35p. Some of this real income benefit might be used to buy more carrots. Such a 'large' reduction in price gives a 'significant' increase in real income, and an insight into the 'income effect' of a price change. Of course here the price has fallen by 50 per cent overall, but this may not be very important if only a small percentage of income is spent on the good in question. However these *income* and *substitution effects* are at the root of the inverse relationship between price and the quantity demanded. They are concepts to which we shall return in Chapter 7.

Taken collectively, in aggregate, within the market some people who were previously unwilling or unable to buy carrots at higher prices, will plan to purchase, as the price is reduced. And those who already buy, even at the higher prices, want to buy more as the good becomes cheaper. The overall result is an increase in quantity demanded, as illustrated by the movement along the market demand curve. A fall in price persuades and enables buyers to change their plans; they aim to purchase more.

Marshall used the demand curve as a starting point when he explained the workings of the market mechanism, showing the hypothetical relationship between price and quantity demanded; a display of imaginary purchasing plans at different prices. The market price is the one thing which we can usually, readily observe in a market, and we are keen to explain what determines that price. It makes sense for our purposes to stress price initially. However, we are not saying that price is the most important single determinant of demand overall, even though price is displayed prominently. Price is only *one* of the determinants of demand. Demand does not hinge on any lone factor. It depends on a whole complex of influences interacting together. The beauty of demand theory lies in its systematic analysis of these determining factors, simplifying in analytical time, so that the impact of each factor can be examined in isolation.

We have seen the impact of a good's *own* price on quantity demanded. Now we can go further to unravel the factors at work, by considering the other *determinants of demand*, one by one. We shall refer to all of these remaining variables as *shift factors*. These bring about a *change in the position of the demand curve*, a complete movement of the price quantity relationship, as shown in Figure 5.2.

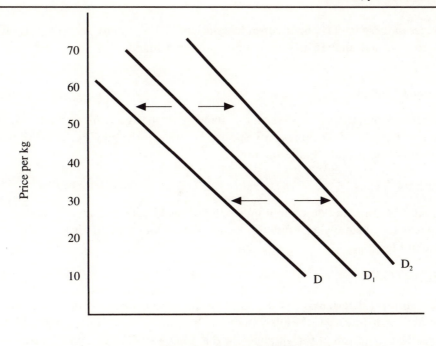

Quantity of carrots in '000s tonnes
per unit of time

Figure 5.2   The shifting demand curve for carrots: a rightward shift to D_2; an increase in demand. A leftward shift to D; a fall in demand

Shift factors: other variables affecting demand

The diagram in two dimensions is convenient for displaying the relationship between just two variables, the independent variable price and the dependent variable, quantity demanded. Yet there are many other potential factors which may affect the level of demand. These include: income, the prices of related goods, tastes, even factors like the weather, a whole gamut of variables. Such independent variables help to determine the exact position of the demand curve. A change in any one such factor will cause the whole curve to shift as illustrated in Figure 5.2. A move to the right means that at every price more will be demanded. A move to the left will mean that at every price less will be demanded. To signify such a shift we talk about an increase or decrease in demand. This is in contrast with an increase or decrease in the quantity demanded, used to indicate a movement along the demand curve.

Prices and income are readily observable and measurable in money terms. Buyers' incomes, the prices of other relevant goods, whether substitutes or complements affect demand. But it is not always as easy to quantify other factors which may affect demand. Nevertheless, that certainly does not render such factors unimportant. Tastes, which affect buyers' underlying preferences, are commonly held constant in orthodox theory. These evolve over time and can have a significant impact on demand. The ability and willingness to buy can be increased or reduced depending on the changes in these underlying independent variables. To simplify we look at each of these factors one at a time to analyse their impact on demand.

The demand function

It is customary practice to express the demand with the following symbolic short-hand where: P, P_o, Y, T, Z, represent respectively: price of the good, price of all other goods, income, tastes and all other factors.

$$Q_d = f(P, P_o, Y, T, Z, \ldots,) \qquad (5.1)$$

Given that all the factors determining demand are held constant we can express the quantity demanded simply as a function of price in equation 5.2. This is the function displayed in Figure 5.1.

$$Q_d = f(P) \qquad (5.2)$$

Income   This is a determinant of demand. An increase in the *level of income* means that the ability of buyers to buy is enhanced. But an increase in the ability to buy does not affect the demand for all goods in the same way. The demand for a *normal good* will increase as a result of an increase in income. The entire demand function will shift to the right. At every price the consumer will demand more. So rising incomes in Britain have led to increasing demands for goods like wine, spirits and kiwi fruits. With more pounds in the pocket, at any given price, the good is more affordable and assuming other things stay the same, more will be demanded. The reverse argument applies to a reduction in income which will induce a fall or leftwards shift in demand.

The demand curves for all goods are not positively affected by an increase in income. *Inferior goods* like pigs' trotters, brains, chicken wings, white sliced bread will be less sought after as income increases. Buyers, as they become better off, may switch their purchasing power to 'superior' commodities like beef steak and prime cuts of lamb. The demand for the chicken wings and the pigs' trotters will shift to the left for they provide less meat per pound and take more preparation, cooking and eating time. People may prefer the flavour of beef and lamb and their relative convenience. Less of an inferior good will be demanded at every price as people substitute preferred foods, a substitution made possible by increased income.

The *distribution of income* can also be an important actual consideration, although a factor implicitly assumed away on the perfectly competitive scene. Small buyers are tacitly imagined to have similar sized incomes, and it is understood that small sellers, each with tiny market shares, do not command unequal income from profits. Nevertheless, distribution is an important issue in perspective time. If there were an increase in income inequality, then the demand for some products may increase whilst that of others could fall. We may see an increase in demand for champagne and truffles and yet a reduction in demand for luxury items enjoyed by those on low income.

Taste   This tells us about the consumer's relative preference for a good. How partial is the buyer to the good? The buyer with a strong liking will demand more than one who is not so keen, other things being equal. An increasing number of vegetarians in the community will bring about a rightwards shift in demand for vegetables. Meat is rejected and vegetables will provide a substitute. Meat demand will fall as a result of changing tastes. Health fears about cholesterol levels will reduce the demand for eggs and red meats and increase the demand for fish and white meat. Buyers change their taste for certain products and this is reflected in the position of the demand curve. In reality, these changes in tastes may occur over a long period as the economy evolves. Indeed, when we relax the strict assumptions of perfect competition and with it, in particular, the assumptions of perfect information, and many small sellers, we find producers often spending large sums of money on advertising. This is targeted to change tastes: to woo new customers and to strengthen the desires of established buyers.

Prices of other goods: substitutes and complements   Economists are always interested in the best alternative forgone. Some goods are *substitutes* for each other. If the price of cabbages were to rise, buyers may well switch their demand to carrots. At every carrot price, after a cabbage price increase, some buyers will switch their demand to carrots. This has nothing to do with the relative tastiness of carrots. It has to do with relative price. Despite a constant money carrot price, carrots become a better buy, in relation to an alternative, like the cabbage. The demand curve for carrots shifts to the right from D_1 to D_2 as shown in Figure 5.2. On the other hand, should the price of asparagus tumble the carrot demand curve might shift to the left. For some buyers will change their plans and switch to asparagus, now relatively cheaper.

Some goods are *complements*, their consumption and hence respective demands are also related. A rise in the price of beef, bringing a fall in the quantity demanded and a decline in beef roasts could induce a fall in the demand for horseradish sauce. These goods go together. A leftward shift in demand for beef, resulting from the fear of mad cow disease, will also impinge on the demand for horseradish. The demand for horseradish will also shift to the left, other things being equal.

Number of buyers   The number of people in the market is also a consideration. If the working population increases, the number of prospective buyers may expand and the demand curve shifts to the right for carrots or wine, for example. On the other hand, a decline in the number of people can bring a reduction in demand. Demographic changes may have significant effects on the demand for particular goods, bringing about shifts both to the right and left depending on the good in question.

Other factors Other factors affect demand. The weather may have an impact on consumption. A cold snap in Britain may induce an increased demand for vegetables, to be eaten in hot dinners. Hot weather, on the other hand, may lead to an increased demand for lettuces and other salad ingredients. Supermarket personnel, the buyers who order stocks, pay close attention to weather forecasts when making their orders. Changes in weather conditions can bring about significant shifts in demand from the shopper.

However, the discussion of the demand side of the market gives only half of the story. We cannot say anything about the price which will prevail in the market, until we examine the supply side. We have to display the intentions of both sides of the market, *before* we can indicate which price will rule. We need to know the supply plans of sellers, what quantities they are willing and able to supply.

The theory of supply

The market supply is simply the amount of a good that all the suppliers, in a particular market, are willing and able to supply over a particular time period. What suppliers offer for sale is dependent on a series of factors: the independent variables. Again, there are many underlying influences at work, often interrelated and pulling in different directions, just as in the case of demand. We need to explain carefully which factors determine the quantities that suppliers plan to produce for sale; and what might cause these plans to change. First, just as with demand, let us examine the relationship between the price of the good in question and the quantity suppliers plan to offer.

Price: the impact on the quantity supplied

The price for the supplier is the amount of cash which will be paid in exchange for the good in question, like a kilo of carrots. Information about *market supply* for carrots can be seen in Table 5.2. Here a list of possible prices is given, with the corresponding quantities suppliers, in total, are willing and able to supply in the particular time period, at each price. This is known as the *market supply schedule*.

Table 5.2 The market supply schedule: carrots

Price per kilo, pence	Quantity supplied (tonnes)
70	14,000
60	12,000
50	10,000
40	8,000
30	6,000
20	4,000
10	2 000

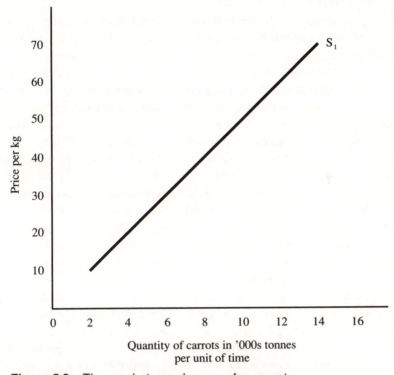

Figure 5.3   The market supply curve for carrots

As the price increases so the quantity suppliers plan to supply increases, in other words, there is a direct positive relationship between price, the independent variable, and the dependent variable, quantity. Price and quantity move in the *same* direction, so if price falls the quantity suppliers are willing to supply falls too. The information in Table 5.2, the supply schedule, is drawn up on the assumption that everything else stays the same. Only then can we isolate the relationship between price and quantity. Any other factors which might influence supply are held still. Remember that we are working in analytical time and so this is a hypothetical relationship. No two prices could co-exist at one point in real time.

We can plot the information in Table 5.2 in a graphical form. In Figure 5.3, on the horizontal axis, the quantity of carrots per unit of time is measured. On the vertical axis the price per unit is displayed. To graph the information from Table 5.2, plot the price and quantity pairs and connect the points. The resulting *supply curve* for carrots in Figure 5.3 shows the quantity which will be offered for sale at a series of possible prices; at every price what suppliers are willing and able to supply. The supply curve slopes upwards from left to right, illustrating a positive or direct relationship between the price of carrots and the quantity firms *plan* to supply. If prices go up suppliers plan to produce more and vice versa.

The 'law of supply' tells us that: the higher the price, the greater the quantity suppliers are willing to supply, other things remaining constant. The lower the price, the lower quantity suppliers are willing to supply, other things remaining constant. We have isolated the impact of one determinant, the price of the good in question, on the quantity that producers are willing and able to supply. Suppliers, in this case farmers, can be induced to supply different quantities depending on the level of price. Some prices are so low that no seller would plan to offer goods for sale; they could not cover costs and make a profit (see Chapter 8 for further discussion). From a price of 10 pence per kilo, suppliers will be persuaded to supply goods because they can cover their costs. Indeed, as prices rise, suppliers will supply a higher quantity because the increase in price will be enough to cover the increased costs of producing additional units of output and will add to profits. On the basis of this perfectly competitive model, prices have to rise to induce existing suppliers to offer more.

In fact, the model we are using is set in a *short-run analytical time period* where it is assumed that whilst it is possible to increase the use of existing firms' capacities, no new firms can enter the market despite the lure of profits. Even in analytical time, economists have to recognize that time has to be taken in order to set up new capacity – it cannot be done instantaneously. Only in the *long run* can new firms enter the market to produce. In the long run the supply curve may be downward sloping or horizontal depending on the assumptions we make. However, this is another story, to which we shall return in Chapter 8. Suppliers will only increase their output if they can cover the additional costs and increase profit. So prices have to rise to make it worthwhile for *existing* suppliers to offer more for sale, producing more with their existing capacity, bringing a movement upwards along the supply curve.

From Figure 5.3 we can see that the supply curve illustrated here behaves quite differently from the demand curve. The supply curve slopes *upwards* from left to right; not downwards as for demand.[2]

Shift factors: other variables affecting supply

Price is not the only factor which affects supply. There are a variety of variables which may affect the ability and willingness of producers to offer goods in the market; these help to determine the position of the supply curve. In analytical time the effect of each factor can be isolated and explained in turn. Indeed, we can move the supply curve backwards and forwards in analytical time, reversing changes – putting things back exactly as they were. Variables, including the prices of the factor inputs, $F_1 \ldots F_m$, the resources used to produce the goods, technology, T, and the number of producers in the markets, G, will have an impact on the position of the supply curve. We can change these independent shift variables in turn, to show how the supply curve will respond; how it will shift its position.

$$Q_s = f(P, F_1, \ldots F_m, T, G) \tag{5.3}$$

$$Q_s = f(P) \tag{5.4}$$

We can start with the prices of the factors of production – the costs which have to be paid for the inputs required in the production process.

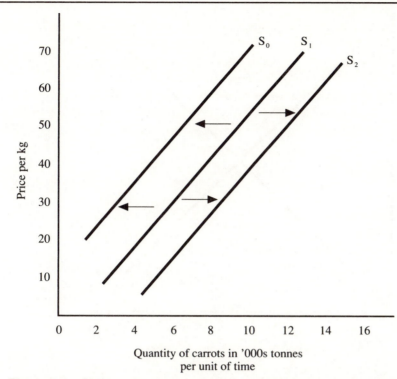

Figure 5.4   Shifting the supply curve for carrots: a rightward shift S_1; an increase in supply. A leftward shift to S_0; a fall in supply

Input prices   The costs of the factors of production are one of the determinants of supply. An increase in labour costs, for example, per tonne of production, because of rising hourly wage rates, will mean that suppliers will reduce planned supply, other things being equal. The supply curve shifts to the left, as shown in Figure 5.4. At each price there will be a fall in supply because it costs more to produce any output level. In other words, any particular quantity will be supplied but at an increased price. A cut in wage rates would have the opposite effect, shifting the supply outwards, to the right. Now every unit of labour can be purchased more cheaply, and so any output level can be offered at a lower price.

Technology   Technology, the existing state of 'know-how' about how to produce, helps to determine the position of the supply curve. The supply curve is drawn on the assumption of a particular state of technology. The discovery and invention of a new process, for example, the introduction of mechanized farm equipment, or a new fertilizer which increases productivity, will shift the supply curve to the right. At every price, more output will be planned because productivity has increased and it is cheaper to produce. Suppliers can make more profit. Of course, in reality, the process of changing technology is much more complex, it continually evolves. Moreover,

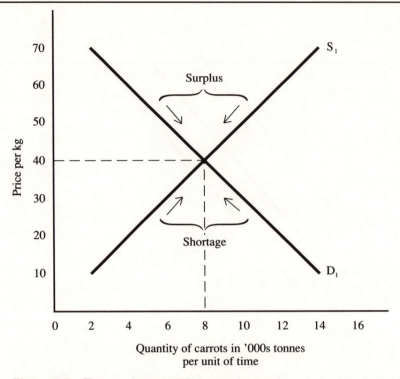

Figure 5.5 The market equilibrium price and quantity determined at the intersection of the supply and demand curves

Table 5.3 Demand and supply schedules and equilibrium price: carrots

Price per kilo, pence	Quantity demanded (tonnes)	Quantity supplied (tonnes)
70	2,000	14,000
60	4,000	12,000
50	6,000	10,000
40	**8,000**	**8,000**
30	10,000	6,000
20	12,000	4,000
10	14,000	2 000

analytical time ignores custom, convention and legal rules. In practice, these can have a significant effect on the nature of production and hence supply.

The number of producers When we draw the smooth continuous short-run supply curve the number of producers in the market is taken as given. If that number increases in the long run when new firms can enter the market, the supply function shifts to the right (see Chapter 8). However, suffice it to say at this point, the more producers – the greater the planned output at each price, other things being equal.

Putting supply and demand curves together: equilibrium price and quantity

The price and quantity which will actually prevail can only be determined by bringing the two sides of the market, represented by demand and supply, together. Only then can we know which of all the possible hypothetical prices will rule and what quantity of goods will actually be traded. In Figure 5.5 demand and supply curves are plotted on the same diagram from the original information given in Tables 5.1 and 5.2, which is displayed in Table 5.3.

Only at the point where the demand and supply curves cross will we find a unique equilibrium where the plans of demanders and suppliers are both satisfied. The *equilibrium price* is the only price where the plans of both buyers and sellers actually match, where the quantity demanded will equal the quantity supplied. At this price the market is cleared, there are no unsatisfied buyers or sellers – no shortages or surpluses. Metaphorically speaking, only then are the scales in balance, the market at rest and the price 'right'. In this case, the equilibrium price is 40p and the equilibrium quantity is 8,000 tonnes.

In addition, the *equilibrium is stable*.[3] There will be no tendency for price and the accompanying quantity of goods to vary. All plans are met and the price set, assuming the demand and supply relationships given. The equilibrium price will only change if the underlying demand and/or supply relationships change. Should anything upset this state of rest, in analytical time, equilibrium will be instantaneously restored. There is complete and immediate *flexibility of price*.

We can illustrate that any other price will not bring an equilibrium. If we take a price of 50 pence then reading from the table or graph, the quantity supplied exceeds the quantity demanded by 4,000 tonnes. This price will not bring a balance, for although suppliers will be persuaded to supply 10,000 tonnes at 50 pence per kilo, they will have goods left on their hands. There will be a *surplus*, an *oversupply*, if suppliers fulfil their plans. The reason for this is clear. Buyers at such a relatively high price are only willing and able to buy 6,000 tonnes. Their plans do not match those of suppliers.

Conversely, if we take 30 pence reading from the table or graph, then the quantity demanded will exceed the quantity supplied. Buyers will not be satisfied by the supply offered in the market. There will be an *excess demand* and a *shortage* of produce. Part of the problem, clearly, is that suppliers at the relatively low price of 30 pence per kilo can only be persuaded to offer a small quantity for sale, 6,000 tonnes. They are not going to meet the market deficiency, for at such a price, it is not worth their while to supply more. But at such a low price buyers are willing and able to buy a lot more than is on offer.

In both of these theoretical scenarios the *plans of either buyers or sellers are frustrated*. This is a *disequilibrium*, although the quantity of carrots actually bought matches exactly the quantity sold, by definition. But buyers' and sellers' plans are not

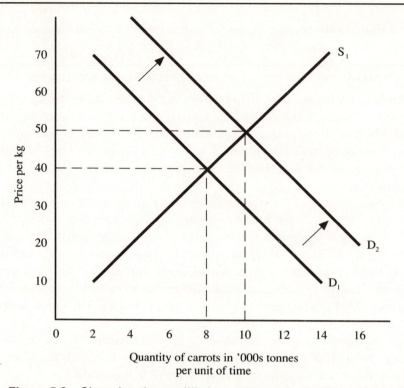

Figure 5.6 Changing the equilibrium price and quantity: an increase in demand – a shift to the right brings an increase in equilibrium price and quantity – disturbing the old equilibrium – a market in motion

harmonized. At 50 pence, suppliers' plans to sell are thwarted, buyers are not able or willing to buy all the supply at this price. At 30 pence, buyers are prevented from fulfilling their plans because suppliers are not willing or able to meet buyers' demands, at this price. A disequilibrium situation exists.

However, the familiar conventional diagram, in Figure 5.5, sometimes called the Marshallian Cross, shows us clearly the equilibrium price. Equilibrium reflects the notion of stability. The neat symmetry of this market, in analytical time, brings us a balanced solution, a harmonious result; everlasting rest.[4]

Changing equilibrium price and quantity: shifting the supply and demand curves

The only way for a change to be brought about in this balanced state, to move the equilibrium price and quantity, is to change at least one of the shift factors, the parameters or conditions of *either* demand *and/or* supply. Only then will the market price and quantity change, moving the system to a new stable equilibrium point. The move comes instantaneously in analytical time.

The market starts at an equilibrium point as shown in Figure 5.6. Imagine that the price of cabbages, a substitute good, increases. The demand curve for carrots shifts to the right, from D_1 to D_2. The new demand cannot be satisfied at the old equilibrium price. Suppliers are only offering 8,000 tonnes and consumers demand more. A shortage arises. The response to this increase in demand and resultant shortage is the bidding up of price as buyers compete for the scarce good. The price has to increase to make it worthwhile in terms of profit for producers to expand their production. This is shown by a movement upwards and along the supply curve. Producers can now make more profit and cover their increased extra or *marginal costs* of production. So a shift in the demand function of necessity leads to a movement along the supply curve. The final result can be seen in Figure 5.6. The price has risen to 50 pence and the equilibrium quantity now stands at 10,000 tonnes.

We can see from the diagram in Figure 5.6 that the price increase is necessary to persuade the producers to supply an increased quantity. But this price increase has choked off some of the extra quantity demanded. As the price increases so a movement along the new demand curve has occurred. Equilibrium is achieved at 50 pence, but at the old equilibrium price of 40 pence, buyers would have demanded a quantity of 12,000 tonnes. Here there have been changes in real magnitudes and relative prices.

Given this demand and supply framework, we can now make predictions about how prices will move, given certain changes. We can foretell the direction of both price and quantity, providing that we shift one curve in isolation. We can compare different static equilibrium points in what is termed *comparative static analysis*. We have little to say about the actual process which is involved in moving from the original equilibrium to the new equilibrium. This process actually takes place in real time, it takes the passage of time for market players to produce and trade. Our model assumes such problems away.

How is equilibrium restored in a disequilibrium situation?

In analytical time little is said about the process of achieving an equilibrium. In equilibrium, buyers' and sellers' plans match exactly. Should there be any mismatch between the plans of market players, reflected in market shortages or surpluses of goods, these are instantaneously removed by an immediate price change. All plans are fulfilled perfectly.

Metaphorically, the market operates as old fashioned kitchen scales. As we adjust the weights on one side, the other will move very quickly into balance. Indeed, the 'ideal type' market always moves in the blinking of an eye, as the weights, the factors determining supply and demand, are changed. With this mechanical analogy we can move backwards and forwards in analytical time, simplifying the complex reality, changing nothing permanently as we vary the weights and observe the impact on price and quantity. However, in this situation nothing evolves, there is no history. We can rerun exactly what went before. Any change can be completely reversed; in real situations this is quite impossible. No account is taken of the continuing evolution of market factors which ensures that we can never go back to an original position.

Moreover, the theory has little to say about the actual time it takes to achieve a balance, how market players have to grapple in perspective time, indeed, how that process actually occurs whether through bids and offers, by trial and error.

Changing demand and supply, simultaneously

We can make a clear and unambiguous prediction about the direction of the price change which follows from a shift in the demand or supply curve in isolation. But when there is a shift in both curves the matter is not so straightforward. Imagine that a new organic fertilizer increases the supply of carrots. Taken on its own, this supply shift, for now more can be produced at every price, would be predicted to lead to a reduction in the equilibrium carrot price. Now assume another separate change occurs at the same time which affects the market demand. There is a rightward shift in demand for all vegetables including carrots, due to an increasing number of vegetarians in the population. Carrot prices would increase and the quantity of carrots on the market would rise as a result of this shift, taken in isolation. However, we have two shifts which lead to changes pulling price in opposite directions. The resultant equilibrium depends on the *relative size* of the shifts. If we draw the diagram in one particular way, with exactly offsetting shifts in both curves, we could show no price change at all. The only impact in this case would be the change in quantity bought and sold in the market, an increase as shown in Figure 5.7 from Q1 to Q3.

If the equilibrium price were to rise then the demand shift would have been greater than the supply shift; its effect would have outweighed the shift in supply. Should the price fall then the supply shift impact would have more than offset the increase in demand as shown in Figure 5.8.

INTRODUCING ELASTICITY

Elasticity simply means the responsiveness, adaptability or 'stretchability' of one variable, like the quantity demanded of a good, to a change in an independent variable, such as the good's own price. Elasticity is a versatile concept which can be used in a variety of contexts in economics. It helps us to explain, for example, the price and quantity changes which occur when the demand or supply curve shifts.

We have actually started with *price elasticity of demand*. This is simply the relationship between a small percentage change in the price of a good and the resulting percentage change in quantity demanded. Price elasticity of demand (PED) is defined and measured by:

$$\text{PED} = \frac{\text{percentage change in quantity demanded}}{\text{percentage change in price}}$$

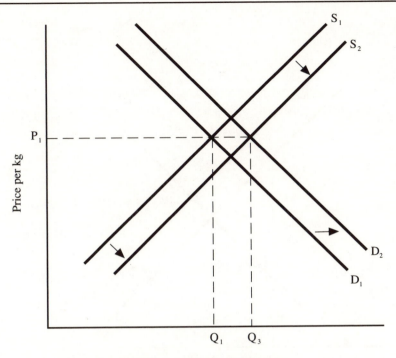

Figure 5.7 Changing demand and supply simultaneously. Given the relative size and direction of the shifts equilibrium price remains constant, the quantity bought and supplied increases

1 If a 1 per cent increase in the price of a good leads to a more than proportional reduction in quantity demanded, for example, 3 per cent, then the price elasticity of demand is categorized as *elastic*. PED is three.[5] This indicates that quantity demanded is highly responsive to a price change.

2 If a 1 per cent price increase is exactly matched by an *equivalent* reduction in quantity demanded, i.e., 1 per cent, then the price elasticity of demand is *unitary*. PED is one.

3 Finally, a 1 per cent increase in price which results in a *proportionally smaller* reduction in quantity demanded, say 0.5 per cent, is categorized as *inelastic*. PED is 0.5: relatively unresponsive to a price change.

Also, there are two extreme positions, one where demand is *infinitely elastic*, that is where any amount of a good will be demanded at the existing price. We shall have more to say about this concept and its use in Chapter 8. The other extreme situation is where demand exhibits a *zero price elasticity*. So far we have worked only with downward sloping functions. But now imagine a demand function for a good, where no matter what happens to price in the relevant range, quantity demanded is *totally*

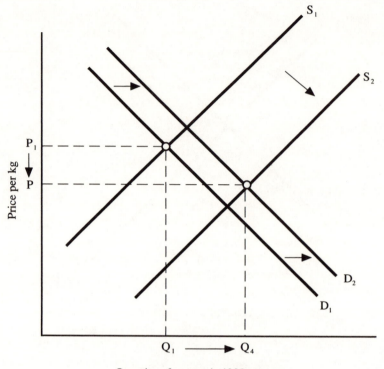

Figure 5.8 Changing demand and supply simultaneously. Equilibrium price falls and the quality bought and supplied increases given a relatively large shift in supply

unresponsive, as shown by D_1, the vertical demand curve in Figure 5.9. Given a relatively small increase in price from P_1 to P_2, consumers here are willing to buy as much as before – they absorb the whole of the price increase. They do not substitute any other goods, neither do they allow the increased amount of real income required to pay for maintaining consumption to deter them from purchasing the same amount. In this case the price elasticity of demand is 0.

Contrast this with the demand curve D_2, depicted in Figure 5.9. Given this demand function, the equivalent percentage increase in price brings a different result. Quantity demanded falls by 50 per cent from Q_2 to Q_1. Here the quantity demanded is highly responsive to the price change and elasticity is greater than unity.[6]

Given that P_1 is the initial equilibrium price displayed in Figure 5.10, then an upward shift in the supply function from S_1 to S_2 would bring differential changes in the equilibrium price and quantities. The largest price increase would occur in the case of D_1, where the price would rise from P_1 to P_3 with no change in equilibrium quantity. However, price would rise by a smaller proportion to P_{1*} given the demand curve D_2 and the equilibrium quantity demanded would fall to Q_{1*}.

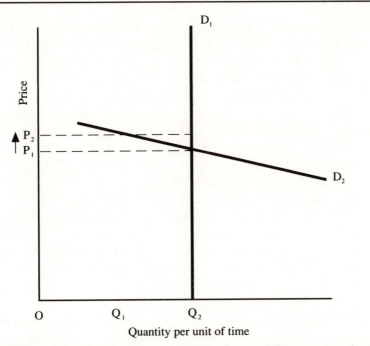

Figure 5.9 Two demand curves displaying different price elasticities of demand

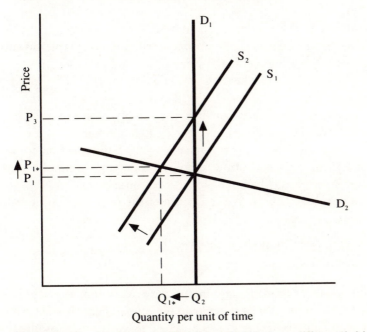

Figure 5.10 A leftward shift in supply brings a differential impact on equilibrium price and quantity given different price elasticities of demand exhibited by D_1 and D_2

What determines price elasticity of demand? Why are there differences in the responsiveness of quantity demanded to changes in price as shown above? There are many factors at work determining demand but price elasticity essentially depends on substitution and income effects. If the price of the good goes up by 1 per cent and there are many very close substitutes in the eyes of consumers, *ceteris paribus*, now relative prices have changed, buyers will switch their purchasing away from this good to a substitute. In the extreme, if there are perfect substitutes, then buyers would immediately switch to them; elasticity would be described as infinite. However, in reality, quantity demanded is not so sensitive to a change in price. Substitutes are usually available – but they are not perfect substitutes.

If the commodity takes only a very small proportion of consumers' income, however, then a small increase in price would not affect purchase plans, quantity demanded might be relatively unaffected and inelastic as in the case of a good like chewing gum or mustard. On the other hand, if the product takes a large proportion of income, then even a small price increase could cause a relatively large fall in real income and a reduction in quantity demanded. However, whilst crack cocaine may take a large portion of an addict's income, there may be no acceptable substitute. Even when the street price increases, more income has to be diverted or acquired to maintain consumption; alternative sources of income may have to be found. In fact, substitution and income effects may pull in different directions and change over time.

The passage of real time is an essential feature determining elasticity, for the longer the time period taken, the more likely that consumers will find acceptable substitutes and be able to use them. For example, if the price of natural gas rises, in the short run, consumers are 'locked into' their heating and cooking systems. They can try to economize on gas use at the margin but they still have to purchase. In the longer term, as heating systems and appliances come up for renewal consumers can switch to a substitute like electricity, other things remaining equal. Of course, an increase in water charges, given water metering, may not have a significant impact on consumption overall for there is no close substitute for piped water in a domestic context, although those on low incomes may be forced to cut back on their use.

Elasticity is a multipurpose concept. We can consider the price elasticity of supply – an analogous concept – defined as:

$$PES = \frac{\text{percentage change in quantity supplied}}{\text{percentage change in price}}$$

Again, time is of the essence. Immediately, in the very short run, the supply of a commodity cannot be increased, for production takes time. The responsiveness of supply to a price change may be greater in the longer term as more resources and producers can be brought into production. Supply functions displaying different elasticities are shown in Figure 5.11 (see Glossary for formal definitions).

Finally, there are other measures of elasticity: income elasticity and cross price elasticity, where the impact on the quantity demanded of a good is set against

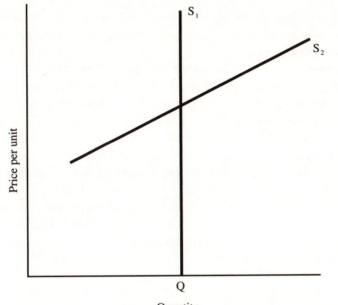

Figure 5.11   Supply functions displaying different elasticities. S_1 represents an inelastic supply, unresponsive to a change in price. An increase in price given S_2 induces an increase in quantity supplied. This is a relatively elastic function. A horizontal supply function would depict perfectly elastic supply

changes in income and changes in the price of other goods, respectively. Income elasticity, how the demand for a good responds to a change in income, determines the size and direction of a demand shift and hence affects the new equilibrium price and quantity.

A REVIEW AND ASSESSMENT OF THE TRADITIONAL 'IDEAL TYPE'

The basic supply and demand analysis enables us to show very clearly the direction of the equilibrium price and quantity in different market circumstances. Moreover, it illustrates forcefully how markets are interlinked. Changes in the carrot price send ripple effects into other markets. People changing their behaviour impinges upon others. The model offers us a clear starting point. It does not describe reality; it is an important aid to thought.

The perfectly competitive 'ideal type' market is the necessary basis for the usual introductory textbook demand and supply cross diagram, set in analytical time. Here perfect information reigns and so there are no search or transaction costs, neither risk nor fundamental uncertainty – all actual features of perspective time. But given this simplified model there are some general observations which we can make about market functions:

a) The market *co-ordinates* the actions of countless small buyers and sellers. No overseer or manager is required to organize market activity. Individual profit and utility maximizers working in pursuit of their own interests have perfect knowledge of the alternatives as reflected by the key information of product price. The basic model provides an outcome where the plans of buyers and sellers are exactly matched at the equilibrium price. All those who plan to buy or sell at this price are able to trade. Prices are the effective *signals* which guide resources to their best uses. When the demand for one product increases, automatically, more resources flow into the production of that 'favoured' good. Resources are drawn away from the production of other goods; these now have smaller demands, other things being equal. The increase in demand for one good, has a knock on effect, a reduction in the price of these other goods. As their prices fall, producers of such goods make reduced profits. Price changes give the signals; they alert and inform producers either to expand or contract production. It is the changes in the conditions of supply and demand which set off these market price beacons.

b) The market mechanism *rations* by price. Limited resources and unlimited desires mean that all wants cannot be met, no matter how necessary. There is scarcity. The market uses price as the rationing device. Equilibrium price is the unique cut-off. Those who are willing and able to buy at this equilibrium price or above, purchase the amounts they desire. But those who, for whatever reasons, are unwilling or unable to pay that price, find themselves 'rationed out', *excluded* from purchasing. The price is too high, given their income and/or desires; their wants will not be met in the market. Price must fall to include them.

   The perfectly competitive market allocates and rations *impersonally*, on the basis of price. The equilibrium price is the watershed. On the supply side those who are unable or unwilling to supply at prices *at or below* the equilibrium price are excluded too. Price rules them out. Those willing and able to buy or sell at the equilibrium price can participate in market exchange. But no individual person or group has to decide who to exclude. The market does this dispassionately.

c) The market price gives *incentives*. Imagine that new information about the intelligence giving properties of carrots hits the headlines: 'Increased carrot consumption enhances IQ'. As a result, at every price people are willing to buy more carrots, *ceteris paribus*. Carrot demand shifts to the right, inducing a response from suppliers as the price of carrots is bid up. Existing suppliers will now find it more profitable to sell greater quantities at the new higher price; a clear monetary incentive to produce more from their existing capacity. Indeed, over the *long run* when fixed physical capital and land inputs can be changed and new plant brought into production, new suppliers will enter the market. As a result of the initial demand increase, and price rise, more resources are drawn into production both in the short and eventually the long run.

The 'ideal type' market in analytical time: an initial assessment of the market mechanism.

The model is a *simplification* helping us to think logically and clearly about the forces which may affect the behaviour of market prices and quantities. It gives an insight into the workings of markets and the possible impact of price changes. But in that process of simplification, inevitably some features have been set aside. The 'ideal type' market in analytical time is sanitized from many important characteristics existing in both perspective and historical time.

The static equilibrium analysis of analytical time does not tell us how an equilibrium actually occurs. There may be a mythical auctioneer who calls out prices. A process of bidding and offering prices occurs until an eventual balance is achieved. But the process must take the passage of real time, it cannot be instantaneous. People making decisions in perspective time do not have perfect information, they often have to proceed by trial and error. Production takes time, plans cannot be instantaneously changed and fulfilled. Our model is not a description of the higgle haggle of trade in many real markets. In the 'ideal type' exchange process there are no impediments, no frictions; property rights are perfectly and costlessly specified; information is perfect and costs nothing to acquire. There are no transactions costs. In an analytical time mode, prices and quantities respond smoothly and effortlessly, moving from one stable equilibrium to another in a system of interlinked markets.

In reality, we cannot hold *ceteris paribus*, other things being equal. Actual price changes are the results of many factors, often pulling in different directions. Whilst the scales always appear to be in perfect repose, a harmonious result, in real markets there may be constant movement and discord. Markets may never reach an equilibrium as circumstances evolve. There may be forces at work which encourage instability. Marshall was always very careful to hedge his arguments with reference to an evolving complex reality, but many of those who have used his diagrammatic presentation have not been so concerned to emphasize this. For Marshall, 'the general conditions of life are not stationary' (1920a: 347), as we highlighted in Chapter 3.

In this perfectly competitive situation, supply and demand curves are drawn to show a neat symmetry, a balanced scale, signalling the underlying theme of this ideal type – equal market power. Buyers and sellers are evenly matched. The neat symmetrical diagram of the conventional model is a soothing construct. But in perspective time, one side of the market, whether sellers or buyers, may have the upper hand. Indeed, supply and demand are not separate in markets where, for example, the impact of advertising, and built-in obsolescence, is engineered by large corporate suppliers who can affect demand. This may make for a set of kitchen scales out of true. Moreover, within groups of buyers or sellers, some may have greater income and power; the market does not operate on the basis of one person one vote. Spending and decision-making power can be very unequally divided. In the introductory model, there is no tradition, no mention of inherited wealth or authority. In the allocation process, the market, in fact, does not consider need or desert. In both perspective and historical time, the outcome may be neither just nor fair, albeit mutually agreed.

In perfect competition there is no discussion of the risks and uncertainties faced by real-world actors making decisions in perspective time. Significantly, buyers and sellers have no long term commitment to each other in the market. People have no allegiances, they can switch their exchange transactions with ease. Whatever the good, a standard carrot or potato, all products are homogeneous; and whoever the buyer or seller, all people are assumed to be the same for the purposes of market trading. It matters not from whom you buy or to whom you sell. Exchange is impersonal, undertaken in the light of all the relevant facts. There is no place for trust, hope or doubt, and no requirement for the necessary institutional features which exist in reality. Essential customs, conventions and laws are wasteful impedimenta in this simplified model, set in analytical time. Labour laws, shops and factory acts, safety standards, consumer legislation, these are held by some to impede the workings of the free market and to cut down on individual choice.

Actual markets are set in a particular historical context; they are not in the ether. The determinants of supply and demand are not ahistorical, 'pure' without alloy. They are fashioned in part by the institutional characteristics of the society in question, its past evolutionary path and social norms. The demand for different types of goods, for example, depends on many things. These include the pattern of inherited wealth and the income distribution which has evolved over historical time, moreover, the custom and practice in society, which mould tastes. There are complex issues underlying our neat curves. Such complexities are vestiges of the past, as much as they are signs of the present. History matters.

COMPETITIVE PRICE MARKETS WHICH APPROXIMATE THE 'IDEAL TYPE'

Nevertheless, there are real-world markets which display many characteristics of the perfectly competitive type. Often agricultural and basic commodity markets, like Hayek's tin market, dealing in standard produce where many small suppliers and buyers meet, approach this ideal (Douma and Shreuder 1991). Each producer's output is a mere drop in the ocean and there are no effective barriers to entry. International stock markets, where vast numbers of buyers and sellers, globally, are looking for the best return possible to compensate them for buying shares gives another example. Here we have to deviate from a riskless world, although we still operate in a standard mode where risk is assumed to be readily measurable (see Chapter 12). Whilst at first sight it might seem that shares in different companies, like Marks and Spencer (M&S), General Motors (GM), London Weekend Television (LWT) are very different, they have standard attributes. It can be argued that the bulk of investors are not concerned about the actual nature of the companies in which they own shares. They merely want to achieve the biggest return for the least risk, standard characteristics to be measured for any share regardless of which company issued it. Modern financial markets are dependent on the most up-to-date information technology, people linked together by electronic means. The prices of financial securities can be shown almost instantaneously, on computer screens around the global market. New information is quickly assimilated by buyers and sellers and reflected in price movements.[7] Whilst the global market and large sophisticated markets like New York, Tokyo and London, have multitudes of market players with good information, not all stock markets display these characteristics. In small emerging markets, for example, in Eastern Europe, there may be very few buyers and sellers, with poor information and ill-defined rules of the game.

The *London Stock Exchange* – a market for financial securities can be used to illustrate a well organized market with clear similarities to the 'ideal type', where prices respond rapidly to changes in supply and demand. There are large numbers of buyers and sellers for the shares quoted on the stock exchange. Each player holds such a small proportion of bonds and shares, that no one seller or buyer can affect market price. There are no significant barriers to entry. Shares in a very large number of different companies are sold (those on the All Share *Financial Times* index). Financial assets can be regarded as homogeneous in important respects – they promise to give a return for a particular risk. Shares differ in terms of the risk and return they offer, and these are the characteristics which interest market players. With modern information technology, prices reflect quickly all new information which relates to the risk return payoff of any particular share. So the market mechanism very speedily responds to news which may affect the market's view of any firm's future earnings capacity. If the market believes a firm is in for a poor trading time, shareholders will sell and potential buyers will be deterred. This will be reflected in a share price fall. Prices can move up or down, swings which may be affected by the overall mood of the market.

Why do all markets require legal rules, customs or convention?

All markets, to a greater or lesser extent, require laws, customs and conventions in order to co-ordinate the plans of buyers and sellers – vital for any market form. To work effectively, markets have to provide security, people need to know that they are not going to be cheated – receive nothing for something or less than they agreed. The London Stock Exchange like other stock markets around the world has a basis of *institutional rules*. Markets have to be organized, to function effectively. As we shall see in Chapter 6, this competitive market is heavily dependent on rules and regulations. There is no such thing as a 'perfect' market, pure, unsullied by tradition or the hand of government. Markets are founded on rules whether set by government organizations or customary practice. Over historical time these rules and regulations evolve, unique in time and place. And as economic interactions, products and markets become more sophisticated the rules and their policing have to develop, to keep pace with or initiate change.

In perspective time the influence of norms and convention intertwine with the price mechanism and economic transactions. Some markets are segregated by tradition, with barriers which are based on past practice. In labour markets custom may lead to discriminatory behaviour, with some groups being preferred to others. Moreover, in perspective time there has to be an element of trust in markets, for once there is a division in perspective time between buying and selling and repeated deals are not expected, trust is very important – the confidence that the other party will fulfil his or her part of the bargain. Where deals are large it may be possible to insure against the risk of default. Institutions like the Small Claims Court have a role to play in enforcing small one-off deals, where trust for whatever the reason has been misplaced. This makes it possible for people to use the law, without great financial cost, to enforce small contracts. The Office of Fair Trading polices many aspects of market trade. Yet at whatever point in historical time, markets require rules of the game.

Fix and flex price markets

Whilst all markets require rules, however basic, a very large number of markets do not approximate the 'ideal type' of perfect competition where prices and quantities respond instantaneously to shifts in the demand and supply curves. Price flexibility is not the hallmark of all markets. In theory, other market forms come under the heading of *imperfect competition*. Whilst they may sound substandard, such markets represent reality. Indeed, whilst some imperfect markets give flexible prices, many market situations are characterized by *inflexible prices – fix prices*.

Whilst we have focused on a real-world highly competitive scenario, there are other types of market. Products in the modern world are usually more complex than the standard, simple innocuous vegetable, like a carrot, which takes little time to consume, needs no after sales service, and has not been differentiated from other carrots by an edible logo or other marketing gimmick. In *oligopolistic* and *monopolistic* markets, we can allow for situations where *prices do not vary* immediately in the event of market changes. The mass of relatively sophisticated goods, which we actually buy in perspective time, are sold in very different market environments from that of perfect competition. In many markets, the very nature of goods perforce, requires production by a large organization, to provide long-term research and development and huge physical and human capital inputs. These are not simple goods produced by the isolated individual artisan, or even the small-scale, low-technology, factory environment which Adam Smith described, where small-scale enterprise could often respond very quickly to changes in demand. In the oligopolistic world of the late twentieth century, many of the items we buy are manufactured and marketed by giant organizations – high-technology, large-scale producers providing highly sophisticated products.

Many markets are dominated by *powerful sellers* who have discretionary power over the prices they charge. Such suppliers are not at the full behest of the market. They can have significant influence over price; they advertise and partially orchestrate market outcomes. As market conditions alter, suppliers may be forced to bow to the impact of long-term changes. However, in the shorter term, they do not jump to change the money price as market conditions vary – they have discretion. Massive organizations, giant suppliers, may be slow to respond to changes in real-world conditions. In fact, in the modern economy, despite the use of computerized equipment, it is often expensive to change prices. It may be cheaper to leave them unchanged. Many building societies decided to leave mortgage interest rates alone when interest rates varied too frequently. They simply altered the rates once a year in order to reduce the significant administration costs. Also, in perspective time, small price changes may be seen as a signal of future changes to come, so sellers prefer to leave prices unchanged. They may be unwilling to set off price wars with their rivals. Large market players may resort to other forms of *non-price competition* like promotional offers or changing quality and product design, rather than competing directly through price. Money prices are 'sticky' and markets are not neatly cleared by price movements. Although changes in inflation rates will change real prices with the passage of time.

In such *fix price markets*, should there be a surplus of a particular good, then rather than reduce price, the sellers may simply store what remains unsold. Money prices remain fixed regardless of market changes. In perspective time sellers do not know how the future will unfold, what, for example, will be the future demand for their product? It costs money to store unsold goods, so the seller has to balance a variety of expectations about costs and revenues. If storage were too expensive, or impossible, then at the end of a particular period produce would be disposed of, for example, either sold to employees at a knock-down price, given away or destroyed. In the next time period, sellers might reduce their planned output. In real situations, wholesalers and retailers simply cut back on their orders. In fact, there may be no reduction of price whatsoever. A reduction of quantity takes all the strain. Output can be reduced through the instigation of short-time working, redundancies or by the multinational company supplying a smaller quantity from another country and closing down the home manufacturing base. In contrast, in some markets even though there is obviously an excess of demand at the current price, firms do not put prices up. A queue of unsatisfied buyers, empty shelves and lengthening waiting lists are the hallmarks of a mismatch between quantities supplied and demanded.

In labour markets there are frequently sound reasons for not engaging in wage reductions. People often do not compete on the basis of lowering the price for which they will work. Many labour markets simply do not feature outright wage competition. People are not homogeneous vegetables or machines – reducing their wages may adversely affect their productivity. People are not perfectly interchangeable, like financial assets with a particular risk and return trade-off. Wage rates and employment levels do not of necessity move in smooth harmony from one equilibrium to another, to accommodate changes in supply and demand as the introductory model would show. Labour markets are more complex than that. Non-price methods are often used to allocate jobs, to choose from the labour queue.[8] This may include competition on the basis of educational qualifications, previous job experience or other personal attributes.

Supermarkets do not operate as auction markets where there is a bidding for goods, there is no higgle haggle of trade at the checkout in Asda or Tesco. But in many parts of the world, for example, in Malaysia and parts of the Far East, the buyer is expected to haggle over price, a custom unfamiliar to the conventional Western shopper. Of course, there are always special deals, cut price offers and a process of trial and error in markets. Prices can be flexible. If the demand for a good increases it may take a short time for suppliers to satisfy this. The quantity they supply is responsive to price changes. But for a good like electricity, where it takes a long time to build capacity to produce extra output, several years may elapse before new equipment can be installed. Changes in the market may not be smooth or rapid. Resources released from one industry need not quickly flow to other productive uses. Labour might need retraining, relocating or capital equipment may require modification. It may not be possible to effect change speedily; moving towards equilibrium may take a very long period of real time. What can be quickly shown on a diagram may be far removed from the practical reality.

MARKETS, PRICES AND ALLOCATION – SUMMARY

- Exchange is at the heart of the market. There has to be a payment at an explicit price and an exchange of property rights. The market requires communication between buyers and sellers – an information system and the rules of the game.
- Markets are organizations, usually linking people in an independent, non-communal way. Markets are not families or firms and do not produce or consume goods. Markets may involve co-operation and rivalry.
- Markets interlink the external relationships of households, private sector firms and public sector trading organizations with money and real goods and service flows.
- A wide variety of markets exist, categorized in a variety of ways, for example, according to the type of final goods, commodities and service to be exchanged, spot or futures markets, legal and illegal markets.
- The key classification is by market structure – the degree of competition. These markets range from the 'ideal type' perfectly competitive market, monopolistic competition, oligopoly to monopoly.
- Demand and supply determine equilibrium price and quantity. Effective demand is determined by the ability and willingness to pay. There is an inverse relationship between quantity demanded and price. Shift factors affect the position of the demand curve.
- The supply curve is a positive function, as price increases, given appropriate assumptions, so will the quantity supplied. Shift factors affect the position of the supply curve.
- The equilibrium price is determined at the intersection of supply and demand. Shifting demand and supply curves bring changes in market prices and quantities.

- Elasticity measures responsiveness. Price elasticity is simply the responsiveness of quantity demanded to a change in price. There are other measures including income elasticity and cross price elasticity.
- Perfect competition is devoid of any institutional features and completely independent of time and place, an ahistorical construct. In perspective time people do not have perfect information and their ability to understand the information available may be limited.
- Markets, in practice, can have fixed or flexible prices. All markets are placed within a particular context of time and place. Their rules and conventions have a historical dimension. Market players perceive the future with a notion of what is normal, based on their experience.

MARKETS, PRICES AND ALLOCATION – QUESTIONS FOR DISCUSSION

1 What are the essential features of any market? Compare the following markets:

   a) the used car market;
   b) the London Stock Exchange;
   c) a wholesale meat market;
   d) the market in your home town;
   e) the marijuana market.

   How do you think that law and custom, and technological change have affected the evolution of these markets over historical time?

2 Explain the difference between a primary and secondary market. Is it possible to have one without the other? Give examples.

3 Why do we draw demand curves which slope downwards from left to right? Discuss the effects on the demand curve for UK eggs as a result of the following:

   a) a new salmonella scare;
   b) an increase in real incomes per head;
   c) a fall in the price of UK eggs;
   d) a significant increase in the number of vegetarians;
   e) a large reduction in the price of French eggs.

4 What are the determinants of supply? What assumptions are made when an upward sloping supply curve is drawn? What factors can bring changes in supply in analytical time?

5 Explain with the aid of diagrams what impact the following events would have on the equilibrium price and quantity of tea:

   a) a link between tea consumption and cancer is suggested;
   b) the price of coffee is reduced;
   c) productivity in tea plantations is improved;

   d) a general rise in real wages in tea producing countries occurs;
   e) poor weather affects tea harvests.

6 'If the amount bought always equals the amount sold – how can disequilibrium ever occur?' Explain.
7 Explain the advantages and disadvantages of using the 'ideal type market', set in analytical time as an illustrative device.
8 What do you understand by the concept of elasticity? Why is it argued that quantity demanded of a good will become more elastic with the passage of time, other things being equal?
9 Why are the prices in some markets inflexible? Give examples. How could relative prices in such markets change, despite the fact that money prices remain constant as time passes?

6

Government, pricing and non-market allocation

INTRODUCTION

The purpose of this chapter is twofold. First, to give further insights into the role and significance of government in a modern economy. Second, to draw attention to the non-market means of providing and allocating resources, goods and services. We have examined the workings of the market mechanism in the last chapter, where buyers and sellers trade well defined products and financial assets. Now our key aim is to highlight non-market procedures of co-ordination and allocation, to show in what situations the market mechanism is deemed to be inappropriate – where markets fail or simply do not exist. In particular, we draw attention to the different activities of government both within non-market and market contexts.

Whilst we are all market players, even in a late twentieth-century modern economy, we have other roles. We are not just buyers and sellers, customers or business people engaged in market transactions. Not all the goods and services we enjoy or need lend themselves to provision by the market, even though they may be costly in terms of resources and vital in the scheme of things. We examine the types of goods and services which do not fit the orthodox neo-classical market paradigm, which do not come to us via a market transaction. The government has a significant role to play in the provision of such goods. Of course, other organizations, particularly the household, have a vital hand in non-market provision, matters to which we shall turn in Part II. As we saw in earlier chapters, the distinct role of the state and civil society and the *mix* of market and non-market allocative processes varies over historical time and place.

In this chapter we emphasize that people can employ different methods of allocation *either* in addition to *or* instead of the market mechanism. We highlight, for example, the role of direct allocation of resources and goods by command, administrative procedures and by traditional means, via custom and practice. Here we work largely within the context of government but, as we shall see in later chapters, such non-market processes are important in other scenarios. Non-market allocative methods play a notable role in the complex modern economy. And there is always the gift relationship, a vital element in any economic system.

Now we take a closer look at the role of government, essentially in its microeconomic dealings, beginning with an orthodox view where government stands outside the system, exogenous, simply intervening in the market process. However, we shall argue that government does more than intercede. It has an important hand not only in the provision and allocation of particular goods but in setting and policing the rules of the game, helping to provide a stable framework for markets. Moreover, it acts as a major market player. More than that, we shall argue that the diverse organizations of the state and civil society are entangled in a complex web of arrangements: the economic system, where market and non-market provision are entwined.

OVERVIEW: GOVERNMENT AND THE NON-MARKET ALLOCATIVE PROCESS

In economic theory government is often portrayed as a monolithic block, an *exogenous* factor, standing outside the market system. It simply intervenes in the market process, interceding by imposing taxes or providing subsidies, occasionally controlling prices or stepping in where markets fail. But government is not a single institution separate from all others, it encompasses many diverse organizations at different levels. In Britain, for example, there are regional and local government bodies, some small, no more than the size of a parish council, others large local authorities presiding over multi-million pound budgets. Contrast this with national central government organizations often linked internationally through supra-national bodies. The state plays heterogeneous roles, in a variety of guises, inextricably involved in the economic system, not separate or apart. We shall continue to argue the case that relationships between civil society and government are interwoven in a complex fashion. There is no rigid dichotomy between them. Whilst organizations of the state have a distinct identity there is a mutual interdependence with other organizations. And through historical time there have been many different mixes of government organizations, families and private organizations, whether business firms or charities.

As we have argued in Chapter 4, at a basic level, the state is a major player in the evolution of the rules of the game (North 1990). Political organizations wielding power have a hand in setting the rules of the game. These organizations provide the overall rules with the power conferred on them or taken by them. State organizations act as co-ordinators; they legitimize and coerce. State organizations tax and spend, they often act as producers and market players. They operate within micro- and macroeconomic contexts, taking on different parts. Sometimes governments may try to achieve social justice through taxation and subsidies, changing the distribution of income and wealth. In some circumstances governments may emphasize economic development and growth. Governments may follow goals which clash, so that they trade off one objective for another.

Economists have long commented on the appropriate role and importance of government in the economy (although the role of the household and non-commercial organization has been pushed to the sidelines). Economists' views differ markedly. Adam Smith saw a limited role for the state, echoed in the laissez-faire views of the nineteenth century, although as we have seen in Chapter 3, for example, Smith saw a role for government in providing education. The sovereign in Smith's terms would have a hand in defence, the administration of justice and the maintenance of certain public works. Marx, in contrast, predicted that the state would eventually wither away in the final stage of development – communism. He was suspicious of the role of the state under capitalism. Keynes, writing in the depression years of the 1920s and 1930s, argued the case for government intervention in the macroeconomy, in a microeconomic context, making a case for expenditure on public works. Other economists, like Hayek and Milton Friedman, have placed emphasis on limited government, with a faith in the workings of the free markets. There is no single view.

Simple solutions about the appropriate role and balance of the market and the state provide handy slogans but the passage of real time shows us complex scenarios. History illustrates that there are many blends of organizations, making up different economic systems which will work. And the role of the complex organizations of state and civil society, including the market, evolve uniquely in time and place. We cannot rerun time past to compare different possible scenarios with or without 'big government'. In fact, it is exceedingly difficult to isolate the impact of governments from all the other related factors in any particular economic system.

In recent years in Britain the predominant mood has been for the state to play a much smaller part in the economy. Since 1979 the objective has been to roll back the frontiers of the state, 'getting government off the backs of the people'. This view has been echoed in other industrialized nations, although not all. Moreover, in what were planned economies, there have been significant changes in the balance of planning and the market, in an effort to move the economic system towards the economies of the rich industrialized nations.

Privatization became the watchword of the 1980s and still rests towards the top of the political agenda in Britain. Privatization has different strands. It includes the sale of state-owned assets to private individuals, households and organizations. Other features include deregulation, encouraging competition, for example, by the contracting out of services previously provided by government organizations, like local authority refuse collection or market testing whereby activities previously undertaken by government departments are put out to tender to private sector firms. Economic prices have been encouraged for services previously provided free or at minimal charge, for eye tests or dental treatments. Indeed, the privatization principle, broadly speaking, emphasizes private ownership, the use of markets and competition. Business firms should supply where they can, competition and the price mechanism should be used more widely. Government failure, it has been argued, required the cutting back of government bureaucracy, inefficiency and waste.

Privatization put into reverse policy measures of previous decades. Beveridge's Welfare State with its universalism was to feel the winds of government change, and those commanding heights of the economy nationalized during and after the Second World War have largely been transferred into the private sector. Public utilities where effective competition was not possible given the essential large-scale production required to achieve minimum costs, including industries like gas, electricity, coal, steel and the railways had been taken into state ownership. Most of these have either been sold off under privatization or are intended for sale. And those business firms previously baled out by government, the 'lame duck' producers, who could not make a profit at a particular time, like Jaguar and Rolls-Royce, have been sold too. Ninety-nine per cent of the shares in Jaguar were sold in 1984 for £294 million. One hundred per cent of shares in Rolls-Royce were sold in May 1987 for £1.3 billion.

However, even after recent changes in Britain, the government still acts as both regulator and market player. Governments set the legal framework, the formal rules of the game. Government organizations operate as purchasers of and competitors with business firms. In Britain, for example, the Ministry of Defence acts as a buyer of weaponry, usually purchasing directly from private sector firms. Yet government also operates in a productive capacity as in a state-run industry like the Post Office – supplying services to households and firms. Moves to privatize the Royal Mail were defeated in November 1994.

Many functions are directly funded and controlled by Government. Organizations of the state operate the legislative process and policing. The civil service, including the Inland Revenue, Department of Social Security and Customs and Excise are important organizations gathering in, for example, tax revenues and paying out social security. Health and education are directly funded and overseen by the state. We shall have more to say about such public sector non-trading organizations in Chapter 10.

In what follows we shall explore the rationale for the state's activity in more detail. The state has a key role to play where markets or other organizational forms, like the household or community group, cannot effectively provide and allocate particular goods and services. The provision of public goods is an important function of government.

Public goods: communal use

Pure public or communal goods, like defence at a national or international level, law and order or public administration, cannot be allocated by the price mechanism. For example, a 'product' like national defence, of necessity, is communally and not individually consumed. Pure public goods do not fit the neo-classical market paradigm for they are not bought and sold in markets. Markets simply do not exist for them. Government at a national and international level provide these. Pure public goods are supplied to the community as a whole without direct charge related to use to the individual, independent of an individual's income or strength of desire. Decisions about the amount of resources overall to devote to these goods are not decided by the workings of the market but by a *political process*.

The following attributes make such public goods impossible to allocate by the market:

Non-excludability

First, no one can be excluded from the protection of Trident missiles, Tornado aircraft or whatever military hardware will displace these as technology changes. Those who do not pay still receive a benefit. Such goods are expensive and 'lumpy'; they cannot be divided up or restricted for individual use. Both the wealthiest citizens and the poorest of the poor have the protection of the armed forces.

However, unless there are enough altruistic people in the modern world, all agreed to look after the common good, narrow self-interest would mean that insufficient resources would be forthcoming to provide such public goods. Too many people might be free-riders, benefiting from the security but without paying for its provision. Indeed, there would be no way of stopping their consumption. Certainly, private business firms could not make a profit, for unlike the ham sandwich or the Coca-Cola, national defence cannot be restricted to those who pay. Although, of course, private suppliers of military hardware and expert systems sell to governments for profit.

Non-rivalry

People are not rivals in the consumption of pure public goods. When defence is supplied, the degree of protection given to one family does not reduce the availability of such benefits for others. There is no need to ration by the price mechanism, even if that were possible. As we showed in the discussion of private property rights in Chapter 4, rivalry exists in the purchase of a private good. If one person buys a pint of beer, that is no longer available for another. But the benefits of a protective nuclear umbrella are nation-wide; consumption by one person does not reduce availability for another. Benefits are for everyone, whether wanted or not. This brings us to a final point.

Non-rejectability

The public good cannot be rejected like a beer for own consumption. Those who do not wish to be defended by a nuclear deterrent and armed forces are not able to opt out. This is quite unlike the provision of a private burglar alarm system where the individual household, given the ability to pay, can choose to reject or accept such protection.

For these reasons public goods are provided centrally by the government at no direct price to people who benefit. In modern economies the costs of producing such goods are paid for largely through taxation receipts, government borrowing or the printing of money. To fulfil the defence function in the modern world, requires a huge input of resources embodying modern technology and often enormous quantities of military hardware and personnel. None but the richest could afford to buy a personal Trident or hire an army. Technological changes and the pooling of large sums of money from a variety of sources have made it possible for the purchase of weaponry by freedom fighters or terrorist groups, but the extent of this is still relatively small compared with the armoury of large nation states. True, some richer elements in society may band together to provide private security, policing for their enclaves, but in the main, overall security is provided by government organizations, at international, national and local levels.

Looking back in historical time, defence has rarely been allocated by a market mechanism. Defence was provided communally at the behest of councils of elders, by feudal knights and princes, latterly national and international government organizations. Although there have been examples of mercenary armies, paid outsiders, usually those being protected did not pay according to the amount of protection they received; central authorities levied taxes and tithes and/or used conscription.

Moreover, the framework of law and order is a public good provided to the citizen at no charge at the point of consumption. The individual, for example, does not pay directly for motorway policing or the workings of the legislature. The costs of such communal services are paid from government funds, whether centrally or locally. Yet not all goods funded and/or provided by the government fall into the category of pure public goods. Quasi-public goods and merit goods, both goods for individual use, are also important.

Quasi-public goods

Quasi-public goods have elements of both a public and private good. Some commodities which potentially could be allocated by the price mechanism are nevertheless provided by the state (and in some circumstances other organizations). These goods are supplied without a specific charge related to the amount used by an individual. The provision of roads, pavements, public parks and recreation grounds are examples of such quasi-public goods. We do not pay directly for a walk in Hyde Park or for our use of the M1, although we pay indirectly through taxes, whether from council taxes, VAT or from road fund licences.

Very often these goods do not display rivalry and excludability, the attributes of a purely private good. But when these facilities are used to capacity and 'over used', then rivalry exists. Consumption for one person reduces what is available for others.

Moreover, there may be the possibility of excluding people although the goods are only partially divisible.

Whilst these goods are allocated primarily by non-market means, in some situations it would be possible to charge a price to exclude those who were unwilling and/or unable to pay. For example, it would be possible to charge for the use of roads, where geographical/physical characteristics made this viable, on some stretches of motorway or on bridges such as the Severn Bridge, where there are limited and clearly defined entrances and exits and where there are no easy alternative routes to choose. People could be readily barred if they would not or could not pay. It would be possible to monitor and control those entering and leaving and charge them accordingly. Payment is made on European toll roads and indeed was a feature of the past in Britain, where toll gates were used on some roads and canals.

However, using the price mechanism is not costless. In the UK most of the road and pavement system may be seen as non-excludable for practical purposes. Imagine the problems created by charging individuals for their use of pavements and suburban roads. In the large majority of situations the transactions costs would be extremely high. There would be far too many exits and entrances to monitor and control effectively. It would cost far more to administer and collect the charges than could be raised, in most cases. Indeed, the very process of revenue collection would cause inconvenience and time wasting for people using the system.

Yet both the use of roads and pavements can in some situations imply rivalry. Often there is a great deal of jostling for limited road space as those in traffic jams and on congested roads can witness. Here the hallmarks of excess quantity demanded over a fixed quantity of road space are traffic jams and queues. These impose external costs on private and business motorists alike, in terms of time lost, poor fuel consumption and frustration. And the wider community suffers pollution and noise.

At certain times many roads, even the pavements in shopping centres are full. Nevertheless, rivalry is not the rule at all times. There are elements of a public good here. The M25 at 2.00 am is relatively empty. Rivalry for road space at that time of the morning does not exist and the cost of an extra motorist is zero, for he or she imposes no burden on other road users. Moreover, many rural roads may be relatively free of congestion at all times.

Although everyone might be in agreement about the need for providing and maintaining pavements and roads, private business suppliers, in general, could not make a profit from their provision. Firms could not effectively exclude users, divide these goods or charge a price sufficient to make profit. Such goods confer external benefits – positive spin-offs over and above any private benefits both in production and consumption. Such advantages cannot be wholly captured by the producer in terms of profit or the purchaser in terms of happiness or utility. The advantages benefit the wider community. If the market mechanism were left to provide and to allocate roads, for example, insufficient of these would be produced for the welfare of society as a whole. Adam Smith saw a role for public works. Without communal provision our road and pavement network would be insufficient to meet the needs of a modern community. Overall resources are allocated for these quasi-public goods by a political decision.

As technology changes there may be the possibility of cheaply metering any individual's use of roads and charging accordingly for limited space, encouraging some to economize on use. Recent experiments in Cambridge illustrate that current technology gives the means to meter road use. Whether this will be economically and politically viable is another matter. And the introduction of motorway tolls is a feasible option. However, on the whole, quasi-public goods are allocated to individuals free or at a nominal charge and paid for by central funds.[1]

Merit goods

Merit goods, like health care, education and, depending on the time and place, housing are consumed by individuals and can be allocated through the market mechanism. They have attributes of the public good. Their acquisition improves the utility of the society as a whole. Certain choices about the acquisition of education, for example, are rarely left in a modern economy to the free choice of the individual. All people are expected to have a minimum level of education. But merit goods are seen as important both for individuals and society as a whole. Left to their own devices, people may have an inability or insufficient desire to buy enough of these goods. Also, of course, parents make decisions on behalf of their children (see Chapter 14). In perspective time people do not have full information and may be ignorant, for example, of the benefits and nature of different types of education. Moreover, they might not be prepared or, just as importantly, be able to buy enough of a good which confers benefits to others. For education provides important spin-offs to third parties. The individual purchaser cannot capture all the benefits. In such circumstances the market mechanism would lead to an insufficient production and consumption. Health care and education could be allocated by the price mechanism, for they are readily divisible, and to a greater or lesser extent, exhibit the characteristics of both rivalry and excludability. To take an example, one person's occupation of a hospital bed means that no one else can simultaneously use the bed. And indeed like private goods people may choose to reject them. Yet decision-makers believe that there is worth in the provision and consumption of such goods. Most countries insist on children receiving education to a certain level or the compulsory treatment of infectious diseases. Education and health care services can provide considerable external benefits, benefits which cannot be captured by the individual who buys these goods, or the producer who supplies them. They are seen as important for the development of the overall economy. The private producer could not capture all the benefits from these, neither does the individual consumer.

So in modern economies, particularly in the case of education, such goods are mostly funded by central authorities and distributed largely independently of the ability and willingness to pay. The market mechanism could be used to allocate education but even where the state does not provide, then charitable organizations often supply education and do not allocate solely on the ability to pay. In modern societies government has an important hand in providing these merit goods which produce such important benefits for society as a whole (*Economist* May 1994). Even where private schools exist they are often supported by public funds as in the case of Holland, Denmark and Australia. Many private schools in Britain have charitable status and thus attract tax relief.

Looking back in historical time, education and health care have usually been provided by non-market means, whether by the family, religious organizations or the state. Indeed, modern societies do not rely extensively on the market mechanism to provide and allocate education, although there are significant differences in provision and allocation patterns between different countries. The bulk of education provision, including university education, is provided in the public sector and paid for out of government funds. It is allocated by non-market means through administrative procedures. Moreover, governments have a major responsibility for the funding of basic research where the benefits cannot be completely captured by the private company and extensive expenditures are required. 'In almost all nations universities now are funded to a substantial degree by governments' (Nelson 1993: 12). This is so even in large market-oriented industrialized countries like the USA.

To reiterate, the provision of vaccines for the individual, for example, gives protection for others; and an educated populace become more productive (and docile) as workers. These matters are too important for the well-being of society as a whole to be left to the vagaries of the market.

The absence of markets: externalities

There are no markets for public goods. Moreover, no markets exist for some things, like pollution, a harmful bad, or a good like clean air. The private car owner and the commercial lorry both create air pollutants, in part responsible for acid rain or the increase in asthma in children. Yet in the purchase price of our vehicles and fuel we do not bear anything approaching the full cost of creating pollution. *Social costs*, adverse externalities, may differ significantly from private cost. 'Third-party costs' are not borne by individuals or organizations who create pollution and congestion. *Social benefits*, helpful externalities, giving rise to 'third-party' agreeable consequences have no markets.

The markets for some commodities do not have a legal basis, for example, for such items as crack, ecstasy, or indeed for endangered wildlife species. Whilst market trade flourishes such activity is illegal. Although private benefits in terms of profit and the enjoyment of some individuals may be great, the negative externalities for society as a whole are considered too significant to allow the legalization of such trade.

THE ALLOCATION OF NON-MARKET GOODS

The quantity and quality of resources devoted to the provision of pure public goods is decided by a political process, not by the interplay of supply and demand and the price mechanism as such. Once provided, the pure public good presents no problem of allocation to an individual. The protection derived from an early warning air strike mechanism needs no rationing. There is enough for all and additions to the population add no extra costs at the margin.

The provision of quasi-public goods overall has also often been decided through the political process. The allocation of such goods may be made on a first-come-first-served basis with no charge. Public parks are free, roads are largely free of charge at the point of use. It is only when such facilities are used to the limit that rivalry becomes an issue. However, in contrast, merit goods display both rivalry and excludability. They have to be allocated on an individual basis.

Non-market allocation of education: school places

There is a dual system for the provision of schooling in Britain, both for primary and secondary education. The largest part is carried out in the state sector although some is undertaken in the private sector. Whilst overall education budgets are decided by central and to some extent local government, resources eventually have to be allocated to districts and individual schools. Primary and secondary education in the state system is provided free at the point of delivery. All children have the right to primary and secondary education. Government in Britain, whilst still funding the school system, has in recent years emphasized the role of parental choice, competition and efficiency. Examination results and league tables have been published to provide information for parents and as a spur to competition. But whilst there have been considerable changes in the state sector, whether schools are in local authority control or have opted out and become grant maintained, responsible to the Department of Education and Science, a means of allocating school places still has to be employed.

In the short run, a fixed number of places exists in any school, as shown by the inelastic supply Oq_1 places in Figure 6.1. In some circumstances a small number of extra places may be made available with the addition of portakabins and extra staff. However, even in the longer term it may not be possible to expand places in a particular school significantly, without altering the characteristics of the 'product or service'. Schooling is of course not one-dimensional, there are many aspects to be considered like the ratio of staff to students, the overall size and the physical environment and ambience, for a complex of factors may affect the experience of education and the final outcome. There is a consideration not simply of the supplier's 'product' but also the nature of the other pupils and their parents, which may significantly affect the overall end 'product' (*Economist* May 1994).

However, given a stock of places at a particular school, parents on behalf of their

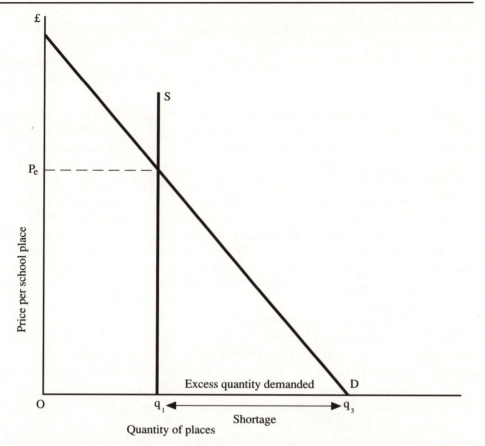

Figure 6.1 School places allocated at zero price, by non-market means: at an over-subscribed school there is excess quantity demanded

children may *express a preference* for that school. If we work in analytical time and draw a hypothetical demand curve as shown in Figure 6.1, we can illustrate the market price which would prevail if we allowed the price mechanism to allocate. State schools allocate at a zero price and for an over-subscribed school there is an excess quantity demanded at this point. There has to be rationing. Once a school is full, for example, it will cost a significant amount to provide an extra place. Where the quantity demanded exceeds the availability of places in a school, there is rivalry. But places are assigned to individuals, so any individual who is not assigned a place is excluded. A method to allocate limited places must be used. Some applicants will have to be rejected given the excess quantity demanded as shown in Figure 6.1.

There are a variety of methods which can be used to allocate school places. These range from the simple to the involved, a straightforward first-come-first-served method, or other administrative procedures based on different criteria. School places could be allocated by price, but the market process is not allowed to allocate here, for social justice, for example, requires that education in a particular school is not allocated on the parent's ability and willingness to pay. Charging the equilibrium price P_e as shown in Figure 6.1 eradicates the excess quantity demanded, and would be straightforward. However, this method is not used in the state sector, whether we examine education systems in France, USA, Holland or Australia, to take but a few examples.

In Britain, non-market administrative procedures are used. The head-teacher and/or local authority may use a variety of techniques and criteria for secondary education selection. These include interviewing children, letters of application, examination results, by area of residence or indeed some combination of these. To allocate places to individuals is a time-consuming and often an administratively difficult task. There are heavy transactions costs. Parents are encouraged to examine a variety of schools. This will be time-consuming. Moreover, the appeals procedures set in motion when a preference is not met are also costly (Le Grand and Bartlett 1993). However, some method has to be used for dealing with a situation where there is the necessity to distinguish between competing claimants. Professional judgement, sometimes backed by examination, custom and practice, all may have a part to play. Parents express a preference; they make a claim. Administrative rules and procedures are used to select whose claims shall be met.

In the catchment areas of successful popular schools, there may be spin-off effects; house prices, for example, may be expected to rise. Good outcomes may lead to increased demand from 'good' students, more resources may follow in a 'virtuous cycle'. The reverse process may occur in the under-subscribed schools. And the overall allocation which is achieved, although independent of income at one level, is determined by a complex amalgam of factors including income, wealth and class at another. Suburban, middle-income home owners may fare better than low-income groups in the overall allocative process. Here we can note that even in private sector schools which often have charitable status, allocation is not wholly by price. Prestigious schools, like Eton, may have long waiting lists which suggests that they could charge more. However, allocation depends not only on the ability and willingness to pay but on custom and practice, class and for some schools, the ability to perform well in exams. Fees are not at a market clearing level. A choice is made from applicants. Moreover, in some private schools bursaries and scholarships are awarded to students with good academic, musical or sporting attainments.

Now we move on from state schools allocating by administrative procedures outside the market mechanism, to the role of the government in the market. Government sets the statutory requirements for education and other merit goods and indeed the legal requirements for the provision of public goods. But it also sets the framework for the market and acts as a regulator. Moreover, government operates as a market player, in some circumstances as a buyer, at other times a seller.

GOVERNMENT SETTING THE LEGAL FRAMEWORK, REGULATING MARKETS AND ACTING AS A MARKET PLAYER: THE LONDON STOCK EXCHANGE

Government has other roles to fulfil beyond the provision and allocation of public and merit goods. The government has a vital role in setting the legal framework for the market and recasting and influencing some of the rules of the game as the economy evolves. Laws are passed regulating the behaviour of firms, outlawing fly tipping, or the dumping of toxic waste for example, to reduce adverse externalities. But also government organizations utilize markets, they may act as buyers and sellers. We can illustrate these roles by using the London Stock Exchange – a market for financial securities, once more as an example. Here government acts in a regulatory role, presiding over the legal basis of the market, but also operates as an important market participant.

The market is made up of a) the Gilt Edged Market for government and local authority loan stock; b) the Companies Securities Market for loan stock and shares. In these markets, government bodies issue financial assets. Local authorities and the national government issue *bonds*, loans – certificates which are transferrable or negotiable, unlike ordinary loans from a bank, where the lender and borrower have a continuing link. Such assets promise an interest and the guarantee of repayment at a future date.[2] Here government organizations are important market players, for example, selling bonds to fund government activities. The selling and buying of bonds are important for the government's monetary policy but are beyond our scope here.

In addition, in recent years the Government has used the securities market to issue ordinary *shares* which give a part ownership in privatized companies, like British Telecom (BT) and British Gas, to act as a seller. The share buyer has an entitlement to future dividends, large or small, issued by Public Limited Companies, *plcs*. The Government uses the market to sell the new privatized companies, and the presence of an active secondary market enables the purchasers to trade their assets if they wish. So the buyers of privatized shares are able to make capital gains (or losses).

Rules and regulations

As we emphasized in Chapter 5, markets require laws, customs and conventions in order to co-ordinate the plans of buyers and sellers. To work effectively markets have to provide security, people need to know that they are not going to be cheated. The London Stock Exchange, like other stock markets around the world, has a basis of *institutional rules*, markets themselves have to be organized. They need rules of the game in order to function in a well ordered fashion. The government sets a legal framework: a) laws defining property rights; b) the legal transfer of such rights; c) laws relating to the provision of market information; d) laws to reduce market restrictions, for example, entry barriers, to encourage many buyers and sellers; e) regulation/policing.

The rationale for this legislation and policing is that people have to have *confidence* in the product or service they buy. Without legal entitlement they could not lay claim to future benefits and would not wish to participate, exposing themselves to an uncertain entitlement. They must also be assured that the legal entitlement can be readily passed to another, for example, in the Stock Market that their money is not 'locked in forever'. In short, that they can readily sell their shares or bonds at a price which reflects their value. Furthermore, for effective and efficient functioning, the market, to raise the most cash at the lowest rates, other things being equal, must give buyers some security and fair treatment. Particular rules are maintained, whereby participants have confidence that they will not be cheated; where there is official recourse to outside bodies should there be a dispute. Scandals and fraud undermine trust and confidence, vital in the sale of financial assets, which by their very nature only promise to deliver benefits in an uncertain future. In particular where consumers are buying complex goods or committing large amounts of money, as is often the case with financial assets, they need protection, for they do not operate in analytical time. As we have emphasized, market players do not have perfect knowledge or the necessary specialized expertise to evaluate the information available.

Government organizations have a vital role in setting the essential framework of rules. Over historical time these rules and regulations evolve. Moreover, as economic interactions, products and markets become more sophisticated the rules and their policing have to develop, to keep pace with change. The Department of Trade and Industry has a major regulatory responsibility for the London Stock Exchange where such regulation is by a mixture of government and self-regulation in a highly complex framework. The legal aspects are set up by the government through various acts of Parliament, like the Financial Services Act 1986. Market players are required to abide by the rules. The law requires, for example, a regular information disclosure from companies. The Stock Exchange has the power to intervene in the case of irregularities or misconduct. To take just one example, insider dealing, buying or selling shares on the basis of price-sensitive information not generally available to all market players is illegal. Insider dealing became a criminal offence in 1980, under the Companies Act, but was specifically defined in the Company Securities (Insider Dealing) Act 1985. The Financial Services Act 1986 gave broad powers to the Secretary of State to investigate insider trading. An objective of such rules is to convince market traders of justice, market fairness, in short, the provision of a level playing field. Confidence is paramount.

There are many different aspects of the regulatory framework which affect the financial markets. The market itself is enmeshed in legalities, customs and conventions. It is worth repeating that the 'perfect' market, pure, unsullied by tradition or the hand of government does not exist. Financial markets, to function efficiently, have to be clearly based on institutionalized rules where governments (and tradition) take an important hand. *Deregulation* as part of the process of increasing competition in the financial markets gave a changed set of rules. After Big Bang, 1986, banks had the right to become market-makers on the Stock Exchange, building societies were able to compete more effectively with the banks and deregulated entry allowed corporate members, both domestic and foreign, to be admitted. Fixed commissions were also abolished. However, whatever the nature of the legislation there is a key role for the government in providing, changing and policing the rules.

The Government acting as a market player: the transfer of assets from the public to private sector

The government acts as a market player. To illustrate this role we can use the example of the privatization sales of the 1980s and 1990s, when assets were transferred from the public to private sector. This was done by selling shares on the London Stock Exchange. We can continue with the Stock Exchange example to illustrate how shares can be sold to the public. Different floatation methods can be used. These can include an element of non-price allocation.

There are several methods available for companies seeking a quotation on the London Stock Market. Here we shall consider:

a) an offer for sale at a fixed price;
b) an offer for sale by tender.

As part of the privatization process the Government used the Stock Exchange to sell state assets, including the nationalized industries, public utilities such as the telecommunications arm of the Post Office, the Gas Industry, Electricity Industry, Water Industry and companies in state ownership like British Petroleum, British Aerospace, British Airways and British Steel. The methods chosen for this process depended in part on the objective of the sale and the relative costs. One aim of Government, to create a share-owning democracy, required that small shareholders were encouraged to buy. As shareholders, it has been argued that individuals would have a greater stake in the economy and that this would enhance economic performance, amongst other things. But at the same time the Treasury wanted to raise money for the Exchequer, to pay-off government debt and to finance tax cuts.

'Offer for sale at a fixed price'

The Government has used this method for most of its privatization issues. A fixed price is announced for the shares on offer and buyers are asked to subscribe to the issue. They make an application for a specified number of shares at the fixed offer price. Before coming to the market, a view has to be taken about what the assets are worth. A decision has to be made about the number of shares and the price at which they will be offered to the public.

In analytical time we can readily draw the demand curve for shares and show how many shares buyers would be willing and able to buy at each hypothetical price.

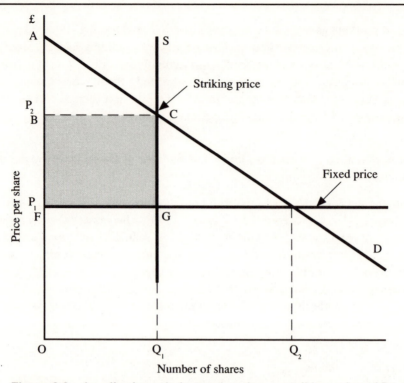

Figure 6.2   An offer for sale by tender gives a striking price of P_2. An offer for sale at a fixed price P_1 brings an over-subscription

Given a fixed quantity of shares on offer, we can display an equilibrium price and give the total value of the company, the rectangle $BCOQ_1$ in Figure 6.2.

In perspective time city analysts advising the Government on the price of privatization issues could not value the company so easily. The sale of British Telecom and British Gas were huge and unprecedented. There were no similar companies quoted on the Stock Exchange to give an idea of company worth. The Government did not know the exact position of the demand curve, how the public would respond to a particular number of shares at a set price. But if we work in analytical time we can see more clearly how a fixed price offer works. The Government sets the price below the equilibrium market price. At the fixed offer price there is a mismatch between the quantity buyers would like to buy and the number of shares on offer.

First, the fixed offer price does not clear the market, because of the difficulties/impossibility of pricing the shares in *perspective time* to ensure that the quantity demanded equals the quantity supplied. Remember that financial specialists advising on the pricing of shares do not have the advantage of a crystal ball. They do not know the precise position of the demand curve. In the case of many of the large privatization issues in particular, no similar companies existed in the market. There were no convenient yardsticks, other plcs already trading in the same line of business and of a similar size, to compare with British Telecom (BT) or British Gas. BT, by any standards, is a huge company; nothing as large as this had ever been floated on the Stock Exchange before. An appropriate market value could not be derived by looking at the price of other companies. Pricing BT shares was quite different from pricing a house in a road full of similar properties, or a chocolate bar with many similar competitors already on the market.

Second, the offer price is usually set below the market clearing price. The price is set somewhere below what might be needed to clear the market, to encourage an active trade in the shares when they trade. *Stags* those who sell quickly for profit, take their gains in the early days of trading, they buy below equilibrium market price and make a gain when shares trade.

At the same time, fixing the price below the market clearing price enables *seller preference* to have an impact. The Government had other objectives in mind, not simply the maximization of the monetary sale proceeds of the issue. The desire to create a share-owning democracy featured prominently. Allocation by price alone would have mitigated against the attainment of this goal, for allocation at a price at or near the equilibrium price gives the seller no leeway to choose between would-be purchasers.

In fact, fixing the price below the equilibrium gives the seller an element of choice. Where shares are over-subscribed, there are not enough to go round to all applicants at the offer price; some alternative measure(s) for allocating are necessarily required. A *non-market price allocation procedure* has to be employed. There are a variety of means to ration the existing shares. Usually, in the Stock Market a common procedure in cases of over-subscription, if the offer is over-subscribed, say by one hundred per cent, is for applicants to be allotted only half of the shares they subscribed for. Some applicants wanting small numbers of shares might enter a ballot and receive none at all, whilst others by the luck of the draw receive their application in full. However, the Government wanted to encourage the small shareholder and those who had never held shares before. Given an excess demand, the Government's agent, say the merchant banks, could decide who would receive what number of shares on the Government's instruction. Often the privatization issues were massively *over-subscribed*. BT was over-subscribed 9.7 times, British Gas 4 times and British Airways 32 times. The first day premiums were, respectively, BT 90 per cent, British Gas 36 per cent and British Airways 84 per cent (Davies and Hillier 1993). Allotments of shares had to be scaled down, but small buyers often had their applications met in full, even if the large financial and corporate buyers were left without shares. At best, the applications for large numbers of shares were scaled down, only a proportion of such applications was met.

We can show in Figure 6.2 that the offer price is set below the equilibrium at P_1. At this price there is an excess quantity demanded over quantity supplied. The shareholders who receive shares gain the *consumer surplus*: the triangle under the demand curve, ABC, above the market equilibrium price plus the rectangle marked BCFG. This rectangle represents the loss in value to the seller. It shows the gain to those who have been allotted shares at the fixed price, when shares are actively traded in the market. '[T]he

Government could, in most cases, have sold the shares at significantly higher prices' (Bishop and Kay 1988: 29). 'The fixed price issues have been sold at substantial – in some cases – absurd discounts' (ibid. 35). But the lower price was used so that share ownership could be encouraged and privatization seen as a success.

Note that in Figure 6.2 we are using the usual concept of a demand curve, a hypothetical concept set in analytical time. In perspective time if people believe that shares will be over-subscribed they may ask for more than they want, for they may fear that their application will be scaled down. The over-subscription is not a true reflection of the exact quantity demanded at the fixed price. If the shares are thought to be under-subscribed then shareholders may ask for none in the hope that they can buy shares at a bargain price when the underwriters trade them. These may be self-fulfilling prophesies in real time. But what we can be clear about is that an offer price below the equilibrium market price leads to excess quantity demanded, *and* the need for additional non-market allocation and a transfer of wealth from seller to buyer.

At this point it is interesting to note that after sale the shares can be traded again. Indeed, shares can be sold on what is termed a 'grey' market before shares officially trade. Many small buyers sold their shares and took quick gains. Stagging occurs when shares rise in price and they are sold on the market. There are profit takers and those who stay with their shares. Initially, the government can decide at the point of sale, where and to whom to sell, but thereafter there is no say in the matter. The state may keep a golden share in order to ensure overall control. There is a transfer of wealth as state-owned assets are sold at less than equilibrium market price. The transfer is to those who bought shares from those who, for whatever reasons, did not. The broader argument for privatization is that in the long run it brings about increased efficiency. We cannot rerun time with and without privatization to test this.

Offer for sale by tender

The tender offer by contrast invites the applicant to tender for shares above a minimum price. When all the bids have been received a *striking price* is set which can match the quantity demanded and supplied. Here the market process can be allowed to work unconstrained. When the seller, or the advisors, are not readily able to value the company this method is used in preference to the fixed price offer. The stock of shares is offered for sale, the demanders make their bids, they say how much they are willing and able to pay for a particular number of shares. The seller does not use this information in order to take from each applicant just what he or she would be prepared to pay. This would remove all consumer surplus. An average price which clears the market, the *striking price* can be set. There is no need for any administrative rationing process, the tendering process can match the quantity demanded with the quantity supplied. The seller receives the full value as assessed by the market at that point for the shares. There need be no gift to the purchasers and no stagging when shares are traded in the market.

The tender method has been used, for example, in the sale of Britoil and Enterprise

Oil. BAA was a mixed sale, part by tender, part by fixed price. This type of offer was made when companies set for privatization were viewed as more suitable for purchase by the large financial institutions. Small shareholders would have little idea about the appropriate price to tender and would have been discouraged from bidding. Not surprisingly, in the great majority of privatization issues, offers for sale were made at a fixed price. In short, the unfettered workings of the price mechanism may not be appropriate for achieving a particular purpose. The Government, seeking to float companies or indeed private sector business firms seeking a stock exchange quotation may not choose to allow the market mechanism to allocate by selling shares to those who are willing and able to buy at the equilibrium price by a tender method. They may have other objectives than simply maximizing money revenues.

GOVERNMENTS INTERCEDING IN THE MARKET

The government sets *taxes* and *subsidies* in order to achieve a variety of ends. The primary purpose for setting taxes in the market is, of course, to raise tax revenue – one important way to finance government expenditure. But taxation may be used to reduce adverse externalities, taxing the polluters, making it more expensive for them to supply. Subsidies may be given to increase the production and consumption of some goods and services, particularly where external benefits are thought to be important. Moreover, governments can directly intercede with *price controls*, setting price above or below the market equilibrium. However, as we have seen, prices which are *lower* than the equilibrium, a price ceiling, require other methods of allocation. And in the long run for private enterprise firms, price controls may have long-term effects which reduce the overall supply and exacerbate the problems of shortage or surplus.[3] Usual examples include the use of price controls in war-time Britain, with ration books to ration excess quantity demanded, and with supplies being diverted to the illegal markets.

Rent controls are another case in point. The rented sector has shrunk given the impact of price controls. In the long run, those renting houses could not earn a sufficient profit and so sold-off their properties or converted them to other use. Seller preference – sometimes discriminatory behaviour to racial minorities or families with children and/or undercover monetary payments in the form of key money or non-returnable deposits for fixtures and fittings, gave suppliers satisfaction and/or better returns.

Finally, the privatization of public utilities, transferring state monopolies into the private sector, has been accompanied by a regulatory framework, which involves *price regulation*. The industry regulator curtails price setting freedom. So, for example, the regulatory body, Ofwat, puts a limit on the percentage increase in water prices allowable. Insufficient market competition is a reason for controlling BT and British Gas, for example, to prevent these private sector companies from increasing prices to levels which the market might bear.

NON-MARKET PROVISION AND ALLOCATION: THE GIFT

Finally, we turn to the very significant non-market activities of households and non-profit organizations, like voluntary groups or charities, which do not fit an orthodox market paradigm. These are often overlooked and with them the allocative processes which lie beyond those at the heart of the basic market story. We shall have more to say about the role of the household in the provision of goods and services for the nurturing and support of rational economic people in following chapters. But household production and the provision and allocation of goods by non-market organizations are important. People are more than simply market players. They can be the givers and receivers of gifts.

Scarce resources and goods: the gift

As we know, not all scarce and valued resources or goods are allocated through markets and rationed by price. Love, blood and human organs for transplant, on the whole, do not come to us via a market process. A significant number of vital items come and go in the form of *gifts*. Whilst the act of giving provides satisfaction and the hope that there might be a return gift at some unspecified date in the future, there is no contract, no expectation of any agreed payment, no *quid pro quo*. Whilst there is reciprocity in gift giving, and often an exchange of property rights, the fundamental basis of the gift is not economic. Of course, that is not to say that gifts do not have important economic ramifications. There is no well defined, nor explicit price ratio. Gifts carry their own messages and motivation even though there may be, as in the case of blood donation 'some expectation and assurance that a return gift may be needed and received at some future time' (Titmuss 1970: 89). But with gift giving there is often no immediate need for reciprocity, and *no* market-like exchange. In some cases, people give with no expectation of a return, for example, donations by elderly pensioners to the British Lifeboat Fund or Romanian orphans.

Here the rational calculating economic maximizer aiming for individual personal gain is certainly an inappropriate starting point for the economic theorist. But we do not have to make such a restrictive assumption. It is perfectly rational for the well-being of others, including strangers, to enter our utility functions. Rational economic people are not of necessity selfish.

Commercial provision and the use of markets are often considered to be ethically unacceptable for the allocation and rationing of many items such as blood, human organs for transplant, which are highly valued by recipients, indeed, often essential to life itself. Although what is ethically acceptable depends on the law, custom and practice in historical time and place. The market sale of blood by blood donors is regarded as legitimate in many parts of the world. The economist has something to give in highlighting, for example, the provision and allocation of gifts, explaining their importance and showing how gifts might be increased. Titmuss showed how the blood donating system in Britain worked well without any significant use of a market mechanism. The collection and use of blood is remarkable. No price mechanism nor central planner is required to collect and distribute the blood. In Britain donors are not paid for supplying the gift. No money changes hands when the blood is given to a patient in the NHS hospital. And yet for the recipient the gift of blood can be as important as life itself. Without this gift a person in need might die.

There is an ethical, moral view that blood should not be marketed, although 'supplied' and 'demanded' by individuals, where, indeed, the possibility of rivalry and excludability exists. If blood were to trade as a commodity in the market place, why not human organs, human eggs, embryos, babies for adoption? Technological change has expanded the range of gifts which can be made. But, as yet, we do not have synthetic blood or synthetic human eggs. We rely on the gifts of others for those things which cannot be manufactured and are not traded in markets.

Why do people believe that it is inappropriate to allocate such gifts through the market mechanism? As we have highlighted, the market allocates according to the ability and willingness to pay. In the provision of health care in this country many people believe that securing treatment should not be dependent on income and wealth. People do not want to see the children of poor parents, for example, being deprived of medical care or the old left without treatment. Income may often be an important determinant of demand and incomes are unequally distributed.

The motivation for gift giving can be complex. But when people give blood or women donate eggs, both of which can be potentially painful and harmful to the giver, the objective is often to help those in need and to give satisfaction to the giver. People do not want their gifts sold and the amassing of private profit as a result, by a third-party. Any scandal in the charity world over the misappropriation or waste of gifts, whether in kind or in terms of money, often leads to a reduction in donations.

If suppliers of blood have to be paid in order to induce them to supply, then the poorer and more vulnerable groups in society are tempted to supplement their incomes by such means. Moreover, they may suppress information about their own health and life-style which might cast doubt on the quality of their supply. The sale of infected blood has harmful consequences, external costs both to society as a whole and to individuals. These go well beyond the costs to the initial seller and recipient. The spread of AIDS and AIDS-related diseases are a case in point. Infected blood products may lead to the death of many strangers. People in poor health, sometimes drug users supplying blood for money, helped to spread the HIV virus. Contaminated blood, often from back street businesses, unregulated 'clinics' in countries like Brazil, was bought in the world market, helping to pass on the virus.

In addition, an over-emphasis on market sales and the pursuit of private gain may mar the development of ethical people. A community's spirit may be increased and secured by the circulation of gifts. That in itself is an important element in encouraging co-operation, sympathy and altruism.

When the need for gifts outstrips the number of donations, 'the supply', then we have an allocation problem. Scarcity is highlighted by the existence of queues and waiting lists. There are not enough organs for transplant given medically-assessed needs. In such circumstances a decision has to be made about who should receive a kidney, lung or heart transplant and who should not. If we were allocating jewellery, we could leave the price mechanism to ration with no qualms. But in these situations a variety of professionals make the decision about who is suitable to give and which individual shall receive that gift. Doctors may rank according to various factors including clinical need, although they do not operate in analytical time, as we shall discuss in Chapter 10. It is assumed that professional responsibility – medical ethics – safeguards against abuse and wastage.

Whilst any system is open to mistakes, wastage and abuse, many argue that non-market allocation and ethical people provide the appropriate solution in the allocation of resources in these circumstances. But how do we increase the supply of gifts both in kind and in terms of money to charities? In perspective time increased information may make people more aware of the need for the gift through education or advertising. Governments and charitable organizations may use moral suasion. Governments can make the money gift tax effective. Clear legislation and the regulation of organizations so that abuse does not occur readily can be very important. People do not savour the thought of gifts being misappropriated or wasted. There has to be an assurance that the rules of the game are adhered to.

CONCLUDING COMMENTS: MARKET AND NON-MARKET PROVISION

Market and non-market provision of goods are often entwined. People consume and produce goods and services in many different contexts and have different motivations. Economists consider the appropriate balance between government and market provision, although the provision of goods within the household and by other private sector non-profit organizations are vital features, even in the late twentieth-century modern economy. Whilst some goods are produced by private business firms and bought and sold in markets, others are allocated directly by the agencies of the State and private non-profit organizations like charities. Some essential goods and services are produced within the household and allocated outside the market as we shall show in Chapter 7. Moreover, we shall point to the non-market allocative processes existing inside business firms in Chapter 9 and the allocative role of non-profit organizations like charities in Chapter 10.

In historical time and place the mix between private sector production and allocation by market and non-market means was different, as we highlighted in Chapter 4. Whilst in the modern economy a large proportion of resources and output is allocated via the market mechanism, we still have a significant volume of collective goods and those items for individual use where non-market patterns of provision and allocation are the norm.

Many goods and services consumed by individuals are not provided and allocated by the market mechanism. They are supplied either free of charge at the point of delivery or at a nominal price unrelated to the volume of individual use. A summary view of the different types of goods is given in Figure 6.3. Decisions about how many

GOODS AND SERVICES

PURE PUBLIC GOOD	QUASI-PUBLIC GOOD	MERIT GOOD	PURE PRIVATE GOOD	HOUSEHOLD NON-MARKET GOODS	GIFTS
Defence Law and order	Pavements Public roads Public parks BBC programmes	Education Health care	Food Clothing Jewellery Cars	Meals Clean Laundry Leisure/Entertainment	Private gifts Human organs for transplant Time: voluntary service
Non-rivalry Non-excludability Non-rejectability	Non-rivalry and non-excludability Non-rejectability → Not fully met		Rivalry and excludability Rejectability		Rivalry Excludability
Non-market allocation	In some situations Rivalry, excludability and rejectability Non-market allocation		Market allocation Ability and willingness to pay	Non-market mechanisms	Non-market mechanisms
Funding from communal/central funds	Free of charge or licence fee unrelated to amount of use Funding: communal/central funds + fees		*Overall quantity and quality services dependent on income and wealth		Funding Private gifts and legacies Central funding Business donations

Figure 6.3 A spectrum of goods and services

resources overall to devote to such goods are not decided by the workings of markets but by a socio-political process.

GOVERNMENT, PRICING AND NON-MARKET ALLOCATION – SUMMARY

- There are different views about the appropriate role of government. Government is not a monolithic block but made up of a variety of organizations inextricably interwoven in the economic system.
- In historical time many blends of the market and state have worked. The impact of government is complex and it is not possible to rerun time to test the impact of different mixes of the state and market.
- Privatization with its aim to, 'roll back the frontiers of the state', has several strands.
- Many vital goods and services are not bought and sold in markets, but provided and allocated by non-market means.
- Public goods are allocated communally. These goods feature non-excludability, non-rivalry and non-rejectability. Quasi-public goods and merit goods are allocated principally by non-market means, although in some cases the price mechanism is used.
- No markets exist for goods and bads – externalities, for example, like pollution.
- The allocation of resources for public and merit goods is decided by a socio-political process – not the interplay of market supply and demand. The non-market allocation of school places involves different techniques and criteria. Administrative procedures are used, not the price mechanism.
- Governments set the legal rules of the game which include the framework for regulating markets.
- Governments also act as market players, for example, selling bonds and shares. In Britain public utilities and state-owned companies have been sold in the market. The price mechanism was not given free reign to maximize the sale value. There were other objectives.
- Governments intercede in markets via taxes and subsidies and through price controls and price regulation.
- The gift is a key factor in all economies. Gifts can be provided and are allocated by non-market means. Where gifts are scarce then a decision has to be made about which needs will be met.

GOVERNMENT, PRICING AND NON-MARKET ALLOCATION – QUESTIONS FOR DISCUSSION

1 What do you consider to be the appropriate role of the state in economic affairs?
2 What are the differences between a public good, a merit good, a private good and a gift?
3 Compare the mechanisms for allocating health care to families in Britain with that used for allocating cars, jewellery and hairdressing. Is there any justification for allocating such goods and services differently?
4 Consider a particular period of historical time in Britain and explain how the provision and the means for allocating education and housing have changed over that period.
5 Why are there different means of charging for and allocating the following:

   a) the BBC television and radio;
   b) the ITV network;
   c) satellite television;
   d) cable television.

   Identify the differences in transactions costs in your answer.
6 Make a case for and against charging an entry fee into:

   a) churches;
   b) museums;
   c) public parks;
   d) motorways;
   e) shopping precincts.

7 What do you predict will happen to the 'A' level grades required for entry to university history courses given that;

   a) universities are required to cut back on Arts courses;
   b) there is an increase in the number of university places for economics and law;
   c) wide media coverage suggests that employers consider that historians make flexible employees.

   Make your assumptions clear.
8 You have seen a rather expensive coat, and after shopping around, have decided that it is just worth buying. On returning to the store you discover that the coat has been reduced in price by a third in a sale.
   Using this example, explain the concept of the consumer surplus and how the price reduction will affect the size of this surplus.
9 [T]o increase share ownership among a risk-averse public unused to share dealing it is necessary to offer tempting discounts; but a large discount means that substantial gains can be made by early sale, in which case wider share ownership has little endurance.

(Bishop and Kay 1988: 34)

a) In principle, what are the different methods by which Government could allocate shares to the public?

b) Explain and discuss the statement.

10 Why do governments resort to price controls in both peace and war time? What are the economic implications of such price controls?

11 Why is the price mechanism seen as an unacceptable means for allocating human organs for transplant, babies for adoption, educational qualifications and sex/ love? Is it illegal to use the market for trading these? What are the implications of allocating these by the market mechanism? Illustrate your answer with *current* examples from television, radio or newspapers.

Part II

THE ECONOMICS OF ORGANIZATIONS

7

The household

INTRODUCTION

This chapter aims to explore the different ways in which economists have used their theories to explain and make predictions about the behaviour of the household and the family. There are alternative approaches to examine which focus on different, although often overlapping issues.

We begin with traditional microeconomic theory, which is concerned primarily with the workings of markets and market behaviour. The orthodox approach treats the household simply as if it were an isolated individual whose clear cut goal is to maximize personal satisfaction on a market stage. Often the family receives no specific mention, but where it does the individual represents the family too. Given this perspective, households operating as rational economic men are buyers, spending on private consumer goods and services, and the owners of resources which they supply in markets, like labour services, including entrepreneurial talent. Rational economic men rent their land and buildings and buy and sell shares in companies, indeed, they are the ultimate owners of capital, playing a market game.

Here we shall consider how this traditional model explains *consumer behaviour* in the context of analytical time. Yet this general approach can be used in a wide variety of different market contexts, from the analysis of labour supply decisions to an explanation of individual investment behaviour. As we shall see, the basic model helps us to clarify key concepts and gives initial insights. It is the fundamental building block of conventional microeconomics.

Nevertheless, there are alternative views of the nature and role of the household, family and individual. People are much more than market players, buying and selling in pursuit of maximum individual gain. The 'new household economics' widens the focus of traditional theory to examine decision-making in non-market contexts. Economists recognize that households/families engage in very important non-market activities. Households can be seen as production units similar to business firms, like mini-factories where people work in a domestic context. They cook, clean and sew, indeed, engage in a variety of activities often thought to be outside the economist's remit, including the 'production' of children. Moreover, households invest, not only in physical items like houses, but also in the human capital of their members. Households can also be thought of as 'leisure centres' where individuals combine together for joint consumption and joint utility maximization.

In particular, Becker (1965, 1981, 1991), using the conventional tools of microeconomic analysis was able to bring together home production, consumption and labour supply decisions. This is in stark contrast to the usual orthodox view which sees little interest in the domestic realm. Becker treated the non-market activities of the household/family as suitable topics for analysis. The fundamental problems of choices relating to personal behaviour in domestic life, reproduction, child-care, the division between 'paid' market work and 'unpaid' non-market work were found to be amenable to analysis in analytical time. Indeed, the traditional neo-classical model has been applied to a variety of issues, including the division of labour within the household, even problems of optimal family size and divorce.

However, the economists' contribution does not end here; the household's internal workings can be scrutinized in greater depth. Becker's view is essentially set in analytical time, but people interact and make decisions in perspective time, where there is imperfect knowledge and uncertainty and the limited human ability to handle real-world complexity. Other approaches to the household and family view them as organizations, not a summation of individuals maximizing joint utility, but a complex of human interactions which exist and evolve over time. Here people have limited information which they may perceive and process differently; they operate in a world characterized by fundamental uncertainty, facing complex decisions. Indeed, the family/household can be seen as a social planning unit with an economic and financial dynamic, involved in a wide range of interlinked market and non-market activities. The household and family change over time and the internal organization and power structure, affected by law, custom, practice and tradition can be seen as important for explaining behaviour. Indeed, the household can be viewed as a complex unit interacting with other social and political institutions in the wider social economic system (Hodgson 1988).

Whilst this approach provides valuable insights, drawing from different disciplines, it gives no neat models like those of neo-classical theory. Yet it recognizes that households and families are much more than the self-seeking, individual market players of basic theory. In this wider context we are faced with the prospect of interdependent utilities, where both altruism and self interest have a role to play and where there are considerations of individual and collective forms of co-operation, competition and conflict.

THE NATURE OF THE HOUSEHOLD AND FAMILY: DEFINITIONS AND OVERVIEW

What do we mean by the household and family? Can these terms be used synonymously? Within economic literature the terms household, family and individual are often used interchangeably, implicitly defined as one and the same. Indeed, one introductory economics text states quite clearly that: 'Households (which is the word we use for individuals) are the consumers of goods and services; they are also the suppliers of labour and various other factors of production' (Sloman 1991: 529).

However, we require distinctions: the *household* is usually defined as a person or group of people living together. The *family* is the kin group living in a single household. The traditional family, that is, a married couple with dependent children, is generally assumed to be the norm in the conventional economic approach. The term family (Government Statistical Office 1991) comprises a married couple either living alone or with unmarried children, or a lone parent with his or her children. In 1994 (Social Trends 1994: 35) a family is defined as a married or cohabiting couple with or without children or a lone parent with children. Definitions of the family change over historical time, for example – cohabitation is now a significant and recognized feature.

We can think in terms of the extended family of the past which included several generations in the same household and the non-traditional family units of the present, headed by lone parents or by two people of the same sex. However, individuals living alone are not considered a family and this category of households corresponds with the traditional theoretical treatment.

The household and family in practice

Over time the nature and make-up of households and families has changed. In a British context, we ask what has been happening to the size of households and the traditional family of a married couple with dependent children? What has happened over time to the proportion of single person households and one parent families? Why has fertility declined? Who does what in terms of market and non-market work?

More than one-quarter of households in 1991 consisted of one person, almost double the proportion in 1961. Economists have an important role to play in analysing and predicting the economic causes and consequences of such changes. Significantly, one parent families with dependent children nearly doubled from 10 per cent in 1976 to 19 per cent in 1991 (Social Trends 1994: 33). Such changes in the composition and nature of households and families reflect economic, social and political changes. They may have important economic consequences for other organizations and for influencing institutionalized rules.

However, the orthodox concern has not been to explain changes in the size and make-up of the household and family or the roles of individual family members.

Conventional theory asks how individuals respond to market price signals and analyses their behaviour in market roles. We start by studying this perspective.

THE NEO-CLASSICAL APPROACH IN ANALYTICAL TIME

In general, the neo-classical orthodox approach has treated the household, family and the individual as synonymous. This provides us with a useful simplification at the outset, allowing us to abstract from a wealth of real-world detail. The family/kin group make-up, the structure of the household and its size and the age/sex of co-residents are ignored. The individual symbolizes the family/household as the convenient basic unit of analysis. It is the representative individual's behaviour which is examined, either playing the role of a consumer buying goods and services for money or as a supplier, for example, hiring out labour services or renting land, receiving an income in return. The household is a 'black box' as shown in Figure 7.1. Goods and services flow in, factor services flow out, each matched by a reciprocal money flow.

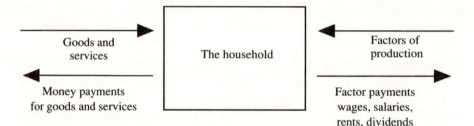

Figure 7.1   The 'black box' household

Often the household is not explicitly recognized and defined by economists and in typical treatments the family is often ignored; only individuals feature. However, Richard Lipsey (1989: 50), a notable exception, acknowledges the household as the important *joint financial decision taking unit*, 'all the people who live under one roof and who take, or are subject to others taking for them, joint financial decisions'. When economists speak of the consumer and the individual they are, in fact, referring to the group of individuals comprising the household. It is also assumed 'that each household takes consistent decisions as if it were composed of a single individual' (ibid.). So the problems about how decisions are reached are ignored, any differences in the internal organization of the household assumed away. Lipsey comments that decision-making 'may be by paternal dictatorship or democratic voting – that does not matter to us' (ibid.). He assumes that such considerations can be safely left to the attentions of other social scientists – they are not the preserve of the economist.

The family and household are often implicity assumed to be the same. However, sometimes the family is recognized explicitly, for example, Samuelson (1956: 9) argues that 'the "fundamental unit" on the demand side is clearly the "family"'. Yet one rationale for treating the family as if it were an individual is that it makes life less complicated. Samuleson postulates 'a consistent "family consensus" that represents a meeting of the minds or a compromise between them'. The preferences of family members are interrelated but disagreements are assumed away. In short, the household in orthodox mode is perceived simply as a 'black box' whose internal domestic workings and decision-making processes can be safely ignored. The household takes in inputs of goods and services produced by firms in exchange for money and is the primary owner of the factors of production, providing factor services for firms in the market place.

The representative person in archetypal treatments is assumed to be a 'rational economic man', whose aim is to do the best possible in terms of personal benefit, by maximizing his own satisfaction or utility. Economists use Mill's concept of a rational economic man but this is of course only a convenient simplification. As we emphasized in the last chapter, people's satisfaction may very well be dependent on the satisfaction of others. We are not saying that only self-interest can or should be *the* determinant of an individual's utility or rationality (Hay 1989). We are simply abstracting from real-world complexity. And rational economic women have an essential part to play.

The behaviour of rational economic man, or as we shall assume, a rational economic person, is illustrated in a variety of *market* contexts. People are market players *par excellence*. They can be assumed to have perfect knowledge in the hypothetical analytical time mode and make rational choices to maximize their individual utility. Given this approach, we shall focus on consumer behaviour with the individual as a buyer of goods for private consumption in the market.

Household/consumer behaviour: the theory of choice

Starting with the individual as the household representative, economists build a hypothetical model to explain and predict how a consumer will react in the face of different market options. How will a consumer choose to spend limited income on different goods? In fact, what will he or she buy and what causes this selection to change? To answer these questions we need to ask:

1 What the consumer would like to buy?
2 What the consumer is able to buy?

But in order to simplify the analysis, given the amazing diversity and complexity of goods on offer in modern markets, and to enable us to illustrate on a two dimensional diagram, picture only two representative consumer products, books and food.

Consumer tastes and utility

To answer question 1 we need to know the consumer's preferences, which are dependent on tastes. Imagine that a consumer knows his or her preferences, likes and dislikes, precisely and with certainty. Moreover, assume that these tastes remain constant in analytical time and independent of income. Indeed, how tastes are determined does not concern us – they are given. Furthermore, assume that the person can *rank* any combination of the two products according to the satisfaction or utility they give. *Utility* is the 'accounting unit' that an individual uses to measure and evaluate the 'well-being' or 'happiness' which different combinations of goods will provide. In analytical time our individual can declare any particular combination of food and books as being:

a) better than,
b) worse than,
c) identical

in terms of the satisfaction which they give, relative to any alternative combination of these two goods. More of *both* goods will be preferred to less. Any combination with more of one commodity and no less of the other, will also be preferred. In addition, it is assumed that the individual is rational – making consistent choices in order to achieve the most utility possible in any given situation.

Ordinal utility

Whilst the preferences for different combinations of goods can be *ranked*, one combination can be picked out as better than another, the individual cannot tell us by how much. Utility can only be ordered and as such is defined as ordinal. Satisfaction or the utility derived from goods is subjective. Satisfaction is locked in the mind of the individual and certainly not open to measurement either by that individual or an outsider. There is no precise objective standard measurement. The individual is simply required to rank all the different combinations of goods, to say whether in terms of satisfaction he or she finds one combination better, worse or the same as another. Like pain, each individual may experience utility differently. Nobody can say whose migraine hurts the most, or by how much, or give a precise measurement of the difference in pain from a migraine or a toothache. Yet in analytical time know-all, rational economic people can state precisely and consistently all preferences, carefully ordering satisfaction levels associated with different combinations of goods. This, of course, is a hypothetical state.

We also assume that the individual's preferences are stable, that no advertising campaign or any other external influence which might occur with the passage of real time, can cause a person's subjective preferences to oscillate. Indeed, rational economic people do not dither. They know their own minds perfectly and the utility which they will certainly derive from any bundle of goods. Given these assumptions we can display the information graphically.

Curves of equal satisfaction or indifference curves

Curves of equal satisfaction or indifference curves are shown in Figure 7.2. On the vertical axis we measure the quantity of books and on the horizontal axis the

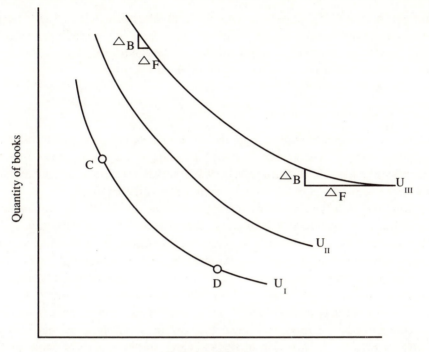

Figure 7.2   Indifference curves
U_{III} represents a higher level of utility than $U_{II} + U_{I}$
U_{III} is better because the individual has at least more of one of the
goods. On the same basis U_{II} is better than U_{I}.
The marginal rate of substitution – how a consumer is willing to trade off
one good for another – changes along the indifference curve

quantity of food. An *indifference curve*, like U_{I} joins up all the combinations of the two goods which give the consumer *equal utility*. Note that the indifference curve construct is not without precedents. Weather forecasters draw curves of equal barometric pressure – isobars – on their weather maps, as abstractions to display ideas. Moreover, map makers draw a contour line to link up points of equal height above sea level. Economists use a similar graphical presentation to display an individual's tastes. But unlike the map maker we have no objective yardstick like metres to measure with. Utility is merely ordered.

The indifference curve represents a boundary line between points preferred to those not preferred. On indifference U_{I} any particular combination of goods represented on the curve gives equal satisfaction, like points C or D. We have no objective *cardinal measurement* as with metres. Here we simply rank alternatives with an ordinal number, we can talk about better, worse or the same, but *not* by how much. In Figure 7.2 indifference curve U_{II}, showing the utility of a particular set of consumption options, gives a higher level of satisfaction than U_{I}, but we cannot say by how much.

The indifference curve U_{III} gives the highest level of satisfaction of any of the indifference curves displayed on the diagram. But there are an infinite array of indifference curves, given infinitely small changes in the quantities of goods involved, although we have chosen for ease of exposition to display just three.

Indifference curves and their shape

1 Given that we are dealing with two goods which give satisfaction, the indifference curves slope downwards from left to right.[1] The negative slope indicates that if a consumer is to be kept on the same level of satisfaction, a reduction in the quantity of books must be matched by some increase in the quantity of food.

2 In addition, the indifference curve displays the rate at which the consumer is willing to trade-off one good for another, the *marginal rate of substitution*. The curve is convex to the origin, that is its slope displays diminishing absolute value as we move to the right – the slope gets flatter. This means for any given marginal reduction of books, say by one unit, there has to be an increasingly large compensatory absolute quantity of food, to keep the consumer at the same level of satisfaction. When the consumer has a lot of books – to give up one unit – requires a small compensation of food. But when the consumer has very few books and a large amount of food, a reduction of books at the margin has to be recompensed by a large quantity of food, see Figure 7.2. The utility trade-off changes as the consumer moves to different bundles of goods.

3 Indifference curves do not cross for an individual at a point in analytical time. It follows logically that a bundle of goods, as in Figure 7.3, labelled A, is preferred to one labelled B, because A has more books and the same quantity of food. A lies on a higher indifference curve. Yet the consumer is indifferent between C and B, for they lie on the same indifference curve. However, C is at the point where the two indifference curves cross in Figure 7.3. How then can the consumer be indifferent between C and A when we know that the consumer prefers A to B.? This is illogical. Preferences may evolve over the passage of real time, but at a point in analytical time they remain stable. Indifference curves do not cross.

The budget constraint and affordable options

Given our consumer preference map depicting the different levels of satisfaction provided by distinct alternative combinations of books and food, the next step is to show what the consumer is actually *able* to buy. We need to draw a line which delineates affordable options from those which are not. This constraint will be dependent on:

a) money income,
b) the prices of food and books.

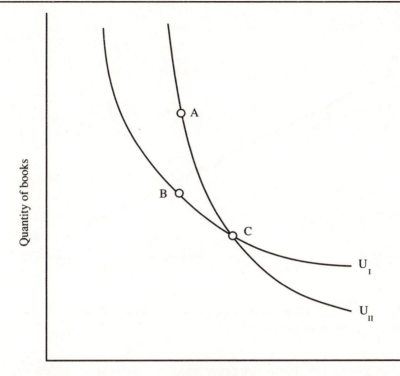

Figure 7.3   Indifference curves at a point in analytical time cannot cross: it is illogical

The theory assumes that the household takes prices as given and cannot affect them. Moreover, income is known and certain. The budget constraint can be seen in Table 7.1. The *budget line* gives the boundary between what is affordable and what is not, the constraint which divides those obtainable positions from the unobtainable. Note that this concept is similar to the production possibility curve and the personal productivity profile introduced respectively in Chapters 2 and 3. The budget line shows all the possible combinations of the two goods which the household can buy

Table 7.1   Affordable options: the budget constraint

Quantity of books Q_B	Expenditure on books £ $(P_b \times Q_B)$	Quantity of food Q_B	Expenditure on food £ $(P_f \times Q_F)$
10	100	0	0
8	80	4	20
6	60	8	40
4	40	12	60
2	20	16	80
0	0	20	100

Note: Spending all income (£100) given that books cost £10 and food costs £5 per unit respectively

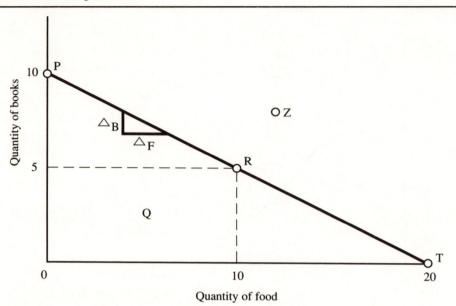

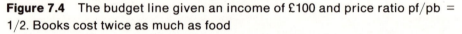

Figure 7.4 The budget line given an income of £100 and price ratio pf/pb = 1/2. Books cost twice as much as food

given a limited income and the prevailing prices of food and books. A budget line can be plotted from the data in Table 7.1, and displayed graphically in Figure 7.4. It is the 'picture' which sets out the household's purchasing constraint in analytical time. Given that money income is £100 and that books sell at £10 each and food is £5 per unit we can map out the alternatives. Take the initial position where all income is spent on books in Figure 7.4 at point P on the axis. This marks the maximum affordable quantity of books, given zero expenditure on food, clearly a hypothetical extreme. Given an income of £100 with books selling for £10 a unit, the household could buy 10 units of books but would then have no money left to purchase food. At the other extreme, point T, all income would be spent on food. An amount of £100 would enable the purchase of 20 units of food at £5 per unit, but there would be no money left for books. Given the initial starting point of P, with all expenditure on books, income could be progressively switched from expenditure on books to expenditure on food. The points P and T set the position of the budget line showing where the line intercepts each respective axis. At point R the household will spend half of its income on books, with 5 units at £10 each and 10 units of food at £5 each unit, so spending all income. Points P,R,T represent different combinations of goods and expenditure patterns.

Any point on the budget line represents a situation where all the income is spent, either on books or food, or on some combination of the two. Points like Z, to the right of and so outside the budget line constraint, represent impossible selections for the consumer. Points within the constraint, like Q, represent bundles of goods which do not exhaust income, where money remains unspent.

Indeed, the continuous line tells us that the individual can make infinitesimally small changes in expenditure on the two goods. There is no 'lumpiness', that is, books and food do not have to be bought in minimum sized quantities. Also, there is no possibility of acquiring credit, a possibility implicitly assumed away. The budget line is fixed in analytical time where the consumer can take up different hypothetical options, *ceteris paribus*.

In summary, at any point on the budget line all income is spent and so to have more of one good requires the consumer to forego some of the other. All points inside the constraint represent situations where expenditure is less than income. Beyond the budget constraint lie the currently inaccessible expenditure combinations.

The slope of the budget line: the price ratio

Assume that the representative consumer is on the boundary at P, in order to buy food, income has to be diverted from books – book consumption must be reduced. We have a budget constraint represented by the downward sloping straight line, which illustrates the trade-off between books and food given the assumption of fixed prices and money income. To acquire an additional unit of food in this example, the individual always needs to have £5, and so always has to give up a half unit of books £10/2, in order to increase food consumption by 1 unit. This represents the price ratio, which is given by the slope of the budget line – the change in the quantity of books divided by the change in the quantity of food, or to put it another way, the price ratio, the price of books divided by the price of food. Here two units of food can be acquired for one unit of books and this represents the opportunity cost.

Moving the constraint: changing the affordable options

Money income changes

A reduction in money income, other things remaining equal, causes the budget constraint facing a household to tighten. The budget line shifts inwards, to the left, towards the origin as shown in Figure 7.5. This income reduction could occur if a full-time wage earner were put on a part-time contract or an increase in income tax left the individual with a smaller take home pay. Providing that the *relative* prices of the two goods remained the same, the slope of the budget line would not change, only its position alters. If the household income were cut by 50 per cent because of the instigation of part-time working, then the available consumption options, shown here, would be reduced by half. Now, with all income spent on books, only 5 units could be afforded. Alternatively, if all household income were spent on food, only 10 units of food could be purchased.

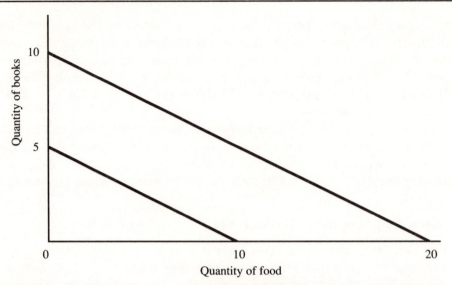

Figure 7.5   The budget line shifts inwards to the left due to a reduction in money income. The money prices of books and food remain constant; the relative price ratio does not change. The same shift would occur if money income remains constant but money prices double

Absolute price changes

By doubling money prices, the same impact on actual purchasing power as in the previous example could be achieved, provided that money income was kept constant at the original £100. If books cost £20 a unit and food cost £10, the results would be as before, with budget constraint shifting inwards. Only a maximum affordable quantity of 5 units of books or 10 units of food could be purchased. In both situations, *real income*, that is, what money income can actually buy, is reduced by 50 per cent. Notice that the *trade-off* or the *price ratio* between the two goods remains exactly the same, 2 units of food can be exchanged for 1 unit of books. Opportunity costs are not affected. Clearly, we can put this process into reverse by reducing money prices, shifting the budget line to the right.

Relative price changes

Changes in the relative prices of the two goods also alters the available possibilities. The slope of the budget line and its position changes as shown in Figure 7.6. If, for example, the price of food were to double, one unit of food is now priced at £10 per unit, holding the price of books constant, then the constraint pivots inwards. Books cost the same as before in money terms. With an income of £100 and a book price of £10 then 10 units can still be afforded, if all income were spent on books. However, if all income were spent on food, then the household could only buy 10 units of food.

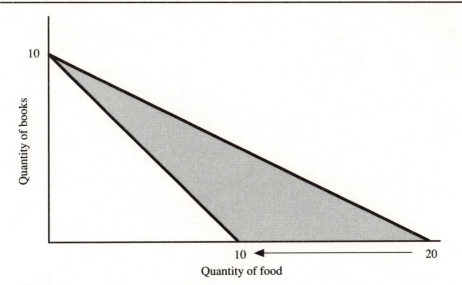

Figure 7.6   Budget line pivots inwards given an increase in the price of food. The shaded area is no longer available. The price ratio given by the slope of the budget line has changed

This gives a reduced set of possibilities, resulting from the change in relative prices. The price ratio has changed, now a unit of books costs the same as one unit of food. Opportunity costs have been affected.

Of course a *reduction* in the price of one good, other things remaining equal, would improve the range of choice, for the budget line pivots outwards, to the right. The quantity of goods available to choose from is increased.

The consumer's choice: the household equilibrium

The individual consumer with free choice is able to reach the best obtainable position selecting that combination of goods which gives the most satisfaction. This will be achieved where the highest obtainable indifference curve has been reached, given the budget constraint. At point E_1 on Figure 7.7, the rational economic individual will purchase 10 units of food and 5 units of books. Here the indifference curve U_{III} just touches the budget line, so at point E_1, the slope of the indifference curve exactly matches the slope of the budget line. It is tangential to the indifference curve. At this point the marginal rate of substitution between the two goods is equal to the price ratio. No better position can be reached in the circumstances. Higher indifference curves, with at least more of one good, would give greater satisfaction – but they are unobtainable.

Consider points Q and S. Both are affordable but non optimum situations, for they

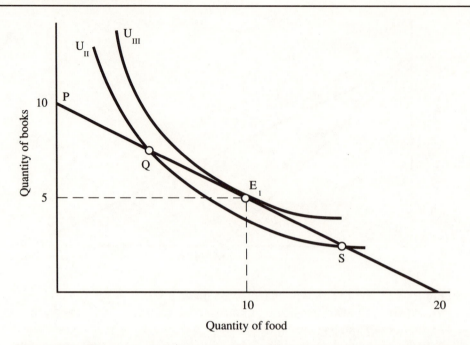

Figure 7.7 The consumer/household equilibrium is shown at E_1, the highest attainable level of utility, where U_{III} is tangential to the budget line. Q and S represent attainable but inferior selections located on the lower utility curve

lie on the lower utility curve U_{II}. They give less satisfaction and represent disequilibrium positions, because by rearranging purchasing plans, the rational economic person could do better. The individual could either move from Q, substituting food for books, or from point S, substituting books for food. The household representative would automatically move from a disequilibrium to an equilibrium position. At the equilibrium, E_1 there will be no revision of purchasing, other things being equal. Only if there were price and/or income changes which affect what the individual is able to do or taste changes which give altered preference maps, and so affect what the consumer is willing to do, will purchasing plans be revised.

Price changes: income and substitution effects

How do rational economic people respond to price changes? This is a key question in the traditional approach. In order to illustrate this clearly take a different situation as shown in Figure 7.8. The price ratio is now such that books are half the price of food, 20 units of books can be exchanged for 10 units of food. The consumer is at equilibrium at E_1. Given a reduction in the price of food, the equilibrium is disturbed. The consumer immediately revises consumption plans and moves to a new

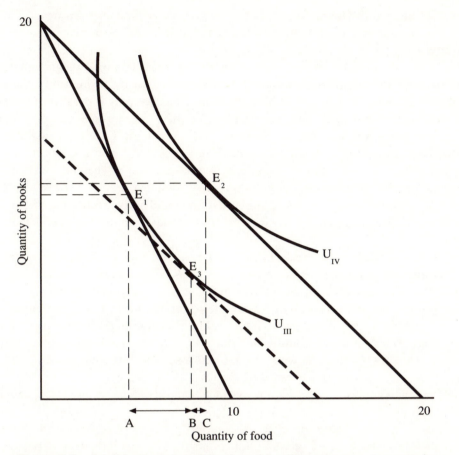

Figure 7.8 A fall in the price of food enables the consumer to move from E_1 to E_2, increasing food consumption by the total quantity AC. This total increase results from a substitution effect, measured by AB and an income effect, the quantity BC.

equilibrium position, in this case, at E_2. In the diagram we can see that the consumer buys more food as a result of halving the price of food. If we think in terms of a demand curve (Chapter 5), the consumer has simply increased the quantity of food demanded. But now we can analyse this formally and in more detail. The change results from two distinct effects:

a) the change in relative prices which induces a *substitution effect*, and

b) the real income change which causes an *income effect*.

The consumer is now able to reach a higher indifference curve, U_{IV}, as a result of the budget constraint pivoting outwards, and buys an increased quantity of both goods. Note that this result depends on the way we have drawn the indifference curves. Positioned differently we could have shown other outcomes. However, focusing our attention on the total effect on the quantity of food chosen we can isolate the two effects.

First, to measure the substitution effect of the price change, imagine that we constrain the individual to the original indifference curve by taxing away the real benefit of the price reduction. Pull back the budget line, keeping it parallel to the new one – the one existing *after* the food price fall – so that the consumer can only attain the original level of satisfaction. Now the consumer is at E_3, buying a different combination from that at the original equilibrium. Given the new budget line – with the new price ratio – E_1, the old equilibrium is unobtainable. The consumer has to move along the indifference curve *substituting* food for books because food is relatively cheaper. The consumer in this situation would stop substituting at E_3. The substitution effect is given by the distance AB marked on the horizontal axis on Figure 7.8.

A measure of the income effect can be found by giving back the real income derived by the price fall, allowing the consumer to move to E_2 to enjoy the higher level of satisfaction. The remainder of the increase in the quantity of food over and above that which results from the substitution effect is shown on the horizontal axis as BC. This is a real income effect of the price change. Note that nothing has happened to the consumer's money income, simply that the pound in the pocket stretches further because of the price reduction which in this case leads the consumer not only to buy more food, but also to spend more on books too. As we can see at E_2, the consumer purchases more books despite the fact that their relative price has actually increased.

In this case, the substitution effect is negative, a fall in price brings an opposite effect in terms of increased consumption of food. The income effect is positive – income and the impact on quantity demanded move in the same direction. Moreover, the analysis can be used to derive a demand curve. Simply by taking lower and lower food prices, in other words, pivoting the budget line outwards, we can find new equilibrium points. The information relating each price with quantity demanded can be plotted to form a demand curve.

Utility analysis can be used for a variety of purposes. Here we have used it to illustrate consumption choices. It gives a theoretical underpinning for downward sloping demand curves, and shows how the consumer would respond to a change in the price of one of the goods, holding all else constant. It shows the total effect on quantity demanded of a fall in the price of food, *ceteris paribus*. This change is a result of two effects, income and substitution. When the price of food falls, the individual buys more because it has become relatively cheaper and so substitutes the relatively cheaper product. In addition, individuals gain an increase in real income, for now money income buys more so an increased quantity of food is purchased.

Purchasing behaviour in analytical and perspective time

The introductory orthodox approach assumes that the representative individual is a rational economic person who:
a) faces a well defined budget constraint, where there is perfect knowledge of all prices and incomes, and no risk or uncertainty, set in a single analytical time period.
b) has a well defined preference map which is stable *and* independent of income.

Given the budget constraint, in this hypothetical situation, the individual always knows the best way to spend money. He or she is certain to know what combination of purchases gives the most pleasure. If the available options change, because of changing prices and/or incomes, the individual knows precisely the best new spending plan and puts that into effect immediately. The hypothetical model, in analytical time implicitly assumes that the consumer is omniscient. This enables us to abstract from a highly complex world and to focus on a particular range of questions, like the impact of budget changes on expenditure given fixed and known preferences.

The orthodox theory assumes that economic agents are either in, or rapidly approaching, equilibrium. Herbert Simon (1976) says that the indifference curve analysis involves 'substantive rationality', given the single goal of utility maximization 'the rational behaviour is determined entirely by the characteristics of the environment in which it takes place' (ibid.: 131) within the limits imposed by given conditions. However, consumers make decisions in perspective time where in practice choices and decision-making are obviously not so clear cut. In reality, nobody could be expected to draw up a utility map, showing infinitesimally small changes in utility derived from infinitesimally small changes in the combinations of commodities. Moreover, price and income information may not always be clear. Yet by using the model we stand aside from events, think in terms of the essential features of a budget constraint – the highly simplified purchasing choices open to the individual/household and an abstract set of subjective preferences. We simplify juxtaposing different situations in analytical time. We have been able to clarify concepts, such as real and money income, and income and substitution effects of price changes. We can make predictions about changes in purchasing plans in the event of revised constraints. But our outcomes are certain and readily deducible given our starting assumptions.

Choices in perspective time

In perspective time, the time of decision, individuals do not think in terms of equating the marginal or extra utility of goods with the opportunity cost/price ratio. To do that for the huge array of goods we buy would be impossible. Moreover, people do not have perfect information about all the options. Where some choices are repeated and happen very frequently, such as making a choice between the purchase of different types of vegetables or meats, *repetition* provides us with a great deal of experience, from which we learn and gain information. The model may not be so far removed from reality in such circumstances. The consumer knows the products intimately and has a very good idea of what satisfaction to expect from them. Well informed consumers buying straightforward goods like apples and pears, peas and carrots may indeed respond in some situations to the marginal price changes as the model predicts. Light is thrown on the reaction of buyers to budget constraint changes.

However, consumption decisions in some situations are 'lumpy', it is not possible to have a little of this or that, a marginal increase – it is all or nothing. In such circumstances price changes may have no affect on the decision at the margin. Prices may change, but purchasing does not within particular bounds. Also, people buy *complex goods*. When they choose to buy consumer durables, like compact disc players, washing machines or cars, they are buying much more intricate products, which promise utilities stretching into the future. The promised utilities arise from a complex series of attributes and the infrequency of purchase renders people *relatively ignorant*. The utility which people expect is very far from certain, particularly when making decisions about whether or not to buy sophisticated new products, where our would-be buyers have no experience. Like firms making investment decisions, people may face considerable uncertainty. Indeed, where there are *unique* one-off decisions to be made, like stating the preference for a particular school, or opting for a particular cancer treatment or a pension plan, the model is much less appropriate. Economic actors may have no experience and little information on these matters. They may seek advice from friends, relatives and professionals, even consumer information magazines like *Which?*. But advice comes as time passes; situations change and information becomes dated. Information may be perceived, presented and evaluated differently, by different economic actors. The pension transfer crisis where inexperienced people bought into inappropriate schemes, encouraged by inexperienced sales people, has been headline news. The Department of Trade and Industry and the Securities and Investment Board have spent considerable time and resources, attempting to clear up the problems. Nevertheless, some people stand to loose considerable sums as a result of ill-advised purchases. And people may not be able to make a rational choice, when, for example, choosing a cancer treatment as we shall discuss in Chapter 10. Indeed, new legislation may render choice more or less difficult depending on the context.

Our conventional treatment illustrates rational economic people choosing between comfortable and safe choices, like books and food, or pizzas and cheeseburgers. These are routine everyday choices. The model does not represent choices, 'as hazardous, expensive to reverse and caught up in the march of structural and technological change' (Earl 1986: 3) where changes occur over the passage of real time. Some decisions are irreversible and may have a significant impact on other purchasing plans. Choosing one particular public or private health care treatment may have a momentous effect on consumption plans and future income possibilities. Similarly, choosing an inappropriate pension scheme can have a very significant impact on present and future well-being. In reality, individuals make decisions in perspective time where there is imperfect information about the present and future, and where people have problems in processing information. The analytical time mode gives a convenient abstraction from a world full of surprises, where change is continuous, and where the options of the future are yet to be created. In the face of these difficulties, straightforward orthodoxy provides neat and comforting equilibriums – a harmonious beginning.

Changing preferences

The orthodox one period choice model tells us nothing about how preferences are determined or the way in which they evolve with the passage of real time. Preferences are *exogenous*, that is, independently determined outside the model. They do not need to be explained. They are ahistorical and fixed. Yet how tastes are determined and evolve are important issues. Laws and customs, the rules of the game, affect preferences and are themselves constraints. Some individual preferences are long lasting and determined early in life, whilst others are acquired tastes gained by continued consumption or through mixing in particular reference groups. Tastes and preferences must be to some extent *endogenous*, determined by a complex of factors including, for example, class, gender, nationality. There are many forms of 'hidden persuaders', subtle forms of social pressure. Sometimes the consumer simply does not know what to do – preferences are blurred.

There is no recognition in the basic model that the outcome of one choice, say to study for an Open University degree or to take a series of holidays in the Far East, might lead to a change in a consumer's preferences, by changing his or her perspectives. Education or foreign travel may well cause an individual's tastes and horizons to change. A change in a person's social class position or peer group may cause desires to change over time. Moreover, advertising may reinforce this. Indeed, people have different life-styles which they want to keep up or they wish to acquire. Their aspirations will be affected – what they want may change. The life-style suitable to a young executive, a retired bank manager or a feminist lawyer will require different consumption patterns and income levels. So the way individuals, and indeed their families, order preferences will vary and change over time.

In the orthodox analytical time mode there are no search or information costs required to make an informed decision, for example, no time or money is required for 'shopping around'. Costs of negotiating and monitoring are irrelevant in our certain world – there are no needs for guarantees or other insurance facilities. Transactions costs are zero. Indeed, the human brain can grapple with the huge range of goods on offer and compare their qualities and prices. But decisions are made in perspective time where search and transaction costs have to be considered, in addition to a straightforward comparison of market prices.

The basic model implicitly assumes that goods to be bought in the market can be consumed without any further time, effort or indeed any input of other resources. These factors are ignored. However, in practice, the choice of purchasing a theatre ticket, for example, or renting a home video, involve different additional costs; these are not confined to the purchase price.

Given the computational complexity of any decision (Simon 1976) it can be argued that especially where uncertainty is involved, the economic (man) person is looking for a *satisfactory* rather than an optimal solution. The knowledge of outcomes may be sketchy so the agent gathers information only up to the point where satisfactory outcomes are identified. Where there is uncertainty the rational economic person will proceed to acquire information up to the point where the extra or marginal cost of obtaining further information is equal to the extra or marginal benefit expected. None the less, the actor needs to know the relevant marginal costs and benefits. This is the subject of further research – yet, again, this needs some knowledge of the costs and benefits of such research. There is an infinite regress, with no reason to believe a person stops searching after a number of steps (Hay 1989). In fact, the use of *routines* and *habits* becomes important for they economize on search and transaction costs. People in perspective time are not always searching for and negotiating the best buy – they may make the decision that it is not worth it. The time, effort and resources expended are simply too great. Besides, sometimes people buy on impulse – moved by whim and sentiment.

To reiterate, the traditional model leaves people firmly embedded in analytical time and within a market economy. The whole thrust of the analysis is centred on a particular range of questions, for example, how the individual consumer will change his or her purchasing plans for private goods, given market price and income changes. The model, an abstraction from horrendous real-world complexities, forces us to think about behaviour, given particular assumptions and fully known constraints. We know in advance exactly what satisfaction the household representative will achieve from any particular combination of market goods. The model helps to clarify concepts such as real and money income, relative prices and the theoretical notions of income and substitution effects of price changes. It is not intended to be an exact replica of reality but rather an analytical tool. Yet when we want to consider the wider problems faced by the household and family in perspective time, the view has to be modified.

WIDENING THE ORTHODOX VIEW OF THE HOUSEHOLD: THE NEW HOUSEHOLD ECONOMICS

The orthodox model casts the household representative in the role of a market player, nothing more. But this is not the only important economic role which people play. The household itself is a key site of economic activity, it can be viewed as a *production unit*. The basic neo-classical approach illustrates individuals as consumers as we have just seen, or as suppliers of labour in the market, choosing to split their limited time between market paid work and all other activities, subsumed under the term 'leisure', illustrated by a trade-off between money income and leisure.

The 'new household economics' departs from this orthodox position by opening the black box of the household and recognizing that *within* the household important *unpaid non-market work* is undertaken. This can be divided into two categories:

1 *reproductive* work – childbirth and child-rearing.
2 *productive* work – for example, 'housework', shopping, DIY activities.

In fact, the household is recognized as a mini-factory, an important locus for housework, DIY; and the production of human capital, where children are raised and socialized. The household is also a complex 'leisure centre' where entertainment, leisure and idleness are produced and consumed. The members of households provide a variety of functions and are more than consumers and factor market suppliers.

The household/family is explicitly recognized in Becker's approach, making important decisions about the allocation of time, effort and other resources including money, in market and non-market contexts. He uses the orthodox neo-classical approach to analyse, household/family decisions of a very different type, questions about family size, the allocation of male/female roles within a family, the split between market and household work. The neo-classical framework is applied to areas traditionally considered to be outside the economist's remit. The 'new household economics' explicitly recognizes households/families as the producers and nurturers of future economic market actors, and the maintainers of rational economic people, with an objective to maximize joint utility.

Alternative uses for time: the household as a production and consumption unit

Time has many alternative uses and is a vital element in both the process of production and consumption. Consumption/leisure activities cover one broad category of activities and in conventional theory they have always been seen as the alternative to market employment. However, it was Becker (1965) who drew a clear and important distinction between time used to earn income in paid employment on the one hand and non-market work on the other. *Non-market work* includes work undertaken for the family/household, including such activities as housework, shopping, and gardening. Also, unpaid work involves 'child production' and 'informal care', the often unpaid caring of the elderly or those with special needs within the family.

Becker's analysis recognized the household as an important *production unit* in its own right. He shed new light on conventional consumption theory by underlining the importance of time as an essential requirement for the enjoyment of market commodities. The amount of actual time needed to consume a good will vary. A can of Coke, for example, might take only a few seconds to drink, the theatre ticket requires a much longer time input, including the time to travel to the theatre. Compare these with a consumer durable such as a compact disc player. This requires the consumer to spend many future listening hours and to buy compact discs and electricity in order to enjoy the product and consume it to the full.

Becker formally recognized that plans to buy commodities in the market required a simultaneous plan to commit time and perhaps other resources too. Market purchases are not simply consumed in isolation but are merely inputs in a production process which transforms them into final goods. Money/resources, time and effort are

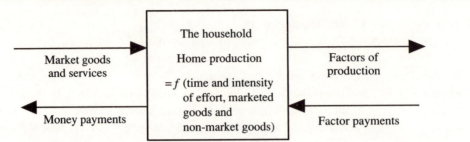

Figure 7.9 The household as a production unit. *Included here non-market goods – gifts not emphasized in the new household approach

required in that production process to achieve a final product. Figure 7.9 illustrates the production function, where output is shown as a function of time, both hours and intensity, and market and non-market goods.

Home production

Just as a commercial restaurant which produces meals for market sale, a variety of inputs including time, are needed to produce a meal within the household. Various ingredients, the raw materials, are required plus household capital, a cooker, saucepans etc., not to mention the scullion and cook. The meal, of course, requires an input of time to consume. Moreover, it is a different 'product' from that purchased in the cafeteria or fast-food chain. The costs and characteristics of the output vary according to the numbers of people involved and the relationship which exists between them (Cigno 1990). Cooking for two is usually cheaper than cooking for one. Unavoidable fixed cost elements like the purchase of cookers and refrigerators, and variable costs from the use of gas and electricity can be spread out over larger numbers of family members. Economies of 'large-scale production' may be reaped as the numbers in the household grow.

So within the household vital decisions are made about the allocation of limited time and resources *both* between *market* and *non-market* uses. Whether to eat at home or in a restaurant may be just one of the many choices which face the family/ household. Although this is not a meaningful choice for all families given their income constraints. Becker's analysis, set largely in analytical time, makes the alternatives explicit. Indeed, we can distinguish between activities for current production and consumption and investment activities, designed to ensure future production and consumption. Human capital theory, which explains how skills are obtained by investing time and resources in, say, education and training, was important in the development of the new household economics. Households, production units, analogous in many respects to firms, could be shown to engage in a variety of investment decisions and processes, including the investment of time, effort and resources in the education and socialization of children. We shall have more to say about these matters, particularly in Part III.

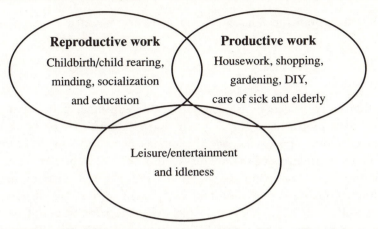

Figure 7.10   Household/family activities. The realm of domestic activity where work and leisure may sometimes overlap. Many 'outputs' cannot readily be purchased in the market place

Becker's family model

Becker's (1981) 'Treatise on the Family' brought *family choices* in terms of consumption, production and investment to the fore. He takes the traditional nuclear family structure as the basic model, a household operating in a modern market economy, and treats the family as a *solitary concordant unit*. Here the aim is to *maximize joint utility*, given that all family income is altruistically placed in a common fund. In analytical time the family's preferences are assumed to be known, consistent and stable. Any individual conflicts between family members are resolved and the objective of maximizing joint utility is achieved when the family head, a male altruist's utility function, is maximized subject to the family's joint resource constraint. The emphasis is on rationale calculation in the neo-classical mould.

The household/family activities are highlighted in Figure 7.10 under the headings of reproductive work, productive work and leisure/entertainment. The categories, which can be made distinct in analytical time, cannot be rigidly separated in reality; they overlap. Some elements of entertainment and leisure activities can have a child-rearing function. A trip to a museum or football match with a child is in part reproductive work, important in the education and socialization process. Shopping is classified as productive work. It ensures the supplies of household 'raw materials' and 'fixed assets' including the capital equipment necessary in the domestic production and consumption process. However, some would include this as a 'leisure activity' in itself, giving recreational value. Productive work is also often coupled with child-minding. But whilst time can be used for several activities at once, it is limited. Choices have to be made for scarcity prevails. Time, effort and energy, along with money incomes are limited.

Given this analytical framework, Becker suggests that explanations can be provided for a variety of behaviour including the demand for children, fertility changes and the sex division of labour within the household and between market and non-market roles.

The demand for children

Becker suggests that children can be treated as durable consumer goods and that economists can analyse the demand for children. Baby 'booms' or 'busts' can be explained with an economic approach, such phenomena brought about by shifts in demand. Fertility choices in terms of the numbers and timing of babies are made by rationally calculating individuals who weigh up the benefits and costs of having children. According to this view, one important component of the costs of having a child is the opportunity cost of the mother's time. As the market wages of women increase the opportunity cost, the price of having children increases. Other things being equal, women therefore have fewer children. Becker cites evidence to support this, for as economies develop, fertility declines. Individuals want to spend more on each child to improve child quality and so they limit the size of their families. Indeed, the analysis sees fertility choices within a general consumption/production framework, where the trade-off between the quantity and quality of children is underlined. As women have fewer children, Becker argues that there is a substitution between quantity and quality. So as the numbers fall, the quality of children increases.

The sex division of labour

The analysis is also used to explain how the sex division of labour is settled. Within an efficient household, Becker argues that joint family income will be maximized by each member practising his or her skills, according to comparative advantage and specialization, concepts which we discussed extensively in Chapter 3. Rationality according to this view, where the aim is to get the most output for joint input, leads women to specialize in non-paid domestic activities and men to concentrate on paid market work. The argument goes that the primary market workers are men, for they can make more money given their higher earnings potential and thus comparative advantage in paid employment. In contrast, women have a home oriented allocation of time and the composition of their human capital reflects this. They will not develop a comparative advantage elsewhere. According to Becker, this is a rational outcome given the lower earning potential of women in the market place. Women will be at home engaging in productive and reproductive work, the primary child-carers and home-makers – men will be the labour market earners.

However, the family will respond to external price changes. For example, an increase in women's wages in paid market work, will change a woman's allocation of time, leading to a substitution of unpaid housework for paid employment and the purchase of convenience foods, such as ready prepared meals or labour saving devices, domestic capital goods – appliances like microwaves, tumble dryers and dishwashers. A change in women's wages might also lead to a change in the make-up of their human capital and reduce their fertility. Women may substitute money income for children or delay the start of a family. However, whatever the market and technological changes, the family will always move to a new equilibrium level. The clear message is that sex roles and family planning can be explained by and are responsive to market forces.

Assessment: the new household economics

New household economics provides a significant change from the usual approach. To view non-market work and the domestic domain as suitable for analysis is in itself a step forward. Becker provides an analytical framework for thinking about issues which had previously been largely ignored. Traditionally and currently, National Income Accounting usually defines women employed in the home as economically inactive, even though the same work undertaken by a paid housekeeper would be valued in the national accounts. Becker, to his credit, does not overlook domestic work.

However, most of the criticisms which are levelled at basic conventional theory can also be applied to the new household economics. The theory is set in analytical time. All family actors have the same underlying and stable preferences which do not vary over time. Moreover, individuals are assumed to be separate with the implication that there is *no synergy*, where two people working together are better than two working independently. In marital production, the partners do not have an impact on each other's productive potential, their own personal production profiles, or preferences. Yet people learn from each other over the passage of time and their preferences change.

A key criticism is the lack of significant insights into situations of imperfect knowledge and uncertainty. People make fertility choices, to take one important example, in perspective time. Would-be parents are making choices with imperfect knowledge of the current situation and imperfect foresight. The decision about whether or not to try to conceive a child may be difficult, made with limited information about the associated costs and benefits; and fraught with uncertainty. Moreover, how many babies are conceived as a result of rational decision-making? The Keynesian view of an investor's animal spirits may be even more appropriate here, than in its original context. This Keynesian notion will be discussed in Chapters 11 and 12. For many, even in a technologically advanced age, the conception of a child is a surprise event, one which sometimes may be unwelcome. In any event, the decision to have children is different in kind from the purchase of a consumer durable. An ill-advised purchase of a car may be expensive to rectify; but there is no sale or return on a child – the decision is irreversible. 'Parents are, at best, guessing about the possible costs of children; weighing these against a set of preferences that are shaped by social norms. Their guesses have long-run implications' (Folbre 1994: 111). To paraphrase Keynes, the full consequences of the conception and birth of a child will be drawn out over many years to come. Babies and children are not like other investments; they cannot be sold or traded if the expected returns are outweighed by the costs. Whilst there is some flexibility, given abortion or adoption, there is considerable evidence that having abortions, or putting children out for adoption have psychological ramifications which people cannot foresee with clarity. Many people are unwilling or unable to follow such paths. Legal rules, customs and religious precepts have a significant part to play – both in forming preferences and constraining choice.

The orthodox approach assumes that individuals in such situations can behave as if they were rationally calculating, not prone to mistakes or passion. Moreover, preference maps are not set in stone, the presence of children may significantly affect parental preferences and the constraints they face, bringing unexpected kaleidic changes.

In the basic model everyone can be shown to benefit by specialization and exchange, a traditional sex division of labour, based on the *status quo*. However, the model ignores the extent to which satisfaction or dissatisfaction is gained from market work directly. It is Adam Smith's notion of *net advantages* resulting from these different courses of action which is important. Utility derives not simply from money wages. Additional attributes of work, including: job satisfaction, status, feelings of self worth are important determinants of satisfaction. Of course, paid work may have negative aspects, it could be difficult or dangerous. However, some forms of non-market work may also have negative aspects such as isolation, repetition and the feeling that such work and effort is undervalued. Of course, child-rearing and domestic duties can provide positive satisfaction from which men are largely excluded by a traditional, rigid division of labour. None the less, the net advantages of different types of activity should be considered, not simply money payments. A more equitable and flexible split of domestic duties could prove rewarding for both men and women in terms of joint utility.

Finally, the family is treated as if it does not change with the passage of time. The family is implicitly assumed to be a permanent indivisible unit, encapsulated in analytical time. Yet families evolve; children grow up and leave home; and parents age. When each person specializes according to comparative advantage, the dependent home-maker is vulnerable in the event of separation, divorce or the death of the primary market worker. The dependent home-worker has not acquired or enhanced marketable skills. The vital on-the-job-training, experience, promotions and connections are missed by the housewife or the woman part-time worker. Redundancy of the market worker can also present problems for the family's human capital risks have not been spread. (See Ben-Porath 1982; Pollack 1985; Okin.)

Differential power

Power is not a consideration in Becker's model. Yet the status of dependency affects the *internal power structure* of the family, where a dominant male worker may make the important strategic decisions. Those who earn the most are generally in a stronger bargaining position and they may have much less to lose by divorce. The dependent partner may have fewer exit options, realistic alternatives to pursue. This puts that person at a disadvantage in any negotiation. Indeed, the altruism of the strategic decision-maker is an assumption. There is limited evidence about the internal division of income and the decision-making process within the family – although this may have an important effect on purchasing and investment decisions.

In addition, the choices about market and non-market work are often effectively constrained for both men and women, by law and custom. 'The rules of the game' apply to the family as much as they do elsewhere. Cultural norms are themselves constraints which restrict choice at one level although giving the benefits of a stable framework on another.

The lack of particular types of labour market skills renders women, widowed or divorced, susceptible to poverty. Moreover, families headed by lone parents are susceptible to poverty. In practice, the family is a changing unit, children grow to adulthood and set up their own households, relatives age and require care, eventually households of several people may reduce to single person status. Often individuals within the family are faced with *conflicting options*, trying to balance traditional responsibilities, market pressures and the changing rules of the game. These are matters not effectively analysed in Becker's approach.

However, the 'new household economics' moves economic theory into the personal realm of family life and the domestic world of the household. This new perspective clarifies and gives important insights into the complex range of interrelated choices which face the household. It opens up the black box, albeit largely relying on the analytical time mode, where all knowing REPs carefully calculate costs and benefits with practised ease. Moreover, individuals and market activity remains an important focus. Yet there are other categories of work, *outside* the home or market. Voluntary activities, effectively gifts of time and effort for non-market purposes, also exist.

HOUSEHOLDS AS ORGANIZATIONS: ALTERNATIVE APPROACHES

Alternative approaches to the household and family provide a different view of human activity and behaviour. These do not lend themselves to the neat modelling of mainstream analysis. Such approaches draw from different disciplines. One shift in focus is from the individual to the interaction of the group and team. The household is viewed as a complex organization where people interact with one another on a long-term basis. Moreover, alternative approaches may emphasize both formal and informal sectors, looking at the family's relationship with the wider community and other organizations which are neither business firms nor households. Such approaches examine the evolving boundaries, structure and internal organizations of households.

Households in perspective and historical time

Institutional and evolutionary theories recognize that families take decisions in perspective time and ask different questions from basic neo-classical theory. They seek to clarify which activities will be carried out within the family; the economic function and social roles of families as compared with other organizations like the market firm and government. These change over historical time and place. The administrative structure of the household and the inequalities of power in the decision-making process, as between men and women, are examined. Insights are given into the changing structure of the family and on the nature of the inequalities, whether in terms of consumption, skills and training, or hours of leisure between men and women. Economists do not normally consider how decision-making within the family is organized. Or what factors might cause families to disintegrate or stick together when there is 'turbulence' and uncertainty. Yet these are important questions, particularly as family members are unlikely to have conveniently identical goals.

People have limited information and understanding, they operate in perspective time where decision-making is quite often characterized by chronic uncertainty. The role of the household/family organization is constrained by formal and informal laws and customs. These provide a framework for building complex long-term relationships, in some part bringing security and stability. Marriage, an important long-term contract, is one such element. People have prolonged commitments to each other in the household and marriage. Bonds are built up, contracts similar in some respects to those which exist in firms, but unlike those in the short-run contracting modes of market exchange (see Chapter 9 for further discussion). Indeed, the household, rather like the firm, provides a 'protective shelter' (Hodgson 1988) a safe space in a world of potential surprise, commotion and competition. Whilst marriage is risky and there may be conflict and power struggles within the family – it may represent a 'safer space' than the alternative, particularly for women. The long-term relationships of the family enable the building up of routines and customs, some unique to each family group, others similar in kind. The role of tradition, custom, habit and *collective* behaviour are important in domestic arrangements. These dominate the domestic family scene – not the individualistic behaviour of orthodox market players. In fact, many of the expenditures of valuable resources including time, made within family groups may best be thought of as gifts. Such resources, for example, spent on education and training, are gifts, motivated by love, rather than investments as such (Boulding 1973), although there is evidence to suggest that women pay for a large portion of these 'investments' in children (Folbre 1994).

The household/family: an institution which mediates between the economic system and individuals

Within the household/family many decisions are made about the activities of all its members and resources. This is an institutional response to the problem of co-ordinating resources for domestic purposes in a continuously changing world – in perspective time. The household – rather like the business firm – uses inputs of human and non-human resources and transforms them into output. But the family specialises not just in affective relationships and, for example, the joint consumption of physical goods, but also in the 'production' of children and their nurturing. Remember that people are *not* procreated or reared in markets, or for that matter by business firms or Government. Although Government, by their policies may significantly affect fertility decisions. In China, the Government decrees one child per family. In Singapore, the Government uses tax advantages to encourage larger families for particular social groups. However, regardless of the rules of the game in any particular situation, infants are not the independent rational adult producers and consumers of orthodox theory. In all economies a large majority of human beings have very limited market activity in their formative years. They are, on the whole, protected from the market, for a considerable time, cared for and socialized within the family or in other non-market organizations. Domestic work and other activities vital for the maintenance and production of people – economic actors of the present and future – are undertaken within the household. Whether family members are in harmony or conflict they usually give some element of protection from the external environment.

The significance of the household's internal organization and family structure

The household/family is not the black box of orthodox theory. The co-ordination of resources requires *co-operation*, both in productive and reproductive work. Indeed, there is a division of tasks within the household, for 'materials' have to pass through a number of different processes; there is a sequential organization of production over real time which requires planning. The market mechanism does not allocate resources, goods and services within the family. Non-price means are required. These include planning, command and mutual adjustment mechanisms, features to which we shall return in later chapters (see particularly Chapter 9).

Moreover, in contrast to the orthodox approach, here individual members are not assumed to have identical goals, or to act as if they did. The institutional approach recognizes *conflict* and *unequal power* relationships. Indeed, we can point to different types of governance structures or authority relationships.

The household viewed as a management or governance structure, decides on policy and action, making both strategic and tactical choices, planning for choices over time. The household may have a very simple hierarchical structure, headed by a boss. Galbraith (1975) distinguishes between the wife, as a crypto-servant, who specializes in the administration of household consumption and production. She makes the *routine decisions*. The husband, in contrast, makes the strategic moves, the *important decisions* relating to career moves, education choice and key expenditures. Galbraith (1975: 48) uses a middle-class example, the household of a 'somewhat senior automobile executive', whose wife has to fulfil the tasks of household management. 'Convention forbids external roles unassociated with [a] display of homely virtues'. Part-time charitable work was acceptable but not full-time employment. Of course, over the passage of time, attitudes have changed.

However, the hierarchical household structure can be seen to operate, for example, in traditional British working-class households. The head of the household may not be planning for upward mobility, although he could be for his children. Yet major strategic decisions on consumption expenditure and saving still have to be made. In the traditional family the male head of the household will decide on these strategic issues, including decisions relating to the labour market participation of his wife. But women from working-class households have often worked in factories, farms and domestic service, in addition to their family roles. In historical time women and children worked long hours in mines and factories or on farms.

Contrast traditional families with the peer group organizational form – *a partnership* – where decisions are made jointly. Perhaps where partners are not bound by a conventional marriage contract. The governance structures of households change over historical time, in response to a variety of interlinked factors. In recent years there has been an increased labour market involvement of married women, for example, as a result of changing education patterns, an impact from feminism and increasing male unemployment. Indeed, over time the relative positions of power have altered as the exit options, the alternative possibilities outside the household, for both women and men have changed. Jane Wheelock in *Husbands at Home* (1990) examines the changing roles of men and women when men become unemployed. In the non-traditional household the man undertakes responsibility for household duties.

As a planning unit the household tries to make predictions, to control and cope with events. It has a continuous complex interplay through markets and via non-market activity with other organizations. It helps to reduce the costs associated with exchange in the market place and can provide incentives, sanctions and its own forms of monitoring. The organization provides gains from specialization and co-operation in a world of fundamental uncertainty. Marriage is one form of contract which can give people a safe and reliable long-term relationship, a secure environment in which to live and rear children, in a world of turbulence (Earl 1986). But as the socio-economic world evolves other forms of non-traditional household develop.

These are complex, multi-faceted issues which do not give us the comfort of unique equilibriums. We shall have more to say about the nature of the household and family in following chapters. We should not forget that households/families are vital organizations in the economic system.

THE HOUSEHOLD – SUMMARY

- Traditional microeconomics treats the household and individual as synonymous. Individuals are merely market players who aim to maximize their utility.
- Consumer behaviour is analysed in analytical time with indifference curves and budget constraints used to find unique equilibriums.
- The analysis shows how consumers will respond in the face of price and

income changes. Income and substitution effects are derived for price changes. Distinctions are made between real and money incomes.

- Choices in perspective time can be complex where repetition is lacking and people are relatively ignorant. Decisions may be hazardous and impossible to reverse. People may simply go for the satisfactory option.
- The New Household Economics opens the black box and sees the household as a production unit where reproductive and productive work are undertaken in addition to leisure and idleness.
- Alternative uses of time are considered – market and non-market. The demand for children and the sex-division of labour can be analysed from the rational perspective of economic people.
- Given the problems of operating in perspective time and the differential power structure which exists within the household, NHE can be evaluated.
- Institutional and evolutionary theories see the household and the people who make them up caught in the march of time and fundamental uncertainty.
- The household can have different governance structures. These have important implications for women and men.

THE HOUSEHOLD – QUESTIONS FOR DISCUSSION

1 Explain the concept of indifference curves. Draw indifference curves for chocolate and chips, for an individual who:

   a) loves chocolate far more than chips;
   b) regards chocolate and chips as *perfect substitutes*;
   c) never eats chips because she dislikes them.

2 Explain the concept of the budget line. Using the indifference curves for books and food as in Figure 7.3, illustrate the impact on consumer purchasing plans of the following:

   a) an increase in money incomes;
   b) a change in relative prices;
   c) a doubling of money incomes and a doubling of all money or nominal prices.

3 What would be the consumer's equilibrium position given the situation where chips and chocolates are perfect substitutes as in 1b)? Hint: there would be no diminishing marginal rate of substitution between the two goods.

4 'Chips and chocolate are safe, comfortable examples for individual choice in traditional analysis. But in perspective time with complex products things are not so straightforward.' Explain and discuss.

5 Why is it argued that tastes and preferences are to some extent endogenous? What factors mould tastes over historical time? Use examples to illustrate your answer.

6 What are the major strengths and weaknesses of the 'New Household Economics'? In what ways can children be regarded as investments?

7 'The law of comparative advantage clearly illustrates the benefits of a traditional sex division of labour between market and non-market work.' Explain and evaluate.

8 What might be the impact on economic behaviour if household governance structures are:

a) hierarchical;
a) peer group?

8

The business firm I

INTRODUCTION

This chapter and the one which follows aim to give an insight into the nature and behaviour of the business firm. Here we examine introductory neo-classical models set in analytical time. However, we also acknowledge other approaches, those which recognize the importance of perspective and historical time, as in the treatment of the household. Nevertheless, whatever the outlook, the business firm is a major area of concern for those seeking to understand the workings of an industrialized nation, set in a global economy. In a modern economic system, business firms supply very many of the everyday items which we consume immediately; and inputs for household production, including consumer durables. They produce inputs for other businesses and non-commercial organizations in the public and private sectors. Firms not only create output for sale but are important providers of paid employment. Indeed, business firms are key components of any modern economy; they are major wealth generators.

However, the economic importance of these business organizations has evolved over time, their initial proliferation came with the process of industrialization. Whilst some enormous firms, like General Motors and giant Japanese corporations rival small nation states in terms of their economic power, historically that was not always so. Giant multinationals, producing and selling globally, are a relatively recent historical phenomenon. Yet whether business firms are large or small, many aspects of their behaviour can be critical to our well being. We need only think of the goods they produce, their employment and investment strategies; and their overall impact on the environment.

In this chapter, to set the scene, we look initially at the firm in practice. Then we develop the introductory neo-classical approach to the firm, in *analytical time*. The firm is a key market player – a self-evident entity – which buys or rents resources from factor markets and transforms them into outputs for market sale. The firm is a *production unit* with the sole objective of making the biggest possible profit. The firm is analysed as a production function, a perfectly specified relationship between inputs and outputs in a world of fully informed rational economic people. Moreover, the firm is an impenetrable entity whose internal organization and legal structure are of no consequence; they can be assumed away with impunity.

The introductory orthodox approach is concerned with a *particular range* of questions. The basic theory seeks to explain the determination of a firm's pricing and output policy in different market settings and, ultimately, to compare the efficiency of firms operating in distinctive market environments. As we saw in Chapter 5, market structures range from the 'ideal type' of perfect competition at one end of the spectrum, to monopoly at the other. Given an introductory view of production and cost theory, we shall concentrate initially on these two market forms. They give the orthodox starting point, where we assume away problems of risk and uncertainty and evolutionary change. We make direct comparisons between these two market extremes. However, in the late twentieth-century modern economy, there are other competitive forms. Often a few producers, oligopolists, are key players, dominating particular markets. A variety of models can be used to shed light on oligopolistic behaviour; the outcomes are not so clear cut. Here we provide an introductory view.

In fact, there are many economics texts which concentrate almost exclusively on explaining and developing the technical intricacies of the theories in this chapter. The purpose here is to give *an insight* into that large amount of material; a short account. For whilst the usual perspective gives particular understandings of business behaviour, there are other significant approaches which are often neglected. In the following chapter we shall take a different and wider focus to emphasize the firm as an *organization* embedded in real time. The neatness of the basic approach with unique equilibriums will give way to alternative treatments. Given a complex reality, no one theoretical system can provide all the insights; different approaches have their parts to play. To underline the diversity of business firms in practice, initially, we give an overview of the business firm 'for-profit', emphasizing important real-world features; then we move to the introductory models of production, cost and firm's pricing and output decisions in different market contexts.

THE FIRM: AN OVERVIEW

The business firm, in practice, uses resources to produce goods and/or services for market sale. In any modern economy there is an enormous range of firms. A current snapshot of all the firms, just in Britain today, would show us an amazingly diverse array. These firms operate in a variety of *markets*, producing a tremendous range of output. Some produce only components of a final commodity or service, and so are simply part of a production chain. Many manufacture the hundreds of different products which are on their order books, and work in different industries. Some are household names, whilst others are virtually unknown. However, there are a number of different ways in which we can classify these firms by, for example, their size and legal status. We shall consider market structure later in this chapter.

Small firms

On the basis of *size* alone, there are those enterprises which can be described as small. Definitions of small firms may use various yardsticks, like the size of a firm's annual turnover or the number of people employed. But definitions of 'smallness' may depend on the industry in which the firm operates; they change over time and vary from country to country. In Britain we can find such businesses advertising in the small ads of newspapers or in BT's Yellow Pages: plumbers (the modern day artisans), corner shops, family restaurants and small private health clinics, to mention but a few.

The *legal status* of the small firm is usually that of a sole trader, a partnership or a small private company. We discuss the economic significance of these forms in the following chapter. But although categorized as small, firms still come in quite different shapes and sizes. Small firms taken together, in terms of sheer numbers, make-up a large proportion of business firms. Very small-scale enterprises could include: garment manufacturers, small building firms or the local newsagent. Certainly, the diversity of goods and services produced by the small business and the range of industries and *markets* in which they operate, whether those markets are local, national, sometimes international, is extraordinary. Moreover, they face different *degrees of competition* and different prospects. Many will remain small but others will grow to become the medium and large companies of the future, significant market players. Others will die, liquidated or wound-up. New firms will be started up as people think they see gaps or opportunities in the market. Yet for any firm currently in business, their past histories are unique and their future prospects are inevitably not certain.

Large firms and multinational enterprise

On the basis of size, at the other end of the spectrum, are those firms which are readily categorized as large. These include the modern day giant corporations, many of them household names – for example, in Britain, those listed in *The Financial Times* Top 100 index. Their legal status is that of a plc, public companies, with shares, the number quoted and traded on the London Stock Exchange. One important measure of their size is by *market capitalization* – the total value of all the company's ordinary shares, the number in issue multiplied by their market price. *The Financial Times* share service publishes the market capitalization values for companies on the market; they vary depending on the daily share price. The figures given here are for 21 January 1994.

British Telecom dwarfs most other British companies, with a market capitalization value of £28.8 billion, more than three and a half times the market value of Sainsbury's, the food retailers (£8.2 billion) and fourteen times the size of TI Group (Tube Investments) (£2 billion), a major British engineering/manufacturing company. Yet in a British context, all of these companies are big by any measure, whether by the market value of their shares, sales volume or the number of people they employ.

In addition, there are also large private companies whose shares are not traded on any stock market, such as the beleaguered Heron Ltd, the property company/petrol station. These are much more difficult to value for there is no ready market for their shares.

Many companies are also classified as *multinational*, like British American Tobacco (BAT), and Cadbury Schweppes. They not only sell in overseas markets but they produce and own production facilities in other countries too. Yet in a global context, compared to the world's largest companies, even large UK companies can look relatively small. Such corporations are *multinational super giants*, owning production facilities and producing on a wide global scale. Indeed, from these immense companies, stand a group who dwarf all others; whose assets and income are greater than those of many poorer countries. These are organizations of immense economic power. They make large varieties of products and operate in many different markets, sometimes wielding monopolistic power, in others, facing competition. But, for example, their decisions concerning production, and the size and location of their activities can touch the lives of millions of people.

The world giants of today, like General Motors, with headquarters in the USA, The Royal Dutch Shell Group and the enormous Japanese Corporations such as the Mitsubishi Corporation, a group of awesome Japanese companies including Mitsubishi Motors, are a far cry from tiny firms buying and selling in local markets. *The Times* 1000 (1994) top 50 industrial companies gives an insight into the size of such big world players with the Itochu Corporation, with headquarters in Japan, as the biggest company and General Motors, with headquarters in the USA as second largest. They are significantly different from small-scale local enterprise, in terms of their size and organizational structure. We shall return to these features in the next chapter.

Finally, some firms can be run for profit on the lines of a business firm, selling their output in markets, although they are not in private ownership. They fall within the realms of the public sector. State-owned enterprise, like the Post Office, whilst different in legal form may be analysed as a business firm. (Plans to privatize the Post Office have been set aside. It will not now join other companies, quoted on the Stock Market like British Telecom and British Gas, which until privatization were nationalized industries operating in the public sector.) We shall have much more to say about the overall evolution, legal and internal organizational features of these different types of firm, whether designated as small at one end of the spectrum or large at the other, in the next chapter.

The business firm and household: a comparison

Whilst we can draw several analogies from the previous chapter, of course there are significant differences between a household and a business firm. The firm usually has quite different objectives and functions – economic motives are paramount. Moreover, the firm can have a much more complex legal and organizational form than any household. In its corporate form, the firm could last theoretically into perpetuity, like a family dynasty, both can outlive individuals. As we shall see in the next chapter, firms and families may overlap in the family firm. Yet the possibilities for the geographical dispersion of the firm are clearly very much wider than those of a nuclear family. However, in terms of analytical treatment, economists can employ similar methods. The introductory approach uses analogous tools for analysing different organizations whether the household, the private business firm or the state-owned enterprise run on commercial lines. We now turn our attention to the basic orthodox approach to illustrate how this dispenses with the layers of real-world complexity in a bid to provide an understanding of business behaviour and to evaluate the performance of business firms.

INTRODUCTORY NEO-CLASSICAL APPROACH USING ANALYTICAL TIME

The firm: the traditional view

Traditional theory stands well back from the remarkable diversity and intricacy of the firm in the actual business world. It directs attention towards a particular typology of firms and asks a particular set of questions using the *analytical time* mode. The firm aiming to maximize profit is viewed as *the basic producing unit*. Its role and actions are examined within a market context where the firm is a key player. The firm supplies marketable goods and buys and rents factors of production, to produce outputs which it sells to other firms, to households or other organizations whether from the public or private sector. The clear focus is on the firms *external market* relationships as illustrated in Figure 8.1. The market structure in which a firm operates is key.

The basic model assumes a single plant, single product and uni-national firm; it could be anywhere in the world and is ahistorical. Moreover, the existence and nature of the enterprise is taken for granted. The firm simply transforms inputs into

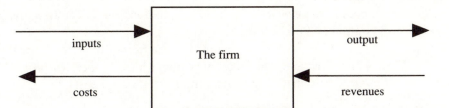

Figure 8.1   The 'black box' firm transforming factor inputs into output

marketable outputs; a 'black box', whose internal workings are hidden and where technology is given. In Figure 8.1 inputs are transformed into outputs. The firm receives a flow of income from market sales and payments are made for the inputs.

The internal organization and structure of the firm is assumed away. As Lipsey says 'we assume that each firm takes consistent decisions as if it were composed of a single individual. . . .each firm's decisions are not influenced by its internal organization' (1989: 51). This is a very convenient simplification. Here there is no significant difference between the complex corporate organization and the individual contractor, for the firm is assumed to behave as a rational individual, by implication a sole owner. Any differences in a firm's legal structure are ignored – the 'rules of the game' do not concern us. In analytical time the economist safely ignores all institutional factors of historical time and place.

Profit maximization

When the firm sells goods in the market it earns revenues – income, by charging a price to its customers. *Profit* is what is left over when all the costs of producing these goods have been covered. *Profit* is the surplus of *total revenues* (TR), the income which accrues from selling goods, over and above their *total costs* (TC) of production. In short, profit is total revenue minus total costs (TR – TC). Rational economic people aim to maximize profit – the straightforward goal of introductory theory. In basic traditional mode the household is seen as a rational utility maximizer choosing between completely known alternatives. Analogously, the firm is seen as a rational individual choosing between completely specified options. The firm always chooses the option which maximizes profit or, in adverse circumstances, minimizes losses. For example, the firm chooses, on the basis of complete information of all the production alternatives, a convenient hypothetical situation.

Key questions raised in the introductory models

The basic model examines several questions. These include:

1 How does a firm determine its price and output, in order to make the biggest profit possible, given the market, production and cost constraints?
2 In what circumstances do firms close down or set up in business, making an exit from or an entry into a particular industry?
3 How do the changes in the *number* of competitors in a market affect an individual firm's price and output and profit levels?
4 Finally, a question which is of fundamental importance to the neo-classical approach. When will a firm and the industry within which it operates provide an *allocatively efficient output*, that is, the most output for the least cost?

To answer these and related questions we must examine: a) production theory, to explain the opportunities for producing output: the firm's production function; and

b)   cost theory to explain the costs of producing these different outputs. Only when we have all the cost information and we know the revenues or incomes from selling different levels of output can we provide answers to the questions posed above.

We shall begin by introducing production and cost theory before we move to examine market conditions which are fundamental for determining what the firm will be willing and able to sell and at what price.

PRODUCTION, COSTS AND TIME

The production of goods requires resources. In Chapter 2 we introduced the concept of a production function, an input/output relationship for the economy as a whole. Now we can apply that concept to the business firm. In basic neo-classical mode, the firm is simply viewed as a production function, a fully known relationship between physical inputs on the one hand and output on the other. In the modern economy many resources are sold or rented in markets; they cost money. Therefore firms incur costs in the process of making an output. To find the cost of producing any particular level of output we have to know:

1 What quantity of inputs of a given quality are required to produce different levels of output?
2 What are the input prices?

Production theory

To answer the first question, for a hypothetical black box firm, we need to understand the technical relationship between inputs and outputs, the overall quantity and mix of inputs required to produce different levels of output. Output depends on the inputs, other things held constant. In a simple production function, as in equation 8.1:

$$Q = f(N,K,) \tag{8.1}$$

where Q is simply the total quantity of all goods which can be produced by our hypothetical firm over a particular time, f means depends on, and N and K respectively represent labour and capital. The equation simply says that the amount of output available in a particular period depends on the labour and capital inputs. Here we are assuming that capital embodies the technology given in that particular time. Of course, there may be other factors of production, such as land and raw material inputs, but for simplicity, we assume these away. There is a positive relationship between inputs and output, if the firm increases all the inputs in the production process we assume that output will increase.

The production function set in analytical time gives us a constraint, analogous to the production possibility curve. It shows the production opportunities open to a firm to combine inputs together to produce a *single output* with a *given* technology. We can move backwards and forwards changing the input mix to see what will happen to output, without changing anything else. In short, we can rerun the firm's options, which are perfectly specified. If we expand one or both of the factor inputs we known precisely how output will change.

The firm could take a *labour intensive* production option, using a small amount of capital and a great deal of labour or a *capital intensive* process using a small amount of labour in relation to capital. In reality, there are a variety of ways of making output or indeed producing a service. Banking 'products', for example, can be labour intensively produced, with manual filing systems and little physical equipment, embodying relatively basic technology; or highly automated processes can be used with high-tech computer facilities, including automated tellers and very few banking staff. The choices of such different production modes in reality evolve over time. In some circumstances the firm may be able to choose between highly capital intensive or labour intensive processes. But remember our model is not a description of the alternatives facing any real firm, it is a simplification. The state of technology differs in historical time and place. There are 'many accidents of geography and history, [which] enter into the choice of technique as well as into the design of "machines"' (Robinson 1975: 38). In perspective time we do not have perfect knowledge of all the alternatives, 'the choice of technique is made by groping amongst incomplete information' (ibid.). We shall have more to say about this process in Part III, when we examine investment. Moreover, here we ignore all the institutionalized rules and their effect on the way in which production is organized.

Time: planning horizons

We have implicitly assumed so far that we can alter *both* labour and capital at will. But now we have to consider different planning horizons. Economic actors performing in analytical time are constrained by different theoretical time periods. We met these in Chapter 5. Economists distinguish between different planning horizons which face the firm, these are distinct time periods in which production decisions and adjustments are made. Here time is explicitly recognized. Although we still assume perfect knowledge, and work in analytical time, the options available, the input–output menu, are critically dependent on the time span under consideration. Economists distinguish between several analytical time periods.

a) The *Long Run* which represents the time scale over which *all* factors of production are variable. There is greatest flexibility assuming a given technology. New factories, machines, highly skilled personnel, all inputs can be varied, either expanded or contracted or substituted for one another. The scale of production can be changed. However, once the firm has committed itself to certain resource inputs, for example, built a particular plant, we have a different situation – the short run.

b) The *Short Run* which is the period during which at least *one* factor input is fixed – incapable of being varied. In such circumstances, if a firm wants to increase output, it can do so only by using the fixed factor more intensively; by adding more of the non-fixed or variable factors of production. The firm is powerless to increase output in any other way. Capital, such as machinery and plant, is conventionally used as the short-run fixed input. The rationale for this is that it takes time to build factories or manufacture machinery and equipment; they cannot be quickly changed.

Labour is usually assumed to be the variable resource which can be changed readily in analytical time. As we shall see in Chapter 14, in reality, labour itself may be fixed in the short run. It may be impossible to employ people with the appropriate skills at short notice, for example, specialist skills unavailable in the market may be required. It takes time for selecting and training people, which makes labour itself effectively a *quasi-fixed factor*. In reality, the input of people cannot be changed at will; and in many instances it may be easier to vary capital than highly trained and specialized labour.

Some economists distinguish the *very long run*, which is said to be that time period over which technology changes. But technology evolves as real time passes; holding technology constant is merely a convenient simplification of analytical time. Finally, at the other extreme, we may think of the *very short run*, a time period so short that all inputs are fixed and so output cannot be varied.

In our hypothetical model we do not put a *calendar time*, on these analytical time runs, in terms of months or years. Although with the passage of real time, what constitutes the long run actually varies from industry to industry. In analytical time it is immaterial whether we are speaking of the long run in oil refining or nuclear power generation, where planning and making capacity changes can take several years. Or whether we examine the long run for estate agents and hair dressers, where planning and making capacity changes can be accomplished in a much shorter calendar time period.

In all of these 'analytical time runs', we are operating with complete knowledge of certain alternatives. Given the complexity of any actual business situation, this is a useful initial simplification, to isolate particular ideas. We shall begin with the simplest situation – the short run – so that we can consider the production possibilities open to a firm.

The short-run production constraint

Imagine that a firm has *already* committed itself to a particular plant capacity and now has a fixed level of buildings and equipment which cannot be changed in the short run. Only labour can be varied in the short run. Moreover, the quality of the labour input does not vary regardless of the number of hours employed. The short run production function is given by equation 8.2:

$$Q = f(N, K^*) \tag{8.2}$$

where Q is a function, f, of labour, N and capital K^*. Note that *capital is fixed* denoted by the asterisk.

Table 8.1   Total, marginal and average product in the short run

Labour	Capital	Total Product	Marginal Product	Average Product
0	1	0	—	—
1	1	5	⟩ 5	5
2	1	12	⟩ 7	6
3	1	16	⟩ 4	5.33
4	1	18	⟩ 2	4.5
5	1	19	⟩ 1	3.8
6	1	18	⟩ − 1	

Table 8.1 gives hypothetical data to illustrate how output changes as a firm adds extra units of the variable factor, measured in labour hours, to a fixed capacity base, like a small factory, which manufactures output.

The data shows how total product or output changes as the labour input is increased. Remember that the quality of labour does not fall with the number of hours employed. In this case, first, note from the hypothetical data:

1 The *total product* (TP) or output *increases* as we add extra units of the variable input up to and including the fifth labour hour. Total output *falls* when the sixth hour is added.
2 The *marginal product* (MP), that is, the extra output (ΔTP) which arises as a result of a one unit increase in the labour input, *varies* as we add additional labour units.

$$MP = \Delta TP / \Delta N \qquad (8.3)$$

Initially, the marginal product increases with each additional one unit increase in labour. The first labour hour adds 5 units of output, the second adds 7 units. But when we add the third labour hour, whilst total output increases to 16 units, the marginal product, although still positive, has started to decline. The extra output from the additional labour hour is only 4 units, a *smaller* amount than was added by the second hour. The fourth labour hour only adds 2 units of output, the fifth a mere one unit increase. Finally, the addition of the sixth labour hour brings no increase in total output. It actually reduces output. Adding labour has become worse than useless, for the marginal output is *negative*, here − 1. Total output falls when this sixth hour is added.
3 The *average product* (AP) varies too. This is derived by dividing total output by the number of labour units employed.

$$AP = TP / N \qquad (8.4)$$

From the table we can see that average product initially rises but then falls. At 3

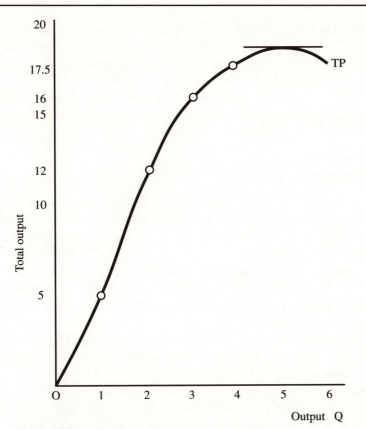

Figure 8.2a Total product curve

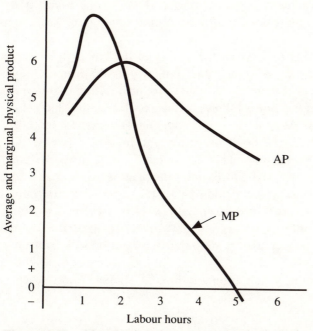

Figure 8.2b Marginal and average physical product curves

inputs of labour, it has passed its peak. We are not going to delve further into the technical details but this type of relationship between inputs and outputs forms a mainstay of the basic orthodox treatment. Total, marginal and average product relationships behaving in this way underpin the short-run *'U' shaped cost curves* which are used extensively in introductory treatments and beyond. We shall explore these short-run costs later in this chapter – they display eventually diminishing returns.

Eventually diminishing returns

The important economic concept of eventually diminishing returns is illustrated by the data in Table 8.1 and Figure 8.2a and b. Given that at least one factor is fixed in the short run, when a firm strives to increase output by adding more units of the variable factor, then eventually the extra or marginal output of additional labour hours declines. At some point both marginal and average output will eventually decline although they will still be positive. In this case, as we see from the table, with an input of more than 5 labour hours, total output actually falls, for the extra output added by the additional labour unit is negative.

Whilst initially, two hours are very much better than one, three even better than two, at some point there are 'too many labour hours' for the fixed capacity. The plant is 'overstretched', used beyond the optimal level. At the point where total product actually declines, we have a situation where 'too many cooks spoil the broth'. In other words, after some point too many variable inputs will actually overload the fixed factor causing *total output to fall*. Clearly, the firm would never operate in a situation of declining total output, this would involve paying for labour hours which actually reduced output. This would never give profit maximization and equilibrium. Even if additional labour hours were free it would be damaging.

This argument has nothing to do with the quality of the labour hours used. The model assumes that the quality of inputs does not vary as the firm employs more labour hours. The decline in the rate of marginal product and the eventual negative product of workers beyond five hours follows because of the relationship between the fixed and variable factors. At first there are *increasing returns*, for initially when hours are added at low levels of plant usage average product rises. At the point of maximum average product, the plant is optimally used, here marginal and average products are equal. But beyond this point the plant is over-utilized. Marginal product is below the average – every addition of the variable factor pulls down the average. If more labour is added, eventually negative returns are made. The message is that a single optimal proportion of variable to fixed factors exists in the short run. Output can be increased beyond this point but only, as we shall see, at increasing costs.

We owe the idea of eventually diminishing returns to Thomas Malthus who wrote in the eighteenth century. Indeed, this is often referred to as the law of diminishing returns. He argued that given a fixed land stock and an expanding population, at some point, extra workers would bring about a decline in agricultural output. There would simply be too many workers for the available land, crops would be spoilt and the land overused, with people trampling on each other and their crops. Over-population would bring famine, pestilence and war, processes by which population would be kept in check. Of course, this is a short-run phenomena where we hold land and technology fixed. In fact, Malthus did not foresee the long-term technical changes which would evolve to offset diminishing returns, shifting the total product curve upwards. Agricultural activity has been revolutionized by widespread changes, including mechanization and more recently, for example, the use of agro-chemicals.

Yet whether we think of the business firm manufacturing output or the farm, the short-run production function illustrates a technical constraint, which divides possible output from the impossible, given the technology and plant level. It shows us efficient situations where more output could not be produced without more of the variable input. And the optimal point for the plant is where average product is at a maximum. At this point we have gained all the increasing returns. To expand plant usage any further leads to diminishing returns.

The long run and returns to scale

The long-run scenario gives us the possibility of changing *all* inputs and the whole scale of production. There are three possible alternative impacts on output following on from these changes in the long run.

Increasing returns to scale   These would have occurred if, when all inputs were doubled, for example, output increased threefold. This is a situation of increasing returns to scale. Several reasons can be given to explain this situation. The production of a greater output makes it possible for people to specialize. Adam Smith's famous pin factory has already been featured in Chapter 3. Small factories were eventually able to produce much greater outputs. Of course, the breaking up of production into small parts encouraged the invention of simple specialized machinery, which could be used for larger scales of production.

The doubling in size of vats, tankers or storage/warehouse facilities will more than double the volume of output which can be processed or stored. Larger scales of output make it possible to benefit from such economies. And higher volumes of output can be overseen by the same supervisors. Within limits, the same management team can co-ordinate larger numbers of workers and output thereby giving rise to economies of scale.

Constant returns to scale   These are straightforward. Here when a firm increases its inputs in a fixed proportion then the output increases by exactly the same proportion.

To illustrate, if inputs are doubled then the output is doubled. Returns are uniform with neither economies nor diseconomies when the scale of production is changed. Output can be replicated.

Decreasing returns to scale   There may come a point where greater volumes of output lead to diseconomies of large-scale production. In particular, there may be managerial diseconomies where management find problems of co-ordination as the scale of activity increases. A firm may have to expand to poorer sites. The optimal production size is important, a firm will not want to suffer from diseconomies of scale. But in perspective time, isolating where such diseconomies will set-in may be difficult and will vary from industry to industry, depending on the nature of production.

Externalities

The emphasis on production for the market often ensures that the *joint production* of *externalities* is ignored. Firms not only produce output, goods for market sale, but also produce waste products, 'bad' side effects and 'goods' for which there is no market. In reality, these can have very important consequences for the satisfaction of people, the profitability of other businesses, and significant impacts on other organizations. The asbestos industry whilst producing a useful and profitable product also produced very harmful side effects from blue asbestos dust, which can cause asbestosis. Many workers and consumers in this industry have been severely affected by this 'by-product', which causes ill health and premature death. Indeed, as the scale of output increases, firms increase the levels of pollution in the form of waste, effluent or noxious gases.

On the other hand, a successful expansion of one firm may have beneficial 'knock-on' effects, positive goods for other firms. One firm may provide training which has desirable spin-offs not completely captured by the firm providing the training. Or, as one firm expands in a locality, it may attract others and lead to an improvement of communal facilities. We shall address these externality issues more fully in Chapter 13.

Technical efficiency

Whether operating in the long or short run the firm requires *technical efficiency*, that is the most output to be produced from any given input of resources, other things being equal. This exists where the firm is unable to produce a particular volume of output with a smaller number of resources. For profit maximization to occur, the firm must be operating at a technically efficient level although whilst many outputs are technically efficient there will only be one which gives profit maximization. To find this solution we need to know the relative input costs for whilst many outputs are technically efficient, different combinations of inputs give different total costs.

Costs and time

Economists use the everyday term, cost, in a precise way. The notion of *opportunity cost* is all important and should be at the heart of decision-making. As we have illustrated in earlier chapters, opportunity cost is the *best alternative foregone*. Given scarcity, a sacrifice has to be made when a firm uses inputs in the production process, the best possibility foregone represents that cost.

In analytical time, the identification of opportunity cost presents no problems. *REPs* have perfect knowledge of all input prices which represent opportunity costs. Economic actors know all costs with certainty. Alternatives can be ranked, effectively isolating the best alternative for any particular product. But the decision-maker operating in perspective time has limited information about present and future input prices. In perspective time opportunity cost may vary, depending on the assessment of the beholder. People may perceive and rank alternatives differently for this depends on judgement; moreover, that judgement can change with the mood of the decision-maker. Nevertheless, the prices of inputs given in our model, set in analytical time, are known and reflect opportunity cost.

Relevant and irrelevant costs in perspective time

It is important to distinguish between other notions of cost to isolate those which are *relevant* for decision-making in perspective time. Sometimes the decision-maker may omit *implicit costs*, for example, the cost of a self-owned resource. The firm might possess land but because this factor of production is already owned, the decision-maker might forget to make any allowance for it when deriving production costs, thus not acting as would a rational economic individual. Indeed, such implicit costs may often be overlooked in reality.

Costs have to be estimated for self-owned resources whether, for example, money capital, buildings or machines. Given that a firm owns land or buildings, using them in the production process is not free, even though there is no explicit cash payment associated with their use. An imputed value for these inputs is required. To decide whether or not to produce, for example, the resource would have to be 'costed' at the value of the best alternative foregone. In the case of land, there might be the possibility of renting the land to other firms. The highest rent possible would be used as a measure of cost for the land in question.

Historic costs and relevant costs

Historic costs represent payments for resources and goods made in the past. These are often mistakenly used by decision-makers in perspective time, when they value resources already owned by the firm. These often bear very little resemblance to opportunity cost. Imagine that a firm already has raw materials required for its current production process, materials bought many months before when competitive market prices were low. Since that time, assume that raw material prices have rocketed, but the firm uses the *original* prices to value the resources. In this case the firm is actually using a cost, which is better than ignoring the value of such scarce resources completely. However, historic cost does not reflect opportunity cost, it merely reflects the money value paid originally and tells us nothing about the value of the resources today. Historic costs are an irrelevancy for decision-making in perspective time.

The essential information for deriving costs in perspective time, is to know, as nearly as possible, what the best alternative use for the resource would be at the current time. If the resource could not be used for the production of any other good within the firm, then it is the disposable value of those resources which is the relevant measure; this represents the opportunity cost. If, on the other hand, the resource has no other use to the firm and the firm would have to pay to dispose of it, using the resource in production would be a positive benefit, a saving for the firm. It should be treated like a cash inflow, like a revenue; in short, a money benefit.

Explicit costs

Accountants and their clients sometimes ignore implicit costs because they do not involve actual cash payments in the current time period. They may consider only *explicit costs*. The accountant uses a narrower definition of costs and sometimes lists expenses or explicit costs. This underestimates costs by ignoring the value of self-owned resources and the result is an overstatement of profit, for all relevant costs are not included. Even if the accountant considers the costs of all self-owned resources but uses inappropriate historic costs to evaluate them, this will lead to an incorrect valuation. Costs may be over or under represented.

Whilst opportunity cost is readily identifiable in analytical time, this is often not the case in perspective time. It may take considerable time, effort and the expenditure of resources to acquire relevant cost information, involving significant search and transaction costs. Only in theory are the market prices of all inputs known and do they accurately represent opportunity cost. In perspective time accountants are constrained by institutionalized rules, the tax laws and laws governing corporate reporting. They often use actual and historic costs paid because law, custom and convention require it.

Short- and long-run costs and the link between production and cost theory

Economists in traditional mode spend a good deal of time and effort mapping out the behaviour of costs categorized in terms of the short and long run. To find out where profits are maximized or indeed whether it is worthwhile to produce at all, we must have essential cost information. We need to know the level of costs and how these are affected as output is varied. In analytical time the firm has the cost information in perfect detail, definitive data, albeit hypothetical.

Short-run costs

The *short run* is the period in which at least one factor is fixed, usually capital equipment. Short-run costs can be categorized as follows. The *fixed cost* represents the cost of buying or hiring such equipment; it does not vary with output and is unavoidable. Regardless of whether the firm produces or not, the fixed cost element has to be paid. The producer is committed to meeting this payment given a decision taken in the past. There is no escaping this cost whether production from the plant is large, small or zero.

Variable costs change with output. These costs reflect the payments required for the variable inputs like labour or raw materials. Additional labour hours are employed in order to expand output in the short run. Variable costs are avoidable for the firm is not committed to any particular level of employment in advance and can hire and fire at will. Whilst committed to fixed costs, variable costs are alterable. Note that the model assumes no fixed costs of employment.

There is an important link between production and cost theory. Economists use a variety of cost calculations but require production data – the input–output relationship from the production function to compute how much production at any particular level will cost. For example, we can calculate a firm's *short-run total variable cost* (TVC) of producing any given level of output, if we know the cost of each labour hour *and* how much that labour hour can produce. Production theory gives us the relationship between inputs and outputs. The production data from Table 8.1 is displayed again in Table 8.2. Now the firm can cost the variable inputs required to make each level of total output given the cost of the variable input. Assume that each labour hour costs the firm £10.

Total costs (TC) are the costs of all the inputs taken together for each possible level of output and are simply derived by adding the *total fixed cost* (TFC) of the fixed factor to the total variable costs. In Table 8.2 total fixed costs are given as £60 as shown when the output level is zero. To produce 5 units of production, for example, costs £60 plus 1 unit of labour at £10 per hour, a total of £70. On the other hand, 19 units of output costs £110, £60 for the fixed costs plus 5 units of labour at £10 per hour, a total variable cost of £50.

Table 8.2 Short-run cost schedules (all costs in £)

Labour	Output	MP	AP	TC	MC	AVC	ATC
0	0		—	60	—	—	—
1	5	⟩ 5	5	70	⟩ 2	2	14
2	12	⟩ 7	6	80	⟩ 1.43	1.66	6.66
3	16	⟩ 4	5.33	90	⟩ 2.50	1.88	5.63
4	18	⟩ 2	4.5	100	⟩ 5.0	2.22	5.55
5	19	⟩ 1	3.8	110	⟩ 10	2.63	5.79

$$TC = TFC + TVC \tag{8.5}$$

Average total costs (ATC), are simply total costs divided by quantity – the level of output.

$$ATC = TC/Q \tag{8.6}$$

Average variable costs (AVC) are total variable costs divided by quantity and

$$AVC = TVC/Q \tag{8.7}$$

average fixed costs (AFC) are total fixed costs divided by quantity. As we shall see,

$$AFC = TFC/Q \tag{8.8}$$

average costs are extensively used to illustrate a firm's cost situation. This information

$$ATC = AVC + AFC \tag{8.9}$$

is displayed in Table 8.2. For example, the average total cost of producing 5 units of output is simply £70 divided by 5 which gives an ATC of £12.

Marginal cost is the change in total cost which arises from a one unit increase in output and is a key element in economic analysis. Marginal cost is also an average

$$MC = \Delta TC/\Delta Q \tag{8.10}$$

from Table 8.2 – if one labour hour costs £10, each additional item made by the first labour hour, on average costs £2, that is, £10 divided by the number of items produced, 5. This information is crucial to the firm for it gives the extra cost of the initial increasing returns producing one additional output.

The average and marginal cost curves are displayed in Figure 8.3. This cost diagram is perhaps one of the most familiar in introductory economics textbooks, after supply and demand. In Table 8.2 we have used very simple figures. The smooth curves displayed in Figure 8.3 are derived from appropriate equations.

The average total and average variable cost curves display a 'U' shape because of the initial increasing returns and then the diminishing returns given by the production function. The marginal cost cuts both of these average relationships at their minimum point. The relationship between the average and marginal curve can be shown mathematically – but a simple way of explaining this relationship is to think in terms of essay grade averages. If your marginal essay grade is below your average, your average essay grade falls, pulled down by a relatively poor result. Your next essay is much better, the marginal grade has improved but still remains below your average – the average is still pulled down. The next essay gives a grade equivalent to your average – the average is constant – no change. However, when the final essay grade is above the average – the average is pulled up. Costs behaviour can be explained in the same way. Economists use the mathematical tool of calculus to explain these cost relationships with greater precision.

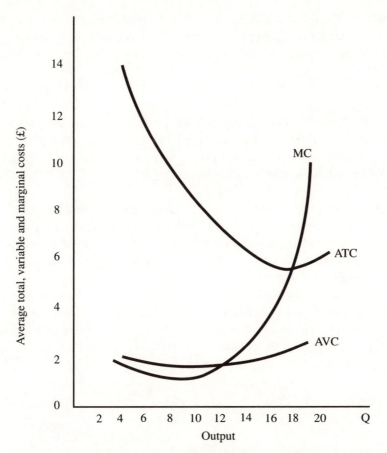

Figure 8.3 Average total costs, average variable costs and marginal cost curves. ATC falls steeply as the fixed costs are spread over larger outputs. ATC reaches a minimum at an output of 18 and then increases. AVC reaches a minimum at 12 and then increases. Marginal cost cuts the average curves at their minimum points. Whilst marginal cost is rising or falling, when MC is below the average cost, the average is pulled down. When MC is above the average, the average is rising

Long-run costs

In the long run, all factors are variable so there are no fixed costs. But how long-run costs behave depends on the nature of the returns to scale. Now there are other possibilities which will affect these cost curves not just the technical factors we have already examined.

Decreasing long-run costs As the firm expands output it may affect the costs of the inputs. It may be able to buy in bulk, thereby forcing input costs down. Marks and Spencer will have special relationships with its suppliers. Supermarkets bulk purchase and so may have favourable deals with their suppliers; and transport and distribution may be cheaper for large-scale outputs. The larger firm may have its own transport fleet or arrange favourable lower rates. Finance may be cheaper to acquire for the large-scale producer. When long-run average costs are falling, long-run marginal costs are below them.

Constant Long-Run Costs   After the benefits of scale economies, long-run costs curves may become horizontal. Output can simply be replicated without changing costs. The long-run marginal cost is equal to the long-run average cost. There are no cost reductions to be had as the firm expands.

Increasing long-run costs   Long-run average costs are upward sloping given diminishing returns to scale, as output is increased – average costs rise. This may occur as the firm grows too large, where management becomes over stretched or where the firm has grown so large that it has forced up input prices. Long-run marginal costs exceed long-run average costs. Figure 8.4 displays these concepts.

   We shall have more to say about how firms and their production and cost relationships have evolved in historical time in the next chapter. However, the U-shape of the traditional short-run cost curves reflects the assumption of eventually diminishing returns and displays the behaviour of costs in a one period, one product

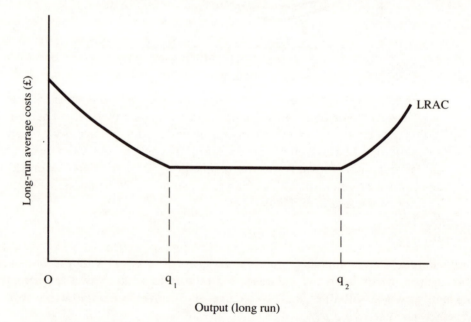

Figure 8.4   A long run average cost curve. Increasing returns to scale and falling costs to q_1. Constant returns to scale and constant costs provide a long flat bottom to the 'U' shape. Diminishing returns and increasing costs set in at outputs above q_2

firm. It tells us at what cost levels the firm can produce; moreover, at what costs it would be impossible to provide any particular level of output. The cost curves give a summary of a constraint which faces any firm, a constraint partly determined by the production function and partly determined by input prices. In analytical time we can vary outputs, juxtaposing different short- and long-run situations to see how costs behave. Long-run cost curves are drawn on the basis of different assumptions although they can be 'U' shaped, horizontal or 'L' shaped, depending on what we assume about the nature of scale economies.

However, costs are only half of the story. Now we must consider the firm's demand curve, what potential customers are willing and able to buy from the firm at any particular price. As we shall see, the price which a firm can charge depends partly on the type of market structure faced by the firm.

CLASSIFYING A FIRM BY MARKET STRUCTURE AND THE NATURE OF THE FIRM'S DEMAND

For traditional theory, the essential categorization of a firm is on the basis of market structure. Competition, or the lack of it, is the key element. This is an important determinant of the demand constraint faced by the firm in both the short and long run. The level of sales at any price is dependent, other things being equal, on the number of existing rivals in the market. Whether sales will remain at any particular level in the long run is in part dependent on whether or not other firms are willing and able to enter the market. But competition comes in different degrees. For example, there are situations where the firm has a monopoly, a sole seller with a market stage all to itself; or an oligopoly, sharing the limelight with a few other big market players.

Given a firm's cost relationships, we have to specify the market structure and the nature of the demand faced by a firm. Only then can we determine equilibrium price and output and how much economic profit, if any, will be made. Moreover, whether or not the firm producing in the short run, will produce in the long run.

In Chapter 5 we introduced the notion of different market structures. Here we shall concentrate initially on firms belonging to opposite ends of the spectrum, the 'ideal type' *perfectly competitive firm*, on the one hand and the *monopolistic firm* on the other. Individual perfectly competitive firms have no market strength, and are simply *price takers* in a sea of perfect competition, powerless to affect the prices they charge. The monopolist, the sole supplier of a good with no close substitutes operates in *imperfect competition* and can affect the price it charges. A monopoly may have power, although the firm is still circumscribed to some extent by the market.

Between these two theoretical extremes are other types of firms which face different degrees of competition and often, like the monopolist, have some considerable ability to affect the price they charge. The *oligopolistic firm*, is one of a *few sellers* in a market where there are barriers to entry and exit. Given the real and increasing worldwide economic significance of oligopolists, we shall consider them in greater detail later in this chapter.

Monopolistic competition stands towards the other end of the spectrum, far closer to the 'ideal type', although still imperfectly competitive. Whilst there are many competitive buyers and sellers and no barriers to entry or exit, their goods and services are not perfect substitutes. Each firm has some influence on the price it charges. Prices can be increased without the immediate defection of all the firm's customers to other sellers. Firms compete by differentiating their products or the services they provide, convincing the buyer that their product is worth 'that little bit extra'. But no firm is sufficiently large enough to stop new entrants in the long run. Its power is transient.

Yet in our introductory models, all firms, regardless of the market structure in which they operate, behave as rational economic individuals with perfect knowledge; rationality is unbounded. All firms aim to profit maximize. However, when we relax the assumption of perfect knowledge and move from the analytical time mode, the analysis becomes more complex.

At this point it is useful to note that despite the accolade of 'perfect', the perfectly competitive state is not in itself inherently ideal. All of these different firm and market models are theoretical abstractions to aid thought. But the loaded language, the nature of the terminology must be appreciated. Perfect competition as we shall see, is only better than imperfect competition in certain theoretical situations, even though imperfect competition somehow contrives to sound faulty or flawed, like a second in a sale. In perspective time all competition is imperfect. Whatever our theoretical results and the hypothetical processes we use to simplify, perfect competition is not a description of the reality that was, is now or will be. With this caveat in mind we turn to the firm as a market player in analytical time, where there are no search or transactions costs and no uncertainty.

I – THE PERFECT COMPETITOR

The perfectly competitive firm provides the conventional starting point, a yardstick to compare other market types. The model helps to shed light on a variety of questions about *output decisions*, a firm's ability to make economic profits in the short and long run; and when a firm will close down. Furthermore, it enables a measurement of efficiency. But no matter what the market form, we assume a single plant, single product firm, and ignore all factors of real time and place. The firm behaves as if it were a rational economic person aiming to maximize profits; and if it cannot do that because of the vagaries of the market, then its target is to minimize losses. The assumptions of the model are as follows:

a) The firm is one of a large number of firms operating in the industry. Each produces a very small fraction of the total industry supply, so that no firm can affect the product price by varying output.

b) All individual firms produce identical products. Goods have strict uniformity, there are no brand distinctions or idiosyncratic differences of any kind; so buyers regard the output of one firm as an exact substitute for that of any other firm in the market.

c) There are no barriers to joining or leaving an industry. No obstacles bar any firm from setting up in production. Barriers such as patent restrictions, licensing laws and the impediments of large investment requirements in plant and machinery, even hefty expenditures on research and development, do not exist. Ease of exit is assured, its capital can be readily used in other industries, movable in the long run.

d) Information is perfect.

The demand constraint

Initially, think of the short-run time period. As our firm is very small in relation to the market as a whole, with a tiny market share, it can sell all it produces at the going market price, but has *no* say in the price it charges. The short-run equilibrium price which faces the firm is given by the market, at the intersection of the market supply and demand curves. The individual producer has nothing unique or novel to sell, output is identical in every respect to that of any other seller. Buyers are perfectly happy to substitute the output of one firm with that of another, in the same market. Whether the product is wheat, carrots or a commodity like tin, it matters not to the purchaser from whom they buy. Homogeneity rules. The individual producer is powerless.

The firm's demand, set by the market price, is a horizontal line, d at p_3, as illustrated in Figure 8.5(a). The horizontal demand shows clearly that the firm can sell everything it produces at the going market price. If the firm tried to raise its price independently of market price, to go it alone and for example charge slightly more than p_3, then it would make no sales. All seeing REPs would make a beeline for the cheaper produce of other firms. The 'maverick' firm would earn absolutely nothing, deserted by its customers, who could do marginally better elsewhere. It would be highly damaging to raise price above that ruling in the market. All sales would be lost to competitor firms. Furthermore, it would be illogical to undercut the market price. The firm which charged a lower price would also be operating against its own best interest; it would earn less money. Profits would be reduced (or losses increased) for the total revenues would be smaller; it simply makes no sense to instigate cut price offers.

The horizontal demand curve shows that when the firm sells an additional unit of output, the price it can charge, the extra or *marginal revenue* earned from selling that unit, is always the same as the price or *average revenue*. The firm does not have to lower price in order to sell more. The quantity demanded is infinitely responsive to price, price elasticity is infinity. The firm can sell any amount at the going price, its output a mere drop in the ocean.

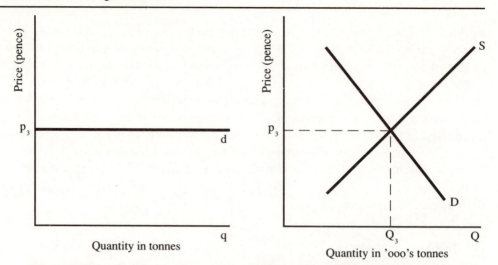

Figure 8.5(a) The firm's demand **8.5(b)** The market demand and supply
The perfectly competitive firm faces a price determined by the intersection
of the market demand and supply curves at P_3. The firm's demand curve is
perfectly elastic at the ruling market equilibrium price

The firm and its market are shown in Figure 8.5 (a and b). Note that the quantity axis is denoted here by Q, measured in '000s of tonnes in Figure 8.5 (panel b) for the market, whilst for the firm, the axis is denoted by q in tonnes. As both price axes are denoted in pence per kilogram, it is possible to read across from the market price to the price ruling for the firm. The firm cannot affect price in this market structure and merely selects what quantity to produce.

The perfectly competitive firm in short-run equilibrium

There are several questions which can now be asked:

What quantity should the firm produce in the short run?

To answer this question the firm can simply follow a 'golden rule or convention'. Optimal output for the firm will be found where *the marginal revenue equals marginal cost*, given that the marginal cost is rising. Provided that the extra revenue, the money earned from selling an additional unit of output, is larger than the extra cost of producing that unit, then it is worthwhile to produce that unit. When marginal revenue equals marginal cost (the marginal cost is rising) the firm is in equilibrium. The marginal revenue is constant and for outputs up to q_3, (the equilibrium), as shown in Figure 8.6 is in excess of marginal cost. The cash which the firm receives from selling each additional unit more than compensates for the extra costs of producing that unit (MR > MC). But the gap which represents the surplus of marginal revenue over marginal cost is closing as output and marginal costs

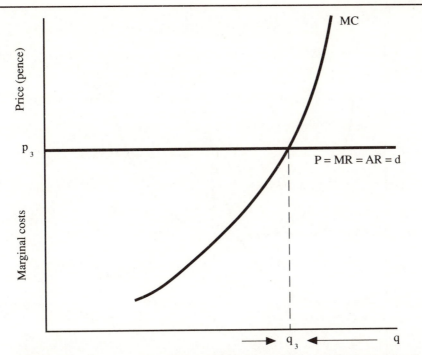

Figure 8.6 The firm equating marginal cost and marginal revenue for equilibrium. At outputs below the equilibrium q_3 the firm forgoes the surplus marginal revenue above marginal cost. MR > MC. At outputs above q_3 marginal costs are greater than marginal revenue. MC > MR. The loss on each unit produced would increase the larger the output above q_3. Only when MC = MR will equilibrium be achieved

increase (see Figure 8.6). Each unit of output sold brings in a surplus over and above the extra production costs incurred and so is worth producing. Remember that marginal costs arise from changes in total variable costs for it is only variable costs which vary with output.

The firm aiming to profit maximize in analytical time, must never produce beyond the equilibrium quantity where marginal revenues equal marginal costs. To do so would involve making goods which cost more at the margin to produce than the extra money revenue they bring in when sold. Should marginal cost *MC* not equal *MR* then a *disequilibrium* exists. Such positions could not possibly give profit maximization (or loss minimization). If marginal revenue exceeds marginal cost, at outputs to the left of the equilibrium point q_3 too little output is produced. If marginal cost exceeds marginal revenue at outputs to the right of the equilibrium q_3, too much output is produced. In either situation output would have to change in order to meet the firm's goal of profit maximization.

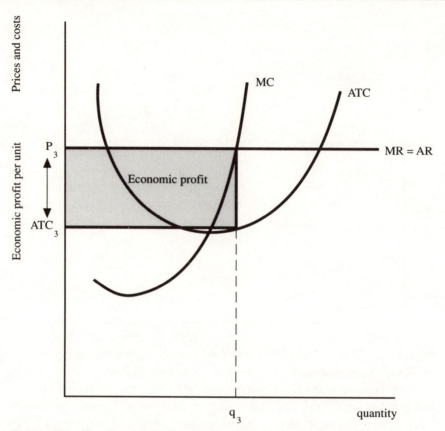

Figure 8.7 The firm making supernormal or economic profit, profit maximizing – more than covering opportunity costs

Does a short-run equilibrium necessarily give an economic profit?

The short answer to this is no. So far we have talked in terms of marginal costs and marginal revenue. However, to know whether or not the firm is making an *economic profit*, we have to show that total revenue more than covers total costs; an overall surplus has to be generated over and above opportunity costs. Economists call the positive difference between total revenues and total costs *supernormal profit* or *economic profit*. We may know that we have covered the variable costs of producing extra units of output, and that MC = MR, but that does not in itself guarantee an overall economic profit, for the firm has also incurred fixed costs which are unavoidable. There are different possibilities as follows:

The firm making a short-run economic profit   Given a price or average revenue of 100p per unit of output, the total revenue from selling any level of output is simply price × quantity. Provided that the ATC of producing output is smaller than the AR from selling that output, then on average the firm makes a profit on the items it sells.

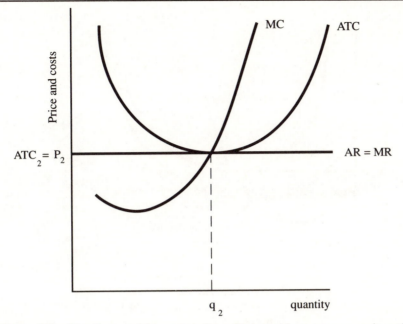

Figure 8.8 The firm making normal profit, breaking even covering all opportunity costs, where $P_2 = ATC_2$

In Figure 8.7, MR equals MC at q_3, assume this to be 100 units of output. The total revenue, if price at P_3 is 100p, is £100. The total cost can be derived from the diagram. Given that the total average cost is 75p at this output, then the total cost is £75, the product of ATC multiplied by quantity. The *profit per unit* is 25p. So, on average, each unit gives us a surplus over cost of 25p. On the diagram we see clearly that this is only an average outcome for the gap between average revenue and average total cost gets smaller as output expands.

The firm breaking even – making a normal profit When the average total cost, ATC, equals the average revenue, the firm simply covers the opportunity costs of producing output and makes no surplus over and above those costs. The firm breaks even, as shown in Figure 8.8 producing q_2. Here the average total cost equals the average revenue and, of course, marginal cost equals marginal revenue and total cost equals total revenue. The firm is producing at the optimum position for the plant, minimizing average total costs.

The firm making a loss in the short run We can show the firm making a loss if we draw the demand curve in a different position as shown in Figure 8.9. When average total costs (ATC) exceed the price (AR), but nevertheless price covers the average variable cost, (AVC), then on average a loss is made on each item sold. The loss minimizing output is given at q_1. The total loss is simply the loss per unit multiplied by quantity. Here then total cost, TC, is greater than total revenue, TR (TC > TR).

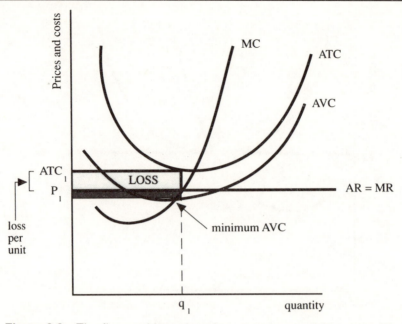

Figure 8.9 The firm making a loss but covering variable costs. The tinted area marks the surplus revenues over the variable costs. The shut down point is marked at the minimum of the AVC curve. Should the demand curve shift downwards – below the minimum – the firm closes immediately. The short-run supply curve is the MC curve above the minimum AVC

This will be an *untenable* situation in the long run when the firm has to replace its capital equipment and reconsider its position. In the short run, continuing to produce gives a money surplus (a quasi-rent) over and above the variable or avoidable costs, to offset against losses incurred and enables the firm to stay in production. Price is actually in excess of the variable costs as can be seen in Figure 8.9. The fixed costs have to be met whether output is produced or not; remember that fixed costs are unavoidable. So long as the price exceeds the variable costs then the firm is making a *contribution* towards fixed costs, although the firm cannot make an economic profit or even break even, by matching TR and TC. The firm minimizes its losses.

When will the firm close down in the short run?

The firm will shut down immediately if average variable costs cannot be covered. In Figure 8.9 this would occur if demand were reduced and price were to fall *below* the minimum point of the average variable cost such that AVC exceeded the average revenue. This shut-down avoids exacerbating losses, for continued production would involve, not merely the loss of the fixed cost which is *unavoidable*, but also the variable costs which could not be recouped by money earned from the sale of goods. Labour inputs, for example, would cost more than could be charged for the goods they produced. These variable costs are avoidable. The firm immediately ceases production, for price cannot cover average variable costs – to continue in production would be 'throwing good money after bad'.

The firm's short-run supply curve

If we take a range of different possible price levels we can show how output will vary. Imagine a series of horizontal demand functions at different price levels. By changing price, and so the marginal revenue and position of demand, you can plot a series of equilibrium points, where price equals marginal cost. You can trace out the relationship between price and the firm's equilibrium output which gives the *short-run* supply curve. As a necessary survival condition, in the short run, the firm must cover its average variable costs. But as demand, price and thus marginal revenue increase, some outputs which were previously loss makers, costing more to produce at the margin than their sale could earn in revenue, now make economic sense to produce. Higher prices cover the higher marginal costs of larger outputs – increased marginal revenues make additional units of production worthwhile. The firm's short-run supply curve is the short-run marginal cost curve, above the critical level of minimum short-run average variable cost. A smooth, upwardly sloping supply curve can be derived for the firm; the marginal cost curve above average variable costs gives the locus of all the possible equilibrium points.

The firm and market in long-run equilibrium

Can the firm maintain economic profits or suffer economic losses in the long run?

Again, the short answer is no. Given perfect competition, economic profits cannot last; they are only short-run phenomena. Moreover, profit maximizing firms cannot endure losses in the long run. In the long run, where all factors can vary, firms will take decisions about resource use which will eliminate both economic losses and profits. The guiding light of economic profit attracts other firms into the market and encourages existing firms to build bigger plants, once plant capacities can be changed over the long run. New entrants can do better in this market than elsewhere for profits are supernormal. Each new firm's marginal cost curve is a supply curve to add to the original market supply, helping existing firms to shift the overall market supply outwards to the right. Given that nothing happens to change the market demand curve, prices are competed downwards in the long run as the market supply increases. Yet as the price level falls, so every firm in the industry faces a lower demand curve. The process comes to rest when all firms break even, just making normal profits, for then the beacon is extinguished, until there is a change in the market affecting either price or costs.

On the other hand, given an initial situation where firms endure losses in the short

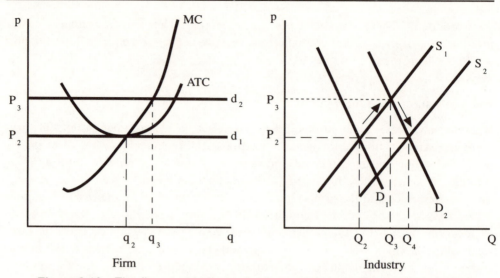

Figure 8.10   The firm and industry in short- and long-run equilibrium. At P_2 the industry and firm is in equilibrium. An increase in the industry demand from D, to D_2 causes the firm's p to rise to P_3. The firm makes supernormal profits. New entrants to the industry cause the supply curve to shift to the right in the long run. Given constant costs, equilibrium price moves back to P_2. Now there are more firms in the industry and output is Q_4

run, then they will leave the industry once there is a need to renew fixed capital, in the long run. Once plant and equipment come up for renewal and total cost exceeds total revenues then the firm must exit. The reduction of firms in the industry will cause a leftward shift in the market supply and this will continue until prices in the industry have risen, such that remaining firms can make a normal profit.

So firms will move into, or leave the market, until firms *break-even* making only a *normal profit*. At this point firms are compensated for nothing more or less than the opportunity costs of their production, where inputs earn only what they could in their best alternative. All costs used in the model reflect opportunity costs, not actual payments. Only when there are no supernormal profits or losses respectively, will entry or exit cease. Prices and output will be in equilibrium.

To illustrate, imagine an increase in market demand from D_1 to D_2. This causes a movement from the initial situation as shown in Figure 8.10 where all firms in the industry are breaking even in the short-run equilibrium position at P_2. Prices will *rise* as buyers compete for limited goods. The short-run response of firms already in the industry will be to expand output, using their existing fixed equipment more intensively, moving up their marginal cost curves. At the new higher prices outputs which would have previously been too expensive to produce, for the marginal costs exceeded the marginal revenues, are now worthwhile; they add to profit because the firm can sell such outputs for more than it costs to produce them. The firm continues to increase output until short-run marginal costs equal the new higher short-run marginal revenue. It now makes supernormal profit, for average revenue, AR, exceeds average total costs, ATC, and what amounts to the same thing, total revenue, TR, exceeds total costs TC. Other firms seeing this profit are attracted in the long run, for there are no entry barriers to keep them out and existing firms can expand. Prices fall as new entrants set up in production and old firms expand, for the industry supply curve has shifted to the right from S_1 to S_2. As output increases, profits are driven back to a normal zero level. When the firm 'costs' its inputs, opportunity costs are used; in equilibrium the firm is earning the return which could be achieved if it were to use the resources in the best alternative.

Given the assumption of constant returns to scale, and so the ability in the long run to increase output at a constant long-run average cost, price is driven back to its original level, in the long run, although now there is an increased output in the market at Q_4. The long-run supply price here is constant. Only when the firm is in short- and long-run equilibrium, making no supernormal profits will entry cease. Prices will cover the marginal cost of production and average total costs will be covered in both the short- and long-run – a perfect state of rest. Every firm will be producing at the minimum point of its short- and long-run ATC and given constant returns to scale, the long-run ATC is horizontal.

In long-run equilibrium *allocative efficiency* exists. This means that no change in resources can make anyone any better off without making someone else worse off. Each firm will produce at the minimum average total cost, equating price with the marginal cost of production. Each buyer pays a price which covers the additional cost of production of the last unit.

However, should there be extensive economies of scale to be reaped in the industry, small firms will not be able to acquire the benefits. It is likely that one or a few firms will grow and dominate to take advantage of these economies; perfect competition will be no more. Indeed, we now turn to the other end of the market spectrum.

II – THE MONOPOLIST

The monopolist is the sole seller of a good with no close substitutes and stands in sharp contrast to the 'ideal type' firm of perfect competition. The monopoly firm in polar position has the whole market cornered and wields market power, unlike the impotent perfect competitor. The Post Office, for example, has a monopoly over the delivery of letters up to the value of £1 – other carriers are prevented from charging less than that to deliver a letter. The Royal Mint has a monopoly on coin production for use in Britain and the Bank of England printing works has a monopoly on the production of British bank notes. The Wellcome corporation has a monopoly on the sale of ATZ, the AIDS drug. Cable TV companies have a monopoly on their service. The new privatized water companies have a monopoly on the supply of piped water. There are many examples.

However, no monopolist has unlimited power; no monopoly is perfect and complete. The buyer can usually find a substitute, no matter how imperfect. Indeed, a buyer may simply be unable to buy, given limited income. So, for example, the telephone offers an alternative to communication by letter, paper money offers an alternative to coinage. Cable TV has competitors from network and satellite television and, of course, broader forms of entertainment. Indeed, it is not always easy to define what constitutes a 'close' substitute and the market.

Sources of monopoly power

The sources of monopoly power are diverse but a key to maintaining a monopoly position is effective entry (and exit) barriers. For a monopoly to exist over time, given that there are economic profits to be made, potential rivals must be blocked. Patents or the ownership and control of vital resources, for example, protect the monopolist's position. They repel the competition which is attracted by economic profit. Often small markets which can only sustain one profitable supplier are the locus of monopoly power. A *natural monopoly* is said to exist where there is room for one firm only to survive, where two or more firms in the industry would face insufficient revenues in total to cover the costs of all firms. For example, a market may only have room to support one producer given the requirement of a very large-scale plant to reap economies of scale. Should the market be shared by a new entrant neither the new firm nor the incumbent could make a profit.

Barriers to entry and exit are a key assumption in the monopoly model and these can be considered in more detail under the following headings:

Technical and cost barriers

The economies of scale may be such that only one large firm can reap them and then undercut others by producing and selling at a lower cost. Often this may be the case in small markets or where very large, expensive capital is an essential requirement. British Oxygen was able to maintain a monopoly position on the provision of oxygen for hospitals because of the relatively high cost of cylinders for storing the oxygen. Moreover, an established firm may be able to produce at lower average cost than any potential new entrant, because as real time passes the firm has learned by experience, knows the most reliable and cheapest ways of producing, and has acquired specialized marketing or financing skills. In perspective time economic actors do not have all the requisite knowledge to compete. High entry costs for the would-be competitor can act as an effective deterrent. In the real world these may include heavy advertising and promotion costs to persuade consumers to change their allegiances and generate goodwill. People making economic decisions in perspective time may need persuading or reminding.

The firm may have the ownership of unique resources, or the benefit of unique managerial talent. A monopolist might own and/or control wholesalers and retailers, key selling points in the market which give power in the market.

Legal barriers

The legal protection of production techniques such as patents and copyrights shields the monopolist. A firm may have an exclusive franchise to serve a market. Professional licensing is used to protect human capital investment returns as in the case, for example, of solicitors and doctors. The imposition of taxes, tariffs – customs duties may be used to protect a monopoly power in home markets.

Threats and predatory behaviour as entry barriers

The incumbent firm in a market may threaten to undercut new entrants or to take them over should they attempt to enter into competition. A firm may engage in *predatory pricing* where it lowers the price it charges to undercut new entrants or to make entry unattractive.

However, many of these entry barriers can be thought of as *first mover advantages*. They arise from a firm being in the market first. In reality, the innovator gains the advantage; it matters at what point in historical time the firm actually starts up. Being first may enable the pre-emption of natural resources, give ownership of patents and the benefits of going through the development process, gaining experience. The entry barriers arise, in part, because of the lack of information and understanding in perspective time. We are compelled to move from analytical time where economic actors have perfect knowledge. The very existence of monopoly power may be due to a secret process and specialist knowledge unavailable to all. *Reverse engineering* is one of the ways in which those who were not first in the race challenge the monopoly power of others. These entry barriers can be breached or smashed. As we shall see in the discussion of investment in Chapter 11, should profits in an industry promise to be very large then others will have an inducement to challenge the monopolist. The possibility of large monopoly profit – a surplus over and above total costs – may make it worthwhile for would-be competitors to invest in the acquisition of knowledge in the *hope* of future gains. On the other hand, the fear of large exit costs, which would occur if the future brings adversity may also act as an effective entry deterrent. Yet whilst monopolists may depend on a mix of protective features, legal entry barriers given by the state and backed by the rule of law (and custom) can often prove to be the most enduring and effective barriers as time passes and firms evolve. The legal 'rules of the game' are often key.

For simplification, the basic monopoly model is set in analytical time, where a sole firm produces a single good with no close substitutes and has the protection of entry barriers in the long run.

The demand constraint

The demand curve facing the monopolist is the market demand for the product; the market and firm's demand are one and the same. This downward sloping market demand curve shows that if the monopolist wishes to sell more output, then price has to

Table 8.3   The demand schedule (average revenue) for a monopolist: total revenue and marginal revenue (all revenues measured in £)

Average Revenue Price (1)	Quantity (2)	Total Revenue (1) × (2)	Marginal Revenue
10	0	0	—
9	1	9	9
8	2	16	7
7	3	21	5
6	4	24	3
5	5	25	1
4	6	24	− 1
3	7	21	− 3
2	8	16	− 5
1	9	9	− 7
0	10	0	− 9

be reduced. However, when price is lowered to gain more sales, the monopolist has to reduce the price of *all* the goods offered for sale; in the market we assume that only one price rules. The monopolist cannot offer the same good to different buyers at different prices, even though some buyers would have been prepared to pay more.[1] The monopolist has to consider how a price reduction affects the total and marginal revenues earned by the firm. What does a price reduction mean for the monopolist's average, marginal and total revenue? We shall see that the average revenue, price and the marginal revenue are *not* equivalent as they were in the case of the perfectly competitive firm. Indeed, the total revenue of the firm does not inevitably increase as the firm sells more. Given the information in Table 8.3, we can see that as the monopolist lowers the price, buyers are willing and able to purchase more. The demand and marginal revenue information is plotted in Figure 8.11. The monopolist's total revenue earned from any level of sales can be found by multiplying the price by the quantity of sales.

Note from the table that, initially, total revenue increases although at a diminishing rate. For example, when the price is lowered from £9 to £8 the total revenue increases from £9 to £16. The extra or marginal revenue gained by making this price reduction is £7. Although the firm lost £1 on selling the first unit more cheaply, for it could have sold that for £9, the extra revenue made on the sale of the second unit, £8, more than offsets the loss of revenue from the first unit. The overall extra revenue is £7. As price is reduced note that the gains in marginal revenue fall. From Table 8.3, if we take a price of £6, for example, where 4 units are sold, then a reduction in price to £5 increases sales to 5 units. Marginal revenue is positive but smaller than the marginal revenue achieved by cutting the price from £7 to £6. When the price is cut from £6 to £5, the price on each of the first four units has to be lowered by £1. The gain in revenue by selling the additional unit is only £5. When this is offset against the loss in revenue via the price cut, it leaves only £1 as the overall gain in total revenue. Indeed, at a price of £5, total revenue reaches £25, the highest level possible given this demand curve. Any further price reductions have the effect of *reducing* the firm's income. At

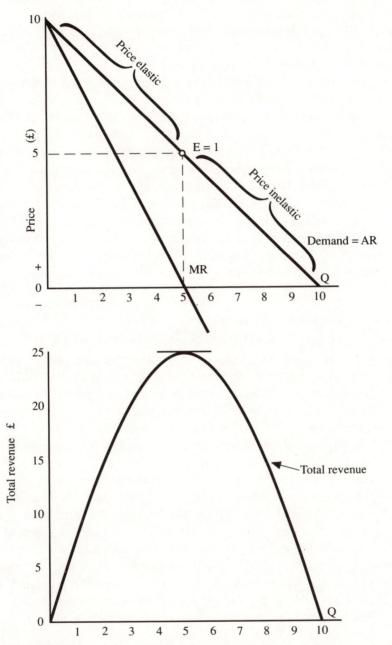

Figure 8.11(a) and (b)   The monopolist's demand, marginal revenue and total revenue. Reductions in price between £10 to £5 bring increases in total revenue. Quantity demanded is responsive to changes in price. Marginal revenue is positive. At £5 elasticity is unitary. TR is maximized. Reductions in price thereafter cause TR to fall. Marginal revenue is negative

the extreme, if the firm lowers its price from £2 to £1, it has to reduce the price on each of the 8 units which it could have sold at £2, giving a revenue loss of £8. This is to gain one more unit of sales at a price of £1. Not surprisingly, this would be a bad move. Total revenue overall would fall to a mere £9.

To reiterate, for the monopolist, the average revenue and marginal revenue are not equal. At 5 units of output, marginal revenue is zero and total revenue is at a maximum. We can explain this in terms of price elasticity. The responsiveness of demand to changes in price, the price elasticity of demand, varies all along the downward sloping demand curve. The demand is elastic above the price £5 and inelastic below. The seller facing a downward sloping demand curve can only increase total revenue by reducing price over the elastic range. Beyond the point at which the price elasticity of demand is equal to 1 at the price of £5, in this case, maximum total revenue will have been reached. Thereafter, total revenue will fall given a price cut, for the quantity demanded is relatively unresponsive to a change in price. This is in stark contrast with the perfectly competitive firm where there is no choice over the price and marginal revenue is equivalent to average revenue.[2] For the monopolist, marginal revenue is not equivalent to price. This has important implications.

Monopoly: equilibrium price and output

What price and what output should the monopolist set? The monopolist can affect price although the monopoly seller can only choose either the price *or* quantity. Whilst there are no close substitutes for the monopolist's product, the monopolist is still constrained by the market demand. There are always alternatives, no matter how imperfect, and limitations on income. When price is increased the monopolist will lose some sales. If the monopolist sets the price, then output is dictated by the market and vice versa. In more complex scenarios where we include advertising, the monopolist may be effective in shifting the demand curve at every price.

Monopolists in the basic model use the golden rule, equating the rising marginal cost with marginal revenue, to achieve a short-run equilibrium. The demand curve, AR, gives the price at which this output will be sold, for price and marginal revenue are not the same here. Moreover, at this profit maximizing output, price no longer equals the marginal cost, the opportunity cost of producing the final unit of output. Price exceeds marginal cost, the consumer of the last unit pays more than the opportunity cost of producing that unit. The equilibrium output is given at Q_m, the equilibrium price at P_m and total profit is given by the shaded area in Figure 8.12, where the area of total revenue is greater than that of total cost.

Do monopoly profits exist in the long run?

Given our assumptions, monopolists can make economic profits which continue in the long run. The profit beacon may blaze but providing that the barriers to entry hold, no other firms can enter to compete profits away. Indeed, even if firms could

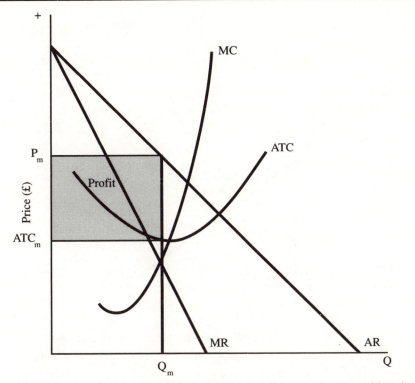

Figure 8.12   The monopolist's equilibrium price and output. Marginal revenue equals marginal cost but price is greater than marginal cost. P ≠ MC. The firm is not minimizing ATC. This situation can persist in the long run given entry barriers

possibly enter they may be deterred by the thought of heavy potential exit costs, say of specialist capital equipment which would have to be written off if the firm were unsuccessful in the industry. So, other things being equal, the monopolist's demand curve stays in exactly the same place. The monopolist is not forced to share its market demand with other firms, so in the long-run equilibrium position, other things being equal, monopoly profits remain untouched. If the monopolist innovates in the long run, other things being equal, monopoly profits will increase for costs will be pushed down. Other firms will not be able to erode such profits provided that entry barriers hold.

Do monopolists always make economic profits?

Not all monopolists make profits, some may merely break even as shown in Figure 8.13. In some circumstances the firm may be unable to cover total costs at any output level. Certain *natural monopolies* fall into this category. Although a firm may not be able to break even, and make losses, the firm may nevertheless produce a vital good

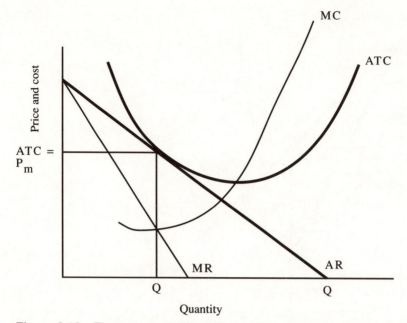

Figure 8.13   The monopolist breaking even, total cost equals total revenue,
ATC = P. Shift the demand curve to the left and losses will be made

or service required for the well-being of people, the profitability of other business firms and the health of non-profit organizations. Important natural monopolies may be nationalized and funded by the state or if they are in the private sector have their losses usually met from the public purse in such situations.

Allocative efficiency: comparison between perfect competition and monopoly

The static case against monopoly   This is that consumers would pay a higher price for a smaller quantity of goods than would have existed given perfect competition. Resources are misallocated. In a situation of perfect competition in the long-run equilibrium, in analytical time, no reallocation of resources could improve production. Prices would all equate to marginal costs and each firm would produce at the minimum level of average costs in the long run, as shown in Figure 8.10. But the monopolist, even if we were to assume the firm in a long-run, break-even situation, in contrast, would be producing in a situation of increasing returns and diminishing costs as shown in Figure 8.12. The monopolist even when earning no monopoly profits, breaking-even, restricts output and charges too much in relation to the perfectly competitive ideal.

But this picture is too simplified. There are *dynamic features* and practical considerations. Economies of scale may be such that only one firm can realistically operate in an industry. Indeed, the monopolist, as a result of economies of scale, would produce at lower cost by pushing long-run costs down. The monopolist could use monopoly profits for research and development to provide new processes and products. Moreover, the monopolist could cut out wasteful competition – unnecessary duplication.

Our view of the monopolist in the basic model is a static illustration set in analytical time. There may be dynamic gains to be had in a world of imperfect knowledge where the search for new processes and products is at the heart of creative enterprise. Monopoly profits may be used for research and development to aid that discovery process, to help create the new ideas for the future. Monopolists take decisions in perspective time where information is incomplete, where there are search and transactions costs. Moreover, in reality we cannot choose perfect competition; this is a hypothetical model. Although that is not to say that competition *per se* is not important in reality, but that blanket condemnations will not do.

III – THE OLIGOPOLIST

The oligopolist is one of a few sellers. Sainsburys, BMW, the Midland Bank are well known names. They can all be categorized as oligopolists. They compete in markets where they are conscious of their rivals, for their future sales and profits hinge, not only on their own actions, but on the policy decisions of competitors. Over historical time, in the UK, for example, manufacturing industry has been progressively dominated by a few large firms with an increasing concentration of economic power. Although the relative extent of concentration varies over time and place, in the UK, for example, aggregate levels of concentration in manufacturing have been continuously greater than those in the USA or in the EU (Moschandreas 1994). Highly concentrated industries in the UK include tobacco, sugar, cars, breakfast cereals, man-made fibres and cement. Production by the five largest firms in any one of these industries is in excess of 90 per cent.

Introducing theories of oligopoly

There are a variety of theories which aim to explain the behaviour of the oligopolist. But there is no overall general theory as in the case of perfect competition or monopoly. The world of the oligopolist is more complex. Interdependency is at the heart of the oligopolistic condition. The oligopolist is neither the monopolist in splendid market isolation considering the demand for whole market nor the impotent perfectly competitive firm with a known given demand.

The oligopolist's sales at any price are dependent on the behaviour of rivals, as well as the position of the overall market demand curve. The action of one firm can significantly affect the others. Indeed, the oligopolist in perspective time may face a good deal of risk and uncertainty – which arise to a considerable extent from the possible actions and reactions of rivals. The oligopolist may take strategic measures in an effort to reduce both risk and uncertainty.

Barriers to entry are an important feature for the oligopolist, just as for the monopolist. It may be that there is only sufficient room in a particular industry for, say four firms – five firms could not produce profitably and so would-be entrants, perceiving this, are deterred. The scale of advertising required to compete could be daunting or the fears of predatory pricing threats or other appropriate barriers discussed under monopoly, including particular rules of the game.

Some theories assume that the firms sell homogeneous products, like oil or petrol, others examine differentiated products such as washing powders or cars. The oligopolist can take a variety of different strategies to handle interdependency. At one extreme, assuming that all rivals will continue to behave in the same way; or by trying to 'outplay' their rivals, 'to steal a march' on them; and finally to co-operate by colluding, either formally or tacitly with their competitors. Models of oligopoly can be split according to whether the firm engages in co-operative behaviour or not. Here we discuss oligopoly models under two broad categories, *non-collusive and collusive*.

Non-collusive behaviour: the model of kinked demand

An oligopolist who does not collude with rivals may conjecture in perspective time that rivals will match price cuts but will not match price increases. The firm believes that at the current ruling price the demand curve is kinked (see Figure 8.14). There will be a very different responsiveness in quantity demanded to a price increase rather than a price reduction, because of the pricing reactions of other firms. In effect, the firm faces two demand curves – one for a price reduction and one for a price increase – these intersect at the ruling price. Indeed, this implies a marginal revenue function which has a gap because it is effectively gleaned from two different demand curves, one for a price increase and one for a price reduction. So the oligopolist is reluctant to change price for this will be disadvantageous. Changes in marginal costs can occur without a change in price – as would follow in the case of monopoly or perfect competition – for there is no longer an equality between marginal revenue and marginal cost as such.

The model may explain why prices are sticky but it does not tell us how prices are initially determined or what will happen should marginal costs shift up beyond the gap. Stability may arise from other reasons as we discussed in Chapter 5. Price changes can be expensive or could simply be the result of collusive behaviour where any change in price might 'rock the boat', calling into question previous agreements. Indeed, prices in oligopolistic industries may well be more variable; there is not always strong evidence to support sticky prices in oligopolistic situations.

Price wars

Although oligopolists may experience relatively stable prices for some periods and compete on the basis of, for example, the quality, packaging, advertising or after sales service of their product, there may be times when price cutting is used for raising or defending their own individual market share. There are many examples of

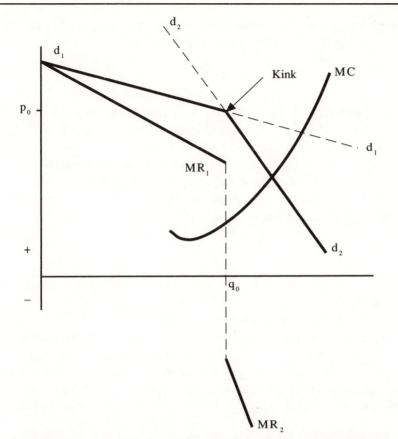

Figure 8.14   The oligopolist kinked demand curve. The oligopolist faces p_0. The belief is that a price *rise* will *not be matched*. The demand is highly elastic. A *reduction* in price *will be matched*. The demand is highly inelastic. The kink represents the intersection of two demand curves; only a portion of each is seen as relevant by the oligopolist. The marginal cost can move up or down in the gap between the two marginal revenue sections. There will be no price change

price wars. These range from supermarket chains slashing the price of baked beans and other grocery items, in an attempt to increase sales, as in the recent past, to fiercer price wars, for example, in home computers in the mid-1980s, when Commodore, Acorn, Sinclair and Amstrad were the main contenders in the market. The home-micro price war was a costly exercise for the producers.

Some prices of national newspapers have been reduced over recent months following the cut in cover price of *The Times* to 20p. Profits in the industry have suffered as a result. Sales of the *Daily Express*, for example, may critically depend, other things being equal, on the cover price of the *Daily Mail*, *The Times* and *The Daily Telegraph*. Sales and profit levels may be particularly uncertain during all out price wars. If the *Daily Mail* reduces its cover price – then many believe that the *Daily Express* would immediately follow suit, exacerbating the situation.

Collusive behaviour

Not surprisingly, oligopolists often co-operate. This may reduce the risk of a price war and bring calm in the face of fundamental uncertainty. However, whether collusion takes the form of the explicit use of cartels or implicit collaboration, both forms are often defined as illegal by the formal rules of the game. In the UK, for example, cartels are prohibited by acts of parliament. The Restrictive Trade Practices Act passed in 1956 made formal cartels illegal, legislation had evolved over time and European Union law now plays a role in competition law and policy.

Cartels

In *cartels*, oligopolists link up to act in concert, collaborating and sometimes acting as if they were a single monopolist. Indeed, any formal deal relating to pricing, output or other aspects of a transaction comes under the heading of a cartel. Nevertheless, despite the law, and inherent problems arising from differences in costs and efficiencies between firms and difficulties relating to the shareout of profit, cartels can and do flourish. And the oligopolist colludes. In Britain, oligopoly firms have operated in cartels in a variety of industries, in particular, in cement manufacture and ready made concrete.

Price leadership

Price leadership involves the oligopolist in *tacit collusion*. Given formal legal rules and their policing, oligopolists may adhere to their own informal rules and customs. These may represent a more effective strategy for co-operation. There are different forms of price leadership – for example:

a) The *Barometric Firm* is a price leader whose leadership role may be conferred by custom or the result of an accident in historical time. Or the firm may be regarded as a good 'barometer' of changing market conditions. When the barometric firm changes prices the other firms in the industry follow suit.
b) The *Dominant Firm* acts as a price leader. Given that the firm has a significant cost advantage, or because of its financial strength, one particular firm dominates the market, with a group of price-taking firms working in its shadow. The small firms follow the leader's price.

Intricate models set in analytical time, based on the assumption of a formal cartel or price leadership are used to show what happens to price and output given changes in demand and cost conditions. *Game theories* have been developed which help us to consider oligopolistic strategies. However, we shall not develop these models here.

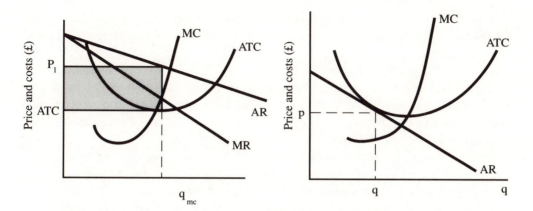

Figure 8.15   (a) The monopolistic competitive firm produces q_{mc} and makes a large supernormal profit in the short run. **(b)** In the long run new entrants compete the supernormal profits away. The monopolistic competitive firm just breaks even in long-run equilibrium, selling a smaller quantity at a lower price

But for the oligopolist acting in perspective time, nothing is certain for the future; there is always an element of *surprise*. Old understandings may change as events unfold. Yet the plethora of oligopoly theories actually underlines the diversity and complexity of reality. Each model gives insights into particular aspects of behaviour.

IV – THE MONOPOLISTIC COMPETITOR

Finally, there are market situations where competition is notable and where market power for firms is very limited. This situation is the closest to perfect competition. Here there are many competitive buyers and sellers and no barrier to entry or exit. However, their goods and services are not perfect substitutes, each firm can influence price. Prices can be increased without the immediate loss of all customers to other sellers, as shown in Figure 8.15(a). Firms compete by differentiating their products. Yet no firm is sufficiently large and powerful to stop new entrants coming into the market and the legal rules do not provide entry barriers.

In monopolistic competition firms, despite facing downward sloping demand curves, where they have some control over price, firms are unable to make profits above what is normal in the long run, for new entrants or enlarged existing rivals compete supernormal profits away. Where economic profits are perceived by outsiders, new entrants quickly move into the market as in the case of video hire shops and small garment manufacturers. The long-run equilibrium position is shown in Figure 8.15(b).

The traditional approach: time and method

The perfectly competitive 'ideal type', in analytical time, provides us with a neat symmetry, a balance of power, giving allocative efficiency, where no reallocation of resources could increase the quantity of output. Here there is a unique equilibrium; any divergence from that equilibrium is quickly resolved by the workings of the market. The balance is automatically restored in a soothing spontaneous movement of resources from one use to another. Prices are equal to marginal cost so consumers simply pay the opportunity cost of production in long-run equilibrium. Sellers respond to the dictates of buyers.

In analytical time, *at the other extreme*, the monopolist also finds a unique equilibrium, a neat solution, but where price no longer equals the marginal cost and monopoly profits can be earned at the expense of the consumer. The balance of power is upset and in static analysis monopoly becomes the villain of the piece.

Yet the model of perfect competition is an aid to thought, it is not part of the real business world which changes over time, where opportunities are to be created. The perfectly competitive firm simply churns out an output in response to the market signal of price, a signal jointly affected by the interaction of supply and demand. There is no place for entrepreneurial flair, imagination or creative effort of any kind on the part of the individual firm. Perfect competition does away with the need for an entrepreneur or any element of luck.

Moreover, whatever the market structure we have considered in basic traditional theory, the firm is a 'black box' whose internal workings, evolution and legal form are essentially of no concern. The process of exchange and production can be met without any search or transactions costs. These basic models are used to show how individual firms and the industry behave in certain carefully specified situations. The models can provide us with useful insights into aspects of pricing, output and efficiency, by abstracting from reality and isolating certain significant features. Perfect competition gives a neat theoretical yardstick, an 'ideal type', to enable the comparison of different and less competitive scenarios. But oligopoly emphasizes the difficulties for the economist working in analytical time, because oligopoly models often require the explicit handling of uncertainty. In perspective time firms may be quite unsure of their rivals' actions and reactions. Firms may simply not know how their competitors will behave in new situations in the present and future, even when they may have colluded in the past. There is no guarantee that the future will behave as the past. Where the action of any one large oligopolist alters the competitive environment for others, then the impact of a price cut or a product change may reverberate through real time, in price wars, promotional battles, the instigation of new products and the take-over and merger activity which we shall discuss in the following chapter. The assumption of perfect information takes us far from the reality of the oligopolistic firm where knowledge about competitors may be limited and uncertain. Here real-world complexity highlights the confines of unique solutions set in analytical time.

Once we consider people making decisions in perspective time, basic neo-classical theory has to be modified. In a world of limited information, change and uncertainty, we require other insights. Indeed, economists have to open up the black box of the firm, relax assumptions and address a range of issues previously ignored in introductory basic models.

THE BUSINESS FIRM I – SUMMARY

- Firms in perspective time are remarkably diverse. They can be categorized in a variety of ways, by size, legal status and degrees of competition. They may operate in different industries and markets. They have unique histories and uncertain future prospects.
- Introductory orthodox models in analytical time assume that the firm is a self-evident entity, a black box production unit with the sole aim of profit maximization. The firm produces a single product, in a single plant and is uni-national. This is a starting point.
- Production theory explains the relationship between inputs and outputs, the production constraints in different analytical time runs – planning horizons.
- Eventually diminishing returns are assumed in the short run. Increasing, constant and diminishing returns to scale can feature in the long run.
- There is a distinction between relevant and irrelevant costs for decision-making. Opportunity costs are key. Historic costs are irrelevant. Economists and accountants use different cost concepts. Accountants are constrained by particular legal 'rules of the game'.
- There are avoidable and unavoidable costs in the short run. All costs are avoidable in the long-run. There is a link between production and cost theory. Production theory gives average and marginal cost curves their particular shapes and relationships in the short run and helps to determine the nature of long-run cost curves and costs constraints.
- Firms face different market structures and thus different demand conditions. Perfect competition gives the 'ideal type'. The model excludes features of perspective time. Monopoly stands at the other end of the spectrum.
- The market sets price for perfectly competitive firms; the equilibrium output which will profit maximize (or loss minimize) is chosen by the firm. In the long run no firm can make supernormal profits for given freedom of entry these are competed away.
- The monopolist at the other extreme is the sole supplier who faces the market demand curve. Prices do not equate with marginal costs and the firm may make monopoly profits in the long run, given barriers to entry.
- Oligopolists compete in markets dominated by the few. Oligopolists, on the whole, are conscious of their rivals for their profits depend on the actions of competitors where other firms produce 'close' substitutes. Interdependence

is a key feature in perspective time. There are several models of oligopoly This is the most complex market form. But the growing importance of the oligopolist in many markets worldwide cannot be ignored.

- Monopolistic competitors can make supernormal profits in the short run, selling differentiated products. Given ease of entry, these profits are eroded in the long run.

THE BUSINESS FIRM I – QUESTIONS FOR DISCUSSION

1 Business firms in perspective time are highly diverse. Explain the key similarities and differences between the following:

   a) a firm of local plumbers (see yellow pages);
   b) a small textile or garment manufacturer;
   c) Tesco or Sainsburys;
   d) Nestlé;
   e) British Petroleum;
   f) General Motors.

2 Why is it argued that the firm in orthodox introductory theory is a black box set in analytical time?

3 Explain the 'Law of diminishing returns'. For what reasons were Malthus' dismal predictions unfulfilled in England? Does the law of diminishing returns have any real world relevance? Distinguish between different points in historical time and place.

4 Distinguish between avoidable and unavoidable costs. Explain which costs are relevant for economic decision-making.

5 Why are the traditional cost curves of orthodox theory 'U' shaped?

6 Despite a large shift in demand over time, the price of personal computers has fallen in real terms. How would you explain that?

7 Explain whether or not a firm in perfect competition would ever:

   a) advertise;
   b) make cut-price offers;
   c) earn supernormal profits;
   d) continue to produce even though making a loss?

8 'Profits at the Royal Mail, the letters operation of the Post Office are on course to rise by a remarkable 25 per cent in 1991–2, despite the worst recession for 60 years.'

(Smith 1992)

   a) How can the theory of monopoly be used to explain this?
   b) What factors would determine the growth of profit in future years?

9 'A monopolist charges higher prices and produces smaller quantities than an industry in perfect competition.' Explain and discuss.

10 Paul has opened a small restaurant. He has signed a lease for one year on the premises and paid rent in advance. Half way through the first year of trading he is making a loss.

   a) Should Paul close the restaurant immediately or keep going until the year end? State what further information you would require.
   b) Would your answer change if Paul tells you that other restaurants in the area are planning to close? Make your assumptions clear.

11 Why is there no single theory for explaining the behaviour of an oligopolist?

12 'The oligopolist faces fundamental uncertainty; much oligopolistic behaviour can be interpreted as a means to reduce that.' Discuss.

9

The business firm II

INTRODUCTION

This chapter focuses on the firm-for-profit as an organization, a complex of people, an entity persisting and evolving over time; no simple black box. To develop our understanding of the firm, we must move from the analytical time mode of basic neo-classical theory, to explore economic behaviour in perspective time. Here the legal structure and internal workings of the firm are important.

As we have seen in the previous chapter, in the late twentieth century, there are in practice an enormous variety of actual business enterprises – firms selling in markets for profit. Looking backwards through historical time, people have often worked together in relatively complex organizational structures. Yet artisans and sole traders, specialist individual producers aiming for maximum profit in the market, often take the pivotal position in economic writing. The firm of the basic neo-classical world, which makes decisions as if it were a single individual, has to be supplemented by a study of more life-like and representative organizational structures, in particular, the modern corporation. Here bureaucratic arrangements are designed to co-ordinate resources and transform them into outputs for market sale. No one individual could cope with the real-world complexity of large-scale production. Moreover, corporate enterprises often have complex links with their major suppliers, largest customers and government organizations. These are a far cry from the anonymous market relationships of perfect competition or the dealings of a black box single product monopoly firm.

Here we shall no longer regard the firm as a mere production function in the neo-classical analytical time mould. Economists have other insights to give. There are a series of significant questions about the nature of the firm-for-profit which are either not addressed or given scant treatment by our orthodox approach. What is the business firm? How is it different from other organizations in general and markets in particular? What determines a firm's existence? Why do firms take different legal and internal organizational forms – what are their economic causes and implications? What determines the perimeter, the boundary between the firm and market and how does that evolve over time? What are the relationships between firms and other organizations in a complex modern economy, where firms are highly diverse and some are global players?

When we consider the problems facing real economic actors, operating in perspective time, such questions become important. When some giant multinational corporations, like General Motors, have a value added per year greater than the GNP of some small countries, then the allocation of resources by the firm takes on a new dimension. Moreover, the strategic and organizational choices made by corporate managers have important consequences for economic performance, whatever the size of the economy (Chandler 1990). Their production, pricing, investment and employment decisions can affect us all. Once the firms' owners/decision-makers are embedded in perspective time and, in particular, where the ownership and control are separate in the distinctive corporate ownership form, the internal organization of a firm and its evolving size and shape are of concern. By recognizing the significance of information problems, risk and uncertainty, economists can give fresh insights into a range of current issues, including corporate restructuring, mergers and internal organizational change.

Alternative approaches to the firm put the value of orthodox theory in context. Traditional neo-classical models provide a very valuable, but partial view. Different outlooks provide new insights. Conflicting policy implications may well follow on from a wider picture of the firm-for-profit. What makes for inefficiency or appears irrational in the traditional analytical time mode, like customs, routines and habits may not be so, given a recognition of the problems which people face in perspective time. These additional theoretical perspectives can be used to examine non-profit organizations and investment decision-making in real-world contexts.

THE NATURE OF THE FIRM REVISITED

What is a firm? There are different perspectives. The traditional view is straightforward: an entity which takes in inputs, transforms them into outputs with the sole aim of profit maximization. In Chapter 8, the firm is treated as if it were a single individual, buying inputs and selling outputs in markets. In contrast here, we shall emphasize that the firm is a complex of human interaction, a purposeful organization, which exists and evolves over historical time, usually set up specifically to achieve economic gains, by seeking profits. This economic objective provides a distinguishing feature.

Of course, whilst economic considerations are dominant they may be supplemented by other ambitions. Sometimes it is helpful to treat the firm as if it were a purposeful entity maximizing profits, at other times we may see no single goal but a compromise of different goals. Coalitions of groups within the firm, with different ends in mind can hold sway. Economists have long recognized that the straightforward goal of profit maximization can be modified. Baumol (1959) argued that firms aimed to maximize sales revenue, not profit, but this was subject to the attainment of a minimum profit level to keep shareholders happy. Managers may be interested in their own prestige, salaries and security. The number of employees under the command of a manager brings prestige: the greater the number, the greater the status (Williamson 1964). Corporate growth may be seen as the best way to achieve these ends (Marris 1964).

Perhaps firms do not seek to maximize anything – but simply to achieve satisfactory results over several goals – to *satisfice*. Profit whilst still important is not the sole end. Institutional approaches acknowledge that people operate in perspective time, where global calculations like the maximization of profit or indeed, sales revenue, are normally impossible because of the lack and/or overload of information and the perplexity faced by those making decisions in an intricate and uncertain environment.

Questions about how business firms evolve and behave are of key interest. The firm's activities can materially affect a wide range of '*stakeholders*', including employees, customers, suppliers, lenders, as well as shareholders and management. Those who live close to a firm or people in the wider society, may be affected by business activities. 'A socially responsible firm considers that it has a moral obligation to its stakeholders' (Ferguson, Ferguson and Rothschild 1993: 8). However, when there are clashes of interest amongst stakeholders, people who have genuine interests in the firm's activities, management and shareholders' interests may be paramount. In the neo-classical view the argument goes that shareholders' interests must come first in order to ensure a supply of funds in the market for investment. Moreover, some argue that in practical terms, to look after what can be conflicting interests of the different groups of stakeholders would be an impossible task, so shareholders and management must come first.

In some circumstances governments constrain the activities of firms in order to protect different groups and the wider society. Legislative examples include laws relating to fly dumping, labour laws concerning employment and fair trading requirements.

A preview: small firms and corporate enterprise – internal and external relationships

Adam Smith observed the pin factory, an organization involving groups of individuals, who worked together, co-operating in the production process. These were not isolated, individual, self-employed, freelance workers, who brought together resources and met to sell their production in the market-place. People interacted with each other *within* the firm. They did not search for others, determine prices, negotiate market transactions. No money changed hands as workers passed semi-finished items to the next person in the production chain. The owner of the factory – the boss – co-ordinated and allocated resources within the firm.

The pin factory was a very small-scale enterprise by modern corporate standards with only ten employees, but it is similar to many modern small business counterparts, in terms of ownership rights and organization. Jack's one man business, producing contact lenses in a small factory, with a handful of workers, operates in a different historical time, but he owns and controls his business in much the same way. There is *direct supervision*. He schedules work – co-ordinates, allocates and makes plans. He decides what and how to produce, and is entitled to the profits, large or small. However, should the firm incur losses, the liability is his.

However, whether we think in terms of the eighteenth-century factory or contemporary small firms, these are materially different from both medium and large sized corporate establishments. Many of the modern giant firms of today evolved through the later part of the nineteenth and in the twentieth centuries. The firm's ownership lies with the shareholders. Unlike the sole trader they do not control and organize day-to-day matters or indeed usually participate in the *strategic management*, where decisions about the scope, long-term goals and overall direction of the organization are made. Professional managers take these strategic decisions and ensure that appropriate actions are taken to carry out these intentions. They do so without the help of the absentee owners, the shareholders. There is a division of labour between those who supply the equity funds – the firms' owners, and those who manage. The factors of production and financial resources are co-ordinated by a complex *managerial hierarchy*. There are large, complex production, marketing and purchasing networks, with recruitment and organization of managers to supervise and co-ordinate functional activities (Chandler 1990). Business operations involve a combined series of interrelated actions over time. This is not only for well practised normal production but also research and development, the distribution of output, advertising, marketing in a complex and evolving world. Decisions on such matters have to be taken both on a day-to-day basis and for strategic considerations.

The firm so pictured presents far more intricate problems than those faced by isolated individuals working on their own account, who simply sell their output in the market or, for that matter, the small business organization, where one boss organizes others. Although firms have common problems, how to turn inputs into outputs for economic gain, all firms do not solve their problems in the same way, they co-ordinate and manage activities by different means.

The firm-for-profit may have close external links with other organizations, symbiotic relationships, for example, joint ventures with other firms, Tesco and Marks and Spencers out of town store sitings and like the close arrangements between Rover and Honda on product design and working practices.[1] The firm is not a household nor a charity, nor a non-profit government organization, although it may have both market and non-market relationships with these organizations. Whilst households and charities bring together and co-ordinate resources, they have very different broad concerns, certainly not the making of profit, as a key feature. However, the *family firm* can illustrate an important overlap between the world of the family, households and business. Many nineteenth- and twentieth-century businesses started as family concerns, some evolving into multinational enterprises (Chandler 1990).

The famous chocolate manufacturer, Cadburys, now a multinational company, with an international business and global sales, a merged enterprise known as Cadbury Schweppes, had its origins as a tea and coffee warehouse, set up in Birmingham in 1824. A sideline in 'Coco Nibs', a breakfast drink prepared by the founder, John Cadbury, was the start of this family chocolate producer (Stranz 1973: 13). The multinational enterprise of today selling its well known branded confectionary and soft drinks, still has a Cadbury as Group Chief Executive although the Cadbury family are no longer prominent in the management of the company. However, firms evolve differently. In the USA, well before the Second World War, founders and their families in many important enterprises, like Standard Oil, had largely been replaced in positions of control by salaried managers. This was a different scene from that unfolding in Britain, where founders and their families often continued to rule the management of business with a relative lack of professional managerial talent, as, for example, in Cadbury's (Chandler 1990). Even when the Cadbury Brothers became a public company in 1912, the policy was to retain family control. It was very much later that outside professional managers came to prominence. In Japan in the late twentieth century, the enormous family firm is still important.

Many current family businesses are still run from home, although the large majority of family firms remains small. An exception, the Redrow company, a building firm begun in the 1970s by Steve Morgan with a loan of £5,000 from his father and run from a spare bedroom, gained a stock market listing in 1994 (*Guardian* March 1994).

Firms may have complex links both with other for-profit-enterprises and public sector non-profit organizations. At times the linkage is via the market mechanism but in some situations it is direct through non-market relationships, as we shall discuss in Chapter 10.

The distinction between the firm and market: features of firms

The distinction between the firm and the market, as drawn by Coase (1937), helps to clarify the nature of the firm and separate the firm from the market. He recognized that firms and markets represent *different* ways of co-ordinating resources for production. The firm has an *internal organization* which co-ordinates resources based on an *authority relationship*. This *governance structure* makes conscious plans and exists to co-ordinate and allocate resources, through formal directions, administrative and bureaucratic methods. This contrasts starkly with the competitive market process where the interplay of supply and demand allocates resources through the market price mechanism, where markets allocate automatically with no overseer or controller, as we discussed in Chapter 5.

Firms, on the other hand, involve a *planning process* where people make non-price judgements. Resources are organized through different forms of deliberate plans, they are not co-ordinated and allocated by the price mechanism even though implicit costs and benefits of different actions may be taken into consideration. (There may be the use of a 'partial price system' within some firms, transfer pricing in the multinational enterprise for example.)

Within firms, prices are not the guiding light for co-ordinating and allocating resources, as in the perfectly competitive market. There have to be overseers and controllers; allocation does not work automatically. Managers have to make strategic as well as day-to-day operational decisions. Non-price mechanisms exist: planning, command, formal instruction and mutual adjustments mechanisms. Resources within firms are allocated by the studied decisions of planners, using an *internal non-price allocative process*.

Williamson refers to the *internal labour* and *financial markets* which function within large hierarchical firms. Here labour and financial resources are allocated via administrative procedures, not by a market price mechanism. Markets are for exchange, they do not produce output. Internal labour markets are simply administrative allocation mechanisms where labour resources are co-ordinated by non-price procedures within the organization. Whilst they are *linked to* and affected by external markets, internal markets work with administrative procedures, rules and customs, not price. On the whole employees in the firm do not compete for jobs internally by offering their services at lower wage rates. Moreover, funds are allocated in perspective time, often in complex organizational structures which necessitate financial controls and the allocation of scarce cash between corporate divisions and departments (see Chapter 11).

Firms and transactions costs

Many economists including Williamson (1975) and Coase (1937), argue that firms bring a saving in transactions costs. In Chapter 3 we explained how these costs, including the costs of negotiating, drawing up, monitoring and enforcing market contracts, are safely ignored in analytical time. But people operate in perspective time. Williamson moves from the basic orthodox model and highlights the notions of complexity, uncertainty and what he refers to as 'information impactedness' – which means that in a transaction, one individual or group has less information than those on the other side of the deal. Williamson puts his faith in markets – but argues that these may fail when transactions involve great complexity or uncertainty and when there are small numbers of buyers and sellers who are able to transact. Firms involve asset specificity and this affects transactions costs. If the firm contracts with an outsider using the market there are transactions costs. Given complex products and production processes and bounded rationality, the firm cannot be sure that the outsider can deliver the goods of the right quality and on time. People may behave opportunistically – that is, have a lack of sincerity or integrity, which 'includes self-seeking and guile' Williamson (1975). They say that they can deliver a component for production – like a vehicle component, for example, an electronic ignition system – but know that they cannot meet the terms of the contract. In such circumstances if the component manufacturer were unable to deliver on time, the car assembler could not go elsewhere at short notice for such a highly specific component. The assembler would have to wait for component delivery. Uncertainty, bounded rationality and the fear that they may be 'taken for a ride', might induce the firm to make the component themselves or to take-over a component company. As we shall see, firms reduce transactions costs by reducing the number of contracts.

However, there are also costs of co-ordinating resources, motivating and monitoring people *within* the firm. This applies whatever the organizational form, simple or complex. For example, information has to be acquired and interpreted in order to formulate and implement plans on time. We shall see how different organizational structures can affect costs and this affects the perimeter of the firm – whether, for example, it will decide to make takeovers or 'contract out'. The view is that firms can minimize transaction costs overall, even though the planning mechanism of the firm itself imposes costs.

The firm: a connected group of contracts, treatises and understandings

The firm can be viewed as a nexus of contracts, treatises and understandings (Alchian and Demsetz 1972) which enables economic actors to co-operate with each other through a system of *bilateral contracts* – whether explicit or implicit contracts. This is seen as an essential feature where the firm is a set of contracts each with a *central authority*. The number of contracts and hence the related contractual costs are reduced. The transactions costs connected with exchange in the market are reduced. Each person comes to an agreement with a *single contractual agent*, the firm. A buyer wanting a particular product, dealing with a firm, rather than a host of individual contractors, saves on transactions costs. Like money, the firm saves people from entering into multilateral contracts with many different individuals (see Chapter 4). We can illustrate this idea by using the example of an individual who wants to go for a holiday in the Far East. Consider two alternatives:

a) The buyer can organize his or her own holiday, seeking relevant information, locating and selecting hotels and by employing various contractors in the market, negotiating and making a contract with a hotel, booking and synchronizing airline flights, arranging travel to and from the airports, arranging insurance, finding information on visa requirements, travel documents and immunization requirements; or

b) The buyer makes a single contract with a package tour operator, specializing in Far Eastern locations, who would supply a package holiday.

Which of these alternatives is the best, other things being equal? Think of the problems which will arise by taking option a. For those with no local knowledge, who do not speak the language, there might be a considerable amount of time and effort needed to contact several hotels, before finding appropriate accommodation. There would be difficulties in acquiring information and assessing the quality of hotels, from the other side of the world. Indeed, the more complex the holiday requirements, a holiday with different locations, for example, the greater the problems of negotiating contracts, organizing and synchronizing. The buyer would have to spend a good deal of time, effort and money in planning, making and co-ordinating individual contracts.

Now add to these difficulties the further problem of opportunism, which may characterize behaviour. For example, hoteliers may act with opportunism, be out for themselves and not looking after the traveller's best interests, particularly as they do not expect to do a repeat deal with the customer. Individual couriers hired by the holiday-maker might shirk, and take the inexperienced for a ride. How much simpler and safer to make an agreement with a single contractual agent, the tour operator who would co-ordinate, organize, monitor and plan the holiday package.

The professional package tour operator organizes such holidays every day of the week. The firm has specialist local knowledge, can negotiate cheaper deals, knows what to do if things go wrong. In short, the firm saves time, effort and money for the buyer. It provides a service which enables many people to travel to the Far East, who might otherwise find that impossible to organize. Figure 9.1 shows how contracts are simplified. The buyer makes one contract with the tour company.

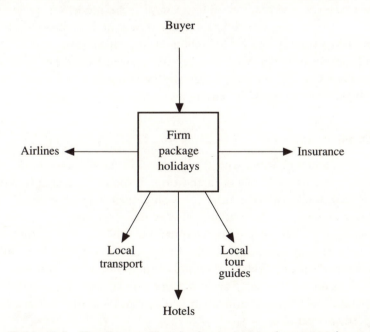

Figure 9.1 The firm as the single contractual agent reduces the number and cost of individual contracts; reduces transaction costs

For the individual the firm can make a custom-made package or a standard package holiday. The firm is the central contractor and makes bookings for large numbers of people, thereby cutting down on the number and cost of individual contracts. The firm can take advantage of economies of scale and scope, so cutting costs. Economies of scope exist where common resources can be used to produce several different outputs. The package holiday firm could diversify into hotels, in some cases airlines, and indeed other leisure activities using existing marketing and administration channels. A cost advantage accrues to a large firm producing a range of services which use related skills, talents and workings.

Buying a package holiday is certainly not the same as buying the ubiquitous vegetable in the perfectly competitive market in analytical time. The once-in-a-lifetime event, even once a year, sees the buyer relatively uninformed. With a small likelihood of repeat purchases, the acquisition of specific knowledge would give a limited return. Moreover, the future may unfold with shocks. In perspective time the firm with its experience is better able to cope with a disaster. The firm has specific mechanisms and networks for dealing with a crisis. Holiday makers are buying convenience and peace of mind, often at a much lower price than could be arranged by their own efforts.

This is a straightforward example in which it is feasible for the individual to buy components of the package in the market, if the expected benefits of a self-made tour look large. However, clearly, there are complex products and services which could not be put together by individual market contracts, where highly specialized equipment and human resources are required. For example, the modern sophisticated camera could not be built by the individual, buying inputs and components in the market-place. Open heart surgery could not be bought in a kit form or readily made-up from individual market dealings. Such surgery is provided by a highly specialist team which it would be extremely difficult indeed for the individual 'consumer' to put together given the highly specialized skills, equipment and knowledge required.

Market-like and firm-like contracts

An employee has *one* bilateral contract with the firm. Individual workers do not have to negotiate formal contracts with others in the organization. They simply have a formal employment contract with the firm to supply their labour services. This contract is a *'firm-like' contract* as opposed to a *'market-like' contract*.

Markets approaching the ideal type involve the interaction of relatively autonomous traders, typically without any long-term commitment towards each other. In the stock or international currency markets, it does not matter with whom you deal. One buyer or seller is as good as another, for prices are known and both shares and currency have common identifiable characteristics. The market contract is short-run and exchange is speedily organized.

The firm-like or non-market contract form is typically longer term, economizing, for example, on contractual costs, and binds the parties together. It ensures continuity.

That makes life easier and facilitates the division of labour, specialization and co-operation. Such long-term contracts are important where repeat dealings matter. A contract for the employee with the firm signifies the agreement to be organized, told what to do, within limits. It has sufficient flexibility to allow for change. Employees can be organized to do different jobs as the need arises; contracts do not have to be renegotiated with small changes. In perspective time the firm needs *flexibility* and non-market approaches. Market-like short-term contracts for employees which have to be regularly renegotiated may mar co-operation and the development of trust and the long-term effective acquisition of skills and expertise. There are pros and cons to the short-term contractual mode – it may, for example, reduce shirking and give flexibility in the face of demand changes. Nevertheless, short-term contracts may not foster loyalty or concern for a long-term view.

In a small business, the single proprietor might be the central contractual agent. But in more complex cases, in the large corporation, separate agreements have to be made, for example, between the firm and its employees, the firm and managers and with shareholders, bondholders and landowners. All these groups have contracts with the firm. Note that the firm is more than a series of formal contracts and agreements for those who work at the firm or who own it. Firms have contracts (like treaties between nation states) with outsiders like banks and landowners.

The firm is a complex tangle of understandings. Given lack of knowledge and uncertainty, people cannot write formal contracts covering every possible set of future events. Written formal contracts have to be supplemented by understandings, unwritten agreements. Different organizations will have different formal and informal 'rules of the game'. These are unavoidable in any real situation and can take time to evolve.

Firms: parcels of generally non-tradable, firm specific assets and human resource teams

The firm develops specific assets, specific knowledge, equipment and capabilities, including technical, managerial and organizational attributes. These are not readily tradeable in the external market. They may have little use to an outsider; their value is hidden, implicit, for example, company specific skills and knowledge (see Chapter 14 for further discussion). The firm may be worth very much less when split into its individual components. Customized machinery for particular processes may be of little use elsewhere. Specific team workers and real assets cannot be readily divided and sold or purchased within the market.

Indeed, *team production* is a key feature of the firm (Alchian and Demsetz 1972). This does not mean a series of identifiable stages through which resources are step-by-step transformed into a final product, like pin production, but a situation where there is co-operation by a team of people all working *at the same time* where the individual team member's effort cannot be readily observed. The team produces an overall result which cannot be attributed to any one team member. And team workers may affect the efforts of others in the team. Each person in the team may perform a range of jobs but will be adaptable and multi-skilled to cope with complex, and often specialized and changing tasks. These are not the simple routine procedures where workers require little expertise and training.

The firm as a social system: an institution

Formal and informal rules guide economic actors (North 1990). The firm provides an institutional environment that induces viable commitments and entails a complex institutional framework of formal rules: informal constraints and enforcement which collectively make possible low-cost transacting. The more complex the exchange through time and space the more intricate and costly are the institutions required to induce co-operative ends. The modern corporation producing a wide variety of sophisticated products and involved in complex marketing, research and development, and investment activities, has to use intricate forms of co-ordination, monitoring and incentive systems.

The firm is a durable *social system* structured internally with sufficient diversity to cope with the intricacy and variety of its environment so people do not have to be continuously renegotiating their agreements in line with small changes (Hodgson 1988). The firm can cope with different situations and change whether in the external market, through competition or technological change or the general vagaries of the macroeconomic turbulence of recession or boom. In fact, the firm is a complex system; a 'safe space', a shelter from the external environment.

Employed people work together in firms for much of their daily life. The firm can produce long-term relationships where loyalty and gift giving are important (Akerlof 1982). Those who spend a large part of their time working together may do more than their contracted work in an environment which encourages trust and co-operation. People may work hard to ensure the success of their work mates, supervisors or manager, or to provide more than the minimum contracted for the customer. Ethical man, as opposed to the selfish economic man, considers reciprocity natural and this strengthens internal markets (Casson 1991, 1993). In the large Japanese firm, with its emphasis on long-term contracts for workers, for life, then trust and co-operation can be encouraged. If these are essential for the efficiency of the firm then the form of organizational structure which will promote this may well be superior in performance.

Habits, traditions and routines, like seniority rights are enduring, they embody skills and information which cannot be easily catalogued and ensure the passing on of such skills and information. These are not readily measurable 'or subject to rational calculus' (Hodgson 1993: 208). Additional mechanisms which may be unconscious, habitual or cognitive are a functional necessity for groups working as teams. To explain how the firm reproduces and develops such habits and routines is important, albeit beyond the normal preserve of the economist.

Such institutional approaches emphasize the requirements of loyalty and trust which are important for encouraging co-operation and reducing transaction costs. Whilst in some circumstances opportunism abounds, there are also examples of people working beyond the call of duty, giving far more than is required by the nature of their work contract. They do not shirk but produce more than obliged. This does not coincide with the neo-classical perspective of the rationally calculating selfish maximizer. However, organizations would run far less effectively without an element of gift giving, where everyone did only the minimum according to their contract; where there was no give and take, where individuals were in constant competition with each other and had little trust.

Why do firms exist?

By examining the nature of the firm in greater depth and, in particular, its relationship with the market, we are now in a better position to consider why firms exist, indeed, why resources are allocated and decisions made in business firms and not markets or other organizations. Economists can give a variety of overlapping explanations for the existence of the firm-for-profit, where output is ultimately traded in markets and where firms have to cover their costs, one way or another, to survive in the long run. Firms are founded and evolve in perspective time where people have limited information and face uncertainty. Indeed, the firm-for-profit, in many actual situations, may be the best way to gain the benefits of the division of labour, specialization and co-operation over time; to deliver both simple and highly complex, technically sophisticated products and services in the modern economy.

We can summarize the reasons for the existence of the firm as follows:

1 Firms facilitate the division of labour, enabling the splitting up of tasks as discussed in Chapter 3. Firms may require sophisticated, complex equipment which is not feasible to have in small amounts. They make possible and improve the utilization of indivisible resources, and facilitate economies of scale and scope, dynamic gains over time.

2 *Transactions costs* are the basis for the existence of the firm (Coase 1937). Firms are constituted and survive because they economize on transactions costs. In a world of costless knowledge and omniscient people, firms would have no rationale, for markets would be as efficient as firms. However, in a continuously changing world in which making agreements between individuals and organizations, co-ordinating activity and motivating are costly, firms may organize resources more cheaply than markets (Ricketts 1987). Where firms exist over time they represent a better alternative.

3 *Specific assets*, both human and non-human resources reside within and are developed by firms. They affect transactions costs. These have little or no alternative uses or users and they *cannot* be hired or purchased in the market-place. Specialist capital equipment developed to produce a particular firm's product, is not available outside the firm. Examples include company-specific storage systems, equipment

for a specialist use, like jacks used for underpinning. Because of specialized requirements, skills are not available nor readily transferable in the market. It is impossible to buy-in specific teams of people, for these develop over time within the firm. Team work is often highly dependent on long-term human relationships. These cannot be developed in atomistic exchange and short-term market contracting. In the firm, it matters who is employed, for individual members affect the productivity of the others, often in ways which are difficult to isolate or measure.

4 Institutional and evolutionary theories emphasize the firm itself exists as a *safe space* to develop research and development, a shelter from an uncertain world. The firm provides satisfaction to people who enter into working relationships with each other in situations of reduced uncertainty. Firms foster and encourage co-operation.

There are several good reasons why resources are allocated and co-ordinated in firms rather than through markets, or indeed within households and charities, where, on the whole, the benefits of large-scale highly complex production could never be effected. In some instances it is impossible to compare the costs of using markets rather than firms for co-ordinating resources. It may be quite impossible to buy a particular 'specialized' resource or input in the market-place. In other instances, of course, the organization may be able to readily substitute in-house manufacture for components bought in the external market, made outside the firm at a cheaper rate.

In summary, economists put different emphasis on the rationale for and the nature of the firm. The transactions cost approach of Williamson and Coase may still be viewed as essentially neo-classical. Here the emphasis is on the individual, opportunism and shirking, the reliance on an ever present calculation of costs and the importance of markets.

For the institutional approach (North 1990; Hodgson 1988) a firm is not just a way of minimizing transactions costs although this is a feature. The firm is a social organization which produces conventions and rules, and loyalty and group gift giving (Akerlof 1982), on a more permanent basis. The firm is a socio-economic system, more than a 'nexus of contracts'. Indeed: 'some concept of radical uncertainty ... either directly or indirectly seems to be a necessary concept to explain the existence of the firm' (Hodgson 1988: 205). 'The nature of the firm is not simply a minimizer of transaction costs, but a kind of protective enclave from the potentially ravaging speculation of a competitive market' (ibid.: 208).

Indeed, whatever the emphasis, the firm as an organization is important in a world of imperfect knowledge and uncertainty. In fact, the legal form of the firm which could be safely ignored in a situation of perfect knowledge in analytical time must now be examined. In perspective time it is an appropriate concern.

THE ECONOMIC SIGNIFICANCE OF DIFFERENT LEGAL OWNERSHIP FORMS

In analytical time the legal form of the firm is irrelevant, given the assumption of perfect knowledge. In Chapter 4 we saw how property rights were a key element in determining the nature of economic production and exchange. Such ownership rights had to evolve to facilitate economic development. In the modern industrialized economy there are different forms of ownership which set the formal rules for business firms. These are: sole traders, partnerships and the corporate form. There are other forms of association: the publicly owned trading organizations, like the post office and co-operatives (see Chapters 8 and 10). Now we can examine the significance of these different legal forms in more detail, looking at their relative costs and benefits. In particular, without the corporate form, in capitalist economies, much of the large-scale enterprise, entailing the collaboration of huge numbers of people, could not have evolved. (In the planned economy of the USSR large, state-owned – collectively owned – organizations developed. These had significant differences but nevertheless were an important mechanism.)

The sole trader The single owner manager, is accountable for the activities of the firm. The owner and controller are one and the same, taking responsibility for decisions and liability for all debts, and receiving all profits. No one can countermand the owner manager about decisions relating to the firms activities.

The partnership People can associate together to run a business. They may co-operate as a partnership, where two or more *joint owners* are each responsible personally for the activities of the firm. The partners have shared rights to the profits and to manage the business but are liable for the firms debts. Each partner has unlimited liability, responsible for all the debts, even if an individual partner had no hand in incurring them.

The joint stock company This is a *collective ownership* form. The company limited by shares is of key importance and a very significant driving force in the modern world. Here decisions about the use of resources are normally made by management on behalf of the owners of the company, the shareholders. Sometimes, particularly in the smaller company, there is no divorce between ownership and control. The joint stock companies come in two major forms:

The private company This is generally small or medium sized, it is unquoted and therefore has shares which are not traded on any stock market.

The public company This is quoted and its shares are traded on stock markets. These are, in the main, large companies, including the global giants – as well as the large national players. Shares in such public companies worldwide were worth more than $13 trillion at the end of 1993 (*Economist* January 1994).

Shareholders in companies where there is a separation between ownership and control, are *principals* and managers are their *agents*. Property rights had to change to enable the development of large-scale, modern enterprise – the single owner and the partnership had to give way to other ownership forms. Why was this so? What advantages did the joint stock company have over other private ownership forms in capitalist economies?

The benefits of the corporate form

a) Limited liability provides perhaps the most important advantage. This protects the shareholder, like a form of insurance, which minimizes potential loss. In the worst scenario, shareholders can only lose the value of their shares, no more. Given the unlimited liability of the partnership or the sole trader, should the worst happen, then the individual might stand to lose more than their stake in the enterprise. All their wealth would be liable to pay-off the firm's debts. In a partnership, where the partners work closely together, each individual could *monitor* the situation. Yet as the number of partners increased to finance larger scale firms, tremendous trust would be required by each partner in the abilities and integrity of the others. The large partnership would impose great risks, for the individual partner would be liable for the actions of others, unless they were able, as in the case of professional partnerships, to purchase indemnity insurance. Fundamental uncertainty is a feature of life.

In the large corporate structure there would be an even smaller chance for shareholders to estimate and contain the risks of their associations. Not surprisingly, limited liability is an essential component of the corporate legal structure, a form of insurance for the owners. Ironically, some of the Names in Lloyds of London, who did not have this cover, found themselves liable for huge losses, and bankruptcy, after recent unprecedented losses in the insurance market. In historical time there are many examples of those who bought shares in companies without limited liability and were ruined as a result when things turned out badly.

However, the benefits of limited liability can be diluted by the propensity of banks and other lenders to take security on the personal assets of the proprietors of small companies.

b) The joint stock corporation principle allows the separation of ownership and control. The company has a legal independence from the shareholders, who are the owners of the company. This means that the supply of managerial talent and/or creative ideas on the one hand and finance on the other, can be separated. There is no reason to expect that these supplies should be embodied in the same people. If the person with creative ideas, or organizational skills, had to rely on their own wealth to use for investment, then this could impose a severe constraint on economic development. Also, the creative ideas and sophisticated, intricate, research and development are generated by teams in the modern world. These are the product of expensive collaborative investment. One way to achieve this is through the corporate form.

In nineteenth-century Britain, the corporation was not so important, for finance in many instances could be readily supplied by the profits of the enterprise. Isolated inventors could still find or become innovators, in relatively small-scale enterprise, where the sole trader or partnership could provide a relatively efficient ownership form. Its utilization did not blossom until the last decades of the nineteenth century when there was a wave of mergers between 1880 and 1914 and the corporate form enabled new methods of finance. Although the corporate joint stock form can also enable people of talent and professional training to rise to the top. It enables flexibility in reallocating property rights, through the purchase and sale of shares.

c) The separation of ownership and control enables an enterprise to enjoy *permanence*, with the *continuity* of a management succession denied to a partnership. Should one partner die or remove his or her share of the business, the partnership is broken and management and organization disrupted. However, a shareholder, one of the collective owners, can sell his or her stake in a *public* company without disturbing the organization. In private companies there is often no division of ownership and management. This is particularly the case in smaller companies, where difficulties can be created when one of the shareholders wishes to withdraw his or her stake.

d) *Large investments* can be financed because the corporate structure enables the pooling of relatively small sums of money by a large number of households and individuals. In Chapter 10 we shall show how this enables people to spread their risks by buying shares in many firms. The passage of the Joint Stock Companies Act in the nineteenth century greatly improved the flow of finance for large industrial developments requiring huge investment outlays, initially, particularly for the building of canals, railways and bridges – public utilities. However, the corporate form was to prove vital for a wide range of late nineteenth- and twentieth-century business. These required immense capital outlays for 'lumpy' investments which could not be undertaken on a small scale.

The costs of the corporate form: principal agent problems

In practice, the benefits of the corporate form do not come free. Agency problems arise. First, the provision of limited liability may have implicit costs. In smaller, less well established companies, sometimes personal guarantees have to be paid to secure finance and the company may face higher input prices in order to cover suppliers' risks. Should a company go into liquidation, a supplier might stand to lose large sums without any hope of repayment from the shareholders' private wealth, so they charge more to supply the firm with resources or other inputs.

However, more importantly, the interests of managers and owners may not coincide, which creates problems since managers may not run the firm in a way that serves the best interests of the shareholders. Adam Smith (1776: 741) made the observation that in joint stock companies, the directors, the managers of 'other people's money' rather than their own, would not 'watch over it with the same anxious vigilance' as would partners in association. Smith believed that 'Negligence and profusion, therefore, must always prevail, more or less, in the management of the affairs of such a company'.

In short, when firms are managed by salaried bosses there are problems in achieving the best results for the owners. In analytical time, with perfect information and an exact match of desires between owners and managers, there would be no problems in achieving maximum shareholder wealth. Any manager who did not work in the shareholders' best interests would be immediately removed. However, complete knowledge and understanding are not the prerogatives of any human actor whether a principal or agent. Therein lies the dilemma.

Principal agent problems exist when people make decisions in perspective time. Whilst no one has perfect knowledge or understanding, people also have unequal knowledge, that is, *asymmetric information*, between shareholders on the one hand and management on the other. Such inequality is the inevitable result of a principal agent relationship, where information is costly or impossible to acquire and difficult to evaluate. There are two key problems in this situation:

Cognitive problems

Bounded rationality ensures that even if the managers, as agents, wished to maximize wealth or profits over the long run, they have to grapple with imperfect knowledge, complexity and uncertainty about the present and future alternatives. In reality, all economic actors face these problems to a greater or lesser degree. Agents may be simply unable to maximize shareholder wealth.

Motivational problems

In addition, managers are likely to have different interests from shareholders. There may well be a conflict between the principals' and agents' objectives. Shareholders are said to want the biggest market value for their shares, the highest market price, *ceteris paribus*, to maximize their wealth, their purchasing power over time. This may not coincide with the best interests of the management. Managers may well be concerned with their own immediate pay and non-monetary rewards of the job including their perks, job security, working conditions or their next career move; the overall *net advantages* of their positions. As agents, they may take decisions which are not in line with the best interests of principals. Managers may, for example, undertake investments which pay back quickly but do not yield long-term benefits (this is a theme to which we shall return in investment decision-making in Chapter 11). Projects which show quick returns, although in the long term are relatively poor, may enhance managerial promotion prospects or ensure career moves to other companies. Managers may give contracts to high cost suppliers in exchange for 'back handers' or favours, behave with *opportunism*. They may award themselves very high levels of remuneration.

Management may take decisions which do not bring strategic advantage, missing opportunities to create wealth, should this entail risk to their own job security or unpleasant conflict. In short, managers may choose alternatives for a quiet or better life for themselves, behaving with opportunism and shirking.

How can principal-agent problems be reduced? How can managers be monitored and controlled – aligned to pursue the shareholders best interests? Managers have direct access to a wide range of company information unavailable to shareholders. The managers have specialized knowledge and experience. Shareholders lack this knowledge. Such agency problems are not confined to shareholders, but are a feature of any principal–agent relationship, for example, the firm and the employee, the client and the estate agent. In human interactions there is often an asymmetry of information and the fear of opportunistic behaviour, shirking and *moral hazard*. It refers to the opportunistic behaviour of individuals after a contract has been made. People reduce the care they take, for example, management borrows money from the bank for a safe project but subsequently uses the funds for a risky venture. Moral hazard is a term originally used in insurance (for a further discussion see Chapter 12). Trust, whilst essential for functioning, can be sorely misplaced, as we have seen in the case of Robert Maxwell and his employees' pension funds.

However, for the shareholder as principal, the monitoring and control of managerial behaviour may come through various means:

Monitoring

This involves overseeing and measuring the agents' performance. This requires information which is costly. Monitoring cannot be perfect given the problems of acquiring and evaluating information in perspective time. Management performance may be adversely affected if they believe that they do not have shareholder trust. Nevertheless, managers are subject to the inspection and probing of specialists.

There are legal requirements: the limited liability firm must have a *board of directors* and provide published information for the shareholders in the form of company reports and accounts. Ordinary shareholders, the ultimate risk bearers,[2] have the right to vote at the *annual general meetings*. Here shareholders may have a say in the appointment or sacking of managers. *Corporate reporting* provides information to the shareholders and the market. Stock exchange rules ensure limitations on managerial activity and require the provision of information.

Dissatisfied shareholders might be able to oust management teams which perform inadequately although in practice this can prove quite difficult, for share holdings are widely diversified, and there is an *asymmetry of power*. Large, institutional players, like pension funds and investment trusts, are more easily able to form pressure groups than the small, individual shareholder. Certainly, there are examples where shareholders' pressure works. In December 1994, Maurice Saatchi resigned as chairman of the global advertising empire which had grown from the business he and his brother founded in 1970. Saatchi had great creative abilities but allegedly did not have the same financial expertise. Some shareholder discontent led to American Fund managers securing his resignation (Bell 1994). In America shareholders were able to fire managers in poorly performing firms like IBM, Westinghouse and Kodak (*Economist* January 1994). If inadequate profit levels are not achieved, shareholders can withdraw their financial capital from the firm. However, many may not move in time. There were casualties from Polly Peck, and Rosehaugh, the property company. Selling shares in the market provides the final vote of no confidence.

There are examples of board room coups, where control is wrested from one group by another, as in the case of Tottenham Hotspur. However, the ultimate discipline/control is the *hostile takeover*. External management teams may purchase shares in a company with a view to taking control. Despite an LWT management fight to convince shareholders not to sell, Granada's hostile bid was successfully completed. Shares, those marketable collective rights, give others the possibility to change the ownership and control of the corporation. But even the threat of a hostile takeover may be sufficient to concentrate managerial minds and work wonders. The company may become the target of a takeover bid as outsiders believe that the physical and human assets of the company are not being used efficiently. The Hanson Group, in 1991, bought a small proportion of the shares in ICI. Perhaps as a result, ICI, a very large chemical company, did its own restructuring and was split into two in 1993. The pharmaceutical divisions were floated off in Zenecon. Although in the case of some giant companies, like GM, it would be exceedingly difficult to mount any takeover bid; the threat would be hollow.

Incentive schemes, like share options and bonus schemes which give benefits if the shareholders gain profits but are valueless if they do not, may be used to spur on management. The principal has to find ways of overcoming problems of managerial moral hazard, to cut down on shirking and induce co-operation. Institutional arrangements have to be made to 'align' managers' and shareholders' interests. But there are other ways to reduce agency problems.

Unwritten rules, customs and practices, ethical codes – wider social conventions are all important for inducing behaviour patterns which cut down on such problems. Casson (1991) points to the need to encourage people to behave ethically as opposed to selfishly, for this reduces the costs of human interactions. It makes transactions cheaper. Often business dealings will be confined as much as possible to those with similar values and outlooks, where trust is paramount. We referred to the Quakers and other religious groups in Chapter 4.

THE FIRM: INTERNAL AND EXTERNAL RELATIONSHIPS

Firms whether they are simple or very complex organizations will exhibit different internal and external relationships. Firms are systems often with complex organizational patterns and intricate webs of external relationships. Firms do not solve their problems in the same way. They co-ordinate and manage activities by different means. This has implications for our theoretical view of the firm and the type of explanations we give. The organizational structure and decision-making process of IBM, Cadbury Schweppes, BT are very different from that of small business enterprise.

Wider approaches to the firm make an important distinction between a firm's external market (and external non-market) relationships where it sells output, the competitive and 'environmental' pressures; and what happens on the inside of the firm, its internal workings. The external environment of the firm may affect its internal workings and vice versa; something which the introductory neo-classical theory, given its own terms of reference, has ignored.

THE INTERNAL ORGANIZATION OF THE FIRM: GOVERNANCE STRUCTURES AND AUTHORITY RELATIONSHIPS

The legal structure of the firm and its competitive environment are relevant for our understanding of the firm-for-profit. However, we must also consider the internal organizational structures of the firm, which are associated with different ownership forms. People operating in perspective time are obliged to spend resources, including time, to co-ordinate their activities. In historical time, non-profit organizations such as the church and the military have long used complex hierarchial organizational structures to co-ordinate human activity and so achieve their survival and purpose. But the development of such intricate structures for business enterprise was innovative. Whilst the East India Company, with its well developed bureaucracy, set a historical precedent, before the mid-nineteenth century, firms-for-profit were structured simply. Changes in internal organization became necessary in an economic environment where business for profit required the benefits of enlarged co-operation – essential to gain the economies of scale and scope of large-scale production. Management required increasing information and their actions had to be taken in a timely fashion, often prerequisites for survival and success, particularly in a competitive environment. We can see how firms like Cadburys evolved over time, taking on different internal forms as they expanded. We begin with the basic organizational form.

The simple hierarchy   This usually has one person, the boss, who co-ordinates the activities of business in a simple hierarchy; a manager overseeing workers, like John Cadbury. Indeed, before the mid-nineteenth century, the personal supervision by the owner, of a limited, small-scale enterprise, was the norm; the owner and controller were one. Such direct supervision gave economies of information in decision-making, ready monitoring and motivating; a flexible, manageable form. Those running the business were able to co-ordinate effectively, near enough to day-to-day operations to make appropriate decisions, in a manageable situation.

Yet as the firm and market evolved in historical time, different organizational forms were required to facilitate economic development. Sometimes people would co-operate in an organization which did not use a hierarchy.

The peer group   This involves a number of people, for example, joint owners of a business collaborating together, where every member is essentially on the same footing. The joint owners participate equally in decision-making. There is no boss, no hierarchy. Often the partnership, the legal form of the peer group, was used when production began to grow and become more complex. The joint owners in partnerships often brought together different skills and financial resources necessary for growth. The partnership had and has advantages. It can bring about economies of scale, given the different talents and financial resources of partners. It enabled risk sharing. Indeed, this peer group form often led to gains through association. Partners felt a responsibility towards each other and were encouraged to give more than they might have done, working on their own account in isolated ventures. Two heads can be better than one, like the Cadbury brothers partnership in the late nineteenth century.

However, this organizational form was and is not without difficulties. Communications had to be good for the partners to arrive at a mutual unanimity. Reaching necessary agreements becomes more difficult as the scope and complexity of the business grows. As the numbers of partners increase, problems of communication and accord could grow at an accelerating rate. The overall difficulties of operating in perspective time imposed increasing managerial costs as production became more involved. In addition, the essential marketing, distribution and purchasing networks of multi-product organizations of the late nineteenth and twentieth century were simply beyond the capacity of the partnership. The growing span of organizations, the increasing numbers of people to be monitored and motivated and the expanding need for financial resources, often placed overwhelming demands on the co-ordinators. The transaction costs became too high. The mutual modifications of the peer group organization were not appropriate for larger firms. In the early days of the Cadbury partnership, Richard and George Cadbury worked in adjoining offices and made decisions as they went along, keeping few records (Industrial Challenge 1964: 9).

Yet the peer group has to give way to more complex organizational forms in order to facilitate economic development. A relatively complex hierarchical form, coupled with joint stock ownership, proves more effective in reducing transactions costs for organizing resources in medium- and large-scale enterprise.

Multi-stage hierarchies: unitary form or U-form   As the scale and scope of the enterprise began to grow, the simple hierarchy or peer group was inappropriate; neither could cope effectively. As firms expanded they had to be organized into manageable parts with *at least two* layers of management. One way to deal with the problem of co-ordinating diverse activities was to run the enterprise on functional lines with a head office, controlled by a general manager who then co-ordinated managers in charge of different areas: production, sales, engineering and finance. This can be found in medium sized companies, with one single activity, or as in the late nineteenth century, for example, when companies engaged in steel making, tobacco or chocolate manufacture (see Figure 9.2).

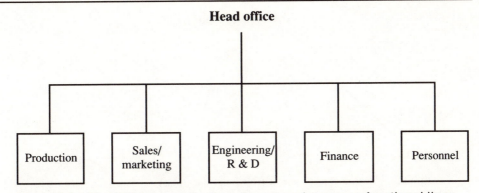

Figure 9.2 The U-form organization. An enterprise run on functional lines

The unitary form enabled companies to grow but it was not without disadvantage. Management could become concerned with pursuing their own goals, like the success of the engineering division, the size of the research and development budget, just the performance of the part they managed. Moreover, with an increase in the layers of management came the impairment of information, managerial diseconomies of scale and loss of control, leading to increased costs.

In the large, U-form organization, only top managers might be concerned with the long-run strategic goals. The attainment of these goals could be frustrated by sub-goal pursuit of the different departments. The firms which grew successfully by diversifying into new products and geographical markets, developed a different hierarchical form, which reduced costs.

The multi-divisional or M-form firm This splits the firm into semi-autonomous operating divisions (profit centres), organized on product or geographic lines, with top management dealing with strategic planning. This M-form enabled the development of current large and giant firms, where sheer variety, volume and complexity made the use of other forms of organization either inefficient or impossible. Managerial diseconomies of large-scale production were offset. Often separate operating companies were set up to ensure more manageable, smaller organizations, linked to a modest number of senior managers and their staff at the top, who co-ordinate and oversee overall operations (see Figure 9.3). By the 1920s this was a key innovatory organizational form in the USA where large multi-product enterprises had developed. Eventually, it was followed by most large multi-product firms in both the USA and Europe.

The M-form firm reflects decision-making requirements in perspective time. Decision-making is devolved down the organization to ensure that those with relevant up-to-date local information can use it to take decisions in good time. This cuts down on information processing and co-ordinating costs. The multi-divisional form gives advantages over the highly centralized organization or one where there is no effective central control. It cuts duplication of effort and improves information flows. Loyalty and a greater feeling of belonging by workers and managers may well follow on. People feel they are less remote from decision-making.

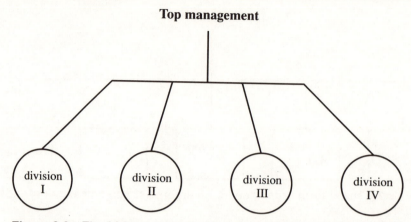

Figure 9.3 The M-form organization. An enterprise split into semi-autonomous divisions – profit centres on product or geographical lines

Top management, responsible for the long-term future of the organization are given time to plan strategy, relieved of the operational and tactical day-to-day decision-making. They can reallocate cash and other resources among the different divisions into those uses which give the best fit to strategic needs. The multi-divisional form is a necessary response to manage large-scale growth and expansion, to cut down on the arterial sclerosis which threatened many large companies. In recent times company structures have been reorganized again with the *delayering* of management, the flattening out of managerial pyramids, pushing responsibility down the organization. Delayering, for example, occurred at British Petroleum (BP) and British Telecom (BT) in the early 1990s. ICI was a huge bureaucracy but had been slimmed down even before the Zeneca split. Employment at ICI's head office has been dramatically cut. In 1955, head office employment was 2,800, by 1991 750, by 1992, it was a mere 150 (*Guardian* 29 April 1994).

The institutional environment and the governance structures of firms is unique in time and place. All of these general organizational forms co-exist today. However, the problem on balance, is to achieve a structure which provides sufficient competitive push with co-operation. The problem of ossified firms comes when internal routines begin to be inflexible where there is no impetus for workers and management to innovate and enhance the productive potential of the firm (Hodgson 1988). The institutional approach is pluralistic. For the firm – what structure is best? The answer is not clear cut, in perspective time it depends on a complex of changing factors.

CHANGING THE PERIMETER AND ACTIVITIES OF THE FIRM

As firms evolve over time they may grow, shrink or, of course, ultimately die. Factors, both internal and external to the firm, may interact with each other to bring such changes about. Firms may grow by reaping the benefits of economies of scale, and/or moving into new areas of production, diversifying into new products and geographical markets. Companies may take the decision to produce within an international context, to be multinational, producing close to their markets in different national locations, sometimes taking the benefit of cheaper labour or government incentives.

The firm may cut down the transactions costs of using the market. The firm may wish to cut back on negotiation and dependence on outsiders, in part, as a means of reducing risk (for further discussion see Chapter 12). There may be incentives for the firm to internalize decisions rather than use the external market or vice versa.

Mergers and acquisitions

Firms may grow by acquiring – 'taking over' or merging with others. A takeover involves the acquirer absorbing the acquiree – a merger is the combining of two companies into a new enterprise. Mergers and acquisitions can enhance the shareholders' position, enabling greater co-operation in gaining economies of scale and scope, creating *synergies*, a situation where 2 + 2 gives a solution greater than 4. But of course, there is the distribution of the gains and costs to be considered. Sometimes mergers and acquisitions may not be in the interest of shareholders, workers or local communities. They may be for management, who wish to secure their own position, reducing their own risks. It would be difficult to make sense of many real-world situations, such as hostile takeovers and corporate restructuring, without accepting the notion that managers have different interests and perceptions from those of the shareholders and, for that matter, the employees and often the wider society. Mergers and acquisitions can be placed in three categories:

1 *Vertical* mergers occur when firms merge with their suppliers or buyers. For example, Inspirations, the travel group specializing in marketing holidays has recently agreed to buy Caledonian Airways.
2 *Horizontal* mergers occur when there is a takeover of competitors at the same stage of production. A recent takeover by BMW of Rover is a case in point or the acquisition of William Low, the Scottish supermarket chain, by Tesco in 1994. Tesco were anxious to expand into the Scottish market.
3 *Conglomerate* mergers enable corporate growth by the acquisition of companies in a variety of different markets. British American Tobacco (BAT) had relatively limited investment prospects in a mature business, so used cash to acquire, for example, Allied Dunbar and Eagle Star. BAT aimed to move into growth areas. The London Rubber Company now the London International Group (LIG) moved into the photoprocessing business in the early 1980s when the company believed that other contraceptive methods would cause declining condom sales. This was a far cry from the group's core activities – condoms and rubber glove manufacture.

The firm may also decide to contract, by pulling out of particular lines of business and closing production facilities in different locations. Indeed, many firms display diseconomies of scale and the advantages of expected synergy turn out to be non-existent. The LIG's disastrous foray into photoprocessing, where the company had little expertise, led eventually to corporate restructuring and the closure of plants in Britain in 1994. Photoprocessing brought large losses to the company. Such radical changes involve corporate restructuring – *divestment*. British Aerospace sold Rover, a company not close enough to its core business interests. Indeed, the wave of *demergers* and management buy-outs have been an important recent phenomenon. Where firms have grown, particularly by acquisition, they have strayed too far from their core business, where they have a comparative advantage or can create one. The unwieldy, sluggish corporate enterprise can be revitalized by hiving-off, and splitting down as in the case of ICI and Zenecon.

At this point it is useful to remember that for the most part companies remain private, they do not have their shares traded on stock markets. Some are too small to meet the listing requirements. But for others there is an option of going public, which is not taken up. By remaining private the companies do not have to bear the costs of stock market regulation or monitoring, they do not face the full scrutiny of city analysts, shareholders and international market players. That enables the managers of such companies to retain control for there is no large increase in readily marketable equity. Avoiding wide share ownership reduces the chance of a takeover; changing the perimeter of the firm by amalgamating it with another. Companies who wish to retain control within the family, like Bechtel, a large US based multinational with interests in oil and construction, do not have their shares traded on any stock exchange and finance their investments from internally generated funds, profits or borrowing. Although, of course, private companies do merge and grow.

Contracting out is another way of changing the boundary of the firm. Companies may contract out their office cleaning, their typing or systems analysis to other firms and small individual contractors. They may sub-contract.

Privatization of the railways gives an interesting insight into transactions costs and the splitting up of an organization. The old BR network will be replaced by some sixty new organizations. A complex system of operations will be put in place, with separate firms, individual private sector train operators, for example, who will negotiate with Railtrack, responsible for the track. Also a new legal framework must be set in place to govern stations and rolling stocks. A whole series of separate contracts must be negotiated, drawn up and monitored. These include station leases, network access, depot leases, maintenance contracts and so on. Some 15,000 individual contracts will be drawn up in the run up to privatization (Smith 1994).

CONCLUDING COMMENTS

Whilst the key message of basic neo-classical market theory was that inefficiencies arose from the imperfections of the market mechanism, including the power and distortions arising from the presence of giant firms, in alternative approaches using perspective time, a favourable case for large enterprises can be made. Other issues take prominence; the rationale for different legal ownership forms, how to explain the different internal organizational forms and their governance structures; how to overcome principal agent problems, for example, to enhance ethical behaviour or to cut down on shirking and opportunism. These approaches make different assumptions about 'human nature'. And they open a very different series of questions from those of the introductory models discussed in Chapter 8. Furnished with these alternative perspectives we now move to an analysis of the not-for-profit firm, organizations largely ignored in the neo-classical market player mode.

THE BUSINESS FIRM II – SUMMARY

- The firm is a purposeful organization which evolves over time.
- Economic objectives are paramount but supplemented by other goals. There are alternative goals to profit maximization. Firms may simply try to satisfice.
- Although firms have common problems they do not co-ordinate and manage activities in the same way. In the small firm, the owner can control. The large firm has a division of ownership and control with a managerial hierarchy.
- The firm and the market are different. The firm has a governance structure. Resources within the firm are allocated by a non-price planning process. There is a difference between market-like and firm-like contracts.
- There are different views about why firms exist. The firm reduces transactions costs, it enables the benefit from economies of scale and scope, using specific assets.
- Firms as organizations are important in a world of uncertainty. They are a social system, a safe space. Habits, traditions and rules are important.
- There is an economic significance of different forms of ownership in perspective time. Ownership forms have evolved over historical time. There are important benefits of the corporate form, although there are also principal/agent problems.
- The firm has different internal forms which evolve over time. These range from the simple hierarchy, peer group, multi-stage hierarchies and the multi-divisional or M-Form forms.
- The firm can change its perimeter through merger and acquisition. The firm may contract out. The large organization can be split up.

THE BUSINESS FIRM II – QUESTIONS FOR DISCUSSION

1 What are the key distinctions between the family firm and the multinational? Why do these two forms of enterprise co-exist at the same time?

2 Sainsburys, Asda, Tesco and Quicksave – are these firms or markets? Distinguish

carefully between these two concepts – illustrating the difference between market-like and firm-like contracts.

3 Explain how a home-owner might organize a home extension by either:

a) hiring individual contractors, or
b) going to a firm of building contractors.

Illustrate what you understand by transactions costs in the context of this question. Which course of action would you recommend and why? Make your assumptions clear.

In either case would you advise the home owner to employ an architect?

4 What are the advantages of a quoted plc status? What disadvantages may arise and how can these be dealt with?

5 Explain why there are different forms of internal organization for the firm. How has the internal organization of Cadbury's changed over historical time?

6 Explain the key reasons for mergers and acquisitions. Use current examples from the media to illustrate your answer.

7 Why do we require different theories of the firm? Compare the orthodox neo-classical approach with that of the institutional/evolutionary view.

10

Non-profit 'firms'

INTRODUCTION

This chapter focuses attention on those diverse organizations which can be described as non-profit 'firms'. Whilst this term is often used to delineate organizations in the private voluntary, 'independent' or third sector, like Amnesty International, the British Heart Foundation or the local playgroup, here we shall also include non-trading, public sector organizations, 'firms' like the Inland Revenue, the National Health Service and the BBC. This multitude of organizations co-ordinate and allocate limited resources to achieve a host of very different ends. However, although they are neither the households nor the business firms of conventional theory, such 'non-profit' organizations play a vital and diverse role in all economies, whatever the institutional backdrop and historical setting. As economies evolve, the roles and significance of non-profit 'firms' change, yet whether in the past or present, they are, as a group, indispensable. For a more formal discussion highlighting the problems of definition see Ricketts (1994).

The goals of non-profit 'firms' are in some cases intangible, not readily definable, let alone measurable in monetary terms. Some provide communal or public goods which do not exhibit the features of excludability, rivalry and rejectability, the hallmarks of private goods. We are not talking about the commercial producers of baked beans or mobile telephones. Many non-profits like Greenpeace or Amnesty International have 'outputs' which cannot be traded readily in markets. Others provide goods and services which could potentially be sold to individuals in the market and rationed by price, like cancer treatments, schooling or some aspects of policing. Yet for a variety of reasons, the organizations spotlighted here co-ordinate resources and allocate 'output' through non-price means. In the main, they are not engaged in market activity.

Indeed, in the normal course of events, most of the non-profits discussed here, unlike the business firm, do *not* rely on revenues from the market sales of goods or services. Funds to cover the costs of their activities come from other sources. Public sector organizations like the NHS are funded largely from the proceeds of taxation. The BBC, a public corporation, is substantially financed by the licence fee. Private sector organizations, like churches, charities or pressure groups are dependent on donations of time and money, on legacies and gifts from individuals and business firms and, in some cases, government grants.

Whilst many non-profit organizations fulfil vital roles in the economic system as service providers, sources of employment and in the overall process of wealth creation, they are usually by-passed by traditional theory. However, these organizations have a variety of important functions, including the provision of direct satisfaction and support for individuals and families, services to business firms and, in some cases, vital roles to play in setting and policing the indispensable 'rules of the game'.

As economists, we can help to enhance our understanding of 'non-profit' firms by using the key theoretical concepts explained in earlier chapters. In situations where wants outstrip limited resources, organizations, whatever their mission, have to find solutions to the questions: What to 'produce'? How to 'produce'? and For whom to provide? Despite the tremendous diversity of 'non-profits', economists can provide insights into the ways in which these questions are addressed. Whilst some organizations may seem remote from economic enquiry and are usually ignored by mainstream probing, economists, none the less, have serious insights to give.

In order to explore and emphasize the economic facets of non-profit organizations, this chapter gives an introductory insight into the following questions: What is the nature of public and private 'non-profit' organizations, and their overall significance? Why do they exist and how are they funded? How do they co-ordinate and allocate resources and distribute 'output'? What are their interrelationships with each other, households and business enterprise? What are their internal structures? How does government policy in general and privatization in particular affect them and their evolving, sometimes overlapping, boundaries?

Given the great assortment of organizations which fall into the 'non-profit' category, our coverage is of necessity selective and aims to provide a beginning. This is an immense field. Initially, we shall consider the definition, nature and historical significance of non-profit organizations and how they are linked. Then attention will be focused on public sector organizations, with particular reference to the National Health Service; a series of related organizations providing a segmented service for a public health care system. Here we use and develop concepts from previous chapters, including non-market allocation and agency theory. Finally, we examine the voluntary sector, a sub-section of the much wider group of private non-profits. Particular attention will be given to charities, for example, in terms of health care 'products'.

THE NATURE AND HISTORICAL SIGNIFICANCE OF NON-PROFIT ORGANIZATIONS: AN OVERVIEW

Neo-classical theory, with its emphasis on autonomous individuals and their market relationships, has given short shrift to the charity, the voluntary association, even the large, non-trading state organizations, like the bureaucracies of the army and the Inland Revenue. These do not fit neatly into a utility or profit maximizing framework or readily lend themselves to exact modelling in analytical time.

A moment's reflection will underline the great diversity of organizations which lie beyond the domestic scene, but which are neither profit-seeking private sector firms nor market trading organizations with commercial interests. In Britain, for example, there are nationalized industries like the Post Office which, of course, do not have shareholders – no private owners to receive the surplus. This heterogeneous group can be categorized into either the public or the private 'independent', or third sector. However, as we shall see, there is often a great deal of similarity in the way some large non-profits work and are structured, whether designated as belonging to the public or private sector. Moreover, there may be a number of similarities with business firms. We distinguish between:

Public sector non-profits These include the government *non-trading* and service sectors of central and local government organizations, including civil service departments, local authorities, the armed forces, the police force, the National Health Service and state schools. In addition, there are public corporations like the BBC. These organizations are, to a greater or lesser extent, creatures of the State, where ownership rests largely in public hands. On a world stage we might think of the global organizations such as NATO and the World Health Organization.

The 'independent' private of third sector This encompasses voluntary organizations, in a British context, charities such as The National Trust, Barnados and National Children's Home. The Roman Catholic church or Islamic religious organizations, for example, are universal, they transcend national barriers. Moreover, pressure groups such as Amnesty International and Greenpeace are international. There are also associations like trades unions and professional bodies. In Britain, mutual organizations and associations, such as the Co-operative Wholesale Society, Bupa, the Automobile Association and most building societies, can be classified in this third sector category. However, the degree of market activity varies and some of these firms can no longer be thought of as non-profit non-market players, whatever their original intent.

The objectives of non-profits

Non-profit organizations can have very different concerns and objectives (Cyert 1975; Leat 1993). In stark contrast to the business firm of orthodox theory, profit maximization clearly cannot be set as the objective for the charity or civil service department. For many non-profit firms there may be no readily definable, measurable objective or an end-product. Broadly speaking, such planning units are non-trading. Their primary purpose is the provision of goods, services or simply money for particular groups; they meet different needs. The 'client' group could be a small local circle, the public, on a national scale, or worldwide. For example, the overall objective of the NHS, could be seen as the provision of health care regardless of the ability to pay, its target, in the main, a national public. The Customs and Excise and the Inland Revenue are revenue generating departments of central government but with other functions. The Customs and Excise, for example, seizes drugs and other illicit materials. The BBC has a remit to broadcast a range of programmes to all licence payers in Britain and to those abroad via the BBC's World Service. Oxfam sees the relief of famine and the alleviation of poverty on a world stage as its mission. In contrast, the trade union or professional association may seek to maximize the well-being of its membership as defined in a broad membership goal, to do the best possible in perspective time, or to satisfice.

Non-profit organizations can make important and far reaching decisions which affect resource allocation in non-market contexts. Moreover, their activities can have significant effects on the workings of markets, households and business firms; sometimes with global ramifications. All, from the smallest to the largest, are part of a symbiotic socio-economic system. Indeed, as taxpayers, funders, donors, 'clients', 'consumers', workers or members, we all play some part and are affected by their activities. We all use the output of public administration, like the services of central and local authorities. Non-profits in both sectors provide essential services, non marketable 'output' which can have a very significant effect on economic well-being.

When goods and services are provided, either no price is set, no payment is made at the point of delivery; or a nominal price is charged, unrelated to use by the individual or the cost of provision. Some goods, public and quasi-public, are unpriced. Other goods and services, as we explained in Chapter 6, are allocated by non-price mechanisms. The costs of provision are not covered by revenues from the sale of goods or services in markets. For, in the main, 'non-profits' rely on other means to fund their activity.

How are non-profits funded?

Funds come from a variety of different sources. Non-trading public sector organizations are largely funded via the proceeds of taxation, licensing fees and government borrowing. In the third sector, funds come from a variety of different sources including the state. Organizations may receive private, charitable, direct contributions, donations and legacies; gifts in kind; government grants; in other instances, as with trades union or AA membership, fees cover costs, although there may be some market activity to supplement incomes, as in the case of the AA selling, for example, books and other publications.

Why do non-profit organizations exist?

Organizations are set up to fulfil needs, to achieve goals through co-operation and solidarity, although competition and conflict may always have a part to play. There are a variety of missions, ends to be achieved, whether: religious, political, educational, the alleviation of poverty, meeting environmental needs and so on. People operating in isolation achieve less or simply cannot provide a complex service or product. Organizations are necessary to achieve non-commercial goals where there is a need for mutual support and where there is uncertainty. There are benefits of specialization and the division of labour, economies of scale and scope to be made in an uncertain world. Isolated individual activity is not enough.

Not all needs can be catered for effectively by families or business firms in the market. As we emphasized in Chapter 4, looking back through historical time, non-profit and household organizations dominated the economic stage. In the beginning, we might argue, there were families, tribes and religion. Certainly, hierarchical religious organizations flourished well before bureaucratic corporate enterprise or the modern state; and before extensively developed markets. In Britain, the church, crown and army, with relatively complex hierarchical structures, were with us long before large, hierarchical business enterprises operating in well organized markets. Indeed, non-profit organizations have a long historical lineage, worldwide. The Roman Catholic church, for example, was like a giant multinational corporation, centuries before the advent of modern nation states. It has a hierarchical network managing extensive resources, planning and allocating over a large geographical area; a universal, global organization with a powerful structure, transcending national and cultural boundaries.

In eighteenth- and nineteenth-century Britain, for example, private associations were founded to achieve goals through co-operation and solidarity. The trades union movement and voluntary organizations committed to political and social reform developed. These grew to meet needs which were not adequately fulfilled elsewhere. Such needs changed and developed as the economy evolved. Sometimes entrepreneurial 'creative altruists' were active. Charity was often linked closely with the entrepreneurial spirit, particularly from religious groups like the Quakers. The private philanthropy of the Rowntrees and Cadbury families provide notable examples. These were people with successful businesses who involved themselves in charitable work and indeed political activity.

Over historical time the roles of private and state organizations have evolved and overlapped; in many cases their functions have been passed between the public and private domain. When Henry VIII ordered the dissolution of the monasteries, their important teaching functions and care for the sick and needy had to be taken by others. The setting up and the funding of grammar schools, by the State, was part of this process. Much later, in the nineteenth and twentieth centuries where private charity was insufficient to meet the growing needs of the developing economy and the social costs associated with industrialization, government stepped in. Indeed, as the economic system has become more complex, with sophisticated technologies, the creation of new requirements and uncertainties, the state has taken over functions where private charity and private business enterprise once held sway.

Public sector organizations today undertake activities in many different fields: administration, defence, education, health care and research and development. As we saw in Chapter 6, they act where markets are either non-existent, unable or deemed inappropriate to provide output. The state supplies services where family support, private philanthropy or business firms, for whatever the reasons, do not give sufficient provision.

There is a continuing debate about the best way to achieve particular ends, either through private or public sector activity. But in the complex modern economy, inevitably there has to be a pluralistic approach; there are no pure alternatives. In the late twentieth century, commercial profit seeking firms form a large and indispensable component of the modern industrialized world as we know it. Nevertheless, for the bulk of human history that was not so. Even now, non-profit organizations of the state and private, third sector, play an essential, significant and evolving role, in modern economies. The relative size and precise institutional make up of these sectors and their interrelationships with families and business firms differ from nation to nation; they always form a unique blend in historical time and place.

Comparing public and private sector non-profits and the business firm

Whilst we can distinguish between the public and private sectors in terms of formal ownership, legal structures, control and accountability, there is often a great deal of overlap, interdependency and similarity between non-profit organizations, whether they are categorized as public or private. Many private charities in Britain, like housing associations, in recent years have been founded and are in part funded by the state. They may take on many of the attributes of public sector organizations, like the local authorities which they were intended to replace.

Nevertheless, some organizations such as building societies and Mutual Life offices are now very much closer to private sector business firms. Building societies began as self-help building co-operatives in the second quarter of the eighteenth century, the first was conceived in a public house in Birmingham, The Golden Cross Inn in 1775. Workmen pooled their skills and resources to provide for housing which was in very scarce supply. Yet modern building societies have come a long way from those roots of mutuality. The Abbey National Building Society, for example, is now a quoted plc, its membership transformed into shareholders, an organization playing under a different set of rules, including company law and Stock Exchange regulation. The aim is now to make profits in the market-place, the Abbey National is no longer a mutual organization seeking to break even.

Size is an important feature, whether measured by income or the number of people involved. We may learn more by comparing large charities, such as Oxfam, with large corporate enterprises like British American Tobacco (BAT) or Nestlé, than with the local voluntary playgroup or the small market trader (Leat 1993). Indeed, government departments like the Customs and Excise or the Inland Revenue, in terms of their internal organization, may have more in common with some large private sector bureaucracies than with small public sector quangos. By and large, there is no neat appropriate theory of 'the firm' or the consumer to apply to non-profit organizations; no straightforward model from the neo-classical world. However, competition between non-profits may be fierce or elements of monopoly power strong. And all of these organizations are faced with economic considerations, the problem of how to allocate limited resources amongst competing ends. Changes in one sector can have considerable ramifications for others. These decision-making units are interwoven in a web of economic and social relationships, formal and informal.

Whether we look at the public or private sector non-profit organizations, we can begin with the assumption that organizations will want to produce their services in the most economical way, given the difficulties of operating in perspective time. An organization's goals should be achieved at the least opportunity cost. However, whilst profit itself is not necessarily an adequate indicator of performance in the commercial sector, in the non-profit sectors, indicators of performance can present us with problems (Leat 1993). The specification of clear unambiguous measurable objectives may be difficult or impossible, where intangible benefits and costs are being considered. Yet all organizations essentially face an economic problem of survival.

However, in order to illustrate non-profit organizations we shall begin with those which have public sector status, and focus on the NHS.

PUBLIC SECTOR NON-PROFIT ORGANIZATIONS

As we have underlined, public sector non-trading organizations do not sell their output, although they may buy and hire resources in the market-place. They are essentially directly funded and controlled by government. In Britain there have been considerable changes within the public sector in recent years. Much contemporary political interest has focused on *efficiency*, although there are also important questions concerning the *equity* of provision.

Government policy-makers have sought to introduce the discipline of the market; to weed out inefficiency; and to provide value for money, to improve accountability. Privatization policies have put a growing emphasis on the use of the market mechanism and commercial practices to achieve these ends. For example, contracting out and market testing have been introduced into public sector organizations to induce competition and value for money. There is an increasing pressure to operate on commercial lines. There are many examples from which we can draw, whether from privatized prisons and prison services by Group 4, the contracting out of local authority refuse collection or school meal provision. Whilst the public sector as a whole provides a wealth of interesting examples, we shall focus on the NHS and health care.

THE NATIONAL HEALTH SERVICE AND HEALTH CARE

First, why choose the NHS as an example for special attention instead of other public sector organizations?

1 The NHS represents a very good example of how Britain provides health care within a unique organizational context, given a particular historical setting of legal rules and custom. Moreover, the NHS represents a popular and ever topical British institution.

2 The bulk of health care is provided in Britain by non-market means within the public sector NHS. Non-price rationing is used to allocate a range of products known collectively as health care.

3 The Government's NHS reforms have as a central tenet the notion that competition and improvement in consumer choice are beneficial. Economists wish to assess whether or not such changes promote efficiency and their impact on the distribution of services. This discussion is especially relevant at a time when several countries are privatizing health care, encouraging competition and consumer choice. And, moreover, when the Clinton administration in the USA, in contrast, wants to reduce reliance on market provision.

4 Finally, and very importantly, health care is essential to all of us at some time, and is used to promote both 'good health' and alleviate 'ill health'. The enjoyment of good health is a vital underpinning to every other aspect of our lives, in whatever roles we play, as: consumers, givers, producers and providers. However, good health is also affected by a range of other 'products' from clean air and a reduction in passive smoking, to better diets and exercise. Good health is what we ultimately want.

NHS: an overview

The NHS provides different kinds of health care products which are produced by segmented although related services. The NHS is a complex of organizations and, in perspective time, we lack comprehensive information about its workings. The NHS at its inception in 1946, aimed to provide comprehensive health care to all citizens regardless of financial means, age, sex, employment or vocation, area of residence or insurance qualification (Maynard 1990: 3). The NHS was set up because of patent dissatisfaction with the system which preceded it, for example, the mix of voluntary and fee paying hospitals. Whilst there were some far-sighted employers, like the Cadburys, concerned with the health of their workers, the provision of health care was patchy and inadequate. The mix of the voluntary sector and market gave inadequate provision overall, with poor co-ordination and planning for the future.

The aim of the new service was to remove price as an allocator and to eliminate the compartmentalizing of decision-making within the system. Although, of course, whatever the system, whether public or private health care, given scarcity, some type of rationing has to prevail, as we discussed in Chapter 6. In addition, very importantly, the aim was to bring about a fairer share of medical care and with that enhanced social benefits. The fragmented, poorly co-ordinated system was expensive in terms of transactions costs. The NHS could facilitate a reduction in transactions costs and the promotion of economies of scale and scope. Its funding was to come from taxation. The overall level of funding was set largely by a political decision-making process of the State, not by the market mechanism or the will of the independent voluntary sector.

The organizational structure

The system has evolved over historical time, with legal changes and the development of custom and practice. The structure was reformed, for example, in 1974 and 1982. Significant changes were made in April 1991 when the NHS and health authorities became purchasers from hospitals and other units and the concept of operationally independent NHS Trusts was founded. These are independent – free to raise their own funds and advertise their services, to bid for contracts to attend patients. A voluntary scheme for general practitioners enables them to control their own funds and to buy particular health and community health services according to their patients' needs. The rules of the game – the institutional framework – changed.

Notably, the NHS has links with the voluntary and for-profits sectors and the support of people in their communities, the informal sector. The complex service provides different types of health care from primary care, to hospital care and care in the community, the suppliers of these are highlighted below, along with the services they provide.

General practitioner

Primary care for routine problems is provided by general practitioners, indeed, we can also include dentists and ophthalmic practitioners. Primary care includes a range of services such as family planning and clinics in addition to routine consultations. However, there is a lack of information about the range of services which is actually provided because there are considerable variations in the provisions and referral practices of individual doctors, dentists and ophthalmic practitioners. These may be dependent, in part, on the nature of 'demand' and 'supply'. For example, the dentist moving from London to the West Country may find little provision of cosmetic dentistry and therefore face a healthy demand for this service.

General practitioners are self-employed contractors. Although there are key differences, we can think of them rather like small entrepreneurs, working as 'sole traders' or in small partnerships. Increasingly, over time doctors and dentists have formed partnerships. The partners decide on how to use limited resources to provide care, given the constraints and demands which they face. They make mutal adjustments and use professional standards, customs and conventions as guides. Given the advantages of the partnership, as we discussed in Chapter 9, it is not surprising that this organizational form has increased in popularity over time. Doctors co-operating share 'lumpy' capital expenditures, and bring economies of scale. Yet in recent years there has been a growth of simple hierarchies with practice managers, nurses, receptionists and administrators co-operating in larger groupings and providing a variety of health care services. However, whilst there are some similarities with entrepreneurial small businesses there are notable differences, which we shall discuss later in this chapter.

Something like 95 per cent of consultations are routine, the rest are referred for specialist diagnostic treatment and for acute care (Maynard 1990: 29). The general practitioner is the first port of call. There have been changes in funding, given government reforms and now doctors are required to have a greater understanding of business and financial issues. The funding of both dental care and ophthalmic care now requires substantial user charges, and pricing has been introduced for some treatments.

Hospitals

Hospital care is an important component of the NHS service. Hospitals are much larger and more complex organizations than the small 'firms' of general practitioners. Hospitals, just like the black box firms of traditional economic theory, can vary the scale of their output in the short and long run. However, they can also change the composition of output – they produce more than one 'product'. Hospitals are diverse in nature. They can be proprietary or non-proprietary, specialized according to function, for example, Elizabeth Garrett Anderson, a women's hospital, Great Ormond Street for children, or, say, specialist orthopaedic or general hospitals. The hospital provides a range of functions, including hotel and catering with out- and in-patient facilities. They may or may not have teaching and training functions. A variety of such features may affect their conduct and performance. It may be difficult to establish who are the key decision-makers, given that managerial and entrepreneurial functions are spread across a number of different individuals. However, the employment of business management teams has become an important feature in recent years. We may think of hospitals as having a U-form organization, according to functional areas, although inevitably there are complexities.

However, for the provision of medical services the consultant in any particular speciality runs a medical 'firm'. He or she is the director with a team of junior doctors organized on hierarchical lines. The firm has internal links with other parts of the organization and external links with, for example, the general practitioners who refer their patients to the consultant.

Community care

This provides a diverse range of services from homes for the elderly, those with mental or physical handicaps, and social support services for those at home. The provision comes from a variety of sources, by the NHS, local government and private sectors. Also, informal support in the community by relatives and friends provides an important complement to the system. The provision here again involves us in complex issues.

Clearly, the NHS has a structure which is compartmentalized with separate decision-making and where the rules of the game may be different (for a more detailed discussion see, for example, McGuire, Henderson and Mooney 1988; Maynard 1990; and Le Grand and Bartlett 1993). Whilst there are no easy answers to intricate problems in perspective time, in order to shed more light on the NHS and the character and implementation of recent government reforms, we need to examine the nature of the product and its supply and demand in greater depth. To do this we shall concentrate further, focusing on the doctor–patient relationship, in order to provide insights into the nature of health care products.

Health care products and provision: analytical and perspective time

The economic analysis of health care is not satisfactorily handled within the analytical time mode or using the yardstick of the perfectly competitive 'ideal type'. As we illustrated in Chapter 7, the demand for health care cannot be usefully treated in a framework where decision-makers are know-all, rational economic maximizers. Health care is not a simple homogeneous good and it is not supplied by perfectly competitive firms or anything approaching them. Although that does not deny the important role of economic analysis for clarifying such a complex and often highly emotive issue as health care products and provision.

The very nature of health care and the way it is provided forces us to acknowledge the realities of decision-making in perspective time. Neo-classical analysis assumes well informed rational economic people, REPs. But in the 'procurement' and provision of health care the assumptions of analytical time and, in addition, the yardstick of competitive ideals can be positively misleading. The good, health care, is not like a carrot or an apple; nor is it a financial asset to be bought and sold in competitive markets. Yet how is health care different from such private goods? Is the patient a customer, the doctor an entrepreneur? How do the economist's notions of demand and supply help us to analyse health care provision? To shed further light on these questions we can consider matters under the following headings:

The consumers and the product

a) Consumers lack knowledge of the commodity. They operate in perspective time with a lack of information and in some circumstances fundamental uncertainty. Often they may be unaware that treatment is needed and so they make no demands. Demand for the product is irregular and often unpredictable. The assumption that individuals can make rational calculations, finely balancing costs and benefits, is misleading. At the point of making a decision, individuals may be far from cool, calculating, rational beings. Sick people may be in pain, discomfort, frightened, experiencing a whole range of emotions which impairs rational thought. They may be irrational with good and understandable reason. Indeed, in some situations the individual may not be conscious or capable of making a choice. The unconscious client cannot be a rational consumer (McGuire, Henderson and Mooney 1988; Mooney 1992, 1994).

b) There is considerable ignorance and uncertainty in assessing the quality of the product, knowing if the professionals have done a good job. A 'quickie' eye test and a cheap set of spectacles might lead to unforseen difficulties. These could take some time to discover and any damage done might be irreversible. Buying an eye test or a cancer treatment is not like buying an apple, a regular purchase of relatively small importance, where the quality can be easily judged. Moreover, if the purchaser is mistaken, in as much as the taste is sour, there is no disastrous impact. The loss is small. But the converse may be true given the choice of an inappropriate eye or cancer treatment.

c) For the consumer the consequences of making the wrong choice can impose severe costs both in financial and non-financial terms in both the short and long term. There are also external spin-offs on the individual's family, employer, and society as a whole. We shall have more to say on these matters in the following section.

d) There are problems of making rational choices even if an individual has the ability to choose. Patients may not want to know of the choices or to do the choosing, but rather have the doctor decide (McGuire, Henderson and Mooney 1988). Choice itself can be onerous and painful, bringing further disutility. Also, a complex set of attributes enter into individuals' utility functions, including *how* they are treated, for example, with respect and dignity; or *where* they are treated, in familiar or unfamiliar surroundings. An operation fifty miles away is not the same as an operation performed in the patient's home town, other things being equal.

e) Finally, the income of the consumer is limited and incomes are unequally distributed. Limited incomes may have important implications for the purchase of health care products where uncertainty about the ultimate size of the health care bill can be significant. People may be tempted to cut back on health care or simply cannot afford it.

The medical profession

Are doctors business entrepreneurs? Do they work in markets which are highly competitive?

a) Different patterns of behaviour are expected from a doctor than the business person (Arrow 1963). The physician does not advertise and openly compete with other physicians. Doctors are supposed not to give advice on the basis of self-interest and treatment will be based on objective needs, not restricted by financial considerations. Doctors are expected to act as experts when certifying to the existence of illness and injuries for various legal and other purposes. They act not to make patients happy as such, but to give the appropriate treatment.

b) Doctors, the suppliers and relevant decision-makers, hold a *near monopoly* on medical knowledge and operate in perspective time. By virtue of the doctor's *specialization and experience*, the patient cannot have the same level of information and understanding. Moreover, gaining a second or third opinion takes the passage of real time – opinions from other doctors can be very costly to acquire. Everything else does not stay the same – medical conditions change. As providers, doctors make decisions in perspective time. They suffer from information overload, relative ignorance and uncertainty. Medical knowledge can be complex and changing. Furthermore, it is open to different interpretations by doctors schooled in particular rules and conventions. Doctors have to judge the probability of particular outcomes in situations of limited information and ignorance. They are not omniscient. Doctoring often requires detective work, with all the consequent search costs. Each individual case is unique and it is potentially difficult to predict the outcome of some treatments. There can be considerable variations in medical practice for ostensibly similar diseases and populations, both between and within countries (Mooney 1994: 115). Not all doctors are following or indeed agree on what is best practice in the treatment of any particular medical problem.

The agency relationship

The doctor is the patient's agent and decides, in consultation, what the individual needs. As we have seen in Chapter 9 principals and agents have different knowledge and interests. There is a major asymmetry between the doctor and patient, which is present under all systems of provision whether private, for a monetary exchange, or public. There may often be 'uncertainty regarding illness episodes and treatment available and effectiveness and the expected loss if things do go wrong' (Mooney 1992: 124). Indeed, the patient and professional health care provider are very aware that there is a differential in the amounts of information that they have; and what they 'know'.

Moreover, there is often a differential in terms of power, status, class, and gender between doctors and patients which can affect the 'bargaining' position. We are not in neo-classical market mode. Even where the patient may have clear, well informed views these may not coincide with those of the doctor which are based on knowledge, experience, custom and practice. For example, there may be considerable differences of opinion about childbirth practice, but male doctors are more likely to determine the methods used even though women might prefer alternatives. Doctors have power and status on their side. They have a strong association which protects their interests. There is no balance of power as in the perfectly competitive market. Consultants, as authoritative decision-makers, not surprisingly, may be swayed by concerns for their greatest professional satisfaction, rather than the maximization of the patients' health care benefit.

Externalities

Health care has some of the attributes of a private good which can be rationed to the individual by markets. Cosmetic surgery and slimming advice are often allocated by price, according to the ability and willingness to pay, in private clinics. However, some treatments have the features of public goods, immunization, for example, not only protects the individual but reduces the likelihood of others catching infectious diseases, positive spillover effects vital to the well-being of society as a whole. There are important beneficial externalities, for infectious disease can be passed from one individual to another like polio, diphtheria and measles. Whilst there is as yet no vaccine to prevent the spread and contraction of HIV and AIDS, it is important on a variety of levels to treat and contain these.

Whilst people may not be at risk from any particular disease, there is nevertheless a concern about the welfare of others. The utility of strangers may enter into the preference function of an individual. Witness the gifts which flow to charities committed to health research and the relief of suffering. Health and special needs charities feature prominently amongst the top charities (see the following section of this chapter). Health care as a good has significant positive externalities, people want to see the suffering of others reduced and prevented. Moreover, individuals give to those charities which might provide for them or their families and friends, if the future should bring them adversity.

Given the complex nature of supply and demand and health care products, we are a long way from the 'ideal type' market of introductory theory. To quote one prominent health care economist,

> [i]nformed choice is the source of the power of the consumer in the private market-place and informed choice is precisely the what the vast majority of patients in the vast majority of circumstances in the market for health care do not have. And it is doubtful even that they want it. It seems more often that patients actively want to rely on an agent whom they hope they can trust.
>
> (Mooney 1994: 102)

> The whole basis of the market is that consumers know what they want, know how to get it and through market forces can let suppliers know what they want.
>
> (ibid.: 103)

Moreover, there is no balance of power in terms of the relationships between consumers and suppliers. And there is an unequal income distribution amongst consumers, each person does not carry equal 'voting' power in the market. Indeed, the most recent evidence relating to income and wealth distribution (Joseph Rowntree Foundation 1995) indicates that 'Income inequality in the UK grew rapidly between 1977 and 1990, reaching a higher level than recorded since the war'. Moreover, 'over the period 1979 to 1992 the poorest 20–30 per cent of the population failed to benefit from economic growth, in contrast to the rest of the post-war period'. See this report for further detailed analysis. Overall, the properties of the competitive market do not exist in the provision of health care. With these caveats in mind we can consider recent issues.

Health care: demand, supply and resource allocation

Recent changes in the overall demand and supply have brought the issue of competition, funding and rationing to the forefront. Whilst state expenditure on health care in Britain has increased in real terms in recent years, the demand for health care services has grown apace. The reasons for such an increase in demand stem from a variety of sources. These include: the ageing population, technological changes which make possible the provision of new types of treatments, the switch to community care for the elderly and mentally handicapped which is more expensive, undertaken in small units, the impact of AIDS, and the programmes of screening for breast and cervical cancer (Maynard 1990).

As we have shown in Chapters 5 and 8, when the quantity demanded exceeds the quantity supplied in perfectly competitive markets, prices rise in the short run and output is increased. In the long run, new entrants come into the market, expanding output; resources flow into the industry. But competitive markets do not exist in the provision of health care. Most societies do not allow the price mechanism to be the major or sole arbiter of allocation, because of the significant difficulties already underlined. Indeed, given the nature of the problems, in perspective time, difficulties occur whatever the system, whether market or voluntary sector. There is no perfect solution.

In the British case, the overall budget for the NHS is set by central government and has been rising modestly in real terms, in relation to the increasing demand pressures on the service. We can expect health care to have a positive income elasticity of demand, a small percentage increase in income leads to a larger percentage increase in demand. Thus when society becomes wealthier we would expect more of the nation's resources to be spent on such goods. Overall, the growing demand for health care exceeds the supply, even though the resources made available have been increasing. People are now more aware of government cash limits and the rationing problem, which shows up in terms of waiting lists and ward closures.

Recent governments have emphasized efficiency savings where more output is derived from the same inputs. The argument goes that public sector provision is inefficient and wasteful because it is isolated from the competitive process. The aim of the government reforms has therefore been to change the institutional framework and to stick to tight cash limits. Competition is to be encouraged by splitting the market up into many different purchasers and providers, and contracting services out to the private and voluntary sectors. Some general practitioners have become fund holders with budgets to allocate between competing ends. They purchase from independent and competing hospital trusts. Elements of privatization have come in the form of competitive tendering for cleaning and catering along with a greater scrutiny of expenditure and the charging for some items which were previously supplied free of charge.

Recent institutional changes: an assessment

The reforms and their effects are complex and it is not possible to explore them in detail here, although we can raise questions about how the reforms have worked. To quote Maynard (1990: 18) 'the NHS like most other health systems is a blackbox whose workings are unknown'. There is a lack of information, the reality is complex and changing. However, we can identify particular features. Some general practitioners have become fund holders, purchasers, given their own budgets to spend with the service providers, for example, the hospitals. Yet there are often few providers in an area, so competition is limited. For purchasing to work effectively, the buyers must have information about the cost, quantity and quality of what they are buying. Additionally, providers should be able to reliably cost their various forms of output. It is patently clear that such information is often lacking or highly imperfect. Moreover, that information is in itself costly to generate; by the time it becomes available it can be out-dated. General practitioners often do not have reliable waiting times for different operations in different hospitals. Searching for such information involves an opportunity cost of resources and time.

Indeed, there are *transactions costs* to be considered. One of the results of the changes is to bring soaring transactions costs in terms of the negotiation and monitoring costs, which are part of using the market. These threaten to wipe out other gains (Le Grand and Bartlett 1993). This may stop the entry of new competitors, for there is an expense and difficulty involved in the drawing up of contracts. Moreover, within the service, information may now be withheld because it is considered to be commercially sensitive (*Guardian* 16 December 1994). Co-operation both between and within units can be significantly impaired. In fact, the Government wants to increase information about services and to put purchasers and providers in closer contact, seeing a role for the state in providing expert skills.

A potential major problem is 'cream-skimming'. If the fees per head are the same for different groups of patients with different needs, those providing health care may only want to take healthy groups in the prime, who will make few and inexpensive demands for treatment and so will be low-cost. In the USA such behaviour exists and it may well become a feature of fundholder behaviour in the UK. General practitioners may turn away those patients who are potentially expensive to treat. Some individuals may find it difficult to find doctors willing or able to take them on their list. These patients may have to rely on their own limited resources, on their family or on private non-profit organizations, in this context, the private charity. Those on low incomes may also find it difficult to obtain provision.

The 'ideal type' market mechanism does not exist for health care. That is not to say that competition and co-operation are not important, but that easy answers will not do. The overall decision about the level of funding is made not by the market but by a political decision-making process. Moreover, within NHS organizations a planning or command process works, as we saw occurring in the firm-for-profit, in Chapter 9. However, the economist can draw attention to the overall provision of funds and their opportunity cost to society as a whole. It is possible to consider the different ways in which resources may be allocated within the service and the implications for efficiency and equity. But we lack information and the introduction of quasi-markets will not necessarily give us the required results. Fragmentation may mar the ability to look at provision overall, bringing with it increased transactions costs and duplication. We are dealing with individuals who operate in perspective time, often within highly complex changing organizations and situations. The simple model of the market is not enough to make sense of a complex reality.

THE PRIVATE, INDEPENDENT OR THIRD SECTOR NON-PROFITS

From our earlier discussions it is clear that there is a large and varied group of non-profit private sector organizations, which include charities, pressure groups, trade unions, mutual organizations, in short, any organization which does not fit into the private for-profit business, public or household sectors. Such non-profit organizations are planning units, of necessity making economic decisions about the use and allocation of scarce resources.

Types of non-profit organizations

Non-profits can be categorized by: their purpose and activity; their source of income or independence from government; or who benefits from them and who participates. They may be organizations for *mutual benefit* where the prime beneficiary is the membership, as in the case of a trade union, like UNISON or sports organizations such as the Volleyball or Football Associations. They may be a *service organization* where there is a 'client group' who benefits, like the 'clients' of the Salvation Army or Save the Children. There is also the *commonwealth organization* where the public at large derives the services or good, from a group such as Greenpeace.

The purpose, historical background and legal status of these organizations may be quite different. They are not all voluntary or charitable. They do not of necessity rely on volunteers or donations, nor are they all independent of government. Quite frequently, governments use charities as their agents to carry out tasks or to channel funds. In recent times in Britain, for example, many new charities result not from the creative altruism of individuals who see unmet needs, whether these result from market, government or family failure. Rather, they are directly or indirectly established by local authorities and central government, like housing associations, to shoulder work previously undertaken by government bodies. Indeed, some charities are wholly funded by central government. Political pressure groups, such as Amnesty

International, do not have charitable status, neither do associations of workers, trades unions or employers' associations, although in Britain most religious organizations do. From this enormous variety of organizations we shall focus attention on a sub-category of the independent third sector in a British context: the charities.

CHARITIES

Definition and different types of charitable organization

What is a charity? Originally, the charity was conceived as an organization for the benefit of others, especially of the poor or helpless. The Poor Law 1597, passed in Elizabethan times, sets the foundation for modern legislation. The Charities Act 1960 defines the charity as 'any institution, corporate or not which is established for charitable purposes and is subject to the control of the High Court in the exercise of the court's jurisdiction with respect of charities'. The purpose has to be defined as charitable by reference to case law. Certainly, the relief of poverty, the promotion of education and religion, indeed to the benefit of the community as a whole, or in sufficient part are important. Charities are for the public good, although of course what is actually defined as a charity varies, dependent on historical time and place. In some societies such organizations do not exist.

The charity is a familiar and significant part of British life, as a group, charities provide important benefits. They have evolved over historical time. By 1990, there were 171,434 charities registered with the Charity Commissioners. The total income of the charities in that year was £16.18 billion – equivalent to 3.4 per cent of Gross Domestic Product (The Charities Aid Foundation 1992). The sector is significant in terms of employment, by the early 1990s, up to 80 per cent bigger than employment in Britain's motor industry and comparable in size with the energy and water supply industries. Moreover, the sector as a whole uses the services of a considerable number of volunteers, who give their time without payment, often on a regular basis. For an up-to-date comparative view of the sector see The Charities Aid Foundation 1995.

Charities are heterogeneous, they vary in size and purpose; they range from very large to small. The majority have no paid staff or significant monetary donations. There are different ways of classifying non-profit organizations like charities (Leat 1993). We can distinguish between them on the basis of income sources and provision. There are:

The fund raisers

These organizations gain a significant part of their income through fund raising, the soliciting of gifts. They provide services rather than grants and have an objective in terms of a particular client group, the old, children or a specific activity such as medical research or famine relief. Table 10.1 gives the ranking by size of voluntary income (£M) in 1992/3 for the top ten fund-raising charities.

Table 10.1 Taken from Table H.5: Voluntary income of the Top Ten fundraising charities 1992/1993 (page 9, Charities Aid Foundation)

Position (previous position in brackets)		Year end	Total voluntary income £000
1 (2)	National Trust	02/94*	78,745
2 (4)	Oxfam	04/93	58,972
3 (3)	Royal Nat. Lifeboat Institution	12/93	56,229
4 (1)	Save the Children Fund	03/93	53,866
5 (5)	Imperial Cancer Research Fund	09/93	48,395
6 (6)	Cancer Research Campaign	12/93	45,352
7 (7)	Barnados	03/93	36,452
8 (10)	Help the Aged	04/93	33,141
9 (9)	Salvation Army	03/93	32,303
10 (12)	NSPCC	09/93	30,818

Source: CAF data
* 14-month accounting period

Trusts or foundations

These rely on investment income from capital endowments and do not solicit contributions. They usually *finance services provided by others*. They have a wide range of purpose and trustees have some discretion. Rather like a financial intermediary, they stand between a company or individual and a particular cause. Many trusts are set up by companies and individuals. These include The Wellcome Foundation and The Joseph Rowntree Trust, a name from the past and the Cliff Richard Trust, one from the present.

Service providers

These make revenues from fees and the charges for providing a service. They include organizations like independent schools and housing associations. In addition, they attract the bulk of statutory support, although from fees rather than grants. We shall have relatively little to say about these organizations but they are significant in the Government's move to encourage private sector provision.

The new *International Classification of Non-Profit Organizations* (ICNPO) uses the primary purpose as the basis for classification, and not the type of organization which receives the income, as given above (see the Charities Aid Foundation 1992). Under primary purpose there are an impressive range of voluntary organizations and charities which deal with: Arts, Culture and Recreation; Animals; Education; Community Development; General Social Services; Housing; International Aid and Activities; Health and Medicine; Environment and Preservation of Heritage; Religion and Spiritual Development; Civil Rights and Advocacy, Grant Making Trusts and Foundations.

The objective of a charity: comparison with the firm-for-profit

By and large, the traditional economic model of the individual consumer or firm, based on utility or profit maximization, is inappropriate here. Whilst for the business firm, the straightforward objective of profit maximization is merely a starting point, it is *inapplicable* in the case of the charity, even as an initial simplification. In the charity we do not have a well defined group of legal owners, the ultimate risk bearers of the neo-classical model, entitled by ownership rights to any surplus produced by the firm. There are *no shareholders* who can sell their stake, they have no counterpart in the charity and the making of private profit is not a goal. In the charity *trustees* are in charge but no group of trustees or directors can decide to allocate net gains to themselves as their own wealth, like directors in the for-profit-firm. Funds have to be spent or retained in the enterprise to further the purpose of the organization.

The theoretical objective of utility maximization, in the context of a charity, is also problematic. Whose utility should be maximized? The donors who give to the charity? The users or 'clients' or the organizers of the charity? How are the charity's goals to be expressed and in what terms? One target is the maximization of the income at the organization's disposal for charitable works, whatever its source. Alternatively, the organizational goal could be stated in terms of a requirement to balance the needs and expectations of the users and the funders. The organization may simply aim to satisfice.

Certainly, it is not always easy to set well defined objectives and as in the case of business firms there are different interest groups who may have *conflicting needs*. For example, there may well be a division between the goals of the volunteers and the management and paid staff. Moreover, the interests of management and staff may not always align with those of the users.

The advantages and disadvantages of charitable status

Again, in a British context, charitable status may encourage people to give, both in terms of money and kind, for they are more likely to believe that their gifts will go to a good cause, if an organization is a registered charity. This gives *confidence* to donors. There are significant tax benefits which accrue to charities. Gifts to charities can be offset against taxation. Tax effective ways of giving can raise the contribution to charity for the charity can reclaim the donor's 25 per cent base rate tax on a covenant, payroll deduction or Gift Aid donation. The Inland Revenue returns the tax paid to the charity. Tax free legacies in the past and present have always been a major source of income for charities (Downing 1993). (However, the charity may have to pay VAT on the services which it provides and is not able to reclaim them as a commercial enterprise.)

However, there are disadvantages. In a charity run by trustees it is often difficult to pay a level of fees which will attract and/or hold the quality of personnel needed to manage what are often relatively complex organizations. These managerial tasks may involve considerable time and effort. Where charities have grown into multifarious organizations with business orientated fund raisers and trading arms, there is often a backlash both from donors and the private companies with whom the charities compete for business. People may not relish the association of charities and business and may be concerned that their gifts are being swallowed up in administration costs.

The external relations and internal organization of the charity

We can think of the charity as a planning unit – a black box – set in analytical time. It has links with individuals, households, business firms-for-profit and public sector non-profits. Rather like the firm-for-profit, in some cases there may be a great deal of competition between different organizations (Leat 1993). In other circumstances, effective barriers to entry exist against others who might be able to provide services more effectively. For the organization there is a necessary requirement to secure income in order to achieve its goals, indeed to survive. That can require competition and the drive to monopolize aspects of 'the market'. Charities are part of the integral economic system.

However, charities, whatever their purpose, make decisions in perspective time where there is limited information, risk and uncertainty. The demands on particular charities can change in surprising ways, making forward planning problematic. Government policy changes can have significant ramifications both directly in terms of changes in the demands faced by charities and on their incomes, whether from private individuals, corporate donors or the government. Major charities may have to run appeals to maintain income. Recently, a downturn in legacy income has hit many charities. Depressed house prices and changes in government policies, such that more elderly people are required to sell their houses to fund nursing or residential care, may partly explain this feature. Corporate sponsorship has, in some cases, also fallen in recession. The National Lottery may now absorb monies previously donated to charities. At the same time, the demands on particular charities like Shelter are growing, as housing benefits change and more people become homeless. The external environment of the charity affects funding and demands.

Just as in the case of the business firm, the organization's internal structure is an important element. In part, this is a function of size. The organization may have one person, the founder, setting the agenda, analogous to a sole trader. Small self-help

Figure 10.1 The 'black box' charity showing gift flows. The charity may have market relationships not displayed here

groups may have peer group structures where information within the organization flows relatively freely and the co-ordination for strategic decision-making and day-to-day running is good. At the other extreme, there is the large complex charity which has more than a prime charitable purpose. It may have a large bureaucracy, organizing and planning for a wide range of activities, like Oxfam and the National Trust. Indeed, such charities may have marketing and financial departments, research and development groups, a complex organization with paid managers and staff and volunteers. So the non-profit organization mimics some of the features of the for-profit, market orientated firm. Whilst trading is not Oxfam's core purpose but a means to an end, it is the largest charity trader with 850 shops. Other large charities, like the National Trust, have trading arms which have significant money turnover.

The problem for the donors is how to ensure that managers' actions, their strategic planning and day-to-day operations align with the donors' objectives. In perspective time there is *asymmetric information and principal agent problems*. For example, there may be little knowledge on the part of givers about what happens to their gifts, for there is a divorce between the giver and the charity user. Measures to provide more effective monitoring and accountability have been set in recent legislation, in the Charities Act 1992, there was a tightening up of accounting procedures: accounts have to be annually submitted to the Charity Commissioners (see Quint 1993 and Falk 1993). If people believe that their gifts may be wasted, then they may be disinclined to donate and users of the charity may ultimately suffer. Donors need reassurance that their gifts will not be used ineffectively or channelled to 'unsanctioned' or illicit purposes.

The key issues are how best to acquire and efficiently channel income; how to align the goals of different groups; how to monitor and control: how to provide an effective, efficient and just distribution of gifts. There are no easy answers.

CONCLUDING COMMENTS

Whether we examine public or private sector non-profits we are often dealing with complex organizations, allocating scarce resources, essentially through non-market means. Decision-makers operate in perspective time – where there are inequalities of knowledge and power. Questions of control and accountability present difficult problems.

NON-PROFIT FIRMS – SUMMARY

- Non-profit organizations are very varied; set either in the public or private sector but interwoven with other organizations, linked by money and goods flows, primarily in non-market relationships.
- Many non-profits are essentially non-trading organizations. They may use markets for acquiring labour services and other inputs but allocate final

goods and services by non-market means. They are essentially funded via private donations or from the public purse.

- Non-profits are an integral part of the economic system, and whether in the public or private sectors they often overlap, evolving over time.
- The NHS is a good example of a public sector non-profit organization set in a particular historical time and place. It is a segmented, related system to provide health care and has evolved over time.
- The health care product is not a homogeneous product of perfect competition supplied in competitive situations. There is often a lack of information and uncertainty.
- Demand by the individual is unpredictable and uncertain. There is ignorance and uncertainty in assessing the quality of the product, yet the consequences of making a wrong choice can impose severe costs. Externalities and unequal incomes are important considerations.
- Health care is often supplied in situations of monopoly. There are possible conflicts of interest and concerns between doctors and patients. The agency relationship and externalities are important.
- Recent reforms are based on the notion that competition and better consumer choice are beneficial. Information is imperfect – often expensive to generate. Efficiency gains can be wiped out by transactions costs. Some groups may be unable to acquire sufficient health care. A greater fragmentation in decision-making may cause difficulties in planning for the future and lead to unnecessary duplication.
- Private sector non-profits are varied. The key focus is on charities, for example: fund raisers, trusts and foundations and service providers. There are comparisons to be made with the firm-for-profit – but no simple orthodox model will fit.
- There are advantages of charitable status – it gives donors confidence and tax effective giving. Disadvantages arise when the organization finds difficulty in paying enough to hold and attract personnel because of legal requirements.
- Internal organization can be very different: small, peer group, democratic organizations or hierarchical with governance structures not too dissimilar from large, bureaucratic, hierarchical, private and public sector organizations. The external environment of the charity affects both funding and the demands made upon it.
- The charity is difficult to monitor, there is a lack of information. There are principal and agent problems.

NON-PROFIT FIRMS – QUESTIONS FOR DISCUSSION

1 What do you understand by a non-trading public sector organization? What are the key differences between this type of organization and the firm-for-profit, such as a corporate enterprise, a plc?

2 Why is uncertainty an important feature for the suppliers and 'demanders' of medical care?

3 How useful is the economists' concept of the market for understanding health care provision? What do you understand by a quasi-market?

4 What do you predict will happen, other things being equal, to waiting lists for NHS operations as:

a) the population ages;
b) new technology, such as key-hole surgery is introduced;
c) AIDS victims increase in number;
d) increased resources are made available for health care provision;
e) private sector clinics increase their throughput;
f) accident and emergency facilities are reduced?

Make your assumptions clear.

5 Is the private charity completely independent from the state?

6 How can charities be categorized? What are the sources of charitable incomes and why might these be uncertain?

7 Why is the giver's trust an essential requirement for the charitable organization, whether the gift comes from a private individual or corporate donor?

8 How do charities allocate scarce resources and by what means can these resources be increased? Illustrate your answer with current examples from your own experience or the media.

Part III

INVESTMENT, RISK AND UNCERTAINTY

11

Investment

INTRODUCTION

Time is essential in any discussion of investment decision-making. Indeed, it is not surprising that the theme of investment is of intense interest to economists, for investment can transform our future options. We make sacrifices now to change the future. Investment is always with us. Read newspapers, listen to radio and watch television, simply look around you. It is not difficult to find examples of new investments planned, or the results of investment decisions taken in the past, which have done perhaps better than expected or very badly. However, those who make decisions about expenditures now have to imagine how the future will unfold.

Organizations whatever their goals, whether large or small, face a wide array of investment choices. The size and potential impact of such investments, whether made by individual households, or public and private sector organizations can be very different. Yet, however diverse the context, all investments have a similar feature. From an array of very disparate examples, whichever we choose, the passage of time is a vital element, for a significant time elapses between the initial investment outlay and the expected receipt of the rewards. Moreover, no investment decision-maker, however experienced or skilled, has perfect knowledge of the current situation or perfect foresight of what is to come.

The major concern in this chapter is to explain how time can be allowed for in the investment decision making process. In short, how we can value gains and costs which are expected to occur at different points in time. For a significant part of the chapter we shall assume away the fundamental problems of risk and uncertainty. Not because they are unimportant but because of the need to clarify the choices for using scarce resources and money over time. To work with the neo-classical analysis in analytical time enables us to develop key concepts and to explain the decision-making rules used to assess different investment alternatives. All this is set out within the context of the profit-seeking firm and utility maximizing individual. This conceptual framework helps us to consider whether investments are worthwhile and which course of cash or resource allocation looks best given the complexities of actual decision-making in perspective time.

This chapter uses and builds upon the concepts from Parts I and II. Here we examine technical ideas, basic orthodox tools of the trade which economists employ to distinguish between different investment possibilities. This material paves the way for dealing formally with risk and uncertainty in Chapter 12. The concepts and techniques presented here and in Chapter 12 are also useful when we leave the world of private enterprise to explore investment decision-making in other contexts. These chapters give the groundwork so that we can move from the realms of profit-seeking firms to other wider scenarios. In particular, where a commercial interest is not paramount to government and private non-profit organizations where commercial investment objectives and criteria are inappropriate. We shall examine investment in these contexts in Chapter 13. Finally, we shall consider the nature of investment decision-making in human resources in Chapter 14.

THE NATURE OF INVESTMENT: AN OVERVIEW

Defining investment

Investment involves the commitment of resources such as capital, labour or cash for the long term. We invest now in the hope of future gains. We make a current outlay with the expectation of receiving future rewards in return. Whatever the form investment takes, for example, whether undertaken in the private or public sector, the passage of time is a key element. For an outlay of resources or cash now, we have to *wait* for the rewards. In analytical time we can know the rewards from any proposed investment with certainty. In perspective time we have to trust that such rewards will materialize in the future. In that real time of decision there can only be promises of benefits to come. Nobody can be certain about the timing and value of future gains; although we may have more confidence in the expected outcome of some investment proposals than in others. The straightforward replacement of well tried equipment may give a firm expectation, considerable confidence, that the future will behave like the past. However, this stands in sharp contrast to very large, new and relatively untried projects with wide uncertain ramifications, some of which may be irreversible. So we can have investment examples which range from the re-building of an Asda superstore to the one-off investment in a new project like the Thorp nuclear waste disposal plant with its uncertain side effects. These are thorny problems and we shall discuss the ways in which they might be addressed in later chapters.

Investment affects our future consumption potential of both goods and leisure. In

Chapter 2 we showed how investment in aggregate pushes out the production possibility boundary for a society, inducing economic growth. Investment also influences the nature of the production process where people spend much of their time, whether in unpaid home-work, in paid market work or unpaid employment. Investments often have differential costs and benefits for people and their communities.

Investment projects and investment choices can fall within the remit of the private, public or third sectors of the economy. Investments from different sectors are often interdependent, part of the complex economic system. But in whatever sector of the economy, with the advantage of hindsight we can see that some investments are highly successful – others disastrous. Often the success of one project depends, in part, on the health of another. There are important links, for example, between private and public sector investments. Olympia and York, the developers of Canary Wharf, the office development complex set to rival the City of London, went bankrupt as a result of the Canary Wharf venture. The future did not turn out as management, shareholders or the bankers of Olympia and York had hoped. The company was also to have contributed to the costs of building the Jubilee Line, an expansion of the infrastructure. This was to be a partnership with the public sector. It was hoped that expanding the public transport network would enhance the private profitability of the Canary Wharf project. Recession, the failure to let sufficient office space, the collapse of property prices and the demise of this company put paid to hopes of private funding for the Jubilee Line from Olympia and York. Now the Government will fund this investment because of its social importance, in short, the hoped for regeneration of Docklands, in part dependent on a well developed public transport network. This investment decision came too late to be of any aid to Olympia and York.

Investment categories

There are various ways of dealing with investment. Attention is often focused on one particular aspect. Economists distinguish between different investment categories in order to concentrate on manageable parts of the complex, interdependent economic system. In this chapter, in the main, we shall focus on the first category of investment as undertaken by the firm-for-profit. But investment can be broken down into the following major categories, by type:

Real or physical investment This involves the purchase of such things as capital equipment, machinery and buildings. These investments can be sub-divided into those for the *replacement* of worn out equipment, investment for maintenance to make good the existing physical stock. The straightforward replacement of old equipment with up-to-date machinery, enhances the quality of the capital stock, for example, the replacement of the 386 computer with the 486 machine, or the dot matrix printer with a laser printer.

Expansion occurs where new additional physical assets add to the capital stock, in a private sector company, additional capacity for existing product lines or increased capacity for new product lines, for example, new cars built by robotic techniques replacing old conveyor line production. However, physical investment is inextricably linked with other aspects of the investment process. In this case it embodies new technology, which is dependent on previous investments in research and development and may necessitate the employment of new labour skills and changed organizational structures.

Working capital   This involves the firm in investing funds for comparatively short periods – not investment long-term as in the previous discussion. The funds are used to pay for production, to maintain stocks and provide credit for customers. Cash has to be spent, for example, to buy-in raw materials, to cover work in progress and any outstanding debts. The more funds are invested in working capital, the less will be available for physical investment. A firm that has liquid short-term funds may take immediate advantage of opportunities in the financial markets – but there is an opportunity cost of so doing. Working capital, cash in-hand, must be sufficient to meet normal expenses. Precautionary balances of money with which to meet the unexpected may bring peace of mind, but that costs.

Investment in research and development   This presents an important category of investment, although one which is readily ignored in analytical time, where information is perfect. In perspective time the investment of resources for the development of creative ideas and the search for knowledge is of key importance for improving the quantity, quality and direction of investment. It includes design and development work, problem solving on production processes, gaining information about the products and processes of rivals. In some situations it may involve 'reverse engineering'. Countries like Japan and Korea have taken apart products, copied their manufacture and then built on them with their own new ideas. How an economy has evolved, the institutional relationships, customs and conventions are important for explaining different amounts of research and development expenditure and its focus (Nelson 1993).

Human capital   This investment involves the expenditure of resources on people. Whilst it is customary in orthodox mode for economists to treat investment in human and physical resources quite separately, changes in the type of capital equipment employed may have considerable impact on human productivity. People and the equipment they use are closely linked in the production process. Within an organization it may take a considerable time and effort to bring new systems into smooth operation. Physical capital can be of little use without the requisite human skills and knowledge. So the study of physical investment gives only one part of the investment story. The decisions which relate to physical investments often have implications for investment in people, whether in their education and training, the way their work is organized and geographical mobility patterns. Physical investment decisions can alter the demand for particular human skills, making some redundant whilst placing a premium on others. Such changes have implications which evolve over time. The decision to generate electricity with gas fired plants and to decommission coal-fired plants has had profound implications for some workers and the wider community. We shall focus on investments in people at a later stage.

Organizational change   This represents a form of investment. When we consider the costs of human interactions, for example, transaction costs in perspective time, then the investment of resources in organizational change becomes significant. At one extreme, one firm may take over another, making a strategic investment. Takeovers are essentially investment decisions. A company buys the assets of another, lock stock and barrel, including goodwill and the names of branded goods. Takeovers involve corporate organizational change. The new corporate structure will be different, as a result of a major strategic decision, changing both the external boundary of the firm and its internal make-up. Indeed, such an investment may have much wider potential ramifications than the purchase of a new photocopier or the go ahead for an in-house training course. As we have seen, the investment decisions of multinational firms can have a global impact.

Whether investment decisions are taken by private companies or government organizations, whether at local, national or international level, they can have important multiplier or 'knock on' effects for people and their communities. A significant investment by a multinational company in one area can bring considerable investment opportunities to others in the locality. The closure of one large company can bring the closure of many other small firms whose trade depends on the level of local business. The analytical model where we can make instantaneous adjustments, may mask the pain of such changes, which bring differential benefits and costs to individuals and families.

However, not all investment is made in real resources whether human or non-human. An important category encompasses financial assets. As we have already shown in earlier chapters, financial investments are linked with real investments.

Financial investment   This involves the purchase of paper claims to future cash flows, including government bonds and shares in publicly quoted companies. In the modern economy, this category includes the purchase of a very wide range of sophisticated 'financial products'. These include such instruments as share options, where the individual pays a 'deposit', a premium, for the option to buy or sell a share after a specified time, if the price proves to be advantageous. Essentially, financial assets enable the purchaser to move cash through time and in a world of uncertainty to make financial gains and losses. The purchaser of a share hopes for future cash rewards, but has no assurance that these will materialize. The original sale of such paper assets, ordinary shares, enables firms to acquire the large pools of cash resources necessary to finance large physical capital investments, research and development, human resource programmes, and the purchase of other companies. Sophisticated financial products are necessary requirements in the complex and changing modern world.

The interdependence of different types of investment and their significance in historical time

In earlier chapters we emphasized the vital role of physical investment in the development of economies through historical time. Physical investment is one of the essential keys to economic development and growth. In Part I we saw the crucial requirement of capital for large-scale industrial enterprise and for the infrastructure of the modern economy. Differences in the quality and quantity of investment provide an explanation for the very different living standards existing amongst nations both in the past and present. But here we need to underline that it is not sufficient to invest simply in physical, real equipment, or in financial paper assets like stocks and shares. *People matter*. Investment also requires the development of human skills and the way we do things, the rules of the game. In times of rapid technological change this becomes even more important.

In discussions of physical investment we must appreciate the essential role of people in the production process. There are many historical examples of investment decisions, where the importance of human skills and custom and practice have been underestimated with disastrous consequences. The forced collectivization of agriculture in the Soviet Union in the 1930s, provided mechanization without changing the skills of the workers to match. The Soviet planners in the early years of planning collectivized agriculture and provided machinery in place of horses (Nove 1980). Human skills and custom and practice could not be quickly changed to coincide with the introduction of this new equipment and new rules of the game. A variety of *complex interwoven factors* led to very poor productivity, with ill maintained and poorly functioning machinery and a consequent fall in living standards, indeed, starvation for many. Over time Soviet agriculture had considerable problems. But these were: 'compounded by shortage of workers trained to use and maintain farm machinery. In the period 1966–75 while the number of tractors on farms increased by 48% the number of trained tractor-drivers increased by only 21%' (Smith 1981: 60). Even then many trained workers migrated to urban areas further exacerbating the problem.

So it is important to emphasize that whilst physical investment may embody new technology, it also requires the appropriate level of human skills to make it function effectively and an appropriate backdrop of institutional rules. It may necessitate organizational changes. The research and development process, the creative search for new ways of doing things and for innovative products is a vital component. At the same time public sector investments in whatever category, are often essential to the success of private sector projects. In the modern economy, expenditures on these interdependent, often inextricable categories of investments, generate cash flows and other benefits in future periods. The rewards from these investments provide us with the means to maintain and increase consumption possibilities over time, one of the factors which ultimately matters for the well-being of people.

Given this overview of investment, we now move to analytical time. We focus on the investment decision-making process at the level of the individual and the profit-seeking firm. The usual practice in traditional theory is to examine the firm's physical investment decision in isolation. We shall start by assuming utility and wealth maximizers, whether individual sole traders or the management of corporate enterprise. We clarify the orthodox investment consumption link and the basic theoretical framework for investment decision-making. This cornerstone ultimately facilitates the handling of investment decisions in a variety of different contexts, including those in non-profit organizations and investments in people. It is critically concerned with the significance of the timing of gains and costs; the impact of timing on their value. The time value of money must be assessed in order to maximize utility.

INVESTMENT DECISION-MAKING IN ANALYTICAL TIME

The one period investment consumption model

Imagine a sole proprietor, the owner manager of a successful private business, Rosa. She faces many opportunities for both investment and consumption, but her current stock of cash, that is, her *wealth*, is fixed. At the present time she has to make choices about how to allocate her scarce cash funds. Rosa is required to answer the following interrelated questions:

1 How much physical investment in total and which specific projects to undertake now?
2 How much to consume now?
3 How to finance investment and consumption expenditure?

The orthodox model can provide unique solutions to these questions and explicitly emphasizes time. Yet this time is not the perspective time of the decision-maker, often faced with complex and uncertain choices. The basic model works in analytical time, abstracting from many real-world details and problems. By using such simplified analysis we can explain key economic concepts used in the appraisal of investment. The model provides the rationale for techniques which can be used to allow for the different size and timing of revenues and costs associated with different projects in the real world. Investment in a lorry may bring returns quite quickly but over a relatively short life, say seven years. In contrast, the investment in a plant for generating electricity from natural gas may take some years before benefits accrue, but then these might last well into the twenty-first century. Techniques which allow for the differential size and timing of gains and costs are used increasingly in the corporate world. In addition, these techniques are often employed by government organizations and non-profit making agencies. The model gives an insight into the way decision-makers may compare different, often seemingly indistinguishable and bewildering options in perspective time.

At the outset the model is stark, with the following assumptions:

a) That there is only the present time, t_0 and one future time period, next year, t_1.
b) There is a rational economic person who aims to maximize utility.
c) Perfect information about *all* the potential physical investment projects is available. Thus all project costs and their net revenues are completely known. *There is neither risk nor uncertainty*.
d) All projects are *independent*, this means that no project affects the cash flow of another and the decision to do one project does not prohibit the undertaking of others. Also, it is further assumed that each project is divisible and so can be divided into infinitely small amounts.

These assumptions do not mirror reality. The assumption of perfect knowledge of both now and the future gives the model a distinct similarity with an undertaking of the production of *The Phantom of the Opera* without the star attraction. But we need such a simplifying assumption to facilitate our initial understanding. The phantom raises awkward issues which come later. The assumptions enable us to display basic concepts with clarity before we address more complicated issues. Given these assumptions, we begin by employing a useful analytical technique akin to the production possibility curve introduced in Chapter 2 to illustrate the basic choices.

The physical investment line: investment opportunities

To illustrate the physical investment and consumption options which face Rosa, now and in the next period, we can draw a *physical investment line* or (PIL), where physical investment might involve the purchase of machinery, warehouses, vehicles etc. This represents a boundary which shows all the possible combinations of consumption and investment expenditure now and consumption in the next time period. This is given on the basis of the owner/manager's current stock of cash and the physical investments available to her given that sum. The boundary between possible and impossible cash flows is shown in Figure 11.1. On the horizontal axis *cash now* is measured, displaying the amounts of money which will either purchase the physical investment or will be available for current consumption. Cash on this axis is in *present value* terms. It represents the current value of money now. Rosa, as we have said, is successful and has an initial stock of wealth in time zero of £8 million, marked at point A.

On the vertical axis we measure cash which comes in at the end of the next period, one year from now at time t_1. This cash inflow is the total cash which can be earned by undertaking different amounts of investment, choices available now in t_0. In reality, most investment projects in the 'for-profit' privately owned company will have net cash inflows, revenues less costs, which will amass over several years, albeit with different project lives. But the fiction of one future time period allows us to

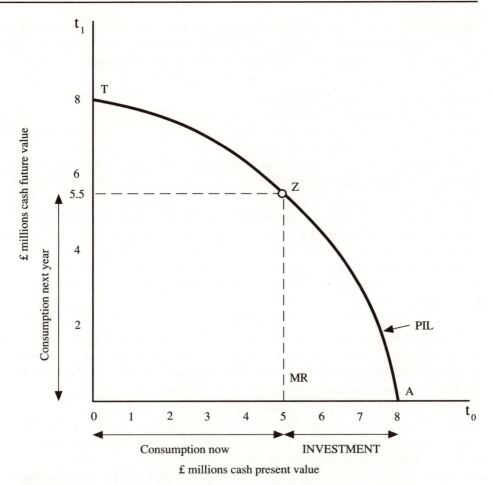

Figure 11.1   The physical investment line (PIL): Rosa's investment opportunities

simplify and to use a two dimensional diagram. Cash values at the *end of year one* are by contrast in *future value*. They do not arrive until next year, and so represent income to come. The PIL is drawn as a smooth curve as shown in Figure 11.1. Rosa, omniscient, can order all the available physical investment projects, from best to worst. There are just two possibilities for spending cash now. Rosa can consume or invest. Given her initial cash holding, her wealth of £8 million in present value terms can be spent on these two options. The PIL displays, graphically, all the options which are available to trade-off cash for spending on consumption now and for consumption in the future. More physical investment expenditure *now* means more consumption next year – 'less jam today means more jam tomorrow'.

Notice that the curve is *concave* to the origin, it has an outward bow shape. This tells us that as Rosa applies additional equal amounts of cash for investment, moving leftwards towards the origin on the horizontal axis, she faces *diminishing returns* in terms of extra future cash generated. Every additional £1 million invested gives a smaller additional cash return next year. The marginal rate of return on investment is falling. This means that the opportunity cost of forgone consumption is increasing as Rosa increases expenditure on physical investment. Every £1 of consumption sacrificed now gives a smaller addition to cash next year. The explanation is analogous to that presented in Chapter 2. A straight line PIL would mean that all projects gave the same return at the margin and thus exhibited constant returns. The best investment, in terms of its ability to generate cash next year, has been marked first, at the far extreme on the horizontal axis with the other projects ranked in order of diminishing returns, the worst, nearest the vertical axis, to be taken last of all.

Just like the production possibility curve the PIL is a *constraint*, a barrier beyond which Rosa cannot reach, given her current investment possibilities. The smooth curve implies that Rosa can split investment projects into infinitely small amounts, there are no 'lumpy' large indivisible investments. Of course, Rosa would not have the information required to draw up such a trade-off curve but the concept helps to clarify ideas.

At one extreme, point A, if Rosa spends £8 million now she will make no investment. There will be no cash available for consumption in the future period. But if she undertakes investment projects then cash will be earned for the future. For example, an investment of £3 million now will generate a certain cash return of £5.5 million at the end of the next period. This level of investment expenditure, £3 million as shown on the horizontal axis, would leave £5 million of cash for consumption now and give £5.5 million next year. Rosa would have the cash combination illustrated at point Z on the boundary. As Rosa increases her investment expenditure, less wealth is available to spend on consumption now. But more cash inflows will accrue in the next period for consumption. At the other extreme, at the origin, Rosa could invest all her current cash, £8 million, consuming nothing now. All her cash would come next year, shown on the vertical axis at T. This represents 'all jam tomorrow, no jam today', a hypothetical extreme.

We can move the constraint and change the position of the PIL, by changing the assumptions. Clearly, if we draw the curve with a steeper slope Rosa's investments would be more productive at the margin; a relatively poor, flat, 'puny' PIL could be transformed into a 'super' PIL, for example, by changing the technology and so enhancing productivity and the future sale proceeds from the investments. This would expand the consumption opportunities open to the investor, by making real investment more productive at the margin. Any given sacrifice of cash now would bring in a larger amount of money next year. If there were a change in technology which affected all the possible investments, the curve would pivot outwards, being fixed on the horizontal, given the same initial endowment of wealth, but reaching the vertical axis at a *higher future value* as shown on Figure 11.2. A 'puny' PIL could also be drawn based on different assumptions of investment opportunities.

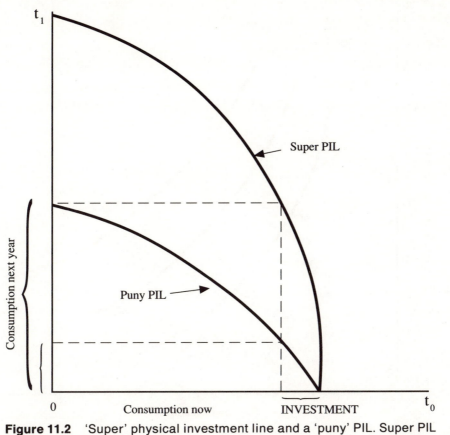

Figure 11.2   'Super' physical investment line and a 'puny' PIL. Super PIL generates more cash next year

Investor time preference – investment and consumption choices

The PIL gives us certain possibilities, choices of physical investment and consumption. Given that Rosa is a rational utility maximizer and we know her indifference curve map, we can easily pick out her optimum situation. There is a unique solution to the question of how much investment and consumption to take now and therefore how much will be available for consumption next year. To find the best mixture we need the investor's preferences, how Rosa will be willing to trade-off consumption now and next year. We can make different assumptions about the way Rosa is prepared to exchange money for consumption now and money for consumption in the future period. In Figure 11.3 Rosa's indifference curve map shows curves of equal utility for combinations of consumption now and in the next time period.

The usual assumption is that an individual will have a *positive time preference*. Money for consumption will have a time value; the nearer in time the better – there has to be a premium for delayed consumption. As Keynes said: 'life is not long enough; – human nature desires quick results' (1936: 157). People may just want instant gratification, to start enjoying consumer goods and durables immediately or

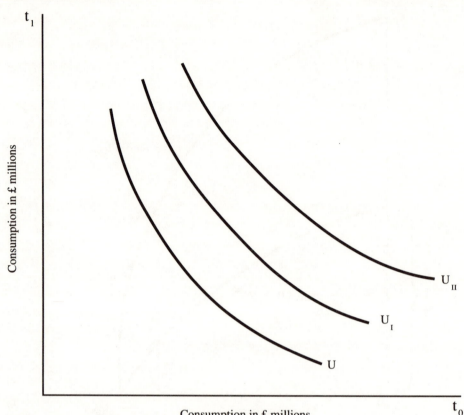

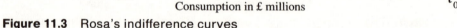

Figure 11.3   Rosa's indifference curves

as soon as possible. After all, death is certain. So even though we have assumed away all risk and uncertainty we can justify a reward for deferring consumption, people have to be compensated for postponing consumption.

However, we could also make a case for a negative time preference – where the person in question likes to look forward to future gratification or expects to require income in the future for retirement. People have been known to save at negative rates of interest to ensure money incomes in their old age. When inflation rates were very high in Britain in the 1970s, in relation to the money rate of interest paid, savings were actually rewarded with negative rates. Moreover, a rational consumer might well wish to postpone a second large meal which must be eaten today, for a smaller meal tomorrow. So it is possible for people to display a negative or, in some instances, a neutral time preference rate, that is respectively to pay for the privilege of saving or be indifferent to a pound today as opposed to a pound next year.

So if Rosa is indifferent between £100 now and £110 next year, her marginal rate of time preference is positive at 10 per cent. Rosa is willing to 'trade' money for consumption between the two periods at a price, an inducement of 10 per cent. If she has the possibility of a 5 per cent return on the extra physical investment project this would give her only £105 next year. She would prefer the money now to spend it on consumption. The premium of 5 per cent would, at the margin, not succeed in tempting her to put off the pleasure of consumption until next year. If, on the other hand, the marginal rate of return on the investment were 15 per cent then Rosa would abstain from spending now and invest so that she would receive £115 next year. The return on the marginal investment would more than compensate her for delaying consumption. At 10 per cent, Rosa would be indifferent to either course of action, equally satisfied by either alternative. By superimposing Rosa's utility map on the PIL, we could show position Z as the optimum situation. If we change the slope of the indifference curves, alter Rosa's time preference, we would get a different result.

In a world where there are no ready sources for borrowing cash, then investment now has to be paid for by reduced consumption. This is often portrayed as the 'Robinson Crusoe on an island' scenario where there is no extended family or other community to borrow from. Abstaining from consumption, *saving*, here is the indispensable price of investment. The highest indifference curve which Rosa can reach given the PIL constraint will be at point Z. No other consumption investment expenditure combination would give a better result. This gives an investment of £3 million, with a consumption now of £5 million and in the next year £5.5 million (see Figure 11.4.) No other attainable indifference curve would provide such a level of satisfaction. To choose a cash flow combination at S would be inferior, for it provides Rosa with a lower utility. By rearranging her consumption and investment pattern she moves to Z with a higher utility. She simply reduces investment, for at a point like S, she is *over investing*. Of course, Rosa would prefer to consume £5 million now and say £7 million next year. But this is an unobtainable option. The production potential of physical assets, as shown by the PIL, does not give this possibility, a combination of cash now and next year. Such a combination lies outside the boundary, beyond Rosa's reach.

The slope of the PIL will equal the slope of the indifference curve at the equilibrium point so that the opportunity cost of forgone consumption exactly matches the extra return on physical investment. Investment in physical projects will continue to be worthwhile, providing the extra return on investment exceeds the utility loss from the forgone consumption of cash. *Given our assumptions*, this cash has to be saved and so not consumed, in order to pay for the project.

However, now let us widen the alternatives open to the decision-maker and bring the model closer to the reality of the modern world. So far, we have emphasized the opportunity cost of investment expenditure in terms of forgone consumption. When we introduce financial markets, where individuals can borrow and lend cash, Rosa has a third option.

Borrowing and lending possibilities: the financial market

The financial market enables lenders, the suppliers of cash or *loanable funds*, to exchange cash with the borrowers, the demanders of loanable funds. With the

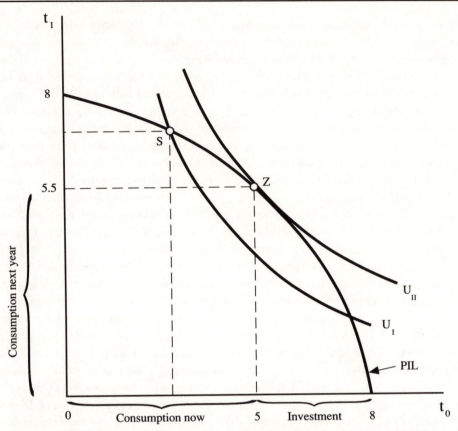

Figure 11.4 The investment and consumption pattern which maximizes Rosa's utility at Z

existence of a financial market, borrowing or lending cash is an alternative possibility for the individual. Imagine now that a perfectly competitive financial market exists. This market has all the familiar attributes of perfect competition. There are many borrowers and lenders. All are assumed to be small in relation to the market as a whole, such that no one borrower or lender can affect the market price. The market price of loanable funds is simply the rate of interest expressed as a percentage.

Furthermore, the assumption of perfect competition reminds us that we still work in analytical time where there is perfect knowledge, certainty and zero transaction costs. No risk is involved in either borrowing or lending. Remember, in addition, that no borrower or lender is big enough to influence the price of loanable funds. The result is a single rate of interest which rules for everyone, whether a borrower or lender.[1] Indeed, people pay differential rates for borrowing and receive differential lending rates in reality. Yet in a world of perfectly competitive financial markets, the reward for lending money is simply a compensation for waiting. No premium would need to be levied by a lender, to compensate for the possibility of things not turning out exactly as expected, a project doing badly or a borrower defaulting. For perfect

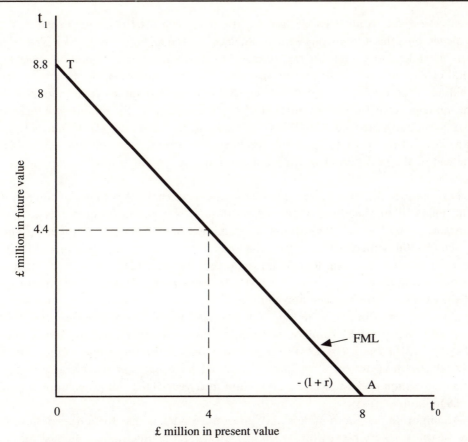

Figure 11.5 The financial market line representing a present value of £8 million given an interest rate of 10 per cent. Change the interest rate and the slope of the FML changes. Change the stock of wealth in t_0 and the FML shifts

knowledge exists. There would be no differential rates of interest charged to individuals and corporate borrowers, indeed no need for limited liability. There would be no difference in the return on fixed interest rate Government Bonds which give a relatively secure return and shares which in perspective time are more risky. In fact, there would be no difference between fixed interest rate debt and the return on equity, in a certain world. And there would be no loan sharks charging high differential rates to the poor. Only one interest rate would exist in this certain, risk free world, moreover, one with no differential market power.

The introduction of such a financial market gives Rosa another set of possibilities. The *financial market line* (FML) shown in Figure 11.5 displays a different constraint, a constant trade-off between money now and money in the future period. To derive this constraint, assume that the market interest rate is given at 10 per cent. Further assume that Rosa lends all her current cash at t_0, at that fixed rate of interest. In the next period she would have £8 million, the repayment of the original cash lent, the *principal* plus the interest payment on that £8 million ($PV(1 + r) = FV$). The principal, her stake and the market rate of interest on that amount, £0.8 million, gives her a total of £8.8 million at the end of year one. So the *future value* of her initial wealth holding, when lent at interest, would be £8.8 million. The future value is greater than the *present value* by the amount of the interest earned. By joining up these two extremes points, labelled A and T with a straight line labelled FML (Figure 11.4), we can show all the available possible combinations of cash, divided between now and the end of the next period which Rosa can have by lending different amounts of her current cash.

Now we can illustrate more forcefully the twin concepts of *present and future value*. The financial market line, a downward sloping straight line, represents a line of *constant present value*. This shows all combinations of income between t_0 and t_1 which give the same wealth. In fact, the financial market line is like a bridge through time for transferring cash. Rosa can rearrange her money between now and next year by borrowing or lending. Along the FML, between points A and T, the present value of the cash flow mix between now and the next period will always be £8 million. Rosa could have, for example, £7 million now and lend £1 million and receive £1.1 million next year. When the £1.1 million is brought to present value, *time discounted*, ($FV \div (1 + r) = PV\ 1.1 \div 1.1 = £1$, all figures in millions) the present value is £1 million. The overall wealth is always £8 million. She could have half her wealth now, lend the other £4 million and so receive £4.4 million next year. This still gives a present value of £8 million.

An important lesson to understand, given the model, is that Rosa does not enhance her wealth stock by borrowing or lending. In perfect competition if she just plays the financial market and makes no physical investment, she cannot hope to have more than £8 million in present value terms. The FML with a present value of £8 million only allows her to move her current stock of cash through time, but not to enhance her wealth.

The rate of interest gives *the opportunity cost of money* consumed or invested today. An extra £1 million spent today has an opportunity cost of £0.1 million, the interest forgone. Or what amounts to the same thing, the opportunity cost of £1 spent today, is 10p in terms of the interest forgone at 10 per cent. This constant opportunity cost can be seen clearly from the straight line FML. There are no diminishing returns as we move money through time, the rate of return on financial investment is constant. So the financial market line is another line of possibility, a constraint, which tells us the trade-off between cash now and in the future, at a fixed rate of interest. Rosa can move money between now and the future period to suit her desired investment and consumption preferences.

If she lends, the interest rate represents her reward for waiting. Alternatively, if she borrows on the strength of future cash, it is the price of enjoying more consumption now. Should the interest rate increase then the FML line becomes steeper, cash today will have a higher future value. At a 20 per cent rate of interest, for example, the £8 million would be worth £9.6 million in terms of future value. If we lower the interest rate then the future value of one pound today will fall. Essentially the interest rate is the price of money and the opportunity cost of cash through time.

In this orthodox model, the market for cash funds, with its interplay of demand and supply, will determine the rate of interest; the price of moving money through time. If people demand more cash now, other things being equal, because, for example, their time preferences have changed, then the market rate of interest will increase. Thus the slope of the FML line will become steeper. This has ramifications for both investment and consumption decisions – for it changes the opportunity cost of money.

The significance of financial markets

In a world with well developed financial markets, physical investment is not constrained by the initial wealth stock of the owner/decision-maker. In the orthodox model, investment, in the absence of borrowing and lending, would have to be financed by cutting back consumption today. The role of the community or a wider family network for providing cash funds is not part of the orthodox perspective. The provision of a financial market makes it possible to tap the savings of others. Savers and investors need no longer be the same individuals. Those with relatively poor opportunities for physical investment or 'puny' PILs, who do not want to invest because of the relatively poor rates of return on their physical investment, can lend surplus funds, those not required for current consumption. On the other hand, those with relatively good investment opportunities, who want to invest but do not want to cut back their current consumption, are able to finance investment by borrowing. So cash funds are traded between individuals in the financial market. Those with a shortfall of funds – borrow. Those with surplus cash – lend. As a result of the existence of a financial market there is no need for an individual or firm to balance the budget in any one year, that is, to be confined by a limited current stock of cash.

Comparing the alternatives: choosing the equilibrium package

We assume that Rosa aims to maximize her satisfaction. In analytical time she knows the best course of action available to achieve this. We have isolated the following alternatives: given a particular sum of cash now, at t_0, our rational decision-maker can either use the cash to:

a) consume – buy goods and services;
b) invest in physical or real assets;
c) lend or borrow cash on the financial markets.

Here it is interesting to note that neo-classical economics does not include the possibility of giving to a charity, a realistic rational alternative. Neither does it include the possibility of hoarding, simply holding cash, storing it without interest. Hoarding would be irrational in a world of certainty but not in situations of uncertainty or ignorance where people may not wish to commit themselves to particular consumption or investment decisions. However, with the set of options given by the model, the secret is to synchronize the opportunity costs of all the alternatives. This approach enables Rosa to achieve the highest level of utility possible, given the constraints. Indeed, to obtain this position Rosa must take the following steps:

Invest in physical projects in order to create and maximize wealth

To find the best solution, Rosa must compare the returns on physical and financial investment. Rosa undertakes that level of physical investment which will enable her to reach the highest line of constant present value, FML in Figure 11.6, she expands her original wealth by moving to the highest FML constraint possible as shown on the diagram. So Rosa would *buy* machines etc., provided they *add* to her wealth, each project undertaken must display a *positive net present value*. This means that the future cash inflow from a project when brought into present value terms by time discounting, must exceed the cost of the investment outlay in t_0.

In this example Rosa will undertake the series of projects which taken together will require an investment outlay of £3 million now and give a total inflow of £5.5 in the next period, t_1. A present value of £5 million is derived by dividing £5.5 million by 1.1. The net present value of these projects would be £2 million.

With £5 million left for consumption after paying for the investment of £3 million, plus the present value of the project inflows £5 million, Rosa has a total of £10 million. Rosa's business firm is worth £10 million. To measure the addition to her wealth, the net present value, the investor must use the appropriate opportunity cost of money. Here Rosa could earn 10 per cent on the financial market, so this is the yardstick against which to measure any project's value. Indeed, through the time discounting process the project's cash flows are automatically compared with the cost of the best alternative forgone.

Inferior wealth outcomes occur if more or less investment than £3 million, is undertaken. The combination of cash flows given at point S would place the investor on a lower FML and so reduce her wealth. If, for example, Rosa invested £5 million in physical equipment, the cash inflow next year would leave Rosa on a lower FML, representing a smaller constant present value. The additional projects undertaken in excess of the £3 million optimum investment which gives Z would *reduce* wealth. The projects beyond Z give a negative net present value, they cost more in present value terms than they bring in and make Rosa worse off. She would be doing too much investment.

The moral of this story is that Rosa should only invest in physical projects if the present value of the returns outweigh the costs, given the opportunity cost of cash. They have positive net present values. This is the same as saying that physical investments should be accepted only as long as the return on the marginal or additional project, that is, the slope of the PIL, is greater than or equal to the return

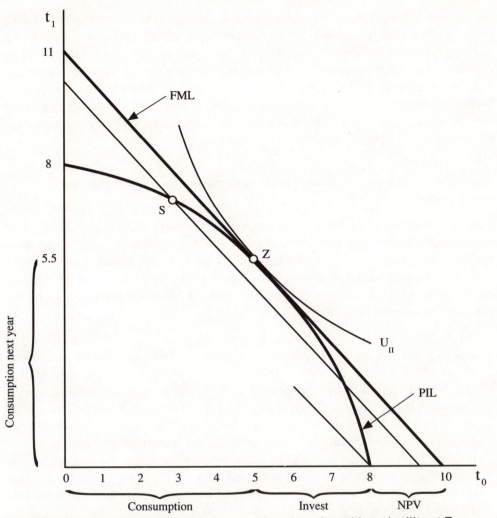

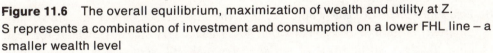

Figure 11.6 The overall equilibrium, maximization of wealth and utility at Z.
S represents a combination of investment and consumption on a lower FHL line – a smaller wealth level

at the margin on the financial market; the rate of interest or the slope of FML. In the assessment of physical investment the key comparison is with the best alternative, the rate of return, forgone in the financial market. If Rosa can earn *more* on the financial market than on physical investments, surplus cash which she chooses not to consume now should be lent at interest, *not* used to purchase physical investments.

In this particular case Rosa is able to increase wealth by physical investment. This net addition to wealth or the *net present value* is £2 million. The present value of Rosa's wealth has expanded from the original £8 to £10 million as a result of physical investment. Now, without physical investment opportunities, Rosa could only play on the financial markets to rearrange her cash through time, according to her time preference for cash now, rather than cash next year, t_1. She would be stuck with a constant wealth. With physical investments which give returns *greater* than could be earned in the financial market, she *expands wealth*. Once wealth has been maximized and the investment level determined, she can attend to the consumption decision. Moreover, remember that the size of the net present value will vary according to the rate of interest. The lower the interest rate the greater the quantity of investment demanded and the bigger the addition to wealth.

The option to rearrange cash through time by borrowing and lending on the financial market

Rosa has maximized wealth but she wants to achieve the highest possible level of satisfaction. The next step is to check whether or not the cash flows which result from the best investment package fulfil this aim. They may not. Whether or not Rosa needs to use the financial market to rearrange cash through time, critically depends on her preferences for consumption now as opposed to consumption next year. We can examine different possibilities:

a) *No financial market trading* would be required given an indifference curve just touching the PIL at Z. Fortuitously, an overall equilibrium would be reached which requires no extra action to rearrange cash in time. With her highest obtainable indifference curve tangential at Z, she has no need for financial market dealings. This situation is shown in Figure 11.6. *All* investment can be financed by Rosa, from her current cash and just leave her with sufficient cash for her consumption requirements in t_0. She balances her budget neither borrowing nor lending. The cash flows from the projects are ideally suited to her relative desires for cash now as opposed to cash next year. Only in the event of her indifference curve intersecting Z will she use the financial market either to borrow or lend, to achieve a better position.

b) *Financial market trading* would occur if the indifference curves are drawn in a different position. First, imagine that Rosa has a very strong penchant for cash now. She is a 'spendthrift' or perhaps terminally ill, someone who just cannot wait. She wants *more cash now* than is available after the optimum investment outlay is determined at £3 million. Moreover, she is prepared to trade-off future cash to achieve this end. At one extreme, if Rosa wants to spend all her wealth now she can do so, by the appropriate financial market strategy. She simply borrows to fund consumption and investment.

She invests in the best £3 million wealth maximising investment package. She finances the investment outlay (£3 million) and acquires the net present value of the projects (£2 million) by *borrowing* on the financial market at 10 per cent. Next year the principal of £5 million plus the interest of 10 per cent owing on that sum will be completely repaid from the certain cash inflow of £5.5 million. So Rosa can consume all her wealth now and have the full benefit of the investment, *immediately*, by borrowing. The financing of the investment outlay *and* the additional consumption, given by the increase in wealth from that investment, is made possible by using the financial market. Of course, consuming all wealth in time zero leaves nothing for next year. Rosa's future earnings are mortgaged to the hilt. None the less, investment and the additional consumption expenditure can be financed through borrowing on the strength of next year's cash flows. It enables Rosa to achieve a better position, instead of utility curve II she reaches the *corner solution* at a higher utility III, as shown in Figure 11.7.

The opposite extreme case can be shown where Rosa is assumed to be a 'scrooge'

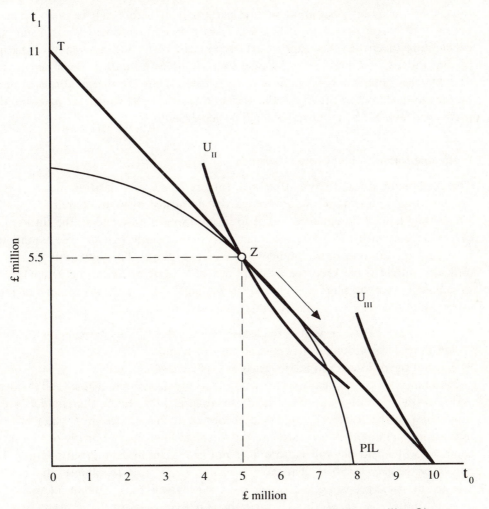

Figure 11.7 Rosa spends all her wealth now and maximizes utility. She borrows to achieve this result, moving down the FHL. She has zero consumption next year (the £5.5 million is owed to the lender) but Rosa consumes £10 million now

who saves and *lends* cash now. First, she invests in the wealth maximizing investment package of £3 million. She is much happier to defer consumption and is prepared to live on thin air in the current period, lending her surplus funds of £5 million, left over after she has paid for the optimum level of physical equipment. She earns £0.5 million next year in interest on the money she lent plus the return of her principal and the earnings from the projects. This leaves her a total of £11 million and puts her on a higher indifference curve; another corner solution at T.

The scrooge and spendthrift scenarios are merely theoretical extremes, chosen to illustrate the importance of the possibility of borrowing and lending. The key point to note is that the financial market option enables Rosa to achieve a greater level of satisfaction, a better consumption time pattern than before. There is no virtue or necessity to balance her budget in the current period. Investment and consumption expenditure taken together can exceed her current cash. She can repay in the next period. Indeed, in a multi-period model she will allocate funds through her lifetime. The different opportunity costs have to be equated. Here the marginal rate of return on the physical investment equals the market rate of interest equals the marginal time preference rate. No better position could be achieved.

From sole trader to corporate enterprise

The example of Rosa is straightforward, for the owner and decision-maker are one and the same. In a situation where companies are owned by many shareholders, all of whom may have different preferences for consumption now and in the future, how can managers, on behalf of shareholders, compare the alternatives? We assume that managers do not know shareholders' preference maps. This situation creates no difficulty provided we keep the assumptions of a perfect capital market, where all shareholders face the same rate of interest. Managers who make investment decisions on behalf of their shareholders are simply required to:

a) maximize shareholder wealth, the total present value of the company by undertaking all projects with a positive net present value, and

b) pay out the residual cash not invested in t_0 as *dividends*.

Cash inflows received next year are paid out as dividends in t_1. These total dividends and investment outlay are illustrated on Figure 11.8. Each shareholder gets a proportion of the total dividend, paid according to his or her proportion of share ownership. Shareholders can then use the financial markets to borrow or lend if the company's dividend pay out pattern does not give them maximum satisfaction. This *separation principle* shows that management merely has to choose the optimal investment package, using the opportunity cost given by the financial market to discount future cash flows. Shareholders then are free to adjust the resulting dividend cash flow profiles by borrowing or lending. However, this principle hinges on the notion of perfect capital markets where the same opportunity cost of capital rules for everyone and where there are no taxes or transaction costs. Managers are then

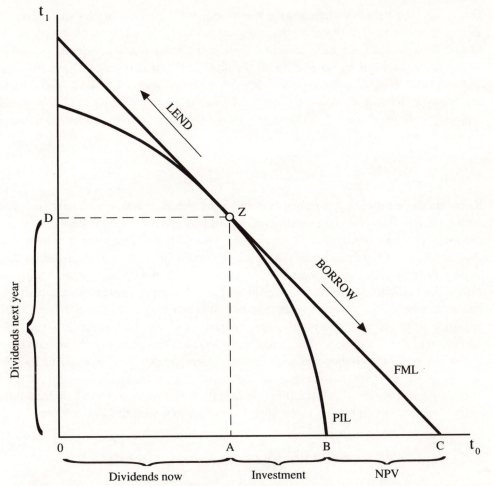

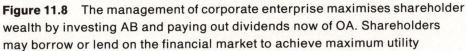

Figure 11.8   The management of corporate enterprise maximises shareholder wealth by investing AB and paying out dividends now of OA. Shareholders may borrow or lend on the financial market to achieve maximum utility

absolved from any concern about the dividend pattern. Managers simply maximize shareholder wealth, the present value of the company. The dividend is then a residual paid out after the investment decision is taken.

We can use this to explain why some companies pay out virtually nothing in dividends, for they *retain* and *plough back*, reinvest cash in the current period. The company has a 'super' PIL where the rate of return on physical investments is very high, exceeding the market rate, in short, giving very many projects with positive net present values. Here management knows that company projects can earn far more than the shareholders can do on their own account, by investing in the next best financial market alternative. Shareholders whilst receiving no dividends in the current period, see the value of their shares rise through an increase in the share price, a capital gain, on the strength of the company's ability to increase dividends in the future. Shareholders are able to make their own 'home-made dividends' either by selling some shares or by borrowing on the basis of future dividends. Companies like IBM, in the 1960s, followed such a policy of retaining funds – for IBM, at that time, had many high net present value projects. There are many examples of high performing companies which attract a clientele who are happy to receive capital gains rather than dividends.

Review

Rosa has chosen a unique combination of consumption, for now and next year, and a physical and financial investment package. In this basic model, the decision-maker, whether the individual owner/manager or the manager operating on behalf of shareholders, aims to maximize the owner's wealth, then to rearrange the owner's money/dividends through time. The decision-maker *compares* the present value of cash to be made from the alternatives of real and financial investment. Cash will be put to the best use by comparing the opportunity costs and returns at the margin. We use logic to choose an optimum strategy which gives the best solution given fully known and fixed constraints. The model provides useful insights into the possibility of moving money through time and gives the theoretical justification for, in particular, the net present value technique of investment appraisal. Here projects are undertaken, given that the present values of future inflows exceed the investment outlay when discounted at the owner's opportunity cost. We shall have more to say on this in what follows.

EXTENDING THE MODEL AND INVESTMENT DECISION RULES

Multi-time periods and the net present value rule

The key ideas derived from the one period consumption investment model in the last section can now be generalized into a wider time context. We can leave the world of one future time period and the two dimensional graph. Consider the much more realistic investment situation where cash flows accrue over many periods, years which stretch into the future. The example of Rosa illustrated the notion that £1 today is worth more than £1 next year. On Figure 11.5, £10 million is worth £11 million in future value at a 10 per cent interest rate. This is not a compensation for risk (or inflation). We assumed these factors away. The time value of money arises because Rosa can spend, lend or invest cash held today, opportunities which are not immediately available from cash to be received in the future. So money now is more valuable than money in the future; it gives valuable options without delay. Money has a time value. The nearer the money arrives in time the better.

The process of time discounting enables us to reduce all sums of cash to a *common present value*, at whatever point in time that cash comes in or is paid out in the future. The use of present value enables a straightforward comparison between projects with different cash profiles and project lives. Some projects, like the purchase of a fleet of trucks, may give high cash inflows in the early years of the project life but give high repair bills as the fleet ages in the later years; other projects may give an even spread of cash over the project life. The following formulas can be used to show how such different cash profiles stretching over many time periods can be brought to a common value:

Future Value This is simply that sum of cash which we will receive if a sum of money is invested now for a given interest rate for a specified number of years. In our example, £100 now, lent at 10 per cent, will have a future value in one year's time of £110. If we save £100 for two years and place it in the financial markets, then the future value in two years time will be £121. The present value of our money now, £100, will have grown to a sum of £121 in two years time. If we expand the number of years over which we lend the money then the future value will grow accordingly. There is a mathematical formula which we can use and there are future value tables which give us ready calculations of future values for both different interest rates and/ or different numbers of years.

$$FV = PV(1 + r)^n \tag{11.1}$$

where FV represents future value, PV represents present value, r is the rate of interest and n is the number of years.

Therefore, the PV £100 saved and invested at 10 per cent for one year is worth $100(1 + 0.1) = £110$ at the end of the year.

Similarly, if £100 is saved and invested for two years at 10 per cent it is worth $100(1 + 0.1)^2 = £121$ at the end of the second year. Note that in the compounding process for $n > 2$ the interest gained at the end of each year is reinvested to earn yet more interest.

Consider the example with n equals 2. At the end of the first year the principal and interest are £100 and £10 respectively. These are reinvested at 10 per cent. Thus the value at the end of the second year is $110(1 + 0.1) = £121$. At the end of the third year, the value would be £133.10.

The Present Value This is simply the money you would have to save now in order to receive a particular sum of money in the future. Present value is found by putting compound interest into reverse. To find the present value of any future sum simply divide the future value by $(1 + r)$ to the power of the number of years that money is lent.

$$PV = \frac{FV}{(1 + r)^n} \tag{11.2}$$

Present value tables, usually found at the end of finance and accounting texts, will give the present value of £1 received at different points in the future and at different interest rates. Remember that other things being equal:

a) the further away in time a specific sum of money is offered, the smaller will be its present value, and

b) the larger the interest rate, the smaller will be the present value.

Indeed, the present value is less than the future value at positive rates of interest, because if we have the money now, for example, we could lend it out at interest and then at the end of the time period have the principal plus all the interest payments. Given a particular interest rate and a specific number of years, a future value always has a 'matching' unique present value. Sums received further away in time are discounted more heavily, there is longer to wait before we have the cash. Given an interest rate of 10 per cent, £100 to be received next year is worth £90.9 now. But if we have to wait for five years before we have the cash in-hand, its present value, given the same interest rate, is a mere £62.1. Also, a future sum will be discounted more heavily when the interest rate is large, we are dividing any future sum by a larger amount. If the rate of interest were 20 per cent, our £100 to be received in five years time would have shrunk to £40.2 in present value terms. If the money comes in ten years time, it will be worth only £16.2 now.

In summary, the further away in time, that is, the greater the number of years before we receive the cash, and/or the higher the interest rate, then the smaller the amount of money will be needed now to generate a particular sum in the future. Given this process of putting compound interest in reverse over many time periods, we can move on from the basic one period model. The net present value rule used to judge the acceptability of independent projects in that one period model can be generalized for multi-periods.

The net present value investment decision rule: independent projects

Independent projects are those which have no impact on the cash flows of any other project and when undertaken do not prohibit the acceptance of other projects. Independent projects stand alone although in reality investment projects may have effects on the cash flows of others. Even what appear to be quite unconnected investments may have implications for the health of other projects. This is a simplifying assumption.

The *net present value* (NPV) decision rule says that the decision-maker should:

a) Accept all those projects with a *positive net present value* when cash flows are discounted at the opportunity cost of capital – the market rate of interest – NPV > 0.

b) Reject all those projects with a *negative net present value*, when discounted at the opportunity cost of capital – the market rate of interest – NPV < 0.

The decision-maker is indifferent to those projects which have a zero net present value when their cash flows are discounted at the appropriate interest rate, for they neither add to nor detract from wealth. The decision-maker is indifferent between

Table 11.1 Project cash flows, discount factors and net present value total

Year	Cash £ (1)	Discount factor (2)	Present value (1) × (2)
outlay t_0	− 100,000	1	− 100,000
net inflow t_1	55,500	0.9091	50,455
net inflow t_2	44,500	0.8265	36,779
net inflow t_3	34,500	0.7513	25,920
net present value			**£13,154**

putting money into such a project and lending the same sum on the financial market. Projects with a zero net present value are break-even projects which simply earn the return on the best alternative forgone, in this case the rate of interest on the financial market.

The net present value can be derived by using the following equations:

$$NPV = \frac{R_1}{(1 + r)^1} + \frac{R_2}{(1 + r)^2} + \frac{R_3}{(1 + r)^3} + \cdots + \frac{R_n}{(1 + r)^n} - C_0 \qquad (11.3)$$

where $R_1, \ldots, R_n$ are the net cash flows at the ends of years $1, \ldots, n$, and C_0 is the capital outlay at the start of the project. n is the project life in years and r is the opportunity cost of capital, 11.3 can be written as:

$$NPV = \sum_{t=1}^{n} \frac{R_t}{(1 + r)^t} - C_0 \qquad (11.4)$$

where $\sum_{t=1}^{n}$ means sum from $t = 1$ to $t = n$.

Given values for capital outlay, the inflows and the project life, the crucial element is the rate of interest. A *positive net present value* shows that a project is worth more to the firm than the forgone financial alternative. This sum represents the addition to wealth which results from undertaking the project. The discounting process enables cash flows received at different points in time to be readily compared with the best alternative forgone.

To illustrate how this works, imagine that Rosa is considering whether or not to invest in a machine. The project has the cash outlay and inflows as given in Table 11.1:

Capital outlay £100,000
Project life 3 years
Opportunity cost of capital the interest rate is 10 per cent.

The discount factors are given in Table 11.1. For example, the discount factor to be applied to the cash flow at the end of year 1 is 0.9091. This is derived by dividing 1 by 1.1.

The net present value profile

The project gives a positive net present value of £13,154 at a 10 per cent interest rate. However, as we vary the interest rate, holding everything else constant, the project becomes a larger NPV earner as the interest rate falls and a smaller earner as interest rates rise. We can display the relationship between NPV and the interest rate graphically by plotting the NPV curve Figure 11.9.

The net present value of the project is plotted on the vertical axis against the rate of interest on the horizontal. The curve illustrates how *net present value is inversely related to the rate of interest*. The highest net present value possible is given at a zero interest rate, where the discount factor is 1. Given a zero interest rate, the money flows are simply added – there is no discounting. In this particular case the sum added to wealth would be £34,500, the best possible surplus for the project. The net present value declines as the interest rate increases. The reason for this is simply that cash inflows are discounted more heavily at higher rates. Future cash flows are being divided by larger amounts – given higher interest rates. Eventually they are so reduced in present value terms that they no longer exceed the initial outlay cost. For this project, a rate of discount of 18 per cent reduces the net present value to zero. At this rate the project just breaks even. At rates of interest above 18 per cent, the net present value becomes negative. The acceptance of the project with a negative net present value reduces wealth. In this situation the project outlay should be lent on the

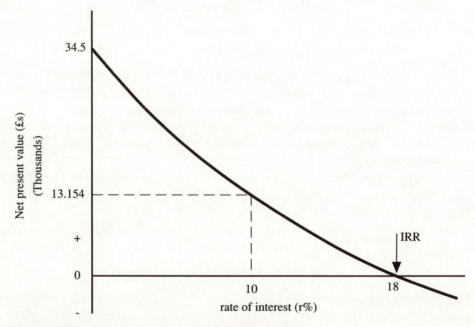

Figure 11.9 The net present value (NPV) curve

financial market or consumed but not invested in this project. The cash profiles, outlay and life span have not changed. Net present value falls because of the increased rate of interest and so the heavier discounting.

In general terms, a *fall* in interest rates, other things being equal, will turn some projects which were marginal, just breaking even, into acceptable wealth makers and increase the wealth to be earned from positive NPV projects. An *increase* in interest rates, other things being equal, reduces the NPV of all projects and tips projects which were just at break-even into the negative NPV, wealth reducing category.

The interest or discount rate at which the net present value curve intersects the horizontal axis, where the project's net present value is zero, has significance. It is known as the *internal rate of return*(IRR) and gives us the basis for an additional discounted cash flow rule.

An additional decision rule: the internal rate of return

The internal rate of return is the discount rate which equates the discounted stream of future net cash inflows to the initial outlay. In short, this is the discount rate (an interest rate) which induces break-even. The decision-maker simply compares the IRR with the interest rate, the opportunity cost of capital. The decision rule for independent projects:

a) *accept* all projects with an IRR *greater* than the opportunity cost rate of interest – IRR > r.

b) *Reject* all projects with an IRR *less* than the opportunity cost rate of interest – IRR < r.

Those projects with an IRR equivalent to the interest rate are break-even. The decision-maker is indifferent to a project whose IRR is equal to the cost of capital. The project just earns the same return as would be achieved by lending funds on the financial market. If the IRR is greater than the cost of capital then the project gives a return better than the alternative. In this case when the cost of capital is smaller than the IRR of 18 per cent the project should be accepted.

In the case of *normal independent projects* where an outlay cost is followed by positive net cash inflows, on an accept or reject basis, the net present value and internal rate of return rules always give the same answer. However, in other situations the rules may give conflicting answers. In general, the net present value rule is the safest to follow, the most likely to give sound advice although evidence suggests that business people favour the IRR rule, perhaps preferring and feeling more comfortable with a percentage value. So far we have only examined independent non-competing projects. Now we move to a different situation.

Choosing between mutually exclusive projects

In some situations only one project is required from competing alternatives. In other words, we have *mutually exclusive options*. Here projects are not perfectly compatible. The acceptance of one project automatically excludes others. Euro Disney only wanted to build one theme park in Europe and had a choice of competing locations, siting Euro Disney in France, Spain or the UK, for example. A choice of competing coal or gas fired systems exists for privatized companies to generate electricity. When there is either a market restriction and/or a physical limitation decision-makers are required to choose one project from alternatives.

The NPV rule is very easy to modify in such a situation. Simply select the project with the largest NPV. As the calculation of the net present value already automatically compares each project with the financial market alternative, the one which adds the most to wealth is selected. On the other hand, projects should not be ranked by the size of their IRRs for this could give a sub-optimum solution, a choice of the project which adds the least to wealth. The IRR rule cannot be so readily modified to cope with mutually exclusive projects, for the IRR is simply the rate of discount which reduces NPV to zero. It has no basis for ranking projects for it does not tell us how much will be added to wealth in absolute terms. Whilst a return of 100 per cent sounds good, if that represents 100 per cent of £100, that return in absolute terms is much smaller than 1 per cent on an outlay of £1 million. Complicated changes are required to make the IRR rule function correctly. Choosing between the alternative projects on the basis of the largest net present value is more straightforward and reliable.

INVESTMENT DECISIONS IN ANALYTICAL AND PERSPECTIVE TIME: A PRELIMINARY VIEW

What lessons can the decision-maker learn from the theoretical discussions set in the context of the individual/firm maximizing wealth and utility in analytical time? The model emphasizes the size and timing of cash flows and the alternative options open to individuals. Money has a time value; this is vital for the assessment of a project's ability to generate money wealth. Whilst wealth is given in terms of cash, it is the stock of tangible and intangible possessions which have market value – so that they are capable of being swapped for cash or other goods. In later chapters we shall have more to say about human capital, to distinguish between human and non-human wealth. However, in order to maximize wealth from physical investment, in *monetary* terms:

1) Only *relevant cash* flows matter, now and in the future. One of the problems when making investment decisions in perspective time is to ensure that only appropriate cash flows are considered. *Only* those cash inflows and outflows which would occur if the project were to be undertaken should be included. There is often an overwhelming temptation to include *sunk costs* – expenditures from the past. Such costs should never be incorporated, for they have already been incurred. (The same argument also

applies for past non-monetary expenditures.) The analytical time model correctly ignores cash flows from any previous time *before* t_0. For nothing that the decision-maker does now can change the past. Money already spent on a project should never be included in current calculations for, as in the old adage, 'bygones are bygones'.

Rosa on the basis of the data in Table 11.1 would go ahead with machine purchase. But imagine that design plans for the special adaptation of the machine for Rosa's business had already been drawn up at a cost of £15,000, paid in the recent past t_{-1}, last year. Should this change Rosa's decision? The answer must be no. Rosa cannot undo that. To include this sum in the net present value calculation would mistakenly shackle the project with a past expenditure. In this case it would bring about the rejection of a project which would, if accepted, actually add to wealth. The subtraction of £15,000 would overwhelm the positive net present value. As a result the project would be rejected and the decision-maker would have forfeited the opportunity to make £13,154 in addition to the loss of £15,000 for the plans which cannot be recouped.

Of course, that is not to say that we cannot learn from the past. With hindsight, Rosa might not have made the initial expenditure on the design plans. In perspective time she might consider more carefully in similar situations in the future, with the advantage of greater knowledge. However, the key step is to isolate whether or not there exists any possibility *now* to retrieve some of the money previously spent on the plans by selling the design information. If the plans could be sold immediately as an alternative to undertaking the project, then this sum must be included as an opportunity cost of the project and subtracted accordingly – along with the outlay costs. If it were discovered that the plans could be sold for £13,500 then this would be the best alternative. The inclusion of this relevant cost in the calculation of NPV would give a negative NPV for the machine project. Everything hinges on the opportunity cost of the plans. But if the plans have a zero opportunity cost, that is, no alternative use, they must not be included.

A project may well have an impact on other schemes, for in reality projects often have spin-offs, both positive and negative. Projects are not completely independent. Any such effects on cash flows should be considered. Sometimes a project may give a negative net present value when examined in isolation, but may have positive spin-offs for the cash flows of other projects. A creche facility considered by a large store in a shopping mall complex might not give a positive net present value when considered as an isolated project. Yet when the impact on the store's overall retailing cash flows are considered, the creche may well boost revenues and induce a wealth generating effect for the store.

The depreciation allowances made by accountants to cover capital outlay, should not be included because they do not represent cash flows. Moreover, these depreciation charges vary according to different accounting conventions. The outlay cost has already been fully considered in the purchase price of the equipment when calculating the NPV. To include depreciation charges would be double counting.

2) The timing of cash flows matters. All cash flows must be considered at the time

they occur and the appropriate opportunity cost used. Timing is vital for working out the time value of money. The time when the work is undertaken or when a money liability is incurred is not the critical point. What matters is not just the size but the timing of the actual payment or cash receipt. Although the liability may be incurred now, an up-front payment of £10,000 is going to cost us more than £10,000 to be paid next year. Deferred payment essentially gives the use of money, like free credit. The time of the cash payment must be included in the calculations. Then the appropriate discounting gives the present value. Given an interest rate of 20 per cent, £10,000 to be received next year is only worth £8,333 in present value terms. Free credit is worth more, the higher the opportunity cost rate of interest and the longer payment can be delayed. Similarly, if we sell output next year but do not receive cash until a year later, then that cash has to be discounted too. What matters is the time when money actually arrives, for only then can we use it for lending, spending or investing; or when money is actually paid out, in other words, when we have to part with these opportunities. Moreover, the appropriate opportunity cost must be used to discount. However, as we shall see, identifying that discount rate in perspective time may be no simple matter. Also discounting the more distant future may lead to difficulties (see Chapter 13).

Why do projects have a positive net present value?

Why do projects have a positive net present value and what is the significance? In a world of perfectly competitive product markets, positive net present values would tend to zero. The attraction of surplus present value over outlay would draw in new firms in the long run; they would want a slice of the gains. For where there is costless entry and exit, undifferentiated products, producers have no power to affect market conditions. Goods which are all the same are sold on the basis of price. No producer has an edge in terms of costs or product. In such circumstances we see a situation of positive NPV only in short-run disequilibrium – the result of a temporary scarcity or hiccup. In long-run equilibrium in the perfectly competitive environment, all net present values of projects under consideration would be zero. Excess returns are quickly eroded by new entrants who are attracted. Any deviation from equilibrium is quickly corrected. As new firms set up in production, bringing their additional capacity, they gain a share of the market, compete and force down the industry price, thereby lowering the returns for all producers. What is crucial in real situations is the ease of entry. The video game market, for example, exhibited ease of entry and high returns in the early 1980s (Shapiro 1993). Competitors flocked into the market and pushed down returns.

In less competitive environments, other things being equal, we might expect significant positive NPVs. Barriers to entry, such things as licences or the ownership of scarce resources, stop or hinder the emergence of competitive rivals in the market. The Wellcome Foundation produces the AIDS' drug with the protection of a licence which effectively bars competition. Time lags in the introduction of substitutes give the market leader the opportunity to make a positive net present value, for high cash flows in future periods are not readily bid down. An important question for the business decision-maker in perspective time is how long can high cash flows last into the future, before competitors are attracted? A prominent ingredient for the successful creation of wealth is the *search* for projects in areas of competitive advantage; and then to *protect* that advantage from erosion. Those who operate in highly competitive environments, commodity type industries, are destined to see their excess returns quickly wiped out. Only by acquiring or creating barriers to entry can the firm hope to protect high excess returns and hence significant positive net present values. Once we relax the assumption of perfect information of now and the future, move from analytical time and step into the real world of the investment decision-maker in perspective time, then choices become much more complex. Here creativity, rules of thumb, fortune whether good or bad, may have a significant part to play in decision-making and the ultimate success of projects. The basic model providing the discounted cash flow techniques is based on a rational economic person, maximizing wealth, operating in 'black box' firms and households. Neat, unique solutions exist in the analytical time mode. This introductory model enhances our understanding by simplifying, emphasizing the importance of the time, alternative gains and opportunity costs. This analysis provides a basic framework and prompts useful questions; but it needs to be seen in context.

INVESTMENT DECISION-MAKING IN PERSPECTIVE TIME: PROBLEMS AND PRACTICE

How widespread is the use of discounted cash flow techniques in practice? Are there other methods for weighing up the pros and cons of investment projects? Finally, how does the usual model, set in analytical time, stand up to scrutiny when we relax its assumptions and take a wider view? The convenient analytical time mode side steps several of the problems faced by decision-makers operating in perspective time. These difficulties essentially result from the human situation, a lack of omniscience and incomplete understanding. Moreover, people perceive information differently, accord data different significance and expect different future scenarios.

How widespread is the use of discounted cash flow techniques in practice?

Pike presents evidence in Pike and Neale (1993:159) which suggests that, in the UK, discounted flow techniques are used and becoming much more widespread in large enterprises. Businesses use more than one method. From 100 large UK firms, 74 per cent used the net present value technique in 1992 as opposed to 32 per cent in 1975. But business people seem to prefer the internal rate of return, 81 per cent of the 100 firms used the IRR method in 1992. The IRR gives a percentage return which business decision-makers, from the evidence, seem to prefer. In fact, the concepts which lie at the heart of these discounted cash flow techniques are not new. In historical time, records reveal an understanding of compound interest, the basis for discounted cash flow techniques, in very early times. In the Old Babylonian period in Mesopotamia, between 1800 and 1600 BC, compound interest was calculated. Indeed, compound interest tables date back to the fourteenth century, and it is said that a recorded reference to the net present value rule was discovered as early as 1582 (Pike and Neale 1993: 158). Evidence from modern times suggests that such techniques are used increasingly in many USA and European companies; they are certainly standard fare for those on management, business and accounting courses. Interestingly, Japanese managers are said to make little use of these discounted cash flow techniques (ibid. 1993:167). However, other techniques, conventional rules of thumb, are also very widely used. One such popular customary technique is the payback rule.

The payback technique versus discounted cash flow approach

Small businesses and large companies alike often simply ask the question, how quickly will we get our money back? If a factory complex costs £7 million now, up-front, how long before the cash flows arising from the project can recoup this initial cost? The firm has a payback target time set by management. Projects which pay back more quickly than or just on the target time are acceptable. Projects which take longer are rejected. In situations where a choice of projects is required, these are ranked according to their payback time. The shortest time is best.

The *payback period* can be found by dividing the capital outlay by the inflow of cash per annum. In our example if the factory pays back £2 million per annum, the payback time is three and a half years, 7 divided by 2. But for a decision to be made, the critical element is the *target payback period*. If the company requires a four year payback the project is acceptable, on the basis of the figures. The project pays back more quickly than the target. A two year requirement, on the other hand, would ensure rejection. Should the cash flow pattern change, if only £1 million per annum is expected, then the payback period increases to seven years. On the basis of a two or four year target the project would be rejected.

The payback rule has wide appeal for it is easy to calculate without computer aid and readily understandable. It gives a measure of liquidity, how soon cash will be received to payback the outlay. In peaceful or turbulent environments it provides a quick, straightforward measure. The payback method is one practical way of coping with uncertainty in situations where decision-makers are just not sure – they may reduce the payback target as a means of coping with uncertainty. Empirical studies in the UK show the payback to be the most popular method of appraisal amongst large companies albeit often used in conjunction with discounted cash flow techniques. In 1992, 94 per cent of the 100 large UK companies surveyed by Pike, employed the payback. Moreover, small companies may often use the payback as the sole arbiter, a cheap unsophisticated rule of thumb.

In comparison with discounted cash flow techniques it has drawbacks.

a) It ignores the time pattern of cash flows. Two projects may have the same payback, but from the example above, factory A has cash flows spread evenly, whereas an alternative factory B might give only £0.5 million at the end of the first year and the rest of the cash in three and a half year's time. Clearly, in net present value terms project A is better, cash flows are received more quickly, despite the fact that A has the same payback as B. Cash received earlier from project A could be lent out at interest, used for other projects, consumed by the owner/manager or paid as dividends.

b) In addition, the payback ignores cash flows after the payback period. Project A might bring in cash flows long after the three and a half year payback time. Project B might provide nothing thereafter. Whilst both projects would still payback over the same time period, project A would clearly be better. The net present value method would give a superior view of both projects, by focusing on the timing of cash flows over the full life of the projects.

c) Finally, there is no clear guideline on how to set the payback target. This is of course a crucial element in deciding which projects are accepted or rejected. The choice of the target does not depend on any clear theoretical basis, any consideration of opportunity costs. Whether as a result of a group decision-making process or the dictat of a single person, the choice is essentially subjective. Even where some large companies enhance the sophistication of the payback technique by discounting the cash flows before working out the payback, the choice of the target is still open to question.

However, business people feel comfortable with this quick, conventional rule of thumb. It ranks as the most popular technique and is often used as a quick screening device before the application of more sophisticated procedures. So even though discounted cash flow techniques are gaining greater popularity as business tools, and computer packages are available to work with complex data, the payback is still used, often employed in conjunction with the discounted cash flow methods. Discounted cash flow techniques have gained greater prominence in the UK and USA over time and they do have an ancient pedigree. However traditional customs still figure prominently in the decision-making process. Such rules of thumb give emotional security to the decision-maker and a quick check, even though they may favour projects which pay back quickly and reject those with good long-term prospects. For the manager who wants to show speedy money returns in order to secure a promotion or a career move, rather than maximize shareholder wealth, this technique may be favoured. That may, in part, be a contribution to short-termism in investment strategies. There is a tendency to pick out the short-term, potentially successful project and the payback acts as a security blanket for the decision-maker. Moreover, the target can be raised or lowered dependent on the strength of confidence.

However, in perspective time, using discounted cash flow techniques, where interest rates are not as clearly defined as in the neat theoretical model, the choice of interest rate may also have some element of arbitrariness and the calculation of net present value is itself a comforting practice. These techniques also rely on data for the future which cannot be known. Discounted cash flow computer print outs may imbue decision-makers with a sense of false security – a delusion of precision.

Investment consumption model revisited: discounted cash flow techniques in a wider context

The discounted cash flow rules and the model from which they are derived are not without limitation. The consumption investment model has to be viewed within a wider context. No matter how sophisticated our decision rules and computer pro- grammes, or how pleasing the equilibrium solution, there are other concerns and still further avenues to explore:

The physical investment line: revisited

a) 'Only in theory is a firm fortunate enough to be presented with no effort or expense on its part, with every available investment opportunity' (A. Shapiro 1993: 77). In practice, the PIL of analytical time camouflages the real position of the business person. The physical investment line assumes all investment opportunities are fully known and ranked in order of the cash return they will with certainty make in the future. But decision-makers in perspective time have limited knowledge. A great deal may be known about routine replacement investments in well tried markets but even there the future is not certain. Yet the block busters of the future, successful new investment opportunities, have to be *discovered* or *created*. They are not definitely known and labelled. In many situations, individual entrepreneurs like Alan Sugar, with the aid of his research and development team, or Paul Allen and Bill Gates, the co-founders of Microsoft, and the research and development teams of giant corporations are searching for market gaps, new ways of doing things; in short, innovative ideas. Useful information is limited and uncertainty about the potential performance of untried processes and products may be significant. Decision-makers have only a limited idea of which projects are available and they may have no precise knowledge for ranking projects by their return.

The physical investment line does not illustrate the need to make sequential decisions or the requirement for overall strategic planning. Investment strategies evolve over many time periods, in part constrained by the laws and custom of the society in question, dependent in part on the institutional backdrop. Finding new investment possibilities generally requires imagination and human effort. The dis- counted cash flow appraisal techniques may improve decision-making, by allowing for the time value of money. But the key to success depends on the quality and quantity of investment proposals and how projects actually perform in relation to those of competitors. This in part depends on luck as the future unfolds, as well as creativity and efficient execution of investment plans and production and the market- ing of products.

We need to remember the importance of *creating* the opportunities which are taken as given in our basic model and the element of luck or chance, assumed away in conventional theory. There are difficulties for the decision-maker who has perforce a limited understanding and no crystal ball. Spurious accuracy and a heavy reliance on precise details may be used to mask a good deal of ignorance or perhaps the *post hoc* rationalization for projects already chosen.

b) The *state of confidence* is a very important element in the perception of potential projects. Different people perceive the possibility that project cash flows will unfold in different ways. The same people can change their view of the future and thus their assessment of any particular project over time. People are quite unable to look at the world with a Spock like detachment.[2] Taking this one step further, it was Keynes who argued that

> a large proportion of our positive activities depend on spontaneous optimism rather than a mathematical expectation, whether moral or hedonistic or economic. Most probably our decisions to do something positive, the full consequences of which will be drawn out over many days to come, can only be the result of animal spirits – of a spontaneous urge to action rather than inaction.
>
> (Keynes 1936: 161)

Human decisions are based according to Keynes

> not on an exact calculation of benefits to come. Thus if animal spirits are dimmed and spontaneous optimism falters . . . enterprise will fade and die; – though fears of loss may have a basis no more reasonable than hopes of profit had before.
>
> (ibid.: 162)

Decision-makers are simply not going to make the rational calculations as assumed in the basic model. Even if the business person were to calculate a precise NPV for a particular project, the money figures included in such calculations may change – affected by optimism or pessimism.

As a result of different states of confidence, the PIL does not remain in the same position. In perspective time we could not draw an exact PIL from real data – it is only a hypothetical tool – the future is unknowable and our view of that future may be more or less fuzzy dependent on how confident we feel about our own knowledge. The PIL can pivot. If optimism reigns, any particular investment may be seen to *promise* a larger cash inflow in the future. In depressed times, if the green shoots of recovery are thought to be withering, then fragile animal spirits are held back – the 'delicate balance of spontaneous optimism' is upset. So net present value curves can shift, for cash flow projections will vary depending on the state of confidence. Moreover, switches in confidence can take place very abruptly before the system has time to reach anything approaching an equilibrium. If animal spirits are depressed even though interest rates are low or falling, investment plans may be postponed or shelved indefinitely. The demand curve for investment, other things being equal, shifts to the left. In fact, people do not abide by a rational mathematical calculus.

Keynes was careful to point out that everything does not depend on waves of irrational psychology: he argued that we can perceive investment decisions as 'our rational selves choosing between the alternatives as best we are able, calculating where we can, but often falling back for our motive on whim or sentiment or chance' (ibid.: 163). Many investment projects might never have been given the go-ahead, if investment depended solely on a narrow monetary calculation. Animal spirits are important. Changes in confidence can have quite spectacular effects (Shackle 1974, Earl 1986). Besides, other non-monetary calculations can matter.

c) In the basic model, changes in the interest rate, the price of cash, had no impact on the position of the PIL. In practice, changes in interest rates may well be taken as a *signal* of the state of times to come, affecting people's perception of the future. An increase in interest rates may depress the view of the future, pivoting the PIL and shifting the investment demand curve to the left. The net present value profile may be *unstable*, shifting as the price of money changes. An increase in interest rates may dishearten business people, making them less optimistic, reducing their expectations of future cash inflows and causing investment demand to shift to the left. A much larger cut back in the quantity of investment demand might come about as a result of increased interest rates, a greater reduction than would be shown in analytical time, where everything is known.

Also, reductions in interest rates may have little impact on investment levels in depressed times for net present value profiles may be shifting downwards at the same time, if people view the future with relative despair. The impact of the interest rate cut could be offset. The state of confidence is a key element.

The goal of maximizing NPV and the division between ownership and control

If owners and decision-makers are not the same people, they may well have different objectives. In a world of imperfect knowledge, this matters. Management may be interested in their own remuneration, promotion prospects or job security, rather than the maximization of shareholder wealth, even assuming management knows how to achieve this. But given the asymmetry of information between shareholders and management there are often very limited possibilities for the owners of the firm to check on the decisions of management. Shareholders, more often than not, take the manager's word that investments are in the shareholders' best interests. Only occasionally do we hear about a shareholder revolt, for example, at Amstrad (and see Chapter 9). Given both the internal complexity of organizations and the environment of the firm, decision-makers with different perspectives and attitudes may simply select projects which achieve *satisfactory performance*. The shareholders are often unable to detect that their agents apply less than 'optimum' strategies. As long as satisfactory profits, a minimum amount of wealth, are earned to keep shareholders happy, all is well. In the corporate organization, investment may be a result of *political bargaining* between different departmental heads for different investment packages, rather than the rational detached analytical calculation of wealth maximizing man. Management seeking a quiet life or the furtherance of their own position may undertake projects which are not in the best interests of shareholders. They may undertake too much or too little investment – aiming to protect and further their own interests.

Unlimited borrowing and lending at a constant interest rate

a) Lack of well developed financial markets may present problems. So far we have assumed the notion of unlimited funds for anyone who wants to invest, within their ability to repay: the perfect capital market. Individuals and companies are assumed to have equal access to funds. This is an unrealistic assumption but one which has enabled us to make an ordered explanation of basic concepts. In some situations financial markets are non-existent or poorly developed. Low-income countries lack well functioning financial markets. Here, to borrow money can involve high transactions costs and large differences between borrowing and lending rates. Cash may be unavailable or *rationed* in these circumstances. This creates a problem for investors who have to seek alternative funds either from friends and relatives, or from other organizations including charitable and government bodies or at times from the equivalent of loan sharks.

b) However, even where there are well developed financial markets, individuals or companies may be constrained by the quantity of cash available to them for borrowing. Capital rationing exists. Whatever the form investment takes we can often observe unequal access to capital. Given limited funds for physical investment, individuals and companies find themselves unable to proceed with all the projects which would add to wealth by providing positive NPVs. The cash constraint blocks the full exploitation of investment potential. Decision-makers have to be wary about spending limited funds in these circumstances. Wealth may not be maximized by ranking the projects by the size of their NPV and allocating cash accordingly. A changed procedure is required to maximize the total net present value.

Capital rationing may result either from an external financial market blockage or from an internally dictated management policy. Moreover, physical investment is itself sometimes constrained by the lack of skilled labour or managerial talent. Investments in human and non-human resources are linked.

External or hard capital rationing   Whether we speak of companies or households, hard capital rationing implies that unlimited amounts of capital are unavailable from external market sources. In perspective time funds are usually not instantaneously available, no matter how large the company. Raising funds through equity sales, selling shares, takes time, often a considerable amount of real time. Even when funds are available, these may be in large lumpy amounts with significant transaction costs, including floatation or rights issue costs, including administrative, underwriting and advertising fees. Bank borrowing may prove to be expensive and involve transaction costs. The financing decision has to be made in good time so it can be argued that a shortfall of capital is, in part, a result of poor planning. But in a world with imperfect information it is not possible to plan perfectly. Nevertheless, for the larger company in the modern economy with developed financial and capital markets, capital rationing is usually considered to be a temporary phenomena.

However, small firms may be unable to raise funds at anything approaching market rates, and with strict terms for repayment. Indeed, those companies which are less profitable, smaller, higher risk, are more severely affected. Although there may be very good potential opportunities, an *information asymmetry* between the would-be investor, the small business and the supplier of loanable funds, ensures that what are considered profitable projects by the small business are not undertaken. Banks distinguish between different borrowers and different risks. Even if each party to the transaction had the same information, their assessments of the risks involved would be different. The small business has no great wealth or proven performance record, factors which may affect a bank's view. Moreover, creditworthiness may be socially constructed with conventional reactions to particular classes of borrowers. However, neither party, borrower or lender, has perfect knowledge; they do not know what will happen. There is a fundamental uncertainty.

Considerable concern has been expressed at various times about the availability of funds for the small business in the UK. Many schemes have been mooted to help the small enterprises to invest in potentially wealth creating projects. Nevertheless, custom and convention play a role in the allocation of capital funds. There are 'rules of the game'. Some groups may suffer discriminatory practices.

Internal or soft capital rationing   In large companies, internal management limit the funds available each year for each section or division as part of the planning process. This internal non-price rationing process emphasizes that companies are not the black boxes of conventional analysis, set in analytical time. In perspective time the human difficulties of understanding and coping with limited information and fundamental uncertainty requires the working of an internal capital market where scarce funds are allocated by administrative procedures. Funds may be limited in any one financial year in each division, enabling investment expenditure to be planned within any large multi-divisional company. Capital rationing may be imposed to cope with fluctuations in short-run demands for investment funds, to save borrowing or acquiring equity capital short term.

Whatever the causes of capital rationing, when it bites, practical solutions have to be found. In the extreme situation the private small business may never get off the ground or the ones that do may simply fail for the lack of cash. When there are too many projects chasing too little money, a ranking and then a choice amongst projects has to be made. In a situation where capital is rationed for one period only and the aim is to maximize shareholder wealth then the net present value rule has to be modified. Those projects which give the biggest increase in shareholder wealth per £ of expenditure should be chosen. Instead of undertaking those projects which give the largest absolute size of NPV we rank and undertake projects according to their benefit cost ratio.[3] The benefit cost ratio measures the NPV per unit of outlay. For example, a project which costs £1,000 and has a NPV of £385 would, per unit of capital outlay, give £0.385 per £ of initial outlay. This is a better project in terms of NPV per unit of outlay than one which gives a much larger absolute NPV, say £800 but costs in terms of limited funds £4,000. This represents a benefit per unit of scarce outlay of only £0.2. Although the second project looks at first sight to be better in terms of its absolute NPV, it gives a poorer result for the shareholder per unit of scarce funds. The question of capital rationing will be considered further in Chapter 13. Here suffice it to say that the result of capital rationing where the constraint is binding is to stop the acceptance of some positive NPV projects. The owner's wealth is lower than it would otherwise be in the absence of rationing.

The problems of constrained capital and choice become more difficult if rationing continues over multi-time periods. The simple benefit cost ratio technique cannot be used, for each period has a separate constraint. This imposes a simultaneous allocation problem which can only be tackled with sophisticated mathematical programming techniques. In fact, for many parts of British industry, for example, capital rationing is not a current problem. Many companies have cash mountains. It is the lack of profitable and innovative, inventive projects which may hold back investment, not constrained capital funds. Capital rationing may not be a binding constraint on many large private sector companies. Recession, competition from rivals and the lack of new ideas for attractive projects are factors which limit the demand for funds for investment. Companies can buy back their shares from shareholders in such circumstances.

However, capital rationing can represent a considerable problem for the small firm where the access to capital markets is restricted. In other organizational contexts, such as some private charities or the public sector organization, capital rationing can present an endemic problem. Public sector organizations facing cash limits may have many worthwhile ventures but are nevertheless constrained as a result of the requirement to keep within the cash limits. We shall return to this theme in Chapter 13.

CONCLUDING COMMENTS

We have introduced the useful concept of the time value of money and the rationale for discounted cash flow investment appraisal techniques. The analytical framework enables us to ask key questions, grasp basic economic insights and look with a clearer eye at actual business situations. Yet the neat simple models have to be viewed in the context of perspective time. Here the tidy determinism and unique answers slip from our grasp. Whilst orthodox neo-classical theory provides some powerful tools for making sense of the highly complex reality, it cannot give us the whole story. Actual investment decision-makers, economic actors are faced with imperfect information and their own limited human abilities. Investment analysis requires us to recognize and consider the role of creativity, ingenuity and surprise, where actual investment strategies and opportunities evolve over time.

Whatever the approach, it is essential to convey the vital importance of time and the different ways in which we can handle time. The conventional neo-classical approach focuses firmly on the problem of investment at the individual, firm and market level, ignoring other organizational contexts. However, the quantity and quality of real investment decisions in the interdependent economic system affect the future prosperity and health of all organizations. Decisions feed back into the wider macroeconomy bringing 'knock-on' or multiplier effects. The investment demand of firms in total, that is *aggregate investment demand* can have profound effects on a nation's health and wealth, where investment expenditure generates both income in the current period and capacity changes over time.

In much of our discussion we have assumed certainty. This enables the display of basic concepts with clarity, before we address more complicated issues in the following chapter – the nature of risk and uncertainty.

INVESTMENT – SUMMARY

- Investment is the commitment of resources now with the expectation of future rewards.
- Different categories of investment are linked – their interrelationships are important as can be illustrated with examples set in historical time.
- The one period investment consumption model set in analytical time shows us how to compare physical, financial investments and consumption alternatives where the goal is to maximize utility. Borrowing and lending possibilities can be considered.
- Given the one period model we can illustrate the concepts of present and future value and choose an equilibrium package of consumption, physical and financial investment.
- We derived the discounted cash flow techniques of investment appraisal – the net present value and internal rates of return.
- This chapter introduced mutually exclusive projects and advised ranking them via the size of the NPV.
- In perspective time several techniques are often actually used. Rules of thumb – payback are very popular. There is a growing use of discounted cash flow techniques in the UK, US and Europe.
- Importance of confidence – animal spirits and the perception of the future hence the assessment of costs and net revenues.
- Capital rationing which binds, involves us in choosing amongst projects according to their benefit cost ratio – where rationing is only in one period.
- Political decision making role – internal capital rationing.

INVESTMENT – QUESTIONS FOR DISCUSSION

1 What do you understand by:

a) the physical investment line;
b) the financial market line;
c) the internal rate of return;
d) historic cost;
e) the payback?

2 Why does the physical investment line have an outward bow shape? What factors could cause the PIL to pivot outwards? Would you classify the following companies' hypothetical PILs as 'puny' or 'super'?

a) Microsoft;
b) British American Tobacco (BAT);
c) Marks and Spencer;
d) British Gas;
e) GEC?

How could companies change their PIL?

3 Explain the concept of positive time preference. Why do people require a premium for delaying consumption? Are there any circumstances in which a person might display a negative time preference?

4 In order to find an equilibrium in the one period investment consumption model what information would you require? Illustrate a borrowing and a lending equilibrium.

5 You are appraising an investment project now. Which of the following costs are relevant and which are not:

a) Research and development costs incurred last year of £1million.
b) Design plans which can be sold for £50,000 if the project does not go ahead.
c) Training costs to be incurred for personnel who will work on the project.
d) Raw materials already in stock which are being costed at their original purchase price.

6 Joe has just been made redundant and with his redundancy money is considering whether or not to set up a small business. He wants to buy a corner store/newsagency. He calculates that he can earn a 'reasonable living' after purchasing the business outright. Moreover, he expects to recoup the purchase price of the business after 5 years. He is very excited at the prospect of being his own boss. However, he cannot run the business unaided. He expects that his wife and young son will help out in the shop in their spare time – it will be a family concern. You are asked to advise the family about this investment decision.

a) What further information, if any, would you require before advising the family?

b) Has Joe considered all the relevant costs?

c) Advise the family making your assumptions clear.

7 What do you understand by Keynesian 'animal spirits' and what are their role in investment decision-making?

8 What do you understand by hard and soft capital rationing? What are the reasons for such rationing?

12

RISK AND UNCERTAINTY

INTRODUCTION

This chapter focuses directly on risk and uncertainty. In Chapter 11 we worked extensively in analytical time to develop a theory of investment appraisal, which emphasized the importance of the timing of cash flows and time discounting. The approach assumed certainty. Whilst very useful for simplifying, this was only a starting point. We introduced the problems of investment decision-making in perspective time where people have imperfect knowledge and have to imagine how the future will unfold. Indeed, in many situations actual circumstances may turn out to be very different from those decision-makers had expected.

Here, we explore more fully the way in which economists analyse risk and uncertainty, illustrating how people cope with these features in different situations. Whilst risk and uncertainty are often rolled into one, terms used interchangeably in conventional treatments, we argue that it is important to distinguish between these concepts. This widens and deepens our understanding of human behaviour and the role of organizations and institutionalized rules in economic explanations.

In Chapter 3 we put risk and uncertainty at different points on a certainty/ ignorance spectrum. Risk was said to be closer to certainty and uncertainty closer to ignorance. Here, initially, we develop the mainstream approach, where risk and uncertainty are treated as synonymous and quantifiable, uncertainty more often than not subsumed under a heading of risk. Then alternative approaches are discussed, those which distinguish explicitly between fundamental, incalculable uncertainty, and risk which can be measured. Yet whatever the approach, it seems that whilst people may enjoy the thrill of some risks, in the main, people do not relish risk or uncertainty. They try to avoid them.

In what follows we ask: what are the sources of risk and uncertainty? What are people's attitudes to these problems? What does the conventional treatment explain and what do the alternative approaches have to offer? Then we can examine how risk and uncertainty can be handled in different contexts. We focus on *insurance* and *diversification* as different ways of coping with the problem of imperfect foresight. We reiterate the importance of institutional rules and organizations. We can think in terms of market and non-market means for coping with our lack of a crystal ball. It is possible to show that a large battery of institutions, technologies, learning processes and strategies, have been developed to minimize the consequences of our inability to know the future. These might include such disparate matters as: money, marriage, weather reports, pocket-sized raincoats, codes of practice, corporate takeover strategies, indeed, a host of cushions in the face of real-world risks and uncertainties.

There is still a good deal of controversy surrounding the questions discussed here. There are no easy unique answers. Nevertheless, it is useful to show the different contributions which economics can make to an understanding of behaviour in perspective time. Whilst no single approach will be best in all circumstances, explicit treatments of risk and uncertainty are very useful, for they compel us to think about the future, plan for contingencies – or hedge our bets.

THE CONCEPTS OF RISK AND UNCERTAINTY REVISITED

In Chapter 3 we argued that *risk* is measurable. Risk falls on a spectrum much closer to the certainty of perfect knowledge than to ignorance. Some activities are repetitive and replicable, where all the possible outcomes are known. To give a basic example, in a game of chance the tossing of an unbiased coin can only give two outcomes, a head or tail. By the laws of probability we can know the likelihood of a particular result. So if it were heads to win, there is a 0.5 or 50 per cent chance of losing, throwing a tail, and, of course, a 0.5 or 50 per cent chance of winning. The two possibilities must sum to an outcome of one or 100 per cent. By flipping the coin we could come up with six heads one after the other but given a sufficiently large number of experiments, the proportion will always average at 50 per cent. This is what can be described as an *objective probability*, for this experiment can be repeated over and over again. It gives us the relative frequency with which particular outcomes will occur if the experiment or choices are repeated. Anyone can check the result.

Insurance companies whilst not being able to repeat experiments with the same 'coin', for they are insuring different people or objects, keep a great deal of information on claims from previous policy holders, and other relevant information. Here risk can be measured on an *actuarial* basis, where probabilities of future events occurring can be estimated on the basis of past experience, information from similar circumstances. So an actuary can work out with a fair degree of accuracy, the probability of giving birth to triplets, or having a heart attack, or confident predictions about the likelihood of unplanned pregnancies, all on the basis of past statistical data. The assumption is that events in the future will behave as in the past.

However, there are many situations where even though we think we know all the possible outcomes, there is less comprehensive information, and we are not as confident about the probabilities we assign to various possible events, for there is little information to go on. People often speak in terms of probabilities when they have insufficient knowledge on which to base such figures. Very often probabilities are not supported by repeated trials from the past. In situations of investment decision-making, for example, the proposed project may be quite different from anything which went before. The probabilities which we assign to potential cash flows in these circumstances are *subjective*. They depend on personal assessment, they cannot be checked by repeated objective trials. They are in the eye of the beholder. Indeed, as we move from the domain of risky situations into the realms of uncertainty it is not possible to assign any probability derived from a repeatable experiment. Gut reaction, based on individual perceptions of a unique historical situation takes over. An actuarial calculation is not available, indeed we may not know the structure of the problem. These are matters to which we shall return.

The sources of risk and uncertainty

What are the sources of risk and uncertainty? To set the scene for our analysis, to help us understand the nature of the problem, we need to address this question at the outset. The main springs of risk and uncertainty are set in the flow of real time; the changing nature of ourselves and the world we inhabit. As Marshall pointed out 'the general conditions of life are not stationary' (1920a: 347). Indeed, Marshall's use of the term general, emphasizes the very broad range of our uncertainty. That applies whatever the context of decision-making, for an individual, the small household unit, a large corporate structure or a charitable enterprise. Moreover, people change too, affected by their environment and their dealings with others.

The world around us changes autonomously *and* as a result of the decisions we make, both individually and collectively. People may want to make the correct choices but these are made in perspective time, where change is on-going. Those making choices are not certain how the future will unfold, what factors might alter between taking a decision and the final outcome. With the passage of real time, to complicate matters, a correct sequence of interdependent decisions may be required. Decisions have to be made in a proper order and often at an appropriate time. These are features which can be conveniently ignored in our one period model set in analytical time.

Economic actors have to manoeuvre in a dynamic and sometimes turbulent world, coping with a *process of events*, where random shocks, unique events may alter the situation radically. A choice made at one moment, may close some doors but open others. The decision to drop the sciences at school in favour of the humanities, effectively constrains future career paths. Opting for the arts makes a career in medicine a non-starter, at least without making time consuming and expensive changes at some later date. However, we are often quite ignorant about which doors we are effectively closing or opening, uncertain what future possibilities may be constrained or created, and what random events may affect our prospects. The decisions of today have ramifications for the future, whether trifling or immense. The world can change independently of our own actions. Without omniscience, making important choices can be very complex and often inherently stressful.

We can think about risk and uncertainty arising under the following broad areas:

a) technological;
b) economic;
c) political;
d) social/psychological;
e) environmental.

In reality, these factors are inextricably linked in a complex system, but they can be separated to highlight the variety of distinct spheres of change. Technological change affects both the process of production and consumption; the nature of goods and services produced. The would-be purchaser of hi-fi equipment is never sure whether a new product is in the pipeline thereby rendering current equipment obsolete. The production manager never knows for certain how a new technology will perform, its spin-offs or when it will be superseded. The purchasers of the Betamax video systems have seen that video format phased out, their video tapes a write-off. The compact disc has displaced the vinyl record. Whether equipment is purchased for the home or firm, similar technological risk and uncertainties may face the decision-maker. This is a problem for people living in the late twentieth century but not of course those living in the ancient world, where technological change was, on the whole, slow. There were no rapid technological changes which rendered feudal serfs redundant or made carts outmoded.

Economic factors in the modern economy, including price changes shown in general inflation rates and exchange rate changes, cannot be foreseen with certainty. Those who bought at the top of the British 1980s' house price boom, did not foresee recession and the fall in real house prices of the early 1990s. Those with negative equity in their homes, owing more to the building society than their property will fetch on the market, with hindsight bought at the wrong time. However, in whatever context decision-makers cannot know the future. Whether we consider the possible actions of business rivals or future reactions of co-operative actors, we do not have a complete view.

Economic actors do not know exactly how government economic policies will change in the future. Yet these may have serious ramifications for household and business budgeting. In Britain, interest rate increases at the end of the 1980s, unexpected by many, had a hand in the collapse of several large corporate empires and myriads of small businesses. Interest rate hikes brought uncomfortable times for mortgage payers, as well as for many of the companies which survived. But whilst some firms did badly, for example some insurance companies and many building firms, others like corporate liquidators saw their profits mount. It is an ill wind . . .

Changes in government economic policy may be linked to wider political and social changes. Political risks and uncertainties about changes in legislation and policy in general, may affect the business decision-maker, the consumer and the charitable giver. The run up to any election usually witnesses an increase in uncertainty. At the extreme, the uncertainties of war are profound. Yet, additionally, changes in the structure of power within organizations and markets may significantly affect economic actors. A company takeover, the entrance of a new market rival, changes the balance of power in ways often unexpected.

Social and psychological factors may bring different scenarios to those expected, such factors held constant in the conventional economic model. Euro Disney, the beleaguered theme park in Paris has not met the expectations of its originators and backers. One explanation is that the French have not taken this pleasure centre to their hearts. The rival Asterix theme park has been much more successful, it is said to accord more closely with the Gallic mood. Perhaps those who decided to build the Euro Disney theme park near Paris believed that cultural differences could be overcome or were unimportant.

Environmental changes may come about autonomously or as a consequence of human actions. The unforseen consequences of Acts of God, the possibility of natural disasters or 'manmade' problems, from the enormity of global warming to the spillage of oil, may have important uncertain ramifications. Yet observers and policy-makers cannot agree or predict with accuracy the outcome of such events. There are those who claim that global warming is not a problem. The disaster of Chernobyl will have effects for many years to come, their nature and extent yet to unfold.

Further away in historical time, people were less able to control and predict their environment. Whilst in the traditional societies of the past, people did not face the risks and uncertainties of the rapid economic and organizational changes of the modern world, their lives were marred by other problems, the vagaries of the weather, untreatable diseases or unrestrained capricious princes.

Economics helps to shed light on what are in fact multi-disciplinary problems. The key point is that people and their environment interact over time, bringing about evolutionary modifications, and sometimes revolutionary change. Our situation can be highly volatile or turbulent. Indeed, Shackle (1965) likened the world of the chooser, to that of a kaleidoscope, where one small change, a twist in its position, could bring a very different pattern of possibilities and constraints, a *kaleidic change*. Indeed, the move from simple, analytical time takes the decision-maker into the fraught world of perspective time, where some choices and their ultimate consequences may be very uncertain. Actual decision-making often involves choosing in the face of a fair degree of ignorance, where choosing is stressful and Keynesian 'animal spirits', that desire for positive action, may prove more representative than rational calculation.

The indelible and positive nature of risk and uncertainty

Before we continue with the analysis, it is important to emphasize that imperfect foresight and change are indelible features of the human condition. As people find the means to cope with or reduce the impact of risk and uncertainty in one area, new elements arise elsewhere, part of a complex process in a changing, intricate system, evolving over time. The modern economy, with all its sophisticated technology and organizations, cannot dispense certainty. But risks and uncertainties do have a positive side (Dawes 1988). They can create challenge, give enjoyment and sometimes pleasant surprises, not simply nasty shocks. To abolish risk and uncertainty would not be desirable, even if it were possible. Fortunately, science and technology have yet to promise, let alone deliver, omniscience. For with perfect foresight, life would be an unbearable certainty with no surprises, pleasant or otherwise; a life without hope or fear. We should appreciate that risk and uncertainty do have a beneficial aspect.

THE ORTHODOX MODEL: RISK

We shall begin with the basic economic model where probabilistic mathematical calculations are used for analysing risk. The mainstream approach treats risk and uncertainty as one, using the terms interchangeably and very often subsuming uncertainty under a heading of risk. The orthodox model examines the behaviour of individuals, making choices between alternatives which are certain and those involving varying amounts of risk.

Broad categories of risk

Two broad categories of risks can be distinguished:

1 Those risks which people or organizations bear because they carry with them a *probability of reward*. These include the gamble, the investment decision, the career choice which promise the likelihood of gain, a gambling or *speculative* risk. Where the individual household member, for example, chooses between buying a well known branded consumer durable, or opting for an untried newcomer's product; buying a share in ICI or saving money in a building society account; or a company choosing between 'safe' or risky investment projects. It can be argued that such risks are taken with an expectation of a reward.
2 Those risks which carry *no possibility of reward*, only of a loss. The hazards of life against which we wish to insure, those risks which no one will pay us to bear – often referred to as '*pure risk*'. These include the chance of having a road accident, being burgled or a factory catching fire.

In this section we shall focus attention essentially on the first kind of risk, comparing physical investment alternatives, where the decision-maker aims to make a gain. This analysis will be useful later in the chapter when we discuss insurance and diversification.

The goals of REPs and attitudes to risk: an introduction

At the core of basic neo-classical economics lies the assumption of REPs, those fully informed, rational individuals; single-minded, know-all, utility maximizers. More advanced neo-classical models include situations where there is no longer one single certain outcome, arising from any particular decision. Although when the assumption of certainty is relaxed, rational economic individuals are still assumed to aim to do the best they can. Their objective has changed, in the risky world, they are assumed to *maximize expected utility*, the average expected outcome from any particular set of risky choices.

Indeed, it is usually assumed that individuals regard risk as a 'bad'; people are thought to be *risk averse*. They need to be rewarded for bearing risk. It seems that most individuals do not see risk as beneficial, except in cases such as gambling, say betting on horses, football pools or the national lottery. The thrill of bingo or the gaming tables, gives positive enjoyment where the outcome is not certain. Particularly where there is a relatively small amount of wealth at stake, people derive positive satisfaction from gambling. True, some undertake risky, potentially hazardous sports, like motorized hang-gliding or pot holing, but such activities are relatively insignificant in terms of overall behaviour. The swash buckling entrepreneur, of course, might be a *risk lover*. The utility or satisfaction derived from such activity, a source of positive happiness, for which he or she would be willing to pay.

Individuals may display different degrees of risk aversion, some may be less risk averse than others, prepared to accept a smaller reward for a particular level of risk. Yet they still need to be compensated for facing risk, albeit by a smaller sum. Only when people have a sufficient thrill or enjoyment from a particular risky venture, they love the risk involved, do they need no compensation and indeed will be prepared to pay for such enjoyment. But at the outset we shall assume risk aversion.

Measuring risk

There are several ways in which risk can be measured, given a probabilistic approach. To make optimal choices, to weigh up the alternatives, REPs must have a consistent yardstick so that they can ultimately decide how much utility to expect, if they chose a particular option.

Initially, we shall examine the concept of the *certainty equivalent*. To explain this concept we ask REPs how they compare the expected outcomes of safe and risky choices. This is a key question in the conventional approach which uses the laws of probability as a basis to provide a risk measure. We can illustrate how to estimate for risk, by taking an example from physical investment appraisal. This continues the theme developed in the previous chapter. Here we compare an investment which gives certain cash flows with an alternative risky proposal. In reality, of course, no investment is certain, nothing is completely safe, not even houses. This is a simplification in analytical time.

Imagine a situation where Rosa is considering two alternative investment projects, one certain in outcome, the other risky; a sure thing and a gamble. For simplicity, assume each project requires the same initial money outlay and that given a limited budget, only one of the projects can be chosen.

1 The first project, A, codenamed 'Well Tried', involves an expansion of the manufacturing capacity of a very well tested, widely sold product. The net sales revenues which would result from this expansion are assumed to be known with certainty. The NPV of Project A is £400, a single, assured outcome, *embodying no gamble*. This certainty is a useful fiction.

2 The second project, B, codenamed 'Novel', the alternative, involves an investment in new manufacturing capacity for a unique, untried product which consumers may or may not like. If consumers take to the product, then Rosa's wealth will increase by £1,000, the NPV of the project. Yet if the product were a flop, with sales reaching a low level, Rosa's wealth would be reduced by £200. Novel is something of a gamble, as was the Euro Disney venture in Europe. Novel might make a loss. But then it could be successful and do very well, rather like the investment in the film *Four Weddings and a Funeral*, which has yielded an enormous return, and is claimed as the most successful British film to date, in financial terms.

How can these two alternatives be compared so that a rational choice can be made? Novel and Well Tried are offering very different outcomes. Should Novel's product actually catch on, it will definitely make two and a half times as much money in NPV terms, as the certain return on project 'Well Tried'. Yet should Novel's product fail to inspire, then Rosa will see her wealth reduced by £200, a negative NPV. Novel could earn so much more than 'Well Tried', but then it could make a loss. To choose Novel is *risky*.

The model uses probabilities to weight future cash flows according to the likelihood of their occurrence. With such a weighting process we can work out a *single expected average money* figure for the risky proposal. To compare the two investments we need to know the probability of each of Novel's two potential outcomes occurring, the chance of its success or failure. Then we can calculate an average expected money outcome, a single value. This simplifies matters, making an easier comparison with the certain sum, the gain from Well Tried. Of course, in perspective time risk estimation would involve:

a) identifying all the possible outcomes;
b) estimating the size of the consequences attached to each outcome;
c) estimating the probabilities of the outcomes.

In analytical time we know all these things with certainty. The resultant sum, given this information, is the *expected monetary value* of the risky project. The Expected Monetary Value, *EMV*, is defined by

$$EMV = (successful\ outcome \times p) + (unsuccessful\ outcome \times (1 - p)) \quad (12.1)$$

where p is the probability of success, and therefore $1 - p$ is the probability of failure.

Table 12.1 Well Tried: certain monetary value

Project (1)	State (2)	Probability (3)	Money (4)	Money * P (3) * (4)
Well Tried	Success	1	400	400
				400

Table 12.2 Novel: expected monetary value

Project (1)	State (2)	Probability (3)	Money (4)	Money * P (3) * (4)
Novel	Success	0.2	1,000	200
	Failure	0.8	− 200	− 160
		EMV		**40**

Indeed, all that is now required to calculate this value, given the information we already have, is the probability of each possible outcome, the chance of success or failure of Novel. Assume that the *probability of success*, p is 0.2 or 20 per cent and the *probability of a failure* (1 − p) is 0.8 or 80 per cent. Remember that the probabilities must always sum to 1 or 100 per cent. These probabilities can now be used to multiply the monetary value of each of the appropriate outcomes, so weighting each possible outcome by the likelihood of its occurrence. Finally, these probability weighted outcomes, are added together to give an average expected outcome for the project. Table 12.1 displays the position for Well Tried. The information for Novel and the calculation of Novel's expected money value is shown in Table 12.2. The details are also displayed in Figure 12.1 panels a and b, showing a simple decision tree diagram for Novel and the certain outcome for Well Tried.

Figure 12.1(a) Project Well Tried with a certain outcome

Figure 12.1(b) Project Novel with two possible outcomes

Clearly, Well Tried has only one outcome as shown in Table 12.1 and Figure 12.1(a). Its money value is certain. In the case of Novel, given that a successful outcome of £1,000, has a likelihood (p) of one chance in five, which is 20 per cent or 0.2, then the weighted outcome is £200. (The probability value in column 3 multiplied by the figure in column 4.) Given that we have specified only two possible outcomes, there are no middling scenarios – it is either success or failure, once we have the probability of success we automatically know the probability of failure, for the probabilities must sum to one. The unsuccessful outcome, a loss of £200 has a higher probability given by (1 − p) or 0.8, a four in five chance of failure. The weighted outcome gives a loss of £160. The expected monetary value, is given at the end of the last column in Table 12.2. This is the addition of the weighted outcomes. The equation 12.2 gives the expected monetary value *EMV*.

$$EMV = 1000p + (-200)(1 - p) \tag{12.2}$$

Comparing (12.1) with (12.2), the successful outcome is a profit of £1,000 and the unsuccessful outcome is a loss of £200, i.e., − £200.

Given these values,[1] the average outcome, *the expected monetary value* for the project is £40.

The expected monetary value

What does this figure tell us? Be warned, the expected monetary value does *not* tell us what will actually happen. It is an *average* based on assumed figures. What happens depends on whether the project is actually a success or a failure. We do not know in advance which will occur. Although we have allowed for two different states of the world and their outcomes, all assumed known. Certainty still plays a large part in the model, for given the assumptions, the decision-maker has a good deal of information about how the future is expected to unfold. To reiterate, *we know with certainty*:

a) all possible states of the world *and* the money outcomes attached to them;
b) all probabilities of these states of the world occurring.

In the case of Novel versus Well Tried, given the data in Tables 12.1 and 12.2, a straight comparison of the expected money value with the certain sum, gives 'Well Tried' a clear victory. A certain sum of £400 would be definitely preferable to the risky alternative weighted average of £40. Rosa would have no difficulty in making a choice, once the expected money value of Novel is defined as a single readily comparable sum in these terms.

Yet how would Rosa choose between the projects if the expected monetary value (EMV) and the certain sum were equal? In other words, what would happen if Novel's EMV, in effect the expected net present value matched the certainty 'reference project' Well Tried, with the assured NPV of £400?

We can create such a situation by increasing the probability of Novel's success.[2]

In this example, other things being equal, a 0.5 or 50 per cent probability of success would give an EMV for Novel equal to the certain money outcome of Well Tried. Improving the likelihood of success for Novel to 50 per cent, automatically reduces the chance of its failure, for probabilities sum to 1. Now the ENPV is £400; a very considerable improvement, a tenfold increase in Novel's EMV. The data in Table 12.3 illustrates this position, and see also Figure 12.2.

However, despite this change, the caveat still stands. The expected monetary value is an average, it does not tell us what will actually happen. Moreover, it is based on the belief that the probabilities will definitely hold and that the number and the money size of the outcomes will be as specified. Of course, if the probability of the

Table 12.3 Novel: expected monetary value

Project	State	Probability	Money	Money * P
Novel	Success	0.5	1000	500
	Failure	0.5	− 200	− 100
			EMV	**400**

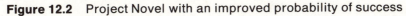

Figure 12.2 Project Novel with an improved probability of success

new product's success is estimated to be greater than 0.5 or 50 per cent, then given that everything else remains equal, Novel would have a higher expected monetary value than Well Tried.

Expected utility maximization and the certainty equivalent

Now we can return to leading questions:

a) How would Rosa choose between the two alternatives if they were to have the same equivalent monetary values? Would she be indifferent between them?
b) Should she always choose the project with the higher expected money value?
c) In what circumstances would Rosa choose a risky alternative in favour of a certain one?

To answer these questions we must make the subtle switch from money to a utility focus, for the ultimate objective in this model is to maximize utility. The essential thrust of the argument is that people seek to maximize *expected utility*, not expected monetary values as such. Moreover, we assume that Rosa receives *no* utility gains or losses from the actions or the mechanisms of actually choosing between the alternatives. Satisfaction arises just from the money outcomes of the projects.

First, we shall see that Rosa is *not* indifferent between the two projects although given a 50 per cent chance of success for Novel, they have the same equivalent monetary values. At a £400 **EMV**, Well Tried would definitely be chosen by any *risk averse* individual. Remember that risk aversion is not an unreasonable assumption. People are generally more relaxed, happier, with a sure thing, safe in the belief, according to the old adage, that 'a bird in the hand is worth two in the bush'. This everyday phrase tells us directly that people prefer certainty and are prepared to settle for something less, provided that it is secure. Whilst not a complete description of people's attitudes to risk, it makes a useful starting point.

Given that REPs aim to maximize expected utility and they are risk averse, then for any risky expected monetary value, there is a smaller but certain sum, known as *the certainty equivalent*, which would leave the decision-maker no better nor worse off in utility terms. In this case Rosa would be indifferent to the ENPV of £400 and a smaller but certain monetary sum.

Why is a certain sum preferred to a bigger, but risky, amount of cash? We can use neo-classical utility theory to answer this.

$$U = f(W)$$

where U is utility and W is wealth.   (12.3)

Utility (U) depends on money wealth (W), other things being equal, as wealth increases so does utility. In Figure 12.3 total utility is shown as a positive function of wealth, with utility displayed on the vertical axis,[3] and monetary wealth measured on the horizontal axis.

For a risk averse individual, as more wealth is received total utility increases, but whilst each additional £1 gained brings with it a positive amount of utility, there is a *declining* marginal utility. Each successive £1 received in wealth adds successively smaller amounts of extra utility. To illustrate, assume that Rosa has a wealth of £2,000. She receives a gain, an inheritance of £1,000. Her total wealth increases as does her total utility. The marginal utility gain can be represented by the distance AB, on Figure 12.3.

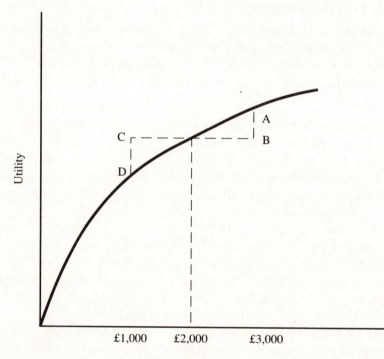

Figure 12.3   The total utility function of a risk averse individual displaying a diminishing marginal utility

However, given her original wealth position, if she loses £1,000 as a result of an uninsured theft, her total wealth and total utility decline. The loss in terms of marginal utility is shown by the distance CD. At the margin the loss of happiness from the theft of £1,000 is bigger than the gain in happiness from an equivalent inheritance of £1,000. But note that we assume no psychological costs arising from the theft. The extra utility gained from an increase in wealth by £1,000 compared with that of the utility lost by a reduction in wealth of £1,000 are not the same. An equivalent money loss is more significant. CD represents a considerably greater utility loss than the utility gain of AB.

With the concept of diminishing marginal utility in mind, return to the example of Novel and Well Tried. It follows that despite the fact that Novel offers the same expected monetary value gain as Well Tried's certain sum, the risk averse would always choose Well Tried. The projects look the same in expected money terms but not in terms of utility. Novel would not give as much utility as Well Tried because Novel is a gamble.

In Figure 12.4, if we take a wealth point of £1,600 an addition of the gain from the certain project, gives Rosa £2,000 on the horizontal axis. We can read off the total utility level, given the acceptance of Well Tried, shown at S. Novel, in contrast with Well Tried, carries a possibility of reducing wealth. Given the falling marginal utility of money, the project does not add as much extra utility for Rosa as does the certain sum from Well Tried. Whilst Novel adds an average outcome of £400 to Rosa's wealth, this does not give the same utility as Well Tried. In Figure 12.4, if the worst happens, Novel brings a reduction in wealth to a total of £1,400 and gives a utility shown at Q. At best, Novel brings a gain in wealth of £1,000, to give a total of £2,600. But increases in total money wealth bring smaller increments in utility. The utility given by £2,600 is shown at T. Now the potential loss from the project bears more heavily in terms of the potential utility lost than the potential gain. Novel will give £400 in expected money terms. On the horizontal axis the wealth will be £2,000. But the utility which would be derived in the event of the average outcome occurring would be shown at point B. This is located on the straight line, QT, which joins the utility levels associated with levels of £1,400 and £2,600 respectively. Given the average outcome at £2,000 based on the probability weights given, note that this EMV is only equivalent to a money utility value of OB on the vertical axis. So Novel gives Rosa a lower total utility than does Well Tried. Novel and Well Tried are equivalent in expected money terms but given the element of risk in Novel, Well Tried wins, hands down.

If we read from Figure 12.4, we can find a certainty equivalent sum which will give the same level of utility as Novel. This certainty equivalent, given Rosa's utility function, is equal to the distance on the horizontal axis between £2,000 and £1,800. In fact, given the way the utility function has been drawn here, a *certain project* which gives a net present value of £200 is equivalent in utility terms to Novel.

It also follows from this, that the expected monetary value of Novel would have to be higher than Well Tried's in order to induce Rosa to select the gamble. Extra

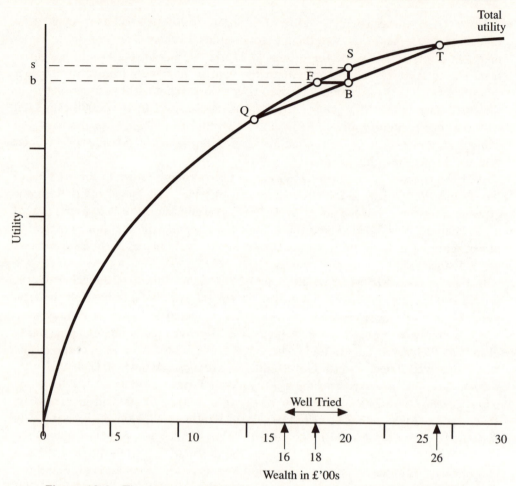

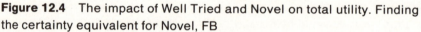

Figure 12.4   The impact of Well Tried and Novel on total utility. Finding the certainty equivalent for Novel, FB

money would be necessary to compensate her for the risk involved. How much higher Novel's expected money value would have to be to induce her to select this risky alternative depends on the risk averseness of our individual.

The analysis provides a framework to illustrate why a risk averse person prefers a certain event, rather than a risky event with the same expected monetary value. The proportionate difference between the expected sum and an equally preferable smaller certain sum, gives a measure of an individual's risk aversion. If Rosa is indifferent between a certain amount of money, £200, and a risky return of £400, then the difference £200 as a percentage or proportion of the safe sum is £200/£400 which equals 0.5 or 50 per cent. At this point the person would require a 50 per cent premium to compensate for risk. The individual who is more highly risk averse would require a greater compensation. An individual with a certainty equivalent of £400, for example, would want a 100 per cent payment, to compensate for risk. People with different degrees of risk aversion will require different certainty equivalents.

Rosa would be able to specify for any event where outcomes are risky, a *certainty equivalent*. The actual size of this will depend on her degree of risk aversion. Rosa may be quite unwilling to accept Novel, for it is not a sure thing. However, there will always be a certainty equivalent project which gives something less than Novel's expected monetary value: and she would be indifferent between the two.

Other measurements of risk: an introduction

The expected money value gives a measure of central tendency – the average value of a proposed project's performance. But risk can be evaluated in other ways. Although these involve more complicated mathematical measures, which are beyond the scope of this book, we can give an indication of these.

One measure would take the extent to which the actual outcome of a decision may diverge from the expected or average value. Risky projects can be compared by the spread of their outcomes around *the mean* – the average. The bigger the spread, the more risky the project.

Imagine a third project C, *Really Novel* with the same ENPV, at £400, but with a different, wider spread of possible outcomes. Statisticians can provide us with this measure of the spread around the average of all the weighted possible outcomes called the standard deviation. Project Well Tried has no expected variation from its certain value. There is just one anticipated outcome, with a probability of 1. So the standard deviation or spread has a zero value. Project B, Novel, in comparison, will have a positive spread or risk. The project Really Novel has the widest range of outcomes, other things being equal. It is the most risky. This measure of spread gives us another way of gauging risk: the larger the standard deviation (or the standard deviation squared which is the variance), other things being equal, the greater the total risk.

Other ways of defining, measuring and evaluating risk exist. What may be important to the decision-maker is the *downside risk* of a project (one measure is the semi-variance), not the overall spread of outcomes. Risk may be better evaluated by taking the worst possible result of a decision and focusing on that. After all, we would not describe the upside, where the project does better than average, as risky, for risk sounds dangerous, a situation where we are exposed to loss or hazard. This is not the flavour of the upside.

Risky choice in different contexts

To explore the nature of risky choice in different contexts, let us change the assumptions and widen our examples. So far we have compared Well Tried, the perfectly safe project with risky alternatives. Now let us make different assumptions about the context of choice:

a) Imagine that only a small amount of wealth is to be spent on a risky project, a very insignificant amount of total wealth. The best scenario gives a high reward but with a very small probability of success. Even if the worst scenario occurs and this has a high probability, the fall in wealth from this is small, a tiny negative NPV. Then Rosa may be quite happy to take a gamble and choose the risky option in preference to a safe project. This is in some ways similar to betting a small amount of money on the pools or the National Lottery, paying a small sum in relation to total wealth, in the hope of making a large potential gain. In fact, people do the football pools and buy lottery tickets with a small expectation of winning.

b) In a situation where there are a very large number of projects undertaken, one project might do badly and make a loss. But that loss would be offset by another project doing well. Given many projects, Rosa can decide on the basis of ENPV alone. Provided that the ENPV were positive, then on the principle of 'what you lose on the roundabouts, you will gain on the swings', Rosa could accept all such risky projects, however wide their spreads and downside risk. A project might have a high downside risk – it could make a big loss. But in the overall scheme of many projects, it would nevertheless be acceptable. Whatever any particular project's future outcome, good or bad, this would be 'balanced out' by the results of other projects. This is essentially a situation of diversification to which we shall refer in more detail later in this chapter.

c) Imagine that a project requires a large expenditure of cash in relation to Rosa's total wealth, but has a very high expected net present value. If the average outcome occurred it would give a sizeable gain. Further assume that the project has a significant downside risk, with a large potential loss. If the worst outcome actually occurred, Rosa would be exposed to bankruptcy. In such circumstances, even if there were only a very small probability of making this large loss, the downside risk might be regarded as too dangerous to bear. In the last analysis, whether such a project would be accepted or rejected would *critically* depend on Rosa's attitude to risk, and the alternative possibilities available.

Attitudes to risk: revisited

People may be prepared to gamble money, where the potential losses are small, or operate on the basis of what is lost on the swings can be gained on the roundabouts. Yet in general we are risk averse, particularly when taking chances, which affect a significant proportion of our wealth. On the whole, decision-makers will pay to keep their options open and to avoid risky situations. They may hesitate to choose a risky project, unless this is one of many similar projects and/or one which uses a very small proportion of total wealth or where the potential worst possibility is insignificant. Then a potential loss is not a serious matter.

Risk attitudes vary for the individual, depending on the context of the choice. A rich person may appear to the outside observer to take great risks, although on closer inspection only a small relative amount of his or her wealth is at stake. The poor may appear very risk averse, for what seem to be small expenditures are relatively large in terms of their total wealth. In addition, any individual economic actor, in some situations, may be risk loving and prepared to gamble a small amount of wealth, like the small investment on the pools, where nothing ventured is nothing gained. At the same time that economic actor may be very risk averse and need a large return to compensate when large amounts of wealth are involved. How much people are prepared to gamble to make potential gains, or to pay to avoid risks as in the case of insurance depends on a variety of factors and contexts, some of which we shall discuss later in this chapter.

Theoretically, it is possible to distinguish the risk averse from those individuals who in some situations are a) risk lovers or b) risk neutral. The risk lover would prefer a smaller expected money sum to a higher certain one. For them, risk is a good in itself to be enjoyed; something that an individual is prepared to pay for. In contrast, the risk neutral person would be indifferent to a certain sum and an equivalent expected money – totally unconcerned by the risk associated with a decision. His or her utility function would be a straight line through the origin. There would be no diminishing marginal utility of money.

The certainty equivalent approach and neo-classical analysis

Neo-classical analysis assumes that the economic decision-maker is in complete charge – sovereign – furnished with all probabilities and outcomes; all the relevant sets of final repercussions and so the complete structure of the problem. Whilst individuals may differ in their willingness to bear risk, they gain no utility from their actions or the processes of decision-making. Satisfaction is only derived from the final outcomes.

The theory treats risk and uncertainty as one. Both inherently involve chance or probability. Risk denotes the exposure to the probability of injury or loss; and it includes the likelihood of being unable to take advantage of a new beneficial opportunity. Risk is measurable, so it follows that people can maximize expected utility, for they have sufficient relevant information to calculate both the expected money values and utilities. They can then simply pick the best unique solution from a set of risky choices. Whilst giving us a useful insight into the factors involved in evaluating risk, this particular way of modelling reality is open to criticism.

Initial criticisms of the expected utility approach and policy implications

The model assumes that people are willing and able to calculate the probability of and apportion a utility to each possible outcome. Furnished with such data, individuals can then act to maximize their expected utility. However, as we have seen, much information is still assumed with certainty. There are several criticisms of this view which question the model's ability to predict (and/or describe) how people respond to risky choices. This has ramifications for government policy (Cooter and Ulen 1988).

Most people have no idea of the expected utility model and would find it too complex to apply in the vast majority of realistic situations. The expected utility is not useful for the actual measurement of risk because no one can measure their utility function in perspective time with any degree of accuracy or assign money values to utility. Simon (1976) points out that given the tremendous intricacy of working out expected utilities, and the limited knowledge of available outcomes, individuals simply gather information up to the point where they achieve a satisfactory outcome. People go for *satisfactory* solutions, not optimal ones. Indeed, satisfactory choices could actually be made with crude rules of thumb, standard conventions and customary responses.

Nevertheless, there are those who argue that the standard model, based on maximizing REPs, should not be discarded. The theory is not intended as a description of reality but a means for organizing our thoughts – something like a parable (Hay 1989). It forces us to think about the structure of the problem in hand and the likelihood of different outcomes. The fact that people do not know of the model, let alone apply it, does not detract from its explanatory powers. As a hypothetical model it helps us to understand a complex reality.

However, more telling criticisms are made by other economists and psychologists. There are some risks where people's judgements are such that they are incapable of giving a reliable estimate of the probability of an event. We have used a business investment context to explain how people could evaluate risk. Here probabilities are often subjective, perhaps based at one extreme on very extensive market research and a great deal of past experience. However, they are not the probabilities of the actuary. By the nature of most investment decisions, we cannot find objective probabilities. Often the entrepreneur gives us a probability based on intuition, guess, hunch or plain wishful thinking. Experiments cannot be repeated because the world is evolving. There is no exact action replay. By the very nature of their subjectivity, such probabilities may well be evaluated quite differently by different actors, depending on the information available and selected, and their 'reading' of such material.

Keynes argued that, most probably, due to the characteristics of human nature:

> a large proportion of our positive activities depend on spontaneous optimism rather than on a mathematical expectation . . . a spontaneous urge to action rather than inaction, and not as the outcome of a weighted average of quantitative benefits multiplied by quantitative probabilities.
>
> (1936: 161).

Animal spirits prevail, not mathematical calculation. Indeed, pessimistic and optimistic personalities may view situations quite differently and frame their comments about a particular investment project in different ways. Two individuals furnished with exactly the same data about the project could behave differently. One might claim that the project has a 50 per cent chance of succeeding, thereby emphasizing the upside. The other might argue that the same project has a 50 per cent chance of failing, a pessimistic view, emphasizing the downside. The average expected outcome is the same either way, but different individuals have different perspectives and will frame their views accordingly. Evidence suggests that the framing of what are probabilistically equivalent choices, will lead to systematic differences in the way people choose. The actual presentation of the options may be very important. The REP may be fooled by presentation (Machina 1987). The project analyst who emphasizes the upside may convince management to accept the project; those who emphasize the downside might convince management to reject it. Finally, as we noted in the last chapter, the same person can be optimistic or pessimistic given a swing of mood. So the project can look different at different points in perspective time.

Individuals may have all their attention focused on one risk out of many, merely because people have been provided a particular set of information. For example, when women are to be given an amniocentesis test, they are provided with official information concerning the risk of having a baby with Down's Syndrome, for different maternal age groups. Other risks may not even be considered.[4]

A variety of research sheds light on the way people view risky events. Psychologists show that despite the available statistical evidence, people may make incorrect judgements about the risks inherent in different situations. In a study by Kahneman, Slovic and Tversky (1982), evidence showed that people overestimated accidents as a cause of death, whilst they underestimated strokes as a killer. Research showed that people believed that accidents caused 25 times more deaths than strokes. From the objective data, in actuality, the stroke killed 85 per cent more people than did accidents. Indeed, often people disregarded statistical evidence, whilst using evidence that seemed more appropriate to them, or was available at first hand – what had happened to somebody they knew. To add to this view, people might not trust the information, particularly if they believe it represents a particular perspective from government or management. They would rather rely on their own belief. Indeed, risk perception 'involves people's beliefs, attitudes, judgements and feelings, as well as wider social and cultural values' (The Royal Society 1992). As the authors of this study point out trust is an important element in risk communication.

The frequency of eye catching, sensational mass media coverage of murders, for example, led people erroneously to believe that they were more likely to die by foul play than from common undramatic causes such as diabetes, asthma or tuberculosis. In some instances where the probability of an event is low then many seem to assign a zero probability to this event. In other cases, individuals may systematically overstate the probability of an event despite objective data to the contrary. Here the difficulty lies not in a lack of information, but the inability to process the statistical evidence. Many underestimate the impact of smoking but possibly overestimate the effects of nuclear power plants. Although this conclusion might be partially modified since Chernobyl. The general public are more fearful of air travel than travel by road, despite the much greater likelihood of a car accident, although the nature of the death in these cases may affect people's views.

If some risks are continuously overestimated and others are underestimated, as the evidence suggests, then this may lead to flawed decisions. People may be fully aware of the structure of the problem and have probabilities to assess expected utility. But the wrong decision could be made if the subjective probabilities used are inaccurate. People misread probabilities and perceive risks differently. There are lessons for the economist. Even if consumers and investors have objective actuarial probabilities at times, they may use incorrect subjective probabilities.

This has implications for the design of public policy. If some risks cannot be estimated faithfully, then there may be little point in making more information available. The state, for example, may pass legislation to enforce the wearing of seat belts, changing the rules of the game. There are those individuals who continuously underestimate the increased exposure to the risk of serious injury, as a result of not wearing seat belts. Although they may believe that an accident cannot happen to them, they are required by law to wear seat belts. The need is then to distinguish an optimal level of precaution (whatever that might be) and directly require decision-makers to take that (Cooter and Ulen 1988).

ALTERNATIVE APPROACHES: UNMEASURABLE UNCERTAINTY

There are alternatives to the probabilistic approach to risk. It is to these we now turn. Whilst in the mainstream view probabilistic risk and uncertainty are terms used interchangeably, some economists make a pointed distinction between these two concepts. Not everything can be measured in terms of unique probability distributions and expected money or utility values. We can separate unmeasurable uncertainty and measurable risk.

Knight (1933) distinguished situations where it was possible to measure risk by using probability distributions, available on the basis of past experience, from situations of uncertainty where no such measurement was possible. Whilst there was no single definition of uncertainty in Keynes's writing (Gerrard 1993: 3), he pointed to several different situations of uncertainty. In some cases it is not possible for the individual to decide which of two events is the most likely or whether equally likely, because of poor information. Even if it were possible to say which event was the most likely, given the existence of better information, knowledge could still be insufficient to give a numerical value to the probability. Uncertainty can be viewed as a situation of *vagueness* without the precise measure of probability.

Keynes also viewed *probability* as a *degree of belief*, given the available evidence. This is different from a numerical relative frequency, as in the repeated trials of the past, from our probabilistic risk measure. Uncertainty mirrors the decision-makers judgement of the *adequacy* of the knowledge on which decisions are to be founded. The more shaky the basis of information, the less *weight* we have in our extrapolations, from the past and present to the future, then the greater is our uncertainty. The degree of uncertainty depends on the vagueness of our knowledge, both in terms of the weight of evidence and the extent to which that evidence corroborates or refutes the chance of alternative explanations. Indeed, in situations where there is little evidence, Keynes argued that probabilities would be unknown because people had little basis on which to form a rational degree of belief. In some contexts they were just ignorant. Many people may believe that there is some likelihood of the collapse of the monarchy or a nuclear war in the foreseeable future. Yet they would not be able to assign a probability to such an occurrence. Indeed, there is a high degree of uncertainty where the probability distribution is very ill-defined.

In some circumstances, ignorance may mean that the decision-maker cannot imagine a complete list of consequences resulting from any decision taken now – let alone assign a probability to them. For Davidson, 'true' uncertainty exists about the aftermath of choices made now, when 'today's decision-makers believe that no expenditure of current resources on analyzing past data or current market signals can provide reliable statistical or intuitive clues regarding future prospects' (Davidson 1991b: 130).

In such circumstances decision-makers may avoid choosing or allow their animal spirits to prevail.

Shackle (1955, 1972, 1983) emphasized non-probabilistic uncertainty and stressed the fundamental ignorance which surrounds economic decision-making, where the focus is on the future. An essential criticism of the usual approach is that it does not take into consideration the possibility of amazement due to an unimagined event. Yet decisions which may lead to potential surprise can be of momentous importance, where people are to make crucial choices. The various scenarios which might follow, lead to very different vistas in the mind of the chooser. Like the pattern in a shaken kaleidoscope, the view of the future may change dramatically.

These different perspectives draw attention to situations of fundamental uncertainty, where we cannot provide precise, neat probability measures. There may be no real idea of the exact structure of the problem, indeed all the possible types of outcome. There may be no component of repetition to provide guidance for the way in which the future might unfold. Uncertainty may be associated with adverse or agreeable surprises in the future (Shackle). People acting in perspective time may have considerable ignorance about the future where they cannot measure the likelihood of an event with any confidence.

Uncertainty is far closer to ignorance on the certainty/ignorance spectrum. It promises a greater degree of sheer surprise, the unimagined outcome against which you therefore cannot insure. As we have seen in earlier chapters fundamental uncertainty requires different and often non-market means of coping.

Transforming uncertainty into risk

Some situations of uncertainty can eventually be transformed into risky ones, given the passage of real time, and the accumulation of information and experience (Kay 1984). The 'explorer' will find new knowledge. Medical scientists will continue to provide more information about the HIV virus and AIDS, so that we may be less unsure about their effects on people. However, some information may increase uncertainty, when observations give conflicting or surprising information. This leads us to reappraise the value of what we think we know, reducing the weight of available information.

Moreover, there will always be the random unique event, the nature and/or timing of which, cannot be foreseen. Such incidents can affect those situations previously considered to be only risky, as well as those which might be described as uncertain. Historical shocks, unique events, such as the outbreak of the Serbian–Croat war, the break-up of Yugoslavia, although perceived by many as likely, had an actual timing, severity and spin-off which shocked people.

The distinction between risk and uncertainty depends in part upon knowledge, or the lack of it. Different people may evaluate and weight that knowledge differently – there may be different assessments of probabilistic risk and what is uncertain. But in terms of knowledge, risky situations embody greater levels of information than uncertain ones. As nobody has perfect foresight, we cannot know exactly what will happen. Even in what are normally relatively safe repetitive situations, we could face shocks. With the advantage of hindsight our categorization of any particular situation could be wrong.

Does this mean that we have nothing to offer in the face of uncertainty? The key point is that economists can make a contribution by asking questions about what *might* happen (Earl 1986). We can inquire what sets of events might either *stop* or indeed *initiate* other events. The essence is to raise awareness about the uncertainty associated with a particular set of measures. It is better to be prepared for a variety of eventualities, rather than to take a confined view, only to find that the future is full of nasty shocks which make for adverse changes and unpleasant surprises, providing opportunities which cannot be grasped. 'The analyst must ... choose which system is more relevant for analyzing the economic problem under study ... for many routine decisions, assessing the uniformity and consistency of nature over time ... may be a useful simplification' (Davidson 1991b: 141). Given problems involving investment or consumption where taking a particular course of action can make large unforeseeable changes over long periods, in what Davidson refers to as 'calendar time', then alternative perspectives are more applicable. Rules of the game, legal constraints, like governments developing institutions to oust 'anti-social results' of uncertainty are necessary (Davidson 1991b: 142). We shall have more to say about this in the next section.

CONTENDING WITH RISK AND UNCERTAINTY IN PERSPECTIVE TIME

How can people contend with risk and uncertainty in different situations? The conventional treatment focuses largely on measurable risk, individual behaviour and the paramount importance of markets for dealing with such problems. It emphasizes, for example, market insurance and private self-insurance, and diversification –

spreading assets in portfolios; not carrying all your eggs in one basket. It lays emphasis on hedging your bets, with assets readily acquired in markets and rationally calculating individuals.

Whilst there are overlaps, alternative views stress the role of institutions, including the importance of custom and convention and non-market behaviour, including state and communal activities. These cushion the impact of risk and uncertainty. In reality, pluralistic approaches are needed for what are many faceted problems.

First, we shall turn to those risks/uncertainties from which we expect to lose, what might be thought of as hazards. Under the heading of insurance we can examine various ways of handling such problems.

Insurance

Insurance is an important element for protecting individuals from loss in the ordinary course of events. We examine the nature of insurance to show how decision-makers in general, both individuals and organizations can set about limiting their exposure to the vagaries of the world, and how far it is possible to do this. Decision-makers, according to the usual neo-classical view, think in terms of either:

a) the purchase of market insurance;
b) self-insurance.

The REP will choose the best alternative or combination of market insurance and self-insurance – aiming to acquire the most expected utility for the least cost. The type of action taken will depend on the decision-maker's objective, indeed from what he or she aims to gain protection, whether that is from a monetary loss or some intangible adverse outcome. However, in addition, we shall also consider non-market forms of insurance, including that of the state.

Insurance – the pooling and sharing of risk

In the modern economy, the market system provides the opportunity for people to buy insurance cover to protect themselves against the unexpected misfortune, for example: the financial loss caused by, premature death, sickness, accidents or the loss of property by theft or fire. Much insurance cover is bought and sold through the market mechanism. *Risk aversion* is at the heart of the individual's demand for insurance. People regularly buy insurance cover for a wide range of items and activities, to protect their cars, homes, holidays in the event of disaster. Insurance can cover a huge range of possible losses: from repair bills on consumer durables, credit card fraud to private hospital bills. Businesses and other organizations also purchase insurance cover. Companies sell insurance cover to individuals, households and other organizations (see Pawley, Winstone and Bentley 1991, for additional institutional material).

Insurance companies

These commercial organizations are *not* risk lovers, taking on other people's risk for fun, nor do they operate as charities. Their aim is to make profit from pooling risk. They take customers' *insurance premiums*, the price for buying insurance cover and combine all the money premiums, to meet claims from those who suffer misfortune. The insurers invest these funds in order to have an appropriate stock of wealth to pay out on claims. The payments of the many, settle the losses of the few. As Smith commented: 'the trade of insurance gives great security to the fortunes of private people, and by dividing among a great many that loss which would ruin an individual, makes it fall light and easy upon the whole society' (1776: 757).

The demand for private insurance

This stems from the desire to protect against the unpredictable hazard. Now, for the individual, particular risks are not readily foreseeable. Buyers of insurance pay a premium, the price of insurance cover for a potential danger, as stated in the insurance policy. To take a simple example, Marks and Spencer, acting as an agent for an insurance company, will insure the individual, against the chance of lost or stolen credit cards. For the payment of a fixed sum, the Card Safe policy, amongst other things, will cover against fraudulent card use, giving unlimited cover on all cards, once M&S has been alerted to the loss. In fact, the policy converts the potential financial loss of theft into a *certain loss* of a small amount, say £7 per annum, to be paid when the policy is taken out.

Health insurance provides another example. Note carefully, however, that it is not ill health *per se*, that the individual insures against. It is financial loss; the insurance cover will compensate for the monetary loss in terms of earnings. To illustrate, imagine a self-employed person, who has an expected working lifetime income of £30,000 per annum. Assume that person has an accident or illness which mars his or her ability to earn, say reducing income to £5,000 per annum. The individual could work out the expected monetary value of these possibilities. Taking out an insurance policy converts the uncertain financial outcome from illness, into a certain money loss – the insurance premium that has to be paid. In return it gives a certain money income. Although this assumes no future shock like the liquidation of the insurance company or the company, for whatever reasons, refusing to pay out. As in the case of the credit card holder, insurance turns an uncertain outcome, into a certain one. In any event, the act of purchase seems to indicate that the insured person gets more utility from a lower but certain income, rather than from the alternative; the option of keeping the insurance premium but with it an uninsured income.

There are limits to the possibilities of insuring against the utility loss arising from adverse events. 'In practice it is important to note that it is only those aspects for which money is able to compensate that can be deemed truly insurable' (McGuire,

Henderson and Mooney 1988: 45). People who have had their homes burgled may suffer psychological trauma and the loss of property, which whilst having little marketable value, holds great sentimental value. In such circumstances financial payments cannot give full recompense. Money cannot buy everything. Health care and health insurance are tradeable goods, but good health is not. It cannot be purchased for the incurably sick. People cannot insure themselves for the loss of their own utility resulting from their own death. No reimbursement to the deceased, either in monetary or utility terms, is possible. Life insurance cover merely is a protection against the financial loss suffered by the relatives or dependents of the insured person, in the event of the insured's death.

The supply of private insurance

This works on the basis of *pooling independent* risks. The impact of a hazardous event for the individual can be reduced by combining what are essentially the independent risks of different people. Mutual companies, like the Equitable Life, started with groups of people who came together to insure risk. The modern insurance companies which have since developed sell insurance cover, write insurance contracts, to make profit. The insurance trade depends on the mathematical *law of large numbers*. An adverse event which befalls an isolated individual – such as a heart attack, might seem indiscriminate, haphazard, down to the vagaries of chance. But the aggregate of such events, when seen in the context of large groups of people or objects, becomes predictable and calculable. When actuaries look at a large set of information, data from the past, they can readily identify such regularities and determine the probabilities of a particular event occurring. So the chance of premature death amongst a particular age and sex group in the population can be objectively estimated. The larger the sample, the more dependable, other things being equal, are the probabilities of such insurable events.

However, the merging of risks of many people, works only if the hazards of one person are essentially independent of the hazards faced by others. Given the aim of profit maximization, insurance companies only want business which will give them a profit, when all claims have been met. The individual's risk of loss is spread over a large number of people and therefore reduced. The individual has paid a fixed premium and in return has insurance cover, in the event of an adverse specified happening.

Does private insurance always work and give profit? When is the efficacy of private insurance marred? If all individuals were affected by the *same* hazard during a particular time, then an insurance company would be swamped by claims. A common disaster affecting a substantial number of policy-holders could be disastrous to insurance companies. Private insurance only works effectively if the events striking individuals are independent of each other. The risk of having a heart attack, by and large, is independent of the risk of someone else having one. An insurance company is therefore willing to sell the customer insurance cover, at a premium. This reduces risks by pooling separate hazards and effectively transfers the risk of a loss to the insurer.

Such calamities which come under the heading of Acts of God, including earthquakes, hurricanes and epidemics, are usually not covered by insurance policies, for they may affect the whole population. In such cases, funds would be insufficient to meet the multitude of claims, leaving the insurance companies to face large losses. In recent times, mortgage indemnity policies, mortgage guarantee cover taken out by those buying homes to ensure the payment of the mortgage in the event of sickness or redundancy, have brought significant losses to the insurance industry in Britain.

Rising unemployment and high interest rates have meant an increasing number of claims. Insurance companies had not foreseen the depth or extent of the British recession of the 1990s. Unemployment, which was once seen as the isolated problem for particular 'disadvantaged' groups or a short-term phenomenon, has become more widespread. The delayering of companies and loss of many managerial and other jobs, previously considered secure, have led to increasing claims. Those insurance companies which set modest insurance premiums were surprised by the size and number of claims.

Insurance companies have also faced increased claims from recession related crimes, for example, theft and burglary. The Sun Alliance and Royal Insurance have by far the largest exposure to the mortgage guarantee business, giving a combined loss of more than £1 billion in the last two years (*Guardian* 8 October 1992). Now there has been a large increase in personal premium rates in an attempt to recover from this.

An increase in subsidence claims in South East England reflects the impact of a prolonged drought coupled with clay soils. Here the risk of subsidence is an independent isolated happening but an event which can affect a large number of households in particular localities. The risk cannot be reduced by pooling. Faced with a growing number of subsidence claims, insurance companies either had to raise premiums or withdraw from the market. Insurance companies may not be prepared to insure against Acts of God or subsidence where everyone will be affected by this. In such circumstances they might not make a profit or may suffer loss.

Lloyds of London: risk sharing

Unlike insurance companies, Lloyds of London does not offer insurance, it is an organization of underwriters with members, not a company with shareholders. Members do not have limited liability. In fact, Lloyds is a market-place where brokers make deals, for those seeking insurance, with the underwriters, who act for the members. Lloyds habitually insures *extraordinary risks*, single events regarded as highly risky, where we move towards the uncertainty zone on our certainty/ignorance spectrum. The sample size of similar events is very small – information is lacking for such events. For the insurer the risk exposure from providing insurance cover is often very considerable.

Lloyds *shares risks* between its members, and so allows people and organizations to off-load risk at bearable premiums. *The Names* are individuals who promise their own personal wealth as security for Lloyds' underwriting activities. This entitles the Names to share in the profits of the business but also requires them to pay up for any losses.

It is possible to insure against most eventualities, providing you are prepared to pay an appropriate premium. The market works by collecting relatively small amounts of money from a large number of people, so that insurers ultimately have a very large sum of money from which to pay out on claims. Risk is spread between many. Profits are made when the revenues from the premiums, received from underwriting, exceed the claims. The insurance policy sets out the conditions and the circumstances in which a claim will not be met, for the buyers of insurance. However, given the great variety of disasters, from adverse weather to accidents and pollution, there have in recent years been record claims and huge losses. Big claims, for example, include Piper Alpha (1988), Exxon Valdez, Hurricane Hugo (1989), Oakland Bushfires, Lauda Air plane crash (1991), CU building bomb in the World Trade Centre and Hurricane Andrew (1992). In 1992, Lloyds had moved into the red with losses of £3 billion and with more losses expected, for many claims from pollution damages may have to be met. Considerable media coverage has been given in recent times to famous Names who have lost large fortunes. The reduction in Names has been stemmed as corporate capital is allowed a limited role in the market (*Guardian* 15 February 1994) and legal rules may change in the future.

The role of private insurance and its problems

Private insurance allows the pooling and sharing of risks, thus individuals, households and companies are able to insure against many risks at manageable premiums. But this is not the full story. Problems can arise both for suppliers and buyers of insurance. Two such problems are moral hazard and adverse selection.

Problems of moral hazard Insurers do not have perfect information about their clients. They do not operate in analytical time. There is a limit to the information which can be gathered and processed and there may be uncertainty about its accuracy and applicability for predicting the future. Once people are insured they may take fewer precautions. They might not lock their cars or smoke in bed, happy in the knowledge that should disaster strike, they are covered by insurance. They might even make false claims. In health care insurance, the doctor and patient may have much less incentive to economize on treatment – the patient may visit the doctor for trifling problems, the doctor recommend expensive branded medicines where cheap generic ones would do just as well. The story goes that insurance cover will foster the very events which people insure against, for they will take less care and have no incentive to economize on costs in the event of loss.[5] This raises claims and lowers insurance company profits, other things being equal. There is also the related problem of:

Adverse selection   At a particular insurance premium, the bad risk client, the one who is most likely to suffer from loss, is more likely to demand insurance than the good risk client. Again, the insurance company making decisions in perspective time, does not have perfect knowledge. It may be very difficult and costly to acquire suitable information, to classify people appropriately according to their risk. Insurance companies may be forced to use broad categories in order to charge according to differential perceived risks. Within a broad band there may be much variation in risk.

To illustrate the problem of adverse selection, think of car-breakdown insurance. The person with a new car is far less likely to purchase such cover, other things being equal, than the driver with an old or ill-maintained vehicle, which has a far greater likelihood of breaking down. If the premiums are increased to allow for these bad risks, then the proportion of bad to good risks may increase. Those who see themselves as good risks are less likely to purchase insurance at a higher price; insurance cover may not seem worthwhile. A vicious circle sets in with a damaging situation for the insurance company – attracting relatively too many bad risks.

In the field of health insurance we can see a similar pattern. People over sixty-five may find premiums too high except for those who know the poor state of their health and have the ability to pay the premiums. Adverse selection would be a problem. Also, as the premiums mount, the relatively healthy, as they age, may be tempted to opt out. This leaves the insurance company with an excessive proportion of poor risks and the possibility of large numbers of claims.

In the USA, group insurance, actually selects the healthier. The insurance goes to the employed and to be employed generally requires good health. The unemployed who may need the insurance the most are least likely to have it. The insurance companies have done their own selection, by choosing the employed. In the USA, a case is being made for the state provision of health insurance as a quasi-public good or indeed a merit good. In Britain, private health insurance is unavailable for many 'high risk' categories and low-income groups. They rely on the National Health Service.

Insurance companies are profit-seekers. The problems highlighted may well reduce the efficiency by which insurance firms operate. How do insurance companies seek to reduce the problems of moral hazard and adverse selection? How are the costs of risk spread? Companies attempt to set their premiums so that approximately, the premium equals the expected monetary value of the loss. But if they do not take account of moral hazard and adverse selection they will underestimate the size of claims, which ultimately could threaten the profitability and survival of the firm. Several ways of reducing such problems come under the heading of:

Coinsurables and deductibles

Coinsurance means that the policy-holder, the buyer of insurance cover, bears a fixed percentage of the loss. Under a deductible plan the insured pays a fixed amount of the loss, with the insurance company bearing the rest, for example, the claimant pays the first £500 for accident damage. This encourages people not to alter behaviour, once they have purchased insurance cover. A *no claims bonus* gives an incentive to take greater care and keep claims to a minimum. There are also policy clauses which aim to minimize moral hazard, for example, non payment on life policies, in the event of suicide or murder. Life insurance companies may influence the behaviour of clients, by charging smaller premiums for non-smokers, lower house insurance premiums for those who install burglar and smoke alarms.

The probabilities used by insurance companies, are those that follow from the law of large numbers, based on data drawn from the past. Such probabilities are only an average figure for within any large group, there will be above and below average risks. The insurance company starts by setting the premium to cover the average probability of a loss. As individuals know more than the company, asymmetric information exists. A person taking out life or health insurance cover, who is a heavy secret smoker; or is planning to commit suicide; or who does not engage in safe sex – all have 'inside' knowledge of their own behaviour past and present, unavailable to the company.

The asymmetry of information and the ability to keep highly relevant information from the suppliers of insurance, may result in mostly high risk people buying insurance. The low risk people, with full knowledge of their own safe behaviour patterns and history, may save their money and buy little or no insurance. Although however low the risk category, no one can be sure how the future will unfold – the reason for buying insurance. There may be markets where no insurance is available because the costs for the insurance companies, of distinguishing low and high risk are too great. They will not be able to make a profit.

The willingness to accept the provisions, such as coinsurance and deductibles, may be used as one way of dealing with both adverse selection and moral hazard. Certainly, in the long run, the insurer can attempt to develop better screening techniques to weed out bad risks, such as medical and psychological tests, to place people into the 'correct' risk category and to share the costs of bearing risks. These activities are of course costly and increase the premiums, other things being equal.

Buyers of insurance cover may also face moral hazard. There may always be the possibility that the insurance company in the small print has hidden away escape clauses, thereby restricting or indeed not accepting liability at all – charging something for nothing. The individual, inexperienced claimant might need expensive legal aid and time to pursue claims through the courts when the fine print is open to different interpretations and the insurance company refuses to pay up (Earl 1986). There is a situation of differential power – the individual policy-holder facing the large company.

The Life Assurance and unit trust regulatory body LAUTRO, oversees the rules of the game.

Self-insurance

There are alternatives to buying insurance cover in markets. Self-insurance is another way in which people cope with risk and uncertainty. The traditional market approach also recognizes the importance of actions taken by individuals, to minimize the probability of an adverse event occurring or to minimize the damage should that event happen. A variety of measures can be classified as self-insurance, where people pay a certain sum now, to reduce the possibility and consequences of various potential hazards. As with private insurance cover they buy peace of mind. People, for example, pay to install burglar alarms and smoke detectors. Consumer groups advise on the purchase of 'safe' cars which help to minimize the impact of damage to their occupants in the event of a crash.

The type and level of self-insurance undertaken depends in part, on the individual's preferences and of course the income constraint, just as in the case of marketed insurance cover. Take the example of self-insurance against ill health.

a) Those aiming to minimize the financial consequences of poor health, could simply set aside a contingency fund to pay for health care treatment and to cover the loss of earnings in the event of being unable to work. This helps to smooth the pattern of income through time, to reduce the impact of a financial loss of earnings due to ill health. Holding *precautionary money balances*, as we discussed in Chapter 4, and other relatively liquid assets to provide *contingency funds*, is an important form of self-insurance, held against a variety of eventualities, imagined and unimagined.

b) In addition, the individual could take a variety of actions aimed at producing good health *per se*, to cut down on the risk of illness. Time consuming activities such as jogging or weight training impose costs in terms of the opportunities forgone and the costs of equipment or sports hall admission fees. In return, such activities promise the benefits of fitness. Self-insurance might involve eating special diets, avoiding exposure to stress, refraining from smoking, taking vitamin supplements or choosing the stairs – a catalogue of measures for those who aim to improve or maintain their health status. Here the individual is actively employed in the hope of ensuring good health. Yet people will be uncertain about the precise impact of such actions. Individuals have difficulty in processing and evaluating the welter of detailed and often conflicting, information about health improving activities. For example, should we eat beef in view of the conflicting views and the uncertainty which surrounds Mad Cow disease? Again the problems of evaluating information loom large – people are often unsure about advice. Moreover, it would be too expensive in terms of resources and *impossible* to eliminate all risks of premature death; there could always be the unforseen accident.

Other activities may be seen as forms of self-insurance. Increasing education levels and improved job market attachment may be a way in which, in particular, women in modern economies, can insure themselves against future adversity. Women may wish to protect themselves, for example, against the consequent loss of income, given the loss of a partner. Their labour market attachment could be viewed as part of an overall strategy for minimizing exposure to risk and uncertainty, over their life cycle, giving them improved access to pensions and other benefits.

Non-market communal insurance

In Chapter 4 we discussed the role of the communal, non-market relationships. In non-industrialized societies the importance of the extended family group or tribe, feudal arrangements, religious organizations, groups, for example, like the Masons, were all important in the provision of protection against loss. Large numbers of children in a family were seen as security for the future and necessary, given infant and child mortality. They would be providers of real goods and services in sickness or old age, and bring other benefits including comfort and status in an extended family or tribal network.

In traditional economies, past and present, communal buffer stocks of storable food would be held to insure against the eventualities of poor harvests. In a religious monastic order there could be insurance from entry to the grave – although uncertainty cannot be eliminated. In sixteenth-century Britain, there was an initial shock at the onset of the demise of the monasteries. Henry VIII's policy was unexpected, previously unimaginable to the general populace. The dissolution sent reverberations through the system as gradually the religious orders were disbanded, their wealth confiscated. Yet as time passed the unthinkable became commonplace and eventually old history.

Even in the modern economy, where much insurance can be provided by the market and/or the state, we should not underestimate the importance of 'family group insurance' both in terms of money and in kind. Although the cover provided by family networks may be very variable. Inequalities of wealth and income amongst different socio-economic family groups, for example, make for patchy, differential cover. The one-parent family, the low-income earner or low skilled, unemployed person may have little, at least in terms of financial gift/loan support, from the extended family group in times of difficulty.

State insurance: public versus private insurance

In Britain, prior to the 1930s private market insurance coverage was widespread for a whole range of eventualities which are now covered by the state. This included insurance against disabilities, unemployment and the chance of living into old age. Indeed, since the 1930s, coverage for these eventualities has been seen as one of the prime functions of the state (Le Grand, Propper and Robinson 1992). But the broader social insurance by family networks and non-profit organizations also covered many areas now under the auspices of state organizations. Evolutionary changes in Britain and other European countries, for example, led to the development of the provision of public insurance.

There are several reasons why the market mechanism fails to provide insurance and why individuals or their family groups are unable to self-insure. Private insurance companies cannot always make a profit from insuring particular groups of people or categories of risk. It is not possible to insure against every eventuality. It is not just that information in perspective time is incomplete, simply because gathering information is costly; but information about future eventualities *cannot* be gleaned. Moreover, people interpret the same information and so perceive risks differently. And 'private insurance cannot cover contingencies such as unemployment, inflation, and important medical risks' (Barr 1993: 127).

Some groups cannot buy private insurance and there is only a limited set of insurance markets, some risky activities are uninsurable at any affordable price. Insurance in the market is provided for well defined contingencies. The state may take on the role of insurer when there are important social benefits, which private insurers cannot reap. Much of the function of social insurance is to provide insurances for eventualities which are unforseen. Barr quotes Atkinson (ibid. 1993: 128) who argues that it is difficult to imagine people taking out insurance for the development of new, expensive surgical techniques or the breakdown of the extended family.

There have been moves to privatize aspects of the Welfare State, for example, by giving the responsibility of pensions to private insurers. However, the inappropriate selling of personal pensions on the basis of incorrect advice has already brought this policy into question. The knowledge gap which exists between the buyer and seller may be exploited. Although, whether the pension is provided by the state or through the market mechanism – nothing is certain. For example, unforseen economic and political changes may render the real value of a pension quite different from what was expected. Unexpected changes in inflation rates or the privatization of state pensions may bring shocks.

Diversification: risk spreading

Insurance is unsuitable for coping with some risks. *Risk spreading* through diversification has a significant role. Given investment decisions in a market context, where people aim to make gains or simply reallocate income through time an element of risk can be diffused by holding a variety of investments.

Our discussion earlier in this chapter considered the risk of undertaking *one* physical investment *in isolation*. We measured the expected monetary values of different investments and commented on the spread of their outcomes around the mean. However, all these calculations related to an individual, single, risky investment project, like Novel. By and large, we ignored the possible *interactions amongst investments*.

The familiar advice, 'don't put all your eggs into one basket', warns people to diversify – to vary or divide their activities so as to minimize risk. That advice may be good, whether we are considering some types of physical investments, or buying financial assets. In fact, it may apply to a variety of situations where people take risks to make a gain. We can show that investments, both in physical and financial assets can be spread to reduce the potential for loss, and therefore evening out rewards. How does this work?

Imagine a company manufacturing chocolate. During the winter months the sales are high. But in the summer, the demand for chocolate is lower, for it may melt. Consumers are more interested in cold soft drinks. The company can diversify by building plant and equipment to manufacture soft drinks or by merging with a soft drinks manufacturer. Then in the event of a very hot summer the company would be unconcerned about sales revenues overall, other things being equal. Should chocolate sales plummet, sales of soft drinks would be expected to rise and so offset any downturn in chocolate sales. This diversification is designed to smooth out the cash flows over time, to offset the seasonal variation in overall demand due to the weather. Moreover, it could make the company more resilient, by increasing the variety of activities within the firm. The Cadburys Schweppes merger gave such benefits.

Can all risk be diversified away?

Whilst diversification reduces the merged company's exposure to risks of abnormally hot summers or cold winters, other factors can change which may affect the firm's costs and revenues. Sales might be hit if a slimmers'/natural food campaign took momentum, a *unique risk* factor affecting both broad categories of goods produced by the firm. Moreover, if there were an overall decline in economic activity, this could adversely affect the sales of both products, and would be an unavoidable feature no matter how widely the firm had diversified into other activities.

Nevertheless, diversification goes some way to reducing risk exposure. Firms which undertake a range of activities, those which have a random or relatively low correlation may well be able, partially, to level out their cash flows. Just looking for unrelated activities and undertaking significant diversification into these different areas could do that. However, such diversification is not without cost. Companies who stray too far from their core business may find that diversification brings an over extension into fields where they have no comparative advantage and little realistic chance of developing one. They begin to lose the benefits of specialization. They may be unable to reap economies of scale or spread themselves too widely, their managements overstretched. Those financial organizations which were 'sticking to the knitting' in the 1980s, some building societies and banks in Britain who did not diversify into a range of different financial activities, emerged more strongly as a result. They were not tempted into areas where they had little expertise, where

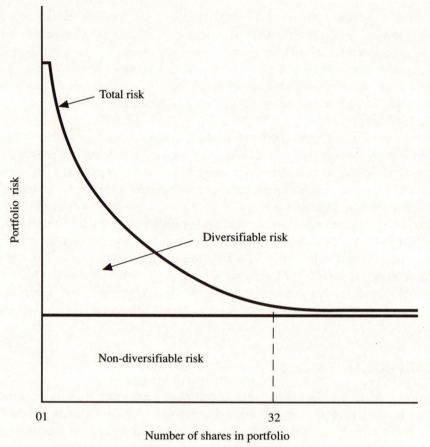

Figure 12.5 Total risk reduction by holding shares in a portfolio; diversifiable and non-diversifiable portfolio risk

the possible benefits of diversification and expansion were far outweighed by the costs.

However, diversification is very important for those buying risky shares and other financial investments, which individuals and organizations purchase for saving and in the hope of making future financial gains. If people invest in one share or in one fund, they are exposed to the total risk of that share or fund. This is rather like the exposure of a manufacturer, who makes only one product. Many pensioners lost all their life savings in the Barlow Clowes débâcle. The media often reports the personal tragedies of those who have not spread their wealth. Indeed, over 50 per cent of private investors in Britain simply hold one particular security in their investment portfolio – for example, a clutch of shares in BT or British Gas. Others have their money in some riskier venture – as it turned out – like Barlow Clowes. They may even have held all their money on deposit in the Bank of Credit and Commerce International (BCCI) which was closed down in 1991 by international regulatory action. Many people lost their money.

There are benefits from spreading wealth amongst a broader range of investments. Even investments which appear to be 'as safe as houses' may behave disastrously. Those with *negative equity*, in their home, owing more for the loan than the market value of their property, as a result of the downturn in house prices, would doubtless endorse this view. For nobody can foretell which investments will prove to be disastrous, although it is easy to be wise after the event. Even where investments look safe the future does not necessarily behave as the past, as those who bought at the top of the housing market know to their cost.

Portfolio theory: an introduction

If we look at risky ordinary shares we can illustrate that it is possible to reduce risk, by spreading wealth over a number of different shares, rather than simply holding the total risk of one company's shares in isolation. By increasing the number of shares in the portfolio, spreading wealth amongst different shares, the total risk of the overall portfolio falls as shown in Figure 12.5.

If an investor were to buy shares in only one company, for example, ICI, then the shareholder is fully exposed to the total risk of these shares. This includes all the risk which arises from the company's productive activities and financial risk which arises from any corporate borrowing. Those who held only Polly Peck shares would have been hard hit by the collapse of that company – for the shares became worthless. Unless they sold at the right time, shareholders would have lost out as the share price declined. Yet holding as little as 12–16 shares in a portfolio significantly reduces the total risk of a portfolio. Although any additional risk diversification effect becomes minimal after approximately 32 shares chosen at random. The risk we can diversify is called *diversifiable risk*, *unique or unsystematic risk*. The risk of adverse unique factors for some companies, like poor investment policies, managerial failures, bad labour relations are offset by favourable unique factors affecting other companies.

Is it possible to eradicate all risk by spreading wealth in a portfolio of assets? From Figure 12.5 it can be illustrated that there is a residue of risk which cannot be diversified away. No matter how widely a portfolio of assets is constructed, even a worldwide basket of shares contains such risk. There is a sizeable element of *non-diversifiable*, *market or systematic risk* which diversification cannot eradicate. Market risk depends on factors which affect the economy as a whole and from which no enterprise can escape, like the impact of tax changes, political factors affecting confidence, global warming or wars. Eggs may be placed in different baskets but if they all go to market in the same vehicle they are all exposed to some common risks. Whilst we can diversify the unique effects of strikes, management problems, singular factors hitting individual company share prices, we cannot diversify away all risk for we have to face exposure to overall market downturns and adverse macroeconomic changes. Investors expect to be compensated for bearing market risk, it cannot be diversified away. Yet given particular assumptions, no one is compensated for unique risks which are readily diversifiable.

Does diversification work in all situations?

Diversification works well in situations where it is possible to split up well identified claims. Investors who divide their wealth amongst a variety of financial assets can reduce their exposure to total risk of shareholding. Shares can be traded in well organized secondary markets and diversified – even by the small investor who can buy shares in investment trusts or units in unit trusts. These financial intermediaries specialize in holding portfolios of shares in a variety of companies. Small investors can gain the benefits of diversification with relatively small amounts of money. They do not pay the high transaction costs associated with small individual purchases; investment and unit trusts economize on such transactions costs and have specific financial and managerial expertise and knowledge which the individual small investor could not match. Investment and unit trusts pool the small bundles of savings from individuals and through diversification reduce risk.

However, whilst it is possible to diversify financial assets with minimal cost, and indeed some physical assets, it can be too costly or impossible to reap such advantages from diversification in other situations. It is not feasible to fully diversify human capital and hold a portfolio of full-time jobs to overcome the risk of redundancy or lack of promotion as we shall discuss in Chapter 14. Moreover, individuals in modern society cannot realistically hold a well diversified portfolio of partners even should they want to. Suffice it to say at this point we only have one life and time is limited.

The role of institutional rules and organizations for cushioning and reducing uncertainty

In previous chapters, we have already emphasized the role and importance of customs, conventions and organizational responses to the problems arising from uncertainty in perspective time. Organizations such as the family, the business, trade union or charity, in part, act as a buffer against uncertainty. The family and marriage are institutions which can provide a 'safe space', where members are protected from a potentially risky and uncertain external world. Here long-term commitments enable individuals to cut down and cope with uncertainty. Business organizations themselves give protection from the vagaries of the market. Businesses undertake takeover activity in an effort to reduce the potential variance in their environment by widening the boundaries of the system.

As Hodgson states:

> in a world of uncertainty, where the probabilistic calculus is ruled out, rules, norms and institutions play a functional role in providing a basis for decision-making, expectation, and belief. Without these 'rigidities', without social routine and habit to reproduce them, and without institutionally conditioned conceptual frameworks, an uncertain world would present a chaos of sense data in which it would be impossible for the agent to make sensible decisions and to act.

(1988: 205)

The notion of custom and practice, the use of rules of thumb and convention, institutionalized responses to cope with an uncertain environment are essential. Habits, rules and conventions frame our actions.

Coping with risk and uncertainty

There is no method to solve a problem which is essentially insoluble. We can never be sure what tomorrow, let alone the more distant future, will bring. But whether we take risk averse individuals, households, business firms, non-profit organizations or nation states, all have to devote resources to handle and reduce the impact of risk and uncertainty. The means for doing this may not always be immediately obvious and the methods used evolve over historical time. Market responses, whether in terms of insurance or diversification, are but part of a wider range of measures which people may employ. Certainly, in any society, institutional rules and organizations are fundamental for coping with uncertainty.

RISK AND UNCERTAINTY – SUMMARY

- The sources of risk and uncertainty are set in the march of real time, where people and their environments change. In perspective time, a correct sequence of decisions is often required.
- Risk and uncertainty are an indelible feature of life; but they do have a positive side. Life would be unbearable if everything were certain, leaving no hope of surprise.
- The orthodox model treats risk and uncertainty as synonymous and measurable. REPs use known probabilities and the structure of a problem to determine expected monetary values and then to maximize expected utility. A good deal of certainty is still assumed. REPs can derive certainty equivalents to compare risky alternatives.
- How people behave depends on their attitudes to risk and the context of the decision. People are usually assumed to be risk averse.
- Other measures of risk include the standard deviation and the semi-variance. The investor may look at the downside – the worst possible scenario.
- Criticisms of the approach argue that people do not know the model and do not use objective probabilities.
- Other views of uncertainty distinguish between probabilistic risk and fundamental uncertainty where there may be considerable ignorance and where uncertainty is unmeasurable.
- Uncertainty may be transformed into risk as knowledge increases. Although the gleaning of new knowledge may bring into question what people believe they know.
- There are a variety of different means for contending with risk and uncertainty in perspective time.

- Private market insurance and self-insurance are key in orthodox thinking. But there is also non-market communal insurance. Private market versus public insurance.
- Diversification presents another way of reducing risk. Portfolio theory illustrates how total risk can be reduced. But diversification does not work in all situations.
- The role of institutional rules and organizations for cushioning and reducing uncertainty are re-emphasized.
- Resources have to be set aside for coping with risk and uncertainty.

RISK AND UNCERTAINTY – QUESTIONS FOR DISCUSSION

1 What do you understand by the following concepts:

   a) 'pure' risk;
   b) speculative risk;
   c) fundamental uncertainty;
   d) expected utility;
   e) the certainty equivalent;
   f) unique risk;
   g) systematic risk?

2 Explain whether or not the measure of the expected monetary value will tell us exactly what Rosa will receive from an investment?
   Given the data for Novel, what would happen to the expected monetary value:

   a) If the probability of success rises to 0.8?
   b) The net present value of both possible outcomes is halved?

3 A small film company is evaluating a proposal for Prankenstein, a low budget film. It will cost £3 million to make and this is to be paid at the start of the project. If Prankenstein were successful, the present value of future net revenues would be £35 million. The probability of such success is given as 0.3. However, the film, alternatively, could be a flop, bringing a present value of net revenues of £2 million. The probability of this occurring is given as 0.7.

   a) What is the expected net present value of Prankenstein and what does this value show?
   b) Distinguish between the concepts of objective and subjective probability. Which type of probability value is used here and how do you think it might have been generated?
   c) Would you advise the acceptance of the Prankenstein project? *Make your assumptions clear* and state what other information you might require. What are the limitations of this method? How might it help decision-makers?
   d) 'If we knew beforehand which films would be blockbusters – we'd be immensely

rich, we'd make no flops. But a key element in this business is surprise.' Comment on this view and explain how the film makers might try to reduce their exposure to such surprise.

4 In analytical time where do we acquire probability values? In perspective time what are the sources of probability information?

5 How does private insurance help people to cope with risk and uncertainty? What are its limitations? Why do we require other important, non-market means to provide insurance for people?

6 Why should *moral hazard* be a problem? What does this term signal about the behaviour of people? What means can be used to reduce it?

7 Explain how diversification reduces risk. Is it possible to eliminate all risk and uncertainty?

8 The total risk of a share is made up of two distinct components, systematic and unsystematic risk. What does this mean and which element can be diversified away by holding the share in a well diversified portfolio?

9 Do you think that risk and uncertainty increase with the length of time between making a decision and the expected outcome? Make your assumptions clear.

10 'The orthodox treatment of risk ignores fundamental uncertainty. But in such situations people require more than marketable insurance for protection; and "inefficient" rules, habits and customs, take on a new light.' Explain and discuss using examples.

13

Investment in non-profits

INTRODUCTION

This chapter aims to highlight investment appraisal in a 'non-profit', non-commercial context, primarily within the public sector. Clearly, public sector organizations make many investment decisions which do have an important impact on the well-being of families and the relative health of private enterprise. Some such investments are deemed essential to the very survival of the economic system. Moreover, 'joint ventures' between profit seeking firms and non-profit organizations are significant. In a variety of national and international contexts, governments, non-profit organizations and private enterprise can be entwined in the provision of research and development and other forms of investment (Nelson: 1993). On a narrower basis, in Britain local authorities and opted out schools make significant investment decisions. After all, they often have budgets which can exceed those of some medium sized corporate enterprises. As well, there are notable investments taken by voluntary organizations in the 'third sector'. In all these situations commercial criteria are largely inappropriate. The maximization of shareholder wealth and utility will no longer do, even as a starting point. The Victoria or Jubilee Lines on the London Underground network, to take but two examples, would not have been given the go ahead on a commercial basis. There were no private profits to be expected. Yet such infrastructure projects can give extensive social benefits.

In such contexts we have to identify a wider community and isolate different objectives, where private monetary returns are an inadequate guide to the real overall effects of investment. A broader view of the costs and benefits is required, sometimes one which looks a very long way into the future, for often the projects under consideration are expected to have very lengthy lives, perhaps with enormous environmental impacts. Moreover, there may be diverse interest groups to consider, sometimes with conflicting objectives. Whilst these issues present us with intimidating problems – none the less, people want to see limited resources used to good effect and not wasted. Moreover, given the enormity of the public sector's investments in all economies – there is a need for appropriate appraisal techniques. Systematic treatments and careful thought may help to avoid a poor decision.

Cost Benefit Analysis (CBA) can provide a basis for deciding on whether to accept or reject such projects and to distinguish between alternative investments. CBA helps us to weigh up the pros and cons, with an aim of maximizing net social gains. Indeed, the central problem is to set up criteria for allocating limited resources between competing uses in the absence of markets or where market price valuations do not reflect all the effects relevant to the utility or well-being of people. This is a complex area where there is a good deal of debate, both at a theoretical and practical level. This introductory view of the CBA technique is intended to alert the reader to the strengths and weaknesses of the approach; it is not a comprehensive treatment.

As we have seen in earlier chapters, organizations have internal procedures for dealing with the allocation of resources, where market prices and a market mechanism are not used, where decisions are taken through a non-price, planning, command process. Given complexity and change, people may settle for satisfactory outcomes in perspective time. Moreover, people may be motivated by 'animal spirits' or simply make decisions by default, for they are not sure what to do. Clearly, over historical time decisions about the amount and type of investments in any sector have not been made by the rationally calculating economic people caught in an analytical time warp. Socio-political processes have a vital hand in determining: how many resources are set aside for investment, where these resources go and for what purpose. Decisions can be made in a variety of contexts, for example, by elected bodies or non-elected quangos.

COST BENEFIT ANALYSIS

Cost benefit analysis (CBA) is a practical decision making tool used, particularly by public sector organizations, for appraising projects in education and health care and in public infrastructure, like motorways and dams or safety projects in underground systems to take but a few examples. However, CBA can also be used to evaluate proposed changes in laws and regulations or pricing schemes (Prest and Turvey 1972: 73). CBA could be used to aid decision-makers in assessing the likely overall consequences of legalizing hard drugs, changing the retirement age for men and women or introducing motorway tolls. The supporters of CBA argue strongly that the technique clarifies and informs, that it prompts appropriate questions and brings about improved decision-making through the use of data provided on a consistent basis – an advancement over arbitrary assessments. Critics and sceptics argue that it is often a *post hoc* rationalization of decisions already taken and readily open to orchestration.

Maximization of social welfare

The goal in CBA is the *maximization of social welfare* or utility which requires *the maximization of a social surplus*, the largest excess of *total social benefit* over and above *total social costs* or *net social benefit*. Total social benefits include all private and external benefits – externalities. Total social costs include all private costs and external costs. Hypothetically, all the repercussions of an investment project will be considered. But concern lies with the welfare of the community as a whole and any investment decision is examined in the light of its addition to the community's net social benefit.

CBA has its theoretical roots in nineteenth-century welfare economics, a particular branch of the subject which uses sophisticated, rigorous models set in analytical time. Here rational economic people aim to maximize utility in a world of 'ideal type' perfectly competitive markets. People pay prices which reflect marginal opportunity costs. They match their marginal utility, the satisfaction which they acquire at the margin from consuming a good, with the price they pay. In a situation of *Pareto optimality* it is not possible to rearrange production – to reallocate resources – so that even one person could be made better off without others being made worse off. The society will not be at Pareto optimality, if by rearranging resources, at least one person could be made better off, without making another worse off. Society would be producing efficiently – on the production possibility curve at Pareto optimality. Only given an inefficient point inside the production boundary could more output of at least one good be produced. Then there would be a gain for some, without others losing out. However, the theoretical condition of Pareto optimality is consistent with a variety of different income distributions. Different points on the production possibility boundary can be associated with different income distributions.

The utility of different individuals cannot be added – or interpersonal comparisons of utility made – given the model. However, we can nevertheless imagine a social welfare function – the utility for the community or society as a whole. Projects are appraised according to their impact on this overall social welfare. There are no difficulties when an investment makes everyone better off and we can point to an unambiguous gain. Problems arise when some people are made better off, whilst others are made worse off. We shall return to these problems.

In addition, *distortions* are said to exist when the marginal cost of producing a good does not match the marginal utility or benefit gained from consuming that good. Imperfections in competition and the presence of taxation are examples of distortions. Then the prices paid for goods by individuals would not equate with the marginal cost of producing them. Consider the discussions in Chapter 8 and recall that in situations of imperfect competition price does not equal marginal cost. In addition, there are *externalities* both of production and consumption which are not fully reflected in market prices. To find an optimal result we should require marginal social cost to equal marginal social benefit. *Marginal social cost* incorporates the private and external costs of production. *Marginal social benefit* includes all private and external benefits.

Originally, the CBA technique was used in the assessment of water projects in the USA and to evaluate military strategy. CBA is more than a text book model – it is used extensively. It could be used to illuminate whether or not the relevant society would be better off as a result of undertaking a particular project, widening motorways like the M1 or M25, building the Narmada Dam in Western India, or perhaps a project for decommissioning nuclear power plants in Russia. The Narmada Dam project, for example, affects up to 40 million people and will have enormous environmental consequences. The potential 'fallout' effects of Russian nuclear power plants are wide. We are not talking about small, marginal investment decisions.

How does CBA differ from investment analysis in a for-profit context?

CBA in the public sector usually involves us in theoretical and practical issues of greater complexity.

1 The traditional neo-classical model requires the maximization of shareholder wealth where only private costs and revenues are taken into consideration. The owner or shareholder can then maximize utility (see Chapter 11). There may be problems with a particular project – a factory might create high levels of toxic waste – but given the basic model, the decision-maker will not include this in the calculations.[1] Yet as the aim of CBA, in theory, is to maximize social welfare, the decision-maker has a broader remit and must take a wider view of costs and benefits. An essential difference lies in the method of defining, identifying, quantifying and considering the gains and costs associated with different projects. Social benefits and social costs include not only private costs and private revenues of the project but in addition, externalities which include *indirect or spillover effects* whether in money terms or in real terms like pollution, a bad or improved safety, a good. These externalities have consequences for the wider community, ignored in the narrow calculus of private wealth. How to evaluate them is a key problem for CBA. Given the evaluation of a project to widen the M1, for example, there has to be an evaluation of 'intangible' benefits like the time saved by those who use the motorway and to those who are affected by the 'spillover', the ripple effects with reduced congestion or increased/reduced noise.

2 CBA may deal with 'one-off' giant projects. In the commercial context, on the whole, analysts are not dealing with projects of such immensity, although the Channel Tunnel is a very large project by any standard and undertaken by a quoted public company. In the public sector, projects can have very wide and far reaching effects over time both in the immediate future and also for very many years after their inception. Critics of the Narmada Dam project, for example, argue

that it will be a human and ecological disaster, having a wide impact, stretching far into the hereafter. Such projects may have *irreversible long-term effects* and as yet *unimagined* economic and ecological implications for the system. Very large 'unique' investment projects can present considerable problems for assessing the potential nature and size of benefits and costs.

3 In the basic model of the firm we simply have to consider one group of beneficiaries – the owner(s). But now there is a wider group – society as a whole. Investment decisions may affect specific groups in the population quite differently. An investment like widening the M1 or M25 motorways will make some members of the society better off, but others worse off. The Narmada Dam may displace up to one million tribal people as the land is flooded. There will be gainers and losers. Decision-makers have to consider the *differential effects on people*, the distributional consequences of the project.

Moreover, there may be the need to consider the possible preferences and consequences for *future generations*. People not yet born may be significantly affected in the future by choices made today. And in the long run we may all be dead but nevertheless may want to consider ethical responsibilities to generations of people yet to come.

The similarities between CBA and business investment appraisal

Time discounting

Whatever the type of investment there will be promises of gains and costs to come in the future. Time discounting enables the analyst to make allowance for the different time patterns of benefits and costs, to bring cash flows which accrue at different points in future time, to a common present value base. The present value of net social benefits less the present value of costs will give the *net present worth*, the addition to 'social well-being'.

Investment decision rules

In CBA, analogous decision rules to those given in Chapter 11 hold. Provided that the appropriately calculated net present worth is positive for an independent project, it should be accepted. In situations of mutually exclusive projects, then the project which adds the most to net present worth will be chosen, given that no capital or other resource rationing exists. So with the knowledge of the size and timing of social benefits and social costs the same discounting rules can be applied as in the business context. Moreover, in perspective time all projects are subject to uncertainty. Benefits will include private monetary benefits and externalities. Costs, similarly, will include all private monetary costs plus externalities. The analyst will attempt to put all costs and benefits in a monetary form. We shall discuss the difficulties of doing this in the following section.

The net present worth will be given by the following:

$$NPW = \frac{B_1 - C_1}{(1 + d)} + \frac{B_2 - C_2}{(1 + d)^2} + \cdots + \frac{B_n - C_n}{(1 + d)^n} - C_0 \qquad (13.1)$$

where

NPW is the net present worth of the project;

$B_1, \ldots, B_n$ are the benefits at the ends of years $1, \ldots, n$;

$C_1, \ldots, C_n$ are the costs at the ends of years $1, \ldots, n$;

C_0 is the capital outlay at the start of the project;

d is the discount rate used to bring cash flows to present worth.

(13.1) can be written as

$$NPW = \sum_{t=1}^{n} \frac{B_t - C_t}{(1 + d)^t} - C_0 \qquad (13.2)$$

An example of a local community project with a four year project life, net cash flows as in (13.3) in £million, a capital outlay as shown in (13.3) and a discount rate of 8 per cent gives a positive NPW.

$$NPW = \frac{10}{(1 + 0.08)} + \frac{10}{(1 + 0.08)^2} + \frac{10}{(1 + 0.08)^3} + \frac{10}{(1 + 0.08)^4} - 20 \qquad (13.3)$$

$$= £13.12 \text{ millions}$$

Cost benefit analysis: assessing benefits and costs in perspective time

How are the costs and benefits to be estimated and valued? For the business firm in perspective time, the estimation of future cash flows often requires extensive research – it may not be straightforward. However, at least revenues and costs can be evaluated in money terms. Although note that there are circumstances in which private sector business firms will want to assess intangibles and use elements of cost benefit analysis. In CBA the valuation of the promises of future benefits and costs is far more difficult and contentious. There are several different dilemmas.

How are externalities, non-marketed elements to be valued?

Externalities – non-marketed elements   How is it possible to put a value on elements such as the saving of time or human life, a reduction in noise pollution or the destruction of a scenic view or the extinction of wild life species, consequent on a particular investment. Pollution, for example, is not marketed. It has no ready price tag. And what is the value of human life? There are no markets for the sale of people. In many instances it is not possible to readily define 'intangibles', but whether it is 'the feel good factor' which arises from particular events or noise conventionally measurable in decibels, such externalities arising from investments may nevertheless be highly significant. The CBA analyst strives to make such elements measurable, readily comparable on a consistent basis, to find a common denominator. Money is that common denominator.

The willingness to pay for benefits

There are different methods for valuing benefits in money terms. We can begin with the *willingness to pay*, *WTP*. This attempts to measure the area under the demand curve – the overall benefit to people from a particular change. If people pay for a particular item we have to add the value of the consumer surplus to achieve the gross willingness to pay. Consider the example of investments in transport. How much would people be willing to pay for improved safety – a marginal change in risk, or to reduce noise pollution or to save journey time? *The Economist* (December 1993) in an article entitled, 'The Price of Life', reported that transport departments in the USA, Sweden and Britain, for example, use the WTP method to value life – to measure the cost of a road accident death. However, not surprisingly the costs of human misery and loss of future output are not easy to measure. The cost of a road accident on this basis in the USA was $2.6 million, more than twice that in Britain where the estimate was $1.1 million on this basis.

In a study which examines WTP for safety projects on London Underground Limited, the state-owned operator of London's underground network, Jones-Lee and Loomes (1994) consider the balancing of social costs and benefits – 'where the measure of social benefits reflects customers' strength of preference for safety' (ibid. 1994: 84). They discuss the difficulties of measuring WTP, the aggregate willingness to pay on the part of people who would be affected by a safety improvement. From their survey findings, including questionnaires and discussions, when comparing a fatality on the underground with a road fatality they estimated that people would be prepared to pay approximately 75 per cent more to avoid death in a London tube accident than death on the road. People fear large-scale accidents where they have little control – it matters how death comes.

Clearly, such methods whilst giving us ideas and information are fraught with difficulties. There may be a difference between the price people say they would be prepared to pay to avoid an event and that which they would actually be prepared to pay. People might tell the interviewer what he or she thinks the interviewer wants to hear. And if it sounds like a good project, the WTP might be inflated because the person knows that if the good is not marketed, i.e., it is a public, quasi-public or merit good, that he or she does not actually have to pay. Jones-Lee and Loomes point out the difficulties of such direct questioning. Passengers, who do pay a fare, when asked about their willingness to pay for safety improvements might believe that this could have an effect on future fare levels and so underestimate what they would pay. The measurement is uncertain. And, as always, those people scrutinizing proposals have to beware of neat monetary figures which could be different if measured on a different basis. Changing the basis of definition, the form of the question and measurement can significantly alter the estimated outcome of a project.

Moreover, there is the problem of weighting the relative social value of £1 gain to different income groups. A rich person will be able to pay more than the poor. A weighting requires us to make value judgements about income distribution. Yet an unweighted approach involves us in accepting the *status quo* income distribution – which also involves a value judgement.

In some circumstances, *WTP* might be estimated in part by looking at people's market behaviour, for example, how much people are prepared to pay to insure themselves. These methods enable the analyst to put a surrogate price on the 'intangible' and give the decision-maker a more informed view. *The willingness to avoid* costs is a method for assessing what people will pay to avoid a particular bad.

An alternative is to abandon any attempt to put money values on externalities but simply to list them. This draws the attention of the decision-makers and relevant others to the existence of such significant items presented in a narrative form. Where should the analyst stop taking into account external economies and diseconomies – the externalities of a project? When should the ripple effects of a project be left out of account? How wide should the analyst cast the net? Inevitably, there is no unique answer to this question that depends on judgement. *Externalities*, those consequences to the wider community are usually only considered where relatively large and obvious costs and benefits are imposed by a particular decision. In perspective time, information costs time and money to acquire. No amount of expenditure can give us a certain breakdown of future events.

The tyranny of discounting

Whilst time discounting has a useful function we may question the discounting advice in the context of large social projects with heavy environmental costs accruing in the more distant future. 'The tyranny of discounting' means that heavy social costs in the distant future are rendered relatively insignificant in present value terms for they occur so far away in time. The process of time discounting reduces the significance of costs in the future (see Turner, Pearce and Bateman 1994). Nevertheless, our grandchildren or great-grandchildren will have to endure these costs, if they eventually have to be 'paid'. There is no simple answer to such problems.

How far do market prices and costs reflect social valuations?

Even where markets exist, prices may not reflect marginal utility and opportunity cost. Given the theoretical ideal, all prices should reflect opportunity costs, and individuals pay a price which matches their marginal utility or happiness. Deviation from the 'ideal type' of perfect competition brings distortions. The analyst could attempt to modify prices to make allowances for the imposition of taxation or the existence of monopoly elements. Because of the theoretical and practical difficulties which this raises, often money prices are used where they are available.

Restricted social surplus

In practice, investment analysts operating in perspective time have of necessity to take as the criterion a *restricted social surplus*. Usually only major social costs and benefits are calculated. In perspective time there is a considerable cost involved in finding and evaluating information. It would be impossible to elucidate all the possible costs and benefits of a particular investment. Some of the consequences of a decision may as yet not be fully understood. Indeed, we shall see that defining, measuring and evaluating the nature of externalities and their extent, can bring problems. Often where projects are very large, previously untried, with irreversible and perhaps widespread consequences, this imposes considerable difficulty for the analyst.

What should be the appropriate 'social rate' of discount?

What rate of interest should we use to evaluate the present worth? Rates of return required by the shareholders in public companies can be estimated in capital markets. But this is not appropriate for a social project. There is a great deal of theoretical discussion about the appropriate derivation of a social discount rate, SDR, but this takes us beyond our scope.

DISTRIBUTIONAL CONSEQUENCES

The theoretical discussions about distributional consequences are interesting. Can the gainers compensate the losers? And if they can, should they? What happens if the gainers are relatively well-off and the losers are relatively poor? However we decide on distributional issues, judgements have to be made – even by ignoring them, maintaining the *status quo*, income distribution is based on the implicit opinion that the *status quo* is acceptable and better than the alternative. Sensible discussions of distributional effects are required. If a project has small distributional consequences, they may safely be ignored. But should they be significant this presents problems and the losers might require compensation. Where the gainers have power there may be pressure to ignore such effects.

CAPITAL RATIONING

Often an organization may have a large number of projects but a constrained funding for financing them. Hard choices have to be made. London Underground has many safety projects which it could introduce but limited funds in any period. The use of a *Benefit–Cost ratio* which examines the net worth per £1 of capital outlay enables a

Table 13.1 Investment projects ranked by NPW and Benefit-Cost Ratios

Project (1)	Outlay (£) (2)	NPW (£) (3)	B–C ratio (3 ÷ 2)	Re–rank (4)
A	800	1200	1.5	6
B	500	800	1.6	5
C	400	790	1.98	4
D	300	700	2.3	3
E	200	500	2.5	2
F	100	260	2.6	1

ranking of projects in situations where cash is limited for one period. This enables the organization to obtain the highest total net present worth. Assume that the following projects are independent and can only be done once with an outlay in year 0. Moreover, the projects are perfectly divisible so that fractional parts of any project can be undertaken. Using a simple example with data illustrated in Table 13.1, assume that cash is limited to £1,000 in year 0, but not limited thereafter.

In this case, ranking by the absolute size of NPW places A first and so on down the list as set out in alphabetical order to F ranking bottom with the smallest NPW. However, when we take into consideration the benefit–cost ratio, the NPW per unit of outlay, the ranking may change. Given the figures here, the ranking is completely reversed. The smallest project in terms of NPW gives the highest NPW per unit of outlay. Project F is now ranked first. In order to choose the best combination of projects we simply go through the list and accept projects according to the size of the benefit–cost ratio until all of the cash is used. Net social benefit will be maximized by accepting the four smaller projects. Projects F, E, D and C would give in total a net present worth of £2,250. This is much greater than the surplus that would be made by accepting projects A and 40 per cent of B which would only give a net present worth of £1,520. Clearly, without the limit on funds, all the projects here show a positive NPW and would be undertaken.

Tightening cash constraints

If the capital rationing constraint were tightened by the imposition of further cash limits, then a modified selection would have to be made. Retain the assumption that all projects are divisible although the capital available is reduced to £700. Projects should again be chosen by ranking via the benefit–cost ratios. But now in this case funds left over after whole projects have been accepted should be used for a fractional part of a project. In this case we would recommend project D, E, F which would use £600 of the available funds. The remaining £100 will be used to undertake 25 per cent of C. Clearly, the net social benefit will be reduced for not as many projects can be undertaken in full. However, the NPW in total would be £1,657.5. On the basis of the figures here again, more can be achieved by opting for a series of small projects than the larger ones.

In situations where the projects cannot be divided then the benefit–cost ratio breaks down and the absolute size of each group of projects has to be checked to see which will give the best result. Given project indivisibility and a cash limit of £700, projects C, E and F now give the best choice with a £1,550 total NPW. Any other possible choice gives a smaller NPW. Although we should have £100 left if we undertake projects D, E and F we would have a smaller total NPW and the discounting process has already allowed for interest we could earn be reinvesting the £100 which we would have left over given this choice.

ALLOWING FOR RISK AND UNCERTAINTY

There are several ways in which the analyst and ultimately the decision–makers might consider the impact of risk and uncertainty. People may be prepared to take account of risk in their WTP – the amount which they would be prepared to pay, for example, to avoid the risk of a particular hazard, for a very small improvement in their own or other people's safety. In projects which are 'well tried' – there are many previous examples for guidance – then probability figures and benefits and costs weighted by the respective probabilities of their occurrence can be used to derive an expected net worth. There are, however, other methods which can be used. These methods are also employed by larger UK and multinational companies, for whether in the public or private sector it is vital for decision-makers and those who produce project analyses to ask, 'what if?' questions. The aim is to cut down on the element of surprise, to make contingency plans and be prepared for corrective action in the event of things going wrong and, moreover, to be prepared with fitting strategies should the future turn out to be better than expected – to make the most of success. Indeed, to quote Brealey and Myers, who were actually speaking in a corporate context, '[t]he greatest dangers often lie in these *unknown* unknowns, or the "unk-unks", as scientists call them' (1991: 216). Those conducting project appraisals need to look for *unidentified variables*. Essentially, we want to *discover* what else might happen.

Sensitivity analysis

Given that there is a belief that all the relevant variables have been isolated, it is possible to conduct a sensitivity analysis with respect to the size of the benefits and costs of the project. The analyst will give an optimistic and pessimistic estimate of the underlying variables taking one at a time and examining what would happen to the NPW given different estimates. If, given a pessimistic estimate for a benefit, the NPW becomes zero or negative, then it may be appropriate to seek further information on that variable. If a small percentage change in an estimate brings about a zero NPW then the decision is sensitive to misestimation of that variable. This should force the analyst to delve more deeply to discover further information – to expose inappropriate forecasts. Underlying variables are interrelated so it is difficult to examine one variable in isolation. Nevertheless, a sensitivity analysis obliges the decision-maker to go further – to give some idea of what will happen if estimates of particular variables are out of 'true'. This is a simple approach which enables the analyst to focus on particular estimates. Sensitivity analysis was used in the analysis of the Channel Tunnel project – a giant, private sector project.

Scenario analysis

The best, middle and worst estimates for the project can be examined. Here the decision-maker could look at different, consistent combinations of factors occurring – estimating particular scenarios. The downside of projects can be considered – what would happen given the worst possible outcome. If we were comparing two mutually exclusive projects the critical comparison might be on that basis – the project with the worst downside would be rejected. This could be used to ponder about the nature and possibility of catastrophic effects. Scenario analysis therefore enables the analyst to consider a range of possible outcomes. But none of these methods gives a measure of risk. They do not provide the decision-maker with rules – to derive precise answers. Computer technology enables costly and complicated simulation techniques but at the end of the day human beings make a decision. Project appraisal is more than crunching out numbers. Experience, feel, intuition have a role to play. Moreover, decisions are not ultimately taken in a power vacuum.

Risk adjusted discount rates

The rate of discount could be increased. This makes risk a compound function of time – which it may or may not be. Net benefits in the future are more heavily discounted. Again, there is no unique guide. By how much should the discount rate be raised? How will we categorize the 'very risky' project from the 'safe' one? Who knows when the benefits of a project may suddenly peter out and the costs spiral?

Any method ultimately involves the decision-maker in making a judgement.[2] There are no unique answers. 'The proof of the pudding will be in the eating' and even here there will be disagreements about the taste. The important point is that people should consider a variety of 'sensible' possibilities and use their imagination in the knowledge that systems evolve.

INVESTMENT: 'THIRD SECTOR' NON-PROFITS

Non-profit organizations are highly varied. In Chapter 10 we emphasized that many non-profit organizations often have no readily specified and measurable objective function, like the maximization of shareholder wealth, which can be expressed neatly in money terms. Nevertheless, in order to use their limited funds effectively, where they have to choose between different investment packages these organizations must have procedures to decide, a) How much investment in total, b) which specific projects to undertake now and c) how to finance them? A clear picture of the mission and these questions aids decision-making.

If we focus on charities once more, in small charities, for example, we would expect the use of relatively simple techniques. The charity may simply do the best it can with the available cash, using customary conventions to allocate amongst competing ends. Here we simply introduce some problems. For example, the appropriate rate of interest may not be readily discernible. In the case of a charity whose opportunity cost of capital should be used to discount benefits and costs. That which relates to the giver's opportunity cost of capital? The rate of return to be earned on ethical funds or the rate of return that a charity could earn by investing funds in Treasury Bills? Or should the charity attempt to measure the rate of time preference for those it seeks to help? There are no simple theoretical answers. But charities find practical solutions, like others they will often use straightforward rules of thumb.

Whilst for some charities, cash is rationed with many more projects than monies to carry them out, others have 'cash mountains', charities with large reserves. There are several reasons which might explain such large reserves. It could well be that some charities have few projects to undertake. The need for their services has perhaps declined or levelled out and been outstripped by donations over the passage of real time. Or the administrative machine might require a large precautionary balance to ensure the smoothing out of cash inflows over time and the long-term survival of the organization. There may be a complex amalgam of factors at work. Some charities amass large reserves whilst others are under severe strain from growing demand and limited cash.

INVESTMENT IN NON-PROFITS – SUMMARY

- Cost benefit analysis is a decision-making tool used for evaluating non-commercial investment decision choices. It has other uses, for example, to evaluate proposed changes in laws and pricing schemes.
- Cost benefit analysis differs from traditional investment analysis. The objective is the maximization of social welfare. It takes a different and wider view of the costs and benefits.
- Cost-benefit analysis may examine very large projects with significant effects over time. There may be many different groups of gainers and losers and unknown inter-generational impacts.
- Cost benefit analysis uses the discounted cash flow techniques.
- There are a variety of difficulties in defining and evaluating the benefits and costs. It may not be possible to put a money value on some. A social discount rate has to be used to bring money values to present value terms. And there are difficulties in allowing for distributional consequences.
- Capital rationing can mean the rejection of some projects which would

yield a positive net present worth. Projects can be ranked by their benefit–costs ratio where rationing is one period.

- There are various methods to cope with risk and uncertainty including the use of sensitivity analysis, scenario analysis and risk adjusted discount rates.
- Third sector non-profits may apply a variety of decision techniques for appraising their investment projects. Not all charities face capital/resource rationing.

INVESTMENT IN NON-PROFITS – QUESTIONS FOR DISCUSSION

1 What do you understand by cost benefit analysis? Comment on its strengths and weaknesses. Does such analysis provide unique answers? Illustrate with current examples.
2 You read the following headline in the local newspaper: 'Proposed investment in local pre-school nursery facility cannot make a profit given realistic prices.'

   a) How would you evaluate a proposed creche nursery facility using a cost benefit analysis?
   b) What theoretical and practical difficulties would you expect to meet in doing this?
   c) How could such a nursery facility be funded and places allocated?

3 What are the difficulties involved in attempting to value human life?
4 What do you understand by the following terms:

   a) the willingness to pay;
   b) an externality;
   c) scenario analysis;
   d) risk adjusted discount rate?

5 How important is the political process in investment decision-making? Why might decision-makers rely on rules of thumb?

14

Investment in people

INTRODUCTION

Now our attention turns directly to the ways in which economists analyse investments in people. The notion of human investment is not new. Adam Smith recognized expenditures on education and training as investments – significant for the wealth of nations in the eighteenth century. In previous chapters we have raised major human capital issues. But whilst a variety of expenditures, including those on health care, represent important investments in people, here we shall give most attention to questions relating to education; and the important training undertaken by firms in the world of paid employment.

Education is a popular and prominent theme. In Britain today more people than ever before go to college and university for further years of study. In the last five years there has been a doubling in the numbers graduating from university and the advantages of a degree are still seen as significant. In addition, training by firms represents a vital feature in the evolving modern economy. The apprenticeships in heavy industry are largely a thing of the past in Britain; but new forms of training are given. To take one example, the fast food chain, MacDonalds, has a 'Hamburger University', where trainee employees are instructed in company procedures and managerial techniques; very different from the apprenticeships of the past, but training nevertheless.

Human capital theory can help us to consider the different investments which can be made in people. The theory uses the techniques developed for evaluating investments in physical capital, which we explored in previous chapters. Expenditures on education, for example, are made today, in the *hope* of benefits to come; future rewards are not guaranteed. The 18 year old school leaver may ask: is it better to take a degree course and a student loan to finance part of the cost which will be incurred by studying; or to look for a job immediately? Of course, choices of subject(s) to study are constrained by previous human investment decisions and these may have significant implications for future career paths. For the older person with skills made redundant by new technology and corporate restructuring, the question might be: is it worthwhile to re-train and if so, what particular new skills should be acquired?

Human investment decisions can also be examined from an employer's position. The business firm might ask how much human investment to undertake, and what proportion of costs the firm will have to bear. The firm wants the best possible return from its investment in people – but how can this be achieved over the passage of real time?

In what follows, we shall explore some of the different issues which relate to investment in people.

HUMAN CAPITAL: AN OVERVIEW

Marshall firmly maintained that '[t]he most valuable of all capital is that invested in human beings' (1920a: 564). Yet despite the insights of Marshall and Smith before him, until relatively recently, economists have neglected the mechanisms by which individuals invest in themselves and their families; how government and firms may invest in people; in short, how different individual and organizational activity can improve the 'quality' of human beings.

Neo-classical economists had long confined their observations to physical and financial investment; labour was implicitly assumed to embody all the necessary skills. Like entrepreneurial talent, education and skill acquisition could be assumed away – irrelevant in basic models set in analytical time. But the development of human capital theory by economists like Shultz, Becker and Mincer, some thirty years ago, heralded an important departure in traditional thinking – although there was still, to a great extent, a focus on rationally calculating, individual market players. The theories provided interesting insights into everyday matters and into unanswered theoretical puzzles. Investment in education and training could provide a plausible explanation for the residual element in the economic growth of nations – which could not be explained in terms of an increased quantity of physical capital or labour inputs. Different types of education and training could *in part* explain the distinct lifetime earnings patterns of individuals and occupational groups and the differential likelihood of suffering unemployment. Much empirical work was undertaken to determine the returns to education. The theory also raised questions about who pays for and who benefits from investment in human assets; significant economic issues. Human capital theory has a wide application; its concerns range from the individual and private returns to human investment to the returns for society as a whole.

However, when we focus on an individual human investment decision, there is a need to emphasize that decisions are taken by people in perspective time – often in situations of relative ignorance where uncertainty looms large; where custom and tradition matter. Indeed, where there are asymmetries of knowledge and power. Choices may be sequential, made in a complex and changing world; not in an analytical time mode where all seeing individuals face known constraints, and where decisions can be costlessly reversed. Moreover, where decisions are affected by what Keynes (1936: 161) termed 'animal spirits' they are not necessarily the result of careful rational calculation. Education can change a person's ability and willingness to undertake different roles, significantly altering current and future lifestyles and aspirations. The very process of investment in human beings may alter preferences – as well as productivity. But now we look more closely at the nature of human capital.

THE NATURE OF HUMAN CAPITAL

Specifying human capital

Human capital can be thought of in different ways. Begg, Fischer and Dornbusch (1994: 198) define human capital as 'the stock of expertise accumulated by a worker. It is valued for its income-earning potential in the future'.

In fact, human capital is often viewed as an individual's marketable productive abilities, talents, know-how – in short, a person's quality as a producer or service provider in the market. This enables a valuation of human assets in terms of present and future *money earnings*.

However, given a broader view, human capital can be defined as much more than that, encompassing an individual's skills, flair and knowledge in non-market activities as well as paid employment. Such activities include *non-paid work* for the household or voluntary group; and increased consumption benefits arising from the investment. An individual's stock of human capital depends on overall utility or well-being, not simply future earnings. Whilst utility does not have an objective measure, that does not render it insignificant.

Different types of human capital investment

Investment in human assets involves creating, enhancing or maintaining the stock of human capital. There are a variety of different types of investment, undertaken in different organizational contexts, like households or firms. In many key situations *decision-makers* are parents, taking decisions on behalf of their children. But whoever the decision-makers, they are constrained by the rules of the game – the laws and customs of the particular society at a point in historical time. Sometimes the decision-maker and the recipient of the investment benefits are one and the same; and they bear the costs. In other situations governments pay for human capital investment because of the important external benefits for society as a whole, benefits which cannot be captured by the individual, as we discussed in Chapter 6. Moreover, the returns to any one particular type of investment like education, may critically depend on expenditures made in other spheres.

Human capital investment can be thought of in the following forms:

Health

Expenditure on maintaining and improving health forms an important part of human capital investment. Without good health all activities may be impaired, reducing the expected returns on other investments. Modern governments usually take actions to promote the health of nations; an essential basis for economic development. Investments differ from country to country reflecting institutional features and different development paths through historical time. But whether, for example, through the provision of clean water or comprehensive antenatal care and immunization programmes, such expenditures on public health by governments have given a longer life expectancy, fewer work days lost or productivity marred, through actual sickness, or simply being 'under the weather'.

Private individuals, non-profit organizations and business firms are also involved in the provision of health care investment. In Chapter 12, we discussed how individuals invest in their own health, by spending time, effort and money, on such activities as keep-fit, healthy diets or regular health check-ups. Investments are made in different contexts. Charitable organizations may engage in research and development to find the causes and cures of disease. Business firms will buy health insurance for their workers and provide health treatment in order to insure the physical and mental well-being of their management and employees; an investment in 'corporate human resources'.

Education

Expenditures on education provide an essential investment in human capital. These can take different forms: pre-school, nursery schooling, formal primary and secondary schooling and further and higher education. Very important educational activities take place within the family unit although through historical time as modern societies have evolved, an increasing reliance on formal education has changed the family's educational role. But the rate of return to education will be smaller if health care investment has been inadequate. Moreover, education and health care provide an essential basis for the third major type of human capital investment.

Training, re-training and experience

Training for skills takes place within different organizations. *Off-the-job* training may be given in general skills, at colleges, educational establishments, usually non-profit organizations. But a significant amount of both formal and informal training is provided in the work place. Formal *on-the-job* training and the provision of informal training and experience takes place within business firms and non-profit establishments. Informal training and experience are also acquired in voluntary organizations and within the household. Women, for example, gain important organizational skills in performing housework and juggling with the multi-faceted demands of child-rearing. Finally, *re-training* also represents an important element in the investment process; unemployed workers, for example, may invest in new skills and companies may retrain their employees.

Information and mobility

Given imperfect knowledge about present and future costs and benefits, people of necessity invest resources to gather, process and interpret *information*. They spend time and money, searching for information about educational and job market opportunities. Employers also incur search costs to identify and gather information about potential employees. Advertising and selection costs may be significant in perspective time.

New information about job prospects elsewhere may lead to expenditures on *mobility*, an important form of investment in human capital. The costs of relocation, the move to a different locality, are met in the hope that existing skills will be employed at higher earnings; or that there will be better opportunities to acquire new skills. The migration of people, whether from rural to urban environments or from one nation to another, has been an important engine of evolutionary change through historical time, although actual compulsion has been an important feature historically. Geographical mobility may often have very high psychic and monetary costs but the hope for those making an investment choice is that the expected gains will outweigh the costs.

Other investments in human capital

Other human decisions have been analysed by some economists as investments, as we saw in Chapter 7. Questions relating to family planning, cohabitation, marriage and divorce have been treated in this way. Whilst these are controversial areas of study for the economist, nevertheless, even in such unlikely subject areas, economics can add a different light.

Human capital and non-human capital: distinguishing features

There are significant differences between investments in people and non-human assets. Whilst Marshall referred to education as a 'national investment' (1920a: 26) and stressed the importance of human capital, he was careful to draw attention to what he termed 'the peculiarities of labour', at pains to distinguish between labour and other factors of production. Human beings have special attributes – they are much more than interchangeable units in a production function, in analytical time.

People are not commodities for market sale. At whatever point in historical time, the essential rules of the game are of human design. The machines and buildings, furthermore the technology they embody, are the result of human creativity and effort (Hodgson and Screpanti 1991). Understanding the importance and the changing nature of the human factor is fundamental to our understanding of evolving economic systems.

The key distinguishing features of human capital can be distilled from Marshall and thought of in the following terms (Thurow 1970):

People and their human capital cannot be separated

The worker may sell or rent his or her work but *retains* the capital. In the modern, non-slave economy the individual remains his or her own property. In these economies human capital is inalienable – there are no slaves as in some economies of the past – like ancient Greece or the states of America prior to the abolition of slavery.[1] Whilst it is possible to separate people from their non-human wealth – individuals and their human capital are inseparable; there can be no divorce between 'ownership and control'. In contrast, the buyer of BT or ICI shares has no necessity to accompany them; and owners are not inextricably tied to their machines. Whilst people may be dispossessed of their non-human assets, no one can take and use the stock of knowledge, expertise and talent embodied in another. No one can confiscate the benefits of another's education and training for their own use.

People experience utility and disutility: a range of emotions

There is a *duality of roles*. When individuals supply their labour services they have to transfer them in person. Inevitably, consumption gains and losses are a *joint product* – an automatic accompaniment in paid employment, unpaid housework or charitable enterprise. In fact, the very process of investment in human capital can bring satisfaction; studying may give considerable enjoyment.

These features have several important implications for economic behaviour; on such questions as: who will be willing and able to pay for investment in human capital? And, how can risk and uncertainty be handled? Certainly, people's productivity and satisfaction are not independent of the ambience of their employment. It matters who people work with and for, their physical surroundings and the pleasantness or difficulty of their work. Self-esteem and status are important. Productivity and satisfaction are dependent on an individual's own feeling of self-worth and the perceived justice of his or her reward. Moreover, the rules of the game, including custom and practice, help to determine views of value, equity and fairness and therefore, in part, how hard people work and how they perform in teams. Other things being equal, this may affect the return to human capital. Labour is far more complex than the homogeneous input in our basic neo-classical model.

Yet in order to help us understand human investment and to consider the significance of these human features, let us turn to the individual's investment decision in human assets and see how far the techniques developed for physical capital may help to shed light on an individual's human investment decision.

HUMAN CAPITAL INVESTMENT DECISION: THE INVESTMENT TECHNIQUES

The human investment decision is part of a wider set of interdependent non-human investment and consumption decisions. Physical and financial investment and consumption decisions are interdependent (see Chapter 11). Similarly, human investment choices are made from an *overall set of opportunities*. Over an individual's lifetime the opportunities for both human and non-human investment and consumption/leisure *evolve*; the result of a complex, interrelated, amalgam of factors. Human capital investment decisions, taken within a family context, require decisions about the amount of money, resources, in particular, valuable time to be allocated between the various options. Human investment decisions for individual family members, have to be set in context of the alternatives, like current consumption, paying off debts, buying shares or paying the mortgage on a house (Earl 1986). We shall have more to say on these matters.

Now we can employ the same procedures and techniques for analysing human capital decisions as we used for non-human investments. If we work in analytical time we can appraise a human investment opportunity as we did for physical capital in Chapter 11. The ultimate objective is to maximize the individual's utility. In practice, the measurement of utility as such is problematic. Often it is customary simply to slip into the notion of earnings maximization (McGuire, Henderson and Mooney 1988). In fact, the individual in a human investment decision would undertake a cost benefit analysis – attempting to put a value on intangibles relating to different options. However, by concentrating on monetary aspects as with physical investment, provided that the individual gains a *positive net present value*, then the human investment project should be accepted. An individual will invest in human capital projects provided that there is a net gain: the discounted private benefits exceed the discounted private costs. Investment will continue until the discounted benefit on the marginal investment project equals the discounted cost of that project: that is, where the net present value is zero. All independent human investment projects should be undertaken given that they add a positive NPV. For example, to continue with an investment decision relating to university education, see the following:

$$NPV_U = \left(\frac{B_4}{(1 + r)^4} + \cdots + \frac{B_{42}}{(1 + r)^{42}} \right) - \left(C_0 + \frac{C_1}{(1 + r)^1} + \frac{C_2}{(1 + r)^2} + \frac{C_3}{(1 + r)^3} \right) \quad (14.1)$$

where NPV_U is the net present value of a three year university degree course undertaken at the age of 18;

$C_0, C_1, \ldots, C_3$ include both direct and indirect net private costs of education with an appropriate allowance for the satisfaction derived from the educational experience;

$B_4, \ldots, B_{42}$ are the net private benefits over and above what can be gained from the alternative option, up to a retirement age of 60.

Benefits are assumed to accrue at the end of each year with one initial payment at t_0. The project is undertaken at the age of 18 at time t_0. (14.1) can be simplified to

$$NPV_U = PV_B - PV_C \qquad (14.2)$$

According to (14.2), the net present value of the university education, NPV_U, is simply the present value of the benefits, PV_B, less the present value of the costs, PV_C, where all relevant benefits and costs have been considered.

Investment in college/university education

To illustrate how the investment theory can be used, consider an investment of 3 years in college/university education, initially for an 18 year old. Assume there are two possibilities, either:

a) to stay at school at the age of 18 and continue in full-time education until the age of 21 *or* to reject this investment option, or
b) to leave school and to join the job market in search of employment.

Human capital theory focuses our attention on the costs and benefits associated with such an investment, their size and timing and the length of time over which such costs and benefits will accrue. Moreover, there has to be an appropriate discount rate to bring future cash flows to present value. In order to evaluate the investment in additional education, and so the alternative choices, all these features have to be identified and measured. We begin by examining the costs.

Private costs

Investing in education, entails *private costs* which occur now and in future periods. The *opportunity cost of time* is a key feature in the human investment decision. The best alternative use for time during the 3 years of study, from 18 to 21, is a relevant cost. Assume that the student choosing the labour market option would be employed full time. The opportunity cost of education is the full-time earnings forgone less taxation. This value will vary depending on the type of jobs on offer to those not formally educated in full-time college, beyond the age of 18 and the level of tax exemptions and tax rates.

There is the possibility of unemployment and the level of unemployment pay to consider. Different assumptions about these will change the opportunity costs associated

with the education option. The opportunity cost of sitting in the classroom, studying in the evenings and at weekends has to be assessed. Opportunity costs rise,
other things being equal, as the job market prospects for workers, not educated
beyond the age of 18, improve or unemployment pay rises. But there are other
relevant costs to be considered.

Direct financial costs

These explicit costs include tuition fees, books and equipment costs and additional
payments for accommodation away from home and extra travelling costs or other
expenditures which arise solely as a result of choosing the education option. All are
relevant. The incidence of such costs is affected by the provisions of grants and
bursaries, which vary in real terms, between different countries and individuals and
over time. In Britain the real value of the grant is falling as the Government changes
the financing mix in favour of student loans.

Private benefits

Private benefits include both monetary and non-monetary gains. The gross lifetime
earnings which stretch into the future are an important feature. If the potential
alternative earnings streams are drawn on a simple stylized picture, as in Figure 14.1,
we can show the individual taking the option of joining the labour force as an 18 year
old worker, facing a lower level of lifetime earnings than the 21 year old with a higher
education qualification. At the same time, jobs give fringe benefits and perks which
would need to be evaluated in money terms where possible and included in the
analysis.

In addition, of course there are other real and psychological benefits and their
converse, including psychological costs – and other disadvantages. Education is, in
part, a consumption good. A college education may bring tremendous enjoyment and
the job which follows interest, good working conditions, possible security and status.
Clearly, it is not an easy matter to put a measure on such attributes. At the same
time, others might find full-time education, for whatever reasons, stressful and see
this as a drawback.

The evaluation of an individual's human capital in terms of market earnings, however,
does not include all the other wider benefits and costs. Individuals have no direct
valuation for their human assets akin to the market value of a share given by its current
price. The model focuses attention on identifying costs and benefits on a market basis.

In order to derive the net present value of the college investment, the individual has
to determine an appropriate *discount rate* to discount future cost and benefit flows.
He or she would have to isolate the rate of return which could be earned on the best
alternative forgone.

When all the appropriate costs and benefits are taken into consideration and
discounted at different rates we can show a net present value curve for the college/

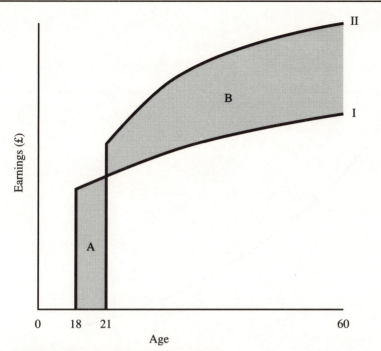

Figure 14.1 Age earnings profiles
Profile I shows the age earnings relationship for the 18 year old school
leaver. Profile II represents the profile for the college/university graduate
who earns the shaded area B, over and above the school leaver after
the age of 21. The shaded area A represents the opportunity cost of
earnings forgone by the university graduate. These earnings include a
return to experience and on-the-job-training. Strictly speaking these
should be excluded to achieve the 'pure' return to a college/university
education

university option as in Figure 14.2. In arriving at this we have included the alternative
labour market option in terms of its opportunity cost. Provided the net present value
is positive and the internal rate of return is greater than the cost of capital, the
individual accepts the education option. Given a negative net present value the
individual rejects the education project and goes to the job market alternative.

The approach is useful in highlighting particular key elements which can affect the
decision to invest in further years of education. These include changes in the levels of
costs and benefit and the number of years over which benefits will accrue.

Cost and benefit changes

Assume that the probability of suffering unemployment rises and/or the value of
unemployment pay falls, other things being equal. The opportunity cost of staying at

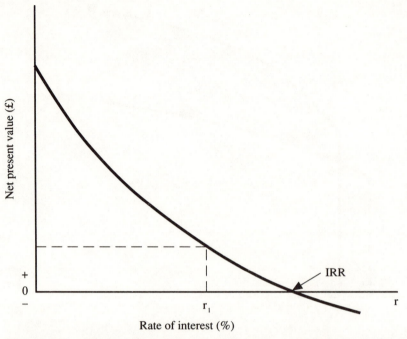

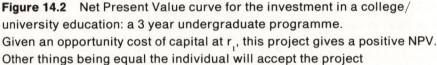

Figure 14.2 Net Present Value curve for the investment in a college/ university education: a 3 year undergraduate programme.
Given an opportunity cost of capital at r_1, this project gives a positive NPV. Other things being equal the individual will accept the project

school and continuing with a college education is reduced. The net present value of the education option increases and individuals will be more inclined to choose this alternative. But if the earnings and prospects of workers without further educational qualifications improve, the opportunity costs of the education option and hence its net present value falls. Tuition fees are not currently paid by UK students, but should they be required to pay these and/or the real value of grants or bursaries falls then the NPV of the education option will fall. The demand for college/university education will decline as individuals choose to join the labour market. The net present value curve would shift to the left – reducing the internal rate of return.

Benefit changes will also affect the net present value and the internal rate of return. Given an increase in graduate demand by employers, other things being equal, and a rise in relative future earnings for those with additional education, the net present value will increase.

Project life

The length of time over which the net benefits of education will accrue is also an important element in determining the size of the net present value and the internal

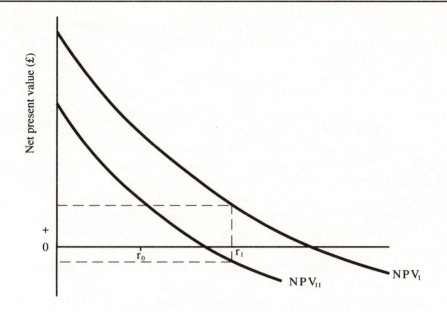

Figure 14.3 Net Present Value curves for the investment in a college/
university 3 year undergraduate programme. NPV_I, represents the
18 year old's net present value curve. NPV_{II}, represents the mature
student's net present value curve assuming *ceteris paribus*. The mature
student has a shorter time span over which to earn. At r_1 the university
education is rejected by the mature student given a negative NPV, and a
smaller IRR or rate of return. The result depends critically on the
assumptions made. At r_0 the mature student would gain a positive NPV and
undertake the course

rate of return. Those who face the alternative of investing in education as a
mature student, at the age of 39, for example, will have fewer years of net earnings
inflows to expect in comparison with those of an 18 year old. Moreover, as earnings
in practice often increase over time with experience and age, the opportunity cost of
forgone earnings will be higher for the mature person. A smaller net present value
may be available to the late entrant to education. In Figure 14.3, two net present
value profiles illustrate that the IRR for the younger person is higher than that for
the mature student. If we assume they have the same opportunity cost of capital, and
all else is the same, the mature student would reject the investment. But of course
there are many other possible considerations here. There are many other non-financial
benefits to education. People may not be simply concerned with the future pay
cheque. And the position of the NPV profile would critically depend on the value
that the mature student places on non-financial benefits and the evaluation of the
alternative uses for time.

Women traditionally may expect to have an interrupted paid employment path, resulting from the demands of child-bearing and rearing; and because of their roles as primary carers of the sick and elderly. If women are culturally led to expect years of domesticity and non-paid work, there is something of a disincentive for them in seeking education and training. They may have lower net present value profiles and lower internal rates of return than their male counterparts. Although it was often the case in the past that women were likely to have fewer years of education and university than men, this difference is being eroded in some countries (*Economist* 5 March 1994), although in many nations significant differences still remain in education and earnings levels between men and women.

A greater provision of pre-school child-care facilities, like nurseries and after school play schemes, would enable women to reap the rewards of their investment in education, in paid employment, over a longer period. A greater availability of good institutionalized care for the elderly and sheltered housing schemes could enhance the return to education and training for women. Effective equal opportunities policies would also have an impact. The net present value curves would shift to the right and the internal rate of return increase. (For further discussions both on human capital and discrimination, see Elliot 1991; and Smith 1994.)

Evidence on the returns from investment in education

There has been a considerable amount of empirical work and evidence generated about the size of the returns to human investment in general and to investment in college/university education in particular. On the whole, more education is correlated with higher earnings, although the size of the estimated returns vary in different national contexts and over different periods of historical time (see Elliot 1991; and Smith 1994 for a detailed discussion of the evidence).

Evidence seems to suggest that the rate of return to education tends to decline as the level of education increases. Smith (1994: 85) cites the average (of private and social) rates of return to full-time study in England and Wales for 1987 as:

9.0 per cent A-level
12.5 per cent Bachelor Degree
3.0 per cent Masters Degree
2.5 per cent Doctorate

However, given the falling real value of the maintenance grant in Britain and the introduction of re-payable student loans and an increased supply of people with degrees in the labour market, there may be a decline in the private rates of return from staying on at school and college. However, should the demand for graduates shift to the right, this might not occur. A recent report suggests that the advantages of a degree are still significant (*Independent* 2 November 1994). US graduates earn 60 per cent more than high school graduates, that is 18 year old school leavers, according to the evidence published by the Institute of Employment Studies. Moreover, university graduates have lower unemployment rates and face better occupation prospects. Whilst there are institutional and other labour market differences between the US and the UK, it is thought that such findings from the US do give an insight into prospects for future UK graduates.

The overall view of human capital theory is that, other things being equal, investment in human capital enhances productivity and increases earnings.

HUMAN CAPITAL INVESTMENT: AN INDIVIDUAL/FAMILY DECISION IN PERSPECTIVE TIME

In our discussions so far we have not addressed a series of important factors, one of which is the fact that adults often make the decisions for their children. Both Smith and Marshall underlined the fact that children have little alternative but to rely on their parents to make important human investment decisions on their behalf. Investment in an individual's human capital 'is limited by the means, the forethought, and the unselfishness of his parents' (Marshall 1920a: 561). Adults take critical actions on the timing and sequencing of human investments for children, before their future preferences are developed or well known. Moreover, these are not the straightforward decisions relating to the one-off purchase of physical equipment by rational economic people operating in analytical time. Such decisions perforce are made in conditions of limited information. And unfortunate decisions may have significant, often irreversible, long-term effects. Much attention is focused on the returns on the number of years of education after secondary schooling and its impact on earnings. Yet the choices made at school prior to this can critically affect future choices and occupational paths for particular individuals and their age earnings profiles.

Human investment opportunities

The range of opportunities for investments in *different* people and the associated rates of return for an individual are dependent on a complex web of factors. These depend, in part, on a child's *abilities and potential comparative advantage*. Yet these are not fully known at the times of decision. Parents have to take decisions which can have life long implications. Not surprisingly, they often take customary or habitual routes. Certainly, governments in modern economies insist on a minimum number of years of education and study in particular areas, given the important social benefits of education. Parental choice is constrained by law and custom.

In part, the returns to education are determined by *human genetic endowments*, gifts of nature, which are not possible to engineer or significantly change.[2] Natural abilities and talents, whether physical or cerebral, vary amongst individuals. Not everyone has the necessary physical characteristics to be trained as a ballet dancer or a shot-putter. Such endowments clearly affect the choices open to individuals and the returns to human capital investment. Other things being equal, those with the most ability will undertake the most education it is argued. However, there is always the difficulty of distinguishing nature from nurture. We cannot identify with any precision, by how much earnings are affected by differences in innate ability.

Gender and *inherited racial characteristics* are important in determining the returns from investment. Moreover, *custom* and *law*, as these relate to gender and racial characteristics, aid, constrain and channel parental choice; all of these factors help to define the opportunity set for any individual. In societies past and present, sons follow fathers in the same occupation; boys and girls are constrained to certain stereotypical choice paths. Looking back through historical time girls were given a restricted and different education from boys. In most countries women were barred from the professions and faced many restrictive rules. But as the rules of the game evolve so new opportunity boundaries emerge. Many women in modern societies, whilst still facing discrimination, now can undertake education and contemplate career prospects which were previously unthinkable. Racial discrimination may have been outlawed in many countries but discrimination still has effects on the labour market opportunities of particular ethnic groups.

Social class has relevance for determining the range of opportunities facing individuals, whatever their gender. In Britain, for example, technological change has seen the demise of the 'smoke stack' industries and alternative employment opportunities have evolved. Yet social class and differential power help to ensure the maintenance of non-competing groups. Class barriers still help to channel individuals into particular paths from which it may be difficult to deviate for much important human capital investment has been made at a young age.

In perspective time, information about opportunities has to be searched out and evaluated. Marshall (1920a) emphasized the importance of parental foresight. Opportunities may be perceived differently by different people. And openings can be created, in some part dependent on *chance* elements, as the future unfolds. Certainly, an individual's start in life is important[3] but however alert some parents may be in identifying opportunities for their children and in encouraging them, even the shrewdest and most knowledgeable will not have perfect vision. The actual returns from human investments may be greater or smaller than anticipated.

Finally, the *financial means* of parents may also significantly constrain the range of choice open to an individual. The financial aspects may be a very important consideration in the human investment decision.

FINANCING HUMAN CAPITAL INVESTMENT

It is often more difficult to finance expenditure on human capital than non-human capital. Capital rationing can be a significant problem. Marshall, pinpointing the importance of parental means and generosity, was well aware of the financial constraints which limited investments in people. Those with insufficient funds from current earnings or savings cannot always borrow to pay for investment in themselves or their children. Much has to be financed when people are young and personal wealth is relatively low. Not surprisingly, many education expenditures are financed by government or charities. But should these sources prove to be inadequate, worthwhile investments, both from an individual's and society's point of view, may not be undertaken.

Imperfect human capital markets

Whilst financial markets are imperfect, human capital markets are acknowledged to exhibit greater imperfection. Banks and other financial institutions are often unwilling to lend on human capital. Human assets cannot be resold or readily mortgaged. Long-term contracts for the use of human capital, except for particular groups like footballers, film stars and pop singers do not exist. (George Michael tried unsuccessfully to break his long-term contract with Sony.) People may be able to mortgage their future salaries to purchase a house but the house can be repossessed if they do not pay. Human capital cannot be repossessed. Moreover, the administration and collection costs of private loans make these unattractive to financial intermediaries like the high street banks.

A portion of the return to human capital investment comes in a non-monetary form, for example, the pleasure derived by an individual taking a degree course, being a student or the satisfaction in acquiring skills through training. Personal delight cannot be used to repay bank loans or indeed other lenders, even though these consumption benefits may be of considerable importance to the individual concerned *and* their training of value to the community. The profit-seeking financial institutions are unwilling to lend cash for investments which, whilst yielding very high non-market returns, both for the private individual and society as a whole, do not promise sufficiently high monetary gains. As a result, some worthwhile human investment projects will not be undertaken unless governments or charitable organizations make finance available. For those wishing to invest in further and higher education in Britain, free tuition at universities and colleges currently exists. Grants are available by means testing. Other forms of payment, like vouchers, enable students to buy education from private sector establishments.

Finally, there are loans where the government acts as the provider of a guaranteed loan scheme for those wishing to invest in relevant education and training. The risks of non-repayment for whatever reason are pooled by society.

Nevertheless, as much investment in human capital is funded by families, income and wealth inequalities ensure that some options are effectively closed for some groups. For example, to become a barrister or doctor requires considerable financial reserves. The medical qualification may promise a high net present value and status but the costs of attending medical school are comparatively high. Those from a low-income, low wealth background will find it difficult to pay for such an investment. The training period is long, the cost of books and incidental expenses substantial. Moreover, high entry grades are required and the appropriate education path. It is not surprising that few medical students are drawn from the working-class environment.

Unequal human investment opportunities

These may be cumulative over time, with an existence of virtuous or vicious circles. Poor quality education and health care may lead to poor job market prospects and low income. This may feed through to the next generation, for example, constraining financial means and aspirations, in a cycle of deprivation. Given a limited supply of particular schools or university courses, and jobs with career ladders, access to these is limited.

Investment as a gift and other issues in perspective time

Investment by the family may be thought of, in part, as a gift, as the resources devoted to child-rearing within the family (Boulding 1973; Hodgson 1988). Human capital investment decisions may be susceptible to Keynesian 'animal spirits'. In analytical time we can map the costs and benefits with certainty. We can also assume rational economic people maximizing individual utility. But in practice, people making such important lifetime decisions are faced with considerable risk and uncertainty. In analytical time we know precisely how many years a person will work, his or her salary, indeed, all costs and benefits with perfect foresight, including their exact timing and the appropriate rate of discount to employ. These assumptions are part of a hypothetical model to aid thought. In perspective time individuals are trying to cope with limited information, risk and uncertainty. People may not maximize but simply do the best they can, aim for a satisficing solution. They can cope with risk and uncertainty by using probabilistic estimates or set out a variety of possible scenarios on the basis of different assumptions. Decision-makers often simply follow a customary route.

COPING WITH RISK AND UNCERTAINTY

Smith clearly recognized the significance of uncertainty for those making investments in human capital. He commented on the 'very uncertain duration of human life' compared with the 'more certain duration of the machine' (1776: 119). From Smith's eighteenth-century perspective, expenditure on the machine was a surer proposition; the investor could not be as confident of the returns on human investment. An individual might simply die; the expenditures on educating and training could never be recouped. However, at a different point in historical time, with a longer life expectancy and more rapid technological change – in different scenarios we might draw other conclusions about the relative uncertainties of human and physical investments. Nevertheless, as with any significant investment decision, risk and uncertainty are important considerations.

Individual owners of financial assets, for example, can reduce total risk by diversifying their portfolios, holding different securities chosen at random. People have only one life of limited length and uncertain duration. Time is strictly rationed. For the individual investing in their own human capital, it is usually not possible or extremely expensive to diversify human assets in order to reduce total risk. No one can undertake several full-time educational courses at the same time; just as no one can hold a diversified portfolio of full-time jobs. An educational course requires a minimum commitment of time and effort. A specific job, an occupational opportunity, is an asset for it is expected to pay a flow of future income payments. But it is also a liability for a person has to meet a variety of commitments in terms of time and effort (Earl 1986). And the gains from specialization may come from specializing in one area and job. A variety of different strategies have to be taken to protect human assets and minimize the impact of risk and uncertainty.

A person may choose education and training for what seems to be relatively secure employment. But shocks and surprises come with the passage of time. Changes in competition, technology and political power, for example, can render some investments in human capital obsolete or enhance the value of others. The new entrant to the civil service or the high street bank, expecting a job for life, twenty years ago, would have been unlikely to imagine the changes which have subsequently occurred. Government cut backs and market testing slim the civil service. Automated tellers, increased competition, institutional change and corporate streamlining wipe out bank jobs. Subsequent redundancies or early retirements eliminate the value of company specific knowledge and skills, concepts which will be explored in the next section.

People gather together in trade unions and professional associations in an effort to gain security; to protect earnings, their conditions of work and employment. They may try to limit the number of training places, for example, to gain a measure of control over their environment, future earnings and job security. Custom and practice may help to guard investment in human assets with rules like 'last in first out'.

Managers of public companies are not indifferent to the value of their own human capital vested in the company. They may take strategies to protect the size of their future earnings, security and status, by choosing what they consider to be safe corporate investment strategies. They may retain earnings and diversify into non-core areas seeing this as a way to reduce their own risk of job loss.

Insurance can be an important feature. The very acquisition of education and the skills required by a variety of employers in different economic sectors may ensure the flexibility to handle change. Education provides a form of insurance. This may secure or improve a person's position in any job market queue for employment, given job scarcity and consequent unemployment. But the decision to leave a secure but stultifying job, in order to re-train may be risky for the older worker or in times of high unemployment. A good deal may depend on the wealth of the individual in question or the income of other family members. Those with few reserves to fall back on might regard the re-training option as too risky to take. Human capital can to some extent be diversified within the family by family members working in different firms and economic sectors. In some societies, children are a form of insurance against sickness and the inability to work.

No one can put the clock back and rerun time in order to compare the outcomes of alternative human investment possibilities of years past. Individuals can only imagine what these might have been with the advantage of hindsight. But the level of economic development, the historical time and place have an important impact on the nature of risk and uncertainty and how people perceive that. In Britain in the 1990s many believe that 'the job for life' has gone. Increased global competition and the rise in skill levels in other areas, can lead to the transference of production to the Third World and Newly Industrializing Countries, like Korea and Taiwan. The London International Group's recent restructuring with the closure of plants making rubber gloves and condoms in the UK is a case in point. The switch in production to Malaysia, Italy and Spain brought job losses in the UK. Job market uncertainties in Britain have forced families to consider investments in skills which give them flexibility – to become 'life-long-learners' – to cope with change. However, now we move to another distinct forum for investment in human capital – the firm.

THE FIRM AND ON-THE-JOB TRAINING

Vital human investments are made by firms; they provide and may pay for training. In Chapter 3 we saw how within the firm the division of labour enabled workers to increase their skills in particular tasks, on-the-job. Moreover, with increasing complexity and technological change over historical time, workers are also required to work together in teams, often engaged in highly specific tasks, as we emphasized in Chapter 9.

Marshall had long since identified the importance of training by business firms and had drawn attention to the 'unselfishness' of firms who gave technical training to workers, which could then be used by other employers. Yet it was not until much later that Becker's (1964) analysis of on-the-job training provided important new insights; prompting innovative questions and explanations. Employees were no longer the uniform inputs embodying all the necessary skills, providing uniform labour hours to be purchased in the market, rather like homogeneous vegetables in ideal type markets. A firm might well require specific skills which do not exist elsewhere, unavailable in the market. Indeed, even where skills can be hired from the market, there are search costs to find appropriate personnel and transactions costs to bear in terms of drawing up contracts.

Becker made a key distinction between *general* and *specific* training and the fixed costs of employing workers. *General training* increases worker productivity in a variety of firms. This was the type of training which Marshall had in mind, for example, the technical general skills which could be used by a variety of employers. Apprenticeships were once a feature of British industry, where firms trained young workers, for example, in general engineering skills. Articled clerks gain general training and junior hospital doctors gain general skills and experience. In fact, the most general of all training would be in the basic skills of literacy and numeracy, vital in the vast majority of jobs in the modern economy.

At the other extreme, completely *specific training* is so distinctive in content, that it can be of no value to any other employer. Given the acquisition of specific skills, worker productivity would not be enhanced elsewhere. As firms use unique techniques and processes, employees have to be trained on-the-job to acquire the requisite associated specific skills and knowledge. A firm of specialist underpinners using unique methods to deal with subsidence and foundation damage would require workers with the appropriate specific skills. Firemen require specific knowledge to tackle fires with different causes in complex scenarios. These skills and knowledge can, in large part, only be acquired on-the-job. UK tax inspectors are given specific training, for example, versed in UK tax law and Inland Revenue procedures, specific knowledge which would be of no use in other countries and in many other jobs.

Of course, no training is completely specific – an element of any training programme will add to general skills and raise the individual's productivity in other employments. But the productivity increase will be greater in the firm providing the training, for it can make use of the specific element. Workers in firms of specialist underpinners add to their knowledge of general building skills. Interviewing, investigation and negotiation are general skills acquired by the tax inspector during on-the-job training. All these are readily transported to a variety of different occupations.

The costs and benefits of training

The costs include the value of the time and effort used by the trainees, the value of the time spent by others providing the training and the equipment and raw materials used. The overall cost depends on the length of training and its type. It costs more to train a doctor or an accountant than a machine operator or a railway signalman. Nevertheless, costs can be significant.

Training raises worker productivity and herein lies its key benefit. Whilst people versed in general skills can be hired in the market-place albeit with recruitment and selection costs which have to be met by the firm, trained workers with firm-specific knowledge are not usually available in the market. Only those people who have previously been in the firm's employ will have the appropriate skills and these may be outdated. Firms have to spend money and time in searching for appropriate workers and raising their productivity by training them in firm-specific skills.

The impact of an investment in training on earnings

Becker argued that investment in general training would raise the workers' marginal productivity elsewhere and so their *wages would be bid up*. Other firms would hire them for higher wages. But investment in specific training would be of no use to other employers. Therefore a worker's earnings in the next best alternative employment would *stay the same*. In fact, as we shall see, the specifically trained worker could achieve an increase in earnings as the firm shared some of the benefits of increased productivity. But the worker with purely specific training could not expect to see his earnings rise outside the firm.

Who pays for training?

Any investment expenditure requires the passage of time to derive expected future benefits. But firms do not buy people – they have no property rights on their employees. Legally and in practice people cannot be committed to work for any substantial time in the future. *Unlike* machines they can walk away of their own accord. Moreover, in perspective time a detailed, long-term contract would be impossible to draw up or enforce; people can, in part, control the effort and certainly the enthusiasm which they supply. Labour is not homogeneous. Hostile workers in poor conditions or those with few alternatives can undermine organizations with indifferent performance, absenteeism or strikes.

People can leave the firm, taking their training and experience with them, *before* the benefits of increased productivity accrue to the firm, either in part or in full. In perspective time job adverts promising higher pay or better conditions lure people with the right skills. Firms of 'head hunters' make profits from searching out people with appropriate human capital, acting as agents for prospective employers. Patent laws stop others mimicking innovatory ideas; this gives *time* to benefit from investment before others can copy. Usually there is no such legal protection for firms which spend resources training their employees.

Who pays for training is an important question with significant theoretical and practical ramifications. Becker's analysis illustrated that a firm's willingness to pay depends on the likelihood of an employee leaving. Labour turnover is a vital issue.[4] The firm whose objective is profit maximization would not be prepared to pay for general training because the employer would not gain from the investment. The rational economic person could leave for a higher salary elsewhere on completion of the training programme; for productivity has been raised in other firms too. Competitors would find it cheaper to poach skilled labour than to invest in training. The firm paying for investment in general skills would make a negative net present value; a loss on training.

However, the employee, a REP who stands to gain by increased wages from another employer on completion of training, would be willing to pay for general training. The person would work for a lower wage than could be earned elsewhere during the training period – less than their worth to their employer in productivity terms. Costs of training are thus borne by employees, for example, lowly paid articled clerks. Articled clerks, junior hospital doctors, both work for low wages for they are acquiring general skills which will be of use to alternative employers.

The rational economic employee would not be prepared to pay for specific training costs. If the employment relationship were severed, for whatever reason, this training would be worthless elsewhere. Yet the employer would also be adversely affected by labour turnover, this could be costly to the firm. Should a worker leave, additional expenditures have to be made on hiring and training a replacement.

In order to reduce costly labour turnover, employers would seek to insulate themselves from the labour market. According to Becker, one way to do this and to encourage workers to use their skills to the full would be to raise their wages; to share the benefit of investment in specific skills. Given a share of the benefits, training costs could also be shared with the worker. (Of course how this is divided depends on information assymetries and the power relationship between employer and employee in perspective time.)

Both firm and employee have a vested interest in maintaining the employment relationship, for the employee is earning more than can be made in alternative employments and the firm a return on investment. Firms would not lay-off workers, in what they saw as temporary demand downturns or if they believed that workers might be permanently lost. Becker argues that it is rational behaviour to provide higher wages, coffee breaks and so forth because these may have a positive effect on morale and hence productivity. Cutting wages would have a negative impact on worker behaviour. Importantly, the firm can use a series of 'locking in' devices like non-transferable pension rights to discourage labour turnover. Of course, in situations of large-scale unemployment it may not be so important to 'lock people in', although some workers are key.

This is essentially an orthodox neo-classical approach, using the ubiquitous calculation of costs and benefits by rationally calculating individuals. Here 'black box' firms provide investment up to the point where the marginal cost of training equals the marginal return to training. Nevertheless, this analysis provides an important departure. Workers are no longer the homogeneous inputs of basic theory. Moreover, skills and worker well-being matters.

In fact, given the acknowledgment of the importance of skills and considering where and at what cost these can be acquired, a number of economists gained an incentive to open the 'black box' firms and households of traditional theory. Questions about investment in training prompted new discussions about the economic functioning of organizations.

INVESTMENT IN HUMAN ASSETS: THE FIRM AS AN ORGANIZATION

Internal labour markets

As we saw in Chapter 9, firms can be complex organizations. Doeringer and Piore (1971) introduced the concept of the *internal labour market*, a set of administrative procedures, rules and customs for allocating labour within the firm; a structured, internal, administrative hierarchy. These are *not* markets as we have defined them. These are generated by skill specificity, on-the-job training and custom. For these authors every job in the organization has specific skill and knowledge requirements. And custom in the form of unwritten, workplace rules based largely on past practice and precedent, results from organizational stability, and a regular, repeated relation-ship between bosses and workers. Doeringer and Piore compare such organizations with the feudal manor of medieval Europe, which they describe as a 'self-contained internal labour market' (1971: 23). In historical time there were other examples of Church and State organization, where stability ensured training and production. In the internal labour market, jobs and rewards are allocated *in part* on criteria viewed as just and fair; defined by past precedent and practice.

The firm takes different organizational structures; but co-ordination of the employ-ees is achieved by a management process. Employees do not compete either with each other or outsiders through wage (price) competition. Wages are administratively set on the basis, for example, of job evaluation, surveys of other employers and other information in the public domain. Whilst external competition outside constrains the wage structure, it does not give a particular wage for each job as the workings of supply and demand might suggest. Management uses non-market mechanisms for motivating and allocating people to jobs and training opportunities. No market clearing mechanism operates within the firm. Customary seniority rights, for example, matter and competition is for training slots on the basis of non-market criteria (Thurow 1975).

External labour markets, like local labour markets or national and international markets are beyond the boundary of the firm. *Insiders*, the firm's workers, are insulated from *outsiders*. It takes a necessary process of investment and the passage of real time before outsiders can become *effective members* of the organization; they are not immediately fully functional within the firm.

Organizations differ in terms of the nature and amount of human investment required and undertaken. Internal labour markets have different structures and links with external labour markets. Some jobs will be filled by internal candidates only, already the possessors of firm-specific skills. *Closed internal labour* markets are relatively shut-off from external markets except at port of entry jobs – where direct access to labour is made from outsiders. Other jobs are filled by existing employees. The *hierarchical job structure* provides a ladder which some employees may climb through internal promotion and training. A job-specific skill shortage, for example, may usually be met by internal promotion and training, *not* by changing customary wage levels. Such highly structured labour markets are found in bureaucratic organiza-tions in both the private and public sector although their structures evolve over time, as we saw in Chapter 9.

Other organizations may engage in very little firm-specific training although they may provide general training. *Open internal labour markets* have jobs which are filled, by and large, from external markets. Their structure is much *flatter, less hierarchical*. The 'Rag Trade', uses a variety of skills, machinists, cutters, designers, pressers. However, there is no clear line of progression, from one job to the next. The retail trade, catering, leisure and entertainment have this type of structure. The lines of promotion may be few or non-existent, with little opportunity to acquire skills on the job. People enter into dead-end jobs.

Nevertheless, even within open internal labour markets there are *primary* jobs, characterized by good pay and conditions, training and internal promotion prospects, with possibilities for further human capital investment. *Secondary* jobs, in contrast, offer poor pay and conditions, with little training or opportunity for advancement.

So workers may be recruited not for the skills that they already possess but for their *potential* to acquire the specific skills required. The transaction costs approach of Williamson (1975) emphasized, for example, the notion of specificity. Human asset specificity was a key reason for the existence of the firm as an organization. The question for Williamson is whether it is more efficient to have market or firm transactions. Yet some skills and knowledge are simply not available for purchase in the market-place. Employees are not owned by the firm, their morale matters, it affects productivity and team working. People learn by doing and because of technical complexity firms have to develop investments in skills of key employees; continuity matters. Williamson emphasized the need to cut down on opportunism and shirking, atmosphere was important. As the work environment becomes more specialized and complex, there is an increasing need to plan and co-ordinate human resource use and investment.

Given the need to *train, retain* and *motivate* key employees, the firm will not use 'Marxian exploitation' (Lazonick 1991: 135). If employers grind key workers, they become demotivated and do the minimum to get by. Retention and motivation comes from the payment of high wages and salaries, the promise of long-term job security and social mobility within the organization; integration for key personnel. The aim is to cut down on these workers' external labour market involvement. Business enterprise may be required to make a long-term commitment to vital employees, who if they leave, inflict heavy replacement costs. The organization will try to reduce uncertainty and plan – it requires a structure which will enable this.

The flexible firm and human capital

The value of a person's human capital may be affected by the changing boundaries of the firm. The boundary and nature of the organization can change – evolve over time through takeovers and investments, changing the balance between full-timers, part-timers, whether on permanent, long- or short-term contracts or simply by sub-contracting work to others outside. There may be *core* workers and those who are *peripheral* (Sissons 1994). Market testing, contracting out are sometimes features of modern administration factories. For some jobs outsiders are hired at cheaper rates and this may lead to redundancy and early retirement for others. Delayering, cutting out levels in the organizational hierarchy, has been a feature of internal labour market evolution in recent years.

Moreover, global competition, made possible, in part, by technological change, means that some large companies in Britain, like British Telecom can send particular aspects of their work to workers in India, who for a fraction of the cost of their British counterparts are designing software solutions for bills. The instructions and information required for work are being sent through advanced telecommunications systems (Jay 1994). Technological and political changes make possible outcomes which were previously unimaginable. For organizations, whether in the public or private sector, for school leavers and employees in different nations, such changes may have important implications for their human capital investment strategies and, of course, the value of their marketable skills. As interdependent economies evolve over time, there is an impact on human investment possibilities for different individuals and groups. Neat equilibrium models with fully known constraints and tastes can only take us so far.

INVESTMENT IN PEOPLE – SUMMARY

- Whilst we can make useful analogies between human and non-human investment, people are significantly different from machines or shares. In modern economies people cannot be bought and sold. People are capable of making choices and significantly modifying their behaviour.

- There are different types of investment in human capital where an outlay of resources in the present is made in anticipation of future long-term gains. Human investment is undertaken in different organizational contexts.

- The techniques derived for analysing physical and financial investment can be utilized for human investments. A college or university education can be treated as an investment and appraised accordingly.

- Evidence suggests positive rates of returns to education although these vary in historical time and place. An investment in college education still offers a substantial return.

- An individual's human investment opportunities vary in perspective time. These depend on a complex amalgam of factors including, ability, race and gender, social class and the rules of the game.

- There are imperfect human capital markets. Inequalities of wealth and income can mean that positive NPV projects are not undertaken. This can lead to vicious cycles.

- Risk and uncertainty are important issues – but human capital cannot be readily diversified.

- Firms engage in on-the-job training. The costs of general training will usually not be met by the employer. Specific training will not enhance worker productivity elsewhere and so firms will share the costs and benefits of such training with workers. Turnover is costly.

- Internal labour markets result in part from the need for specific on-the-job training. The key workers are required to be trained, motivated and retained. But in the flexible firm there is a reliance on short-term contracts for 'peripheral workers'.

- Technological and political changes make it possible to alter the boundaries of the firm. This has implications for those investing in their human assets.

INVESTMENT IN PEOPLE – QUESTIONS

1 Why can the following be regarded as investments? Explain the key similarities and differences between investing in:

a) a university education;
b) shares in ICI or BT; or a unit trust;
c) shares in a small, private company;
d) a home computer;
e) a re-training course.

2 Who finances and who directly benefits from the investments in question 1? By what means might you allow for risk and uncertainty in your decision as to whether or not to undertake such investments?

3 Twelve months ago, Sid inherited a part share in a property and used his portion of the sale proceeds to purchase 50,000 ordinary shares in XYZ plc, the company for which he works. This represents Sid's total life savings. He has just read in the newspaper that the company is making a rights issue. He would like to buy the shares on offer to him and is thinking of borrowing from the bank in order to do this. However, a friend is dubious about Sid's overall investment strategy. She believes that the new cash will be used to fund redundancies and pay for new manufacturing facilities abroad for the company is moving into the red. In short, he should re-consider his overall strategy.

   How would you advise Sid? Would you require any further information? Make your assumptions clear.

4 How can discounted cash flow techniques be used to appraise investments in human capital?

5 Distinguish between specific and general training. Illustrate these concepts with your own examples. Explain why it is said that all jobs have an element of specific skill or knowledge.

6 In what circumstances is labour turnover costly for the firm?

7 In what circumstances might an employer pay for general training? Who pays for specific training and what types of action will an employer take to protect investment in human capital? Will workers ever be persuaded to pay for specific training?

8 Why do internal labour markets arise and evolve over time? Use an example chosen from your own experience or from current media discussion.

9 'Short-term contracts make it possible for the individual to hold a portfolio of jobs and be flexible, in short, to enhance their human assets – in the entertainment business they are often the norm; they are increasingly used in the UK.'

   Evaluate this statement. What do you think are the benefits and costs of short-term contract working, for a) the employer b) the employee?

   Consider different commercial and non-commercial scenarios in addition to the entertainment business. What are the wider consequences for society?

Conclusion

The overriding purpose of this book has been to introduce you to economics – to pass on a knowledge and an appreciation of what is just a small part of its subject matter. Time has been the recurrent theme of this particular beginning. Joan Robinson (1962: 73) maintained that Keynes: 'brought back *time* into economic theory. He woke the Sleeping Princess from the long oblivion to which "equilibrium" and "perfect foresight" had condemned her and led her out into the world here and now'. That is the world you and I actually inhabit – where we cannot reverse the past or precisely preview the future; where we are no strangers to uncertainty.

A quarter of a century ago Joan Robinson believed that the Princess was still 'dazed and groggy'. So many years on some of the Princess's retainers are still deeply sleeping; for the 'equilibrium lullaby' silences further probings. Yet economics is more than a study of equilibria, neat diagrams and precise answers; more than an exercise in narrow technicalities or mathematical calculations, no matter how engaging and satisfying the solutions. Economics has no single song and no flawless bland tune for the goods and ills around us.

We can understand much from our forays into analytical time, where we assume perfect foresight and abstract from so many real-world difficulties. Yet this alone is not enough. We cannot pretend to ignore our values or ignore the fact that our view in perspective time is constrained and coloured by those necessary 'rules of the game' and our relative position in historical time and place. Moreover, we make choices in situations where change is ongoing, where with the passage of real time, a correct sequence of interdependent decisions are frequently required – decisions made in a proper order often at an appropriate time. Furthermore, as Galbraith (1993:1) warns us:

[t]he lessons of history are not to be taken too readily or without question. Life, in particular economic life, is in a constant process of change, and in consequence the same action or event occurring at different times can lead to very different results.

Moreover, Sheila Dow (1995) reminds us that we may be 'uncertain about uncertainty'. Indeed, in an uncertain world, in a constant process of change, how we need the truths and rituals to which we cling. How important are laws and customs – the rules of the game.

I have underlined the fact that economists study social mechanisms – social relations. Indeed, as economists we can be unashamed to speak of community, power, status, loyalty, sympathy, love and trust; or to recognize the ambiguities, contradictions, inequalities and uncomfortable dilemmas in the messy uncertain world of everyday life – where markets are certainly not the only means or ends. Where you and I are more than individual customers or the purveyors of marketable commodities. To highlight this truth, I have emphasized the importance of the gift. Boulding (1973) spotlights the variety of gifts which circulate and their importance in the scheme of things. Influenced by Titmuss, Boulding's insights provide us with a very valuable added view. This is not to deny the importance of the market exchange process but it helps to put that into perspective; and to juxtapose opportunistic behaviour with generosity. Human beings are capable of both.

The ideas of many economists have been used here – too many to review in a short conclusion. But perhaps times are changing. Whilst we may wish to be cautious in taking lessons from history, we should not always ignore the past. Between writing the early chapters and completing this final conclusion, Douglass North has been given the Nobel prize in economics, one of two economic historians to be so rewarded. This is the first time economic historians have been formally recognized in such a way, breaking the twenty-four year tradition of awarding the prize to economic theorists and mathematically orientated economists. Can it be that historical analysis is no longer the Cinderella to be dismissed so summarily? Will a new generation of economists be encouraged along different paths? Time will tell.

Finally, when I am asked: what has economics to offer? I can say without hesitation to those who doubt, that it gives a great wealth and breadth of intellectual interest, a sheer practical relevance and an excitement which stands without question. And to the additional query: what do you need for further successful study in economics? I am mindful of Shackle's view and choose clarity. I would like to believe that for many of you this is a beginning – not the end.

Vicky Allsopp

Notes

2 SCARCITY, CHOICE AND TIME

1 Data from Social Trends 1994 (Government Statistical Office) shows that access to consumer durables like cars, telephones and computers is much smaller for those in the bottom quintile of income (Social Trends 1994: 19).
2 This is only a prediction based on particular assumptions. The future may unfold in a different way.
3 Information and knowledge are often used interchangeably. However in perspective time the *same* information may be perceived differently – people may 'know' different things from the same 'data'
4 Historical time enables the analyst to take a perspective on the past.

3 SPECIALIZATION, EXCHANGE AND UNCERTAINTY

1 Black Wednesday became known as Golden Wednesday by some observers as events unfolded and Britain withdrew from the ERM. Different people view circumstances differently and individuals may change their view as time passes.

4 LAW, CUSTOM AND MONEY

1 The notion of fair treatment is still important today where buyers and sellers have long lasting relationships and particularly in the context of the labour market (Solow 1990: 7).
2 Anthropologists cannot be sure whether this was merely a gift exchange or purposeful trade.
3 We are assuming that the promise of a goat next season is not acceptable.

5 MARKETS, PRICES AND ALLOCATION

1 Mathematicians will note that our graph is set out in an unorthodox way, with the dependent variable on the horizontal axis. Marshall, who gave us the demand curve, did not use the mathematical convention which places the dependent variable on the vertical axis. Economists habitually follow Marshall's practice when graphing the demand function.

2 Note that the way we draw the curves depends critically on the premises which we build in our models. Here we are assuming that both the supply and demand curves are linear over the range we are examining.

3 Not every equilibrium is stable. Economic modelling can give explanations of situations where equilibria are unstable.

4 The result depends critically on the way the curves have been drawn, which in turn depends on the underlying assumptions built into the model. By assuming different relationships, for example, where there are time lags in supply, it is possible to show unstable equilibria. Here any deviation from the equilibrium could bring a movement away from balance.

5 In order to achieve positive price elasticity values, given the inverse relationship between quantity demanded and price, the value of PED has been multiplied by -1.

6 Note that price elasticity is not given by the slope of the demand function. Elasticity varies all along the length of a straight line demand curve from infinity at the point where the demand curve intersects the vertical axis to 0 at the point where the function intersects the horizontal. Price elasticity is the product of the inverse of the slope of the demand curve and the ratio of p to q. See Chapter 8 for futher discussion.

$$PED = -(\Delta Q/Q)/(\Delta P/P) = -(\Delta Q/Q) \times (P/\Delta P) = -(\Delta Q/\Delta P) \times (P/Q)$$

where $(\Delta Q/\Delta P)$ is the inverse of the slope of the straight line downward sloping demand curve and (P/Q) is the price divided by the quantity. On a downward sloping straight line demand curve i.e., with constant slope, the value of elasticity changes with the changing ratio (P/Q).

7 Or so the story goes, there are questions raised about these conclusions.

8 For futher discussion see L. C. Thurow (1975) and R. Solow (1990).

6 GOVERNMENT, PRICING AND NON-MARKET ALLOCATION

1 Note that some goods and resources are owned by charities, like The National Trust. The National Trust parks and coastline, for example, may be free to all or to members and at a charge to non-members. These are quasi-public goods.

2 There are bonds which have no redemption date, but which pay interest into perpetuity.

3 Surpluses can result when governments impose price floors – minimum prices supported by subsidies. Common market wine lakes and butter mountains result from such intervention.

7 THE HOUSEHOLD

1 Indifference curves can slope upwards from left to right, for example, a risk averse individual, choosing a portfolio of risky assets (see Chapter 12) will need to be compensated for bearing extra risk, by a greater return. This can be shown on an indifference curve. Risk, a bad, would be measured on the horizontal and expected return on the vertical axis.

8 THE BUSINESS FIRM I

1 Price discrimination, selling essentially the same good at different prices may be practised by some monopolists, who can sell to different groups of buyers, where the resale of goods cannot take place. However, for simplicity we shall assume that this does not occur here.

2 Total revenue would increase at a constant rate as sales were increased in perfect competition, the total revenue function is a straight line through the origin.

9 THE BUSINESS FIRM II

1 These relationships have changed given BMW's takeover of Rover.

2 Other interest groups also bear risks, like workers, management and customers, but the usual approach assumes the shareholders to be the ultimate risk bearers.

11 INVESTMENT

1 This is not a description of reality where borrowing rates may exceed lending rates in markets where there are transactions costs, risk and uncertainty.

2 The Star Ship *Enterprise* is appropriately named – but the first officer Spock was of course half human.

3 The benefit cost ratio should not be confused with cost benefit analysis which will be examined in Chapter 13.

12 RISK AND UNCERTAINTY

1 From (12.2)

$$EMV = 1,200p - 200$$

If $p = 0.2$, $EMV = 1,200(0.2) - 200 = 240 - 200 = £40$.

2 In order to achieve an EMV of £400, an outcome equal to that of the alternative certain project, and maintaining the same money sums associated with success and failure as before and using an equation derived from (12.2), we can solve for p to achieve an EMV of £400.

Substituting into (12.2)

$$400 = 1,200p - 200$$

$$1,200p = 600$$

$$p = \frac{600}{1200} = 0.5$$

3 We are 'measuring' utility in units here. For further discussion see Alchian (1953).

4 Sheila Dow brought this point to my attention.

5 Moral hazard may be a feature of other forms of insurance such as insurance from the state. When a third party pays there may be little incentive to cut down on costs. Patients may use the service unnecessarily and not take necessary precautions to promote good health. In addition, the doctor may prescribe expensive drugs where cheaper generic forms would work just as well. Although altruism and the promotion of a common good in a system like the NHS may mitigate against this.

13 INVESTMENT IN NON-PROFITS

1 In reality firms will be concerned that there might be a consumer backlash or government legislation or taxation implications. They may well consider these factors to some extent.
2 All of these techniques can be used in both a private and public context for handling risk and uncertainty.

14 INVESTMENT IN PEOPLE

1 Although there are situations in some parts of the world where, for example, prisoners are forced into veritable slave labour. And there are adults and children sold in illegal international markets.
2 Although technological change and medical developments, for example, now make it possible to change sex.
3 Marshall drew attention to 'the start in life', he saw that '[m]uch of the best natural ability in the nation is born among the working classes, and too often runs to waste now' (Marshall 1961a: 212).
4 This is in stark contrast to the basic market model of labour supply and demand where it matters not who is employed, where labour can be treated like any other homogeneous commodity such as a simple vegetable. Whether the same or different workers from day to day, it would be of no consequence.

Glossary

Absolute advantage A person has an absolute advantage in production, if he or she can produce more of all goods than another individual. One country has an absolute advantage over another if that country can produce more of all output.

Absolute price The price of a good or service expressed in money terms. This does not tell us the real price. A knowledge of money income is required for that.

Acquisition The takeover of one independent firm by another which involves the acquirer absorbing the acquiree and creating a new, larger enterprise. See Mergers and Hostile takeover.

Adverse selection At a particular insurance premium, bad risk clients, most likely to suffer from losses, are more likely to demand insurance, than good risk clients. Insurance companies, in perspective time, are unable to classify people appropriately according to their risk and may attract too many bad risks. This term, originally used for insurance, is now applied to any situation, where before a contract is drawn up and signed, one party has private information which suggests that the contract will be disadvantageous to the other but withholds that information. See Opportunism.

Age earnings profile The relationship between age and earnings, illustrated graphically.

Agency relationship Where one person, the agent, acts on behalf of another, the principal. For example, the manager acts on behalf of the shareholder. See Principal/agent relationship.

Allocative efficiency This is achieved at an output where no change in resource allocation can be made such that one person can be made better off without making someone else worse off. See Pareto optimality.

Analytical time This concept of time abstracts from experiencing events. This assumes full information of all possibilities available before, now and afterwards. The analyst moves backwards and forwards to different points without changing anything which could occur afterwards, taking a series of hypothetical positions in order to consider patterns of causes and consequences. An abstract, logical, pre-reconciled time.

Animal spirits   The Keynesian term used to refer to the individual's 'spontaneous urge to action rather than inaction', closely associated with 'spontaneous optimism'. He used it in the context of investment decision-making, where he emphasized spontaneity, not exact rational calculations. Animal spirits can be dimmed by changes which are interpreted as adverse.

Asymmetric information   People have different amounts and types of information about each other and the world at large. There is uneven information available to different parties. People may also interpret information differently. People have unequal knowledge, for example, shareholders and management. Such inequality is the inevitable result of a principal agent relationship, where information is costly or impossible to acquire, and difficult to evaluate.

Asymmetry of power   There is often a want of proportion and inequalities in power relationships. For example, large institutional players, like pension funds and investment trusts, are more easily able to form pressure groups than the small individual shareholders. People have different amounts and kinds of power which they may employ differently.

Average fixed costs   The total fixed costs divided by quantity – the number of units. This gives a per unit fixed cost.

Average product   This is total output divided by the number of labour units (the variable factor) employed.

Average revenue   The total revenue divided by the quantity – the number of units. This is also the price in perfect competition, for example.

Average total costs   Total costs divided by quantity – the number of units. This gives a per unit cost of production.

Average variable costs   The total variable costs divided by the quantity – the number of units. This gives a per unit variable cost.

Barometric firm   This is a price leader whose leadership role may be conferred by custom, result from historical accident, or the firm may be regarded as a good 'barometer' of changing market conditions. When this firm changes prices the other firms in the industry follow suit.

Barriers to entry   A variety of barriers stop free entry into industries and markets. These include technical and cost barriers, for example, large investment requirements in plant and machinery. Also, legal barriers, like patents and copyrights, licensing laws or exclusive franchises to serve a market. Professional licensing is used to protect human capital investment.

Barter   This is exchange without money, the direct swapping of goods where the price of one good is expressed in terms of another.

Benefit–cost ratio   This is the net present value (or worth) of a project divided by its initial capital outlay. It gives the net present value (or worth) per £1 of initial capital outlay and enables a ranking of projects in situations where cash is limited for one period only.

Big Bang   The changes in the institutionalized rules affecting the London Stock Market in 1986. For example, banks were given the right to become market-makers on the Stock Exchange, building societies were enabled to compete more effectively with banks and stock market entry was deregulated. Fixed commissions were abolished.

Black box   This is a term used to describe the analytical treatment of households and firms whose internal workings and decision-making processes are ignored. This is the conventional way of perceiving firms and households, a simplification which ignores their organizational structures.

Bonds   These are certificates, issued by borrowers, loans which are transferrable or nego-tiable, unlike ordinary loans from a bank, where the lender and borrower have a continu-ing link. Such assets promise an interest and the guarantee of repayment at a future date. They can be issued by governments, local authorities and corporate borrowers. See Gilt edged securities.

Bounded rationality   People make decisions in perspective time, where they face imper-fect information, complex masses of detail and uncertainty. They find difficulty in under-standing and processing such complex information and are said therefore to face bounded rationality.

Break-even   This occurs where total revenues equal total costs. See Normal profit.

Budget line   This gives the boundary between what is affordable and what is not. Points on the line show the options available to the consumer, what he or she is actually able to buy when spending all income. This constraint is dependent on the level of money income and the prices of the two goods. Its slope is given by the price ratio.

Calendar time   This is time in terms of days, months or years.

Capital   The factor of production, capital is the produced means of production, physical capital which includes plant and equipment, factories, warehouses or the infrastructure, including roads, schools and hospitals. Capital is required as a physical input in the production process and embodies a particular level of technical 'know-how'.

Cartels   Firms acting in concert, collaborating and sometimes behaving as if they were a single monopolist. Indeed, any formal deal relating to pricing, output or other aspect of a transaction comes under the heading of a cartel.

Certainty   This is the starting point of the basic traditional model, where all outcomes of any decision are known completely and in advance given perfect information.

Certainty equivalent   Given that individuals do not like risk, for any risky expected monetary value, there is a smaller but certain sum, which would leave an individual no better or worse off in utility terms. People with different degrees of risk aversion will require different certainty equivalents. See Risk aversion.

Certainty ignorance spectrum   Between the extremes of certainty and ignorance lie situations which embody different degrees of knowledge on which to base forecasts about the future. Situations of risk fall nearer to certainty. Uncertain situations are closer to ignorance.

Ceteris paribus   This means holding everything else constant or all other things being equal. It is the assumption which enables us to see the impact of a change in one variable on another. Rather like a freeze-frame facility.

Circular flow relationship   Money flows as the payments for goods and services and money rewards earned by the factors of production, like wages, salaries, rents and dividends. These are matched respectively through market exchange, by a flow of real goods and services, resources and factor services.

Closed economic system   An economic system which has no international transactions.

Closed internal labour   These internal labour markets are hierarchical and are relatively closed-off from external labour markets except at port of entry jobs, where outsiders are taken on. Other jobs are filled internally by existing employees. See Internal labour markets.

Coinsurables and deductibles Coinsurance means that the policy-holder, the buyer of insurance cover, bears a fixed percentage of the loss. Under a deductible plan, the insured pays a fixed amount of the loss, with the insurance company bearing the rest, for example, the claimant pays the first £500 for accident damage. A no claims bonus gives an incentive to take greater care and keep claims to a minimum.

Collateral The security on a loan, property of a borrower which has to be forfeited to a lender in the event that the terms of a loan are not met.

Collective property rights These property rights are not concentrated in a single holder but there is a *sharing* of rights as in a joint stock company. A collective right involves decision-making on behalf of the group, where shareholders leave managers to undertake the day-to-day running of the organization.

Collusion Oligopolists often co-operate and such collusion takes the form of the explicit use of cartels or implicit collaboration.

Command economy See Planned economy.

Commodity markets Markets for raw materials and produced items.

Communal buffer stocks In traditional economies, past and present, for example, storable food would be held to insure against the eventualities of poor harvests.

Communal goods See Pure public goods.

Communal property rights These exist where people hold the rights to use a resource in common with others. If none can be excluded from the use of a resource it is by definition communal. Decisions about the use of resources are left to the individual within circumscribed limits.

Comparative advantage An individual or country has a comparative advantage where they have the greatest relative efficiency; where production is made with the smallest opportunity cost. Resources can be concentrated in the best activity, where there is relative efficiency or where there is the least disadvantage.

Comparative static analysis This analysis compares different equilibrium points before and after changes in analytical time. It has little to say about the actual process which is involved in moving from the original equilibrium to the new equilibrium.

Complementary good A good which is used together with, or complements another. When the price of good A goes up and the quantity demanded of good B falls, there is a negative cross price elasticity. Good B is a complement of A.

Conglomerate mergers These mergers enable corporate growth by the acquisition of companies in a variety of different markets, in unrelated business activities.

Constant long-run costs Output can simply be replicated in the long run without changing costs. There are no cost reductions to be had as the firm expands.

Constant returns to scale These occur when inputs are increased in a fixed proportion and output increases by exactly the same proportion. For example, if inputs are doubled then the output is doubled. Returns are uniform with neither economies nor diseconomies as the scale of production is changed.

Consumer goods markets These are markets where consumers buy from sellers items as diverse as vegetables, personal computers and package holidays for consumption purposes.

Consumer surplus The triangle under the demand curve above the price that consumers pay. The difference between what the consumer has to pay over and above what he or she would be prepared to pay.

Contracting out Firms contract out aspects of their work to others. In particular, public sector organizations contract out work previously undertaken by their own employees internally, like office cleaning, their typing or systems analysis to other firms and small individual contractors. See Privatization.

Contribution A firm makes a contribution towards fixed costs provided its revenues from sales cover its variable costs. A contribution is made even though the firm cannot make an economic profit or break even.

Cost benefit analysis This is a practical decision-making tool used, particularly by public sector organizations, for appraising investment projects. It considers the consequences to the wider community ignored in the narrow calculus of private wealth. It can also be used to evaluate proposed changes in laws and regulations or pricing schemes. It aims to achieve the largest excess of total social benefits over and above total social cost. See Restricted social surplus.

Countertrade This is exchange without money and occurs between countries where at least one of the traders has a currency which is either non-convertible (of little value in relation to hard currencies) or has insufficient money to exchange.

Cream-skimming In the context of health care, if the fees per head are the same for different groups of patients with different needs, those providing health care may only want to take healthy groups who will as a result be low-cost.

Creative altruism The creative altruist spots areas of need, not met by other organizations, inadequately catered for by market, government agencies or family. This requires 'entrepreneurial' type talents of innovation, organizational skills and energy but which are channelled into non-commercial areas, pressure groups or charities.

Cross price elasticity The impact of a small proportional change in the price of one good on the quantity demanded of another, for example, compact disc players and compact discs. See Substitutes and Complementary goods.

Currency markets Markets for trading foreign currency.

Decreasing long-run costs As the firm expands output its long-run, average costs fall. This may result from technical factors. Another reason is that as the firm expands output it may be able to buy in bulk, thereby forcing input costs down. The larger firm may have its own transport fleet or arrange favourable lower rates. Finance may be cheaper to acquire for the large-scale producer.

Decreasing returns to scale These occur when inputs are increased in fixed proportion and output increases by a smaller proportion.

Delayering Hierarchical organizations reduce the tiers of management, the flattening out of managerial pyramids, pushing responsibility down the organization.

Demand This is effective demand, the desire to buy, backed by the ability to pay.

Demand curve   This shows graphically the hypothetical relationship between price and quantity demanded; a display of imaginary purchasing plans at different prices.

Demand function   A functional relationship between the quantity demanded and the different factors which affect that, like the good's own price and the prices of alternative goods and income distribution.

Demand schedule   The series of possible prices with the quantities which buyers plan to buy at each price in a particular time period, in a tabular form.

Demand shift factors   These are the independent variables which bring about a change in the position of the demand curve, a complete movement or shift of the price quantity relationship. They include, for example, income, tastes and prices of other goods.

Demergers   The splitting up of corporations into smaller parts.

Depreciation   The wearing out of capital equipment. The fall in the value of assets. Also, an accounting charge, a convention to allow for the wear and tear on capital.

Deregulation   Changing the institutional rules, aiming to increase competition. For example, removing restrictive entry barrier rules, or particular product standards.

Derivatives   For example a share option, a security whose existence depends on the existence of another security.

Diminishing returns   See Eventually diminishing returns.

Disequilibrium   A state of unrest where there is unbalance and a tendency to change.

Disequilibrium price   A price where the plans of buyers and sellers are frustrated where the quantity demanded does not equal the quantity supplied. There will be a surplus or shortage.

Disequilibrium quantity   A quantity where the plans of buyers and sellers are not matched where there is a shortage or surplus.

Diversification   Some risk can be diffused by holding a variety of investments. By varying or dividing activities, risk can be minimized. Investments, both in physical and financial assets, can be spread to reduce the potential for loss.

Divestment   This occurs when a company sells-off parts of the business, thus restructuring the organization. A company may sell-off those areas not close enough to its core business interests.

Dividends   The payments which are made to shareholders from the profits the company earns.

Division of labour   This can involve specialization by function – the butcher, the baker – into different trades. Also, a job can be split into a series of mini-tasks, basic steps in production to be undertaken by different people, involving further specialization and the division of labour.

Dominant firm   One particular firm dominates the market and may act as a price leader. This occurs because the firm has a significant cost advantage, or because of its financial strength.

Double coincidence of wants   This means that two traders can deliver goods of the requisite quantity and quality so that each party is satisfied.

Downside risk   This is the worst possible result which could occur from a particular decision.

Economic growth   The increased output for a nation over the long term, the increasing capacity to produce.

Economic profit   This is the surplus of total revenues, the income which accrues from selling goods, over and above their total costs of production. This is a surplus above opportunity costs, also referred to as supernormal profit.

Economically inactive   Not defined as in the labour force, e.g. *not* employed, self-employed or unemployed. Traditionally and currently, National Income Accounting defines women employed in the home as economically inactive even though the same work undertaken by a paid housekeeper would be valued in the national accounts.

Economies of scale   The reductions in average cost, the cost per item as the scale of output increases.

Economies of scope   The reductions in average cost which can be achieved when a group of different products which require some common inputs, are made by a single firm rather than by several independent firms.

Efficient production   Production is efficient where there is most output for given inputs, using resources to their best. It can only be defined with reference to the state of knowledge.

Elasticity   This is the responsiveness, adaptability or 'stretchability' of one variable, like the quantity demanded of a good, to a change in an independent variable, such as the good's own price.

Elasticity of supply   The responsiveness of quantity supplied to a change in price, as measured by the percentage change in quantity supplied divided by the percentage change in price.

Endogenous variable   This is a variable which is explained within the model; the dependent variable, for example, quantity demanded.

Entrepreneurs   People who organize and co-ordinate factors of production. They innovate, take risks, have energy and foresight to overcome individual and institutional resistance to change and to move into uncertain situations.

Equilibrium   A state of rest or balance at which there is no tendency to change. This equilibrium is stable.

Equilibrium price   The only price where the plans of buyers and sellers actually match, where the quantity demanded will equal the quantity supplied. At this price the market is cleared, there are no unsatisfied buyers or sellers – no shortages or surpluses.

Equilibrium quantity   The only quantity where the plans of buyers and sellers actually match, where the quantity demanded equals the quantity supplied. There are no shortages or surpluses.

Eventually diminishing returns   Given that at least one factor is fixed after some point as additional units of a variable factor are added, the marginal output of added labour hours will decline. The extra output from the additional hour is smaller than the previous hour employed. This is also referred to as the law of diminishing returns.

Exogenous   Any factor which is determined independently, outside the model or system, e.g., tastes or government activity is exogenous, a given which does not have to be explained but yet affects the outcome of the model.

Expected monetary value   This is a weighted average, where the money outcomes of different events are weighted by the probability of their occurrence.

Expected utility   This is a weighted average, where the utility attached to different possible events are weighted by the probability of their occurrence.

Explicit costs   These include expenses and may underestimate opportunity costs by ignoring the value of self-owned resources, thus not including all relevant costs.

Extended family   This includes several generations of a kin group who may live in the same household.

External capital rationing   See Hard capital rationing.

External labour markets   Markets which are beyond the boundary of the firm, such as local labour markets or national and international labour markets.

External pecuniary economies   These bring a reduction in the cost per item of goods as the scale of production increases – they arise from sources outside the firm, for example, the advantages of bulk buying inputs at lower prices or raising large amounts of finance at cheaper rates.

Externalities   These are by-products of the production and consumption process, external costs met or external benefits received by people other than the consumer and producer. These are not fully reflected in market prices or necessarily considered by those who create them. See Social costs and benefits.

Factor income payments   These include wages, salaries, rents, interest payments and dividends.

Factor markets   Markets where factor services, inputs in the production process, like labour or capital are rented or bought and sold.

Factors of production   These are the inputs used in the production process. They include the broad categories of land, labour and capital. Entrepreneurship is sometimes treated as a separate factor not included in labour. Technology and the rules of the game have an important bearing on the quantity and quality of these factors.

Family   The kin group living in a single household. A family can be defined as a married or cohabiting couple with or without children or a lone parent with children.

Financial capital   This includes securities issued by governments, local authorities and companies. The funds raised by the issue of such paper claims can be used for different purposes including the financing of investment.

Financial investment   This is the purchase of the paper claims to future cash flows, for example, bonds and shares.

Financial markets   These are markets where the paper claims to future cash flows are traded – like government bonds and shares.

Financial market line   This is a constraint, a constant trade-off between money now and money in the next period – all combinations of income now and then which give the same wealth or constant present value.

Firm   This is a planning unit which takes in factors of production and transforms them into outputs.

Firm-like contract   An employee has one bilateral, formal contract with the firm to supply labour services. This contract is usually relatively long-term, implying a continuing relationship between the employer and employee.

First mover advantages   Such advantages arise from a firm being in the market first. The innovator gains the advantage, enabling the pre-emption of natural resources and specialist knowledge, unavailable to all.

Fix price markets   These are markets with inflexible prices which do not respond to changes in demand and supply conditions in the short run as do markets which approximate the 'ideal type'. Prices are set by individual firms and are administered. Money prices are 'sticky' and markets are not neatly cleared by price movements.

Fixed cost   Those costs which do not vary with output and which are unavoidable. Regardless of whether the firm produces or not, it is committed to fixed costs, given a decision taken in the past.

Flex price markets   These are markets where prices respond quickly to changes in the conditions of supply and demand.

Formal rules   These institutional rules can include written constitutions, common and statute laws or the legal contracts between individuals. Formal rules incorporate taboos, custom and tradition of simpler societies. Formal rules are altered by studied action.

Function   An f is functional notation, a mathematical convention, it signifies that there is a systematic relationship between a dependent and an independent variable.

Fundamental uncertainty   Where there is no idea what the future will bring, for example, where there is no real knowledge of the structure of a problem, no idea of possible outcomes let alone probabilities to assign to particular possibilities. Sometimes referred to as true or radical uncertainty. See also Uncertainty.

Future value   This is the money which will be received in the future, in a specified number of years, if a sum of money (the principal) is invested now at a given interest rate for that number of years.

Futures and options markets   In these markets there is an exchange of forward contracts which enable the trade of physical commodities, currencies or the options to buy and sell shares at some future date. These contracts are exchanged for money. The futures markets enable dealers to buy and sell a product for delivery at some time hence; not now.

Game theories   Theories which have been developed in an effort to understand strategic behaviour – for example, in oligopolistic situations.

General training   This training increases worker productivity in a variety of firms. The most general of all training would be in the basic skills of literacy and numeracy required in most jobs in the modern world.

Gift   A gift involves no contract, no expectation of any agreed payment, no *quid pro quo* and no market-like exchange, although there is reciprocity in gift giving and often an exchange of property rights.

Gilt edged securities Securitites issued on behalf of the British Government which have fixed interest payments and will be redeemed (where appropriate) at a particular date.

Global markets These are markets which are worldwide – buyers and sellers are linked by information and transport networks, and exchange on a global basis.

Grey markets These are unofficial markets. People can trade shares before they have received their allotment of shares in privatization issues. Dealing is risky for there is no guarantee that the sellers can deliver the shares.

Gross domestic product (GDP) This gives a measurement of the total amount of goods and services produced by an economy over a particular time period, usually one year.

Hard capital rationing This occurs where unlimited amounts of capital are unavailable from external market sources – also known as external capital rationing.

Historic cost This is the original money value paid for goods and resources. It says nothing about opportunity cost and is irrelevant for decision-making.

Historical time This is the time of history, time past over which economies have evolved. People and their organizations change with the passage of time. Different points in historical time can be compared.

Home production This includes the production of a variety of goods and services within the household, many of which could not be acquired through market exchange. Also see Reproductive and Household productive work.

Horizontal mergers This is the merger or takeover of competitors at the same stage of production in a related activity.

Hostile takeover The management team of the acquiring company takes control without the co-operation of the management team in the takeover target; made possible by the purchase of sufficient shares to gain effective control.

Household This is usually defined as a person or group of people living together. The introductory neo-classical approach has treated the household, family and the individual as synonymous.

Household productive work This includes housework, shopping, DIY activities. See also Reproductive work.

Human capital An individual's marketable productive abilities, talents, know-how, a person's quality as a producer or service provider measured by the present value of future earnings. A broader view encompasses an individual's abilities in non-market activities as well as paid employment. Such activities include non-paid work for the household or voluntary group; and increased consumption benefits arising from the investment.

Illegal markets These are illegal but nevertheless function as markets – they include, for example, the international heroin market or illegal sales of goods circumventing government price controls as in war time.

Imperfect competition All forms of market structure are imperfect with the exception of the ideal type, perfect competition. See Market structures and Perfect competition.

Implicit cost The cost of a self-owned resource, used in the production process is not free, even though there is no explicit cash payment associated with its use. This is a relevant cost for decision-making.

Inalienable rights   These include the rights to 'goods' which are not sold on markets but are allocated to an individual by non-market means, at a zero or nominal price, like a university place, the right to adopt a child or citizenship granted to an immigrant. These cannot be exchanged, sold to someone else or in most cases given to another.

Incentive schemes   These include share options and bonus schemes used to spur on management. They give benefits if the shareholders gain profits but are valueless if they do not. Performance related pay for workers is another example.

Income effect of a price change   This is the impact on quantity demanded of a real change in income which results from a change in relative prices. See also Substitution effect of a price change.

Income elasticity of demand   Measures how the demand for a good responds to a change in income. It is measured by the percentage change in quantity demanded divided by the percentage change in income.

Income inelastic   This is where a small proportional change in income leads to a smaller proportional change in quantity demanded.

Increasing long-run costs   As output is increased in the long run, average costs rise. This may occur as the firm grows too large, where management becomes over stretched, or where the firm has grown so large that it has forced up input prices.

Increasing returns   This occurs when additional units of a variable factor are added to a fixed factor, when, for example, at low levels of plant usage, average product rises. At the point of maximum average product, the plant is optimally used, here marginal and average products are equal.

Increasing returns to scale   These occur when all inputs are doubled, for example, and output increases more than proportionately. Doubling the size of storage/warehouse facilities will more than double the volume of output which can be stored. This gives rise to economies of scale.

Independent risk   This is the risk of a hazardous event for the individual which is not related to other similar events affecting others. These risks can be reduced by combining the essentially independent risks of different people. See also the Law of large numbers.

Independent project   A project whose acceptance would have no impact on the cash flows of other projects and where the decision to accept that project does not prohibit the undertaking of others.

Indifference curves   These are curves of equal satisfaction which enable us to see all combinations of two goods which give an individual equal utility.

Individual productivity profile   This is the production possibility boundary for an individual, displaying that person's productive potential given their human and non-human resources.

Inefficient production   Output levels which are feasible, within a society's or firm's capacity to produce but do not use resources to their best. More output could be achieved by using resources efficiently and to the full.

Inelastic demand   This is where a small proportional change in price results in a proportionally smaller reduction in quantity demanded. Quantity demanded is relatively unresponsive to a price change.

Inferior good   A good whose demand falls, shifts to the left, as income increases. It has a negative income elasticity.

Infinitely elastic   A demand curve, for example, is infinitely elastic when any amount of a good will be demanded at the existing price. The demand is a horizontal straight line. A supply curve is infinitely elastic when any amount of the good will be supplied at the existing price. The supply is a horizontal straight line.

Inflation   This is the general tendency for prices to rise.

Informal rules   These are institutional rules which include conventions, norms of behaviour and codes of conduct, often ingrained as habit and routine. They are culturally determined and may be modified through group pressure, changes in cultural or religious climates.

Infrastructure   This includes fundamental facilities like roads, communication systems, schools and hospitals.

Insurance   This is the pooling and sharing of risk. The provision and protection against loss. In the modern economy, the market system provides the opportunity for people to buy insurance cover to protect themselves against unexpected misfortune.

Insurance premium   The price for buying insurance cover.

Intangibles   These are factors which often are not readily definable or measurable but which can nevertheless be important to well-being. These include 'the feel good factor' which arises from particular events or the beauty of a scenic view. Some intangibles, like noise, can be measured.

Interest rate   This is the sum of money paid each year on a loan, the principal. This is usually expressed as a percentage.

Internal capital rationing   See Soft capital rationing.

Internal economies of scale   These are economies which occur within the firm. For example, the costs of increasing VAT or warehouse sizes do not rise proportionately with production.

Internal financial markets   These function within large hierarchical firms. Here financial resources are allocated via internal administrative procedures, not by a market price mechanism.

Internal labour market   This is a set of administrative procedures, rules and customs for allocating labour within the firm; a structured internal administrative hierarchy. Labour resources are allocated internally within the organization via administrative procedures, not by a market price mechanism.

Internal rate of return   This is the interest or discount rate which reduces the net present value of a project to zero. The project just breaks even.

Investment   This involves the commitment of resources such as capital, labour or cash, a current outlay for the long term in the hope of future gains. Whatever the form investment takes, the passage of time is a key element.

Investment trusts   Financial intermediaries, companies quoted on the stock market, which specialize in holding portfolios of shares in a variety of other companies. Small investors can gain the benefits of diversification with relatively small amounts of money. See Unit trusts.

Joint stock company   A company limited by shares with a separate legal identity from its owners; a collective ownership form. Decisions about the use of resources are normally made by management on behalf of the owners of the company, the shareholders; there is a divorce between ownership and control. The joint stock companies come in two major forms, see Private and Public companies.

Just price   In times past, this was perceived as a fair price, a fair transaction, where to make a profit at someone else's expense was regarded as sinful. People still have a view of a just price.

Labour   People, the human resource, embodying different physical and mental talents, innate abilities and, more importantly, large variations in the type and levels of education and training, investments in human capital. Unlike capital in the production process, labour can provide services to satisfy wants directly.

Land   This factor of production includes land but also, minerals underground, resources like oil and natural gas, even fish stocks in the sea.

LAUTRO   The Life Assurance and Unit Trust Regulatory Organization is a self-regulating organization which oversees the rules of the game in the retail marketing of life assurance and unit trusts.

Law of large numbers   This is a mathematical law upon which the insurance trade depends. An adverse event which befalls an isolated individual such as a heart attack, might seem indiscriminate, haphazard, down to the vagaries of chance. But the aggregate of such events, when seen in the context of large groups of people or objects, becomes predictable and calculable.

Limited liability   Any loss is limited to the value of the capital invested. A shareholder is protected by limited liability, like a form of insurance, which minimizes potential loss. At worst, the shareholders can only lose the value of their shares. They are not held responsible for all debts.

Liquidity   Cash is the ultimate liquid asset. An asset's liquidity depends on its nearness to cash.

Lloyds of London   This is an organization of underwriters with members, not a company with shareholders. Members do not have limited liability. Lloyds is a market-place where brokers make deals, for those seeking insurance, with the underwriters, who act for the members. Lloyds habitually insures extraordinary risks, single events regarded as highly risky.

Loan stock   This is a form of security, bonds issued by government, debentures issued by companies. These are traded in the market. See Gilt edged securities.

Loanable funds   This is cash which lenders, the suppliers of loanable funds, exchange with borrowers, the demanders of loanable funds.

London Stock Exchange   This is a market for financial securities. It includes the Gilt Edged Market for government and local authority loan stock and the Companies Securities Market for loan stock and shares.

Long run   This represents the time scale over which all factors of production are variable. There is the greatest flexibility assuming a given technology.

Macroeconomics   This studies the workings of an economy as a whole, dealing with broad aggregates, such as national income, output, employment, inflation and economic growth. It examines the system as a whole rather than its parts in isolation.

Management buy-outs   The managers purchase the firm. These are often financed by significant borrowing.

Managerial diseconomies   Diseconomies where management find problems of co-ordination as the scale of activity increases leading to increased costs.

Managerial economies   Economies resulting from the ability of managers to oversee large outputs just as well as small ones, thereby reducing costs.

Marginal cost   This is the change in total cost which arises from a one unit (or a small) increase in output. The extra cost of producing one additional output.

Marginal rate of substitution   This is the rate at which the consumer is willing to trade-off one good for another, keeping at the same level of satisfaction. It is given by the slope of the indifference curve.

Marginal rate of transformation   This reflects the opportunity cost of the production of one good in terms of another.

Marginal social benefits   These include all private benefits and external benefits which arise from an additional unit of output.

Marginal social costs   The extra cost of producing an additional unit of output which incorporates both private and external costs of production.

Marginal physical product   This is the extra physical output which arises as a result of a one unit (or small) increase in the labour input.

Marginal revenue   The extra or additional revenue earned from selling an additional unit of output.

Market capitalization   The total market value of a company's ordinary shares. *The Financial Times* share service publishes market capitalization values.

Market economy   This type of economy solves production and distribution problems by using market mechanisms, based on private ownership. There is no pure market economy. See Mixed economy.

Market-like contract   A short-term contract where the buyer's and seller's identity does not matter where there is no continuing link between the individuals or organizations.

Market-makers   Dealers in bonds and shares as principals – being responsible for the risk in their own name. British banks after Big Bang were allowed to be market-makers.

Market rate of interest   This is the rate of interest expressed as a percentage. It is determined by the interaction of the demand and supply of loanable funds in a perfect capital market.

Market risk   See Systematic risk.

Market structures   These are different categories of markets, based on their relative competitiveness. These range from perfect competition, through monopolistic competition, oligopoly to monopoly.

Market supply   This is the amount of a good that all the suppliers in a particular market are willing and able to supply over a particular time period at each price.

Market testing   In the public sector, organizations putting out work previously done internally to outside firms after a process of competitive bidding.

Markets   These are organizations for the exchange of goods or services and property rights. A set of social institutions in which large numbers of exchanges regularly take place. Organizations of the market give information about products, prices, quantities and buyers and sellers, both actual and potential.

Medium of exchange   This is a means of payment – money.

Mergers   Firms may grow by merging, the joining together of previously independent firms, combining two companies into a new enterprise. See also Acquisitions, Horizontal, Vertical and Conglomerate mergers.

Merit goods   Goods like health care and education are seen as important both for individuals and society as a whole; but people may have an inability or insufficient desire to buy enough of them. The market mechanism would lead to an insufficient production and consumption. Government ensures that more of them are made available.

Microeconomics   The study of people and their organizations, including households, firms and markets. The analysis of economic behaviour whether on the domestic scene in an individual market context, or, for example, within the business firm, government organization or charity.

Mixed economy   All economies, in practice, are mixed, meeting the problems of production and distribution with elements of tradition, market and planning albeit with different emphases.

Money   This can be legal tender or some customary form. It is a social invention and what functions as money depends in part on historical time and place. Any generally accepted medium of exchange which serves as means of payment. Money also acts as a single unit of account, a store of value and can be used as a standard of deferred payment.

Monopolist   The sole supplier of a good with no close substitutes.

Monopolistic competition   This market form has many sellers and buyers with ease of entry. Each individual firm produces a differentiated product or offers a slightly different service, not exactly matched by competitors.

Monopoly market   This has one seller, a monopolist. Would-be rivals are kept out by entry barriers.

Moral hazard   Involves opportunistic behaviour of individuals after a contract or agreement has been made. People reduce the care they take, for example, money borrowed from the bank for a safe project may be subsequently used for a risky venture. The term was originally used in insurance. Given imperfect information, insurers cannot be sure that, once insured, people may take fewer precautions. They will take less care and have no incentive to economize on costs in the event of loss. The buyers of insurance may also face moral hazard from policy changes or the interpretation of fine print.

Multi-divisional or M-form firm   The firm is divided into semi-autonomous operating divisions (profit centres), organized on product or geographic lines. Strategic planning and co-ordination among the units is made by head office but day-to-day running is done by the divisions.

Multilateral barter   Swaps which include more than three traders.

Multinational enterprises   These are organizations which produce and own production facilities in a variety of countries. They may produce on a wide global scale with large varieties of products and operate in many different markets, transnationally.

Multi-stage hierarchies: Unitary form or U-form   The firm has an organizational hierarchy with at least two layers of management. The firm is split up on functional lines.

Mutual companies   These started with groups of people who came together to insure risk on a mutual non-commercial basis. The modern insurance companies which have developed to sell insurance cover, write insurance contracts, to make profit.

Mutually exclusive projects   Only one project is required from competing alternatives. The acceptance of one project automatically excludes others.

Names   Individuals who promise their own personal wealth as security for Lloyds' underwriting. This entitles the Names to share in the profits, but also requires them to pay up for any losses. See Unlimited liability.

National Health Service   A complex of organizations providing different kinds of health care products, produced by segmented although related services, involving general practitioners, hospitals and community care.

Natural monopoly   Where there is room for one firm only to survive, where two or more firms in the industry would face insufficient revenues to operate. Where one firm can supply at a lower price than two or more.

Negative equity   When more is owed on a home loan/mortgage than the market value of the property in question.

Negative returns   Total output will actually fall after some point when additional variable inputs are added to a fixed factor.

Neo-classical   The dominant school of thought in microeconomics. At an introductory level this focuses on rational individuals involved in market exchange, maximizing utility and profits, operating with perfect foresight. Firms and households are black boxes to be analysed as individuals.

Net advantages   Originally Adam Smith's term for the net benefits derived from employment. These include money wages and non-monetary benefits including perks plus additional attributes of work, like job satisfaction, status, feelings of self-worth. Paid work may have negative aspects, it could be difficult or dangerous.

Net present value   This is the present value of all the future net cash inflows from a project less the capital outlay, the initial cost of the project. It is the addition which the project brings to the owner's or shareholder's wealth.

Net present value curve   This is a graphical relationship showing how the net present value of a project is inversely related to the rate of interest. As the rate of interest increases the net present value of a project falls and eventually becomes negative.

Net present worth   The present value of net social benefits less the present value of social costs.

Non-diversifiable risk   see Systematic risk.

Non-market communal insurance   Insurance not bought in the market but provided communally. The importance of the extended family group or tribe, feudal arrangements and religious organizations, were all important in the provision of protection against loss. Non-market mechanisms provided contingencies.

Non-market work   This includes unpaid work undertaken for the family/household including such activities as housework and shopping. It involves 'child production', caring for the elderly or those with special needs within the family. It also includes all other forms of unpaid work outside the household, for example, for the charity or voluntary group.

Non-price competition   This includes factors such as promotional offers or changing quality and product design, rather than competing directly through price.

Non-traditional family   These are headed by cohabiting parents, lone parents or by two people of the same sex.

Normal good   The demand for this good will increase as a result of an increase in income. The entire demand function will shift to the right. Income elasticity is positive.

Normal profit   This is the profit which is what could be earned in the best alternative forgone. The firm just covers all opportunity costs.

Objective probability   See Risk.

Offer for sale at a fixed price   This is one method for bringing (launching) a company to the stock market. A fixed price is announced for the shares on offer and the public are asked to subscribe to the issue. A prospectus giving the details of the sale must be placed in a national newspaper. Then applications are made for a specified number of shares at the fixed offer price.

Offer for sale by tender   This is an alternative means for making a stock market launch. The Tender offer invites applicants to tender for shares above a minimum price. When all bids have been received a striking price is set which can match the quantity demanded and supplied.

Oligopolistic market   This is dominated by a few sellers and characterized by entry barriers.

On-the-job training   This is informal training and the acquisition of experience which takes place within business firms or non-profit establishments and is acquired on the job.

Open internal labour markets   These have jobs which are filled, by and large, from external markets.

Opportunism   A lack of sincerity or integrity which 'includes self-seeking and guile' (Williamson 1975).

Opportunity cost   The cost of using resources, including time, in their best alternative forgone. This benefit forgone does not have to be expressed in money terms.

Options   These are the rights to sell or buy, for example, shares, bonds, foreign exchange by a specified time in the future at a price set now. The premium is the price for buying or selling the option. Options will be exercised if the price is right. Options may be traded.

Ordinal utility   This utility or satisfaction can only be ordered, it is not measurable. Preferences for different combinations of goods can be ranked, one combination can be picked out as better than another, but the individual cannot tell us by how much.

Ordinary share   This is equity capital, a share which gives a part ownership in a joint stock company.

Over-subscription   There are not enough shares to meet the quantity demanded by applicants at the offer price; some alternative measure/s for allocating are necessarily required. A non-market price allocation procedure has to be employed. Some schools are over-subscribed.

Pareto optimality   A situation where it is not possible to rearrange production, i.e., to reallocate resources, so that even one person can be made better off without others being made worse off. A society would be located on the production possibility curve.

Partnership   A legal form of ownership where two or more joint owners are each responsible personally for the activities of the firm. The partners have shared rights to the profits and to manage the business. Each partner has unlimited liability, responsible for all the debts, even if an individual partner had no hand in incurring them. See Peer group.

Payback period   This is the number of years that an investment will take to pay back its initial capital outlay. The cash inflow per annum is divided by the initial outlay. But for a decision to be made, the critical element is the target payback period chosen by management.

Peer group   An organization which involves a number of people, collaborating together, where every member is essentially on the same footing as, for example, joint owners of a firm, participating equally in decision making. There is no boss, no hierarchy. The partnership is the legal form of the peer group.

Perfect competition   The 'ideal type' market structure where many buyers and sellers, both actual and potential, trade a homogeneous good. Perfect information rules and no single small buyer or seller can possibly affect the market price. There is freedom of entry and exit.

Perfectly competitive firm   This firm has no market strength and is a price taker powerless to affect the price it charges.

Perfectly elastic demand   Here the quantity demanded is infinitely responsive to price – any amount can be sold at the going price, elasticity is infinity. The perfectly competitive firm faces such a demand.

Perspective time   This is the time of decision where events are seen as people experience them, without perfect foresight or an ability to rerun the past. Choices in this real time have to be made on the basis of limited and sometimes ill-digested information where people may view the same information differently. Here only one option can be taken which may well have ramifications for future choices and decision-making may be stressful.

Physical investment line (PIL)   This is a graphical representation showing a boundary with all the possible combinations of consumption and investment expenditure now and consumption in the next time period, given the owner/manager's current stock of cash and the physical investments available. It shows the boundary between possible and impossible cash flows.

Planned economy   This type of economy solves production and distribution problems through a planning process. There are different brands of planning and in recent years many have moved towards mixed economies on Western lines.

Positive time preference   Money for consumption will have a time value; the nearer in time the better – there has to be a premium for delayed consumption.

Precautionary money balances   These provide contingency funds held against a variety of eventualities, imagined and unimagined.

Present value The money which must be saved now in order to receive a particular sum of money in the future given the interest rate. The present value of a future sum is found by putting compound interest into reverse.

Price controls Governments can directly intercede setting price above or below the market equilibrium price. It may also control or regulate the prices of privatized industries.

Price leadership Occurs where oligopolists operate in tacit collusion and may adhere to their own informal rules and customs. See, for example, the barometric firm.

Primary jobs These are characterized by good pay and conditions, training and internal promotion prospects, which offer possibilities for further human capital investment.

Primary markets Markets for the purchase and sale of new products.

Principal (a) The original sum of money lent out at interest; (b) The person/s whose interests are to be cared for in the agency relationship.

Principal/agent relationship For example, the relationship between shareholder and manager, patient and doctor. Problems arise when principals and agents have different objectives in perspective time.

Private company A company which is unquoted, that is, it has shares which are not traded on any stock market and they are not offered for sale to the general public.

Private property rights These bring the right to exchange or to give away private property. The decision about the use of private property, whether it has been bought, is a gift or has been inherited, is left to the individual – within circumscribed limits. The sanctity of private property and the traditional rules of private inheritance underpin the market mechanism.

Private sector non-profit firms Firms, organizations in the private voluntary, independent or third sector which on the whole are not producing output for market sale and are non-commercial. These include, for example, charities, voluntary associations and pressure groups.

Privatization This refers to a group of policies which emphasizes private ownership, the use of markets and competition. It includes the sale of state-owned assets to private individuals and organizations. Also, deregulation, changing the rules of the game, encouraging competition. Also, the contracting-out of services previously provided by government organizations. Also, economic prices have been introduced for services previously provided free or at minimal charge.

Production function This shows the functional relationship between inputs and outputs, the maximum amount of output for every level of input. See Function.

Production possibility curve This gives a range of production options, or choices open to a society at a point in analytical time, given fixed factors of production. It shows the best possible output combinations given a society's limited resources, the boundary between the possible and impossible.

Profit The surplus of total revenues over and above total costs.

Profit maximization The straightforward goal of introductory neo-classical theory – to acquire the biggest surplus of total revenues over total costs.

Property rights These institutional rules specify what people are entitled to do with resources and goods. Formal and informal rules which give rights over use, ownership and disposal may be more or less clearly defined. There are different property right structures. See Private, Communal and Collective.

Public Limited Companies, plcs A public company, limited by shares – which can offer shares for sale to the general public. A company which is quoted on the London Stock Exchange where its shares are traded must be a plc. These are, in the main, large companies, including global giants and national players.

Public sector non-profits These organizations include government non-trading and service sectors of central and local government. Organizations including civil service departments, local authorities, the armed forces, the police force, the National Health Service, state schools and public corporations like the BBC.

Pure public goods Goods like defence, a core of law and order services or public administration, cannot be allocated by the price mechanism. Markets simply do not exist for them.

Pure risk This risk carries no possibility of reward, only of a loss. The hazards of life against which people wish to insure, those risks which no one will pay people to bear. These include the chance of having a road accident, being burgled or a factory catching fire.

Quasi-markets For example, in the NHS, quasi-markets have been introduced with purchasers and providers. Some general practitioners have become fund holders, the buyers, and independent hospital trusts are the providers competing to supply services.

Quasi-public good These goods have elements of both a public and private good, commodities which potentially could be allocated by the price mechanism but are nevertheless provided by the state (and, in some circumstances, other organizations). Roads, pavements, public parks and recreation grounds are examples of such quasi-public goods.

Rational economic man A fundamental building block of traditional neo-classical theory, where rational men maximize their own utility.

Rational economic people Men and women who maximize their own individual utility.

Real or physical investment This involves the purchase of such things as capital equipment, machinery and buildings.

Relevant costs Those costs which are relevant for decision-making, opportunity costs.

Reproductive work The work of childbirth and child rearing.

Restricted social surplus In practice, only major social costs and benefits are calculated in cost benefit analysis. The aim is to maximize a restricted social surplus.

Reverse engineering Taking apart the product and processes to see how they work. Studying the technical development of products produced for some time. A way in which newly industrializing economies can challenge market leaders.

Risk This is measurable where activities are repetitive and replicable, where all the possible outcomes are known, as in the tossing of an unbiased coin. By the laws of probability we can know the likelihood of a particular result. Insurance companies measure risk on an actuarial basis, where probabilities of future events occurring can be estimated on the basis of past information from similar circumstances. These probabilities are described as objective.

Risk averse Individuals who regard risk as a 'bad' are risk averse. They need to be rewarded for bearing risk, which gives a disutility.

Risk adjusted discount rates   The rate of interest or discount can be increased to make an allowance for risk. This makes risk a compound function of time – which it may or may not be. Net benefits in the future are more heavily discounted.

Risk lover   The utility or satisfaction derived taking a risk is positive, therefore a person would be willing to pay to take risk.

Risk neutral   An individual is indifferent to risk and does not have to be compensated for bearing risk and will not pay to take a risk. Risk has no impact on utility.

Rules of enforcement   These are rules required as a means to oversee and regulate formal and informal institutional rules and to measure the extent of any breaches in these rules.

Rules of the game   These are institutionalized rules, essential requirements for the functioning of any society/economy. See also Formal and Informal rules and the Rules of enforcement.

Satisfice   Individuals or firms may simply aim to achieve satisfactory results over several goals – to satisfice.

Scarcity   All wants cannot be met. This arises because the factors of production and time are limited whilst wants are unlimited.

Scenario analysis   A technique for coping with risk, used, for example, in investment appraisal. The best, middle and worst estimates for a project are examined, enabling the analyst to reflect on a range of outcomes.

Secondary jobs   These jobs offer relatively poor pay and conditions, with little training or opportunity for advancement.

Secondary markets   These are for the exchange of second-hand goods. The London Stock Exchange acts mainly as a secondary market, almost all of the trading is in 'second-hand' shares, not new share issues.

Self-insurance   A way in which people cope with risk by particular behaviour, for example, cutting down on the risks of ill health by eating a healthy diet, exercising.

Seller preference   Given a price below equilibrium, sellers can exercise a choice as to who will receive goods. Allocation at the market clearing price gives the seller no leeway to choose between would-be purchasers.

Semi-fixed factor   Labour may take time to acquire as does capital. The need to select and train people means that labour is not a variable factor but quasi-fixed.

Sensitivity analysis   A technique for dealing with risk in project appraisal. Estimates of changes in underlying variables are taken one at a time, examining whether net present value or net present worth is sensitive to changes in each variable.

Separation principle   This says that given a perfect capital market, management should choose the optimal investment package which maximizes shareholder wealth, paying out dividends as a residual. Then shareholders are free to adjust the resulting dividend cash flows they receive by borrowing or lending on the financial market.

Sex division of labour   This term is used to refer to the division of labour between men and women in market and non-market activities.

Share option schemes   Management may be given the option to buy shares in the company at a particular time in the future at a price set now. This option will be valuable if by that time the share price has risen. Managers buy at the old set price and can sell at the higher market price, making a gain. This is a means for providing incentives, attempting to reduce agency problems. Workers may also be offered such schemes.

Shareholders   The owners of a company. Where there is a separation between ownership and control, shareholders are principals and managers are their agents.

Short run   The time period during which at least one factor input is fixed.

Short-run supply curve for the firm in perfect competition   This is given by the marginal cost curve above average variable costs.

Short-run total variable cost   The total variable cost of producing any given level of output in the short run.

Simple hierarchy   An organizational form where usually there is one person, the boss, who co-ordinates the activities like a manager overseeing workers. The owner and controller are one.

Social benefits   Private benefits *plus* beneficial externalities. Sometimes the term is used simply to refer to beneficial externalities.

Social costs   Private costs *plus* adverse externalities. Sometimes the term is used simply to refer to 'third party costs' not borne by the individuals or organizations who create them, for example costs of pollution and congestion.

Social rate of discount   The rate of discount used for appraising a social project.

Soft capital rationing   This occurs where management limit the funds available internally every year for each section or division as part of the planning process. Internal, non-price rationing is used to allocate scarce funds. This is also referred to as internal capital rationing.

Sole trader   A single owner/manager accountable for the activities of the firm. The owner and controller are one and the same, taking responsibility for decisions, liability for all debts and receiving all profits.

Specific assets   Both human and non-human resources are used within and are developed by firms. These may have specific attributes which cannot be acquired elsewhere. The value of such assets is much greater than in their best alternative use. See Specific training.

Specific training   As firms use unique techniques and processes, employees have to be trained on-the-job to acquire the required specific skills and knowledge. Given the acquisition of completely specific skills, worker productivity or rewards would not be enhanced elsewhere.

Speculative risks   Risks which carry a probability of reward. These include the gamble, the investment decision, even the career choice which promises the likelihood of gain.

Spillover effects   These are externalities, consequences to the wider community, ignored in the narrow calculus of private wealth. See Externalities.

Spot market   A market where goods and payment are exchanged, with people taking delivery immediately.

Stags   Those who sell shares quickly for profit, take their gains in the early days of trading, they buy below equilibrium market price and make a gain when shares trade.

State insurance   For example, in Britain, National Insurance coverage. The state is responsible for a whole range of eventualities including insurance against disabilities, unemployment and the chance of living into old age.

Strategic management   This involves managerial decisions about the scope, long-term goals and overall direction of the organization. Strategic decisions are taken in other forms of organization like the household.

Striking price   The price at which shares are allotted in an offer for sale by tender.

Subjective probabilities   Very often probabilities are not supported by repeated trials from the past for this is not possible. Probabilities are based on the personal assessment of the information available. See Uncertainty.

Substitute good   A good which is an alternative. Some goods may be close substitutes for each other. Cross elasticity of demand for a substitute will be positive.

Substitution effect of a price change   This is the increase in quantity demanded which arises purely from the change in relative prices, when the real income effect of the initial price change has been removed. The buyer is constrained to the original indifference curve.

Supernormal profit   This is an economic profit where total revenues exceed total costs. The firm more than covers its opportunity costs and therefore the return in the best alternative foregone.

Supply curve   This shows graphically a hypothetical relationship between the quantity which will be offered for sale at a series of possible prices; at every price what suppliers are willing and able to supply.

Supply function   A functional relationship between the quantity suppliers are willing and able to supply and the different factors which affect that including, for example, the price of the good in question, input prices and the level of technology.

Supply schedule   A list of possible prices with the corresponding quantities suppliers are willing and able to supply in a particular time period at each price.

Sympathy   Adam Smith argued that people would be moved by mutual sympathy, being helpful to each other and avoiding causing pain. Sympathy may be an important feature in accounting for some externalities.

Synergy   This is where the whole is greater than the sum of the parts, two people or two firms working together are better than two working independently.

Systematic risk   The risk which cannot be diversified away. All shares are exposed to some common risks, from tax changes, macroeconomic factors, global warming. Investors expect to be compensated for bearing this risk. Also known as market risk or non-diversifiable risk.

Technical efficiency   most output to be produced from any given input of resources, other things being equal. This exists where the firm is unable to produce a particular volume of output with a smaller number of resources.

Technology   The level of technological know-how, from sophisticated computerized equipment of the 'best practice' plant, just brought into production, to primitive techniques.

Terms of trade   These are the relative prices at which traders exchange their goods. The price ratio will determine how much each person actually gains from a deal, *ceteris paribus* or whether or not trade will take place.

Third Sector   This encompasses voluntary organizations, charities, religious organizations, pressure groups, associations like trades unions, professional bodies, mutual organizations and associations such as co-operatives. These are also referred to as the independent sector. Used to cover organizations which do not fall neatly into the public or private sectors.

Time discounting   This process enables the analyst to make allowance for the different time patterns of benefits and costs, to bring cash flows which accrue at different points in future time, to a common present value base. It puts compound interest calculations into reverse.

Total costs   The costs of all the inputs taken together for each level of output. The addition of total fixed and total variable costs.

Total fixed cost   The cost of the fixed factor, a constant sum which does not vary with output and which is unavoidable.

Total product   Total output.

Total variable costs   The total costs of all the variable inputs for each possible level of output.

Traditional economy   Pre-industrial societies solved problems of production and distribution by traditional means with limited use of the market although in some cases with a significant reliance on the planning process.

Traditional family   A married couple with dependent children. This is generally assumed to be the norm in the conventional economic approach.

Transaction costs   These arise from the organization and co-ordination of specialization and exchange. According to North these include the cost of measuring valuable features of what is being exchanged, protecting rights and policing and enforcing agreements. Transactions costs include negotiation and monitoring costs, which are part of using the market. They also result from the activities of the firm. In a world of costless knowledge and omniscient people in analytical time, there would be no transaction costs.

Transfer payments   These are not related to current labour market work. They include payments such as old age pensions, student grants and social security benefits.

Triangular trade   This occurs where three people are involved in joint swaps.

Trust   The belief, faith, conviction that people will behave and the future will unfold in a particular way. Trust is essential for the functioning of an economic system for in perspective time, of necessity, some things have to be taken on trust.

Uncertainty   This cannot be measured, unlike probabilistic risk. There may be no real idea of all the possible types of outcome and objective probabilities cannot be assigned. People speak of probabilities when they have little knowledge on which to base such figures. Information is lacking and expectations are unclear. Uncertainty mirrors the decision-makers' judgement of the adequacy of knowledge on which decisions are to be founded. Unique historical events cannot be predicted. Uncertainty cannot be eradicated. See Fundamental uncertainty.

Underwriters   Financial institutions will agree to underwrite an issue of shares for a fee, to buy up any shares which the company cannot sell. They underwrite the risk that the shares will not be sold. Insurance companies underwrite the risk of property, aircraft, ships being damaged.

Unique risk   This is diversifiable and arises from unique factors affecting a company, such as poor management or other singular adverse factors affecting a company's share price. People are not compensated for unique risks which are readily diversifiable. Also called specific risk or diversifiable risk.

Unit trusts   Financial intermediaries, trusts which sell units. They are not companies quoted on the stock market with shares. These intermediaries specialize in holding portfolios of shares in a variety of other companies. Small investors can gain the benefits of diversification with relatively small amounts of money.

Unitary elasticity of demand   This is where a proportional change in price is exactly matched by an equivalent reduction in quantity demanded. The percentage change in quantity demanded divided by the percentage change in price has a value of -1.

Unlimited liability   A partnership or sole trader has unlimited liability. If the worst happens, then an individual might stand to lose everything for they are liable for all the debts.

Unpaid non-market work   See Non-market work.

Team production   This involves the co-operation of a team of people all working at the same time, where the individual team member's effort cannot be readily observed.

Usury   This arose from money lending, making a profit from industry or trade and was viewed in the past as unacceptable. Earning interest at someone else's expense was regarded as 'unlawful'. Some religious groups still disapprove of earning interest.

Utility   This is well-being, happiness or satisfaction.

Variable costs   These change with output and reflect the payments required for variable inputs like labour or raw materials. They are avoidable. The firm is not committed to any particular level of employment in advance.

Vertical mergers   These are mergers of firms with their suppliers or buyers. They bring successive stages of production and distribution into the single firm.

Very long run   The time period over which all the factors of production, including technology, changes.

Very short run   Sometimes called the market period, time period so short that all inputs are fixed and so output cannot be varied.

Voluntary sector   A sub-section of a much wider group of private sector non-profits including charities and small voluntary groups.

Wealth   This is the stock of an individual's or country's assets both human and non-human. Wealth may be divided into marketable and non-marketable forms. Wealth can be defined in money terms as the present value of all net cash inflows.

Willingness to pay   Cost benefit analysts attempt to measure how much people would be willing to pay for an improvement, for example, improved underground safety – a marginal change in risk.

Working capital   This involves the firm in investing funds for comparatively short periods to pay for production, to maintain stocks and provide credit for customers. Cash is spent to buy raw materials, cover work in progress and any outstanding debts.

Zero price elasticity   No matter what happens to price in the relevant range, quantity demanded is totally unresponsive, a 1 per cent increase in price, for example, leads to no change in quantity demanded.

Bibliography

Akerlof, G. A. (1970) 'The Market for Lemons: Qualitative Uncertainty and the Market Mechanism', *Quarterly Journal of Economics* 84: 488–500.

—— (1982) 'Labour Contracts as Partial Gift Exchange', *Quarterly Journal of Economics*, 97(4) 543–69.

Alchian, A. (1953) 'Utility Theory and Consumer's Surplus: The Meaning of Utility Measurement', *The American Economic Review* (March 1953) 26–50 reprinted in Breit, W. and Hochman, H. M. (eds) (1968) *Readings in Microeconomics*, 69–88, London: Holt, Rinehart and Winston Inc.

Alchian, A. A. and Demsetz, H. (1972) 'Production, Information Costs, and Economic Organization', *American Economic Review* 62: 777–95.

Alden Mason, J. (1964) *The Ancient Civilizations of Peru*, Harmondsworth: Penguin.

Arrow, K. H. (1963) 'Uncertainty and the Welfare Economics of Medical Care', *American Economic Review* 53: 941–73, reprinted in Cooper, M. H. and Culyer, A. J. (eds) (1983) *Health Economics, Selected Readings*, Harmondsworth: Penguin.

Atkinson, A. B. (1989) *Poverty and Social Security*, Brighton, Sussex: Harvester Press.

Bain, K. and Howells, P. (1988) *Understanding Markets; An Introduction to the Theory, Institutions and Practice of Markets*, Hemel Hempstead: Harvester Wheatsheaf.

Barr, N. (1993) *The Economics of the Welfare State*, 2nd edn, London: Weidenfeld and Nicolson.

Baumol, W. J. (1959) *Business Behaviour, Value and Growth*, London: Macmillan.

—— (1961) *Economic Theory and Operations Analysis*, Englewood Cliffs, NJ: Prentice Hall.

Becker, G. (1964) *Human Capital*, New York: National Bureau of Economic Research, pp. 7–36, 37–66 reprinted in Burton, J. F., Jr, Benham, L. K., Vaughn, W. M., III and Flanagan R. J. (1971) *Readings in Labour Market Analysis*, New York: Holt, Rinehart and Winston.

—— (1965) 'A Theory of the Allocation of Time', *Economic Journal* 75: 493–517, reprinted in Burton J. F., Jr, Benham, L. K., Vaughn, W. M., III and Flanagan R. J. (1971) *Readings in Labour Market Analysis*, New York: Holt, Rinehart and Winston.

—— (1981) *A Treatise on the Family*, Cambridge, MA and London: Harvard University Press.

—— (1991) *A Treatise on the Family*, enlarged edition, Cambridge, MA and London: Harvard University Press.

—— (1993) *Human Capital Theory: A Theoretical and Empirical Analysis with Special Reference to Education*, 3rd edn, Chicago: The University of Chicago Press.

Begg, D., Fischer, S., and Dornbusch, R. (1994) *Economics*, 4th edn, London: McGraw-Hill.

Bell, E. (1994) '"Hello", And Goodbye, Say Saatchi Enemies', 18 December, London and Manchester: *Observer*.

Bellos, A. (1994) 'Uganda Determined Not To Be AIDS Victim', 13 November, London and Manchester: *Guardian*.

Ben-Porath, Y. (1982) 'Economics and the Family – Match or Mismatch? A Review of Becker's *A Treatise on the Family, Journal of Economic Literature* XX: 52–64.

Bishop, M. and Kay, J. (1988) *Does Privatization Work? Lessons For The UK*, London: Centre For Business Strategy, London Business School.

Boulding, K. E. (1973) *The Economy of Love and Fear*, Belmont, CA: Wadsworth.

Brealey, R. A. and Myers, S. C. (1991) *Principles of Corporate Finance*, London and New York: McGraw-Hill.

Brindle, D. (1994) 'Legacy Fall Hits Some Charities', 15 December, London and Manchester: *Guardian*.

Bryant, W. K. (1990) *The Economic Organization of the Household*, Cambridge: Cambridge University Press.

Carvalho, F. (1983–4) 'On the Concept of Time in Shacklean and Sraffian Economics', *Journal of Post Keynesian Economics* 6(2): 265–80.

Casson, M. C. (1991) *The Economics of Business Culture: Game Theory, Transactions Costs, and Economic Performance*, Oxford: Clarendon Press.

—— (1993) Ethics mark East–West divide', 13 September, London and Manchester: *Guardian*.

Chandler, A. D. Jr (1962) *Strategy and Structure: Chapters in the History of the Industrial Enterprise*, Cambridge, MA: MIT Press.

—— (1977) *The Visible Hand: The Managerial Revolution*, American Business, Cambridge, MA: Belknap Press.

—— with the assistance of Takashi Hikino (1990) *Scale and Scope: The Dynamics of Industrial Capitalism*, Cambridge, MA and London: Harvard University Press, Belknap Press.

Charities Aid Foundation (1992) *Charity Trends 1992*, 15th edn, Tonbridge, Kent.

—— (1993) *Charity Trends 1993*, 16th edn, Tonbridge, Kent.

—— (1994) *Charity Trends 1994*, 17th edn, Tonbridge, Kent.

—— (1995) *Dimensions of the Voluntary Sector: How is the Voluntary Sector Changing?* London.

Chew, D. H. J (ed.) (1993) *The New Corporate Finance: Where Theory Meets Practice*, New York: McGraw-Hill, Inc.

Cigno, A. (1990) 'Home Production and the Allocation of Time', in Sapsford and Tzannatos (eds) *Current Issues in Labour Economics*, Basingstoke: Macmillan.

—— (1991) *Economics of the Family*, Oxford: Clarendon Press.

Coase, R. H. (1937) 'The Nature of the Firm', *Economica* 4: 386–405.

Cole, K. Cameron, J. and Edwards, C. (1983) *Why Economists Disagree: The Political Economy of Economics*, Harlow, Essex: Longman Group UK Limited.

Cooter, R. and Ulen, T. (1988) *Law and Economics*, United States of America: HarperCollins Publishers.

Cyert, R. M. (1975) *The Management of Nonprofit Organizations*, Lexington, MA, Toronto, London: Lexington Books, D. C. Heath and Company.

Davidson, P. (1991a) *Controversies in Post Keynesian Economics*, Aldershot: Edward Elgar.

—— (1991b) 'Is Probability Theory Relevant for Uncertainty? A Post Keynesian Perspective', *Journal of Economic Perspectives* Winter, 5(1): 129–43.

Davies, G. and Hillier, P. (1993) 'Effectiveness and Efficiency in Privatisation Advertising', *International Journal of Advertising Quarterly Review of Marketing* 12(3): 211–21.

Dawes, R. M. (1988) *Rational Choice in an Uncertain World*, San Diego, New York: Harcourt Brace Jovanovich, Publishers.

Dean, M. (1993) 'Fading Faith and Hope in Charity', 6 October, London and Manchester: *Guardian*.

Doeringer, P. B., and Piore, M. J. (1971) *Internal Labor Markets and Manpower Analysis*, Lexington, MA: D. C. Heath and Company.

Douma, S. and Schreuder, H. (1991) *Economic Approaches to Organizations*, Hemel Hempstead: Prentice Hall International (UK) Ltd.

Dow, S. C. (1993) *Money and the Economic Process*, Aldershot: Edward Elgar.

—— (1995) 'Uncertainty about uncertainty', in Dow, S. and Hillard, J. (eds) forthcoming (1995) *Keynes, Knowledge and Uncertainty*, Aldershot: Edward Elgar.

Downing, H. (1993) 'Raise Your Standard of Giving' 3 October, London and Manchester: *Observer*.

Driscoll, M. (1991) 'Deregulation, Credit Rationing, Financial Fragility and Economic Performance', Department of Economics and Statistics Working Papers, No. 97, OECD, February.

Earl, P. E. (1986) *Lifestyle Economics: Consumer Behaviour in a Turbulent World*, Brighton, Sussex: Wheatsheaf Books.

—— (1990) *Monetary Scenarios*, Aldershot: Edward Elgar.

—— (1990) 'Economics and Psychology: A Survey', *The Economic Journal*, September, 718–55.

Economist (1993) 'The Price of Life', 4 December, London *Economist*.

—— (1994) 'A Survey of Corporate Governance: Watching the Boss', 29 January, London: *Economist*.

—— (1994) 'Schools Brief: the War Between the Sexes', 5 March , London: *Economist.*

—— (1994) 'Investing in People', 6 March, London: *Economist*

—— (1994) 'Parent Power', 7 May, London: *Economist*.

—— (1994) 'The Smack of Firm Government', 8 October, London: *Economist*.

Elliot, R. F. (1991) *Labour Economics: A Comparative Text*, London: McGraw-Hill.

Falk, F. (1993) 'Accountable to whom, for what and how?' *The Henderson Top 1000 Charities 1993: A Guide to UK Charities*, 28–30, Hemmington Scoot Publishing Ltd.

Ferber, M. A. and Teiman, M. L. (1981) 'The impact of Feminism on Economics', in *Men's Studies Modified: The Impact of Feminism on the Academic Disciplines*, Spender, D. (ed.) Oxford: Pergamon Press.

Ferguson, P. R., Ferguson G. J. and Rothschild, R. (1993) *Business Economics*, Basingstoke and London: Macmillan.

Fine, B. (1992) *Women's Employment and the Capitalist Family*, London: Routledge.

Folbre, N. (1994) *Who Pays For The Kids? Gender And The Structures Of Constraint*, London: Routledge.

Fourie, F. C. v. N. (1991) 'The Nature of the Market: a Structural Analysis', in Hodgson, G.M. and Screpanti, E. (eds) *Rethinking Economics: Markets, Technology And Economic Evolution*, European Association for Evolutionary Political Economy, Aldershot: Edward Elgar.

Frank, R. H. (1992) 'Melding Sociology and Economics: James Coleman's Foundations of Social Theory', *Journal of Economic Literature*, March 1992, XXX: 147–70.

Galbraith, J. K. (1975) *Economics and the Public Purpose*, Harmondsworth: Pelican Books.

—— (1993) *The Culture of Contentment*, London: Penguin.

Garcia Moreno, C. (1989) 'Women and AIDS', *Gender and Development Unit PACK 9*, June, Oxford: Oxfam.

Gerrard, B. (1993) 'Keynes on Probability, Uncertainty and Expectations: A Constructive Interpretation', Leeds Conference Paper, in Dow, S. and Hillard, J. (eds) forthcoming (1995) *Keynes, Knowledge and Uncertainty*, Aldershot: Edward Elgar.

Giarini, O. and Stahel, W. R. (1993) *The Limits to Certainty: Facing Risks in the New Service Economy*, 2nd edn, Boston and London: Kluwer Academic Publishers.

Glyn, A. and Miliband, D. (eds) (1994) *Paying for Inequality: the Economic Cost of Social Injustice*, London: IPPR / Rivers Oram Press.

Government Statistical Office (1991) *Social Trends 21*, London: HMSO.

—— (1992) *Social Trends 22*, London: HMSO.

—— (1993) *Social Trends 23*, London: HMSO.

—— (1994) *Social Trends 24*, London: HMSO.

Guardian (1994) 'Builder Cements £250m Fortune', 3 March, London and Manchester: *Guardian*.

Hannan, M. T. (1982) 'Families, Markets, and Social Structures: An Essay on Becker's *A Treatise on the Family'*, *Journal of Economic Literature*, XX: 65–72.

Harcourt, G. C. (1992) *On Political Economists and Modern Political Economy: Selected Essays of G. C. Harcourt*, edited by Claudio Sardoni, London: Routledge.

Hay, D. A. (1989) *Economics Today: A Christian Critique*, Leicester: APPOLOS, Inter-Varsity Press.

Heilbroner, R. L. (1986) *The Essential Adam Smith*, Oxford: Oxford University Press.

—— (1993) *The Making of Economic Society*, 9th edn, Englewood Cliffs, NJ: Prentice-Hall Inc.

Heinsohn, G. and Steiger, O. (1984) 'Marx and Keynes – Private Property and Money', *Économies et Sociétiés* 18(4), Grenoble: Pressess Universitaires de Grenoble.

—— (1985) 'Technical progress and monetary production: an explanation', *Économies et Sociétiés* Volume 19(8), Presses Universitaires de Grenoble.

Henderson, R. (1993) *European Finance*, Maidenhead, Berkshire: McGraw-Hill.

Hirshleifer, J. (1958) 'On the Theory of Optimal Investment Decision', *Journal of Political Economy*, August, 329–52.

Hodgson, G. M. (1988) *Economics And Institutions*, Cambridge and Oxford: Polity Press in association with Basil Blackwell.

Hodgson, G. M. (1993) 'Evolution and Institutional Change: On the Nature of Selection in Biology and Economics', in Maki, U., Gustafasson B., and Knudsen C. (eds) *Rationality, Institutions and Economic Methodology*, London: Routledge.

Hodgson, G. M. and Screpanti, E. (1991) *Rethinking Economics: Markets, Technology and Economic Evolution*, European Association for Evolutionary Political Economy, Aldershot: Edward Elgar.

Independent (1994) 'Advantages of a Degree are Still Substantial', 2 November, London: *Independent*.

Industrial Challenge: the Experience of Cadburys of Bournville in the Post-War Years (1964) London: Sir Issac Pitman and Sons Limited.

Jay, P. (1994) 'Panorama: The Age of Fear', broadcast on BBC, 10 October.

Jones-Lee, M. and Loomes, G. (1994) 'Towards a Willingness-to-Pay Based Value of Underground Safety', *Journal of Transport Economics and Policy*, January, 83–97.

Joseph Rowntree Foundation (1995) *Inquiry into Income and Wealth*, Chaired by Sir Peter Barclay, 1, York: Joseph Rowntree Foundation.

—— (1995) *Inquiry into Income and Wealth: A Summary of the Evidence*, by John Hills, 2, York: Joseph Rowntree Foundation.

Joshi, H. (1989) *The Changing Population Of Britain*, Oxford: Basil Blackwell.

Kahneman, D., Slovic, P. and Tversky, A. (eds) (1982) *Judgement Under Uncertainty: Heuristics and Biases*, Cambridge: Cambridge University Press.

Kay, N. M. (1984) *The Emergent Firm: Knowledge, Ignorance and Surprise in Economic Organisation*, London: Macmillan.

Kerr, C. (1969) *Marshall, Marx and Modern Times: the Multidimensional Society*, London: Cambridge University Press.

Keynes, J. M. (1936) *The General Theory of Employment, Interest and Money*, London and Basingstoke: Macmillan Press Ltd, 1973.

King, J. E. (1992) *Labour Economics*, 2nd edn, London: Macmillan Education Ltd.

Knight, F. H. (1933) *Risk, Uncertainty and Profit*, 2nd edn, London: London School of Economics.

Lavoie, M. (1992) 'Towards a New Research Programme for Post-Keynesianism and Neo-Ricardianism', *Review of Political Economy* 4(1): 37–78.

Lazonick, W. (1991) *Business Organization and the Myth of the Market Economy*, Cambridge: Cambridge University Press.

Leat, D. (1993) *Managing Across Sectors: Similarities and Differences Between For-Profit and Voluntary Non-Profit Organisations*, London: City University Business School.

Le Grand, J., Propper, C. and Robinson, R. (1992) *The Economics of Social Problems*, 3rd edn, Basingstoke and London: The Macmillan Press Ltd.

Le Grand, J. and Bartlett, W. (eds) (1993) *Quasi-Markets and Social Policy*, Basingstoke and London: The Macmillan Press Ltd.

Lipsey, R. G. (1989) *An Introduction to Positive Economics*, 7th edn, London: Weidenfeld and Nicolson.

Loasby, B. J. (1976) *Choice, Complexity and Ignorance*, Cambridge: Cambridge University Press.

McGuire, A. Henderson, J. and Mooney, G. (1988) *The Economics of Health Care: An Introductory Text*, London: Routledge, Keegan and Paul Ltd.

McQuillan, J. (ed.) (1993) *Charity Trends 1993*, 16th edn, Tonbridge Charities Aid Foundation.

Machina, M. J. (1987) 'Choice Under Uncertainty: Problems solved and unsolved', *Economic Perspectives*, Summer: 1(1) 121–54.

Macrae, C. (1992) 'Troops Must Retain Problem Rifle to Keep Arms Firm in Business', London: 6 September, *Observer*.

Mair, D. and Miller, A. G. (eds) (1991) *A Modern Guide to Economic Thought: An Introduction to Comparative Schools of Thought in Economics*, Aldershot: Edward Elgar.

Marris, R. L. (1964) *The Economic Theory of Managerial Capitalism*, London: Macmillan.

Marshall, A. (1920a) *Principles of Economics*, 9th (Variorum) edn, with annotations by Guillebaud, C.W., 1, Text, London: Macmillan and Co Ltd. 1961.

Marshall, A. (1920b) *Principles of Economics*, Ninth (Variorum) edn, with annotations by Guillebaud, C. W., 2, Notes, London: Macmillan and Co Ltd, 1961.

Marx, K. and Engels, F. (1872) 'Manifesto of the Communist Party', reprinted in *Selected Works* , (1968) London: Lawrence and Wishart.

Matthews, R. C. O. (1993) 'Political and Economic Causes of the Economic Slowdown', *Scottish Journal of Political Economy*, 40, 129–42.

Maynard, A. (1990) 'The United Kingdom' in Rossiter, L.F. and Scheffler, R. M. (eds) *Advances in Health Economics and Health Services Research, Supplement 1: Comparative Health Systems*, Greenwich, CT and London: JAI Press Inc., 1–26.

Meek, R. L. (1971) *Figuring Out Society*, London: Fontana, Wm Collins Sons and Co. Ltd.

Milgrom, P. and Roberts, J. (1992) *Economics, Organization and Management*, New Jersey: Prentice Hall International.

Mooney, G. (1992) *Economics, Medicine and Health Care*, 2nd edn, Hemel Hempstead: Harvester Wheatsheaf.

—— (1994) *Key issues in Health Economics*, Hemel Hempstead: Harvester Wheatsheaf.

Moschandreas, M. (1994) *Business Economics*, London: Routledge.

Nelson, R. R. (ed.) (1993) *National Innovation Systems: A Comparative Analysis*, Oxford: Oxford University Press.

North, D. C. (1990) *Institutions, Institutional Change and Economic Performance*, Cambridge: Cambridge University Press.

—— (1993) 'Institutions and Economic Performance' in Maki, U., Gustafasson, B. and Knudsen C. (eds) *Rationality, Institutions and Economic Methodology*, London: Routledge.

Nove. A (1980) *The Soviet Economic System*, 2nd edn, London: George Allen and Unwin.

—— (1992) *Economic History of the USSR*, 3rd edn, London: Penguin.

Okin, S. M. (1989) *Justice, Gender, and the Family*, New York: Basic Books.

Parkin, M. (1990) *Economics*, Reading, MA: Addison-Wesley.

Pawley, M., Winstone, D. and Bentley, P. (1991) *UK Financial Institutions and Markets*, Basingstoke, Hampshire and London: Macmillan Education Limited.

Pike, R. and Neale, B. (1993) *Corporate Finance and Investment: Decisions and Strategies*, Hemel Hempstead: Prentice Hall International (UK) Limited.

Pollack, R. A. (1985) 'Transaction Cost and Families', *Journal of Economic Literature*, XXIII: 581–608.

Prest, A. R. and Turvey, R. (1965) 'Cost–Benefit Analysis: A Survey', *Economic Journal* 75: 685–705, also reprinted in Layard, R. (1972) *Cost Benefit Analysis*, Harmondsworth: Penguin Books Ltd.

Quint, F. (1993) 'The Charities Act 1992', *The Henderson Top 1000 Charities 1993: A Guide to UK Charities*, 28–30 Hemmington Scoot Publishing Ltd.

Raphael, D. D. (1985) *Adam Smith*, Oxford and New York: Oxford University Press.

Ricketts, M. (1987) *The Economics of Business Enterprise: New Approaches To The Firm*, Hemel Hempstead: Harvester Wheatsheaf.

—— (1994) *The Economics of Business Enterprise: An Introduction to Economic Organisation and the Theory of the Firm*, 2nd edn, Hemel Hempstead: Harvester Wheatsheaf.

Robinson, J. (1962) *Economic Philosophy*, Penguin Books Ltd.

—— (1975) 'The Unimportance of Reswitching', *Quarterly Journal of Economics* 32–9.

—— (1978) *Contributions to Modern Economics*, Oxford: Basil Blackwell.

Rohlf, W. D., Jr (1989) *Introduction to Economic Reasoning*, Reading, MA: Addison-Wesley Publishing Company.

Royal Society (The) (1992) *Risk: Analysis, Perception & Management*, London: The Royal Society.

Samuels, J. M., Wilkes, F. M. and Brayshaw, R. E. (1990) *Management of Company Finance*, 5th edn, London: Chapman and Hall.

Samuelson, P. A. (1956) 'Social Indifference Curves', *Quarterly Journal of Economics*, February, 70 (1): 1–22.

Shackle, G. L. S. (1955) *Uncertainty in Economics*, London: Cambridge University Press.

—— (1958) *Time in Economics*, Amsterdam: North-Holland.

—— (1961) *Decision, Order and Time in Human Affairs*, Cambridge: Cambridge University Press.

——(1965) *A Scheme of Economic Theory*, Cambridge: Cambridge University Press.

—— (1972) *Epistemics and Economics. A Critique of Economic Doctrines*, Cambridge: Cambridge University Press.

—— (1974) *Keynes on Kaleidics*, Edinburgh: Edinburgh University Press.

—— (1983) 'The Bounds of Unknowledge', in Wiserna, J. (ed.) (1983) *Beyond Positive Economics?* London: Macmillan.

—— (1984) 'To Cope With Time' in Stephen, F. H. S. (ed.) *Firms Organisation and Labour: Approaches to the Economics of Work Organisation*, London: Macmillan.

—— (1990) *Time, Expectations and Uncertainty in Economics*, Ford, J. L. (ed.) Aldershot: Edward Elgar.

Shapiro, A. (1993) 'Corporate Strategy and Capital Budgeting Decision', in Chew, D. H., Jr (ed.) *The New Corporate Finance: Where Theory Meets Practice*, London and New York: McGraw Hill.

Sharp, C. (1981) *The Economics Of Time*, Oxford: Martin Robertson and Co.

Sheng, P., Chang, L. and French, W. A. (1994) 'Business's Environmental Responsibility in Taiwan – Moral, Legal or Negotiated', *Journal of Business Ethics*, November, 13(11): 887–97.

Simon, H. (1976) 'From Substantive to Procedural Rationality', in Lastis, S. (ed.) *Method and Appraisal in Economics*, Cambridge University Press.

Sisson, K. (ed.) (1994) *Personnel Management: A Comprehensive Guide to Theory and Practice in Britain*, 2nd edn, Oxford: Blackwell Publishers.

Sloman, J. (1991) *Economics*, Cambridge: Harvester Wheatsheaf.

Smith, A. (1776) *An Inquiry into the Nature and Causes of the Wealth of Nations*, vols 1 and 2, edited by Campbell, R. H. and Skinner A. S., textual editor Todd, W. B. Oxford: Clarendon Press, 1976.

Smith, G. A. E. (1981) 'The Industrial Problems of Soviet Agriculture', *Critique 14 A Journal of Socialist Theory* 41–65.

Smith, M. (1992) 'Profits at the Royal Mail', 9 February, London: *Observer*.

—— (1994) 'Rail sell-off fuels legal bonanza', 23 October, London and Manchester: *Observer*.

Smith, S. W. (1994) *Labour Economics*, London: Routledge.

Snooks, G. D. (ed.) (1993) *Historical Analysis In Economics*, London: Routledge.

Solow, R. M. (1990) *The Labour Market as a Social Institution*, Oxford: Basil Blackwell Ltd.

Stranz, W. (1973) *George Cadbury: An Illustrated Life of George Cadbury 1839–1922*, Aylesbury, Bucks: Shire Publications Ltd.

Teece, D. J. (1993) 'The Dynamics of Industrial Capitalism: Perspectives on Alfred Chandler's Scale and Scope', *Journal of Economic Literature*, March XXXI: 199–225.

Thorniley, D. and Reed, J., (1993) 'Trade and Payments: Adventures in Countertrade' *Business Eastern Europe*, 16 August, London: The Economist Intelligence Unit.

Thurow, L. C. (1970) *Investment in Human Capital*, Belmont, CA: Wadsworth Publishing Co., Inc.

—— (1976) *Generating Inequality,* London: Macmillan.

Titmuss, R. M. (1970) *The Gift Relationship: From Human Blood To Social Policy*, Oxford: George Allen and Unwin.

Turner, R. K., Pearce D. and Bateman, I. (1994) *Environmental Economics: An Elementary Introduction*, Hemel Hempstead: Harvester Wheatsheaf.

Walker, W. (1993) 'National Innovation Systems: Britain', in Nelson, R. R. (ed.) *National Innovation Systems: A Comparative Analysis*, Oxford: Oxford University Press.

Wheelock, J. (1990) *Husbands At Home: The Domestic Economy in a Post-Industrial Society*, London: Routledge.

Williams, A. (1993) *Human Resource Management and Labour Market Flexibility: Some Current Theories and Controversies*, Avebury: Business Research Library, Ashgate Publishing Limited.

Williamson, O. E. (1964) *The Economics of Discretionary Behaviour: Managerial Objectives in a Theory of the Firm*, Englewood Cliffs, NJ: Prentice-Hall.

—— (1975) *Markets and Hierarchies: An Analysis and Antitrust Implications: A Study in the Economics of Internal Organisation*, New York: Free Press.

Winston G. C. (1988) 'Three problems with the treatment of time in economics: perspectives, repetitiveness, and time units', in Winston, G. C. and Teichgraeber, F., III (eds) (1988) *The Boundaries of Economics*, Cambridge: Cambridge University Press.

Wittington, R. (1993) What is Strategy and Does it Matter? London: Routledge.

Wray, L. R. (1990) *Money and Credit in Capitalist Economies: The Endogenous Approach*, Aldershot: Edward Elgar.

Index